JUSTICE THROUGH APOLOGIES

In this follow-up to *I Was Wrong: The Meanings of Apologies*, Nick Smith applies his theories of categorical apologies to law. State agents determine punishments for millions of offenders by consulting gut feelings and rendering unappealable decisions regarding the defendant's contrition. Findings of remorse can determine whether an offender lives or dies, yet we expect reviewers to "know it when they see it": look into the defendants' souls, intuit the depths of their evil, and punish accordingly. Smith argues all major theories of punishment should typically endorse "apology reductions" *only if* offenders demonstrate moral transformation by satisfying rigorous standards for apologies. Smith also explains how apologies have become pawns for civil defense attorneys who consider them cheap and low-risk litigation strategies to appease victims. Recent legislative trends increase the likelihood that offenders will gain the many financial and public relations benefits of "saying sorry" even when they do not accept blame, provide redress, or reform behaviors and policies to prevent additional injuries.

Nick Smith is an associate professor of philosophy at the University of New Hampshire. Formerly a litigator and a clerk for the U.S. Court of Appeals, he specializes in the philosophy of law, politics, and society. Smith is the author of *I Was Wrong: The Meanings of Apologies*. He regularly appears in the media, including *The Wall Street Journal, The New York Times, The Chronicle of Higher Education, The Guardian UK,* and *Fortune*, and on NPR, BBC, CBC, CNN, and others.

Justice through Apologies: Remorse, Reform, and Punishment

Nick Smith
University of New Hampshire

CAMBRIDGE UNIVERSITY PRESS

CAMBRIDGE
UNIVERSITY PRESS

32 Avenue of the Americas, New York, NY 10013-2473, USA

Cambridge University Press is part of the University of Cambridge.

It furthers the University's mission by disseminating knowledge in the pursuit of education, learning, and research at the highest international levels of excellence.

www.cambridge.org
Information on this title: www.cambridge.org/9780521189453

© Nick Smith 2014

This publication is in copyright. Subject to statutory exception and to the provisions of relevant collective licensing agreements, no reproduction of any part may take place without the written permission of Cambridge University Press.

First published 2014

Printed in the United States of America

A catalog record for this publication is available from the British Library.

Library of Congress Cataloging in Publication Data
Smith, Nick, 1972 January 14– author.
Justice through apologies : remorse, reform, and punishment / Nick Smith.
   p. cm.
Includes bibliographical references and index.
ISBN 978-1-107-00754-3 (hardback) – ISBN 978-0-521-18945-3 (paperback)
1. Law – Psychological aspects. 2. Apologizing. 3. Remorse. 4. Punishment.
5. Law – Philosophy. I. Title.
K346.S65 2014
340'.19–dc23   2013037437

ISBN 978-1-107-00754-3 Hardback
ISBN 978-0-521-18945-3 Paperback

Cambridge University Press has no responsibility for the persistence or accuracy of URLs for external or third-party Internet Web sites referred to in this publication and does not guarantee that any content on such Web sites is, or will remain, accurate or appropriate.

*To my parents, Carol and John Smith,
in part for helping keep me on this side of the law and
for teaching me compassion for those on the other side.
In their words: "No one is better than anyone else."*

Contents

Acknowledgments	*page* xi
Introduction	1
1 **The Categorical Apology Revisited**	17
A. The Elements of a Categorical Apology	17
B. An Applied Example: Elliot Spitzer 2008	23
C. Collective Apologies Revisited	34
Part One. The Penitent and the Penitentiary: Apologies in Criminal Law	
2 **Against Court-Ordered Apologies**	51
A. The Dark History of Court-Ordered Apologies	54
B. Humiliation Will Compensate for the Offense: Kant's Retributive Justifications for Court-Ordered Apologies	58
C. Contemporary Kantians and Apology Rituals	62
D. The Middle Ground between Involuntary and Voluntary	65
E. Consequentialist Considerations Regarding Court-Ordered Apologies	71
The Importance of Consequentialism to a Comprehensive View of the Value of Court-Ordered Apologies	71
Rehabilitation and the Analogy to Ordering Children to Apologize	74
Deterrence and Incapacitation	83

		Consequentialist Benefits to Victims and Communities	86
	F.	Freedom of Speech and Conscience	88
		Conclusion	92
3	**Apology Reductions in Criminal Law**		**94**
		Introduction	94
	A.	In Principle: Why Apologetic Offenders Deserve Reductions in Punishment	99
		According to Consequentialist Justifications for Punishment	99
		According to Leftist Social Justice Theories	118
		According to Retributive Justifications for Punishment	148
		Becoming Apologetic versus Already Apologetic	175
		Symmetry: Increasing Punishments for Unapologetic Offenders	185
	B.	In Practice: Applying Apology Reductions	189
		The Institutional Framework	190
		A Practical Framework for Evaluating Apologies in the Criminal Context	202

Part Two. **Apologies in Civil Law**

4	**The Institutional Framework: Economic Outcomes and Noneconomic Values**		**243**
		Introduction	243
	A.	A Prominent Distinction Between Civil and Criminal Law: Money	249
	B.	Why We Would Not Expect Apologies in Civil Law	251
	C.	The Economic Value of the Semblance of Noneconomic Value: The Enduring Desire for More than Money	253
5	**A Practical Framework for Evaluating Apologies in Civil Contexts**		**259**
	A.	Guiding Questions: How Should We Evaluate Apologies in the Civil Context?	259
		1. Has the Civil Offender Corroborated the Factual Record?	262
		2. Has the Civil Offender Accepted Blame?	266
		3. Does the Civil Offender Possess Appropriate Standing to Apologize and Accept Blame?	286
		4. Does the Civil Offender Identify Each Harm?	296

5. Does the Civil Offender Identify Principles
 Underlying Each Harm? 297
6. Does the Civil Offender Share a Commitment to
 the Principles Underlying Each Harm? 299
7. Does the Civil Offender Recognize Victims as
 Moral Interlocutors? 300
8. Does the Civil Offender Express and
 Demonstrate Categorical Regret? 304
9. Has the Civil Offender Performed the Apology? 307
10. To What Extent Does the Civil Offender
 Demonstrate Reform? 310
11. Has the Civil Offender Provided Appropriate
 Redress? 316
12. What Intentions Motivate the Civil Offender's
 Apology? 323
13. Does the Civil Offender Demonstrate
 Appropriate Emotions? 326
 Conclusion 329

Concluding Call for Collaboration 330

Notes 333
Index 397

Acknowledgments

This book is about righting wrongs, but, to quote a friend, we can also make the rights even more right. Appreciating the people who have helped you walk a long path is one small way to do this.

One of the pleasures of researching apologies has been how the interdisciplinarity of the work emphasizes the collective nature of thinking clearly about such complex issues. This book is one link within an expanding web of research, and I benefited immeasurably from the work of many others across disciplines and fields. I attempt to acknowledge these debts in my notes, but a few deserve recognition here.

Many people have nurtured my work: colleagues in Justice Studies, Public Health, the UNH Center for Humanities, the UNH Honors Program, the UNH College of Liberal Arts, the UNH Graduate School, the UNH Law School, the UNH Provost's Office, UNH Advancement, the UNH President's Office, NHPR, New Hampshire Humanities Council, and the National Endowment for the Humanities. My students breathed life into many of the ideas on these pages, and I appreciate the effort that many of them – and their families – must put in behind the scenes in order to take a philosophy class.

My department colleagues treat me like a member of the family and give me every opportunity to succeed. I have been incredibly fortunate to land in a place that has been such an obviously good fit and that appreciates me for all of my oddities. Bill deVries, in particular, deserves special thanks for his help with drafts – and for generally being such a *mensch*. Working with all of these colleagues is a great privilege.

Guyora Binder, Markus Dubber, and John Kleinig continue to serve as role models for thinking clearly about practical problems in criminal law without sacrificing philosophical rigor. Mitch Simon helped process these ideas into a form that could be useful for practitioners. His good sense extends far beyond the discussions of bar admissions. The Honorable Richard Lowell Nygaard wrote about many of these issues well before people like me began to study them, and clerking for him was a profoundly formative experience for me. In his chambers I learned that even though reasonable people can disagree about resolutions to legal disputes, we need to find the best argument and side with it. Jennifer Robbennolt's writings were especially helpful as I organized my thinking about social scientific research on apologies. Michael O'Hear guided me through the Federal Sentencing Guidelines. Philosophers of punishment too often ignore the role of plea bargaining, and I follow down the path of Richard Lippke's trailblazing work. Cesar Rebellon, Chris Colocousis, and Stefan Sobolowski contributed at many levels. Philadelphia attorneys David Shapiro and Steven LaCheen deserve special recognition for their zealous advocacy for not only their clients' legal interests but also for their moral development. For the reasons discussed throughout this book, this is a difficult position to sustain. I recommend them to remorseful offenders seeking guidance through the process of apologizing within the legal system.

I learned quite a bit regarding court-ordered apologies and the analogy to requiring children to apologize from conversations with thoughtful friends and family as well as academic colleagues. In particular, I am grateful for the practical wisdom of Albert Chang, Drew Christie, Andy Colby, Alix Handelsman, Michelle Holt-Shannon, Rebecca Johnson, Tom and Jonti Rodi, Bob Scharff, John and Keena Smith, and Charlotte Witt.

Many others planted seeds that continue to grow in my work, including Jay Bernstein, Danielle Celermajer, Zach Davis, Margaret Gilbert, Charles Griswold, Gregg Horowitz, Zohar Kampf, Christopher Kutz, Jeffrie Murphy, Glen Pettigrove, Linda Radzik, and Bruce Waller.

I also thank participants at several venues where I presented portions of these materials, including the American Philosophical Association Eastern Division, the Law and Society Association, the Northern New England Philosophy Association, the American Bar Association National Conference on Professional Responsibility, the Straus Institute for Dispute Resolution at the Pepperdine University School of Law, University Centre Saint-Ignatius Antwerp, Case Western Reserve Law School, John Jay College Department of Philosophy, Wayne State University Law School, St. John's University Department of Philosophy, Connecticut College Department of Philosophy, UNH Law School, and my own UNH Department of Philosophy.

Previous attempts at these ideas appeared in various venues, including my first book, *I Was Wrong: The Meanings of Apologies*. Given that this current book builds on and applies my previous work, readers will find some redundancies between the texts. Editors for these earlier publications helped me crystallize the content and form of this book over the years. John Berger at Cambridge has been the ideal editor, always present but never hovering. His wisdom allowed me to write two books on apologies rather than hastily cram everything into one volume. Other editors pushed and pulled on early formations of these ideas appearing in: "Political Apologies and Categorical Apologies," in *On the Uses and Abuses of Political Apologies*, eds. Mihaela Mihai and Mathias Thaler (New York: Palgrave Macmillan, 2013): 29–43; "An Overview of Challenges Facing Collective Apologies," in *Public Apologies Between Ritual and Regret*, eds. Daniel Cuypers, Daniel Janssen, Jacques Haers, and Barbara Segaert (Amsterdam: Rodopi, 2013); "Against Court-Ordered Apologies," *New Criminal Law Review* 16–1 (2012): 1–49; "Apologies in Law: An Overview of the Philosophical Issues," *Pepperdine Dispute Resolution Law Journal* (2013); "Apologies and Fitness to Practice Law: A Practical Framework for Evaluating Remorse in the Bar Admission Process," 37 *ABA Journal of the Professional Lawyer* (2012) (coauthored with Mitch Simon and Nicole Negowetti); "Kantian Restorative Justice?" *Criminal Justice Ethics* 29–1 (2010): 55–70 (review essay); "Commodification in Law: Ideologies, Intractabilities, and Hyperboles," *Continental Philosophy Review* 42/1 (2009): 101–29; "The Penitent and the Penitentiary: Questions Regarding Apologies in Criminal Law," *Criminal Justice Ethics*, Summer/Fall (2008): 2, 82–85; and "The Categorical Apology," *The Journal of Social Philosophy* 36/4 (2005): 473–496. I genuinely appreciate all of their patience and dedication to the details that add credibility to scholarship.

But my wife Nicole is the best editor – as well as the best person – I have ever worked with. She has many talents, and I must resist breaking into verse to declare my appreciation for her here. Our house overflows with love thanks to her. As with apologies, my gratitude to her cannot be expressed merely in words. It orients me every day.

My three young children contributed to this book in ways I hardly understand. Because they are little for so short a time, every experience becomes endowed with such significance. Children amplify the significance of life, which is why I refer to them as my "meaning machines." Caring for such beloved children as I thought about the examples in this book brought all of it home. The people I discuss – the worst offenders and the most sympathetic victims – were once young and just wanting to play and cuddle. Then something terrible happened. As we analyze these cases we can become desensitized to the suffering of these people and their struggles. We risk treating them as cases, abstractions we never look in the eye. The fragility of my own children reminds me of the humanity and finitude they share with all victims and offenders. I note this here because the cold lens of analysis risks obscuring the respect I intend to afford everyone involved in the injuries considered in this book. The following pages document much pain, and I hope my arguments perform a bit of alchemy to convert those losses into a future with less suffering.

Finally, my mother and father continue to provide unwavering support for everything I do. That is a great gift – the foundation of my spirit – that I try to always pay forward.

I have been surrounded by such love and opportunity. Thank you all.

Introduction

In 1984, William Beebe drugged and raped eighteen-year-old Liz Seccuro at a University of Virginia Phi Kappa Psi party. Seccuro awoke the next day wrapped in a bloody sheet on the couch of the deserted fraternity house. She confirmed Beebe's identity by the mail on his dresser. Still bloodied and bruised, Seccuro reported the attack. Campus authorities and Charlottesville police treated her claim dismissively and obstructed her access to a proper investigation. Beebe claimed she had consented. Feeling stonewalled and hoping to move forward with the rest of her education and life, Seccuro stopped pursuing legal recourse.

Twenty-one years later, Seccuro pulled out of her driveway en route to a vacation with her spouse and young child. She stopped at the mailbox and found the following letter:

Dear Elizabeth:

In October 1984 I harmed you. I can scarcely begin to understand the degree to which, in your eyes, my behaviour has affected you in its wake. Still, I stand prepared to hear from you about just how, and in what ways you've been affected; and to begin to set right the wrong I've done, in any way you see fit.

Most sincerely yours,
Will Beebe[1]

In a subsequent exchange of e-mails where Beebe explained that he was undergoing a twelve-step addiction recovery program, he confessed to a decades-old crime for which he was not under investigation and that carries a maximum sentence of life imprisonment. "I want to make clear that I'm not intentionally minimizing the fact of having raped you," he wrote, "I did." Seccuro took this opportunity in 2005 to contact Charlottesville police. This time they properly investigated her claim. She pressed charges against Beebe.

Despite his confession, Beebe hired a Charlottesville criminal defence attorney who rigorously contested Seccuro's account of events and claimed in Beebe's defense: "This was bad behaviour, poor judgment, immature, and all those other things, but it was not a rape."[2] Further investigation revealed that three men raped Seccuro while she was unconscious that night. This complicated the case, and the state agreed to a plea arrangement whereby Beebe admitted guilt to aggravated sexual battery.

At sentencing Beebe stated:

My only purpose in contacting Ms. Seccuro was to make amends for my conduct twenty-two years ago. I am not trying to excuse my behaviour, but I was a different person then. I was an immature nineteen year old with a drinking problem that I did not yet fully understand.... It was not until thirteen years ago when I became willing to address all my mistakes in accountability using these tenants [sic] that I could even stay sober, let alone find the inner freedom that I have today. Since that time, in adopting a new way of life, I have a purpose and that gives life meaning. I didn't have that then.[3]

Beebe's peers from Alcoholics Anonymous testified to his commitment to sobriety and his exceptional service to others struggling with addiction. Judge Edward L. Hogshire found that Beebe had "been a leader in the recovery community" in ways he had "never seen before."[4] Hogshire asked himself: "Is he remorseful? I think so."[5] Beebe received a 10-year sentence, with all but 18 months suspended on the condition that he perform 500 hours of community service in the area of sexual assault and substance abuse on campuses. He served five months.[6]

This extraordinary example captures many of the complexities regarding the role of apologies in law. Contemporary prisons in the United States descend from eighteenth-century penitentiaries, to which society sent its outcasts to study their bibles, experience quiet self-alienation, hear the word of Christ, and repent. Although we wince at the idea of secular states engaging in such soul crafting, this institutional DNA lives on in modern rituals of penance as we expect judges to divine the essence of the offender's nature. Approximately one in every thirty-four adults in the United States is under correctional supervision of the criminal justice system.[7] In many if not all of these 7 million cases, state agents determined punishments in part according to impressions of whether the offender appeared remorseful or apologetic. These numbers do not include the millions of crimes that never reach the justice system because authorities – for example, parents, teachers, police, or prosecutors – exercise discretion to avoid formal charges because of an offender's apparent contrition.

Although it can seem as if the bureaucracy of justice accounts for every detail in criminal procedures, decisions regarding findings of remorse occur in the star chambers of intuition. State officials consult their gut feelings, evaluate a few emotional cues, and render unappealable decisions regarding the offender's character. They usually do not explain why they find an offender's remorse compelling, nor do they offer insight into or defend the standards of contrition that orient their decision. They often rely on instincts, allowing a variety of explicit and implicit biases to color their intuitions. Officials rarely mention that the offender's attitudes impact sentencing, and when they do flag these elements they typically invoke arguably the most overused, opaque, and imprecise term in law: remorse. The Federal Sentencing Guidelines attempted to add some substance to the cultic concept by allowing for reductions in sentences for those who "accept responsibility," but in practice accepting responsibility has come to mean agreeing to a plea *even while denying guilt*. The U.S. Supreme Court has recognized that findings of remorse can determine whether an offender lives or dies, yet we entrust such determinations to "know it when I see it" standards as if judges and juries can look into the eyes of offenders, intuit the depths of their evil, and punish accordingly.

Return to Beebe in the context of these traditions. On the one hand, Beebe's confession and expressions of remorse speak to core issues of justice. An act of voluntary confession inviting life in prison in order to make amends bespeaks such reform that ordinary punitive measures seem inappropriate. His story seems more at home in religious parables than in a prosecutor's statement of facts. Denigrating this as "*just* an apology" – a vacuous "legalogy" uttered in service of the offender's strategic interests – avoids difficult issues regarding how acts of contrition can advance objectives of justice and require us to reconsider how to respond justly to apologetic offenders.[8] The criminal justice system seems like such an unnatural habitat for such acts that we do not know what to make of Beebe. If he confesses, what is the role of his attorney? Why does she deny the rape and minimize its significance? If Beebe appreciates the seriousness of his offense, should he serve the maximum sentence rather than accept a plea? Should he tell the full story regarding the identity of the multiple attackers rather than leverage this knowledge to reduce his sentence? How should we view the apparent self-serving nature of Beebe's act of contacting the woman he raped? Completing his recovery program seems like his primary motivation for contacting Seccuro, even though this caused her considerable pain in forcing her to again confront her rapist on his terms. Is he so clueless about the seriousness of rape that he only realized the potential penalties after he confessed? Did he mistakenly believe a statute of limitations would protect him?

Somehow Hogshire resolved these rather complex moral and factual questions into an eighteen-month sentence. How did he come to this conclusion? What does remorse mean for this judge? Why exactly does Hogshire find Beebe genuinely remorseful? Precisely how does remorse warrant such a considerable reduction in punishment? Does such a light sentence belittle violence against women? If Beebe confessed to a rape, should courts treat him like all other rapists – repentant or not – lest they violate basic principles of equality under law? As in the vast majority of cases, we do not get to see the judge's evaluation here beyond a few words finding him remorseful. With no analysis to evaluate, appellate courts and courts of public opinion have little to scrutinize.

We also do not know whether Hogshire considered the broader context and the various other individuals and institutions involved in this case. Beebe knows the identity of the other rapists but refuses to implicate them. How did Hogshire reconcile this refusal to cooperate with his finding of Beebe's remorse? Did the justice system pursue the associate dean who gave Seccuro false legal information, seemingly to discourage her from pursuing a legal claim and tarnishing the school's reputation? In 2010, University of Virginia lacrosse player George Huguely beat his ex-girlfriend Yeardley Love to death after school officials missed multiple warning signs that Huguely presented dangers.[9] Huguely also appeared before Hogshire, and he hired the same defense attorney that negotiated such a light punishment for Beebe. Seccuro spoke at the university's Take Back the Night events three weeks *before* Love's murder, calling on administrators to do more to prevent violence against women on campus. At the time of Love's death the university did not require students to undergo any education in sexual assault, dating violence, or substance abuse.[10] Should the justice system hold the university and Charlottesville police accountable for their roles in these offenses? What sorts of meanings could apologies from such institutions hold? Should views change if instead of a privileged college student the apology comes from someone like Dumisani Rebombo, a black South African who now works as a national manager for the Sonke Gender Justice Network and who received no punishment when he apologized for gang-raping a woman twenty years after the crime?[11] Did Hogshire think through any of these issues of race and class? To what extent did he see Beebe as a brethren University of Virginia alumnus – Hogshire attended the school as both an undergraduate and a law student – to whom he afforded benefits of the doubt? Would he have been more skeptical of apologetic gestures from a defendant who did not share his race, gender, and educational pedigree?

The case of Conor McBride raises different sorts of questions regarding the extent to which apologies should reduce punishments.[12] Nineteen-year-old McBride had been arguing with his girlfriend Ann Grosmaire over the course of two days. As McBride tells the story, the exchanges escalated. In the drama of an overwrought teen romance, Ann said "I just want you to die." McBride took his father's gun, loaded it, and pointed it under his own chin. Ann came into the room and McBride put the gun down but entered into what he described as a "wrathful anger." Emotionally exhausted, Ann said in weeping convulsions that she wanted to die. McBride retrieved the gun claiming that this would "scare her" so that "maybe she would snap out of it." Finding her on her knees and "not thinking straight," he pointed the gun at her: "Is this what you want? Do you want to die?" He fired, tearing through the hand Ann raised to protect herself. An hour later he drove to the Tallahassee police department. "You need to arrest me," he told the officer. "I just shot my fiancée in the head."

Prosecutor Jack Campbell charged McBride with first-degree murder, which usually carries a mandatory life sentence in Florida. Campbell explained to Grosmaire's parents that he had considerable discretion in determining McBride's punishment. Before the murder, the Grosmaires treated McBride as a member of the family and expected him to become their son-in-law. In the throes of grief, Ann's father Andy believed he heard his comatose daughter tell him to forgive McBride. Andy Grosmaire recounts when he "realized it was not just Ann asking me to forgive Conor, it was Jesus Christ," explaining that "I hadn't said no to [Christ] before, and I wasn't going to start then." "It was just a wave of joy, and I told Ann: 'I will. I will.'"

Commanded to forgive by their god and murdered daughter, the Grosmaires embarked on a mission of restorative justice. With Prosecutor Campbell's reluctant permission, they enlisted a facilitator to conduct a pre-plea conference that would bring them together with McBride, his parents, a reverend, attorneys, and a photo of Ann along with a few of her belongings. The meeting began with McBride hugging his parents and the Grosmaires. They went around the circle to give participants the opportunity to speak without interruption. Campbell summarized the police reports. The Grosmaires spoke of Ann's birth, her childhood, her passions, her life plans, and their devotion to her. "You worked so hard to send her off into the world," said Ann's father capturing some of every parent's existential horror, "what was the purpose of that now?" Campbell found Grosmaires' testimony excruciating: "as traumatic as anything I've ever listened to in my life."

McBride had expressed his sorrow to the Grosmaires previously, but on this occasion he confessed to the details of the events leading to Ann's death. Despite not remembering a decision to pull the trigger, he accepted blame. In a later interview McBride explained his crime as "inexcusable." "There is no why, there are no excuses, there is no reason." He did not plan to shoot Ann, but he did not see her death as an accident: "[O]n some subconscious level, I guess, I wanted it all to end. I don't know what happened. I just – emotions were overwhelming."

After McBride finished speaking, the facilitator asked the participants for their views regarding restitution and punishment. In addition to a sentence of between five and fifteen years, Ann's mother wanted McBride "to do the good works of two people because Ann is not here to do hers." McBride's parent's agreed with Ann's father that ten to fifteen years was an appropriate sentence. McBride recognized that he should not weigh in regarding his punishment. Against the usual restorative justice protocol where such conferences end with a resolution, Campbell wanted time to think through the emotional process and to discuss the issues with community leaders and experts in violence against women. Campbell thought his supervisor would require a minimum sentence of forty years, but their office offered McBride twenty years plus ten years of probation. He now works in the prison library and enrolled in an anger management class. The Grosmaires say they have forgiven McBride, primarily as a means of what Ann's mother describes as "self-preservation." They visit him about once per month. Upon release, McBride plans to volunteer in animal shelters and to speak publicly about dating violence.

At first glance, McBride's case seems to tell of a remorseful offender who turns himself in and thereby earns deserved mercy from both the state and the victim's family – although readers unaccustomed to sentencing in the United States may still find a twenty-year sentence rather long and difficult to characterize as merciful. But notice troubling issues beneath the surface of this *New York Times* story of apology and forgiveness. Like Beebe, McBride turned himself in and confessed to the crime. But unlike Beebe, McBride surely would have been caught and convicted. Investigators discovered a history of McBride abusing Ann. Ann had written "The List" for McBride, seemingly to correct a history of mistreatment: "No aggressive cursing, no negative comments on physical appearance, no negative comments on relationship, no falling asleep on the phone while talking to me, no running away from our problems." Under the heading "Never Again" she listed "physical (sic) harm me, look at porn, cheat, try ending us due to anger, yell at me, keep me in the dark." McBride had hit Ann several times during their relationship. Investigators found an apology card stating "I'm sorry doesn't begin to cover how horrible I feel or how much I am going to make it up to you. I love you, Conor." A few days before her death, Ann texted Conor: "I'm starting to think it's a bad idea if we live together."[13] With this information the situation begins to look like a typical cycle of domestic violence characterized by a treadmill of contrition and abuse: abuse, apology, escalating abuse, intensified histrionics of remorse that convinces the victim to stay, and further escalation of abuse. A victim's attempt to break off the relationship can bring about the gravest threats, and this abusive relationship ends with nineteen-year-old Ann on her knees near the door pleading for her life. Her first serious boyfriend shoots her in the head. McBride recounts his side of the story in a manner that accepts responsibility while describing the shooting as almost-but-not-quite-accidental, says he is sorry, and sees his punishment effectively halved. Difficult questions abound.

Despite knowing that their relationship was toxic and subject to "wild swings," Ann's parents seemed to encourage it and embraced McBride. Should we wonder that the man who emotionally devastated Ann also manipulated her parents, both before the murder and after? Their remarkable mission to forgive McBride begins with Ann's very religious father literally hearing voices – both of his comatose daughter and of Jesus Christ – as he stands at her deathbed in incomprehensible grief. Should the state allow such impassioned and explicitly Christian motivations to guide its hand in punishment for murder? When a murderer silences a victim of domestic violence, should standard retributive and consequentialist penological objectives be overridden by the wishes of family members who put words of forgiveness into her mouth in order to advance their own interests? While we can feel great empathy for their desire to mitigate their pain and guilt for not intervening in what retrospectively appears to have been an abusive relationship, did these proceedings overvalue their interests at the expense of public objectives such as reducing violence against women?

Ann mistakenly believed Conor's apologetic promises to reform his behavior. Why should the state now believe in his transformation? The restorative justice facilitator asserts with remarkable ease that she is "not worried about him getting out in 20 years at all."[14] She explains that the process examined "more deeply at the root of where this behavior came from than we would have had it gone a trial route – the anger issues in the family, exploring the drama in their relationship, the whole conglomeration of factors that led to that moment." These important points emphasize the strengths of restorative justice over assembly line incarceration. But if she believes "there's no explaining what happened," how do we know that McBride deserves the sentence reduction? Do we have sufficient confidence in prison anger management programs to allow him to resume dating before he turns forty? What evidence do we have that he can control his impulses toward violence? How does the prosecutor weigh these factors? Campbell knows that "if Conor gets out in 20 years and goes and kills his next girlfriend, I've screwed up terrible." As an elected official, he also worries about political "backlash" against a light sentence. What convinces him that McBride has not put on a show of contrition because he realized that was the best way to play his legal hand? With Beebe, the court could review a twenty-year record of reformed behavior within civil society. Although far from providing certainty that Beebe would never reoffend, he presented a long and compelling record of staying clean.

How convincingly can we extrapolate McBride's future behavior based on what we know at the time of sentencing? He has been incarcerated since the day of the murder, so we have no evidence that he has learned to control his anger in the context of intimate relationships. Removed from the temptations to abuse other women, McBride offers little more than promises that decades from now he will publicly address dating violence and volunteer in animal shelters. Apologetic actions speak louder than apologetic words, and beyond turning himself in and confessing – powerful but ambiguous acts because of the likelihood that he would have been convicted even if he tried to flee – we have very few data points on the extent of his contrition. Expecting a prosecutor, judge, or jury – however thoughtful and fair – to peer into McBride's soul and decide his fate seems unreasonable if not delusional. Even if we could prove that McBride has undergone a genuine moral transformation and that he provides a categorical apology for murdering Ann, does that entail that the state should reduce his punishment? Where did prosecutor Campbell look for the answer to that question?

Like Beebe's story, McBride's case makes for a gripping magazine article on the alchemical abilities of remorse and forgiveness to transform a brutal attack against a defenseless woman into a narrative of grace. These stories attract us, in part, because they remind us that humans can be simultaneously the ugliest and the most beautiful of creatures. But these situations raise far more questions than they answer about the relationship between apologies and justice, and I fear that our desire to find a silver lining of redemption in the most inhumane actions – as if all of the horror happens for some cosmic reason – clouds our ability to think clearly about how we should treat apologetic offenders. It has taken me two books to identify and address these questions. In 2008, I published *I Was Wrong: The Meanings of Apologies*.[15] I originally intended to establish a conceptual framework for apologetic meaning and apply that framework to criminal and civil law in *I Was Wrong*. That proved naively ambitious. One book became two as I realized the richness of the subject. The first book developed a framework for apologetic meanings. This book applies that framework to law.

I Was Wrong argued that our beliefs about the moral substance and social functions of apologies are honeycombed with deep confusions. Rather than asking the binary question of whether a speech act "is or is not" an apology, I attempted to account for the many ways that acts of contrition succeed or fail to achieve various objectives. I argued that apologies have evolved from a confluence of diverse cultural and religious practices that do not translate easily into pluralistic secular discourse, but I made the case for a robust core of meanings conveyed by what I named a "categorical apology." I summarize that argument in Chapter 1 of this book, but in general a few questions guide my thinking: Did the offender explain what she did with an appropriate degree of specificity? Does she accept blame rather than merely express sympathy? Does she resist casting the offense as an accident or otherwise deny that it was her intention to harm? Does she make clear why her actions were wrong and identify the principles she violated? Does she promise not to do it again? Does she keep that promise? Does she provide appropriate redress? Does she understand apology as an ongoing process, a kind of treatment for wrongdoing rather than a cure? Veblen's quip that researchers should seek "to make two questions grow where one question grew before" describes my experience with the subject, as a complex second set of questions sprouted regarding apologies from collectives. Although apologies from corporations, governments, and other groups can be profoundly significant, *I Was Wrong* flagged the kinds of meaning that collective apologies often do not convey and warned of the dangers of collective acts of contrition that allow individual wrongdoers to obscure their personal blame. This comparatively high-resolution conceptual framework allows me to look a bit deeper into the dark corners of apologies in legal contexts.

The Two Faces of Apologies in Law
I Was Wrong argued that much of our private and public moral discourse occurs in the giving, receiving, or demanding of apologies. Daily headlines feature someone apologizing or calling for someone to apologize. We understand that certain kinds of apologies can amount to life-transforming events for both victims and offenders in crisis situations, and we also appreciate that apologies serve as the daily bread of our moral discourse as we develop social habits. Whether teaching our children when and how to say they are sorry, expecting contrition from our spouse when we feel wronged, or lobbying for an apology from institutions responsible for historical injustices, apologetic rituals provide one of the most familiar and significant occasions when we think explicitly about our shared values. Yet we rarely consider precisely what we expect from a gesture of contrition. As a result, apologizing has become a vague, clumsy, and sometimes spiteful ritual. We all know that some apologies can be worse than none at all. Empty gestures may masquerade as soul-searching apologies, sometimes because this seems like the least burdensome means of returning a relationship to the desired state. Sometimes apologies become weaponized in various social conflicts, for instance when an offender intentionally wishes to deceive and manipulate a victim with an apology. Such duplicity occurs not only between adversaries but also among friends, relatives, and lovers. Whether an unrepentant executive orders her attorney to feign contrition so that an injured party will settle a claim or an abusive partner with no intention to reform claims to be "sorry that" a lover is upset, victims stand to suffer further injuries if they attribute more substance to an apology than warranted.

Whereas religion and its practices of repentance and perdition once provided the backdrop for apologies, a legal environment driven by adversarial procedures and oriented toward economic outcomes increasingly frames our apologies. This creates a tension. Apologies bring people together. Adversarial law typically pushes legal combatants apart in high-stakes competitions. It might therefore seem like apologies would play a minor role in modern legal proceedings, but the situation is decidedly more convoluted. On the one hand – and as we might initially expect – apologies seem out of place in most modern legal contexts. What I describe as categorical apologies, for instance, admit guilt. Whether in criminal hearings, corporate settlement negotiations, or malpractice litigation, admitting guilt in an adversarial justice system can amount to legal suicide.[16] As the American Medical Association once warned physicians: "Anything you say can and will be held against you."[17] Some medical malpractice insurers will void their policies if doctors provide too many details to injured patients.[18] Corporate executives and directors of various institutions resist apologizing not only because they fear personal exposure to liability but also because they risk breaching fiduciary duties to their constituencies. Criminal defense attorneys typically advise clients to resist apologizing to victims, even if the defendant feels a moral compunction to "come clean" early in the proceedings. Skepticism for the efficacy of rehabilitative techniques, increased support for standardized sentencing, a desire to avoid state involvement in an offender's religious awakening through repentance, and a refusal to fund the sorts of therapeutic programs that might promote moral development all point away from early views of penance as the primary objective of the penitentiary.

For some, the problem is metaphysical rather than strategic. Blackstone wrote in his eighteenth-century *Commentaries on the Laws of England* that law concerns fallible humans but repentance is a matter "left to the just determination of the Supreme Being."[19] As Leszek Kolakowski phrases it, "legal punishment is for transgressions of law, but sin is part of the moral order of the universe." As such, "ideas of sin, of evil, of guilt, of repentance, are beyond the scope of the legal system; the law can function well without them."[20] Given that contemporary secular apologies inherit much of their meanings from religious rituals and these practices do not always translate into the legal vernacular of the liberal state, we might interpret the many complexities regarding apologies in law as a sign that their logics stand beyond our mortal capacities. In all of these respects, the sorts of morally rich apologies that I describe in *I Was Wrong* seem antithetical to the very spirit of modern adversarial law. Legal battlegrounds hardly provide a natural habitat conducive to reconciliation through moral transformation.[21]

On the other hand, current legal trends point toward a rise in the prevalence of certain kinds of apologies in law. Building on findings in the social sciences,[22] legal scholarship and legislation now reinforce the belief that strategically timed and worded apologies can prevent litigation altogether, reduce damage payments and jury awards by considerable amounts, or shave years from prison sentences.[23] The U.S. Federal Sentencing Guidelines permit judges to reduce punishments by considerable amounts for defendants who "accept responsibility" for their crimes.[24] Expressions of remorse can be the difference between life and death in capital sentencing procedures.[25]

In civil law, research suggests that apologies provide an astoundingly successful means of mollifying disputants.[26] Many suggestive social scientific studies have appeared in the past twenty years, but consider a few of the more striking recent arguments for increasing the role of apologies in law.[27] Michael Woods, a physician and leading advocate for apologies as a means of reducing medical malpractice litigation, claims that the "likelihood of a lawsuit falls by 50-percent when an apology is offered and the details of a medical error are disclosed immediately."[28] Evidence from nineteen medical malpractice cases indicates that 91 percent of cases in which the defendants offered an apology settled, whereas only 38 percent settled when the defense did not apologize.[29] Jennifer Robbennolt reached similar conclusions in her experiments, finding that receiving an apology that accepted responsibility increased the likelihood that a respondent would agree to a settlement offer by 21 percent.[30] A team at the Nottingham School of Economics' Centre for Decision Research and Experimental Economics claimed in a 2009 study that apologizers received considerable benefits even for obviously insincere apologies.[31] Another 2009 paper argues that those who apologize for corporate transgressions should pay special attention to the shape of the spokesperson's face – a "baby face" is best for minor offenses, but a mature face better conveys seriousness in light of grave wrongdoing.[32] Apology consulting has become a cottage industry.

Apologies came to thrive in such a seemingly hostile environment in large part because of a rather audacious adaptive strategy: the campaign to define apologies as something other than a confession and admission of guilt. Contrary to my arguments in *I Was Wrong* and without any serious consideration of the moral features and cultural histories of repentance, various attorneys and legal scholars repeat versions of the convenient assurance that "an apology is specifically *not* synonymous with an admission of guilt," as they advise legal parties to exploit the ambiguities of apologetic language to their advantage.[33] Once divorced from blame, apologies emerge as tactical defense that "should be part of the arsenal of resources brought to bear in addressing and resolving legal disputes."[34] Attorneys can deploy such apologies as an "attitudinal structuring tactic" to "lubricate settlement discussions" and "influence an opponent's bargaining behavior."[35] Apology becomes a wolf in sheep's clothing.

The medical field embodies these two faces of apologies in law, as it underwent a dramatic transformation by evolving from an "admit nothing" culture to a profession that routinely advises physicians to apologize for adverse outcomes to minimize the costs associated with medical malpractice litigation.[36] Indeed, apologies have become so institutionalized in law that many states now provide evidentiary "safe havens" for certain types of apologies, with some of these laws explicitly encouraging physicians to offer gestures of contrition in the hope that apologetic doctors will be sued less and thereby advance the objectives of tort reform its corporate backers. Prompted by a legislator who sought an apology from the driver who struck and killed his daughter, Massachusetts's version of this statute provides that statements or writings expressing "sympathy or a general sense of benevolence relating to the pain, suffering or death of a person involved in an accident and made to such person or to the family of such person shall be inadmissible as evidence of an admission of liability in a civil action."[37] Whether spoken by a convict or a practicing physician, a sympathetic expression that "I am sorry your daughter died" conveys very different meanings from an admission that "I deserve blame for killing your daughter." Although this distinction seems rather obvious on reflection, legislators, attorneys, and academics routinely describe such expressions of sympathy – and the even more vague "general sense of benevolence" – as "apologies." Laws of evidence have transformed in the wake of these findings as tort-reforming lobbyists support legislation that maximizes the benefits of apologies for wrongdoers while protecting them from the legal disadvantages of admitting wrongdoing. "Safe apology" legislation sends mixed messages, with some states protecting only expressions of sympathy, whereas others protect various sorts of admissions of wrongdoing.[38] Some statutes apply only to cases of medical error.[39] Other states provide general protection for apologies while leaving the term ambiguous.[40] Airlines have been early adopters welcoming apologies into corporate culture. Southwest Airlines employs a full-time "apology officer" who sends out roughly 20,000 letters – which all include his direct phone number – to dissatisfied customers per year.[41] Continental attributes more than $150,000 in new revenue to its practice of sending apologetic letters to customers experiencing adverse "transportation events."[42]

A History of the Tension
Repeating some of the philosophical genealogy of apologies from *I Was Wrong* provides some context for the conflicted existence of apologies in law.[43] Consider Plato's *Apology* in which Socrates does not offer anything like what we would now consider an apology.[44] Instead, he provides an *apologia* as was customary in the classical Greek legal system in rebuttal to the prosecution's accusations. Rather than accept blame or even express sympathy, Socrates' *apologia* argues for his innocence and righteousness. *Apologia* still finds use in this sense of offering a defense of one's position, and the field of apologetics has come to be associated with the tradition of defending and reinforcing religious doctrine – particularly Christian beliefs – through argumentation. In modern parlance we consider an "apologist" to be a sort of spokesperson who promotes and defends causes by using various rhetorical strategies to spin facts and influence an audience, sometimes performing this service for pay. The modern use of apology as an admission of wrongdoing rather than a defense seems to have gained momentum around

the sixteenth century, when Shakespeare used it in *Richard III* to imply a kind of regret.⁴⁵

The etymology of apology pulls in two directions. On the one hand, we associate apologizing with repentance, confession, remorse, blame, and moral *defenselessness*. On the other hand, a considerable period of history understood the practice precisely as a *defense*. A third convention came into usage around 1754 and defined *apology* and *sorry* as a poor substitute, as in a "sorry excuse for a friendship" or "crackers served as but an apology for dinner." The *Oxford English Dictionary* recognizes each of these forms as acceptable definitions of "apology."⁴⁶ Given this plurality of occasionally competing meanings, consider an attorney acting as a paid apologist in the old sense as she instructs her client to offer something like an apology in the modern sense because this may be her best rhetorical strategy for the optimal legal outcome. Now imagine the attorney calibrating the apology to avoid admitting wrongdoing to maximize the strategic benefit of her client appearing to have undergone a moral transformation while minimizing legal exposure. The legal landscape becomes still more inscrutable when we appreciate that most criminal cases result in pleas and most civil cases result in settlements. A public apology within formal sentencing proceedings presents different issues than confidential statements of contrition protected by settlement agreements. Thus various legal parties may hold very different understandings of the meanings of an apology on the table. The public may have another reading altogether.

These legal and cultural environments coevolve. Legal institutions and strategies structure our conceptions of the moral components of apologies, and our moral traditions of apologizing for blameworthy behavior shape our legal practices. This dialectical interplay between moral norms and legal institutions requires us to make sense of apologies as they transform from the ancient notion of a legal defense to the modern notion of contrition for wrongdoing but then occasionally return to their roots as a kind of concealed legal, political, or personal rhetorical stratagem. Given that so many of our conversations about our deepest values occur in the context of apologizing and so many offenses within modern culture become legal disputes, the feedback between apologies and law resonates throughout modern moral discourse.

I do not wish to overstate the significance of apologies in law. If one doubts the law's influence over our culture of apologies, however, place any example from *I Was Wrong* within the context of the victim having already brought a legal claim of some sort against the offender. Notice how the fear that an apology may void our insurance coverage influences our interactions at the scene of an automobile accident or how we might give extra thought to the wording of an apology for infidelity if it might be used against us in divorce proceedings. We often act as if we expect the lawyers circling overhead to descend at the first sign of contrition, and this can have a chilling effect on apologetic discourse and our everyday moral interactions.

Thesis and Methodology
With all of this in mind, we can appreciate the complexities of finding these highly nuanced rituals of contrition within the labyrinths of modern legal institutions and culture. This book attempts not only to make explicit the various kinds of meaning hidden in acts of contrition by legal agents but also to empower those parties by providing them with tools to evaluate the apologies given and received.

After reviewing my theories of categorical and collective apologies, I will make three core arguments. Chapter 2 argues that court-ordered apologies add very little value to the meanings and functions already present in contemporary legal proceedings and punishments. They also present considerable costs. I evaluate Kant's infamous advocacy for court-ordered apologies as retributive humiliation as well as arguments from contemporary Kantians who support court-ordered apologies on somewhat less divisive grounds. I then consider various consequentialist arguments for and against court-ordered apologies. Any value we might derive from court-ordered apologies, I conclude, can probably be better realized through less problematic means.

Second, I argue that, in principle, the state should in most cases significantly reduce punishments for categorically apologetic offenders. This holds true, I claim, across a range of underlying justifications for punishment that includes both consequentialist and retributive theories. Although categorically apologetic offenders typically deserve reductions in punishment, implementing such a principle presents numerous practical issues that threaten to undermine the feasibility of my view. Distinguishing the "truly repentant" from the disingenuous, for instance, requires considerable theoretical nuance as well as sophisticated institutional procedures. However, just as the criminal justice system routinely evaluates the credibility of various legal agents and judges the mental states of its subjects, so too can it develop methods for evaluating contrition. Particularly in the context of the dark history of confessions in law, vast social and economic inequalities and the procedural mechanisms that compound these injustices complicate any general claim that those who apologize well should be punished less. I identify and address these practical issues.

Third, Part II identifies what I consider the most significant and worrisome issues regarding the role of apologies in civil proceedings. I first explain the counterintuitive situation whereby apologies come to have considerable financial worth in legal contexts because their deep moral associations appear to transcend economic matters. Apologies become so expensive in civil cases, in other words, in part because people associate them with *priceless* matters of the soul. Because of their ability to save wrongdoers millions, apologies and their knock-offs flood markets in dispute resolution. Gaming the new economy of apologies becomes an element of legal representation. Incentives arise to create and control the narrative that apologies "have nothing to do with fault" because this allows offenders to appear contrite – thus gaining the benefits of seeming like they underwent a moral transformation – without exposing them to the risks associated with accepting blame. Manipulative offenders pool ambiguity into the soft spots of our desire for justice and dignity. We want to believe that they really are sorry and will not do this again, and we want to believe so badly that we are vulnerable to deception. I argue that understanding these dynamics will empower legal agents to understand the sorts of meanings actually conveyed in civil apologies and to insist on the meanings they desire. If a victim of an oil spill, for example, wants the offender to admit fault and change safety protocols, she should be wary of a spokesperson claiming to apologize for the harm by merely "expressing sympathy to everyone harmed." Has anyone, we should ask, said anything like "I was wrong"? I find it especially important to raise awareness of these dynamics so that sophisticated offenders do not manipulate ambiguities of apologetic language to deceive disadvantaged victims. Because so many civil matters address harms caused by institutions such as governments and corporations, readers will find the bulk of my analysis of collective apologies in law in Part II.

I will not spend much time here discussing my methodological choices, and I refer those interested in such questions to the early chapters of *I Was Wrong*. In addition to avoiding a binary approach that would define what "is" and "is not" an apology, *I Was Wrong* looked to other disciplines for help identifying the many forms of meaning that apologies can convey. This book takes a similar "kitchen sink approach" and aims to synthesize research from the humanities and sciences into a unified account of the role of apologies in law that might serve as a conceptual framework for further research in legal apologies across disciplines. This became especially important to me after I spent time digesting empirical research on apologizing and realized that many of these studies operated with – and perpetuated – deeply problematic definitions. Some studies would simply stipulate a controversial definition without attempting to explain, for instance, why an apology did not require an acceptance of responsibility or a demonstrated commitment not to reoffend. Some researchers simply "counted" every utterance of "sorry" as an apology, even in cases of "I'm sorry your grandmother passed away" or "I'm sorry you feel that way." Considering that I am interested in empirical questions related to apologies – such as whether women apologize more frequently than men or whether apologies track recidivism rates in juvenile criminal offenders – I hope the conceptual work in this book proves useful for those who try to measure such things.

I should note here my reasons for building these arguments around apologies rather than various related terms such as remorse, contrition, penance, and atonement. As I discuss elsewhere, legal circles tend to favor *remorse* as the operative term.[47] As I understand it, apology offers a much more capacious and multifaceted concept because of its ability to accommodate a range of mental states, behaviors, and traditions. Remorse, in contrast, tends to describe primarily one aspect of a wrongdoer's mental states – typically an emotional state. Discussions of remorse tend to cluster around *feeling bad* and pay insufficient attention to post-offense behavior, which strikes me as especially confusing because the term derives from the French for fine and compensatory redress.[48] Other terms have a similar narrowness. *Contrition* typically refers to a mental state. *Penance* emphasizes ritualized remedial activity. *Repentance* probably offers the broadest analogue to apology, but – like penance, atonement, and contrition – it conjures religious rituals. Apology offers a secular umbrella concept covering many additional features of post-offense identity. Apology is also far and away the favored term in contemporary Western culture, although perhaps less so in more theocratic cultures.

As a final pragmatic point, we need a reasonably compelling and consistently applied standard against which to measure apologies. What sort of apology does the state or victim seek? Does the offender provide those meanings? What sort of apology deserves what sorts of legal consequences? Confusion about such questions, as I will argue at length, tends to benefit wrongdoers – especially powerful wrongdoers with the facility to manipulate apologetic exchanges. Apologies in legal settings dredge up an unconscious sludge of biases, emotions, and conditioning in our reptilian brains. They can also summon the better angels of our nature. The absence of a common language of apologies makes reconciliation all the more difficult and contributes to the sorts of post-offense confusions that escalate conflicts. The prescriptively stipulated notion of a categorical apology provides a moral landmark. When we confront an offender like Beebe, McBride, or British Petroleum, it marks where we should look to evaluate the substance of the transformation. Otherwise we will find ourselves adrift in the fog of apologetic spin.

CHAPTER ONE

The Categorical Apology Revisited

A. The Elements of a Categorical Apology

I Was Wrong considers a wide variety of apologetic meanings and warns against thinking of apologies in binary "all or nothing" terms. The following benchmarks guide my standards for categorical apologies and serve as touchstones for our thinking about apologies in law. Categorical apologies, which I understand as a regulative ideal for acts of contrition, address the following concerns:

1. Corroborated Factual Record: A categorical apology will corroborate a detailed factual record of the events salient to the injury, reaching agreement among the victim, offender, and sometimes the community regarding what transpired. The parties will also agree regarding what amounts to such salient events, leading them to share an understanding of the relevant aspects of the context in which the injury occurs. Rather than providing general and vague descriptions of the events ("I acted badly"), the record will render transparent all facts material to judging the transgressions. Such a record will often include honest accounts of the mental states of the apologizer at the time of the offense when such information would prove relevant, for example by describing the offender's intentions when committing the transgression.
2. Acceptance of Blame: In accordance with prevailing notions of proximate causation, the offender accepts causal moral responsibility and blame for the harm at issue. We can distinguish this from expressing sympathy for the injury or describing the injury as accidental or unintentional. We can maintain a binocular view of wrongdoing that attributes individual blame while appreciating environmental and structural contributors to wrongdoing such as systemic inequality.
3. Possession of Appropriate Standing: The categorical apologizer will possess the requisite standing to accept blame for the wrongdoing. The offender can and does accept proximate responsibility for the harm and

she – rather than a proxy or other third party – undertakes the work of apologizing described herein.
4. Identification of Each Harm: The offender will identify each harm, taking care not to conflate several harms into one general harm or to apologize for only a lesser offense or the "wrong wrong."
5. Identification of the Moral Principles Underlying Each Harm: The offender will identify the moral principles underlying these harms with an appropriate degree of specificity, thus making explicit the values at stake in the interaction.
6. Shared Commitment to Moral Principles Underlying Each Harm: The offender will commit to the moral principles underlying these harms (again with an appropriate degree of specificity), vindicating the value at issue and finding the victim's offense at the apologizer's breach of this value justified. Here the phrase "I was wrong" will better convey this meaning than the traditionally favored "I am sorry," as the former accepts personal blame for wrongdoing whereas the latter may provide no more than an expression of sympathy or a displeasure with a state of affairs.
7. Recognition of Victim as Moral Interlocutor: Through this process the offender comes to recognize and treat the victim as a moral interlocutor. The offender treats the victim as a moral agent worthy of engaging in moral discourse and abandons the belief that she can disregard the victim's dignity, humanity, or worth in pursuit of her own objectives.
8. Categorical Regret: The offender categorically regrets the actions in question, meaning she believes that she has made a mistake that she wishes could be undone. We can distinguish this from continuing to endorse one's decisions but expressing sympathy regarding what the offender perceives as the justifiable consequences of her actions: I wish I didn't have to cause you such pain, but you deserved it and I'll do it again if I need to.
9. Performance of the Apology: The offender expresses the apology to the victim rather than keeping her thoughts of contrition to herself or sharing them only with a third party such as a judge or member of the clergy. She addresses the apology to the victim as a moral interlocutor. She expresses the content required of a categorical apology explicitly. The apology reaches the victim. The victim may exercise reasonable discretion regarding whether the offender must present the apology only to the victim or also to a broader community. We should generally defer to the victim's reasonable discretion regarding whether the apology should be committed to writing.
10. Reform: The apologizer will reform and forbear from reoffending over her lifetime and will repeatedly demonstrate this commitment by resisting opportunities and temptations to reoffend. A categorical apology

allows the victim to isolate the cause of her suffering, apportion blame for her injury, and take some security in the offender's pledge never to repeat the offense.[1]

11. Redress: The apologizer takes practical responsibility for the harm she causes, providing commensurate remedies and other incommensurable forms of redress to the best of her ability. The offender provides a proportional amount of redress, but she need not meet excessive demands from victims with unreasonable or inappropriate expectations. I leave questions regarding what constitutes unreasonable or excessive demands to be determined in consideration of cultural practices, and I appreciate that such deliberations will often be contentious. The apologizer accepts legal sanctions for her wrongs, although she may protest these penalties to the extent that she finds them unjustifiable as disproportionate to her offense.

12. Intentions for Apologizing: The categorical apology also requires certain mental states. Rather than promoting the apologizer's purely self-serving objectives, the offender intends the apology to advance the victim's well-being and to affirm the breached value. Benefits the offender receives from her apology – such as restored social standing or reduced punishment – arise as the by-product rather than the primary objective of the apology.

13. Emotions: As a result of her wrongdoing, the apologizer experiences an appropriate degree and duration of sorrow and guilt as well as empathy and sympathy for the victim. I leave questions regarding the appropriate qualitative and quantitative emotional components of categorical apologies to be determined in consideration of cultural practices and individual expectations.

I defend each of these benchmarks at length in *I Was Wrong*. Conceived as such, categorical apologies are demanding acts that indicate a kind of moral transformation that resonates with thick conceptions of repentance within religious traditions. A categorical apology in the legal context can begin the process of turning one's life around. With a categorical apology, the crisis becomes the offender's finest hour as contrition steers her toward walking a different path. The categorical apology relegates the offense to a chapter in their lives rather than allowing the misdeeds to define them.

I could have adjusted the standards up or down, but I find that these criteria capture what we might think of in Iris Murdoch's terms as a "highest manifestation" of the practice as opposed to a "lowest common denominator" between anything that might arguably be classified as an apology.[2] We should recognize when apologies fall short of this standard and pursue their full meaning or understand them as less than categorical. This is not to say that all apologies must be categorical or that all noncategorical apologies are meaningless, insincere, inauthentic, or otherwise deficient for their purposes. I detail and classify many kinds of apologies in *I Was Wrong*, and the categorical apology offers but one possible arrangement of such meanings.[3] These principles identified in the categorical apology should, however, help us organize our thinking as we consider the role of apologies in law. When an abbreviated account is useful, we can refer to the *four corners of apologies*: explaining what happened with sufficient detail, accepting blame as deserved, not reoffending, and providing appropriate redress.

With a standard in place, we can measure particular examples against it. Not all injuries call for categorical apologies, and we can seek more or less apologetic meaning depending on the circumstances. The elements of categorical apologies involve multiple and sometimes discrete meanings, and occasionally only one of the meanings will concern us. If someone steps on my toe, I may be satisfied with any expression that simply conveys that the harm was not intentional. If someone dents my car, I may seek little more than a fulfilled promise to pay for repairs. This also applies to culturally divergent conceptions of apologies.[4] Some groups emphasize different aspects of apologies, for instance deeming an apology satisfactory even if the offender feigns remorse or does not accept fault for the harm. I am less concerned with whether such interactions should be properly understood as an "apology" or some translation of the term than I am with deciphering how such statements convey or omit various meanings. A fine-grained conception of apologies helps us make sense of the range of possible meanings that a categorical apology can convey so that we can better compare the apologies we receive with the meanings we desire.

Parties could agree to depart from the standards provided by the categorical apology, adjusting the apologetic substance they seek to their situation and desires. Indeed, we might worry that a gesture that followed my script for a categorical apology might appear too rehearsed. If an offender appears to provide a paint-by-numbers apology, we might question her intentions and the depth of her clichéd understanding of the gesture she enacts. In some cases, diverging from the script could prove especially important. If an offender has extreme difficulties expressing emotions, for example, the victim might appreciate this idiosyncrasy and be entirely satisfied with something other than a categorical apology. Again, the point is not that every expression of apologetic meaning must satisfy the elements of a categorical apology. Nor do I mean to make the best the enemy of the good or imply that "imperfect" apologies are necessarily flawed in some way. Instead, the categorical apology provides a touchstone against which we can interpret and compare all apologetic expressions.

A few points of clarification may be useful for the subsequent discussions. Notice that we could not categorically apologize for an accident unless somehow we could consistently accept blame for the harm. Disagreements about the worth of the underlying breached value – if a drug offender believes in legalization, for instance – also block categorical apologies. Unless we consider them moral interlocutors, we cannot categorically apologize to children, animals, or inanimate objects. The death of the victim or the offender forecloses the possibility of a categorical apology in all but the most exceptional cases. Deathbed apologies will likely prevent the offender from demonstrating reform or completing redress.

Because forbearance, reform, and redress present an ongoing task for the offender, we cannot conclusively measure her contrition against the standard of the categorical apology at the moment she offers it but rather will judge it over the course of her lifetime. In this respect we should view apologies as a form of treatment rather than a cure. This presents something of a problem in that we cannot immediately declare a gesture or ceremony to have "categorically apologized" because so much work remains. We can consider apologies at this declarative stage to be a kind of promise. A categorical apology keeps its promises, and therefore we might describe the gesture before the offender has completed reform and redress as a "promissory categorical apology." If the offender breaks her promise to reform and provide redress over her lifetime, her gesture would not rise to the level of a categorical apology. Because categorical apologies are usually works in progress, in the strict sense we should refer to even the most exemplary apologies between the living as promissory categorical apologies. Some may find this inability to definitively judge an apology at the moment it is offered to be a nuisance. The sorts of moral development associated with categorical apologies do not typically occur over a news cycle or even a few weeks of court proceedings.[5]

Emotional requirements present especially difficult issues. How much emotion is required, what is the necessary intensity and duration of those emotions, and how might we measure such quantities? Max Scheler describes the "simultaneous peace and contentment which may rise to the height of bliss" that can accompany repentance.[6] How should we evaluate negative emotions associated with apologies when concurrent with the positive emotions of moral improvement? Just as I do not provide restitution schedules for every possible sort of injury, I leave parties to negotiate such potentially intractable questions in accordance with their customs and sensibilities.

Although we may desire instant and conclusive gratification from a gesture of contrition, categorical apologies require patience from both the offender and the victim. We should meet urges to prematurely judge apologies with suspicion and scrutinize the motivations behind such haste. We should be especially wary of those who attempt to simplify the exchange so that they can "put it behind them," "find closure," or "turn the page." Such sloppy metaphysical language betrays a clear understanding of the many vectors of apologetic meanings. I repeat the mantra: *Apologies are treatments rather than cures. We should view initial apologetic gestures as beginnings rather than conclusions.*

I attempt to flag questions that would benefit from further empirical research, and I make efforts – to the best of admittedly novice ability – to engage and learn from social scientific literature across a range of fields. Apologies present genuinely interdisciplinary questions; no single methodology corners the market on insights in this field. Although I appreciate the difficulties of conducting social scientific research on highly nuanced and context dependent phenomena, I typically find definitions of apologies utilized by social scientists too oversimplified to capture significant aspects of conciliatory behavior. Some studies simply "count" utterances of the word "sorry" as apologies rather than evaluate the substance of the speech act and its meaning in context.[7] Such findings will not distinguish between expressions of sympathy and admissions of blameworthiness and, therefore, do not account for significant variance in meaning between the utterances. *I Was Wrong* considers related issues with respect to Deborah Tannen's widely cited claim that women apologize more frequently than men. Tannen's claim may be true, and there are many intuitive reasons to suspect that she is correct, but we can appreciate how such research would benefit from revising the concepts on which these studies were built.[8] Jennifer Robbennolt has become the leading figure in the empirical study of apologies in law, and she has made considerable contributions to our understandings of how legal agents understand apologies in both civil and criminal settings. Robbennolt's evenhanded evaluation of existing social scientific literature as well as her own findings pays close attention to distinctions between expressions of sympathy and admissions of guilt, and she explains the limits of her findings with some care.[9] From my view, however, even Robbennolt's definitions suffer from blind spots precisely where I most want to see.

Following sociologist Nicolas Tavuchis, Robbennolt claims that an "apology is a statement offered by a wrongdoer that expresses acknowledgment of the legitimacy of the violated rule, admission of fault and responsibility for its violation, and the expression of genuine regret and remorse for the harm done."[10] From this definition, Robbennolt asks her subjects to respond to this example of a "full apology": "I want to let you know how sorry I am. The accident was my fault. I was going too fast and not watching where I was going until it was too late. I am so sorry."[11] This example captures the distinction between an expression of sympathy and an acceptance of blame, but notice how various sorts of meaning that I identify as significant for a categorical apology operate beyond the scope of such a study. Most importantly, the example meant to illustrate a full apology tells us almost nothing about reform, redress, or other future behavior.[12] On Robbennolt's account, the offender could provide no redress for the injury and commit the same offense the following day and this would have no bearing on whether the apology is "full" or otherwise. The offender could remain unreformed and untrustworthy yet receive full credit by Robbennolt's measurements. If a prosecutor evaluates a defendant's contrition during plea allocutions or a judge weighs a convict's statement of remorse at sentencing, the relationship between the specific elements of the apology and the likelihood of recidivism should be one of her primary concerns. We should similarly distinguish between an apology from a hospital in response to a medical malpractice claim that commits to undertaking structural reform to correct the problem and one that fails to reform the root cause of the injury. Regardless of one's disciplinary perspective, it seems uncontroversial that one of the most substantive aspects of just about any apology lies in its relationship to the offender's future behavior.

I appreciate the difficulty of measuring these aspects of apologetic meaning, as it is more feasible for researchers to limit definitions of apologies to the words spoken than to study the full range of an offender's future behavior and moral transformation over her lifetime. We should be careful, however, not to allow facility in empirical research and the halo of data to distort our understanding of these complex concepts. Ill-formed empirical studies in such an emotionally and politically charged topic like apologies and justice can produce more darkness than light. Inversely, philosophical theories of apologies disregarding empirical findings suffer from a different set of weaknesses. I aim for an appropriately dialectical balance between the disciplines, but this is easier said than done. Hopefully representatives from the various perspectives working in this area can keep each other honest and integrate the most sensible contributions regardless of their methodological origins.

B. An Applied Example: Elliot Spitzer 2008

For elaboration and defense of these positions, readers can review the relevant sections of *I Was Wrong*. As an example of the theory in practice, consider Elliot Spitzer's March 2008 statements regarding his relationship with an escort service. I choose this example both because of its interest as a criminal matter that straddles public and private concerns and because my view of the situation has evolved since I publicly commented on Spitzer's apology.[13]

As Democratic governor of New York after winning 69 percent of the vote over incumbent Dennis Vacco, Spitzer enjoyed such popularity in large part because of his service as New York attorney general. In successfully prosecuting cases relating to securities fraud, mutual fund fraud, price fixing, predatory lending, excessive executive compensation, and other white-collar crimes, Spitzer made many enemies as the "sheriff of Wall Street." His bare-knuckle approach to economic reform and his fiery disposition led several of the most powerful financial leaders to publicly feud with Spitzer and to vow to bring about his demise. Alex Gibney's documentary suggests that these interests – supported by Republican officials and operatives – trailed Spitzer, identified his suspicious money transfers, and leaked the information to the media. After the *New York Times* identified Spitzer as "Client 9" in a federal affidavit, he held a press conference on March 10 with his wife Silda Wall Spitzer at his side. In front of more than 100 reporters in a briefing room at the governor's office, Spitzer read the following statement:

Good afternoon. Over the past nine years, eight years as attorney general and one as governor, I've tried to uphold a vision of progressive politics that would rebuild New York and create opportunity for all. We sought to bring real change to New York and that will continue. Today, I want to briefly address a private matter. I have acted in a way that violates my obligations to my family and that violates my – or any – sense of right and wrong. I apologize first, and most importantly, to my family. I apologize to the public, whom I promised better. I do not believe that politics in the long run is about individuals. It is about ideas, the public good and doing what is best for the State of New York. But I have disappointed and failed to live up to the standard I expected of myself. I must now dedicate some time to regain the trust of my family. I will not be taking questions. Thank you very much. I will report back to you in short order. Thank you very much.

Spitzer expressed little emotion during the sixty-four second statement – he appeared glassy-eyed but otherwise seemed quite composed – and he did not take questions regarding his political future. Two days later he expanded his apology in his resignation speech. Again with his wife beside him, he stated:

In the past few days I have begun to atone for my private failings with my wife, Silda, my children, and my entire family. The remorse I feel will always be with me. Words cannot describe how grateful I am for the love and compassion they have shown me. From those to whom much is given, much is expected. I have been given much: the love of my family, the faith and trust of the people of New York, and the chance to lead this state. I am deeply sorry that I did not live up to what was expected of me. To every New Yorker, and to all those who believed in what I tried to stand for, I sincerely apologize.

I look at my time as governor with a sense of what might have been, but I also know that as a public servant I, and the remarkable people with whom I worked, have accomplished a great deal. There is much more to be done, and I cannot allow my private failings to disrupt the people's work. Over the course of my public life, I have insisted, I believe correctly, that people, regardless of their position or power, take responsibility for their conduct. I can and will ask no less of myself. For this reason, I am resigning from the office of governor. At Lt. Gov. Paterson's request, the resignation will be effective Monday, March 17, a date that he believes will permit an orderly transition.

I go forward with the belief, as others have said, that as human beings, our greatest glory consists not in never falling, but in rising every time we fall. As I leave public life, I will first do what I need to do to help and heal myself and my family. Then I will try once again, outside of politics, to serve the common good and to move toward the ideals and solutions which I believe can build a future of hope and opportunity for us and for our children. I hope all of New York will join my prayers for my friend, David Paterson, as he embarks on his new mission, and I thank the public once again for the privilege of service.

Upon Spitzer's resignation, former New York Stock Exchange director Ken Langone gloated that he played a role in Spitzer's downfall and stated that "we all have our own private hell; I hope [Spitzer's] private hell is hotter than anyone else's."[14]

In November 2008, the U.S. Attorney in Manhattan announced that as a result of "insufficient evidence to bring charges against Mr. Spitzer" and in "light of the policy of the Department of Justice with respect to prostitution offenses and the longstanding practice of this office, as well as Mr. Spitzer's acceptance of responsibility for his conduct, we have concluded that the public interest would not be further advanced by filing criminal charges in this matter."[15] Spitzer released the following statement minutes after the announcement:

I appreciate the impartiality and thoroughness of the investigation by the U.S. Attorney's Office, and I acknowledge and accept responsibility for the conduct it disclosed. I resigned my position as Governor because I recognized that conduct was unworthy of an elected official. I once again apologize for my actions.

Given this context, what should we make of Spitzer's apology? Working through the elements of the categorical apology helps organize our analysis.

1. Corroborated Factual Record: Spitzer admits very little by speaking abstractly of "violating obligations" to family. I am not aware of any occasions where Spitzer explicitly admits to patronizing a prostitute. Rather than "coming clean" and confessing the details of his wrongdoing, he leaves us to speculate. How long had he engaged in such behavior? The affidavit suggests that he was a repeat customer and that the woman appearing in the media was not his regular prostitute at the Emperor's Club, but he does not volunteer this information. Nor does he explain the illegalities of his money transfers to the Emperor's Club.

   By describing this as a "private matter," he implies that certain facts are not appropriate to the public forum. Although a justifiable position regarding certain facts – for instance with respect to various lies he may have told his wife to cover his misdeeds – he overextends this position. As the governor and former attorney general accused of multiple federal crimes, he untenably attempts to stretch the privacy argument to cover his public crime. Beyond his status as a public official and in particular as a former prosecutor of prostitution, he violated a public law by patronizing a prostitute. This distinguishes his offense from non-criminal infidelity, but he never admits to the crime of patronizing a prostitute and implies that his wrong was more like a Clintonian extramarital tryst. However unconvincing the argument that Spitzer had an affair of some sort rather than committed a crime, this position may have legs if repeated often enough. Alan Dershowitz, for example, claimed that Spitzer "was a great political figure who made one mistake and we're a forgiving country, and the mistake he made was a private mistake."[16]

Spitzer could have "come clean" on all of the relevant facts, but instead it may require years of investigations and legal proceedings to disclose the extent of his transgressions. Because the U.S. Attorney never charged him, Spitzer avoided a highly publicized trial that would have likely revealed very private information as well as facts more obviously relevant to his public offense. As time passed, withholding these facts appears to support his legal strategy. Prosecutors found "insufficient evidence to bring charges against Mr. Spitzer," likely a result of the efforts of his assembly of elite New York attorneys working to protect incriminating information.

Insufficient evidence to support prosecuting a former governor differs from sufficient evidence to establish moral turpitude or to destroy a marriage. Beyond the role such information could have played in his prosecution, it would bleed into divorce proceedings, future campaigns for office, and his attempts to carve out a career as a media commentator. History will probably never know the full story, and this factual deficiency introduces ambiguities throughout the other meanings of his apology.

2. Acceptance of Blame: Spitzer sets an appropriate tone in his resignation: "Over the course of my public life, I have insisted, I believe correctly, that people, regardless of their position or power, take responsibility for their conduct. I can and will ask no less of myself. For this reason, I am resigning from the office of governor." As someone who built his career prosecuting others and holding them responsible, these lines from Spitzer resonate. Spitzer accepts some blame by admitting that he acted in a way that violates his obligations to his family. He does not deploy a version of "sorry if anyone was hurt" or the like. He has wronged. However, because of the limited facts he provides, for what specifically does he accept blame? What are the harms at issue? His primary admission relates to the private harms, and we might understand his desire not to provide a detailed account of how he deserves blame for harming his family.

With regard to his public wrongs, however, does he accept blame? He states, "I apologize to the public, whom I promised better. I do not believe that politics in the long run is about individuals. It is about ideas, the public good and doing what is best for the State of New York. But I have disappointed and failed to live up to the standard I expected of myself." This suggests that he deserves blame for failing to "live up to the standard" he expects of himself. Important ambiguities result. He admits no criminal activity. Does he deserve blame for illegally paying for sex and attempting to cover it up, or only for some more vague inability to live up to his own lofty ideals? What exactly does he perceive as the harm for which he deserves blame? He apologizes to the public to whom he "promised better," but what is the content of those promises and how did he breach them? For precisely what does he accept blame? We do not know.

Spitzer does not attempt to deflect blame in these initial statements by mentioning the possibility that these allegations result from attacks by his political enemies. Spitzer's downplaying the element of political assassination contrasts with Clinton's strategy of characterizing Kenneth Star as a political hit man who abused federal power, allowing Clinton to cast himself sympathetically as a lone soul seeking redemption while being pilloried by vengeful opponents.[17] Spitzer deployed a bit of apophasis in a later interview by saying "I will not try to blame others or excuse my behavior.... If [enemies] were involved in unearthing it, so be it. That isn't my concern right now." Spitzer can avoid making this particular excuse for his downfall in part because Gibney's documentary makes that case so strongly on Spitzer's behalf.

Note that in the midst of accepting blame, Spitzer helps himself to some praise in reminding the audience of his "vision of progressive politics that would rebuild New York and create opportunity for all." An apology can appropriately distinguish between blameworthy and praiseworthy behavior, and here we can recall New Jersey Governor Jim McGreevey's apology for his infidelity but not for his homosexuality.[18] For some, such a reminder of Spitzer's agenda may render his apology even more painful. Others may find it self-congratulating and setting an insufficiently contrite tone.

Regardless of these contours of Spitzer's acceptance of blame, the U.S. Attorney cites his "acceptance of responsibility for his conduct" as support for the conclusion that "the public interest would not be further advanced by filing criminal charges in this matter."[19] If Spitzer and his attorneys calibrated his contrition as a legal gambit – accept just enough to appear remorseful but not so much to admit criminal wrongdoing and serve up an easy trophy conviction to a political rival – then it worked as a means to that end.

3. Possession of Appropriate Standing: Spitzer issues the statement himself rather than through a spokesperson. He also does not attempt to deflect responsibility by hiding behind his office or some institutional collective.

Nor, again, does he invoke the shadowy activity of his enemies, for instance by stating that he is "sorry that I am a casualty of Wall Street's war against the American people."

4. Identification of Each Harm: Without establishing a factual record or indicating for what exactly he deserves blame, various harms go unidentified. Such spectacular moral failings often result from the aggregation of many lesser offenses, and such an accounting would provide insights into the character of Elliot Spitzer and the nature of this offense. What does Spitzer see as the harms at issue? Consider a few possibilities:

> Committing marital infidelity
> Lying to his wife
> Causing his wife to suffer pain of various kinds
> Visiting various harms on his children
> Using the name of his friend as an alias at the hotel where he met the escort
> Objectifying or otherwise harming the escorts
> Contributing to an economy of sex trafficking
> Using campaign funds to pay for the hotel
> Secretively wiring money to an illegal organization
> Throwing his political party into crisis
> Undermining the moral authority of his party and his elected office
> Contributing to public skepticism toward politicians as hypocrites by soliciting prostitutes after prosecuting similar crimes
> Wasting tax dollars on this investigation
> Causing such a distraction to – and rendering the "Sheriff of Wall Street" a bystander in – efforts toward financial reform just prior to the economic crisis of 2008

Rather than identifying any of these particular harms, he speaks of "failing to live up to the standard" he set for himself. This sounds like apologizing for the "wrong wrong," like the clergy member who apologized for breaking his vow of chastity when accused of molesting children.

5. Identification of the Moral Principles Underlying Each Harm: Because of the vagueness regarding the harms, we remain unclear about the values underlying these harms. Again, he speaks of violating his "standards," promising to "do better," and violating "any sense of right and wrong," but he does not make these principles explicit. What, exactly, are the values at stake? We would benefit from some precision here. Why was it wrong? Because he disrespected his wife in so many ways? Because he exposed his children to this ordeal? Because he repeatedly lied? Because he paid a financially vulnerable woman twenty-seven years his younger to have sex with him? Because he supported an industry that he publicly

denounced? Because his hypocrisy after claiming that he wanted "ethics and integrity to be the hallmarks" of his administration contributes to public cynicism toward government officials? Because he weakened the Democratic Party? Because he violated the rule of law, an especially grievous offense for a public official of his stature? Or was his primary failing, in his eyes, getting caught or being outfoxed by his adversaries? His apology would have considerably more substance if he explained what he did and made explicit why he believes it was wrong in these regards.

6. Shared Commitment to Moral Principles Underlying Each Harm: Identifying the principles at issue differs from actually sharing those principles. Perhaps Spitzer does not personally find prostitution morally objectionable. Perhaps he sees the sexual escapades of international leaders as increasing their popularity – Spitzer's sympathizers joked that this scandal would have increased his electability in France – and thus finds the U.S. electorate unfortunately puritanical. Or perhaps he finds his actions constitute a genuine moral failing. We do not know.

Compared with other public figures in similar situations, Spitzer does not strike a particularly religious tone. He speaks of "atoning" and of praying for his successor, but this is quite retrained when compared, for instance, with Clinton's deployment of Southern evangelical tropes to disarm his opponents.[20] Whereas Clinton spoke of his "sins," surrounded himself with conservative clergy, held a prayer breakfast, and was shepherded through penance by an "accountability group" of renowned church leaders,[21] Spitzer – who is Jewish but did not have a bar mitzvah or an otherwise particularly religious upbringing – avoids the Augustinian rendering of his flawed soul that led many to sympathize with Clinton.[22]

7. Recognition of Victim as Moral Interlocutor: Spitzer undertakes an egalitarian gesture in answering to the public rather than refusing to comment.[23] Unlike an authoritarian leader who can scoff at popular judgment, Spitzer recognizes that he does not stand above moral or political law.[24] Who Spitzer views as his victims depends on what he thinks he did wrong. Victims might include his family, the escorts, his colleagues, his constituents, or others. Does he recognize them as moral interlocutors? This is difficult to discern with respect to his family. We see his wife beside him, and he speaks as if they deserve his full attention – indeed he claimed that he resigned because he could not simultaneously attend to his family and serve as governor. We are not, however, privy to his private treatment of his family, and "spend more time with family" has been a euphemism for retreating from scandal for some time. I speculate that he has not offered much of an apology to the escorts. We know little of how he handled the events with his colleagues and

staff. Regarding his treatment of "the public" as a moral interlocutor, the notion of treating such a collective with dignity stretches the concept. Having said that, he did address the media rather than denying the claims and remaining silent. Not taking questions at the time of his initial statements blocked moral discourse, but with the emotional and political intensity of those moments – as well as a potentially legitimate distrust of the kinds of questions that might arise in that context – it would be difficult to blame Spitzer for stepping away from the media. Although always cautious, Spitzer has since been somewhat candid discussing these events.

8. Categorical Regret: Unlike those who claim that they regret the consequences of a difficult but justified decision, Spitzer does not suggest that he continues to endorse his behavior. It seems clear that in light of the various consequences, he believes he made a mistake. The particular activities he wishes could be undone and the reason he believes this, however, remain vague.

9. Performance of the Apology: Spitzer stands before cameras and delivers his statements onto public record, but because of the uncertainty regarding who he believes are the victims of his offense, we should wonder about additional "performances." Presumably this public statement did not also serve as his apology to his family or his staff, but if it did, we could walk back through each of these elements to identify additional issues.

10. Reform: First note the timing of his apologies. Spitzer first apologized within hours of initial reports of the scandal. He resigned while further apologizing within forty-eight hours. He arranged for a prostitute less than one month earlier. Spitzer leapt from one peak to the next in his career, and he was by all measures a rising star. His political career came crashing down. His family will never be the same. Here we should recognize a truth that often conflicts with our media culture: moral development does not occur with a news cycle. Spitzer has a great deal of work to do, and he will account for this for the rest of his life.

A categorical apology promises forbearance over a lifetime. A new offense from Spitzer would drain meaning from his apologies accordingly. Resistance to repeated temptation and successful redress would add meaning to his 2008 apologies. In my view, the best apologies are essentially promises to change. They are treatments, not cures. Like promises, we cannot judge them fully in the moments they are spoken. We need time to search for the deepest values that orient our lives and begin rebuilding our futures with habits that honor those principles. Although it may not make for good television, this sort of persistent moral growth creates good people. Spitzer's statement that our "greatest glory consists not in never falling, but in rising every time we fall" – a line delivered to him by Ethel Kennedy – indicates an appreciation for the work ahead of him.

What did Spitzer promise and what has he done in these regards? Spitzer promised efforts to "regain the trust" of his family and states "I will first do what I need to do to help and heal myself and my family." We know neither what this entails nor the extent to which he has followed through on this promise. Much of his reform will occur privately, and we have little information to evaluate his efforts in this regard. The best current evidence of his reform is probably (a) his avoidance of divorce and commitment to couples therapy and (b) the lack of evidence of repeat offenses.[25] These are both rather weak inferences because although the media reports that he rededicated himself to family matters soon after the scandal, we lack insight into the evolving state of his marriage and commitment to it. He could abandon his marriage at any time.

The increased scrutiny he now faces makes it highly unlikely that he would attempt to solicit a prostitute again. Does he deserve his family's trust? I imagine this is a continual question for them, and one that will linger for the rest of their lives.

Uncertainty regarding what exactly he did wrong in his official capacities leaves us to wonder how exactly Spitzer intends to reform his public behavior. What exactly does he promise not repeat? We do not know.

Like an imprisoned drug offender who lacks access to her vice, Spitzer no longer serves as a public official, and therefore he does not face certain temptations to abuse public trust and authority. Although we have no evidence that he has reoffended, he does not – as Maimonides requires to corroborate repentance – face and resist temptations similar to those that led to his downfall. Does he deserve the public's trust? We have limited data to evaluate in making such a determination.

11. Redress: We also know little about the sorts of redress he provides for his private offenses. He paints his resignation as itself a kind of redress ("I must now dedicate some time to regain the trust of my family"), but what else has he done? Does he, for example, still travel alone? What sorts of efforts has he made to redress harms against his three daughters? We do not know.

With regard to redressing the public, has Spitzer "paid the price" as a certain stripe of retributivist might demand? We could understand his resignation of the governorship as a kind of hard treatment. Is this enough? As early as 2008 Spitzer stated, "I committed my sins, and I've paid for them." Whether Spitzer has paid for his offense depends on how one perceives the extent of his misdeeds and the pain of his punishment. Certainly resigning the governorship was a great loss, but he did not face criminal charges or fines. He remains a very wealthy and very well-connected person. He has not to my knowledge worked to address harms associated with prostitution.

If he ever attempts to regain public office – I do not discount this possibility given the litany of other politicians who resurrected their careers after sex scandals – he might make additional efforts to demonstrate his reform and rehabilitate his image. In part he understands his redress as serving "the common good and to move toward the ideals and solutions which I believe can build a future of hope and opportunity for us and for our children." This is well underway with his gradual reemergence into public life through various media appearances. He succeeded Keith Olbermann as host of a popular news program and has once again become a major voice in debates regarding economic reform.

Insofar as these efforts are sufficient to offset the harms he caused his party, his political legacy remains an open question. Perhaps Spitzer has a long political career and the scandal will wither in historical memory because he makes such significant contributions that they exceed any redress one might expect of him. He could also fade from the public eye, leaving history to mark the Spitzer scandal as a momentum shifting defeat in the twenty-first century battle to reform banking.

12. Intentions for Apologizing: Although discerning intentions may seem like mind reading, justice systems routinely evaluate offenders' mental states. What motivates Spitzer's apologies? Does he merely promote his self-serving interests, for example going through the motions of apologizing as a strategy to maximize his chances of receiving favorable treatment from prosecutors, public opinion, and his family? Or does he primarily intend the apology as a means of caring for his family? Perhaps in light of his identity as a prosecutor he really does take primary orientation from a desire to honor the values he breached and sees his apology as a self-sacrifice on the altar of the rule of law. This seems unlikely in light of his legal defense, but it may contribute to the story he tells himself and others. Spitzer's intentions may include a combination of these possibilities, and even he may be unclear about what motivates him. Humans have a remarkable ability for self-deception. If he had been more explicit regarding his commitment to the moral principle underlying his offenses, this could offer insight into his intentions. Instead, we are left to read his mental states through the lens of his other inscrutable actions and words. He appears to have dedicated time to his family, but is this primarily because of newfound free time resulting from his exclusion from public life? Think here of the shameless boyfriend who apologizes primarily to maintain a sexual relationship with his current lover while looking over his shoulder for someone better to come along. It is not unusual for politicians to attempt to get their own houses in order primarily as a means to the end of restoring

their public image, and his wife would be wise to reevaluate the motivations for his apology if he does return to prominence. In this respect an apologizer's intentions can become more apparent over time.

13. Emotions: Appreciate the difficulty of determining whether Spitzer has experienced emotions of contrition with sufficient intensity. Has he felt badly enough? Spitzer helps himself to various "emotional amplifiers" in his statements, indicating that he is "deeply sorry" and that he "sincerely apologizes." He also states that "the remorse I feel will always be with me." These statements do little to provide us with a window into his emotional states. I later discuss in detail the idea that apologetic emotions are retributive in nature – the apologizer *deserves* to suffer acute humiliation – but his remarks about "rising every time we fall" and having "paid for" his sins seem so self-assured that they risk minimizing the badness of his actions. Spitzer's suggestion that he need only pull himself up and pay his dues asserts that now he controls his future rather than, for example, his spouse or the public – a sentiment boldly lacking humility in this context, but in character given Spitzer's personality. Rather than a shameful resignation, at times his statements sound like a celebration of a hard fought campaign when honorably conceding to a formidable foe.

"I look at my time as governor with a sense of what might have been," reflects Spitzer, and this conveys interesting emotional content with respect to his public ambitions. Spitzer, commonly referred to as "the first Jewish president of the United States," appreciates not only the height of his personal fall but also the damage to his causes. By resigning from office, he removed himself as a general in the campaign for Wall Street reform just as its bloodiest battles commenced. He appears to take no joy in being right, for example, about the impending crisis at Allied Investment Group. As the *Guardian* put it, "the man who had voiced more problems than virtually any other public figure was turned into a discredited punchline to a political joke just as those warnings came true." He has referred to his downfall as a kind of Greek tragedy, and I cannot fathom the complex emotional pain this must cause him even beyond what he suffers in the context of his more personal failings. We do not see much of this emotion, and therefore we extrapolate from various behaviors and statements to determine if he experiences an appropriate degree and duration of sorrow and guilt as well as empathy and sympathy for the victims.

Note as well the complexities regarding the positive emotions Spitzer expresses at what should presumably be his most painful moments: "Words cannot describe how grateful I am for the love and compassion they have shown me." The negative emotions associated with apologies often coexist with positive emotions, whether gratitude in this case or other feelings such as pride in one's moral transformation. One can justifiably enjoy a bittersweet sense of satisfaction of moral growth while simultaneously confessing a heinous moral failure. For those with retributive tendencies, this may prove frustrating. In Spitzer's case we have a child of extreme privilege who attended elite Manhattan preparatory schools, Princeton undergraduate, and Harvard Law – all paid for by his real estate mogul father who also funded his early campaigns for public office. He betrays his family and supporters with grossly poor judgment. Consider what he receives in return: the love of his family, a posh Fifth Avenue office building in his father's empire, and the trappings of wealth and fame. Those inclined to ask such questions will wonder if he has suffered enough.

From this discussion we should draw a few conclusions to carry forward through the subsequent chapters. Apologies have many moving parts, and the binary question of whether Spitzer "apologized or not" tells us little about the meanings and functions of his contrition. Ambiguities remain even after we break it down. Again, I think of the analogy of someone telling you that they love you on the first date. Such a statement could well be a life-transforming proclamation, but we would need to know much more before we could make a well-informed judgment. We will have a much better sense of the substance of Spitzer's March 2008 apologies if we check in with him in ten years or perhaps longer. As Dershowitz advised Spitzer, "this incident will be a footnote to a great life lived greatly" and one of his "goals has to be to make this a footnote in his obituary, and not make it the lead."[26] We will consider throughout this book how such optimistic sentiments apply to the majority of apologetic convicts in the contemporary United States.

The Spitzer example also demonstrates how apologies in legal contexts straddle public and private matters. Like Spitzer, a typical drug offender has often wronged her family as well as the state. The sorts of contrition one might express to her mother after conviction will share quite a bit with what she should convey to the sentencing judge. Although many of the meanings are entwined, sometimes they can and should be pulled apart for moral as well as practical reasons.

C. Collective Apologies Revisited

I devoted nearly half of *I Was Wrong* to collective apologies, arguing that apologies from groups of people add layers of complexity to nearly every facet of apologetic meaning. Collective apologies often address serious harms against classes of victims by multiple offenders, many of whom will have very different attitudes toward and roles in the harm. In addition, collective apologies often arise in the context of political and governmental bureaucracies, making it especially difficult to determine who deserves and who accepts responsibility. Apologies from individuals are complicated; apologies from collectives exponentially compound these complexities. For a variety of reasons discussed later, U.S. laws tend to view harms caused by institutions as civil rather than criminal offenses. Readers will therefore find most of my discussion of collective apologies in Part III of this book, but those interested in these issues should review Part II of *I Was Wrong*. A few general and brief points warrant repeating in advance of the ensuing analyses.[27]

First, we should not discount the possibility of a collective providing a categorical apology. Although rare and most likely to occur in small groups bound by considerable solidarity, each member of the group could individually satisfy the elements of a categorical apology and perform the gesture communally. The group would speak and act from a consensus regarding all relevant elements, and it would clearly define the group's membership. In essence, a collective categorical apology would be an aggregation of coordinated individual categorical apologies supplemented by various sorts of synergies achieved by unifying the acts. Many obstacles may prevent collective apologies from reaching the status of "categorical," but such meanings are possible and highly desirable in many cases.

If a collective does not attempt to provide a categorical apology, we can ask whether it serves as a poor substitute for categorical apologies from individual members of the group. To restate a few of the questions that recurred throughout *I Was Wrong* in this regard: Does the collective offer a noncategorical apology *instead of* the categorical apologies that the individuals most directly accountable for the harm should provide? Charles Tilly claims that "war stimulates collective attributions of credit and blame more than any other human activity."[28] Crime must be a close second. Do individuals who should apologize for their personal wrongdoings conceal their culpability in the collective and allow it to shoulder blame that they alone should bear? Does the collective apology avoid naming those who deserve blame and shield them from facing the consequences of their contemptible actions? Do leaders invoke individualist conceptions of responsibility when accepting praise but shift to collective theories and speak in the passive voice when deflecting blame? Does the collective apology exploit ambiguity and prey on our desperation for the sorts of thick meaning provided by categorical apologies? Does it attempt to parlay undeserved moral credit into some self-serving benefit? Do those who most deserve blame outsource the work of contrition? Does every member of the collective, a slight majority, or only a powerful minority vow to uphold the values expressed? Does the apology come from those with the authority and resources to make good on promises to reform? Who foots the bill for redress? Who undertakes the reform? Does the collective honor the principle selectively or does it uphold its promise without exceptions or excuses? Such questions drive Part III, for instance as we consider apologies for the Deepwater Horizon spill, birth defects caused by thalidomide, or Chisso Corporation's poisoning of Minamata Bay.

It often makes more sense to understand collective acts of contrition as value-declaring rather than categorical apologies.[29] Instead of accepting blame for past wrongdoing, a value-declaring apology can announce or renew its commitment to a policy. A group can endorse a principle in this sense without any current members admitting personal culpability. It can also avoid attributing blame to the collective in an aggregate or conglomerate sense. The group can use the gesture to denounce the acts of others or even as a means of parrying an accusation against it by insisting on its unwavering commitment to the principle. Value-declaring apologies can insist that someone else or some other group should categorically apologize. When victims and communities worry less about apportioning blame for the past but instead primarily seek an assurance that a group will not commit an offense in the future, value-declaring apologies may suffice.[30] Declaring values in this way can advance public normative discourse by articulating a community's values and recognizing the violation. Collectives can stabilize such progress by building solidarity around the declared value and investing resources in a shared vision of the future. At times, the limitations of value-declaring collective apologies may even provide an asset, as a community may realize that it cannot survive a fine-grained causal analysis that finds so many of its members guilty.

Despite these important functions, we should remain aware that some forms of meaning central to categorical apologies may or may not accompany value-declaring collective apologies. Representatives uttering collective apologies may endorse the value in the context of establishing a historical record in some detail, or they may prefer to avoid discussing the past. They may choose which victims they wish to recognize as interlocutors, which offenses they acknowledge, and which values they wish to endorse. Because they need not accept blame for past injustice, they may have nothing to regret. They could even claim that although a course of action was justified in the past, it would not be in the future. A declaration that promises not to breach the value in question need not necessarily provide redress for past injuries. They may support relief efforts in a variety of ways, but members of the collective will probably describe their efforts as charitable contributions rather than payments of moral debt if they do not accept blame for the harm. Even so, we should pay attention to whether a declaration pledges resources to the cause, who it expects to fund these efforts, and whether it has standing to commit the supporters and financiers. For a variety of reasons, intentions and emotion can play a less central role in value-declaring apologies. Institutional members who provide value declarations can also avoid suffering any of the punitive consequences of apologizing.

In short, collective apologies raise many serious issues. These concerns drive a healthy skepticism for collective apologies, but critical evaluation need not lapse into cynical disregard for collective acts of contrition. Collective apologies can provide distinctly meaningful and indispensable supplements to individual apologies, especially in their ability to mobilize structural reform. As we will see repeatedly throughout this book, however, collective apologies are often not what they seem.

PART ONE

The Penitent and the Penitentiary: Apologies in Criminal Law

[T]he concept "punishment" possesses in fact not one meaning but a whole synthesis of "meanings": the previous history of punishment in general, the history of its employment for the most various purposes, finally crystallizes into a kind of unity that is hard to disentangle, hard to analyze and, as must be emphasized, totally in-definable. (Today it is impossible to say for certain why people are really punished: all concepts in which an entire process is semiotically concentrated elude definition; only that which has no history is definable.).[1]

Nietzsche, *Genealogy of Morals*

Introduction: Central Debates in Philosophy of Punishment Relevant to Apologies in Criminal Law

The subsequent chapters make two interrelated arguments. First I argue against court-ordered apologies. I then argue in favor of reducing sentences for categorically apologetic offenders. Considering the interdisciplinary nature of this book and my extensive reference to the central debates in the philosophy of crime and punishment, a brief overview of this literature may be useful for some readers. Those well versed in such arguments may want to skim this section. All readers, however, can take a moment to appreciate an obstacle confronting my arguments: the contemporary United States, I think it is fair to say, has no coherent or consistent set of principles guiding its massive criminal justice system. Instead, we have an ideological storm of highly contestable beliefs blowing in various directions – although most often toward increased incarceration. The push of political currents and pull of economic tides present various difficulties for analyzing the role of apologies. Very few questions regarding why the criminal justice system's ultimate objectives – for instance, why we punish drug offenses with lengthy sentences – are met with sensible answers. Attempting to carve out a sensible treatment of apologies within such Kafkaesque institutions can feel like a fool's errand.

Beyond the challenge of trying to make sense within an often senseless system, apologies can become ammunition in various struggles in the justice system. I therefore attempt to identify the most common means of weaponizing apologies in the hope that these explanations help diffuse the most unjust uses of the power of contrition. In particular I worry that the privileged will wield apologies most effectively as but another means to increase their advantage within the status quo of criminal justice. Moreover, attempts to determine effective roles for apologies within such institutions risk providing bandages for a hemorrhaging system. Although primarily a palliative treatment for injustice, I will argue that systematic study of apologies can occasion a radical reconceptualizing of crime and conflict resolution.

With those concerns flagged, a few statistics should frame this theoretical overview. According to the U.S. Bureau of Justice Statistics, 2011 ended with about seven million people on probation, in jail or prison, or on parole. The U.S. incarceration rate of 743 per 100,000 of national population is by far the highest in the world.[2] Americans represent approximately 5 percent of the global population, but 25 percent of the world's prisoners are incarcerated in the United States.[3] Commentators typically attribute the rise in U.S. incarceration rates to changes in drug policy. The Nixon administration promulgated the Comprehensive Drug Abuse Prevention and Control Act of 1970, commonly understood as the opening battle in the modern War on Drugs. The Reagan administration presided over subsequent offensives in the battles against recreational drug use, including the Sentencing Reform Act of 1984 and the Anti-Drug Abuse Act of 1986, both of which resulted in steeply increasing incarceration rates. As a result, nearly half of all federal inmates are now incarcerated for drug offenses,[4] and the United States has experienced a 1,110 percent increase since 1980 in inmates in jail or prison on drug charges.[5] The racial consequences of these policies have been well-documented, with Michelle Alexander describing drug policy as the "new Jim Crow" in which the "United States imprisons a larger percentage of its black population than South Africa did at the height of Apartheid."[6]

We can loosely – and with the usual caveats accompanying such definitions – define judicial punishment as an intentional infliction of harm by those vested with political authority to do so against an individual for an offense against law. Unlike conflicts that occur privately between offenders and victims, judicial punishment and the criminal law involve offenses against the *public as such*. Even though a criminal offender may harm an individual person, *the state* becomes her legal opponent. We title cases accordingly, with the conventional form being *The United States v.*

Smith rather than *Victim v. Smith*. This dynamic becomes more prominent in arguably "victimless crimes" such as drug possession in which the state prosecutes the offense even though the offender did not directly harm any particular person. Whereas the state brings the charge and administers the case in criminal matters, civil law requires injured parties to pursue their own efforts toward receiving redress. Civil claims are public in the sense that they reference a community's formal law and are subject to various degrees of publicity, but we typically consider the offense in civil cases against the individual rather than the state. A breach of contract, therefore, presents a matter between the contracting parties. They should turn to civil legal action to resolve their conflict as a matter of last resort. It may strike readers as odd that criminal law understands an assault, for instance, primarily as an offense against the abstract state rather than against the person harmed and that the victim usually plays very little role in criminal proceedings. I later consider this debate, sometimes described as the state's usurping of injuries from victims. Here we can simply note the conventional but contested spectrum from the public to the private nature of injuries: criminal offense as most public, civil offenses as less public, and non-legal offenses such as infidelity between unmarried lovers as private.

Punishment harms offenders in ways that require justification: what, for example, allows the state to capture and detain a person? Without good reasons, such aggression rather uncontroversially offends our sense of justice. State-sponsored punishment suspends the freedom of millions every year and intentionally subjects them to pain and suffering. How could such a resource-consuming institution have a place in modern life? This leads to the core philosophical questions in the field. What justifies punishment? What are its moral principles and practical objectives? How should we honor these principles and accomplish those objectives fairly? How important are those objectives when compared with other objectives, such as personal liberty or public safety? Who deserves punishment? What methods of punishment should the state employ? How much should it punish? Who administers the punishment? Various theories debate these questions, but they endure as the central issues for all attempts to create a compelling theory of punishment. Arguments against court-ordered apologies and for reductions of punishment for apologetic offenders require us to confront these traditions.

Prior to the eighteenth century, punishment for criminal offenses typically consisted of sporadic public displays of spectacular corporal violence. We would now consider much of this to qualify as torture. Such punishments served several objectives, including demonstrating the authority of the rulers, exacting revenge on the convict, and issuing a warning to anyone entertaining the idea of committing similar offenses. Historians typically cite Cesare Beccaria's 1764 *On Crimes and Punishments* as the seminal systematic study of punishment.[7] Contrary to the ad hoc and often religious rituals of punishment that prevailed at the time, Beccaria argued that deterring offenders could be the only legitimate function of punishment.[8] According to Beccaria, a state deters most effectively by standardizing penalties, publicizing the penalties so that everyone understands and has notice of the harm they could suffer, and enforcing sanctions regularly and fairly. Beccaria further found excessive punishments inhumane and unnecessary for deterrence. English philosopher and reformer Jeremy Bentham developed Beccaria's insights into a comprehensive theory of law governed by the central premise of what has come to be known as "utilitarianism": legislation should promote the greatest good (utility) and the least suffering for the greatest number of people. Unlike the primal urges to exact revenge and somehow correct the past, utilitarian punishment looks forward and seeks primarily to prevent crime. This generates three possible justifications for punishment: deterrence, incapacitation, and rehabilitation.

Deterrence functions as a disincentive to committing a crime. It may be in my interest to steal something. If no penalty exists for stealing, I have little reason not to other than my moral convictions or perhaps fear of disapproval of my peers. Utilitarian penologists generally find it insufficient to rely on moral beliefs to prevent people from doing things that would decrease a community's overall happiness. Humans are, from the utilitarian perspective, sophisticated animals. Punishment trains us by altering incentive structures so that it becomes in each individual's best interests to obey the law. If I risk burdensome fines or jail time, I am less likely to steal. Breaking the law becomes unworthy of the risk. For a state to realize the benefits of manipulating risk/reward ratio, the public must understand the laws and their sanctions, believe there is an adequate degree of likelihood that they will be apprehended and subjected to the punishment, and view the punishment as not so extreme that levying it would produce suffering outweighing the happiness it was designed to promote. For these reasons, punishments that intend to deter cannot be too harsh, must be proportionate to the crime in that more serious crimes trigger more severe punishment, and must be only as severe as required to accomplish the penological objective. Excessive punishment causes more suffering than required and therefore runs against the utility principle. These arguments presume that a substantial portion of potential offenders engage in something like a rational cost-benefit analyses to determine whether criminal activity outweighs the risks of punishment, and some critics question the extent to which potential criminals undertake such deliberations.

Utilitarianism also finds incapacitation to be a legitimate strategy for reducing crime. Incapacitation renders the convict less capable of committing further crime against the general public, typically by either incarceration or physical debilitation. Incapacitation can include methods such as execution or castration for sex offenders. The belief that individuals who commit crimes will continue to commit crimes unless incapacitated underlies recidivist statutes such as three strikes laws that impose more severe punishments for repeat offenders. Justifications for prison as incapacitative would weaken if serving time increased a convict's likelihood to commit crimes upon release, for example if she became further acculturated to criminal life while living among other convicts during her sentence or if she found her opportunities for success in non-criminal life worse upon her release from prison than when she entered the criminal justice system. Although warehousing convicts in prisons will, to some degree, prevent them from committing offenses against civilians for the duration of their sentence, crimes occur *within* prisons at rates higher than in the general public. A consistent utilitarian cannot discount the pain caused by these offenses; however, most popular advocates for incapacitating criminals pay little attention to this consequence of segregating our most troubled populations into such dangerous conditions. Some add the dangers of incapacitative incarceration to the deterrent effect, for instance suggesting that the fear of being raped in prison will increase the disincentive to commit crime. At first glance, the worse the prison conditions, the greater the deterrent value. Consistent utilitarians must, however, calculate the impact of such suffering into the overall utility calculus by designing prison conditions to strike a balance that make punishment a deterrent but not so terrible as to create unnecessary suffering in the inmate or in society (for instance, by subjecting offenders to experiences so damaging that they reenter civil society more likely to commit crimes).

Utilitarians who emphasize rehabilitation view criminal behavior as symptomatic of a disease requiring a cure rather than punishment.[9] Many convicts suffer from problems that increase the likelihood that they will engage in criminal activity, for example mental and physical illness, drug addiction, or limited opportunities for economic success. If we incarcerate the convict while she "pays her debt to society," she will likely return with all of the obstacles that drove her to crime still in place. She will also contend with additional difficulties: a criminal record will impact her employment opportunities, she will be older and still without marketable skills or education, her social relationships may have deteriorated while she was in jail, and she may have become further acclimated to criminal culture. Incarcerating offenders could actually make them *more likely* to reoffend upon release. Instead of exacting revenge against criminals and making their lives worse, rehabilitation treats offenders more like patients needing help than prisoners deserving punishment.

U.S. prisons such as those at Auburn, Ossining, and Pittsburgh during the 1820s developed rehabilitative principles.[10] These programs isolated convicts to remove them from the temptations that had driven them to crime. Solitude provided time to reflect on their deeds while studying the Bible. This belief that convicts would listen to their conscience and return to their inherently good natures when removed from the corrupting influences of society gave way to more aggressive forms of treatment informed by the rise of social scientific studies into criminal behavior. Research in psychology, criminology, and sociology provided reformers with new theories and sharper tools for excising deviance. Evolving rapidly from pre-modern rituals of redemption, rehabilitation became a science of reeducating criminals with the values, attitudes, and skills necessary to live lawfully. Contemporary rehabilitation techniques take many forms in practice, including psychological counseling, drug and alcohol treatment, educational programs, vocational training, relationship counseling, anger-management therapy, religious study, and other services required to meet the needs of particular offenders. Because supporters of rehabilitation believe offenders have different problems to overcome, they individualize reform accordingly, just as a doctor prescribes treatment for a sick patient. Two convicts committing the same crime may receive distinct sentences. Someone driven to steal to feed her drug addiction, for example, will require different treatment than an immigrant who shoplifts because she cannot find work adequate to feed her family. Rehabilitative punishment thus tailors sentences to the offender rather than to the crime. "Hard treatment" inflicted for retributive reasons should be avoided when counterproductive to rehabilitation. In addition, prison may not provide the optimal venue for achieving rehabilitative objectives because it isolates offenders from the realities of life with which they must learn how to cope. Incarceration can also cause offenders to become dependent on the prison system. From a rehabilitative perspective, noncustodial sentences such as parole, probation, community service, and deferred sentences can help keep the offender functioning within her ordinary life while helping her learn how to manage the responsibilities she will face after her sentence has expired. Advocates for rehabilitation typically find it especially appropriate and effective for young offenders.

Critics of the rehabilitative model question its effectiveness and express skepticism regarding our knowledge of the causes of crime and our ability to reform criminal behavior. Many doubt that any amount of therapy would change the worst offenders. Others find rehabilitative objectives vague, difficult to measure, and unclear regarding the point at which a subject is "rehabilitated." This raises issues concerning the principle of proportionality: those who commit similar offenses should endure similar punishments. If two people commit the same crime but one responds well to treatment and is easily rehabilitated, it may seem unjust that one's sentence ends before her less malleable counterpart's. Further, some fear that rehabilitation blurs the line between treatment and punishment and thus results in extended criminal detention of those needing only therapy. The mentally ill, for example, may have difficulty ever leaving the criminal justice system. Perhaps the most determinative practical concern has been economic in nature: it is expensive (at least in the short term) to administer an effective rehabilitative system. Politicians reluctantly devote funds to helping such an unpopular and disenfranchised group.

Retributivists level the most trenchant moral criticism of rehabilitation. They disagree with the entire utilitarian view of punishment and find that coddling rehabilitative methods suffer from a fundamental confusion: criminals simply deserve to suffer punishment. Retributivists find it morally imperative to punish murderers, for example, regardless of whether doing so would reduce crime rates. From the Latin "to pay back," retribution traces its Western origins to the Biblical *lex talionis* or "eye for an eye." Unlike the forward-looking orientation of utilitarianism, retributivism seeks to address the wrongs of the past by forcing the offender to pay her debt to the victim and society. In other words, the retributivist believes punishment should balance the scales of justice by causing the offender to suffer pain commensurate with that of her victim. In this sense, retribution exacts pain in proportion to the moral desert of the offender.

Secular retributivist theories usually owe their origins to Kant's eighteenth-century arguments that the ability to reason enables humans to think freely. By determining moral truth from our own reasoning rather than from the authority of another, employing our will to rise above the corrupting influences of culture and desire, and performing the good, we become self-governing and dignified. Because humans have dignity, Kant argues, we must always treat them as ends rather than as mere means. The "practical imperative" names his requirement that we not use others exclusively as tools, and utilitarian justifications for punishment violate the practical imperative by using offenders merely to reduce crime rates. By the Kantian account, the justice system must hold offenders responsible for their crimes and treat them as if they freely make moral choices. The law must address subjects as rationally persuadable by moral reasons rather than mere self-interest. Thus "positive retributivists" argue for a moral obligation to punish the guilty.[11]

By attributing her behavior to forces largely beyond her control – as some consider mental illness or poverty – rehabilitative techniques can treat offenders as if they are not ultimately accountable for their decisions. This, according to the retributivists, reduces offenders to animals or children and leads to techniques that strip offenders of their dignity. As we inject drugs that will decrease libido in sex offenders or perform psychosurgery to reduce violent tendencies in convicts, we create humans effectively unable to choose between right or wrong. Because choice anchors our understanding of what it means to be fully human, retributivists find such punishment inhumane. Utilitarian forms of punishment risk denying dignity in this respect. Rehabilitation seeks to cure them of their disease, deterrence treats them like rats needing shocks to keep them from eating the cheese, and incapacitation compromises their ability to make moral choices. Retributivists also claim that because preventing crime presents the primary objective of utilitarian punishment, utilitarian's would permit grievous injustices such as framing innocent people if such sacrifices furthered this goal.[12]

Critics find that retributivism minimizes practical justifications for punishment: reducing future crime and generally improving behavior. We punish children, for example, to foster their development rather than to balance metaphysical scales of justice. Most would find it reprehensible if a parent administered corporal punishment because the child "deserved to suffer" for her misbehavior. This raises the suspicion that the retributive demand for "just deserts" provides a thinly veiled excuse for a lust for vengeance or even sadism.

In response, pacifist critics of retributivism offer the warning that "an eye for an eye makes the whole world blind." Others object that retributive theories claim that punishment must be proportionate with the offense, but they do not offer convincing explanations for how to go about matching offenses with crimes. How, for instance, might *lex talionis* determine punishment of a drug offender? In addition, sentencing decisions also raise problems of incommensurability. In what respect does a term of imprisonment *equal* the crime of selling controlled substances? Even if we execute a murderer, it seems like a wicked conflation to view the death of the murderer as equivalent to the death of an innocent victim. Death, suffering, and loss endure regardless of the pain we inflict on the offender. Retributive metaphysicians that think in quantitative terms of balancing the scale seem to overstate the ability of punishment to compensate for losses.

Debates between utilitarian and retributive theories of punishment produced hybrid theories, with the most common calling for a consequentialism constrained by deontological boundaries. These attempts to synthesize the best of both theories, however, typically fail to resolve their incompatible foundations. The "restorative justice" movement offers an alternative to retribution, as it emphasizes repairing the damaged relationships between offenders and victims through reconciliation programs rather than punishment. Still others advance the increasingly popular "restitution" theories of punishment that follow the law and economics movement to argue that offenders should pay their debts to society and their victims with financial compensation rather than through conventional penalties such as prison sentences.

Perhaps the greatest shortcoming of philosophy of punishment as a field has been its limited focus on *responding* to crime rather than considering justified means of *preventing* crime. Following the spirit of Marx's definition of crime as "the struggle of the isolated individual against the prevailing conditions," progressive versions of utilitarianism emphasize crime prevention by addressing social causes and "rehabilitating" the broader culture as well as individuals.[13] If drug abuse, poverty, or racial discrimination cause harm, then utilitarian-minded reformers may want to uproot criminality by eliminating these conditions rather than by incarcerating post-offense. From this perspective, we should diagnose and cure the social diseases that cause crime rather than simply treat individuals once they express symptoms of criminal behavior. Elliot Currie provides an analogy between public health and criminal law in this regard:

> Suppose we live in a society that tolerates abysmally primitive sanitation and that, accordingly, suffers from predictably high levels of preventable disease. Under these conditions we will "need" to build a lot of hospitals to care for the most seriously ill and to keep them from infecting other people – which, to some extent, they will do. In that sense 'hospitals work.' But most people would now regard such an approach to illness as thoroughly irrational. Hospitals 'work,' but they cannot substitute for preventative measure, and continuing to rely on them while ignoring the need to do something about the sanitation problem is both self-fulfilling and self-defeating. So it is with violence. If we simply accept the conditions that predictably breed large amounts of violent crime, then we will "need" a lot of prisons – and building a lot of them is likely to prevent some crime.[14]

George Fletcher explains that focusing attention on root causes of crime carries a strong political charge because "the belief that poverty causes crime is usually associated with liberals."[15] "Conservatives," he claims, "are more inclined to locate the ultimate cause of crime not in the offender's surroundings but in the personality of the offender."[16] Thus, there "is no need, the conservative argument runs, to look behind the evil person who acts in an antisocial way. The will to do evil is manifested in the deed and that is all the explanation one needs."[17] Within the current political climate, the decline of rehabilitation provides the right with an occasion to extend its anthem of "personal responsibility" in matters of distributive to retributive justifications for punishment. Just as the poor deserve their poverty and can rise from destitution by working harder, conservatives argue, criminals deserve to be held accountable for their actions because they alone caused their plight.

For the left, such arguments for individual autonomy obscure the injustices that segregate a racial and economic underclass behind prison walls. In Angela Davis's words, the prison "functions ideologically as an abstract site into which undesirables are deposited, relieving us of the responsibility of thinking about the real issues afflicting those communities from which prisoners are drawn in such disproportionate numbers."[18] Davis and others thus advocate for various versions of prison abolition. Rather than asking why we should abolish punishment, they argue, we should shift the burden of proof: given that punishment uses state authority to cause suffering, the onus lies on those who argue for punishment to convincingly make their case.[19]

Because no generally accepted justification for incarceration has emerged after hundreds of years of debate, we should retire the antiquated practices. In its place, some abolitionists would understand crimes as conflicts requiring resolution rather than the infliction of more pain. Abolitionists share many ideological commitments with pacifists and are subjected to similar criticisms, including the charge that it fails to adequately protect victims from aggressors.

Jeffrey Reiman similarly claims that the ideological agenda of contemporary criminal justice serves to compound the advantages of the rich and the disadvantages of the poor. By excessively emphasizing "one-on-one" crime, Reiman argues that the criminal justice system fails to protect populations from the greatest dangers to their well-being such as environmental and occupational hazards. Because the rich tend to cause such harms, Reiman argues, we punish such dangerous activities lightly when compared with crimes committed by the less powerful. According to Reiman, media and political forces combine to convey the "message that the real danger to decent, law-abiding Americans comes from below them, rather than above them, on the economic ladder" and this "image sanctifies the status quo with its disparities of wealth, privilege, and opportunity, and thus serves the interests of the rich and powerful."[20] Electoral politics has driven this trend, as few politicians find advocates for anything but longer sentences because doing so would expose them to "soft on crime" attacks. The disenfranchised – often by felony drug convictions – suffer most from these policies and find their interests comparatively underrepresented. Trends toward increasing incarceration appear entrenched for these reasons.

Although greatly simplified, this overview provides a map of the theoretical and practical geography in which we find apologies in criminal law. My following arguments cover a lot of ground. Hopefully the preceding paragraphs provide some orientation for visitors to this territory.

Ethical Pluralism in Punishment Theory

The theories of punishment summarized earlier and their various nuances have been debated for at least 200 years. Support for consequentialism, retributivism, and Marxism as the underlying justification for punishment has surged and retreated with changing social and political trends. No clear victor has emerged. In this context I find compelling what John Tasioulas describes as "ethical pluralism" with respect to punishment theory. Skeptical of a "top-down" ethical justification for punishment, Tasioulas argues for "a form of pluralism that recognizes an irreducible plurality of ethical values that are prone to conflict in individual cases."[21] Such an ethical pluralism "had better not simply present us with a jumble of distinct and conflicting considerations accompanied by the well-meaning but hollow instruction to exercise 'judgment' in discerning their practical import" but should instead "tell us something about the nature of the operative values, how they relate to each other and why they have the salience they do for the justification of punishment."[22]

I argue that all of the major theories of punishment should endorse "apology reductions" for remorseful offenders. Retributivists, for example, should agree with this conclusion according to their own internal logic. I also argue, however, that a compelling theory of apologies in law will consider, explain, and refine the various ways that apologies can simultaneously advance and even synthesize objectives from multiple perspectives. A convict who becomes categorically apologetic can satisfy the highest deontological ideals of punishment while also providing consequentialists with compelling reasons to find her less likely to recidivate. Alternatively, deterrent or incapacitative motivations for imprisoning a dangerous offender can provide occasion for the sort of moral reflection and transformation sought by communicative retributivists. The threat or experience of retributive hard treatment can stimulate and reinforce genuine moral reform; genuine moral reform can prove the most effective deterrent. Even the most compelling moral transformation can benefit from the threat of punishment in the backdrop should temptations arise.[23] A theory of apologies in law need not label criminal offenders either beasts requiring social control or moral agents only to be rationally persuaded toward the good. Apologies in law convey many meanings. Our task should be to understand how these meanings can both supplement and complement the major punishment theories without generating further inconsistencies, incoherencies, and contradictions.

This pluralistic view conveys a major benefit. Analyses of apologies limited to the presuppositions of one punishment theory will typically preach to the converted and thereby limit their audiences. A retributivist theory of apologies that does not consider the social utility of remorse in criminal law, for instance by testing the relationship between an apology and the likelihood of reoffending, will hold little appeal for policy makers. The big but partitioned tent created by this book hopefully promotes coalition building among the range of interested parties.

I find this position in the spirit of H.L.A. Hart's *Prolegomena to the Principles of Punishment* wherein he argues that "any morally tolerable account" of the modern criminal justice system must be a "compromise between radically distinct and partly conflicting principles."[24] Hart summarizes his position:

What is needed is the realization that different principles (each of which may in a sense be called a "justification") are relevant at different points in any morally acceptable account of punishment. What we should look for are answers to a number of different questions such as: What justifies the general practice of punishment? To whom may punishment be applied? How severely may we punish? In dealing with these and other questions concerning punishment we should bear in mind that in this, as in most other social institutions, the pursuit of one aim may be qualified by or provide an opportunity, not to be missed, for the pursuit of others. Till we have developed this sense of the complexity of punishment... we shall be in no fit state to assess the extent to which the whole institution has been eroded by or needs to be adapted to new beliefs about the human mind.[25]

Written in 1968, the "new beliefs about the human mind" Hart mentions refer to various rehabilitative methods then under development. Contrast the sorts of neuroscientific findings that promise and threaten to transform understandings of culpability in the twenty-first century. Hart's guiding method, however, seems more relevant today than ever: "In the case of Punishment the beginning of wisdom (though by no means its end) is to distinguish similar questions and confront them separately."[26] This is a helpful mantra. Apologies and remorse speak to many interrelated but distinct values. We find them within complex and dynamic environments. Contexts add layers of nuance while introducing additional and sometimes conflicting values. It requires effort to pull the issues apart to get a good look at them, which is why the elements of a categorical apology provide helpful landmarks through apologetic meanings. Sometimes we learn that a few parts intertwine inextricably. Some meanings serve primarily functional ends. Others speak to our highest spiritual commitments. A theory of apologies and criminal law should attend to the substance of these details within the configurations of contemporary criminal justice systems, conflicted as they may be regarding justifications for punishments.

CHAPTER TWO

Against Court-Ordered Apologies

> They wanted a statement saying that I was sorry for the crimes that I had committed against North Vietnamese people and that I was grateful for the treatment that I had received from them... I held out for four days. Finally, I reached the lowest point of my 5½ years in North Vietnam. I was at the point of suicide, because I saw that I was reaching the end of my rope. I said, O.K., I'll write for them. They took me up into one of the interrogation rooms, and for the next 12 hours we wrote and rewrote. The North Vietnamese interrogator, who was pretty stupid, wrote the final confession, and I signed it. It was in their language, and spoke about black crimes, and other generalities.... I kept saying to myself, "Oh, God, I really didn't have any choice." I had learned what we all learned over there: Every man has his breaking point. I had reached mine.
>
> Senator John McCain

Consider the case of Rickey Sharratt.[1] A Washington state jury found twenty-nine-year-old Sharratt guilty of the misdemeanor crime of destroying state land by illegally driving his four-wheel drive truck through protected forests. In an effort to "get its message out" regarding the penalties for illegal off-roading, an official from the Department of Natural Resources suggested requiring Sharratt to apologize and upload the video of his statement. YouTube seemed to be an especially appropriate forum because off-roaders often post videos of their outings, and having Sharratt's apology appear alongside clips that glorify the illegal activity could reach the targeted audience. Clark County District Court Judge James Swanger offered Sharratt a choice: serve five days on a work crew or apologize on video.

In the two-and-half-minute video, Sharratt sits behind a table reading from a statement and responding to questions from off camera. Between clips showing off-roading damage overlaid with heavy metal music, he explains that he was caught driving around a locked gate and held liable for approximately $2,000 in damage. "I learned that it's important for all of us to operate our motor vehicles in a safe manner and to observe all the rules," he

51

states. "Illegal off-roading damages habitat that fish and wildlife depend on," and "that's pretty important to me as a sportsman." Upon being prompted to explain why he offers this message, he states: "I thought it would be worth doing this public service announcement to make other recreationalists aware of the situation and of how important it is to observe the road signs." He does not utter the word "sorry" or otherwise describe his statement as an apology. The judge believed ordering the apology would be "therapeutic" for Sharratt and that if "the word gets out about the problems with illegal off-roading, that's a benefit to all of us."

Once the video appeared online, however, Sharratt made his actual opinions clear: "It's just a bunch of baloney." Compared to serving the work sentence, he "just thought that was an easier route to go." "The jurors," he explained, "were all a bunch of tree-hugging hippies." As judged by popular off-roading discussion boards, the intended effect may have been lost on the target audience.[2] Commenters argued that damage caused by off-roading "is nothing" compared to natural erosion and that such court-ordered apologies are akin to the forced statements of U.S. prisoners of war in Vietnam. One commenter derided Sharratt for not choosing five days of labor over "an eternity of being mocked on the internet."

Sharratt's case exemplifies the confusion regarding the meanings and uses of apologies and their role in criminal law. Obvious questions arise. What exactly is the apology meant to accomplish beyond conventional penalties? How, for instance, does the apology contribute to notifying potential offenders when compared with clear signage and public notices of convictions and punishment? If Sharratt chose the apology over five days of penal labor, will potential offenders perceive the apology option as easier and thus less of a deterrent than other penalties? Do we have compelling reasons to believe that making the video would provide "therapeutic" benefit? Given his description of the apology as "a bunch of baloney," Sharratt does not seem rehabilitated. Nor does his description of the jurors as "tree-hugging hippies" bode well for his future of environmental stewardship. Might such a coerced expression of remorse prove more likely to humiliate the offender and make him even less compliant? Did the state agents intend to humiliate him as part of his punishment, perhaps because of a retributive view that he deserved to suffer for his moral turpitude? Should the state put words in the mouths of offenders, requiring them to parrot beliefs under threat of violence? Should a government compel its citizens to lie about their beliefs in such a manner?

This chapter considers these questions by first placing the repentance of criminal and civil offenders in the context of a long and dark history of forced confessions. Court-ordered apologies, I argue, share many features with coercive practices of authoritarian states and religious institutions. We should view them with appropriate suspicion. In this light, I evaluate Kant's advocacy for court-ordered apologies as retributive humiliation as well as arguments from contemporary Kantians who support court-ordered apologies. I then consider various consequentialist arguments for and against court-ordered apologies. Clean distinctions between voluntary and involuntary apologies deteriorate throughout these discussions. I ultimately argue that compelled acts of contrition add very little, if anything, to the meanings and functions already present in contemporary legal proceedings and punishments, and they come at considerable costs and present serious dangers. Any value we might derive from such practices can be better realized through other means. I emphasize ordered apologies in criminal contexts, but the analysis applies to civil matters as well.

I should clarify some terms before proceeding. *I Was Wrong* organized various kinds of meanings associated with apologies and argued against understanding apologies primarily as something like a speech act or utterance of words like "I am sorry." Mental states such as the apologizer's moral beliefs, intentions, and emotions contain central meanings for acts of contrition. A person's actions after she utters apologetic words – whether she reoffends, for example – provides important information for evaluating the exchange. Some transformative apologetic acts may lack the speech act altogether, believing that talk is cheap and instead focusing on providing redress and undertaking reform. I mention this here because nearly all court-ordered apologies of which I am aware understand the apology as little if anything more that the utterance of words. This, I believe, accounts for many of their limitations.

Despite blurring boundaries between free and compelled acts of contrition, I will consider the subtleties that distinguish voluntary and involuntary apologies. For the purposes of this argument, we can stipulate a loose definition of court-ordered apologies as a written or spoken *speech act* conveying contrition (which includes statements of guilt and blameworthiness rather than only expressions of sympathy) that is compelled by state agents and in which a threat or an offer significantly compromises the subject's decision to utter the apologetic words. To alleviate my worry that someone will cite this definition as my conception of a *good* apology, I repeat: court-ordered apologies under this definition convey very different meanings from categorical apologies. I emphasize the speech act in this definition because I devote so much attention to understanding apologies as *more than speech acts*. Much of my resistance to court-ordered apologies lies in the failure of legal agents to appreciate the meanings of apologies beyond the words uttered. I describe the definition as loose because it leaves unresolved many important questions considered later. How, for instance, are compelled statements of guilt and blameworthiness different from those freely offered? Who is the intended recipient of the apology, who needs to hear it, and how public must it be? Given that apologies usually involve losses and gains for apologizers, what sort of threat or offer "significantly compromises" the apology? An especially confused court might understand itself to be ordering an apology but require only a statement of sympathy. This technically would not fall under the earlier definition, but I will consider such examples because they fall within the spirit of the legal phenomena with which I am concerned. Little hangs on this definition other than identifying a loose constellation of practices for the subsequent discussions and emphasizing courts' focus on the speech act as the core of the order. This misplaced emphasis, we will see, lies at the heart of problems with court-ordered apologies.

Additionally, note that I speak of court-ordered apologies rather than remorse. Remorse plays a considerable role in my discussion of voluntary apologies. I take it as evidence for my argument that the prospect of a court ordering remorse will immediately strike readers as misguided. Courts can subject offenders to a variety of punishments, but they cannot yet – barring the discovery of a biomechanical trigger that the state could press to produce the desired emotive state – make offenders *feel* remorse. The state can compel speech acts, by contrast, in the sense that it can require someone to pledge allegiance even if they do not *feel* patriotic.

A. The Dark History of Court-Ordered Apologies

The practice of inducing convicts to apologize has a long and often repugnant history. I will not reconstruct that history here other than to remind readers of the major events that fill in Linda Radzik's claim that the "history of atonement is in large part a history of degradation."[3] Although apologies may seem antithetical to modern adversarial criminal justice systems, in many respects they provided the foundations for these institutions.

Foucault describes confessions and repentance as the primary objective of widespread medieval practices of state-sanctioned torture, underwritten by the codification of penance as a sacrament in 1215 by the Lateran Council.[4] Investigation techniques of the Middle Ages led the accused to participate in their own incrimination and to testify to both the legitimacy of the state's authority and the veracity of the charges against them. According to Foucault: "The only way that [the state] might use all its unequivocal authority, and become a real victory over the accused, the only way in which the truth might exert all its power, was for the criminal to accept responsibility for his own crime."[5] Such punishment techniques ultimately created subjects who "judge and condemn themselves" and participate in the rituals of publicly declaring their own guilt by carrying their cross or wearing the placard announcing their sentence.[6] The very fact that one was *suspected* of a crime meant that she deserved some degree of punishment just for raising suspicion. Inducing confessions advanced judicial economy by streamlining investigative work – little need for detectives if the subject will eventually confess – while simultaneously administering punishment.[7] From this perspective "every possible coercion would be used to obtain" the highly valued act of confession.[8]

On Foucault's account, the details of the suffering of those burned alive contributed to the narrative of penance:

> The eternal game has already begun: the torture of the execution anticipates the punishments of the beyond; it shows what they are; it is the theatre of hell; the cries of the condemned man, his struggles, his blasphemies, already signify his irremediable destiny. But the pains here below may also be counted as penitence and so alleviate the punishments of the beyond: God will not fail to take such martyrdom into account, providing it is borne with resignation. The cruelty of the earthly punishment will be deducted from the punishment to come: in it is glimpsed the promise of forgiveness. But, it might be said, are not such terrible sufferings a sign that God has abandoned the guilty man to the mercy of his fellow creatures? And, far from securing future absolution, do they not prefigure imminent damnation; so that, if the condemned man dies quickly, without a prolonged agony, is it not proof that God wishes to protect him and to prevent him from falling into despair? There is, therefore, an ambiguity in this suffering that may signify equally well the truth of the crime or the error of the judges, the goodness or the evil of the criminal, the coincidence or the divergence between the judgment of men and that of God. Hence the insatiable curiosity that drove the spectators to the scaffold to witness the spectacle of sufferings truly endured; there one could decipher crime and innocence, the past and the future, the here below and the eternal. It was a moment of truth that all the spectators questioned: each word, each cry, the duration of the agony, the resisting body, the life that clung desperately to it, all this constituted a sign. There was the man who survived "six hours on the wheel, and did not want the executioner, who consoled and heartened him no doubt as best he could, to leave him for a moment"; there was the man who died "with true Christian feeling, and who manifested the most sincere repentance"; the man who "expired on the wheel an hour after being put there; it is said that the spectators of his torture were moved by the outward signs of religion and repentance that he gave"; the man who had shown the most marked signs of contrition throughout the journey to the scaffold, but who, when placed alive on the wheel, "did not cease to let Forth the most horrible cries"; or again the woman who "had preserved her calm up to the moment when the sentence was read, but whose wits then began to turn; she was quite mad by the time she was hanged."[9]

Torture, confession, and repentance intertwine into a gruesome spectacle of justice, divining a subject's blameworthiness from the contours or her anguish. Spectators read each contortion as somehow indicative of the offender's soul. Each scream introduces new ambiguities. Does immediate death signal God's wishes to limit suffering of the innocent, or the Devil's hunger to take the guilty? As Foucault famously goes on to claim, confession becomes integrated into our daily rituals – religious and otherwise – as a means of normalizing behavior in others and ourselves. "Confession," he writes, "has become one of the West's most valued techniques for producing truth." He explains in *The History of Sexuality*:

> It plays a part in justice, medicine, education, family relationships and love relations, in the most ordinary affairs of everyday life, and in the most solemn rites; one confesses one's crimes, one's sins, one's thoughts and desires, one's illnesses and troubles; one goes about telling, with the greatest precision, whatever is most difficult to tell. One confesses in public and in private. To one's parents, one's educators, one's doctors, to those one loves; one admits to oneself, in pleasure and in pain, things it would be impossible to tell anyone else, the things people write books about. One confesses – or is forced to confess. When it is not spontaneous or dictated by some internal imperative, the confession is wrung from a person by violence or threat; it is driven from its hiding place in the soul, or extracted from the body. Since the Middle Ages, torture has accompanied it like a shadow, and supported it when it could go no further: the dark twins. The most defenseless tenderness and the bloodiest of powers have a similar need of confession. Western man has become a confessing animal.[10]

Like our ancestors, we read the cries of offenders: do those tears bespeak genuine remorse or manipulative devilry? For us, however, the boundaries between criminal procedures and private conflict blur, allowing authorities to colonize further reaches of our psyches via the inroads of confession.[11] The cultural ascension of confession and remorse, on Foucault's view, enables increasing normalization and becomes a weapon in the consolidation of power.[12]

Authorities deployed court-ordered apologies to compound inequality and increase social control in many contexts. In eighteenth-century England, the privilege of prosecuting crimes was typically reserved for victims with sufficient resources to afford such legal processes. In such contexts, wealthy victims would threaten to prosecute unless the accused apologized and provided restitution.[13] According to Lawrence Friedman, trials in the colonial United States shared many features with those described by Foucault and served as "an occasion for repentance and reintegration: a ritual for reclaiming lost sheep and restoring them to the flock."[14] Here the "condemned were expected to play the role of the penitent sinner; it was best of all if they offered a final confession, a prayer, and affirmed their faith, in the very shadow of the gallows."[15]

Authoritarian states have long coerced public statements of "rehabilitation" from resisters. Soviet political dissidents underwent treatment in the *psikhushka* or "psychoprison" where they were to be cured of their reformist delusions and thereby experience a transformation in consciousness to embrace the state's objectives.[16] The English usage of the term "brainwashing" originates from *xǐ nǎo*, a collection of Maoist-era practices of coercive persuasion to party doctrine typified by public apologies.[17]

Coercive persuasion as a means to repentance arguably served as the foundational principle of the prison system in the United States. Leading penological theories once imagined the penitentiary as refuge where the offender could be removed from the temptations of criminal life and shepherded back to her true conscience when left to study her Bible. David Rothman elaborates:

> The functioning of the penitentiary – convicts passing their sentences in physically imposing and highly regimented settings, moving lockstep from bare and solitary cells to workshops, clothed in common dress, and forced into standard routines – was designed to carry a message to the community. The prison would train the most notable victims of social disorder to discipline, teaching them to resist corruption. And success in this particular task should inspire a general reformation of manners and habits. The institution would become a laboratory for social improvement. By demonstrating how regularity and discipline transformed the most corrupt person, it would reawaken the public to these virtues. The penitentiary would promote a new respect for order and authority.[18]

Theories disagreed regarding the extent of isolation and silence to be observed by inmates, but from the 1770s to the 1850s an international formula for the modern penitentiary emerged: the isolation in prison would turn the inmate's thoughts to God, reform, and penance.[19] The convict would leave prison a penitent and "morally cleansed Christian."[20]

Such lofty views of penitentiaries as retreats for spiritual redemption have lost ground to the belief that prisons should be, as Jeffrie Murphy describes the popular sentiment, "fortresses in which we warehouse an alienated underclass."[21] This history, however, provides a cautionary context for current debates regarding crime, repentance, and restorative justice. Despite my arguments throughout this book for an increased role for apologies in criminal justice, we should be mindful that historical traditions of repentance often seem, in retrospect, like thinly veiled justifications to compound the suffering of the disadvantaged. In this regard Radzik warns that "society's most vulnerable groups are likely to suffer disproportionately under atonement systems."[22] Elevating suffering to a criterion for redemption can also encourage submissiveness within vulnerable populations, leading them to accept various harms as legitimate aspects of atonement when they should be questioning and fighting these injustices. The powerful can also manipulate conceptions of atonement to their advantage, for instance when institutions like churches hypocritically call for retribution against sinners but call for forgiveness when finding their own members embroiled in a scandal such as the case of forced labor for "fallen women" in the Magdalen asylums of Ireland.[23] When we add banal *Schadenfreude* to our concerns that court-ordered apologies spring from suspicious motivations, we have good reason to be wary of atonement in criminal justice.

In many of these examples we see the most coercive techniques known to humans employed as means to the ends of religious repentance or secular conversion. How does this long history inflect the actions of a contemporary judge who requires an offender to publish a letter in the newspaper apologizing for a DWI conviction? Should we understand a federal sentencing judge reducing a prison term for a remorseful drug offender as inheriting this long legacy of states coercing moral transformations with the threat of violence? Can we distinguish between contemporary requirements that convicts express remorse for drug offenses or receive the full sentence and Soviet era demands to repent or face the Gulag? Should we understand court-ordered apologies as innovative forms of restorative justice, an additional deterrent for future offenders, a retributive or even vengeful attempt to humiliate convicts, or some disoriented hodgepodge of punishment theory?

Unfortunately, all of these questions arise within the baffling ideological context described earlier. Elliot Curie claims that "short of major wars, mass incarceration has been the most thoroughly implemented government social program of our time."[24] Despite these massive investments – both in terms of money and human life – in incarceration, the United States lacks a coherent theory of punishment.[25] Attempting to provide clear answers to even the most basic questions about the purposes of simple initiatives in the U.S. criminal justice system can prove fraught with political battles firing at practical cross purposes. Given the underlying confusion regarding the basic objectives of punishment, legal agents rarely make explicit the intentions of court-ordered apologies. As we evaluate the worth of court-ordered apologies in contemporary law, the history of coercive persuasion should remind us of the relationship between atonement systems and various problems of social justice. Beyond clarifying the moral concepts at issue in apologies in law, a compelling theory of apologies in law should appreciate the boots on the ground role of such ideology in culture.

B. Humiliation Will Compensate for the Offense: Kant's Retributive Justifications for Court-Ordered Apologies

If an offender recognizes her transgressions as a moral failure, something like a sense of blameworthiness and a concern for the victim will motivate her categorical apology. I argue in *I Was Wrong* that an ultimatum from someone with power to cause significant harm to the offender leads to coerced apologies. If we momentarily set aside the difficulty of maintaining clean distinctions between voluntary and involuntary gestures of contrition, voluntary apologies hold very different sorts of meanings from expressions of contrition ordered by courts. Beebe's initial letters, for example, would seem far less remarkable if he did not provide them so freely and against his legal interests. The legal process can accomplish many objectives without apologies from offenders. For one, it can undertake factual discovery of varying degrees of breadth and depth to establish an official state-sanctioned account of what happened. This corroboration of their stories and memorialization of their injuries may constitute the primary benefit of the legal action for some victims. Would an ordered apology add anything in this respect? Likewise, legal proceedings can also assign blame, excuse accidents, identify and affirm the values breached, recognize the victims as members of the moral community, levy penalties, and oversee the completion of sentences and efforts at redress. It can accomplish all of this without recourse to apologies. What, then, does a court-ordered apology add?

Like so many issues, we can trace much of our thinking about court-ordered apologies to Kant. Kantian ethical theory pulls in two directions. On the one hand, we find in Kant arguably the most inspiring secular articulation of the meaning and significance of humanity. In the Kantian framework, the rational human agent deserves respect above all else. Anything that prevents us from orienting our lives by our duties to care for each other (or at least not treat each other as mere means) should be understood as a lie that must be exposed in the radiance of enlightenment thinking. Despite the arguably racist, sexist, or speciesist undercurrents in his corpus, the central Kantian message rings true for many: clear thinking teaches us that humans deserve respect. People or institutions violating human dignity must be reformed. This informs much of the spirit of the restorative justice movement and its efforts to humanize modern legal practices.

Given this, one might expect a kind and empathic theory of punishment from Kant. His retributive theory of justice, however, feels very different in spirit from his general ethical theory. From his endorsement of capital punishment to his approval of humiliation as a retributive sanction, Kant hardly seems *progressive* to many advocates of restorative justice. His sternness and absolutism throughout his works make it difficult to sustain a clean separation between the "two Kants," but the rift between the humanitarian Kant and the punitive Kant continues to trouble modern Kantians.[26] R.A. Duff massaged this tension more than twenty-five years ago by describing his theory as "Kantian" while refusing to "call it Kant's principle," and two recent books – Radzik's *Making Amends* and Christopher Bennett's *The Apology Ritual* – use different strategies in their efforts to reconcile Kant and restorative justice.[27] These issues become especially prominent in the context of involuntary apologies in law.[28]

Immediately following the passages setting forth his most famous summary of retributive punishment and before his arguments for capital punishment, Kant provides this scenario in his 1797 *The Metaphysical Elements of Justice*:

Now, it might seem that the existence of class distinctions would not allow for the [application of the] retributive principle of returning like for like. Nevertheless, even though these class distinctions may not make it possible to apply this principle to the letter, it can still always remain applicable in its effects if regard is had to the special sensibilities of the higher classes. Thus, for example, the imposition of a fine for a verbal injury has no proportionality to the original injury, for someone who has a good deal of money can easily afford to make insults whenever he wishes. On the other hand, the humiliation of the pride of such an offender comes much closer to equaling an injury done to the honor of the person offended; thus the judgment and Law might require the offender, not only to make a public apology to the offended person, but also at the same time to kiss his hand, even though he be socially inferior. Similarly, if a man of a higher class has violently attacked an innocent citizen who is socially inferior to him, he may be condemned, not only to apologize, but to undergo solitary and painful confinement, because by this means, in addition to the discomfort suffered, the pride of the offender will be painfully affected, and thus his humiliation will compensate for the offense as like for like.[29]

This passage makes evident not only the retributive tenor of Kant's call for apologies in law but more specifically the value of humiliation as a counterweight on the scales of justice. Kant justifies court-ordered apologies because offenders – at least the sorts of offenders in such cases – *deserve to suffer the negative emotions* associated with such rituals. An apology produces the proportionate and commensurate negative emotions in such a situation. This should also apply, Kant argues, for offenses against the dead.[30]

For some readers the prospect of a court siding with the poor by humbling a mean-spirited aristocrat might seem both fair and inventive. I find Kant's position here peculiar, however, even by Kantian logic. For one, Kant – the great advocate for the unconditional value of truth telling – implies that the state can punish an unrepentant offender by requiring her to lie about her beliefs, values, or feelings in a court-ordered apology. If I find you worthy of insult and stand by my words but the court requires me to pretend that I believe you deserve my apology as I bow to kiss your hand, then *the court orders me to lie*. The source of the humiliation is twofold: not only must I admit wrongdoing publicly, but I must participate in my own degradation by lying and denouncing my views to comply with court orders. I am lying and suffering the indignity of being forced to lie. Rather than reintegrating offenders into the moral community of dignified moral interlocutors, such practices seem more likely to alienate convicts by dehumanizing them. The Minnesota Supreme Court reached this conclusion in the context of an order requiring police officers to write letters of apology to a young victim of their assault and racial discrimination. The court reasoned that such punishment is "calculated to humiliate and debase its writer and will succeed in producing only his resentment – an emotion not particularly conducive to the advancement of human rights."[31] In such cases the offender becomes a puppet of the state that speaks through her, a very un-Kantian predicament.

We can add an additional layer of humiliation in Kant's account. Categorical apologies convey various forms of emotional significance for victims and offenders, and we can appreciate the obvious shortcomings of emotionless apologies for serious offenses.[32] Our intuition that the apologizer deserves to suffer some emotional pain in apologizing resonates to some extent with the Kantian position that humiliation associated with court-ordered apologies serves appropriate punitive ends. Notice, however, an essential distinction. In my view, the emotional content of an apology typically consists of guilt and shame, feelings attached to the wrongness of one's behavior. These emotions convey an acceptance of blame and *motivate reform*, particularly in the context of the other transformative aspects of categorical apologies. Humiliation when ordered to kiss the hand of an inferior holds quite different content. I am humiliated because I am paraded as a subject of the court. Rather than reintegrating me into the moral community, such degradation seems more likely to stoke resentment and alienation. Instead of the state helping to understand my blameworthiness and cultivating the appropriate constructive emotions and actions that should follow, it drags me down a path of humiliation through the spectacle of my punishment.

Notice that Kant does not limit this position to cases of defamatory injuries that cause the victim humiliation and that, from the eye-for-an-eye perspective, call for commensurate humiliation of the offender. Broadening the class of offenses that deserve humiliating punishments, Kant writes: "[I]f a man of a higher class has violently attacked an innocent citizen who is socially inferior to him, he may be condemned, not only to apologize, but to undergo solitary and painful confinement, because by this means, in addition to the discomfort suffered, the pride of the offender will be painfully affected, and thus his humiliation will compensate for the offense as like for like." Kant's example speaks of the "higher class" attacking the "socially inferior," but it is not clear if or why such punishments should apply only when the rich injure the poor. Not all attacks against the underclass result from the sort of excessive pride best countered with humiliation, and some crimes of poor against rich do result in part from egocentric disregard for others. Most crimes arguably commit a disrespect of some kind – whether disrespect for a person or disrespect for the law – which leaves us to wonder if all criminal offenders in the Kantian system deserve the sort of humiliation accomplished by court-ordered apologies. Add to these considerations the underlying fact that I am being publicly censured because I have done wrong and we have four intertwined sources of suffering: I am an offender; I am a tool of the state displayed as an example of its authority to control the speech of its citizens; I am forced to publicly lie; and I experience emotions that may be damaging to my moral development.

In addition, the emphasis on emotions seems otherwise out of place in a Kantian framework given that he minimizes the significance of feelings throughout his ethical philosophy. From a Kantian perspective, one's motivation for apologizing should not be to reduce one's negative emotions or minimize one's sentence. On the contrary, we should expect cognitive intentions – whether to honor the violated value or the harmed person – to be central to a Kantian account of apologies.

The emotional component of apologetic meaning also adds to the difficulties facing binary theories of court-ordered apologies. Which emotions, with what intensity, and for what duration must they be experienced? If the reluctant apologizer feels no remorse, just how much humiliation must she experience for her punishment to be proportionate to her offense? What if I am a hardened criminal or from a particularly stoic culture, and therefore the compelled apology does not generate sufficient negative emotions in me? Can a court look to other ways of humiliating me? Given that humiliation already seems contrary to Kant's requirement that we treat convicts with dignity, the boundaries between legitimate and illegitimate humiliation begs for clarification. One might argue that Kant does not intend the sort of debasing humiliation that I suggest but rather suggests humiliation as a pedagogical means of promoting humility. Such a sympathetic interpretation seems implausible given his characterization of humiliation as proportionate suffering: "equaling an injury done to the honor of the person offended." Retributive debasement seems like Kant's intention here.

All of this is rather confusing. The central point, however, deserves emphasis: for Kant the primary justification for court-ordered apologies is not only retributive but retributive in the especially problematic sense of forcing the offender to suffer humiliation by state coercion.

C. Contemporary Kantians and Apology Rituals

Later chapters discuss various issues related to restorative justice with respect to my arguments for reducing punishments for voluntary and categorically apologetic offenders. Here I consider several contemporary Kantians writing on court-ordered apologies from the perspective of restorative justice but distancing themselves from Kant's own position. Without citing the humiliation passage, for instance, Radzik claims that the "suggestion that suffering is an intrinsic good that may be offered by way of compensation is too bloody minded to be acceptable."[33] Unlike Kant's understanding of the negative emotions associated with retributivism as a form of suffering inherent to just punishment, Radzik argues that the "wrongdoer's suffering should not be seen as an intrinsic good" but rather as the side-effects of the appropriate attitude toward one's wrongdoing.[34] She describes experiencing guilt after wrongdoing, therefore, as a byproduct of right thinking – a kind of "moral hangover."[35] Radzik prefers to understand negative emotions as not "valuable for their painful nature per se but as indicators that the wrongdoer has the proper attitudes about morality and his relation to it."[36] She therefore understands her "moral hangover" position as a "defense of suffering [that] is not retributivist."[37]

Following "right to punishment" principles inspired by Kantian and Hegelian retributive arguments that assert that legal sanctions must respect an offender's autonomy and her right to be punished like a rational member of the moral community rather than a mere object of social control,[38] Bennett advocates for what he calls the "apology ritual."[39] Bennett argues that "by requiring offenders to undertake the sort of reparative action that they would be motivated to undertake were they genuinely sorry for what they have done, the state condemns crimes in a way that is symbolically adequate and hence more meaningful than simple imprisonment or fining."[40] On Bennett's account, a court-ordered "apology restores relationships and redeems wrongdoers because it expresses emotions that are appropriate to wrongdoing."[41] These court-ordered apologies would be "artificial and symbolic"[42] but would fulfill what he considers the primary objective of punishment: "the expression of symbolically adequate censure."[43] Arguing that it is "not part of the remit of the state to pursue the full-blown moral reconciliation that comes with repentance" and that "the state has no duty forcibly to rehabilitate the offender, or even to aim to induce repentance in any way other than through the symbolically adequate expression of condemnation," Bennett believes governments have "no business giving out sentences the explicit aim of which is to make offenders genuinely penitent."[44] Following fellow Kantian Andrew von Hirsch's belief that penalties cannot disregard the offender's dignity by engaging in "compulsory attitudinizing,"[45] Bennett argues that whether the offender is "genuinely remorseful or not is not relevant to his relations with the state."[46] Bennett emphasizes that his court-ordered apology ritual "does not require offenders to undertake these amends in a spirit of remorse or even to put on signs of such remorse." "A person should be judged to have completed the sentence perfectly well," he argues, "simply by carrying out the level of amends, regardless of the spirit in which they do it."[47] For Bennett, forcing an offender to go through the motions of an apology is punishment enough. Requiring offenders to apologize regardless of their actual beliefs, Bennett argues, protects his position against objections that it violates freedom of conscience because the apologizers can ritualistically enact the appropriate contrition without *actually being required to undergo a moral transformation.*[48]

We should ask again what such apology rituals contribute to the legal process. Even with the conflicting principles underlying criminal proceedings in the contemporary United States, a conviction can accomplish many objectives that I claim are associated with apologies. To repeat, legal processes can establish a factual record, assign blame, excuse accidents, identify and affirm the values breached, recognize the victims as members of the moral community, levy penalties, and oversee the completion of sentences and redress. These processes express censure from various perspectives, and it is not clear how ordering an apology provides additional significance in this regard. We might appreciate the value of a court's demand for an apology as an especially powerful expression of authoritative condemnation: you have wronged and we command you – whether you want to or not – to bow your head in respect for our laws and your victims. Does demanding an apology convey this message better than a conviction and sentence?

Bennett holds a distinctively punitive conception of restorative justice, claiming that his theory of "apology will give us an answer to the question of why hard treatment is a necessary part of a response to wrongdoing."[49] He claims that "apology restores relationships and redeems wrongdoers because it expresses emotions that are appropriate to wrongdoing."[50] If the offender enacting the apology ritual need not *actually experience the negative emotions* associated with apologies, however, how does she suffer?

Although Bennett does not say this explicitly, my worry regarding Kant's original justification resurfaces: ordering the apology causes the offender to suffer a particular kind of submissive humiliation aiming at retributive rather that rehabilitative ends. Bennett believes that allowing offenders to undertake the order to apologize without sincerity protects their dignity and honors their freedom of conscience, but his apologetic ritual might prove even more dehumanizing. If the community believes I speak the court's words against my beliefs, my autonomy will be more compromised than if I am allowed to serve my sentence without the additional degradation of puppeting the court's words. Such humiliation could be especially acute in situations where the accused insists on her innocence or where she disagrees with the statute under which a court convicts her – for instance, if she advocates for marijuana legalization, for instance, while convicted of possession. These are not trivial examples given the number of criminal cases devoted to drug offenses that rest on deeply contested justifications. Imagine if Martin Luther King Jr. were alive and considered drug laws as the front lines in the march toward racial justice. Imagine if instead of his sequel to *Letter from a Birmingham Jail*, we had a court-ordered apology from King denouncing his planned campaign for drug reform.[51] Requiring such a person to contradict his beliefs under the threat of punishment evokes the most authoritarian examples of forced conversions.

Bennett intentionally excludes just what seems most absent from and needed in current criminal processes: the genuine moral transformation of offenders toward compliance with just laws. We should hope that offenders will experience negative emotions – that they will feel guilty, remorseful, and so forth – because this speaks to their moral transformation and their recognition of laws as just. An apology without experiencing the requisite negative emotions lacks central meanings. If offenders can successfully complete apology rituals "regardless of the spirit" in which they enact the amends, it seems unclear what the ritual adds beyond the sort of humiliation identified by Kant.

Perhaps more importantly, an offender ordered to apologize on Bennett's account need not accept blameworthiness. This strikes at the heart of my problem with court-ordered apologies: if the offender does not wish to admit wrongdoing and accept blame, describing her court-ordered actions as an apology invites misinterpretation. If she does not accept blame, explain what she did wrong, attempt to provide redress, experience apologetic emotions, or otherwise offer a categorical apology, it is best for all parties to understand clearly the meanings that are and are not expressed. Courts cannot, without an offender's considerable cooperation, cause someone to internalize their blameworthiness and thus spark their transformation. Courts can lead us to the fountains of virtue, but they cannot make us drink.

Moreover, if I have undergone a genuine moral transformation and seek to express this in an apology, a culture that practices apology rituals akin to Bennett's will probably be more skeptical and unlikely to understand me as truly reformed and thus deserving of moral credit of various kinds. The apology ritual might, in other words, create yet another obstacle for offenders to realize the sorts of robust apologetic meaning that we might view as the ultimate indicators of reform.

Thus far, retributive justifications for court-ordered apology seem unconvincing. Duff's Kantian "middle" position suffers from similar shortcomings.

D. The Middle Ground between Involuntary and Voluntary

Bennett's apology ritual originates in Duff's influential argument that punishment is best understood as a form of penance meant to bring about genuine repentance in the offender. According to Duff, "punishment should be understood, justified, and administered as a mode of moral communication with offenders that seeks to persuade them to repent their crimes, to reform themselves, and to reconcile themselves through punishment with those they have wronged."[52] Duff imagines a mandated sentence awakening the offender by concentrating her attention, explaining why her actions are wrong, and causing her to realize that she should voluntarily repent and accept her sentence as deserved. Duff explains:

If [an offender] is brought to repent his crime and to see the need for some reparative apology to reconcile him with those he has wronged, he will also come to accept his punishment as the formally prescribed way in which that apology is to be made. What began as punishment inflicted on him in order to induce repentance becomes a punishment (a fully fledged penance) that he accepts or wills for himself as an expression of that repentance. This is the proper aim of punishment as penance. The offender comes to recognize and repent his crime as a wrong and to realize that he must, and how he can, so reform himself as to refrain from such crimes in the future. He also comes to accept his punishment as a justified response to his crime – as an appropriate means of inducing that repentance and as an appropriate way in which he can express that repentance to others.[53]

Some terminological clarification may be helpful. By penance, Duff means some kind of burdensome act undertaken in response to a wrongdoing. Penance can be self-imposed or commanded, but in the criminal context he imagines courts will order the penance. Ideally, Duff argues, undertaking the work of penance leads the offender to see this work as deserved. The offender thus becomes repentant and now sees the penance as a burden she should carry willingly: "Penance, as vehicles of repentance, are at the same time vehicles for the self-reform that repentance motivates."[54] Duff appreciates that his model shares features with early U.S. penitentiaries and the "Quaker view of imprisonment as the appropriate mode of punishment: prison removes the criminal from his corrupting peers, and provides the opportunity for and the stimulus to a reflective self-examination which will induce repentance and self-reform."[55]

Although Duff writes from a Kantian perspective, he understands the "hard treatment" aspect differently than those views discussed earlier. His view appears more compatible with my conception of the role of emotions in categorical apologies: "Repentance is necessarily painful, since it must pain me to recognize and admit (to myself and others) the wrong I have done."[56] Rather than generate humiliation, this process attunes offenders to the emotions an appropriately apologetic person should feel: "In aiming to induce repentance, punishment thus aims to bring offenders to suffer what they deserve to suffer – the pains of repentance and remorse."[57]

Throughout this process, Duff argues, we must maintain a thoroughly Kantian disposition toward the offender as a moral interlocutor:

Penitential punishment that censures criminal wrongdoers, aiming to persuade them to repent their wrongdoing and to embark on the necessary tasks of self-reform, constitutes a mode of moral communication that addresses them as autonomous moral agents. It aims, not to coerce them into conformity with the law, but to appeal to their consciences – to their moral understanding. Like any mode of moral communication, it leaves it in the end up to them to be persuaded (to accept the message it communicates) or to remain unpersuaded.[58]

On this account, legal proceedings attempt to convince the offender via rational dialogue to accept punishment as just and to understand it as a form of penance "through which he can express his repentance and restore himself to the communion from which his sin separated him."[59] Self-reform therefore offers the ultimate aim for punishment. Such "a respect for autonomy will preclude any attempt to *force* a citizen to change her moral attitudes, or to bring about such a change by any means other than those of rational moral persuasion."[60] Unconvinced or otherwise noncompliant offenders still serve their penance, but Duff finds this coercion justified as long as the process treats the offender as an autonomous moral end rather than a mere means. Duff does not support extending sentences until offenders experience transformation because doing so would violate principles of proportionality and "turn punishment into an attempt to coerce offenders into submission rather than to appeal to them as moral agents."[61] Directly inspiring Bennett's apology ritual, Duff argues that we should treat those who remain remorseless upon completion of their sentence "as if" they are apologetic:

> How can his punishment reconcile him to his victim and the wider community if it is obvious that he is unrepentant and unapologetic.... The offender has been subject to what would constitute an appropriate reparative apology if he undertook it for himself. His fellow citizens should therefore treat him as if he has apologized. This is not a matter of pretending what they know to be false – of pretending that he has apologized when they know he has not. Instead, it is another aspect of treating him as someone who can redeem himself – as someone who can, and to whom we owe it to hope that he will, refrain from crime in the future. He might not have *paid* the apologetic debt he owed, if his punishment was simply inflicted. But something like that debt has been extracted from him, and those who extracted it should now treat him *as if* that debt has been paid.[62]

With this, Duff's position drifts toward advocating for the court-ordered apology: You will undertake penance, we will attempt to persuade you to repent and apologize, and you may choose to apologize or not. If you do not apologize freely, we will force you to undertake your penance but treat you as if you voluntarily apologized.

I find Duff's theory both important and problematic. Generally, it seems unclear what Duff means by apology and repentance. This creates confusion regarding how these practices map onto the various nuances of the meanings and functions of apologies that I attempt to identify. The Kantian tenor of his argument also leads him to ignore the sorts of consequentialist costs and benefits of ordered apologies discussed later that account for much of their potential value. This severely restricts the attractiveness of his theory for most policy makers. In addition, and as we would expect from a Kantian, his emphasis on the autonomy of the rational individual actor pays little attention to the underlying conditions that breed crime and contribute to the sorts of transgressions that require apologies. Duff does, however, offer a compelling and humane ideal of punishment: we should treat offenders as moral agents to be convinced of the wrongness of their transgressions such that they experience an awakening that leads them to repent and voluntarily undertake their sentence with a spirit of desert. Duff also begins to map the "middle category" between voluntary and involuntary apologies by understanding contrition as an evolving process. Such a moral transformation could result in a hybrid apology that begins as coerced but ends as a categorical state of contrition. An offender might also have an authentic desire to apologize or generally "become a better person," but she may be uncertain of how to proceed. Like an addict wanting to come clean, the contrite but confused offender may need considerable help before she understands how to provide and maintain a categorical apology. The justice system can either facilitate that process by treating the offender as a moral interlocutor in need of guidance or hinder the convict's development by treating her as a remorseless animal to be caged.

Once we understand the relationship between apologies and punishment as a dialectical process – punishment can occasion remorse that in turn speaks to the amount of punishment deserved – the boundaries between voluntary and involuntary apologies in the criminal justice system become difficult to sustain. Various incentives and disincentives inform a criminal offender's decision to express repentance or not. Distinguishing voluntary from involuntary activity generally presents notoriously thorny issues, and I will not detour into that rich literature here.[63] We can, however, recognize a spectrum of voluntariness without obvious thresholds between degrees of coercion. If I am subjected to medieval torture and told to repent or suffer disembowelment, few would consider my repentance voluntary even though I could have chosen to die. A threat to confess or board the next train to the Gulag would similarly compromise the voluntariness of my reform. In the contemporary United States, expressions of remorse can be the difference between a death sentence and life imprisonment.[64] Findings of remorselessness regularly and directly impact sentences. Restorative justice programs may view unremorseful offenders as uncooperative and not suited for alternatives to imprisonment. All of this creates a considerable incentive to appear repentant. Does such an incentive – express remorse and receive a discounted sentence – differ in its impact on voluntariness from a threat that you will receive the full sentence if you do not express appropriate remorse? Courts do not order apologies in these cases, but they do provide a powerful system of rewards and penalties around an offender's decision to apologize.

Although such considerations complicate matters and generate what Michael Moore describes as the "tournament field of competing doctrines" of criminal causation, we can recognize these incentive structures without abandoning notions of choice and voluntariness.[65] As I argued in *I Was Wrong*, we may disagree with commonsense individualistic notions of personal responsibility and their cognates, but many of our social practices rely on these ideologically charged terms. Without a relatively narrow notion of proximate causation, for example, criminal justices systems would attribute blame very differently. If we understood poverty or neurochemical activity as the primary causes of criminal behavior, then many of our customs of assigning praise and blame would lose traction. Apologetic practices certainly rely on rather strong notions of individual self-determination, perhaps excessively so. My basic point here is that we find our conceptions of voluntariness embedded in contested cultural and theoretical histories. *I Was Wrong* settled on a definition of coerced apologies as those offered in circumstances in which a threat or an offer significantly compromises someone's ability to choose not to apologize. The apologizer's recognition of her blameworthiness or desire to increase the well-being of the victim does not lead to her apology. Rather, an ultimatum from someone with power over her drives a coerced decision to apologize. This does not include cases in which the alleged offender risks only disapproval from others who wish for her to apologize but who lack the desire or ability to cause her serious harm.[66] Otherwise, we might view all disagreements as potentially coercive for apologizers.

Within this context, an offender's *intentions* for apologizing can inflect her gestures with very different significance. In my account of categorical apologies, we should distinguish between an apology given to reduce a sentence or even to win the favor of peers and one motivated by a desire to affirm the breached value or advance the victim's well-being. In this regard, von Hirsch goes so far as to claim that an offender subjected to Duff's model and "browbeaten" into apologizing offers "no real apology at all."[67] Questions of intention therefore influence discussions regarding voluntariness and involuntariness in significant ways. Even a voluntary instrumental apology – an obviously disingenuous statement offered freely to curry favor with authorities, for instance – has value as an expression of the state's commitment to the breached principle and its ability to bend the will of its subjects to honor such laws. Acts of contrition in criminal law fail and succeed in ways that defy binary conceptions of apologies, and these issues provide a sense of the work required for a comprehensive treatment of the subject.

Duff's accounts of penance, repentance, and apology would benefit from more precision in mapping the sorts of meanings conveyed along the spectrum of voluntary and involuntary apologies. Duff appreciates that apologies entail reformed behavior[68] and that such reform requires time and effort.[69] He also helpfully distinguishes between morally persuaded offenders, shamed offenders, already repentant offenders, and defiant offenders. The categorical apology, I argue, captures still more salient nuances. In addition to matters of intention, questions abound regarding the meanings conveyed by Duff's repentant offender. Consider a few: Does she explain the full story of her offense? Has she understood and confessed the related non-criminal but immoral activity where appropriate? Does she understand how her seemingly innocuous behaviors lead to criminal activity? If drug or alcohol abuse contributed to the illegal activity, has this been satisfactorily addressed? To what extent and with what degree of clarity and commitment does she assent to the moral principles at issue? Does she refrain from the activities because they are illegal or does she honor these values as central to her life independent of the law? Has she repeatedly faced and overcome temptation to reoffend? The lack of answers to these questions leads me to doubt Duff's claim that we should treat the unrepentant offender ordered to apologize as if they have apologized. We can treat even unrepentant offenders with dignity and as capable of "redemption," but we should exercise care in distinguishing between categorically apologetic offenders and others. We already suffer from considerable confusion regarding the significance of apologies, and such an "as if" approach will likely create even more uncertainty, danger, and injustice. With the categorical apology we have some assurance that offenders have undergone the sort of transformation that will make them less likely to reoffend. We have no such assurances from the unrepentant and should take the necessary precautions.

In light of these considerations, retributive justifications for court-ordered apologies seem weak. To review, Kant's call for apologies as retributive humiliation seems steeped in the dark history of coerced confessions and undermined by serious objections even internal to Kantian arguments. Contemporary Kantians modernize his views, but claim that the state should require offenders to repent and then treat them as if they have provided a morally thick voluntary apology generate dangerous confusions about offenders' attitudes. I have difficulty understanding what significance court-ordered apologies add to more traditional criminal processes and punishments, and the retributive accounts of court-ordered apologies do not help us clarify the precise kinds of meaning that apologetic offenders do or do not provide. Instead, court-ordered apologies strike me as remnants of premodern punishment. Unlike Bennett and Duff, I find the "ritualistic" nature of court-ordered apologies to be an argument against rather than for their perpetuation. Kantians should heed Nietzsche in this regard: "[I]t is not long since princely weddings and public festivals of the more magnificent kind were unthinkable without executions, torturings, or perhaps an auto-da-fé [burning penitents at the stake as was common during the Inquisition], and no noble household was without creature upon whom one could heedlessly vent one's malice and cruel jokes."[70] "Without cruelty there is no festival," continues Nietzsche, "thus the longest and most ancient part of human history teaches – and in punishment there is so much that is festive."[71] The humiliating rituals of court-ordered apologies remind us that for most of human history we punished not because the offender deserved it in some metaphysical sense – a view that Nietzsche believes is "in fact an extremely late and subtle form of human judgment and inference" – but rather from a more primitive reflex to lash out in anger.[72]

We can distinguish Duff's claim that forced penance can serve as a means to the end of transformation from other retributive justifications for court-ordered apologies, but this requires us to recast that claim in more consequentialist terms than Duff intends. Consequentialist arguments supporting court-ordered apologies, to which I now turn, are only slightly more compelling.

E. Consequentialist Considerations Regarding Court-Ordered Apologies

The Importance of Consequentialism to a Comprehensive View of the Value of Court-Ordered Apologies

Duff gives little consideration to consequentialist issues, explaining that although his "account is non-consequentialist, in that it does not make the justification of a penal system depend upon its contingent efficiency as a means to some independently identifiable end, it is not a purely retributivist account that justifies punishment solely in terms of its relationship to the past crimes." Because punishment attempts to "protect citizens from crime and to preserve the political community by persuading offenders to repent their crimes," it should have crime-reducing side effects.[73] Although consequentialism may appeal to practical-minded reformers, Duff insists that "using punishment as a deterrent is inconsistent with a proper regard for actual potential offenders as members of the normative political community."[74] Radzik's and Bennett's Kantian dispositions similarly prevent them from systematically considering the consequentialist value of restorative justice or apologies in law.[75]

I imagine most legal agents and reformers will be dissatisfied with a theory of reconciliation or punishment that does not address the concrete issues of deterrence, rehabilitation, recidivism, and the like. One of the most powerful reasons to give serious consideration to apologies in law, for instance, lies in the strength of an offender's promise to refrain from reoffending. If we learn from compelling studies that court-ordered apologies provide powerful indicators of recidivism – with regard to either less reoffending because they occasion moral growth or more reoffending because they further alienate offenders by humiliating them – I would not want to ignore such evidence. A holistic view of the relationship between punishment and apologies requires us to consider such objectives.

Having said this, Bennett clarifies an important point of contention:

Even if we see deterrence or preventative punishment as necessary, why see it as part of punishment rather than as a quite different type of social agency, something more akin to welfare or housing, that aims at the eradication of serious and avoidable harms? This insistence on the distinctiveness of punishment "proper" might look like a valid but uninteresting point until we see that it is only by insisting on that distinction that we get a clear picture of the moral costs of some aspects of crime prevention – the way in which sometimes what we need to do to prevent crime involves us wronging individuals to whom we owe better treatment.[76]

I agree that we should aim for precision regarding the distinct retributive and consequentialist aspects of both punishments and apologies and we should exercise care when we label state action as "punishment" rather than education, reform, or otherwise. My view of apologies in law attempts to account for the range of meanings and functions of acts of contrition so that we can conceptualize and evaluate their full spectrum of moral and practical significance. In addition to gaining "a clear picture of the moral costs of some aspects of crime prevention," we should understand the benefits of voluntary and involuntary apologies in criminal law to assess their worth as humane and effective policies. Unlike other forms of utilitarian punishment that Hegel describes as akin to "man who lifts his stick to a dog," thus treating "a man like a dog instead of with the freedom and respect due to him as a man," we have reason to believe that categorical apologies can go some way toward satisfying both retributive and consequentialist justifications for punishment.[77] We are, however, most likely to realize the benefits of apologies in criminal law from the sorts of voluntary gestures of contrition addressed later.

Before turning to voluntary apologies we should consider the consequentialist aspects of court-ordered apologies in more detail. As a methodological note, one can generally build strong deontological arguments without empirical data. Utilitarian arguments, by contrast, can speculate about the likely outcomes of proposed policy, but compelling social scientific studies support the most convincing consequentialist claims. With a few exceptions, the ensuing discussion unfortunately relies primarily on the speculative costs and benefits of court-ordered apologies.

With that disclaimer, what sorts of consequentialist benefits might court-ordered apologies contribute beyond those already accomplished in standard legal proceedings? I admit that this question proves more complicated than I initially understood. Prima facie, I suspected that court-ordered apologies did not add much other than perhaps some marginal deterrent value via humiliation. As I have repeatedly asserted, the legal process can establish a factual record, assign blame, excuse accidents, identify and affirm the values breached, recognize the victims as members of the moral community, levy penalties, and oversee the completion of sentences and redress. This appeared to leave little work for a court-ordered apology to accomplish. I now realize that traditional legal proceedings *can* achieve all of these objectives associated with apologies, but they seldom do so in criminal justice systems like that of the United States where approximately 95 percent of criminal cases conclude in plea agreements.[78]

Return to Beebe's plea. Beebe provides a rather exceptional example of a voluntarily apologetic criminal defendant, yet the legal process leaves so many gaps. Important facts about the assault – both regarding Beebe's actions and those of others – remain unknown. The legal proceedings and plea do not corroborate the morally salient details from the factual record. We will probably never know the details of what happened that night. Likewise, Beebe admits guilt and presumably accepts blame for aggravated sexual assault, but the plea removed charges of rape and object sexual penetration. Beebe admitted to rape in his e-mails to Seccuro, but the legal proceedings do not capture this fact or require Beebe to accept blame for these more serious offenses. Seccuro questioned even Beebe's acceptance of blame for the lesser charge because of his understanding of the offense as a byproduct of youthful addiction. In her words, "Blame Youth. Blame alcohol. Blame the victim."[79] What values do such legal proceedings identify and affirm? Whenever a criminal justice system prosecutes a crime, it denounces those activities as unacceptable and confirms its intent to enforce those underlying values. The court expresses its commitment to the wrongness of sexual violence in these proceedings, yet the ultimate penalty – recall that Beebe served five months and community service – arguably does not affirm that value strongly enough. Rape and object sexual penetration, by contrast, carried a maximum life sentence.[80] Further, although we might believe that the criminal justice system recognizes Seccuro as a moral interlocutor by prosecuting the offense committed against her, victims play a very small role in the proceedings and have little, if any, say in plea agreements and sentences. Seccuro not only found the prison sentence too short, but she also took issue with the requirement that Beebe speak about sexual violence on campuses. Besides the "fox in the hen house" element, she thought he would send the message that "rape could land you in jail" rather than what she considered the more important points regarding the horrific impact of rape on its victims and the need for students to protect themselves and others.[81] This example underscores that even in cases of voluntary apologies, a considerable gap exists between the sorts of meanings that formal trials and punishments *can* convey and what they actually *do* convey given the realities of criminal justice systems, especially given the predominance of pleas. When assessing the utilitarian value of both voluntary and court-ordered apologies, therefore, we should avoid idealizing legal proceedings and consider the significance of acts of contrition within such environments.

Notice first what a court-ordered apology cannot add. If the accused does not confess and is not found guilty of the most serious charges – as a result of exoneration or a plea agreement – a court-ordered apology is highly unlikely to order the accused to confess details not already in the record or to accept blame beyond that determined by the court. Imagine if the judge accepted Beebe's plea to aggravated sexual battery and punished him accordingly, but then required him to apologize and accept blame for rape as he did in his initial communications to Seccuro. If the formal process cannot or does not establish guilt regarding the more serious charge, a court-ordered apology requiring confession to that offense would flout the legal process and its basic standards for proving blameworthiness. Court-ordered apologies can establish a backdoor for assigning culpability in this regard. Now imagine a far more typical example in which the accused admits no criminal wrongdoing and either pleads to a lesser offense or receives a not guilty verdict. How could a court then order her to apologize, explain what really happened, accept blame for her wrongdoing, and undertake appropriate redress? For this reason I reject arguments that court-ordered apologies require wrongdoers to "accept public responsibility for violating legal norms" in some sense beyond that conveyed by the legal ruling.[82] Again, civil and criminal courts can find a defendant guilty in various ways and declare this finding publicly. They cannot, however, cause defiant offenders to accept blame or endorse the state's account of events. Even those who are obviously guilty may deny responsibility. Sometimes they blame others, sometimes they suffer from delusions, and sometimes they find the law unjust. Requiring such offenders to read an apologetic statement will not convince them of their blame.

Rehabilitation and the Analogy to Ordering Children to Apologize

One promising consequentialist benefit parallels Duff's retributive vision: the process of requiring an offender to apologize may bring about not only repentance on a deontological register but also rehabilitation from a utilitarian perspective. Compelled apologies could create opportunities for the sort of moral reflection that triggers personal transformation – or at least a kind of behavior modification – and thereby reduces recidivism. The question becomes whether an ordered apology provides more effective rehabilitative benefits than other forms of punishment. As noted earlier, a court-ordered apology could also prove contrary to rehabilitative and normalizing goals by antagonizing the offender and entrenching a sense of hostility toward the justice system. Empirical research regarding whether ordered apologies do more harm than good would need to control for the particulars of the process. A procedure requiring a convict to read a statement prepared by the prosecutor and that demonizes the offender or contains contested information, for example, will likely produce different results from a state-mandated apology authored by the offender after a period of effective therapy and treatment.

In the absence of sufficiently nuanced social scientific studies of the rehabilitative effects of court-ordered apologies, we can look to the analogue of requiring young children to apologize.[83] Rather than merely reprimanding a child for hitting a sibling, for example, many parents require their children to apologize. Understanding whether we should endorse this practice deserves consideration because it illuminates the shortcomings of arguments claiming that ordering adult criminal offenders to apologize will facilitate their rehabilitation.

Requiring children to apologize can serve several purposes. First, it identifies principles at issue and names them for a child in the process of learning the rules of the community, their subtleties, and the consequences for violating those expectations. A rule has been violated, and we notify the child that the rule exists and that we will enforce it. Second and third, the parent not only names the principle and the wrong but also delivers a kind of verdict that assigns blame: you hit your brother and hitting your brother is not acceptable. Notice two distinct issues. This first provides a finding of fact that states what happened: you hit your brother. The child may deny it, but the parent sets the record straight. With this in place, she can assign blame. Such a finding of blame can help the child learn the basics of moral responsibility and causation. As many parents know from experience, children experiment with exculpatory arguments: "I didn't hit him – he ran into my first," or "He made me hit him because he took my toy." At three years old, one of my children even tried "my brain made me do it," an argument that may be correct but not a justification in our house. Declaring who deserves blame teaches not only the principles at stake but also how we assign blame and how we must take responsibility for our actions. We cannot force children to accept blame – they may defiantly refuse or insist on their innocence – but we can explain why they *should*. Our normative notions of moral causation hopefully begin to make sense and become internalized with enough repetition.

This leads to the fourth potential benefit of requiring the child to apologize: it provides an occasion for the child to reflect on and adopt the principle at issue. Although repeatedly stating "do not hit" names the principle and issues a command that may socialize via rote learning, requiring the child to apologize hopefully leads her to make the principle her own. This process can benefit from some version of a "time-out," not as a punitive measure but to "think about what you did and why it is unacceptable" and thereby undertake the sort of guided reflection that helps integrate the child into a normative community. If the child hears the principle often enough and if we repeatedly require her to apologize for violating it in a manner that helps foster understanding why we enforce these rules, we hope that repetition will not only condition her behavior but also lead her to appreciate why the principle is a good one.

Fifth, requiring an apology also provides opportunities for various lessons in emotional development. Most basically, it can cultivate empathy. Although obvious to most adults, children must learn that others feel pain and that we cause pain of various kinds and intensities when we harm others. By asking the child to consider how she would feel if she were the victim and to imagine what would make her feel better in such a situation, we invite her into a moral dialogue that hopefully brings her to realize that she should apologize and help the other child "feel better." We also teach the child that her victim is a moral interlocutor, what most parents will recognize as reminding the child that she has injured a *person*. Thus parents may find themselves repeatedly saying "she's a person" or "I'm a person" in order to lead a child from brute egocentrism into an empathic appreciation of people as fundamentally unlike the other objects they come into contact with and deserving of different treatment. This empathy training promotes additional emotional education. When you do something wrong and make someone suffer, you should feel bad. We teach and model appropriate emotional responses, and requiring an apology hopefully helps a child understand that causing suffering in others creates suffering in oneself. Because we care about and look after each other, we should feel both empathy and guilt when we cause harm. Parents can also teach children not to feel excessively bad for their misdeeds, training them not to experience continuous shame for minor infractions and to appreciate that apologies can relieve both the victim and the offender of negative feelings. Here lies a more advanced lesson regarding intentions: we apologize not because we want to avoid further punishment but because we have wronged and we care about the other person and the principle at issue. Because the apologizer should *feel bad* about her misdeeds – and the worse the deed, the worse she should feel – a certain tone should animate the apology. A reluctant grumble or flippant manner bespeaks insincerity, and we infer that the child has not achieved the appropriately contrite mental state. Although it may invite disingenuousness to require a child to repeat an apology until she adopts the proper tone, children require coaching in the proper expression of emotions. In addition to teaching children moral principles, we also model emotional responses to violations of those principles. Subtleties of apologetic tone, facial expression, body language, word choice, and other cues all contribute to a child's socialization.

By teaching the child how to provide redress to the person she injured, she gains experience thinking empathically with regard to what might set things right with the other child. Depending on the offense, this may range from simply checking on the other child to devoting allowance money to repair a broken object. Undertaking supervised redress teaches consequences in this respect. Learning how to provide redress also empowers the child with conflict resolution skills – she made a mistake and she has the ability to make it better rather than wallow in shame or lose a companion. This constellation of moral lessons hopefully impresses on the child from a variety of angles that she should not reoffend. The apology contains an expression that the child has learned, or she is in the process of learning how to handle the next situation differently as well as a promise not to reoffend. If she does not change her behavior, we can explain how this drains her previous apology of substance and that she was not truthful when she said that she would not do it again. Even very young recipients of apologies seem to understand this distinction. Some two-year-olds can explain that older siblings are "not really sorry" if they continue the offending behavior. This provides an important lesson: just because someone says "sorry" does not necessarily mean that you should trust her. Whether giving or receiving an apology, children should learn that meaningful apologies entail reformed behavior.

Redress also benefits the victim, providing her recognition as well as an assurance of reform and restitution. If an elder sibling hits a younger sibling, requiring an apology from the offender indicates to the younger child that the adult ("the authoritative law") understands that she has been unjustly harmed, the adult will not tolerate it, the offender has been censured, and the victim can feel secure that the adult will protect her from future transgressions. The apology also creates an occasion for the victim to express how she has been made to feel, an important process not only for the offender to appreciate the pain caused but also for the victim to practice expressing complex emotions while having those feelings validated. The younger child in this example also receives some secondary normalizing – although she may not be guilty on this occasion, she knows the principles apply to her as well. Commanding the child to apologize also, for better or for worse, conditions children to submit to authority whether they want to or not.

All of this provides an occasion not only to internalize rules but also to practice moral reasoning and various social skills, including accepting blame and resolving conflicts. The child learns how to apologize, itself a valuable lesson. Thus, even coerced apologies – apologize to your brother or suffer X deprivation – provide important tools in the process of moral development. This resonates with Aristotelian arguments for the necessity of habituation during childhood for the formation of ethical life: one becomes a good person by practicing virtuous behavior. We learn to become the kind of person who apologizes when appropriate. An Aristotelian would argue that someone improperly trained in childhood faces reduced possibilities for developing good habits and for living well as an adult. Over time and with practice, we hope that children become habituated to and explicitly endorse the principles at issue such that we no longer need to order them to apologize because they do so voluntarily. As we mature, apologizing can mark an occasion when we pause and self-consciously honor our abstract moral beliefs – we have wronged or have been wronged and we must denounce the trespass or risk losing the value jeopardized by it. If a child apologizes before the parent raises the issue, this can signal a significant development in the child's moral education because it suggests that she has internalized the norms at issue and has engaged in something like autonomous moral deliberation. Without prompting – or sometimes reminding the child with a question such as "What do you do when you hurt someone?" – the offender realizes that she breached a value that she endorses and thus finds internal motivation for engaging in apologetic behavior. As discussed earlier regarding the difficulty of drawing bright lines between voluntary and involuntary apologies, apologies from children often populate the middle ground. Given the nature of their subjection to various adult authorities, children experience a spectrum of control exercised over them as adults order, request, strongly encourage, remind, reward, and take pride in the apologies of the young. The general points here seems uncontroversial: we hope children learn to voluntarily apologize well at some point in their development. With so many potential benefits derived from properly requiring a child to apologize, it appears to deserve its status as a time-honored parenting technique.

Less constructive uses of ordering children to apologize also warrant attention. Some parents may force children to apologize for the parent's self-serving social reasons, hoping that such an authoritative display sends the impression to other adults that the parent is not overly permissive or otherwise culpable for the child's misbehavior. Ordering an apology can, in other words, provide a comparatively easy reactive response to minimize embarrassment when preventative measures fail. Overreliance on this strategy may not only prove ineffective but may teach the child that apologizing offers a license to misbehave. Here we should worry about encouraging the treadmill of contrition: offend, apologize, offend, apologize. As long as I apologize after I do it, all will be forgiven. The opposite maladjustment can occur when parents seize a child's apology as an admission of wrongdoing and continually harp on it long after the issue has passed. This can teach a child to never apologize unless forced because – as John Wayne advised to "never apologize" because it is a sign of weakness – contrition can damage one's social position and be weaponized against the contrite.

For these reasons some parenting experts advise against ordering children to apologize. Jane Nelson, author of numerous books on positive discipline, argues that you should not "force anyone to apologize at any age." Doing so, she believes, is "teaching kids to lie. If they're not sorry and we make them say sorry, just to make us feel good, that's not about empathy."[84] According to this view, authentic apologies, like heartfelt love, cannot be ordered. In this respect we might worry that instead of teaching children how to apologize well, we train them to fake their emotions and simulate whatever sentiments produce the desired outcome. Although arguably a valuable skill in its own right, I doubt many parents intend the social utility of inauthenticity to become the primary lesson of forced apologizing. Nelson argues that instead of forcing the child to apologize, we should speak to the child about what triggered her misbehavior, for example asking "what made you so angry that you hit your brother?" Once we make this "connection" and empathize with the offending child about her feelings, then you undertake "correction" by asking them to consider how the victimized child feels. As you lead her to empathize with the other child, this will awaken the offender's empathy and feelings of contrition. Once she actually "feels sorry" you can then coach her toward providing an honest apology and undertaking remedial behavior. Such a technique may also reduce the child's potential resentment for authority while enhancing self-esteem via internally motivated moral behavior. This technique offers a promising method of shepherding a child toward apologizing voluntarily, but the child may not reach this realization for any number of reasons. By the time she becomes "ready" to apologize on her own terms, the victim may have forgotten the offense. Attention spans are short in conflicts between young children, leaving less voluntary apologies to serve important time-sensitive functions.

Advocates and critics alike should note the importance of developmentally appropriate treatments of apologies from children. Some aspects of categorical apologies exceed the cognitive capacity and emotional maturity of young children. We should not expect a two-year-old, for instance, to appreciate nuances of empathy and intentionality central to apologetic meaning. Young children may genuinely not understand why their actions were wrong or that they caused suffering in another. Forcing a child to undertake tasks that are not developmentally appropriate will likely do more harm than good, and we should calibrate our expectations and how we teach accordingly. We may confuse, discourage, or frighten a four-year-old if we demand categorical apologies from her. Rather than teach young children how to apologize thoughtfully, developmentally inappropriate expectations may primarily train children to comply with what might look to them like arbitrary demands: dessert comes after dinner, do not pick your nose in public, apologize when I say, and so forth.

Excessive expectations for apologies can introduce additional unproductive struggles if the child refuses to apologize, perhaps from confusion or inability to control emotional outbursts. If we demand an apology from a young child clearly unwilling to provide it or incapable of doing so at that moment, we risk escalating a dispute when we should instead model less confrontational conflict resolutions. Prudence may also require a parent to treat scraps between young siblings – an ongoing process with thousands of iterations evolving over a lifetime – differently than altercations with strangers on the playground. Thus instead of using apologies as an all-purpose and one-size-fits-all tool of moral education, disentangling the lessons and identifying when our children will be most receptive to these discussions will likely teach children – especially young children – most effectively. Rather than requiring an apology with all of its complexities from a three-year-old, for example, we should sometimes isolate the basic lesson that the child hurt another person. Once the child becomes consistently competent with the building blocks of contrition, we can introduce more complex aspects of contrition without overwhelming her. We will find older children receptive to sophisticated lessons such as the realization that even though in the "real world" people often receive credit for patently disingenuous apologies, we should aspire to become a person with the strength of character to apologize well even in such an imperfect and unfair world.

Difficult questions arise regarding which expectations are reasonable at what ages. Should a four-year-old know to apologize for hitting his brother? If so, what sort of apology can we reasonably expect? How should such expectations evolve by age twelve? By what age should they learn the subtleties of apologetic meaning such that we should raise the bar all the way to expect categorical apologies? I leave the particularities of these questions to experts in child development, but again the general point seems uncontroversial: effectively teaching children to apologize requires developmentally appropriate techniques and expectations. Developmentally appropriate techniques for teaching children to apologize include methods across the spectrum from involuntary to voluntary, with the objective that over time and with considerable practice children develop the values and strength of character to apologize categorically when appropriate.

As we return to the analogy between requiring children to apologize and court-ordered expressions of contrition, a few major distinctions between the practices illuminate the problems with coercing apologies from adult convicts. First, young children are not full moral agents. Just as we tell a four-year-old that she cannot have ice cream for breakfast, we might command that she cannot go to the playground until she apologizes to her sister. Advocates of requiring children to apologize typically consider this justified paternalism because it presumably benefits the child's long-term well-being. The child's adult self will appreciate the restrictions we placed on her in childhood because they helped teach her beliefs and practices that she, as an adult, values as her own. This reduces our concerns, somewhat, regarding the coercive nature of ordering apologies from the young. As children mature, this concern increases because we generally afford adults more autonomy. If my fifty-year-old adult child wants ice cream for breakfast, I might disapprove but ordering her to eat her oatmeal becomes fraught with difficulties. Parallel issues arise if I tell my adult child that I will write her out of my will if she does not apologize. Because we expect adults to know when they should apologize, requiring them to do so under threat emphasizes that they do not feel as they should and highlights the distinctions between voluntary and involuntary acts of contrition. The absence of central forms of apologetic meaning only becomes more obvious.

This leads to the second distinction: because we do not understand young children as full moral agents, we do not – at least I hope we do not – punish them for retributive reasons. If a preschooler hits her sister, we do not strike her back to administrative proportionate suffering and thereby balance the scales of justice. If anything, corporal punishment of children is a misguided attempt to achieve consequentialist objectives with harsh deterrents.[85] Although we might appreciate Kant's argument that forced apologies from certain kinds of adult offenders can provide commensurate redress for certain kinds of insults, retributive justifications for ordering young children to apologize as a form of justified suffering or humiliation seem irredeemably problematic.

The effectiveness of ordering a child to apologize presents various empirical questions, and I know of no systematic study of such parenting techniques. We do, however, have good reasons to expect that ordering apologies proves more successful with young children than with convicts. Apologies have an important role to play in child development, but adult offenders have presumably already undergone the most formative periods in this process. Whatever benefits children experience when ordered to apologize, these seem less likely to reach adults. This is not to say that adults cannot reform, but only, as Aristotle suggests, that the process will likely become increasingly more onerous as the offender ages. Juvenile criminal offenders may therefore receive more benefits from court-ordered apologies than adult offenders.

Notice also that the effects of ordering children to apologize aggregate over time. Training a child to express contrition appropriately can require hundreds if not thousands of consistent repetitions before she internalizes the values and rituals. Like teaching a child to speak a foreign language or to brush her teeth, the initial attempts may require considerable coercion, but with practice and understanding the child becomes a proficient and self-motivated apologizer. By comparison, I doubt that ordering an adult offender to provide a single apology will have an effect similar to an entire childhood of moral training in contrition. In the context of various other influences – both positive and negative – one forced apology delivered at sentencing is probably a drop in the ocean of a convict's socialization. Perhaps an adult's cognitive abilities and her increased awareness of the various costs and benefits of apologizing enhance its value for her beyond that for a child, but this should point toward the offender offering the apology voluntarily.

In addition, the gravity of offenses at issue also distinguishes the cases between child and adult offenders. A fracas between children experimenting in the moral laboratory of the playground differs from an adult offender who knowingly violates an obvious moral principle and seriously injures another. Note how Beebe's statements invoke these distinctions. From his adult perspective he views his college self as morally juvenile and in the throes of alcoholism. This recognition in part motivates his contrition. Even considering the shortcoming of his voluntary apology, his acts indicate maturation. I doubt that ordering Beebe to apologize – either as a college student or twenty years later – would bring about instant maturation of this sort.

Significant moral development rarely happens over the course of a court proceeding or a news cycle.

Although a child may dislike being required to express contrition, the parental objective is presumably social integration. Requiring the criminal offender to apologize, by contrast, risks increasing her alienation in several respects. First, consider the warning by John Braithwaite – whom I discuss at length in the context of voluntary apologies – regarding punishments causing social disintegration: "[W]hen individuals are shamed so remorselessly and unforgivingly that they become outcasts, or even begin to think of themselves as outcasts, it becomes more rewarding to associate with others who are perceived in some limited or total way as also at odds with mainstream standards." "Once labeling and rejection have occurred," he continues, "further attempts at admonishing association with the group which provides social support for deviance has no force."[86] From Braithwaite's consequentialist perspective, court-ordered apologies will usually stigmatize and shame offenders and thereby drive them toward criminal subcultures in which they will gain social approval from criminal peers. Braithwaite argues that "the way we respond to deviance, particularly crime, in the West, gives free play to degradation ceremonies of both a formal and informal kind to certify deviance, while providing almost no place in the culture for ceremonies to decertify deviance."[87] If Braithwaite is correct, coerced rituals of contrition make it more difficult for offenders to reintegrate. In this regard, humiliation via compelled apology may actually increase recidivism and, as Martha Nussbaum suggests, reduce confidence in one's ability to make reparations.[88]

Moreover, the convict can understand the ordered apology as a particularly humiliating affront in an unfair system that already undermines her dignity in so many ways. Considering that 90 percent of prisoners for drug offenses in many states are black or Latino even though people of all races use and sell drugs at similar rates, we can appreciate why a black drug offender might feel especially resentful toward the justice system if forced to apologize.[89] If I experience my conviction as arbitrary and unjust – perhaps because I face a life sentence for selling drugs in my impoverished neighborhood while rich college kids use the same drugs with little risk of capture – forcing me to apologize will likely escalate my sense of injustice and hostility toward the system.[90] Nearly half of federal inmates in the United States serve sentences for violations of drug laws that lack clear moral authority, so this is not a trivial point.[91] This should also help us appreciate the potential counterproductivity of practices like those of Ted Poe, the Texas judge and U.S. congressman, who finds shaming sanctions most suitable for offenders with "an attitude" or "contempt for the system."[92]

Murphy makes an important related claim in response to Duff's position that punishment separates offenders from their communities and in so doing causes offenders to realize the *value* of their communities. As the offender comes to realize through punishment that she deserves this separation from a community she values, in Duff's account she should understand why she should feel repentant: the offender wants to return to society because she understands society as basically just and of value to her. Murphy notes serious difficulties with this view. If an ordered apology should encourage the sort of reflection that leads one to accept blame while coming to appreciate the fairness and value of society, modern incarceration practices in the United States hardly provide such conditions. According to Murphy:

It is not at all clear to what degree there is a genuine community of values in our society; and, even where there may be a community of values, it is sometimes the case that those who flout those values feel so alienated (perhaps because of poverty or racial injustice or cultural exclusion) that they could not reasonably see reintegration into the community as a good to be secured by their punishment because they never felt truly integrated into the community in the first place.[93]

To continue with the analogy of ordering a child to apologize, imagine such a practice in the context of an unfair and abusive family. If the child believes she will continue to suffer violence and insecurity regardless of how well she apologizes, we have little reason to believe that her acts of contrition contribute to healthy moral development. Rather than teaching her to appreciate the community's values, the apologies will remind her that no matter how well she bows before parental authority things will not change – so too with the criminal offender. Until prevailing community values deserve her respect by treating her fairly and serving her interests, she will likely view the forced apology as adding legal insult to social and economic injury.

In light of these considerations, I find limited rehabilitative potential for court-ordered apologies of adult offenders. Future empirical data may teach us otherwise, but until then we should be wary of retributive and humiliation-based arguments for court-ordered apologies disguised in rehabilitative speculation.

Deterrence and Incapacitation

Several commentators assert, without much argument, that ordering offenders to apologize provides some deterrent effect.[94] Prima facie, this strikes me as farfetched. If I already risk suffering serious penalties for an offense, what is the likelihood that tacking on the prospect of a forced apology will tilt my cost-benefit calculations toward lawful behavior? Measuring the deterrent effect of various punishments has long proven notoriously difficult, and I am aware of no study evaluating the differential effect between a sentence with a mandatory apology and one without. The data could someday suggest otherwise, but I have difficulties imagining that a drug offender – undeterred by lengthy mandatory minimum sentences – would be scared straight by the threat of being required to read a statement of contrition.

One might argue that although prison sentences may not successfully deter offenders who view serving time as a means of enhancing their street credibility, the threat of the humiliation of a court-ordered apology provides a different kind of disincentive to a certain demographic of offenders. Some consider this deterrent effective because it requires "offenders to swallow their pride and go through a potentially embarrassing, uncomfortable experience."[95] Congressman Poe goes so far as to baldly assert that "the greatest deterrent to criminal conduct is public humiliation" via court-ordered apology.[96] Once again, however, how does the suffering associated with this humiliation add to the various penalties inherent to convictions in modern criminal systems? In the context of lengthy incarceration and the associated deprivations, the possibility of suffering sexual and other violence while imprisoned as well as alienation from family, a generally diminished life prospect on release, and so on, a few minutes of humiliation at sentencing seems comparatively insignificant. This appears true with respect to both specific and general deterrence. Braithwaite argues that court-ordered apologies can be particularly effective deterrents for institutional offenders such as corporations, but it remains unclear what the ordered apology adds to the more obvious deterrent effects of the penalties resulting from convictions. If courts offer an offender a choice between an apology and some other penalty – recall Sharratt's options of five days of labor or a video apology – presumably many who choose the apology will do so because it seems in some respects *easier*. If so, the apology option may actually undercut the deterrent value of other penalties.

An advocate for the potential deterrent value of court-ordered apologies might respond that we could increase their value by intensifying the associated suffering, perhaps by requiring the offender to write out the statement thousands of times before a global audience. Courts could find inspiration in the Malaysian settlement agreement that required a social activist to post his ordered apology via Twitter 100 times.[97] Although a consequentialist could be open to such possibilities, why would we derive the most utility from "intensifying" mandatory apologies rather than other aspects of punishment such as simply lengthening a prison sentence or increasing a fine? What is the comparative utility value of such techniques? How does publicizing a court-ordered apology differ from widely broadcasting the conditions of a sentence generally? Or tattooing the offense and sentence to the offender's forehead? Or requiring the convict to publicly self-flagellate? At some point we drift from attempting to squeeze deterrent value from apologies into using apologies as a platform for various tactics approaching torture. Consequentialists place no taboo on such practices, but most sophisticated utilitarians doubt that the benefits of such extreme measures outweigh their costs.[98] Those tempted to "pile on" ordered apologies to current sentences in the hope that they might have some deterrent effect must remember to subtract from the utilitarian register the costs of doing so.

Rather than (or in addition to) viewing court-ordered apologies as a means of increasing the negative consequences post-offense, we might consider the value of such an event as a means of placing potential offenders on notice. Deterrence theory requires populations to be notified of the laws and the penalties for breaching them so subjects will conform their behavior accordingly in light of the potential costs and benefits. Harsh penalties have little deterrent value if few know they exist. One spectacular punishment can have more deterrent value than many unknown punishments of equal severity. When a judge orders someone convicted of driving under the influence to apologize in the local newspaper, this publicity can remind the community of both the law and the consequences for violating it.[99] If we seek to amplify notice, we can consider any number of options such as parading offenders through streets, locking them in town squares' stockades, or posting the severed heads of capital offenders at the city gates. It seems dubious, however, that ordered apologies provide more notification value than prominently posting the laws, offenses, offenders' personal information, and the punishments administered. In addition, most apologies ordered in criminal contexts do not reach audiences beyond the courtrooms, sentencing hearings, or offices hosting plea negotiations. One could argue that courts should both order more apologies and undertake greater efforts to publicize them – recall the YouTube and Twitter examples – but again this requires an argument that doing so most effectively maximizes utility (or retributive value) in this regard. For the reasons discussed throughout, that seems generally unlikely. However in some cases – such as when the offender occupies a prominent public position or controls media outlets – the balance could shift toward requiring an offender to broadcast her apology to populations that she can reach easily. We need to do the math to determine whether the utility calculus points toward ordering the apology, but the equation seems generally weighted against coerced contrition.

Whether broadly publicized or not, court-ordered apologies are not value-declarative in nature. *I Was Wrong* argued that a value-declaring apology primarily serves to announce the values of the speaker (or to denounce the acts of others) and to commit her to honoring those principles. The apologizer does not accept personal blame for the past wrongdoing but instead proclaims that actions committed by others were somehow wrong and she vows not to commit similar offenses. A criminal court's determination and the very promulgation of criminal laws declare values by identifying illegal behavior. Value declaration in this respect notifies populations of the rules governing them. In a publicized court-ordered apology, by contrast, the offender does not add much, if any, declarative value. The population presumably already knows the law. The finding of guilt reinforces the system's commitment to the declared value. If the public is not aware of the laws, ordered apologies are probably not a particularly effective means of providing such information. A voluntary statement can declare an offender's values. She may even assert the value while insisting on her innocence, for example announcing that "sexual assault is wrong and we should strictly punish it, but I am innocent." An offender's reluctant utterance of her guilt and contrition does not declare the values she holds but rather expresses the court's values through her.[100]

We can be brief regarding incapacitative aspects of court-ordered apologies. As discussed at length in later chapters, I find that one of the most powerful reasons to give serious consideration to voluntary apologies in law lies in the categorically apologetic convict's fulfilled promise to refrain from reoffending. Although rather different from typical conceptions of incapacitation that literally seek to render reoffending impossible – for instance, by killing the convict so that she can never again break the law – I will argue that the promise to reform that is central to categorical apologies provides some incapacitative value. I see no reason to believe that ordering an apology from an offender incapacitates her in any way. An involuntary apology does nothing to prevent her from reoffending, and the fact that she requires coercion to express contrition should increase suspicion that she will reoffend.

Unlike the definition I offer at the outset of this chapter, we could imagine situations in which a court conceives of an ordered apology not only as a requirement to utter a few sentences in a courtroom or to publish a contrite statement in a newspaper, but also understands the redress and punitive elements as constitutive of the sentenced "penance." In Duff's sense, a convict's "penance" might include a term of hard labor. In such cases, a court might require the convict to announce her own sentence. Courts could further revive the spectacle of requiring the convict to repent on the gallows and declare her death as deserved, perhaps with a modern analogue of forcing the capital offender's hand to flip the switch for her own electrocution as her final act of court-ordered penance. We could attribute a range of incapacitative value to apologies ordered by the court if we conceive of them in this broader sense, but typically contemporary courts conceive of the apologetic speech act – perhaps accompanied by some public humiliation, outreach, or service – as the extent of the apologetic nature of the sentence. As such, court-ordered apologies have little, if any, incapacitative value.

Consequentialist Benefits to Victims and Communities

In addition to whatever retributive or vengeful satisfaction a victim might receive from watching her perpetrator being forced to apologize, commentators find various consequentialist benefits for the victim in this process.

We can first attribute value to the satisfaction enjoyed by some victims upon experiencing pleasure in the suffering or humiliation of their offenders.[101] This counts for something, even on the consequentialist register. Some victims may, however, experience the opposite. Contrary to studies suggesting that even apologies that do not accept blame can mitigate anger, an offender's refusal to voluntarily apologize might *increase* a victim's frustration with the offender and add insult to injury: you did this to me, and the court must *force* you to apologize? The spectacle of the ordered apology can also increase the victim's, offender's, or community's disappointment with the law because it is perceived as a grotesque display of state authority that does nothing to advance justice or prevent future crime.

In the civil rights context – where we find many such examples – Brent White advocates for court-ordered apologies "to help injured individuals get the apology that they need to begin to put their lives back together."[102] White further claims that apologies can "prospectively heal psychological wounds of victims."[103] Another commentator claims that "even a coerced apology can mitigate anger, shame or educate the offender, or improve prospects for settlements" and "may heal the victim and/or the community in some way."[104] An Australian tribunal asserted that requiring the publication of an apology in local newspapers would be valuable to the victim "so that she might feel some mitigation of the distress she has suffered as a result of the conduct to which she was exposed."[105] "Somehow, mysteriously," White claims of witnessing offenders being forced to apologize, "this makes us feel better."[106]

I find it difficult to evaluate such impressionistic claims because they do not defend their conceptions of apologies nor do they explain what they might mean by notions such as "healing the community." Even if we could clarify these terms and marshal evidence for the claim that court-ordered apologies promote something like community healing, I would wonder why this is the case and whether the benefits outweigh the costs of such coercive punishments. Given my analyses of apologies, I worry that much of the value results from a victim's and community's *misunderstanding* of the meanings conveyed by ordered apologies. In the long term, I suspect their lack of substance would undermine the perceived value from the ordered apology. A victim's mistaken belief that a court-ordered apology conveys meanings akin to those found in categorical apologies can be not only confused but also dangerous. If I take a court-ordered apology from a sex offender as evidence of a transformation of character and enter into a relationship with this misunderstanding, the long-term costs will likely outweigh whatever "healing" benefits the community experienced from the forced contrition. I am therefore wary of assertions that court-ordered apologies have "mysterious" powers to heal or "put lives back together."

Some courts have taken the position, again particularly in discrimination contexts, that ordered apologies provide uniquely valuable remedies in certain cases. In *De Simone and Ors v. Bevacqua*, the Australian Court of Appeal ordered an employer found guilty of sexual harassment and discrimination to publish an apology to all employees because it would vindicate the victim's humiliation and denounce gender stigmatization.[107] The court reached a similar conclusion in *Skellern v. Colonial Gardens Resort Townsville & Anor*, ordering the complainant's general manager to publish, in a prominent position in a local newspaper, an apology for wrongfully dismissing a pregnant employee.[108] Australian courts have similarly ordered public apologies from unrepentant defendants found to discriminate against indigenous peoples[109] and HIV-positive tenants.[110] The Court of Appeals of New York upheld an order requiring a corporate executive to apologize for "uttering obscene and anti-Semitic remarks," reasoning that "it cannot be said that ordering an apology was not essential to eliminate the particular discriminatory practice the commissioner had found."[111] In each of these cases, the court found that the wronged parties had been publicly stigmatized and that an apology sanctioned by the court was the most direct means of expressing the court's position and reversing the offense. According to this view, an insincere apology held meaning because what mattered was not the offender's contrite mental state but the court's disapproval of the offense. As I have repeatedly noted, however, whatever consequentialist benefits result from such commands seem to be accomplished at least equally well by findings of guilt and the resultant penalties. For this reason the Hong Kong Court of Appeals explained in the context of a disability discrimination claim that if a defendant is not "contrite or repentant," requiring him to apologize "would be nothing more than a meaningless and empty gesture and it should not have been ordered as it would not... have constituted redress to the plaintiff's loss and damage."[112] When we add the variety of costs associated with court-ordered apologies, it is difficult to imagine them providing a net gain of consequentialist benefits to victims and their communities.

Finally, approximately half of federal offenders in the United States commit what many understand as "victimless" drug crimes. Who receives the consequentialist benefits of these court-ordered apologies? If we claim that we should understand "the community" as the victim in need of the sort of "healing" best administered by involuntary apologies, then I refer readers to the various complexities presented by apologies to and from collectives.[113] In general, I would view involuntary apologies to or from collectives with considerable skepticism and find it unlikely that they would provide noteworthy consequentialist benefits.

F. Freedom of Speech and Conscience

Court-ordered apologies also raise issues regarding freedom of speech and conscience in that such rights include the right *not* to say something as well as the ability to express oneself freely.[114] Ordering an offender to issue an apology thus implicates what is often referred to as the "compelled speech doctrine," a broad theory central to discussions ranging from FDA provisions regarding warning labels on cigarette packages to school districts requiring students to recite the Pledge of Allegiance. Several commentators contend that first amendment protections do not prevent criminal courts from compelling apologies because of the broad discretion granted to trial courts to fashion probation conditions.[115] Civil cases – including those protecting the rights of the "consciences" of corporations – face stiffer First Amendment challenges when attempting to compel apologies.[116] Courts arguably provide greater First Amendment protections for the freedoms of the legal fiction of the corporate mind than they do for actual human criminal offenders. Government actors receive fewer protections than corporate actors.[117] Thankfully I need not consider the intricacies of First Amendment jurisprudence to note the free speech objections to court-ordered apologies. My concern is not whether courts can compel apologetic speech under the first amendment, but whether they generally should do so.

Freedom of speech – including whether to say or not to say something – is not an absolute right but instead identifies a cluster of values within the context of a variety of other values. Sometimes these values conflict, requiring us to sort out the comparative importance of these goods and to determine how to best balance them. As Stanley Fish puts it, "speech, in short, is never a value in and of itself but is always produced within the precincts of some assumed conception of the good."[118] Freedom of speech secures profoundly important values for a variety of reasons, but in some cases other objectives – such as protecting national security or eliminating child pornography – take priority. For Fish, this means that "we must consider in every case what is at stake and what are the risks and gains of alternative courses of action."[119] David van Mill captures this succinctly: "[T]here have to be reasons behind the argument to allow speech; we cannot simply say that the First Amendment says it is so, therefore it must be so."[120] Compelled speech requires a parallel balancing of interests. Although requiring citizens to say things they otherwise would not can cause considerable harm and can drift toward the worst of the dark authoritarian practices discussed earlier, it can also provide a legitimate means of achieving an important end. When a government compels citizens to complete tax forms even though they might prefer not to convey this information, we may disagree regarding how much taxes each should contribute, but few object to the forced nature of the financial statements.

No absolute right against interfering with speech prevents courts from ordering criminal offenders to apologize. Instead we ask what is lost and gained from state-compelled speech. As we have seen throughout this analysis, the social, political, and moral benefits of court-ordered apologies seem minimal. The costs, however, are many. Free speech considerations add to this list. Several factors might motivate an offender who refuses to apologize. She might insist on her innocence, even in cases of overwhelming evidence to the contrary. She might protest drug policies, for instance, by admitting to breaking the law while rejecting the law's moral authority. She might believe that she is guilty of violating a just law but refuse to apologize until that law is fairly enforced (consider again the disparate conviction and punishment of minorities for drug violations). She might refuse to see the value in the "empty words" of an apology and prefer to provide the victim with more significant redress. In any of these situations, ordering her to apologize would extend the reach of the state rather deeply into her conscience. If I maintain my innocence, for instance, requiring me to proclaim that I deserve blame for committing what may be a life-defining transgression demands that I publicly forswear my beliefs regarding the very core of my self-understanding. This resembles the worst in the dark history of coerced confessions. Court-ordered apologies seem very difficult to justify given that they provide so little benefit, all of which can be accomplished by less invasive means.

In the context of the Constitutional Court of Korea's finding that court-ordered apologies as remedies for defamation violate freedoms of conscience, Dai-Kwon Choi argues from a retributive perspective that "an apology is an apology whether or not it is made voluntarily, even if the apology seems degrading now that the defendant must 'even the score' by publicizing his wrong."[121] As a result, "a court-ordered apology has nothing to do with an apologist's conscience (except perhaps for his extreme sensitivity)" but rather "amounts to nothing more than a simple refusal to offer an apology, perhaps because [the defamer] thinks of such an act as degrading."[122] If I read Choi correctly, an ordered apology is not truly a matter of conscience because everyone understands that the court does not and cannot require the offender to believe that she deserves blame or to feel remorseful. Instead, the ordered apology only mandates that she act apologetically – an external presentation separable from constitutionally protected internal mental states. Because courts cannot make me *feel* remorseful, my conscience remains free while the community enjoys the retributive value of my comeuppance. This mirrors Bennett's claim that apology rituals do not violate freedoms of conscience because apologizers can ritualistically enact the appropriate contrition without actually being required to undergo a moral transformation.[123]

If we understand the ordered apology as retributive humiliation in part because it requires the offender to submit to state authority by uttering words that she does not believe or feel (and that the community knows she does not believe), consider extending this argument to other compelled speech situations. Consider compelling school children to recite the Pledge of Allegiance not because we seek to influence their consciences by providing a daily reflection on patriotism, religion, and justice, but rather to train youth to submit to state authority even if doing so offends and publicly humiliates them. The pledge presents such a political and legal battleground in large part because it cultivates our values. Children do not merely listen to the pledge. Nor do they recite it, as they do the alphabet. They perform the speech act of *pledging allegiance*. Coercing such a pledge of allegiance presents especially significant challenges in school settings because it reaches impressionable children in the very classroom where they learn reading, writing, and arithmetic. Schools can regulate student speech in a variety of ways, leading one federal district court to reason that if "the school board can determine what manner of speech is inappropriate in the classroom, it can also dictate what speech is proper when fulfilling its charge to inculcate the habits and manners of civility."[124] I argue in some detail that apologies are not merely speech acts because so much of their meaning occurs beyond a declaration that "I am sorry."[125] They do, however, include such declarations. Ordering an offender to apologize will in most cases require her to undertake speech acts declaring, pledging, and committing her to principles of conscience. We should justify such practices only if we can demonstrate that they provide clear and significant benefits.

Questions regarding freedom of conscience require us to balance the extent of the infringement against the benefit gained by the infringement. Here I agree with what White describes in the civil context as a sliding scale: "[T]he greater the burden on core First Amendment rights, the more compelling the government interest must be."[126] Requiring a citizen to report her income to the tax bureau provides a great benefit (the maintenance of a government, even an ultraminimal government) at a comparatively low cost (mandatory reporting of financial data). Requiring a student to recite the Pledge of Allegiance comes with a greater imposition on her freedom of conscience – in large part because the "under God" phrase added in 1954 speaks to fundamental questions of ultimate belief and value. Because the benefits of mandatory recitation are unclear, we tend to err on the side of freedom of conscience. Court-ordered apologies can present deep infringements of freedom of conscience, even requiring convicts to describe themselves as violent criminals despite their insistence of innocence. Compelling justifications for such serious harms should require some certainty that such violations will confer considerable benefits. The considerations throughout this chapter identified few such benefits.[127] In my view of court-ordered apologies, the benefit is small and the price is high. I will later consider how voluntary apologies for criminal offenses also present concerns regarding freedom of conscience, but they typically cause considerably less significant impositions and convey greater benefits.

Conclusion

Writing in the context of the trial court's order that a corporation provide an apology for its negligence in causing an oil spill in the Hudson Bay, the Supreme Court of the Northwest Territories of Canada sensibly captures many of the nuances:

> Extracted on demand... a grudging so-called apology is plainly no more than a reluctant concession to an opponent possessing, for the time being, an overwhelming advantage of some sort. It is all too likely to be regarded primarily as a form of unjust humiliation and not necessarily as a vindication of what is right. In consequence, it has little of the value of the apology freely given out of genuine remorse. It is seen by the offender, and no doubt by others, as a form of punishment and not of contrition.... [A]n apology can be a constructive and positive step in the rehabilitation of the offender and the restoration of peace in the community. This is particularly important in the many small communities of the Northwest Territories. I do not wish to be thought to say that a public apology should never be made, whether as recognized in the terms of a probation order or otherwise. The point I make is that no apology should be coerced, whether by Court Order or otherwise, as part of the sentencing process. After all, an apology which is not freely given lacks all the characteristics of a genuine apology and is surely worthless as such. If judicially coerced, it will undoubtedly tend, sooner or later, to bring the administration of justice into disrepute.[128]

Numerous international courts express similar doubts regarding the value of court-ordered apologies.[129] Other jurisdictions express the opposite view. The South African Promotion of Equality and Prevention of Unfair Discrimination Act, for instance, confers the ability for Equality Courts to do something that may be impossible: "*[O]rder* that an *unconditional apology* be made."[130] In both theory and practice the situation is, frankly, quite confused.

To summarize my view, court-ordered apologies in criminal and civil contexts produce many costs and few benefits. The consequentialist benefits potentially include very marginal deterrent, rehabilitative, and notification value. Even these benefits are speculative and potentially counterproductive, for instance if an offender finds offering an apology less of a deterrent than an alternative sentence or if the ordered apology alienates rather than reintegrates a convict. One might argue for a potential "amplifier effect" by requiring broad dissemination of the ritual – by publishing the apology in media outlets, for instance – and thus increasing the reach of such benefits, but publicizing convictions and sentences without the apology component appears likely to produce similar results with fewer problems. I expect that empirical studies using appropriately nuanced concepts of apologetic meanings would corroborate consequentialist arguments against the utility of court-ordered apologies. Retributivists who understand punishment as a backward-looking punitive measure meant to cause proportionate suffering in the offender will find value in court-ordered apologies to the extent that they cause justified humiliation in the offender. Non-retributivists and retributivists who reject humiliation as a primary objective of punishment will find such degradation of offenders among the greatest costs of court-ordered apologies both in terms of the wrongness of humiliation as such and the counterproductiveness of further alienating offenders rather than attempting to reintegrate them into the community. Although voluntary apologies work to resolve conflicts in various respects, apologies reluctantly issued under threat of state violence seem more likely to increase hostilities. An emphasis on compelled apologies will also likely come with an excessive emphasis on the personal responsibility of the offender at the expense of addressing the underlying conditions that contribute to criminal activity like drug offenses. Court-ordered apologies also risk causing considerable confusion in populations that misattribute significance to involuntary acts of contrition and fail to differentiate them from voluntary apologies that accept blame or indicate personal transformation. Given my research on the subject I would personally find little value in a court-ordered apology from an offender who victimized me or my family, but these complex issues invite misunderstanding and the resultant dangers. In addition, court-ordered apologies can seriously violate a convict's freedom of speech and drift toward authoritarian displays of a state's power to bend a citizen's conscience against her will. Notwithstanding thoughtful arguments from Bennett and other theorists, in practice court-ordered apologies seem driven more by grandstanding retributivist judges attempting to appear tough on crime than from considered ethical, social, and political arguments.

On balance, I find arguments favoring court-ordered apologies unconvincing. Compelled acts of contrition add very little if anything to the meanings and functions already present in contemporary legal proceedings and punishments, and they come with considerable costs and present serious dangers. The value we might derive from such practices can probably be better realized through other means. I do not reject outright the possibility that some court-ordered apologies may be more valuable than others and that principled procedures could be constructed to maximize these benefits. I doubt that such arguments will ultimately prove compelling, but this is something about which reasonable people may disagree when confronted with the evolving data and arguments. The sorts of ad hoc and under-theorized uses of court-ordered apologies that populate contemporary courts, however, seem especially untenable. Voluntary apologies in criminal contexts, to which I now turn, present potential for far greater benefits.

CHAPTER THREE

Apology Reductions in Criminal Law

> But if he has done wrong, then he must, if he really wills one thing and sincerely wills the Good, desire to be punished, that the punishment may heal him just as medicine heals the sick.
>
> Kierkegaard[1]

> It is precisely among criminals and convicts that the sting of conscience is extremely rare; prisons and penitentiaries are not the kind of hotbed in which this species of gnawing worm is likely to flourish: all conscientious observers are agreed on that, in many cases unwillingly enough and contrary to their own inclinations. Generally speaking, punishment makes men hard and cold; it concentrates; it sharpens the feeling of alienation; it strengthens the power of resistance. If it happens that punishment destroys the vital energy and brings about a miserable prostration and self-abasement, such a result is even less pleasant than the usual effects of punishment – characterized by dry and gloomy seriousness.[2]
>
> Nietzsche, *Genealogy of Morals*

Introduction

U.S. Court of Appeals Judge Richard Lowell Nygaard makes explicit what many justices only imply: "Repentance and correction are the real, albeit unacknowledged, often unexpressed hopes of sentencing."[3] Throughout my work in these areas I have been struck, time and again, by the fact that state agents rendered determinations regarding remorsefulness or remorselessness for more than seven million offenders in the contemporary U.S. criminal justice system. They often made these determinations informally, never mentioning that remorse played a role. They rarely explain or defend the relevance of apologies to punishment. I find it staggering: millions of offenders, millions of state agents with diverse views, an infinite variety of contexts, and hardly any guidance on the proper relationship between apologies and punishment. The words from Beebe's judge cited in the introduction – "Is he remorseful? I think so" – haunt this book.[4]

The preceding chapters offered Beebe as an example of a voluntary apology in the criminal context. Beebe provides a problematic example for many reasons, leaving us to wonder if he selfishly went through the motions of confession in the context of addiction treatment. His post-confession backpedaling by describing the crime as a youthful indiscretion and allowing his attorney to deny the rape suggest that his initial apology failed to understand the gravity of his offense and the potential punishments. Imagine a fictional reconstruction that removes some of those shortcomings. Suppose that Beebe – we can call him Categorical Beebe in the example – wrote the following letter to Seccuro:

Dear Elizabeth:

I write to you from within custody in the Charlottesville jail, where I turned myself in last week for the crimes I committed against you. I write to attempt to apologize to you as I am terribly, terribly sorry. This sorrow has defined much of my life since that night. As you have long known, I drugged and raped you in 1984. I will confess every detail I can remember to the authorities and to you should you want to know them. I deserve all of the blame for this crime. I lied to you and deceived you into drinking an incapacitating drug. I disregarded your clear refusals of my sexual advances. I forced you into sexual intercourse against your will. I then fled, leaving you injured, alone, and vulnerable. I subsequently lied to authorities and others by denying my assault against you, causing you further pain as officials and peers doubted your credibility. I willingly perpetuated the rape culture that persists on campuses and throughout society to this day. I hid my crime for over two decades, leaving you to fear that I might reappear and denying you knowledge that I had been brought to justice. I violated values that I now find central to my beliefs and faith. I did not treat you with respect and dignity. I committed violence against a person. I caused you to suffer in ways that I can scarcely begin to understand. I lied. I was a coward. I now realize, in part through my years of addiction recovery, just how wrong I was in all of these regards. I deeply regret my actions and the harm I caused you. My life has been full of persistent shame and guilt as I have grappled with my deeds. Over twenty years later, I often cry in bouts of terrible emotions. I cry for both my failures and for the suffering I brought into your life.

I built my life over the last ten years around ensuring that I do not commit a similar offense. I dropped out of school. I have been sober for over a decade. I have spent twice as long in therapy. I spend most of my time working with addicts and sexual offenders to help them to avoid the mistakes I made. I never again committed a sexual assault and I have been celibate for over ten years. I turned myself in to the police because I came to realize that despite progress I have made, I have focused on my own self-improvement and helping other potential offenders. This is not enough. I should not be free to choose how to handle this situation. I have a responsibility to the law and I submit myself to its procedures to determine my fate. I will deserve whatever punishments I receive and I understand that I may spend the remainder of my life in prison. I have asked my public defender to fully cooperate with prosecutors, to concede all facts, and to accept their proposed sentence. I also have a responsibility to you. I do not know how I might best and most respectfully attempt to redress my harm against you without making things worse. If you wish, I will never contact you again and I will serve whatever penalties the justice system determines are appropriate in light of my confession. But if you would like to direct my efforts, I stand prepared to hear from you regarding how I might address the wrong I've done in any way you see fit. As painful as they are, these words are only one part of a lifelong process of apologizing to you. I am a rapist and that will follow me to my grave and beyond. But I hope that is not all that I am, and that my life since 1984 can somehow lessen the pain I caused you.

Although an embellishment of an already extraordinary example, aspects of this situation commonly arise in criminal contexts. Some criminals turn themselves in. Some confess and apologize when caught. Some experience remorse years into their sentence, only after long stretches of sobriety, reflection, and treatment. Harkening back to the early justifications for the modern penitentiary and as Judge Nygaard continues to find at the heart of sentencing, we might hope that all offenders will achieve such apologetic conversions. Perceptions of prisons have changed. Lofty views of penitentiaries as retreats for spiritual redemption have lost ground to the view of prisons as punitive warehouses. Modern legal institutions hardly foster a culture of apologetic convicts. Apologetic convicts do, however, appear in the criminal justice system. How should it treat such people?

I appreciate that lenience for apologetic offenders creates incentives for various sorts of "inauthentic" apologies. If a jurisdiction reduces punishment for convicts who express contrition, it invites a parade of purely instrumental apologies and risks rewarding the best actors rather than the most transformed. One U.S. federal appellate court warned that reducing sentences for the contrite will result in "lenience toward those who cry more easily, or who have sufficient criminal experience to display sentiment at sentencing."[5] These are serious issues. Such concerns require us to consider difficult questions regarding whether we have good reasons for reducing punishment for "genuinely" apologetic offenders, how we might differentiate between the sorts of apologies that should be rewarded and those that amount to little more than gaming the system, and what sorts of procedures would promote a morally sensible and criminologically sound administration of such principles.

Two distinct sets of questions arise. First, note the issue in principle: Should we reduce punishments for categorically apologetic offenders? Many jurisdictions codify this sentiment into the "mitigation principle," holding that "if the existence of genuine remorse in an offender is proved to the sentencing court's satisfaction, then that remorse should be treated as a mitigating factor in sentencing."[6] The U.S. Federal Sentencing Guidelines appear to believe that apologies warrant lighter sentences, allowing judges to reduce punishments by considerable amounts for defendants who "accept responsibility" for their crimes and "express remorse."[7] We tend to judge remorseful offenders less deserving of execution.[8] Why do we believe this? What do these terms signify, how do cases interpret this language, and do the provisions capture the sorts of meaning that they should? Are these consequentialist sentiments? Is it that an apology signifies a kind of successful rehabilitation given the fulfilled promise to refrain from reoffending? How, in this regard, do various aspects of apologies predict recidivism rates? Is recognizing the victim as a moral interlocutor, for example, a better indicator of the offender's future behavior than the emotional content of her apology? Do voluntary apologies serve specific or general deterrence? Might exercising lenience toward the repentant undercut the deterrent value of some penalties if offenders believe they will not suffer full consequences if they can stage an adequate apology?[9] Is the belief that remorseful offenders deserve less punishment and remorseless offenders deserve more retributive in nature? Bennett argues for the retributive value of court-ordered apologies, but what deontological significance can we attribute to voluntary acts of contrition? When we consider Beebe's apology, how can we reconcile the intuition that he deserves moral credit for his confession with the sense that he also deserves serious punishment? Does lenience in this respect minimize the wrongness of his deed or diminish the justice due to the victim? Might voluntary categorical apologies present a regulative ideal for a form of punishment that maximally honors the Kantian and Hegelian traditions of recognizing the dignity of both offenders and victims? If we believe that an apologetic offender deserves less punishment, must we inversely believe that unapologetic convicts deserve more harsh treatment? Unlike my comparatively simple work on remorse in bar admissions cases in which the American Bar Association clearly sets overarching consequentialist objectives regarding the applicant's ability to follow codified standards for ethical conduct, the criminal justice system lacks explicit or coherent justifications for punishment.[10] Arguing that apologetic offenders deserve reductions in punishment proves especially challenging when retributivism and consequentialism uncomfortably coexist alongside "tough-on-crime" political grandstanding,

In addition to the threshold questions regarding whether we should punish apologetic offenders less, a second set of morally laden practical issues arises. How can we read hearts and minds to distinguish offenders who offer rich apologies from those who feign contrition to reduce their sentences? What criteria should reviewers use to judge an offender's beliefs, values, emotions, or intentions? Must the apology satisfy the rigorous categorical standard to warrant leniency, or can we calibrate reductions by degrees? If a categorical apology honors a promise to never reoffend, how and when do we evaluate commitment to such reform? Apologies promise change. As with promises, we cannot fully judge apologies in the moments they are spoken. Offenders need time to search for the values that orient their lives and to begin rebuilding their futures with habits honoring those principles. This seems especially important in criminal matters. Just as I would need to know much more before I could make a well-informed judgment regarding someone saying "I love you" on a first date, apologies during sentencing offer limited insight. Longitudinal data offers the best vantage of the offender's apology, and the longer the duration of reform the stronger the evidence of remorse. This creates considerable logistical problems for a justice system. The stakes are high for both offender and the community, and we want to get this right. Waiting until death to evaluate the apology to see if it warranted a reduction in punishment, however, defeats most of the purpose. At what stage in the proceedings should an apology occur, and when should reviewers evaluate it? Must certain elements, like admissions of guilt, come during plea allocutions or otherwise early in the proceedings? Early confessions reduce inclination to apologize after convictions but before sentencing to maximize the benefit but reduce the risks of accepting blame. If we reserve restorative justice practices for the sentencing phase rather than for the prosecution, we can appreciate that apologies at that stage may lose much of their significance because a confession comes too easily after one has been found guilty. Who should best judge the quality of the apology? Should an apologetic offender accept full punishment rather than seek to reduce her sentence? To what extent can she mount any sort of legal defense or enter into the plea bargaining process? Many offenders may seek to apologize but lack understanding of how to go about doing it well. Should the state coach her in contrition? Should the state actively promote remorse or only respond to it as it appears? How can the state promote remorse without further inviting inauthenticity or interfering too deeply with the subject's consciousness? These and other issues demonstrate the entwinement of ethical and practical aspects of voluntary apologies in criminal law.

In response to all of these questions I argue that, in principle, strong arguments exist for significantly reducing punishments for categorically apologetic offenders. I call applications of this principle "apology reductions." Categorically apologetic offenders meet such high standards that reducing their punishments presents the easiest case: they accomplish so much with their apologies that they render redundant much of the work associated with state-sanctioned sentences. Given that categorical apologies provide regulative ideals and are rarely achieved, however, much of my analysis will address cases that do not reach this standard but still warrant reduction because of the meanings they provide and functions they accomplish. If, an offender voluntarily confesses her crime before she is suspected or apprehended, accepts blame, and undertakes proportionate remedial efforts, for example, this is relevant to how a criminal justice system should treat her. Considerations will arise that may defeat the general principle, but my underlying assertion holds true across a range of underlying justifications for punishment that includes both consequentialist and retributive theories as well as various leftist views. Variants of apology reductions have appeared over time and across cultures, and even children recognize the intuitive sense of punishing the remorseful less than the remorseless.[11] The subsequent discussions attempt to explain why this intuition has such durable appeal and how we should integrate it into contemporary justice systems.

Implementing apology reductions presents numerous practical issues that threaten to undermine the feasibility of my view. Distinguishing the "truly repentant" from the disingenuous, for instance, requires considerable theoretical nuance as well as sophisticated institutional procedures. However, just as the criminal justice system routinely evaluates credibility of various legal agents and judges the mental states of subjects, so too it can develop methods for evaluating contrition. Particularly in the context of the dark history of apologies in law, vast social and economic inequalities and the procedural mechanisms that compound these injustices complicate any general claim that those who apologize well should be punished less. I identify and address each of these practical issues, ultimately recommending the means of ensuring fair applications of apology reductions.

A. In Principle: Why Apologetic Offenders Deserve Reductions in Punishment

According to Consequentialist Justifications for Punishment
Rehabilitation
Consequentialist arguments overlap and resist neat categorization because of their shared emphasis on reducing recidivism, but we can begin with rehabilitative justifications for punishment. For the sake of argument, stipulate the example I constructed for Categorical Beebe as distinguished from Beebe's actual response with its various shortcomings. Such a voluntary confession corroborated by years of reform and redress provides an undoubtedly exceptional example, but it offers a touchstone for evaluating more typical cases. By just about any conception of rehabilitation, Categorical Beebe is effectively rehabilitated by the time he confesses. Some may contend that his rehabilitation would benefit from additional redress directed

more specifically toward Seccuro and the community. Others may require him to undergo various tests and experiences before declaring him rehabilitated. Just as we tend not to think of alcoholics as "cured" but rather as "effectively treated," some may resist thinking of rehabilitation in terms that suggest that one can be definitively rehabilitated. Regardless of how we define rehabilitation, however, categorical apologies appear to cover its meanings and functions. Categorically apologetic criminals undergo verifiable moral transformations that reorient their behavior. Setting aside for a moment disclaimers regarding how we can establish with a sufficient degree of certainty an offender's contrition and reform, *a categorically apologetic person is more or less a rehabilitated person*. It is therefore tempting to declare the categorically apologetic offender as having satisfied rehabilitative objectives for punishment. Several issues – both in principle and in practice – require attention before closing that case. I address the issues of principle here while flagging the practical issues discussed in more detail later.

First consider "hard treatment" and related retributivist objections. If one views rehabilitation as the primary objective of punishment, the categorically apologetic offender satisfies this objective. Categorical Beebe undertook the bulk of his rehabilitative efforts outside of the criminal justice system. If he arrived at his current state through comfortable means – perhaps through the best therapy and education money can buy – he may have undertaken rehabilitation without *suffering*. Although difficult to imagine someone undergoing a profound transformation without some discomfort, the negative feelings of therapy, Alcoholics Anonymous meetings, and self-criticism probably do not equal the pain wrought by an extended prison sentence. For a retributivist, rapists deserve to suffer hard treatment commensurate with the crime. Self-reform looks too easy to balance the scales of justice and express the seriousness of the offense, especially when contrasted with the life sentence facing Beebe. Retributivists will also expect apology reductions to violate rules regarding proportionality in punishment. Imagine Categorical Beebe serving minimal jail time while one of his fraternity brothers who attacked Seccuro refuses to accept blame and therefore spends decades incarcerated. According to principles of proportionality, both men committed similar offenses and should suffer similar consequences. Reducing punishment for Beebe because he apologizes creates unfairness, and retributivists find such disparities endemic to indeterminate sentences. Some offenders will confess before even being suspected, some will take years to become repentant, and others may never come around. Those who quickly learn how to apologize well will benefit. Those who refuse to accept responsibility or express contrition for offenses that would otherwise carry short sentences may find themselves imprisoned indefinitely. If crimes of equal seriousness should receive equally harsh punishments regardless of the convict's subsequent attitude toward the deed, this presents a serious retributivist objection to apology reductions.

Retributivists and consequentialists have long argued about hard treatment, proportionality, and indeterminate sentencing. Those generally sympathetic to rehabilitative justifications for punishments will probably support an increased use of apology reductions. Those with general grievances against rehabilitation will rehearse them here. I argue, however, that retributivists should endorse apology reductions according to their own logic. If sufficiently apologetic offenders *deserve* reductions in punishment, as I later claim, this dissolves the primary retributivist arguments against apology reductions.

Practical issues present more serious challenges for rehabilitative applications of apology reductions. First, how can we know that the offender is genuinely apologetic rather than manipulating a system that rewards remorse? Evaluating the authenticity of contrition proves difficult enough in everyday matters. Criminal contexts amplify the complexities and stakes. Serious offenses have occurred, often with life-altering consequences for victims and offenders. Mistakes evaluating remorse in such situations can result in grave injustices. For this reason, even supporters of apology reductions such as Jean Hampton worry that we should "be very reluctant to endorse such a policy" because "it is difficult to be sure that a seemingly repentant criminal is truly repentant, and thus because a policy of suspending or shortening sentences for those who seem repentant to the authorities could easily lead the criminal to fake repentance before a court or a parole board."[12] Such concerns warrant appropriate skepticism, but judgments regarding mental states pervade the criminal justice system. State agents continually evaluate the not-quite-black-box of criminal minds, for example, with respect to establishing mens rea and reviewing mental health to determine eligibility for parole, probation, or even death. Uncertainty pervades law. The point is not to abandon such judgments – reject apology reductions because we can never know if they are really sorry – but to maximize our ability to evaluate apologies fairly and consistently. My efforts are twofold: to explain *why* we should usually reduce punishments for apologetic offenders and to offer solutions for *how* we can go about this sensibly. I work through the practical considerations systematically in "Applying the Apology Reductions," but in the rehabilitative context the why and how interrelate so extensively that the major practical issues deserve introduction here.

In particular, we should treat apologetic offenders as rehabilitated primarily because of their demonstrated commitment not to reoffend. Because forbearance, reform, and redress present ongoing tasks, we cannot immediately declare a gesture or ceremony to have "categorically apologized." Apologies take time to earn and prove their value – often a long time while the offender comes to understand her blameworthiness, internalizes the wrongness of her deeds, rebuilds her life around newly embraced values, and undertakes redress. Apologies make promises; a categorical apology keeps its promises. If the offender recidivates and/or fails to provide redress, we should revise our views accordingly. As much as we might desire instant and conclusive gratification from a gesture of contrition, apologies require patience from both the offender and the victim. This may be inconvenient, but we should meet urges to prematurely judge apologies with suspicion and scrutinize the motivations behind such haste.

In the criminal context, this temporal issue presents serious practical concerns that I address later but that merit noting here. How much time must pass from the moment of the offense in order to view the apology as warranting a reduction in punishment? The longer the record of reform, the stronger the evidence will be. Waiting until her death to decide if she was truly rehabilitated, however, obviously diminishes the value of reducing her punishment. In Beebe's case, are twenty years – including a decade of sobriety – long enough? Duration alone seems insufficient to answer this question because a promise not to reoffend will carry more weight if the convict regularly confronted and resisted the temptation to reoffend. The prison environment, however, typically removes convicts from opportunities to reoffend. Good behavior behind bars offers limited insight into the strength of conviction once exposed to the challenges of civil society. Tempting the offender to test her reform – by allowing Beebe unsupervised interactions with intoxicated and vulnerable women, for instance – is obviously problematic.[13] Even if we accept the risks of such diagnostic tests, any appearance of reform will appear contrived if the offender knows that she acts within a fishbowl of state diagnosis. Similar issues arise with respect to redress. If arrested soon after offending, the state limits and controls my opportunities for providing remedies. How can courts evaluate my commitment to autonomously take practical responsibility for the harm I caused unless I already provided commensurate redress while incarcerated or before? Timing becomes further complicated when offenders become apologetic at different stages of the criminal process. Beebe confesses while not under investigation. As discussed in the introduction, McBride turns himself in rather than committing suicide. Some embrace the rehabilitative process only once they stare down the barrel of their sentence: "This is serious, I am not getting away with it, and I really need to change my life." The imminent threat of suffering can coerce compliance, a sentiment captured in Flannery O'Connor's *A Good Man is Hard to Find*: "She would of been a good woman," The Misfit said, "if it had been somebody there to shoot her every minute of her life."[14] Some may require only a short shock of hard time to focus their attention on their blameworthiness, whereas others need the entire sentence to learn their lesson.[15] Some may find the process of "paying their debt to society" therapeutic in a manner that inspires rehabilitation. In addition, the "age-crime curve" provides one of the few relatively uncontested transcultural principles in criminology. Delinquency peaks in late adolescence and offenders typically "age-out" of crime as they become older.[16] Thus the very passage of time, regardless of contrition, will rehabilitate most offenders to some extent. If an apology comes years after the offense, as in Beebe's case, how much credit should he receive for his contrition when considered in the context of his now middle-aged life? What proximately causes his rehabilitation: his moral reform or the rather unintentional trajectory of aging that reduces his temptations to criminal activity and provides greater disincentives to indulge his waning criminal appetites? We also know that some offenses have higher recidivism rates than others and that socioeconomic status provides an important variable. Such data should inflect how we read the rehabilitative value of apologies for different kinds of offenses. I respond to these issues in later sections when suggesting procedural means to support apology reductions, but these concerns deserve mention here because they defy simple formulas like

Apology = Rehabilitation = Punishment Reduction.

Concerns regarding definitions and data used to support correlations between apologies and rehabilitation also warrant mention here. Common sense suggests that remorse should correspond to reduced recidivism, and prosecutors routinely invoke the inverse belief that remorseless offenders present the greatest threats.[17] The social scientific research on the issue, however, remains conflicted in large part because of the disagreement regarding what exactly should be measured. One group recently provided a longitudinal study arguing that feelings of guilt lower recidivism, but shame increases it.[18] Another study found shame-prone individuals "more likely to feel anger and to manage their anger in an unconstructive fashion."[19] Such findings appear to challenge reintegrative shaming as a centerpiece of restorative justice, but the definitions of shame and guilt driving these studies are so far from settled that different authors reverse meanings of the terms. Braithwaite has a particular view of shame; others complicate matters by differentiating between kinds of shame and identifying normal and pathological varieties.[20] Guilt and shame also seem to vary across cultures, with the Japanese example garnering the most attention in criminological literature.[21] If academics and clinicians have difficulty defining and identifying these emotional states, imagine the confusion of judges and other legal agents attempting to look into the mind of a convict to determine how her mental states predict her future behavior. Is she ashamed or feeling guilty? Can these mental states exist concurrently? Is it shame or guilt that merits reduced punishment? Is she faking it?[22] Michael O'Hear justifiably worries about the judiciary's ability to make such determination, asking us to compare "the picture of a single, untrained judge attempting to discern emotions from a defendant's in-court performance with the way emotional states are studied by academic researchers: subjects are videotaped (which permits repeat viewing), trained teams of coders seek to identify specific responses from the videotapes, and reliability is quantitatively assessed across teams of coders."[23] Not only are state reviewers likely to get it wrong, but such impressionistic judgments also invite racial and other biases as well as provide an advantage to well-coached defendants.[24]

Even if the social scientists agree regarding what to measure and how to measure it to establish a correlation between apologies, rehabilitation, and recidivism, attempts to date tend to overemphasize emotional states. Although emotions provide an important aspect of apologetic meanings, other elements seem simultaneously more central and less studied. Has the offender, for example, confessed all of the morally and legally salient facts? Does she accept blame and explicitly endorse the breached values? Does she understand and denounce various behaviors that are not illegal – alcohol abuse, for instance – that contributed to her offense? Does she view her victim as a moral interlocutor? Questions of this sort raise the possibility that an offender's emotional state may be, when considered among the other aspects of a categorical apology, comparatively ineffective at predicting recidivism. An offender's sobriety, for instance, may tell us more about her future than does the intensity of her shame. Similarly, the sort of person inclined to express remorse may also be the sort of person less likely to reoffend. Contrary to the assertion that apologies and rehabilitation cause reduced recidivism, psychological predispositions may drive the process as well. Consider this from an Aristotelian perspective: If I am generally virtuous and offend in a bout of weakness, remorse will come more naturally to me because I will immediately recognize my mistake. My subsequent remorse would seem more reliable than that of a person who offends in disregard and disrespect for the law and offers remorse only once captured and reprimanded.[25] However, the habitually weak-willed – I know this is wrong but I cannot help myself – can be as dangerous as the sociopath. Compelling data should attempt to account for these variables.

To review, apology reductions rather obviously compliment rehabilitative justifications for punishment. Serious practical issues remain to be addressed in "In Practice: Applying the Apology Reductions." These considerations require us to distinguish between rare cases of apologetic offenders arriving at the gates already repentant and varieties of contrition that tend to take root in the cracks of the justice system. As with court-ordered apologies, hybrid cases will be most common and the state will preside over offenders undergoing varying states of remorse. It may even actively promote and oversee such moral development. Although rehabilitative theories typically embrace state efforts to shepherd offenders toward personal transformation, concerns arise regarding governmental intervention into its citizens' most private beliefs and values. Critics express these concerns most powerfully in the context of restorative justice, to which I now turn.

Restorative Justice and Consequentialist Benefits to Victims and Communities

Reviewing recent work in restorative theories of justice makes clear why it, like rehabilitative views, provides a natural habitat for apology reductions. The restorative justice movement does not subscribe to exclusively consequentialist theories of punishment, and some of its philosophically sophisticated practitioners such as Duff and Radzik find inspiration in Kant. As an early consequentialist leader in the field, however, Braithwaite set the tone:

> I argue that in the conditions of late modernity our retributive values are more a hindrance to our survival and flourishing than a help. Hence restorative justice should be explicitly about a values shift from the retributive/punitive to the restorative. Retributive emotions are natural, things we all experience and things that are easy to understand from a biological point of view. But, on this view, retribution is in the same category as greed or gluttony; biologically they once helped us to flourish, but today they are corrosive of human health and relationships.[26]

In contrast to rehabilitative theories focusing on the offender, restorative justice generally attends to the victim and community as well as to the offender. Radzik's "social conception of wrongdoing" thoughtfully captures the spirit of restorative justice wherein the *relationship* between the offender, the victim, and the community – rather than any one of these entities in isolation – provides the primary focus of responses to wrongdoing.[27] Drawing an important distinction between moral *status* and moral *standing*, Radzik explains that one's moral status – what we can roughly understand as dignity in the Kantian sense – does not diminish when one transgresses. Our moral status transcends our specific actions; our moral standing depends on the quality of our relations with others.[28] Atonement, in Radzik's view, seeks to restore one's diminished moral standing by "reforming... the relationships among the wrongdoer, the victim, and the community."[29] Thus, unlike retributive or restitutive theories, Radzik encourages us "to attend to all of the parties who are negatively affected by wrongdoing and to identify the various kinds of harms that wrongs might cause."[30] Radzik's "ideal" of atonement "includes both the hope that the wrongdoer will come to merit restored standing in the moral community and that other members of the community will have good reasons to grant or recognize that standing."[31] Rather than isolating and treating the offender, restorative justice reaches into the community and understands relationships of trust, care, and responsibility as pillars of lawful society requiring public maintenance when eroded.[32] Braithwaite similarly explains that unlike the adversarial attitude where "the criminal trial assembles in a room those who can do maximum damage to the other side," restorative practices attempt to rebuild lives and communities.[33] Warning that attorneys trained in adversarial methods will attempt to game restorative processes, Braithwaite explains that "lawyer domination" of the process results in restorative practices being "used tactically and cynically to extract as much truth as possible from any noncycnical truthful engagement by the other side while communicating deceptively to them in an attempt to put them on the wrong scent." "Silencing lawyers," he claims, "is a more productive path than reforming them."[34] Braithwaite therefore proposes a "bottom-up face-to-face dialogue among a plurality of stakeholders before any lawyers start collecting fees."[35]

Victims contribute little to the typical criminal justice process. Although they may provide information, testify, and offer statements at sentencing, for the most part victims passively observe the state's prosecution of the offender. Victims have little if any say in the process and may not even know whether the offender has been charged, offered a plea bargain, convicted, or sentenced.[36] As Bibas explains, "the right to punish belongs to the state, not the victim," and the state may disregard the victim or her surviving family members' opinions regarding the most suitable punishment.[37] By contrast, restorative justice brings victims – often referred to as survivors to emphasize their agency – as well as offenders to play active and prominent roles in restorative justice. The prosecutor's unusual decision to engage in restorative practices in a murder case allowed Ann Grosmaire's parents to play such a central role in sentencing Conor McBride.

Restorative justice purports many benefits. Living victims can articulate their desires and participate in the process of satisfying them. Setting aside for a moment how they define apology and forgiveness, several studies argue that victims want apologies more than anything else and that restorative justice practices are more likely than conventional punishment to produce contrite offenders and provide them with procedural opportunities to apologize.[38] Interactions between victims and offenders can heighten the offender's awareness of the harm she caused and humanize the offender for the victim. The victim can gain a better understanding of why this happened to her, potentially leading her to feel more secure. This strengthened relationship increases the likelihood that the offender will apologize and that the victim will respond positively to expressions of contrition.[39] Studies suggest that recipients of such apologies experience mitigated anger and reduced aggression toward offenders, which in turn contributes to their general recovery.[40] Granting the victim authority to forgive or otherwise determine the offender's fate also offers a means of overcoming feelings of disempowerment occasioned by the crime against her. This also suggests a "broken windows" element of apologies: the longer the victim goes without having her status restored by an apology, the longer the temptation for others to see her as damaged and to pile on similar offenses against her.[41]

The restorative process views convicts with a high degree of particularity and individualizes punishments according to the needs of the offender as well as the victim. Just as it transforms victims from passive observers into active participants, restorative justice tends to address offenders as moral interlocutors capable of transformation rather than as animals shuttled through a bureaucratic process. Again, this counters the dehumanizing aspects of justice systems that treat offenders as abstract numbers to be processed according to governing penal metrics. Ideally this cultivates responsibility in the offender and a sense that the offender can work toward her own reform.

Victims, offenders, and communities each have a voice in tailoring remedies in a manner that best meets their needs. Proponents of restorative justice argue that such dialogue strengthens community bonds and support systems, which in turn prevents crime more effectively than unraveling the fabric of a community by over-incarcerating. In addition, the fruits of the process – be it in the form of financial restitution or community service – go to the victim and the community rather than siphoning public resources into the prison system. Offenders can therefore contribute to solving the problems they cause rather than serving sentences at taxpayers' expense.

Various procedures typify restorative practices: victim-offender mediation, opportunities for the offender to provide redress prior to sentencing, presentencing conferencing, and generally increased participation by the victim, offender, and community in the process from investigation to post-sentencing.[42] George Fletcher even argues for allowing victims to veto plea bargains.[43] Most envision restorative justice supplementing rather than replacing traditional punishments.[44] Bibas, for example, advocates for a generally more "forgiving system" that would "emphasize less the state's abstract right to exact punishment and more the rights, or at least interests, of offenders, victims, and community members."[45] Here, Bibas argues, criminal law "could once again resemble private law, in which tort victims may prosecute, settle, or waive their shares of claims."[46] Forgiveness and all of its benefits, Bibas imagines, would flow more easily from such a system.

Rejecting the description of these theories as a recent development, Braithwaite argues that "restorative justice has been the dominant model of criminal justice throughout human history for perhaps all of the world's peoples."[47] However, by "progressively casting the deviant out," most contemporary justice systems stigmatize and channel "offenders toward criminal subcultures."[48] From here, Braithwaite argues, "a self-fulfilling prophecy unfolds":

Once a person is stigmatized with a deviant label, a self-fulfilling prophecy unfolds as others respond to the offender as deviant. She experiences marginality, she is attracted to subcultures which provide support for deviance, she internalizes a deviant identity, she experiences a sense of injustice at the way she is victimized by agents of social control, her loss of respectability may push her further into an underworld by causing difficulty in earning a living legitimately. Deviance then becomes a way of life and is rationalized as a defensible lifestyle within deviant subculture.[49]

Further punishment accelerates the downward spiral, and Braithwaite believes this explains the exceptionally high incarceration rates in the United States. We punish millions, removing them from their communities in dramatic spectacles of state authority. When sentences expire, we drop them on the other side of the gate without any gesture of forgiveness or welcome to civil society: we give "free play to degradation ceremonies of both a formal and informal kind to certify deviance, while providing almost no place in the culture for ceremonies to decertify deviance."[50] The time served will have stretched, if not broken, the ties to the communities most likely to shepherd them toward non-criminal life. Mass incarceration becomes "a policy both for breaking down legitimate interdependencies and for fostering participation in criminal subcultures."[51]

Rather than creating a "class of outcasts," Braithwaite's reintegrative shaming follows "expressions of community disapproval" with "gestures of acceptance into the community of law abiding citizens."[52] These "gestures of acceptance" *de-label* the offender as criminal and "vary from a simple smile expressing forgiveness and love to quite formal ceremonies to decertify the offender as deviant."[53] Drawing from positive reinforcement parenting theories[54] as well as criminological statistics identifying crimes as disproportionately committed by young, poor, unmarried, urban males who have high residential mobility and poor relationships with their families and schools, Braithwaite argues that reintegrative shaming works best in strong communities.[55] The possibility of being shamed in communities with strong ties and deep interdependencies creates a potent deterrent, as the "loss of respect weighs more heavily for most of us than formal punishment."[56] The more I care about and respect someone, the more I suffer if they disapprove of me.[57] Likewise, reintegrating into a valued community provides an incentive to reform. Weak communities suffer on both ends: potential offenders perceive being shamed as less of a deterrent because they have little respect for those judging and may not care if they forgive them or not. If I reject those who shame me – judges, police, parents, teachers, and so forth – their disapproval means little and may serve only to enhance my status in the criminal communities where I am now more at home.[58]

Reintegrative shaming presents a lifelong communal effort to teach children acceptable behavior through shaming disapproval while strengthening social bonds. This work of developing both a conscience that will regulate behavior and a community that reinforces norms occurs long before formal interactions with the criminal justice system. These pillars of conscience and community provide "the most important backstop to be used when consciences fail to deliver conformity."[59] Braithwaite believes reconceptualizing punishment in this way should have crossover political support: "The appeal of restorative justice to liberals is a less punitive justice system," whereas the attraction for "conservatives is its strong emphasis on victim empowerment, on empowering families (as in 'family group conferences'), on sheeting home responsibilities, and on fiscal savings as a result of the parsimonious use of punishment."[60]

Apologies and restorative justice work hand in glove toward the common objective of repairing social bonds. By confessing and accepting blame, apologies strengthen commitments to community values while recognizing victims as valued community members. Victims and offenders – along with their respective supporters – come together to solve shared problems rather than allowing anger to escalate. By demonstrating reform and providing redress, apologetic offenders earn trust. They work to repair and improve their communities rather than worsening them by diverting resources toward punishment and neglecting responsibilities to families and neighborhoods. Rather than leaving families separated and facing the economic disadvantages caused by having a loved one in prison, apology reductions can strengthen character, bonds, and communities. Apologetic offenders can break a community's downward spiral and become models of successful reintegration for others. In general, the collaborative and supportive tone of restorative justice creates an environment conducive to voluntary apologies fundamentally different from the "admit nothing" attitude of adversarial punitive justice. Predominant criminal justice practices seem designed not only to isolate and punish the offender but also to push her toward legal strategies that minimize the victim's harm and deny any responsibility for it. Restorative justice seeks to avoid this by placing victims in dialogue with their offenders and communities and maximizing the support available to all parties working toward redress and reconciliation. Few convicts within U.S. penal institutions have the opportunity to interact with their victims after harming them, and punitive justice systems do not have time and resources for the sorts of elaborate rituals characteristic of meaningful apologies. Restorative justice, however, was built precisely for these sorts of interactions and provides procedural mechanisms to create opportunities for offenders to recognize victims as moral interlocutors and to convey the various forms of meaning expected from categorical apologies. Unlike routinized criminal justice bureaucracies, proponents of restorative justice believe communities can determine more compelling sentences. Apologies and forgiveness provide obvious *components* of that process. Apologies and forgiveness provide obvious *conclusions* to that process.

A few issues require attention before endorsing the relationship between apology reductions and restorative justice too strongly. First, the theories tend to lack precise understandings of key terms such as apologies, forgiveness, and even restoration. Braithwaite, for instance, says of his central term:

Shaming means all social processes of expressing disapproval which have the intention or effect of invoking remorse in the person being shamed and/or condemnation by others who become aware of the shaming. When associated with appropriate symbols, formal punishment often shames. But societies vary enormously in the extent to which formal punishment is associated with shaming or in the extent to which the social meaning of punishment is no more than to inflict pain to tip reward-cost calculations in favor of certain outcomes. Shaming, unlike purely deterrent punishment, sets out to moralize with the offender to communicate reasons for the evil of her actions. Most shaming is neither associated with formal punishment nor perpetuated by the state, though both shaming by the state and shaming with punishment are important types of shaming.[61]

Braithwaite goes on to define reintegrative shaming as "shaming which is followed by efforts to reintegrate the offender back into the community of law-abiding or respectable citizens through words or gestures of forgiveness or ceremonies to decertify the offender as deviant."[62] Reintegrative shaming "labels the act as evil while striving to preserve the identity of the offender as essentially good" while she undergoes a finite period of punishment, which distinguishes the practice from stigmatization "in which no effort is made to reconcile the offender with the community."[63] These are immensely important distinctions, yet shame on this account captures such a range of activities that it becomes difficult to identify and analyze. "Of what then, does shaming consist," asks Braithwaite? "It can be subtle: a frown, a tut-tut, a snide comment, a turning of the back."[64] How would we measure such a nebulous concept of shame? Likewise with reintegration, where an offender can be "shamed by a tear and reintegrated with a hug."[65] What does reintegration mean and how much value can it have if accomplished with a momentary gesture? What is its relation, for example, to the complex notion of forgiveness? Vagueness here runs risks parallel to the dangers associated with identifying the full range of apologetic meaning with a quick utterance of "sorry." Braithwaite claims that "apology is the most powerful and symbolically meaningful form of shaming"[66] and that the "deeper the evil, the more profound the comparative advantage of rituals of repentance and forgiveness over rituals of degradation."[67] What exactly does apology and repentance mean within the reintegrative model? Must the offender apologize before being reintegrated, or do even the spitefully unrepentant deserve to be welcomed back? Should victims treat all apologies as sufficient to reintegrate the offender even if they doubt their sincerity?[68] To what extent does forgiveness and reintegration require a full resumption of relations between victim and offender? Without compelling answers to these questions, overemphasis on apologies as reintegrative invites deception and abuse.

In addition, many of the general criticisms of rehabilitative approaches apply with even greater force to apologies in the restorative justice context. Most generally, does restorative justice work and to what ends? Parallel to skepticism regarding our ability to know if an offender is truly rehabilitated, how can we be certain that the apology sincerely conveys the sorts of meanings that it should? If an offender restores a relationship with an apology, to what extent should this exempt her from hard treatment? Does reducing punishment for apologetic offenders through a restorative process fail to meet the state's responsibility to publicly condemn the offense with appropriate severity? Does reintegrative shaming and similar approaches provide sufficient deterrence? Whatever the benefits of reintegrative shaming and other uses of apologies in restorative justice, do they justify violating the principle of proportionality by punishing similar offenses with more or less painful responses depending on the offender's contrition or the victim's willingness to forgive? Should we subordinate equal treatment of offenders to the restorative utility of apologies? To preview issues I discuss more thoroughly in the context of Marx and social justice, restorative justice can disrupt the balance between achieving context sensitive sentences and administering equal, fair, and consistent punishments. Offenders have considerable incentive to coalesce to the views of victims; we can imagine the consequences of McBride refusing to participate in a sentencing circle. Radzik worries that the accused "might agree to the negotiation even if they believe their rights are not being properly respected"[69] and further notes that such processes can compound inequalities in "race, gender, class, education, physical strength, or linguistic abilities."[70] Here she reminds us of Martha Nussbaum's notion of "adaptive preference formation" in which the disadvantaged come to expect less and the privileged expect more. A resident of a wealthy community may arrive at a sentencing conference believing she has suffered a grave injustice if the offender picked her pocket, but a victim who lives in an impoverished area might see such an offense as a fact of life in her own community. Such disparate views of similar crimes can lead to further inequality when the disadvantaged expect and demand less justice than the privileged and thus crimes against the poor result in lighter sentences than crimes against the rich.[71] Although restorative justice rightly criticizes routinized treatment of all offenders, eliminating these safeguards invites even greater inequality. Discretion, in other words, risks inconsistency and unfairness. Similarly, Braithwaite explains that reintegrative shaming works best in healthy interdependent communities. Impoverished communities seem least likely to meet this standard. Should privileged communities be the first to adopt the kinder and gentler techniques of reintegrative shaming? We have good reasons to worry, therefore, that the emphasis in restorative justice on specificity and particularity in sentencing risks undermining the values of equality and consistency.[72] These concerns drive my attempts to articulate the standards and procedures governing apology reductions such that similar apologies receive similar reductions in punishment.

"Objections from liberal neutrality" form a set of politically oriented criticisms of apologies in restorative justice. Bennett describes the "laissez-faire conception of restorative justice" as advocating for procedures that largely exclude the state from the restorative process and that empower the relevant parties to determine – usually face to face – how to best respond to particular cases.[73] This raises several concerns. First, we might worry with Radzik that restorative justice's ultimate "goal is the offender's internal improvement – a change in her point of view, values, or motivations, where those are judged to be lacking according to some moral standard."[74] Here, a libertarian or like-minded critic might argue, the state coercively enforces certain moral positions and thus infringes on its citizens' freedom of conscience. Rather than offering a progressive and humane method of dispute resolution, increased use of apologies in the restorative justice context expands the state's power into the most private regions of our values and identities. In the sheep's clothing of deregulating public control of punishment comes the wolf of the state deeper into our "business," as both Bennett and von Hirsch describe it.[75]

These objections have increasingly less force as we move along the spectrum from court-ordered to court-encouraged to freely offered apologies. Responding to the fully repentant presents minimal worries about state coercion; ordering apologies is most problematic. Most cases will fall in the middle ground where the state encourages remorse, for instance by using restorative justice as a vehicle for promoting moral transformation via apology. If someone undergoes the transformation on his own, like Categorical Beebe, the state takes the offender as she comes. The ordered apology also takes the offender as she comes, but finds her defiant. A justice system's attempt to lead her toward apologizing – to actively promote genuine apologies from those who arrive unrepentant – does not take her as she comes. It seeks to alter her moral fabric. This sort of deep intervention into a citizen's conscience under threat of punishment raises concerns.[76] As I will discuss in the retributive context, Duff's model of voluntary repentance as the outcome of punishment produces similar concerns, but his theory is limited by pervasive Kantian concerns that we respect the offender's dignity and appeal to her as a reasonable moral agent throughout the process. A consequentialist view of restorative justice that understands repentance as the goal of punishment would not be so restricted in meeting its ends. Given that these objections are most common and complex in situations wherein offenders become apologetic during the process of state-administered punishment, I address them in detail in "Becoming Apologetic versus Already Apologetic."

A second objection from liberal neutrality claims that restorative justice imposes a certain brand of moral transformation not only on offenders but also on victims by requiring them to adopt and practice a generally forgiving attitude toward justice and apply it to particular offenders. For those whose gods advocate for a more vengeful brand of punishment, restorative justice may seem against their faith. It is not the state's place, the argument contends, to require citizens to adopt a view of punishment contrary to their moral beliefs. In response to this criticism, all systems of punishment will likely offend some. Current incarceration practices conflict with many views of justice held in the population. Restorative justice may be more in line with prevailing views, or perhaps less. That is an empirical question. Restorative practices do, however, offer a greater range of possibilities beyond incarceration, and victims and communities can participate to a greater extent in that process. Some victims and contexts may be well-served by restorative practice and others may not. The ability to tailor criminal procedures and outcomes to the needs of involved parties seem, at least prima facie, beneficial. Moreover, forgiveness is as complex and multifaceted as apology. Apology reductions surely do not require victims to forgive offenders.

Incapacitation and Deterrence

A straightforward compatibility exists between apology reductions and both rehabilitative and restorative conceptions of justice. Incapacitation and deterrence require a bit more unpacking. A categorical apology incapacitates an offender, but not in the usual sense. In the categorical apology I promise to never reoffend. The extent of my incapacitation is as strong as my promise. Such a promise does not physically deprive me of the capacity for reoffending as would executing me or locking me in a cell, but it does establish a bond. If an unfaithful spouse apologizes to her partner and promises that she will never cheat again, this obligation should govern her behavior in the face of future temptation: I promised and I am morally bound to honor that duty. I disqualify myself from the forbidden activity. A categorically apologetic offender does not reoffend and is incapacitated in this sense – so too with criminal behavior. I apologize and promise the victim, the community, the state, and myself that I will not reoffend. My apology self-incapacitates, like an addict flushing her stash.

Of course neither prosecutor nor a betrayed spouse should place naïve trust in apologetic promises alone. Short of execution, few forms of incapacitation guarantee prevention against recidivism. Some promises are more reliable than others, and I offer means of evaluating apologies in this regard later. Note here that effectively incapacitating apologies will do more than utter promissory words. Apologies should appreciate how seemingly minor behaviors contribute to the harm at issue, and promises to reform will embed the commitment within changes to related behavior. This will include prudential measures meant to minimize temptation to reoffend. The unfaithful husband can increase credibility by honoring a promise to get sober, undergoing therapeutic treatment, no longer traveling for work, or discontinuing problematic relationships. Demonstrated commitments to these corollary promises create an incapacitating environment by minimizing, if not eliminating, opportunities to reoffend. Voluntary apologies for criminal offenses can be similarly fortified with incapacitative measures and will often include demonstrated commitments to therapy, sobriety, and avoidance of temptations. Extreme examples of apologies committing to incapacitative measures could include an offender's own desire for physical incapacitation: I understand my weakness of will and to fulfill my promise to never reoffend I wish to be imprisoned or killed to eliminate all temptation. Additionally, as should be clear, apology reductions do not suggest that all apologetic offenders should receive no punishment. Incapacitation via incarceration or other means can remain a legitimate response to crime, and some apologetic offenders may require reductions in certain kinds of punishments while presenting such a risk of recidivism that non-punitive incapacitation would best maximize utility. We might, for example, find that Beebe deserves a reduction in punishment while still banning him from campus and requiring him to register as a sex offender.

This discussion of incapacitation demonstrates the interdependencies of the strains of consequentialist theories with regard to voluntary apologies. Rehabilitation functions best within a restorative environment where the justice system works to build and preserve strong bonds and social networks. An offender working toward self-reform will likely fare better within a reintegrative context. As her treatment evolves and she becomes reintegrated, the offender gains an understanding of the behaviors that contributed to her offense and learns to avoid temptation. The more rehabilitated she becomes and the more she values her community, the more credibility we should attribute to her self-incapacitation. Voluntary apologies strengthen all of these fronts. Now notice the ties to specific deterrence.

A categorically apologetic offender will experience all of the negative emotions associated with her wrongdoing. She will accept blame for injuring others. She learns a painful lesson in accountability. She explicitly commits to honoring the breached values, promises not to reoffend, and provides redress. She knows the suffering associated with being shamed by those she most respects.[77] Beyond the bare commitment not to reoffend that can be corroborated in the aforementioned ways, all of this should lead her to a heightened appreciation of the consequences of her choices. She will both understand and feel these consequences more than an unrepentant counterpart. She will have a richer negative experience than a stoic and unrepentant peer who serves her time without "letting it get to her." Apologizing should *hurt*. This should amplify the specific deterrent effect for the contrite offender because she acutely feels the pain of sanction and contrition. She will not want to do it again.

Throughout the process leading up to categorically apologizing, the offender undergoes a process of *moral development*. This should strengthen her conscience in terms of both her awareness of her values and her mechanisms for honoring those values.[78] For the vast majority of people, the internal deterrence maintained by one's own beliefs functions far more effectively than external legal threats. An effectively socialized person does not typically think "I want to attack that person but I won't because it isn't worth the legal penalty." Instead, we do not even consider violence as a serious option because our moral habits steer us toward other choices. Hampton explains the bridge between moral education and specific deterrence:

> The ultimate goal of the punishment is not merely to deter the child from performing the bad action in the future, but to deter her by convincing her (as well as the other children) to renounce the action because it is wrong. And the older and more ethically mature the child becomes, the less the parent will need to resort to punishment to make her moral point, and the more other techniques, like moral suasion, discussion, or debate, will be appropriate.[79]

Posner similarly suggests that the "person who is conscious of having done wrong, and who feels genuine remorse for his wrong, ... is on the way to developing those internal checks that would keep many people from committing crimes even if the expected costs of criminal punishment were lower than they are."[80] A categorical apology recalibrates the moral compass both in terms of guiding the repentant person toward core principles and alerting her to the dangers and temptations leading off course. Such a morally reoriented and experienced person should require less deterrence. Murphy even notes in this regard that "controlling crime by provoking repentance is just another way of describing the idea of special deterrence."[81]

One might question the argument that apologies provide specific deterrence along a few lines. As with most of these issues, one can remain skeptical of our ability to distinguish genuine categorical apologies from "jailhouse conversions."[82] I later make the case for our ability to do this with sufficient accuracy to warrant including specific deterrence as a benefit of voluntary apologies in criminal law. If we can make such determinations, if apologies do provide a specific deterrent effect, and if we reduce sentences of contrite offenders, exactly how does this compare with the specific deterrent value of the full sentence? Criminology has notorious difficulty measuring deterrent effects, to the extent that debates continue regarding whether capital punishment prevents crime. If such comparatively simple correlations prove difficult to establish, imagine the difficulties social scientists will face providing convincing empirical evidence that explains the relationship between the varieties of apologies and recidivism rates. Perhaps sophisticated methods will eventually provide conclusive data, but until then speculation points toward the conclusion that the serious repentance will be painful enough that it provides more deterrent value than *some* portion of common sentences such as incarceration. The categorical apology provides more specific deterrence than does the threat of an additional day on a multi-year sentence. How much reduction is it worth? I doubt that we would want to treat even a promissory categorical apology as providing as much specific deterrence as a life sentence for a major offense, but we can appreciate that apologies have potentially substantial value as specific deterrents.

If the threat of hard treatment by the state deters potential offenders unmoved by moral arguments against illegal activity, lightening the treatment for apologizers would seem to reduce general deterrence. If someone learns that an apologetic offender receives a discounted sentence, she may come to think that the posted punishments only apply to the remorseless.[83] As long as she apologizes, she might believe, she will be subject to a lesser punishment. She may think this with little understanding that only the most demonstrably sincere and painful repentance warrants reductions. Exercising leniency toward the repentant may undercut the deterrent value of some penalties if offenders believe that they will not suffer the full consequences if they can stage an adequate apology. Additionally, even if she requires no specific deterrence, an apologetic offender may wish to have her punishment serve as a general deterrent to others. She may therefore insist on *no* reduction to make herself a maximally useful example.

Apology reductions can meet these objections. First, intentions motivating apologies play a central role in evaluating their meanings. According to my guidelines, courts can distinguish apologies driven by the desire to reduce punishment from those seeking to honor the offender and the violated principle. If the public understands that courts rigorously evaluate acts of contrition and do not reduce sentences for a few remorseful words, this disabuses them of the idea that they can get off easy with a quick apology. Sentence reductions must be earned, and apologizing may be more difficult than serving time or other penalties.

Second, apologies can provide dramatic spectacles in which the public witnesses the suffering of remorse. Rather than conveying that apologetic offenders get off easy, the message can be that criminal activity causes deep emotional pain and upheaval. The categorically apologetic offender will probably look like she suffers more than an impassive inmate. A potential offender may witness the extent of the shame and distress of an offender and find the prospect of a categorical apology a greater deterrent than a run-of-the-mill prison term.

Third, and as with specific deterrence, questions of marginal deterrence value arise. Exactly how much deterrence is sacrificed by reducing a sentence by X? In most cases of serious offenses this is not a matter of an apology *or* a prison term, for example, but an apology *plus* a reduced term. Sentence X plus Z pain from the apology minus Y reduction per the principles of apology reductions seems likely to add up to more general deterrence than simply sentence X. It depends on the amount of the reduction.

Fourth, both punishments and incentives modify behaviors. If the general criminal population witnesses an offender undergo a moral transformation of this magnitude, it may inspire them to walk a similar path toward treatment. Like recovering substances abusers who visit schools to tell their stories, apologetic offenders can provide examples of how to turn one's life around and explain with credibility the incentives for doing so. A culture of genuinely apologetic offenders – as opposed to penal warehouses of defiant and unrepentant inmates – will support and inspire those amenable to rehabilitation. For some, the incentive to be good can provide a more powerful motivator than the fear of being bad. All these potential general deterrent effects vary depending on the amount of publicity given to the apology as well as the effectiveness of notification procedures indicating the roles of repentance in criminal law. Finding the appropriate balance of sufficient publicity without excessive shaming requires a longer discussion supported by data that does not yet exist, but in principle the general deterrent value of apology reductions seems strong enough to warrant serious consideration as a supplement or alterative to more traditional means of behavior modification.

Conclusion

I have argued that, in principle, various consequentialist theories of punishment should support apology reductions. Retributivists can offer "ideal theories of punishment," but consequentialist arguments are only as compelling as the policies and procedures they suggest.[84] With Bentham in mind, H. L. A. Hart warns of the dangers of evaluating mental states: "Any increase in the number of conditions required to establish criminal liability increases the opportunity for deceiving courts or juries by the pretence that some condition is not satisfied."[85] "When the condition is a psychological factor," he cautions, "the chances of such pretence succeeding are considerable." This includes "embolden[ing] persons who would not otherwise risk punishment to take their chance of deceiving a jury in this way" and allowing those who successfully game the system to remain on the loose.[86] I am well aware of these legitimate concerns, and I attempt to work out these details in "In Practice: How to Reduce Punishment for Apologetic Offenders." We can note here, however, that consequentialist punishment requires trade-offs when doing so promotes the overall good. Apologies may prove to be an excellent means of rehabilitation, but broad application of apology reductions may diminish general deterrence to some extent. We should measure these costs and benefits not against perfection but against the current situation characterized by lengthy sentences infantilizing inmates who live under constant threat of degradation and violence and reenter civil society with weakened self-control, reduced prospects for employment, and increased likelihood of recidivating.[87] I expect that practices informed by a measured application of apology reductions would prove comparatively more utility maximizing.

Apology reductions may provide additional consequentialist benefits beyond the issues considered here. In addition to the various benefits discussed earlier, for example, a confession will also reduce investigative efforts as well as various administrative costs associated with an adversarial judicial system. Additional unforeseen costs and benefits would arise. Holistically evaluating such costs and benefits raises complex empirical questions requiring sophisticated social scientific methodology that utilizes nuanced concepts of apologies. I am not qualified to answer these empirical questions. I am fairly confident, however, that findings regarding the social benefits of reducing punishments for voluntary apologies will mitigate some of the disutility of mass incarceration. As Currie notes, "the rush to incarcerate has been both indiscriminate and conducted with an astonishing absence of serious evaluation." It remains shocking that those who "scrutinize every penny of spending on, say, a job-training initiative or a rehabilitation program for delinquents have been more than willing to throw money at untested and unevaluated sentencing reforms that collectively amount to one of the largest governmental efforts at social engineering of our time."[88] Apology reductions offer a morally defensible and resource-efficient countermeasure.

According to Leftist Social Justice Theories
The View of Criminal Justice from the Left
Contemporary leftists tend to prefer rehabilitative and restorative policies to retributive policies, but many view this as a matter of choosing the lesser evil. Rather than simply reintegrating offenders back into a fundamentally unjust society, leftist arguments tend toward concentrating efforts on building a more just society that results in not only less crime but also more social justice beyond the criminal system. In this view, the disproportionately high rates of criminality in the United States are a *symptom of an underlying disease*. So long as we continue to treat the symptoms of individual criminals – whether with hard treatment or increasingly effective rehabilitative techniques for reforming individuals – we do little to cure the root social problems. Without structural change, leftists will assert, even the most thoughtful applications of apology reductions risk amounting to little more than a bandage on a hemorrhaging body politic. Using a different analogy to describe the "moral and administrative mess" of the U.S. justice system, Murphy worries that "spending a lot of time tinkering with the small corners of the present system that might be affected by remorse and apology is rather like, as the saying goes, rearranging the furniture on the decks of the Titanic."[89] Notwithstanding these issues, I argue that leftists should support apology reductions.

It bears repeating: as of 2011, about seven million people in the United States are on probation, in jail or prison, or on parole, with the incarceration rate by far the highest in the world.[90] Americans represent approximately 5 percent of the world's population and 25 percent of its prisoners.[91] In the absence of a unified theory of punishment guiding the criminal justice system, policies drift toward more incarceration. A "heads I win, tails you lose" situation arises. If crime rates rise, politicians claim that we need more prisons. If crime rates decline, politicians claim that incarceration works so we should build even more prisons. Afraid of being labeled soft-on-crime bleeding hearts, even progressive candidates tend to avoid questioning overreliance on imprisonment. Rather than addressing underlying causes of crime such as inequality, addiction, under-resourced educational systems, inadequate job opportunities, and insufficient mental health policies to help those facing all of these stresses, we respond with more convictions and longer sentences. As Reiman puts it: "Whatever the news – whether crime goes up or down – we need more cops arresting more crooks and putting them behind bars for longer amounts of time."[92] About 50 percent of federal inmates are serving for drug offenses.[93]

Leftists view these statistics from a historical perspective mindful of class, race, and justice. For Marx, of course, the structures of capitalism cause the rich to get richer and the poor poorer. This happens, in broad strokes, because those with money control the means of making more money. If only in the form of interest accumulating assets in the bank, wealth tends to compound and concentrate over time. Whether money, land, machinery, intellectual property, or otherwise, those who own the means of production employ those who have nothing to sell but slices of their own lives in the form of labor. The rich profit, in effect, by making more money off the laborers' toil than they are willing to pay them. With this profit, the rich buy more capital, employ more labor, make more profit from these workers, collect more interest on these profits, and so on. Again, the rich get richer.

This long-debated description of capitalism rests on Marx's less discussed account of the "primitive accumulation of capital." If money begets money, why do certain people have money at the beginning of the process and, therefore, the overwhelming advantage in the competitive game of capitalism? Why do some enter into transactions privileged and others disadvantaged? If somewhere down the line the capitalist or her ancestor earned wealth by fairly making a valuable contribution to society, then the chain of intergenerational inequality will seem more defensible because the current distribution of wealth correlates with a lineage of moral credit. The rich would deserve wealth; the poor would deserve poverty. To rebut the belief that contemporary inequality has its origins in historical desert, Marx recounts the myth usually told to justify the origins of inequality:

In times long gone-by there were two sorts of people; one, the diligent, intelligent, and, above all, frugal elite; the other, lazy rascals, spending their substance, and more, in riotous living.... Thus it came to pass that the former sort accumulated wealth, and the latter sort had at last nothing to sell except their own skins. And from this original sin dates the poverty of the great majority that, despite all its labor, has up to now nothing to sell but itself, and the wealth of the few that increases constantly although they have long ceased to work.[94]

In other words, the legend tells us that we owe our economic fate to the heroism or sins of our ancestors. "Such insipid childishness," Marx cautions, "is every day preached to us in the defense of property." According to Marx, "in actual history it is notorious that conquest, enslavement, robbery, murder, [and] briefly force" best explain how we arrive at our current economic arrangements. Rather than the "idyllic" story of primitive accumulation where "right and labor were from all time the sole means of enrichment, the present year of course always excepted," Marx believes the rich should trace their wealth to mass systematic violence. On a Marxist account, the primary determinants of North American wealth are the confiscation by force of Native American land and the use of African and other slave labor to cultivate and render that land profitable, for example through farming and mining.[95] Once conquerors and their descendants divvied up the land, set into motion the means of extracting profit from it, and accumulated interest-bearing wealth, then the slaves could be freed – typically to work that same land for subsistence earnings. With the spoils from conquest and slavery providing a systematic advantage over those with "nothing to sell except their own skins," the colonizers could abolish slavery and protect negative liberties. Only after the conquerors had appropriated the land would they promulgate property rights and enforce them as if natural law.

A few points connect this account of the origins of the United States to our current condition in which we imprison a larger percentage of our black population than did South Africa at the height of Apartheid.[96] Petchesky argues in this regard that "the involuntary confinement of social deviants on a systematic, massive scale arose and developed along with capitalism."[97] Sheldon similarly claims that the transition from corporal punishment to incarceration created an unintended consequence of the Civil War: slave owners preferred to punish their subjects with beatings because a term of imprisonment cost them the labor time of their human commodity, but emancipation allowed an employer to easily replace an imprisoned worker with another worker.[98] Slave owners, in others words, can have a greater investment in their individual workers than do capitalists. Meanwhile capitalism compounds and concentrates both wealth and poverty over time, leading disparities between rich and poor to grow. Even as the United States progresses through the Emancipation Proclamation of 1863, *Brown v. Board of Education* of 1954, and the Civil Rights Act of 1965, increasing formal social and political equality does not correlate with increasing economic equality because of the intergenerational reach of money begetting money. For a Marxist, the initial conditions of slavery lead to the modern condition in which white households in the United States average $113,149 in median net worth and black families average $5,677.[99] If one color starts the game on third base, color-blind rules will not result in fair outcomes.

Many see criminal justice as hardly color-blind. Although not from an explicitly Marxist perspective, Michelle Alexander asserts that the War on Drugs – which escalated just as the Civil Rights Act gained traction as an equalizing force – effectively transfers the children of slavery from the plantation to the prison. "Ninety percent of those admitted to prison for drug offenses in many states were black or Latino," writes Alexander, "yet the mass incarceration of communities of color was explained in race neutral terms, an adaptation to the needs and demands of the current political climate."[100] This occurs despite the fact that "people of all races use and sell drugs at remarkably similar rates."[101] On Alexander's account, differential enforcement and preferential treatment explain these disparities. Unlike most crimes with clear victims, neither the buyer nor seller in drug transactions has reason to report the offense. Moreover, more than one in ten individuals in the United States violates drug laws in any given year.[102] Authorities must make strategic choices about how to police this common and consensual activity. Rather than spreading efforts equally across jurisdictions, law enforcement concentrates efforts on poor urban neighborhoods instead of college campuses even though both environments show similar rates of drug activity. Alexander claims that police make this choice, in large part, because of the political impossibility of enforcing drug laws equally against young white men:

Can we envision a system that would enforce drug laws almost exclusively among young white men and largely ignore drug crime among young black men? Can we imagine large majorities of young white men being rounded up for minor drug offenses, placed under the control of the criminal justice system, labeled felons, and then subjected to a lifetime of discrimination, scorn, and exclusion? Can we imagine this happening while most black men landed decent jobs or trotted off to college?[103]

We cannot envision the War on Drugs fought with equal aggression against wealthy white and poor blacks primarily because of the comparative enfranchisement. The powerful would not tolerate such penalties against their children and would force drug law reform. For the poor, however, increased police presence in their neighborhoods contributes to the feedback loop of poverty, disenfranchisement, and incarceration. Considerations that seem racially neutral such as prior criminal history and three strikes laws become tools of segregation according to Alexander because a "black kid arrested twice for possession of marijuana may be no more of a repeat offender than a white frat boy who regularly smokes pot in his dorm room." Thanks to "his race and his confinement to a racially segregated ghetto," however, "the black kid has a criminal record, while the white frat boy, because of his race and relative privilege, does not."[104] These factors and others lead Alexander to claim that with the War on Drugs "the New Jim Crow was born." The black underclass migrates from slave to sharecropper to felon. The felon label cements underclass status, diminishing prospects for employment, education, and reintegration.[105]

We can expand this view of racial injustice with Reiman's argument that the rich get richer and the poor get prison. According to Reiman, criminal justice in the United States creates a "carnival mirror" that distorts our understanding of the dangers facing society. Instead of focusing on dangers statistically most likely to harm us such as environmental and occupational hazards that cause chronic illness and death but that generate profits for the wealthy, the criminal justice system and the media amplify threats from violent crime and drug offenses.[106] Reiman claims that this results from overemphasizing the sort of "one-on-one crime" typically committed by the poor while minimizing risky profit-making activities that cause the most harm to the most people. An arguably victimless crime such as marijuana distribution can result in life in prison, but it seems unlikely that anyone will serve jail time for the Deepwater Horizon oil spill that resulted in the deaths of eleven laborers and massive property and environmental damage.

For Reiman, laws favoring the wealthy provide only the first level of funneling the poor toward and the rich away from prison. When Reiman asks why prisons are filled with the poor, he resists the answer that poor people commit more crime. Instead, he sees a sequence of stages filtering the wealthy out of the justice system and thereby concentrating the poor. First, those with political power criminalize primarily one-on-one crimes but relegate harms typically committed by the wealthy to civil disputes. When legislatures do criminalize white-collar offenses, the penalties tend to be comparatively light and call for fines rather than prison time. Given that the law focuses primarily on one-on-one crimes, we would expect to find the poor offending at greater rates. Even if rich and poor offend at similar rates, the poor are more likely to be caught and arrested. With more police in poor neighborhoods and with these areas often more densely populated and with less private space than rich neighborhoods – wealthy teenagers, for example, can use drugs in their yards or basements, but urban youth typically lack these spaces and end up in public areas – the poor face a greater risk of detection. When caught, police discretion favors the wealthy. On many elite college campuses, for instance, campus police seem more concerned with the safety of students experimenting with drugs than with making arrests. Compare this to the attitude of a beat officer on the west side of Baltimore. Now imagine a wealthy person and a poor person committing the same crime, getting caught for the same crime, and being arrested for the same crime. Who is more likely to be convicted? Setting aside matters of prosecutorial discretion and bias throughout the pleading process, we distribute legal representation according to wealth. Just as some can afford luxury vehicles and some only have money for the bus, some pay for the undivided attention of teams of elite attorneys. Others rely on public defenders suffering from staggering case loads. We object to the principle of selling justice outright, leading Reiman to find it "sheer hypocrisy to acknowledge everyone's right to equal protection under the law by the police and then to allocate protection under the law by lawyers on the basis of what individuals can pay."[107] Class drives some away from the justice system and others toward it. Disparities continue after sentencing, with the poor being more likely to serve their full sentence in large part because they typically present a greater threat of recidivism than the wealthy. Money, contacts, education, therapy, and all the trappings of wealth point toward successful reintegration. Poverty herds the felon back toward prison. Reiman cites Scythian: "Laws are like spider webs: they catch the weak and the small, but the strong and powerful break through them."[108] This explains, on Reiman's account, why we find our prisons filled with the most disadvantaged.

As to be expected from a tradition of critical theory following Marx's call for the "ruthless criticism of the existing order – ruthless in that it will shrink neither from its own discoveries, nor from conflict with the powers that be," these perspectives on criminal justice systems give rise to several challenges facing the role of voluntary apologies in criminal law.[109] Given the dark history of court-ordered apologies and their disparate impact on vulnerable populations, do apology reductions similarly compound disadvantages and suffering of the poor while advancing interests of the powerful? Will the poor be most commonly subjected to a system of apology reductions? Might a steady stream of apologies from poor black urban youths reinforce perceptions of this demographic as dangerous – and as inferior to those who do not apologize because their privileges allow them to avoid the justice system? Does emphasizing voluntary apologies reinforce the ideology of personal responsibility by requiring the offender to accept blame when we should instead understand crime as symptomatic of unjust structural conditions? By focusing on repentant *individuals*, will increased emphasis on apologies draw attention away from treating the underlying conditions contributing to crime? Will the rich receive greater benefits from reduced sentences for voluntary apologies? If apologies and reintegration work best in strong communities, how will this work in areas damaged by generations of poverty? How might such a practice introduce new biases and further compound inequality, for instance, in light of the much discussed "demeanor gap" that causes members of some social groups to appear uncooperative and unrepentant? I examine each concern in some detail after first setting out the general case for progressive support of apology reductions.

The Case from the Left for Reductions in Punishment for Apologetic Offenders

Marxist perspectives tend toward radical critiques aimed at *structural* issues. Despite Marx's many criticisms of Bentham and Mill, much of the preceding discussion should sound consonant with various utilitarian perspectives on punishment. Arguments for preventing rather than reacting to crime, for instance, tend to view structural conditions rather than individual actions as proximate causes of crime. Ideological considerations belong more narrowly within Marxist analysis, although here too consequentialist considerations arise. Ideology refers to the set of beliefs and values held within a culture that result from the dominant material relations in that culture.[110] Ideas, in other words, track how civilizations meet their needs. A hunting and gathering culture will likely worship animals and have little sense of private property because of its nomadic lifestyle. Agrarian societies will pray for rain, develop notions of private property as individuals invest labor by cultivating land, and value various personal traits that support agrarian production. In Marxist terms, structural relations (our primitive or advanced "markets") give rise to our superstructural beliefs (religion, morality, culture, etc.). Markets evolve over time, and our lifestyles reflect the markets in which we find ourselves. Regardless of the extent to which one agrees with economic determinism – to what extent is my vision of a good life a product of capitalist markets? – the basic point is that economic systems determine a great deal about not only obviously economic matters but also how we understand and value the world. Those who control the means of production also control the production of ideas. They will cultivate ideas that legitimate and increase their power. Here material conditions root intellectual work like all other labor. Culture manufactures concepts of morality, religion, and metaphysics while attempting to give them the appearances of having descended from the heavens. These concepts provide the background for normative discussions and feel instinctual, so much so that Marx describes these tendencies as the "ideological reflexes" of our body politic. Wealthy Western institutions produce the vast majority of analyses of punishment, and we have reasons to wonder about their independence from and complicity with ideology production. One need not be a full-fledged dialectical materialist to notice that Kantianism and utilitarianism – the two ethical philosophies most often applied in punishment debates – came to prominence with the development of industrial capitalism in Germany and England in the eighteenth century.

The economic structures of capitalism, Marx argues, generate an ideology that includes beliefs such as

1. a tendency to convert valued things into commodities exchangeable for private profit;
2. a strong view of personal freedom and individual responsibility;

3. an emphasis on competition over cooperation;
4. a high tolerance for inequality justified through quasi-religious beliefs that the rich deserve their wealth and the poor deserve their poverty.

Apology reductions require us to consider four corresponding tendencies:

1. A habit of converting valued things into commodities prepares the way for viewing harms as quantifiable into durations of prison terms.
2. A belief that individuals rather than structures proximately cause crime.
3. A desire to cast out rather than reintegrate offenders, leaving imprisonment a favored means of conflict resolution.
4. A sense that the current laws protect populations equally from the greatest dangers facing society and that the poor present the gravest threats.

These beliefs run through the following discussions, and I discuss them with differing degrees of attention as I work through the various reasons why leftists should support apology reductions. Richard Quinney argues that under current conditions the "objective task of the criminologist is to transmit bourgeois ideology to the working class as a whole, to ensure harmonious relations between the working class and the capitalist class according to the interests of the latter."[111] From this perspective some may worry that apology reductions serve up a red herring while sanctifying unjust laws and endemic inequality. I defend against this objection throughout the following sections.

Against Incarceration

In the most basic sense, apology reductions lessen imprisonment. This alone will curry favor with leftists who oppose trends toward increasing incarceration and punitive responses to crime. Although versions of the anti-incarceration position face many serious criticisms – surely incarceration is not worse than alternatives such as torture and execution on the one hand or a kind of pacifism that refuses to incapacitate the most obviously dangerous criminals on the other – they carry an emotional charge that energizes leftist critiques of the justice system. For social conservatives, such impulses will appear symptomatic of the bleeding-heart liberal excessively sympathetic to offenders. Leftists will in turn describe the opposing desire to exact revenge as symptomatic of any number of pathologies. Such exchanges dominate popular debates but do little to clarify the issues. Here I identify the leftist reflex favoring reducing punishment and how it corresponds to apology reductions.

For some, apology reductions open a backdoor toward abolishing prisons altogether. Angela Davis describes our perception of prison as an "inevitable fact of life, like birth and death."[112] Prison now seems like the "natural" response to crime, with the burden of proof shifted to alternatives. Inconclusive arguments against prison default back to more incarceration, even though arguments for incarceration are hardly compelling. Considering that we very rarely reach definitive conclusions when debating philosophical problems, pro-incarceration arguments can usually force a draw. Ties go to the home team. In this context a categorically apologetic offender stimulates our imagination by occasioning reflection on the fundamental and neglected questions regarding the purpose of incarceration. If this person has demonstrably reformed, why should the state expend such resources to imprison her? What is the point of sending this flesh and blood person – a person with parents and children and addictions and debts and talents and feelings and regrets and challenges and opportunities – into a cell paid for with funds that could be used for public education or public health? If poverty or other disadvantages contributed to the likelihood that this person would offend, why would we want to pile on additional disadvantages by labeling her a felon and sentencing her to a prison term? What, ultimately, is the point of such punitive measures? A repentant individual embodies troubling questions regarding the nature of justice. Just as it is much easier to ignore theoretical questions about global poverty than it is to deny food to a starving child at your table, the apologetic offender interrupts the machinery of criminal justice. Administrators of justice can go about their work feeling justified as they perceive millions of convicts as remorseless animals, but the apologetic offender raises questions. *Why are we doing this to her?* Juvenile offenders can pose similarly radical questions because of our inclination to attribute their criminality to structural disadvantages – "that kid didn't have much of a chance growing up in that environment" – and thus we tend toward treating rather than incarcerating juveniles. Apologetic offenders stimulate similar sensibilities.

The path toward increasing incarceration may now appear inevitable, but Currie describes the debates between left and right as recent history:

Thirty [now 40] years ago, we stood at a crossroads in our response to urban violence. One path ... called for a balanced approach to crime. They wanted a strong and efficient criminal justice system, and they thought the system we had needed both more resources and better management. But they also insisted that we could never imprison our way out of America's violent crime problem, already the worst in the advanced industrial world. In the long run, attacking violent crime meant attacking social exclusion – reducing poverty, creating opportunities for sustaining work, supporting besieged families and the marginalized young. It also meant making a real, rather than a merely rhetorical, commitment to reintegrating offenders into the community and protecting local communities form serious crime.

The other road led toward a much greater emphasis on incarceration, coupled with a waning commitment to rehabilitation and the reduction of social disadvantage. The approach was rooted in three related ideas: that we had become insufficiently punitive with offenders, that most rehabilitative efforts were useless, and that the social conditions often said to be breeding grounds for violent crime really weren't important after all. At the extreme it was argued that the rather timid programs launched in the 1960s against poverty, joblessness, and racial discrimination were part of the problem, not part of the solution. We had coddled criminals, weakened the resolve of the poor to better themselves, spawned a climate of permissiveness, and provided excuses for crime.

In the 1970s, we made a choice: we took the second road.[113]

Against this trend, attention to apologies points toward the first direction described by Currie. If "reintegration over incarceration" fairly describes a mantra of the left, apology reductions combat rather than increase social exclusion. Apologies work toward reintegration on at least two levels: by fostering individual rehabilitation and by repairing and developing community relationships. Leftists should not simply compare more incarceration with less incarceration – a caricature drawn by conservatives to argue that the bleeding hearts would open the prison gates and let chaos reign. Rather, as Currie writes, the "real choice was between an approach emphasizing prevention, reintegration, and strategic social investment versus one that accepted – or encouraged – widespread social neglect and relied on vastly increased incarceration to contain its consequences."[114] Contrary to arguments for increasing incarceration that exclusively consider an individual's personal choice to commit crime, I now discuss how apology reductions work to eliminate underlying conditions of crime and view the offender and her community in a dialectical relationship.

Commodification, Imprisonment, and the Ideology of Reductive Equivalence

What sorts of things should and should not be reduced to the pecuniary value in legal disputes? Consider a traffic violation, a breach of contract, racial discrimination, sexual assault, a wrongful death. I discussed elsewhere the various ideologies, hyperboles, and intractabilities regarding issues of commodification in law.[115] Here, I wish to bring attention to the ideological parallel that Marxists will draw between the drive to convert valued goods into quantifiable commodities and the drive to convert criminal wrongdoing into quantifiable prison sentences.

Soviet legal scholar Evgeny Pashukanis makes the following claims:

Deprivation of freedom, for a period stipulated in the court sentence, is the specific form in which modern, that is to say bourgeois-capitalist, criminal law embodies the principle of equivalent recompense. This form is unconsciously yet deeply linked with the conception of man in the abstract, and abstract human labour measurable in time. It is no coincidence that this form of punishment became established precisely in the 19th century, and was considered natural.... Prisons and dungeons did exist in ancient times and in the Middle Ages too.... But people were usually held there until their death, or until they bought themselves free. For it to be possible for the idea to emerge that one could make recompense for an offense with a piece of abstract freedom determined in advance, it was necessary for all concrete forms of social wealth to be reduced to the most abstract and simple form, to human labour measured in time.[116]

Here Pashukanis attributes the increasing historical prevalence of incarceration to the type of cognitive habits encouraged by and developed within capitalist modes of production and exchange. "In becoming an exchange value," Marx writes, "a product (or activity) is not only transformed into a definite quantitative relation, a relative number – that is, a number which expresses the quantity of other commodities that equal it, which are its equivalent, or the relation in which it is their equivalent." The commodity must also, he continues, "be transformed qualitatively, be transposed into another element, so that both commodities become magnitudes of the same kind, of the same unit, i.e. commensurable." Capitalist ideology suffers from a kind of fetish of equivalence, unifying all things through the lens of money.

As we become accustomed to treating goods as reducible to the common denominator of money, we increasingly understand a broad range of things previously understood as belonging to different spheres of value as commensurable. Because of the force of global markets, commodifying a good allows it to spread. Such products can then supplant traditional goods and ways of life, leading to a global monoculture that replaces diverse systems of meaning. Citizens of market cultures tend toward certain personalities, and Simmel predicts that we will become calculating time managers. The modern mind will demand from social relations "the same precision, reliability, and...lack of ambiguity" that we expect in the natural sciences.[117] We come to share a "matter of fact attitude in dealing with men and with things" and take up "a formal hardness" in our relations. For Simmel, the "whole heartlessness of money mirrors itself" in the commodified personality as we become cold and calculating people.[118] We cram into cities, but most of our interactions occur over distances in which "man is reckoned with like a number, like an element which is in itself indifferent."[119] We apply our overdeveloped instrumental rationality toward means disguised as ends. Unlike the desire for particular kinds of wealth in the form of jewels, fine food, and other concrete goods, the quest for money is not limited by our ability to use, store, or even see it. More is always better, leading Marx to claim that money is not only an object of greed but the object of greed – "the fountainhead of greed" – that makes possible unprecedented degrees of hoarding.[120] In Marx's terms, the more we commodify, "the more egotistical, antisocial, and alienated from his own essence man becomes."[121] The market cultivates a kind of economic creature: cold, calculating, greedy, materialistic, selfish, individualistic, disconnected, lacking compassion, and worshipping the money god.

In this context, courts routinely convert the value of human life, limbs, sexual intimacy, companionship, and emotions into the same cash nexus. For Pashukanis, the abstraction of labor into wages leads to understanding life in financial terms. This, in turn, paves the way toward thinking of a duration of freedom deprivation by prison sentence as the commensurate means of paying debts for injuries inflicted. *Lex talionis* processed through the one-dimensional mind results in something like the Federal Sentencing Guidelines. X offense *equals* Y sentence. For Marxists, the outright commodification of criminal offenses as endorsed by restitutive theories of punishment – commit X offense and pay Y amount – represents the next stage of the abstract reduction of value to money. In contrast, apology reductions engage a plurality of beliefs, objectives, and solutions. A categorical apology trains our attention on blame but also on causes, effects, moral principles, future behavior, redress, emotions, relationships, and other values. A justice system attuned to the meanings of apologies will appreciate incarceration as a simpleminded and often ineffective response to multifaceted problems. Having said that, mechanized apology reductions could perpetuate and even advance a kind of reductive commensuration if X apology equals Y reduction in incarceration. As I will argue, we should instead reduce sentences for apologetic offenders in a manner that recognizes their significance across multiple normative registers.

Attention to Underlying Causes: Prevention over Reaction

As criminal justice focuses on the relationships between victims, offenders, and their communities, attention toward underlying conditions causing crime increases. Faced with a repentant offender, we ask what pushed such a person – a person with a moral capacity demonstrated by her ability to apologize so fully and appreciate the wrongness of her behavior – toward criminal activity. As Marx describes crime as "the struggle of the isolated individual against the prevailing conditions," the apology tells the story of life under such conditions.[122] Unlike the view of criminal offenders as generic undesirables who arrive in the criminal justice system because of their bad decisions, we confront a person undergoing a life-defining transformation within the context of various challenges, disadvantages, and outright injustices. The offender's wrongdoing is but one event in a life. That life takes place within structures and institutions. The apology simultaneously humanizes the offender and places her in relief against the various structural determinants framing her crime.

Here leftists can state full-throated versions of arguments advocating for preventing rather than reacting to crime, captured by the aforementioned analogy between preventative criminology and preventative medicine. A society with poor sanitation that breeds disease will need a lot of hospitals in reaction to these illnesses. Fixing the sanitation thereby preventing the majority of outbreaks, however, would remove the underlying cause of the diseases and provide a more humane and efficient means of controlling the problem – so too with crime. Instead of treating the criminal symptoms of a sick society with incarceration, cure the society of the underlying disease causing crime. Bruce Waller makes a version of this claim in *Against Responsibility* without invoking Marx anywhere in the book:

> [B]y keeping the focus on the individual who did wrong and "deserves punishment" (end of inquiry), we block careful attention to the causes of wrongdoing – the deeper sources of violent behavior. Thus we draw attention away from the root causes in poverty and social neglect. This destructive system of moral responsibility harms those who are punished and hides the problems that we could start to solve; instead of seeking to justify it, we should focus on controlling this deep inclination and pushing society to look harder at real causes and how they could be corrected.[123]

Social psychologists describe a similar issue in "the fundamental attribution error," which leads us to believe that the root causes of a person's behavior lies in her natural "disposition" rather than various situational factors.[124]

Approaches emphasizing social prevention over moralistic reaction can take various forms, from radical to incremental. Early twentieth-century Marxist criminologist Willem Bonger considered endemic inequality within capitalism as the primary cause of crime, arguing that capitalism generates vast relative deprivation while simultaneously promoting greed. A culture that celebrates egoism systematically erodes social bonds in favor of competition, creating a perfect storm of desperate desire unchecked – and even encouraged by – community values. In Bonger's words, within capitalism "compassion for the misfortunes of others inevitably becomes blunted, and a great part of morality subsequently disappears."[125] Murphy compares punishing the poor for acting out of the egoism taught to them by society to satisfy their needs with prosecuting some war crimes: "When you have trained a man to believe that the enemy is not a genuine person... it does not seem quite fair to punish the man if, in a war situation, he kills indiscriminately."[126] Like punishing a warrior for failing to make fine moral distinctions in battle, Murphy claims in the criminal context that "there is something perverse in applying principles that presuppose a sense of community in a society which is structured to destroy genuine community."[127] From this perspective treating criminality requires broad reform of the structural inequality of capitalism. For Murphy, alienation presents the root problem. If we restructure society to solve that issue, then "crime itself and the need to punish would radically decrease if not disappear entirely."[128] Bonger argued that any crime that remained in a properly reformed society would be a matter "for the physician rather than the judge."[129]

Preventative measures can take two basic forms: (1) the reform of the social conditions causing crime and (2) the reform of the individual. Consequentialist criminology tends toward the latter, for instance by emphasizing deterrence or rehabilitation for individuals rather than economic structures. From a radical perspective, such "correctional" views on prevention risk reinforcing excessively individualist conceptions of crime and can therefore become "instruments of oppression."[130] Social programs designed to prevent crimes adopt a variety of implicit and explicit stances regarding individual or structural reform. Such programs include initiatives such as reducing poverty and inequality within free markets,[131] improving educational opportunities, enhancing meaningful job prospects,[132] building strengths and capabilities of families and children, increasing access to quality child and medical care,[133] decreasing access to guns,[134] preventing child abuse and neglect,[135] intervening early and intensively with juvenile offenders, and offering comprehensive rehabilitation and reentry programs that prepare offenders to live lawfully and productively in civil society.[136] Less encumbered by the sorts of objections from liberal neutrality, this preventative perspective offers a holistic combination of social programs designed to erode the roots of crime. Given the previous discussion of socialist states utilizing court-ordered apologies and Bonger's suggestion that criminals belong in the hospital rather than the prison, one might worry that leftists might embrace apology reductions *too enthusiastically*.

I should emphasize the general point regarding prevention over reaction. Like so many ethical issues, questions regarding punishment typically adopt a reactive attitude: How should we punish an offender? But like attempts to theorize the proper response to abortion, organ sales, terrorism, or any number of conundrums, philosophers tend to look at the egg after culture scrambles it. We ask questions that try to unscramble: Is abortion moral? Should we allow markets in human organs? How do we distribute limited health care resources? How can we justly fight terrorism? Philosophers train to address these sorts of questions, but we might provide more benefit by asking how to prevent such eggs from scrambling: How can we prevent unwanted pregnancy without unduly interfering with reproduction autonomy? How can we improve the economic conditions leading people to be so desperate as to sell their innards? Should the state prevent people from getting sick? How might we avoid actions that lead people to want to terrorize us? – so too with punishment. How might we create an environment that prevents people from committing criminal offenses that require apologies? If they have already offended, what might prevent them from reoffending? If prevention is the best medicine, voluntary apologies provide one of the most effective diets against recidivism by foreswearing the proscribed activity and undertaking the relevant lifestyle changes. In addition, just as we should attribute the bulk of the improvements in collective well-being not to medicine but to public health – for example in sanitation, vaccination, safety regulations, and so forth – a culture that engages its apologetic offenders simultaneously works on individual and systemic reform of conditions breeding criminality. In the general ecology of crime and culture, apologies foster an environment that appreciates the interdependencies between choices of offenders, harms suffered by victims and communities, and the social structures framing these interactions. Unlike systems that cast out offenders and leave them and their families facing diminished intergenerational opportunities for success, apology reductions offer a foothold for the reformed to climb out of the downward spiral.

Minimizing Social Exclusion and Alienation

Unlike systems characterized by denial, prosecution, ostracization, severed bonds, and lifelong stigmatization, a justice process creating space for apologies and encouraging repentance works to lift individuals and communities out of this destructive cycle. Apologies address social exclusion by building both individual character and community bonds in all of the respects previously identified in the context of rehabilitating individual offenders: offenders admit wrongdoing, accept blame for their acts, understand and endorse community values, empathize with and reach out to victims, reform their behavior, and work to provide redress to the victim and community. Rather than engaging in admit-nothing legal battles generating resentment from all parties, the categorically apologetic offender undergoes a transformation in attitude toward her community. These efforts improve not only the offender but also her relationship with the community because community members will likely feel more bonded to a convincingly apologetic offender than to an alienated and unrepentant convict warehoused in a prison. When compared with the prevailing alternative of ever-increasing incarceration, reducing sentences for voluntary apologies presents a significant means of fostering personal reform and community solidarity. Rather than viewing alienation as a form of punishment, apologies work toward overcoming alienation.

One might worry, however, that apologies in criminal justice could *increase* alienation by compounding inequality in a variety of ways. Recall Radzik's warning that the "history of atonement is in large part a history of degradation"[137] and that "society's most vulnerable groups are likely to suffer disproportionately under atonement systems."[138] Imagine, for instance, a drug offender: born into poverty, raised in a fractured home with family members often absent as they try to make ends meet, subject to low-quality housing, education and health care, without legal employment or much in the way of job prospects, and continually harassed by the police without being afforded much in the way of protection from the dangers of his community. As Murphy notes regarding a similar example, it seems rather unfair to describe the punishment this person serves as "repaying a debt to society."[139] To the extent to which it makes sense to speak in such terms, a drug offense hardly leaves this citizen with an overall debt to society because society has provided her with so little. If anything – and I think this colors some leftist sentiments regarding punishment as rehabilitation – society still owes the criminal for its neglect. Because benefits of the law go primarily to elites and underclasses bear a disproportionate share of its costs, the law will look like but another tool of oppression. From this perspective disadvantaged apologetic offenders suffer from something like Stockholm syndrome, having so internalized the objectives of their captors that they feel remorse upon violating them. A Marxist approach to apology reductions must distinguish between apologies that bespeak transformations toward the offender's true class interests – and thereby a reduction in her alienation – and those ritualizing false consciousness. Otherwise apologies risk becoming an ideological reflex adapted toward assimilating offenders back into exploitative relationships when they should instead refuse to acquiesce to injustice. In line with the previous discussion of adaptive preference formation whereby the poor come to expect a considerable degree of suffering while the rich take grave offense to small infractions, those without power learn to apologize in subservience. The rich can afford defiance or standing on unfounded principles.

Much of the appeal of restorative and reintegrative theories of punishment rests on the assumption that offenders exist within a community of shared values that serve the interests of all. From a communitarian perspective, punishment teaches the offender that she should respect these principles and value the community. This sort of paternalistic moral education through punishment – whether with hard or soft treatment – relies on the assumption that the community values are generally in the interest of the offenders. Separation from the good community causes suffering, and the offender comes to realize that she has made a mistake for which she should repent. This is, however, highly dubious from a Marxist perspective. The alienation experienced by many offenders results not from failure to see the error in their ways, but rather from a realistic appraisal of the structural conditions in which they live: this community and its law unjustly benefit others while harming me. If I feel alienated by the prevailing norms and blame them for my oppression, it seems unlikely that I will feel moved by criminal punishment to take these principles into my heart.[140] Instead of moving me to apology, I would feel further alienated and perhaps radicalized to bring about a community that truly advances the interests of people like me.[141] A paternalistic theory of apology and remorse would be compelling in a society where those who broke the law mourned not only their incarceration but also their failure to honor principles they find central to the meanings of their lives. I doubt we can say this of the majority of current criminal populations.

Consider additional ways that apology reductions could increase alienation. For all of their faults, mandatory sentences go some way toward achieving proportionality: similar offenses should be met with similar punishments. As discussed in the context of restorative justice, apology reductions require tailoring punishments to individuals. Although this has benefits, allowing such discretion invites various implicit biases into the process. Individualizing punishment introduces a range of judgments regarding the offender's attitudes, character, disposition, and prospects. Value attributed to an offender's remorse may track her privileges. Various studies suggest that judges discount apologies from racial minorities because they find them lacking credibility for a variety of reasons.[142] The attitude of certain demographics of offenders may conflict with expectations for repentance. Some anthropologists claim, for example, that members of subordinated groups tend toward developing coping mechanisms that include "concealment, dissimulation, noncooperation" when confronted with their oppressors.[143] Disadvantaged youth often adopt a "hard pose" to cope with disintegrative shaming by defining themselves against the criminal justice system. Such attitudes inhibit expression of contrition.[144] Moreover, the wrongness of some crimes such as drug trafficking may not be obvious for those who experience such activities as a way life for friends and family. Denouncing a mainstay of one's social network can cause missed feelings. Alienated by continual surveillance and criticism from the justice system, offenders may also feel like their punishment is more than they deserve. Like someone who was planning to apologize but then recoils when the victim exaggerates the offense or demonizes the offender, a stigmatized convict may hesitate or not fully commit to the process because of feelings of self-respect and a desire to save face among her peers.

For those who overcome the hard pose and experience contrition in various forms, their acculturation within criminal subgroups – in the form of clothes, speech patterns, posture, and so forth – creates what has been described as a "demeanor gap" between races and classes.[145] If a person looks and acts like those associated with criminals, they must overcome powerful implicit biases before judges consider their repentance convincing. From a Marxist perspective, credibility determinations allow judges to evaluate class signifiers for indications of the offender's future compliance with bourgeois norms. In contrast to the earlier point regarding the underclass learning to apologize as a submissive reflex, remorse from those without the cultural education or linguistic skills to provide sophisticated apologies will probably seem less credible than contrition from someone who shares an education and enculturation with judges and attorneys. Even if the disadvantaged apologize *more*, therefore, they probably will not apologize *as well* in the eyes of the court. Similar concerns arise for mentally ill offenders – about half of all of those incarcerated according to the Bureau of Justice Statistics – as their conditions may impair their ability to achieve the requisite apologetic mental states and adopt the appropriately contrite demeanor.[146]

Such biases need not result from discriminatory intentions. One study, for example, argued that the facial shape of corporate executives influences responses during public relations crises, with "baby-faced" spokespersons evoking better responses during minor crises but "mature-faces" producing better results for serious offenses. All of this reflects unconscious judgments by the participants, leading the authors to advise: "While there is no panacea for a company suffering a PR crisis, putting the right face on a response might just help save some face."[147] Consider in this regard how faces of criminal offenders influence perceptions of their remorse. Four judges from the U.S. Court of Appeals for the Ninth Circuit expressed concern in the context of reducing sentences for white-collar criminals because of their perceived remorse. Dissenting to the court's decision to deny en banc review, the minority addressed what they viewed as the court's practice of "affirming unreasonably lenient sentences for white-collar criminals."[148] Appellate courts grant considerable deference to district courts' findings of facts with respect to offenders' remorse; decisions are very unlikely to be overturned. The dissent worried that "white-collar offenders are uniquely positioned to elicit empathy from a sentencing court" because they share a socioeconomic background with judges. Citing research that judges extend more understanding and sympathy "for the person whose position in society may be very much like their own" and that "factors intimately related to the defendant's social status do receive weight in sentencing,"[149] the minority opinion warned of the "latent risk in the case of white-collar sentencing that an 'it's only money' rationale will result in undue leniency for serious offenses."[150] In this regard judges may rationalize a classic in-group bias, favoring those whose high-status lives look most like their own.

Beyond such clearly unjustifiable biases, judges have arguably compelling reasons for finding remorse from wealthy offenders more credible. Offenders with resources can undertake any number of measures prior to sentencing to corroborate sincerity, for instance enrolling in state-of-the-art inpatient treatment and providing victims with considerable redress. The rich can throw money at the problem, but a poor repentant offender may languish in jail, unable to make bail, receive treatment, or provide much for her victims. In addition, the path to transformation will seem easier and more direct for the affluent offender given her resources, social networks, and advantages. Credibility determinations require estimating the likelihood that repentant offenders can keep promises not to reoffend. The fewer the obstacles and temptations, the better the odds. The playing field is not level, even in such matters of the soul.

Finally, so long as we distribute legal representation according to wealth, it seems likely that those with the most resources will benefit from the counsel of attorneys best able to guide their clients through the intricacies of remorse within criminal law. Experienced attorneys will coach defendants regarding how to best positions one's remorse – how to express it, when to express it, when to avoid it – to maximal strategic benefit. Inexperienced attorneys risk not only failing to earn their client a reduction but also may not appreciate when confessing and accepting responsibility will result in longer sentences.

In all of these respects we risk not just violations of the principle of proportionality but more specifically injustices of race, class, gender, disability, and so on. Discretion tilts toward power. Informality invites the casual injustices of implicit biases. If the disadvantaged come to realize that the rich take the lion's share of benefits even in matters of repentance, this would only deepen a sense that the laws governing them and the punishments they endure are unjust. This is not, of course, a problem singular to apology reductions. At every stage of criminal justice – recall Reiman's explanation regarding why we find the poor disproportionately represented in prison – we attempt to combat inequality with varying degrees of success. The goal is to identify sound principles of justice and to devise methods of applying those principles fairly. Individual judges applying their vague and privileged sensibilities regarding contrition to disadvantaged offenders present considerable danger. Excessive discretion regarding complex moral phenomena situated within networks of bias predictably leads to discriminatory effects. I seek a means of making explicit the criteria for the sorts of apologetic substance warranting reductions in punishment as well as outlining formal and institutionalized methods for identifying these meanings. Such guidelines attempt to maximize our ability to reduce punishment when appropriate in the fairest possible way and in a manner subject to reasoned analysis and public scrutiny.[151] Such careful coding of apologies in accordance with accepted criteria by experienced administrators, I believe, is more just, effective, and fair than allowing sentencing judges to render an impressionistic – and often implicitly biased – "examination of the criminal's soul," as one court put it.[152]

The Ideology of Personal Responsibility

My account of categorical apologies will likely appear excessively individualistic to some leftists because it expects wrongdoers to accept blame. As Pashukanis would describe it, the understanding of guilt and blame at work in my theory "corresponds to the radical individualism of bourgeois society" and thereby reinforces the belief that individual actors rather than social conditions proximately cause crime.[153] Marx held sympathies for Kantian and Hegelian retributivism as the "one theory of punishment which recognizes human dignity in the abstract," but he found "something specious" in Hegel's elevation of the criminal "to the position of a free and self-determined being."[154] Marx saw the metaphysics of punishment philosophy as a byproduct of evolving sensibilities toward freedom and responsibility that develop alongside capitalism. Marx writes:

> German idealism here, as in most other instances, has but given a transcendental sanction to the rules of existing society. Is it not a delusion to substitute for the individual with his real motives, with multifarious social circumstances pressing upon him, the abstraction of "free-will." ... This theory, considering punishment as the result of the criminal's own will, is only a metaphysical expression for the old '*jus talionis*,' eye against eye, tooth against tooth, blood against blood. Plainly speaking, and dispensing with all paraphrases, punishment is nothing but a means of society to defend itself against the infraction of its vital conditions, whatever may be their character. Now, what a state of society is that, which knows of no better Instrument for its own defense than the hangman, and which proclaims... its own brutality as eternal law?... Is there not a necessity for deeply reflecting upon an alteration of the system that breeds these crimes, instead of glorifying the hangman who executes a lot of criminals to make room only for the supply of new ones?[155]

On this account, prevailing views of freedom amount to intellectual smoke from the fire of economic development, screening our view of the actual causes of crime by reinforcing built-for-capitalism notions of personal responsibility. It therefore makes sense, from a Marxist perspective, that neoliberal countries demonstrate the strongest desire for punitive responses to crime.[156]

Apology reductions, from this view, can ritualize the "transcendental sanction," locating the origin of sin in the offender's will and evangelizing for the theology of individualism. The historical evolution of modern secular apologies from religious traditions of repentance adds force to this view. A bourgeois notion of freedom will produce a bourgeois notion of responsibility, which will in turn lead to bourgeois theories of blame and apology.[157] By emphasizing the centrality of acceptance of blame, some radical criminologists will argue that my theory of apology reductions amount to another "liberal reform" that reinforce capitalist ideology.[158] This tendency toward assigning individual blame might result in part from our desire to reduce multifaceted and even chaotic situations into stories, what Tilly describes as "explanatory narratives incorporating limited numbers of actors, just a few actions, and simplified cause-effect accounts in which the actors' actions produce all the significant outcomes."[159] Such stories typically highlight choices of a few individuals and discount structural causation, making it easier to assign credit and blame and to read crime in terms of good guys and bad guys. The narratives reinforce ingroups and out-groups rather than cultivate cross-group empathy or consider underlying causes of conflict.

There is indeed something grotesque about expecting the disadvantaged to bow in apology before agents of the laws that oppress them.

Contemporary debates between personal responsibility and structural causation side too strongly with and thereby reinforce individualist ideology. Reducing prison sentences for apologetic offenders guilty of breaking oppressive laws is probably not a particularly effective technique for reforming structural inequality. Like all contemporary social, political, and moral concepts, my theory can be said to rely on the kind of "embourgeoisment of language" that we all inherit.[160] A revolution of the sort Marx envisions would require a revolution in moral language, and apologies might be radically reconceptualized in a world of transformed material relations combined with increasingly deterministic understandings of human behavior.[161] A few points should soften these objections.

First, as discussed in *I Was Wrong*, the sorts of acceptance of blame that I expect from categorical apologies may seem excessively individualistic and wedded to unjustifiably voluntaristic notions of responsibility.[162] For better or for worse, these notions of blame dominate our everyday discourse not only in the context of crime and punishment but also in how we raise our children, grade our students, interact with our friends and lovers, or hold our politicians accountable. P. F. Strawson claims that the practice of holding people responsible does not depend on a commitment to a metaphysical belief that people are free, but rather arises according to the degree to which we value the actions of others.[163] Our notions of responsibility spring from our experiences of concrete interpersonal relationships as well as from a quest for intellectual consistency. If we cannot reconcile our commonsense view with theoretical debates about determinism, lived practices of ascribing culpability typically win out.[164] Competing notions of the intricacies of proximate causation vary within the cultural traditions, but the practice of attributing blame in some sense appears to be an enduring feature of human experience. Without this broadly held commitment to human agency, apologies would be devoid of a central aspect of their significance. Certain kinds of apologetic meaning make little sense without relying on a rather thick notion of personal responsibility. In the absence of blameworthy individuals, apologies drift toward expressions of sympathy or declarations of values. Our temptation to cast blame widely may serve numerous social functions, but if we erode the relationship between proximate causation and moral responsibility, then we risk losing a considerable portion of the possible substance of apologies. Without some notion of blame predicated on individual moral responsibility, we might understand all injuries as unintentional accidents or excusable consequences of structural coercion. Dennett describes this as "creeping exculpation" resulting from research that increasingly identifies biological causes for human behaviors.[165] Describing all injuries as proximately caused by economic structures or biomechanics exonerates all of us equally – from the white-collar criminal to the homeless addict. From within such a perspective, the old narratives of responsibility begin to look mythological. Traditions built around these stories break down. I am not arguing that "this is how we do it and therefore it must be right" – a position that would smack of ideology – but rather that these practices still make good sense across diverse cultures and viewpoints. Even the thoroughgoing determinist wants an apology that accepts blame when someone wrongs her and the most reductive neuroscientists hold individual people personally accountable.[166] Just as apologies meant something different within deterministic religions in which God ultimately chose both whether I would sin and whether I would repent, there may come a time when we understand a misfiring neural pathway or a relation to the means of production as the proximate cause of wrongdoing. Apologies might become socially vestigial in such a world. I, however, do not know anyone living fully in such a world yet. Even those such as Derk Pereboom who believe that growing evidence in the physical sciences demonstrates that we lack the sort of free will required for moral responsibility tend to think that this should "not be devastating to morality or to our sense of meaning in life."[167] This is not to say that we must necessarily analyze all moral questions solely in terms of individuals, but rather that many kinds of apologetic meaning require us to think in this particularly durable normative vocabulary. Apologies have been cultural fixtures for thousands of years. I expect that they will endure in a recognizable form for some time beyond the next economic and scientific revolutions.

Second, I also argued at length in *I Was Wrong* in the context of collective apologies that shifting blame away from individuals and toward structures, as Marxists tend to do, can have serious negative consequences for matters of social justice.[168] Whether in the context of torture at Abu Ghraib, the British Petroleum oil spill, or the 2008 financial crisis, attributing responsibility to collectives often results in effectively exonerating the individuals within these institutions who have clearly committed culpable acts. If we can blame most everything on capitalism as such, how can we place blame on corporations and their leaders who administer its structures? We often help ourselves to the theory of causation that best advances our interests. Our strongest opinions regarding individuated personal identity surface when it comes to accepting benefits: I deserve praise for my hard work, I should receive credit for that idea, I earned the highest grade in the class, or I merit a promotion. When things go wrong, we shift to collective notions of responsibility: we made mistakes, our policies failed us, or market forces are unpredictable. When accepting praise, we shorten causal chains. When deflecting blame, we extend them indefinitely and even question whether moral responsibility makes sense given any number of metaphysical conundrums. When we seek a raise, we emphasize freedom and responsibility. If faced with punishment, we invoke determinism. Having it both ways provides a boon to institutional actors within democratic capitalism because leaders and executives can maximize the benefits of individualism while minimizing personal risk. This should provoke suspicions regarding the motivations for simplifying many individual offenses into one conglomerate wrong.

Third, sustaining precision in moral causation provides one means of preventing collective attributions of responsibility and collective apologies from supplanting individual apologies for the sort of institutional harms of great concern to leftists. We can often trace what may at first glance seem like collective wrongdoing to the culpable actions of individuals. Malefactors may hide within shadowy institutional structures, but with some investigation we can expose their misconduct and hold them accountable for it. Such research requires fine-grained moral analysis. If one blames harm on corporate rules or policies, for instance, we can typically track how such features of organizations result from the choices of individual institutional agents. Institutional objectives and the structures designed to achieve them are not somehow prior to human choice but rather represent the sediment of individual agency. Just as executives and politicians take credit for their roles in an organization's progress, they can accept blame and apologize for how their decisions cause harm. Even if an institution's stated policies appear morally sound, there are many ways that members of the group can be culpable for breaching or failing to enforce those rules. As we pay closer attention to how individuals behave and misbehave within collectives, we should become more skilled at connecting the dots between what initially appears to be collective wrongdoing and the actions of those accountable. We can then pair our expectations for apologies with the gestures of those most suited to give them. With these distinctions in mind, we can watch for those who obfuscate lines of moral responsibility. Such subterfuge can take a variety of forms, including the most audacious tactic of declaring that one accepts all responsibility while transferring all blame to subordinates. Attributions of credit and blame rest on dubious metaphysical assumptions and appear justified only if we collectively permit certain normative slights of hand. We should ask whose interests such illusions serve and who is being fooled most of the time.

In addition, failing to trace moral responsibility to individual wrongdoers leaves important gaps in the historical record. Speaking in generalities about the responsibility of the collective will likely fail to create a record of the multitude of faults that we should ascribe to individuals in cases of large-scale harm. Consider the degrees and kinds of contributory responsibility for which individual members of the "international community" should apologize for the Rwandan genocide. Despite numerous obvious culprits – most obviously himself – Clinton blamed no one in particular. If the history books only explain how the international community in general erred, they do not tell the story of how the actions and omissions of individuals aggregated to produce an atrocity. This fails to teach a crucial lesson regarding how seemingly minor offenses can compound and contribute to mass murder. In this respect, not individuating wrongdoing can minimize the scale and breadth of harm. The assertion that the "international community failed" Rwanda seems both more innocent and more isolated than a detailed account of the many different ways in which thousands of political leaders and billions of global citizens share blame for genocide. The former description gives the impression that the policies of the United Nations would benefit from reform; the latter points toward the ubiquity of racism and indifference. Racism and indifference can be understood in individual and institutional senses, and we can address these ills at both levels. Structural features of modernity make it likely that Western nations will respond similarly to future crises in Africa, as the Darfur conflict demonstrated. If we blame only Clinton, Albright, and others for the failures in Rwanda, we will not understand or treat the institutional diseases that repeatedly produce such gruesome symptoms. If we address only the institutional features, however, we fail to identify those who infect us or exacerbate our condition. Apologies can and should reflect these complexities.

I should again emphasize that I do not intend my preceding comments to suggest that we should disregard structural causation. Indeed, I find structural considerations essential to understanding the social meanings of apologies. We can hardly make any sense of apologies in contemporary life without placing them in the contexts of our religious traditions, legal cultures, and global markets. These structures can cause harm. Blaming capitalism rather than capitalists, however, often disfigures the current moral vernacular beyond recognition in the case of apologies. We can make little sense of the idea of "capitalism apologizing." We might first think of corporations as the faces of capitalism, but the notion of British Petroleum apologizing seems equally anthropomorphizing even if it is a "legal person." Just as a person would be misguided if she sought an apology from the rock rather than the person who threw it at her, we should ascribe blame to those who set corporations and governments into motion rather than narrow our investigations to the institutional features at the point of impact.

Optimally, we should maintain a binocular view of apologetic practices by keeping structural causation in mind while attributing individual moral culpability when appropriate. Responsibility is a historical concept and the dialectic swings between excessively individualist and excessively structural understandings. Bruce Waller and Lucian Leape provide an interesting example in their advocacy for reducing, if not eliminating, the notion of personal moral blame in medical error situations that result in an estimated 100,000 deaths per year in the United States. Leape explains that medical schools socialize physicians to strive for perfection by teaching that "mistakes are unacceptable."[169] Demanding infallibility and overemphasizing personal responsibility of physicians "creates a strong pressure to intellectual dishonesty, to cover up mistakes rather than to admit them."[170] By placing blame on individual doctors, the medical system de-emphasizes the structural conditions that contribute to such high error rates: ineffective training, insufficient staffing, brutal schedules, inadequate procedural safeguards, and financial conflicts of interest. "When the focus is narrowed to finding and blaming an individual," writes Waller, "the systemic causes of individual errors are left in place to produce repeated failure."[171] Moreover, writes Waller, if "blame is focused on the individual who was the last link in the chain that produced the mistake, then individuals who make errors are reluctant to admit their mistakes, striving instead to hide the problem."[172] Unlike cultures that punish individuals and treat the problem as solved, Waller argues that "we must stop *blaming* individuals for mistakes, and instead focus on what caused the mistake and how to correct it."[173] Waller makes a useful analogy to air traffic control, which benefited from shifting from a culture that blamed individuals for accidents to one that worked with controllers to develop a safer system. To reform the culture of hiding errors and near accidents, air traffic management encouraged employees to bring structural weakness to light and to collaborate in devising systemic reform. Waller extends his arguments "against moral responsibility" to apologies, claiming that we should cultivate "sincere apologies without moral responsibility."[174] "When I acknowledge my mistake and apologize to you for the harm I did, I am not saying that I deserve blame," he writes. Instead, "I am saying that you deserve to be treated with decency, treated as a person who should not be harmed, regarded with concern and regret when something goes wrong, and respected as a person whose welfare matters and with whom we must deal honestly."[175]

Waller goes so far as to claim that under my theory "denial of moral responsibility is consistent with, and contributes to, full categorical apologies" and that "moral responsibility abolitionists can consistently make such categorical apologies, and the denial of moral responsibility will facilitate sincere full apology."[176] Eliminating blame from apologies, in my view, overcompensates. We should undoubtedly pay more attention to structural causation and the underlying conditions of wrongdoing. In matters of apologies, however, I am inclined toward attributing more rather than less blame to individuals. For all of the reasons discussed in *I Was Wrong*, an apology that does not accept blame invites deception, further injury, and injustice. In most cases such duplicity compounds disadvantages as the powerful leverage ambiguity to their advantage. An undifferentiated minimization of individual blame, we should remember, would apply to the corporate executive as well as the homeless drug addict. Instead, we should confront injustice on both the individual and structural level. If we practice preventative justice, we should increase rather than decrease the accountability of those with authority to build structural components of culture. Whether setting economic policy, promulgating drug laws, overseeing wars, or failing to prevent environmental catastrophes, we should be wary of the powerful who claim to be victims of forces larger than themselves. Consider, for example, bankers who reap the benefits of economic collapse while blaming inhuman "markets" for any misfortune.

I am concerned not only with apologies from criminal offenders who cause harm and undergo a subsequent transformation but also with repentance and reform from police officers, prosecutors, judges, or lawmakers for wrongful convictions or otherwise unjustifiable treatment of those within the criminal justice system.[177] For the wrongfully convicted, receiving an apology from such agents can go a long way toward restoring faith in the justice system and demonstrating to the communities into which they attempt to reintegrate that their exoneration is more than a "technicality."[178] Given my view on collective apologies I am reluctant to consider legal opinions such as *Brown v. Board of Education* or *U.S. v. Furman* as "apologies for historical racism" by the Supreme Court, but I do believe we should derive greater benefits from various individual actors apologizing and accepting blame for their roles in systemic injustice.[179] This would represent an ideological inversion not in the dissolution of blame but in the attribution of blame to the powerful rather than the powerless.[180]

We can maintain notions of proximate cause and individual blame while refining the legal standards regarding what should qualify as justifications or excuses for illegal activity. This requires determining how poverty or other disadvantages impact agency and how serious a deprivation must be to consider it exculpatory. In revising such notions of moral causation – a concept continually subject to revision – we need not abandon individual blameworthiness. If we maintain a sense of personal responsibility while appreciating a degree of structural causation, we can appeal to normative frameworks that rely on individual agency while using those notions to reform unjust social conditions. I hope such a binocular view of justice would seem sensible to both collectivists and individualists.

My position does not, like many punishment theories, consider offenders abstracted from economic conditions. It occasionally proves useful to isolate moral questions from the complexities of their social context to draw conceptual distinctions, but ignoring inequality in favor of parsing the finer points of ethical theory has become the rule rather than the exception in punishment theory. Interesting questions arise in farfetched case studies, for instance if we consider a privileged student selling illicit drugs and donating the proceeds to charity. Stipulating complete global equality makes it easier to think about just punishment. Stacking the hypotheticals in such a manner to argue that punishment could *in the abstract* be justifiable can divert our attention from the brutal realities of the situation on the ground. It might also be possible to imagine an alternate universe in which racial segregation resulted in better education for minorities or prostitution empowered women, but we should be mindful of the political ends that such thought experiments might serve in this world. I hope that my theory of apologies in law attends to these realities without unwittingly reinforcing the ideological status quo of punishment theory.

Also note here several additional issues discussed more thoroughly in the civil context. If the collective as such is blameworthy, who must undergo reform? Who, ultimately, bears the cost of remedial efforts? If categorical apologies have some punitive content, who or what will be punished? Additionally, we typically consider the intentions and emotions of agents when assigning blame. Does it make sense to speak of the mental states of collectives in these senses? Similarly, collective responsibility can present serious difficulties in defining the membership of a group. A nation, for instance, is a complex arrangement of overlapping organizations and individuals. Membership at all levels is in constant flux. How, then, do we identify who belongs within such a collective? What substance do collective apologies provide beyond an aggregation of individual categorical apologies? Instead of accepting blameworthiness by stating "we were wrong," collective apologies often serve as declarations of the values and intentions of members of a group. Such meaning can be momentous, but we can clearly distinguish between the significance of categorical and value-declaring apologies. Likewise, ambiguity within apologies occasionally serves important ends. Some ambiguity regarding distributing blame across a group might allow, for instance, a group to move forward with remedial efforts without undergoing the kinds of protracted analyses that fine-grained accounts of blameworthiness can require. Given the damage that such investigations and finger-pointing might cause to group solidarity, situations may arise wherein leaders would be well advised to forgo the sorts of meaning associated with findings of individual guilt. In some contexts, it may be wise to emphasize the prospective significance of apologies over retrospective components. Although those administering truth and reconciliation tribunals often make this choice, I hope to have provided some sense of the costs and dangers of such strategies. Collective apologies can also, in certain circumstances, pave the way for individual members of the group to provide categorical apologies for their own wrongdoing. If a collective offers an apology, for example, individuals can worry less that they will shoulder all of the blame if they offer a personal apology or that their admissions will conflict with accounts provided by their superiors. Additionally, an apology from an institution is often best situated to provide the sorts of "synthetic" meanings that account for and attempt to reform a collective's structural failures. In some respects, this allows collective apologies to foster solidarity around the breached principles and mobilize remedial efforts.

I should also remind readers that collectives can, in principle, offer categorical apologies if they provide sufficiently detailed accounts of the aggregate responsibility of the members of the group. Parsing moral responsibility in this respect becomes increasingly difficult as the size of the group expands or its membership spans over long periods. In general, however, I worry that it is far more common that collective apologies simply dodge questions of culpability to protect individual members from bearing the cost of their wrongdoing. Both collectivists and individualists should appreciate the cost of such trends.

Race, Class, and the Ideology of Threats
Incautious apology reductions risk reifying prevailing ideologies of race and crime. Douglas Hay argues that in eighteenth-century England, mercy and pardon served an important ideological role.[181] In an era of extreme inequality and draconian punishments, landholders would expect their subordinates to plead for mercy. Rather than enforcing the laws, massacring the offending working class, and potentially inciting rebellion, the wealthy could demonstrate their generosity and moral authority by sparing the lives of their servants. As a purported act of grace, the powerful could exercise mercy at their discretion and thus torment the underclass with the uncertainty of punishment or death. Reductions of punishments drew attention away from the oppressiveness of the laws and cast the powerful as godlike saviors. According to Hay, mercy "allowed the rulers of England to make the courts a selective instrument of class justice, yet simultaneously to proclaim the law's incorruptible impartiality, and absolute determinacy."[182] Discretionary mercy permitted "a prosecutor to terrorize the petty thief and then command his gratitude." Maintaining this magisterial appearance enabled "the class that passed one of the bloodiest penal codes in Europe to congratulate itself on its humanity."[183]

We would similarly expect contemporary apologies to come primarily from poor minority drug offenders. From this, the public will likely draw conclusions that reinforce their ideological framework: poor minorities find themselves in these situations because they are inferior and dangerous. Note two mutually supporting ideological pillars. The first lies in the belief that the real dangers to society come from drug and related typical one-on-one crime rather than various economic, occupational, and environmental harms presenting the greatest statistical dangers.[184] If we witness a steady stream of apologetic drug dealers but rarely see repentance from fraudulent bankers or executives overseeing commercial disasters, this confirms a sense that the real threats come from the sorts of things that are policed, prosecuted, and repented. Reiman describes this as the carnival mirror of criminal justice:

> The criminal justice system is like a mirror in which society can see the face of evil that is in its midst. Because the system deals with some evils and not with others, because it treats some minor evils as grave and treats some of the gravest evils as minor, the image it throws back is distorted, like the image in a carnival mirror. Thus, the image cast back is false, not because it is invented out of thin air but because the proportions of the real are distorted: large becomes small, and small large; grave becomes minor, and minor grave.... If criminal justice really gives us a carnival-mirror image of "crime," we are doubly deceived. First, we are led to believe that the criminal justice system is protecting us against the gravest threats to our well-being when, in fact, the system is protecting us against only some threats and not necessarily the gravest ones. We are deceived about how much protection we are receiving, and thus are left vulnerable. The second deception is just the other side of this one. If people believe that the carnival mirror is a true mirror – that is, they believe the criminal justice system simply reacts to the gravest threats to their well-being – they come to believe that whatever is the target of the criminal justice system must be the greatest threat to their well-being. In other words, if people believe that the most drastic of society's weapons are wielded by the criminal justice system *in reaction to* the gravest dangers to society, they will believe the reverse as well: that those actions that call forth the most drastic of society's weapons *must* be those that pose the gravest dangers to society.[185]

Apologies can provide another reflective surface in these respects, magnifying current distortions even further. This creates a feedback loop with the second ideological theme: racial ideology. The more minorities apologizing for criminal activity, the more dangerous and inferior they appear. The more dangerous racial minorities appear, the more they will be policed. The more they are policed, the more they will be prosecuted. The more they are prosecuted, the more they will be disadvantaged and the worse their reputation and demeanor will become. Dramas of sin and repentance play out in the ghetto rather than the board room, confirming the moral authority of the powerful and their laws as we train our attention on drug crimes rather than policing economic reform. Ideologies of race and crime become self-fulfilling reifications.

Taken together, all of the previous considerations should assuage these concerns. Notice how, in principle, my view would impact drug sentencing. Leftist reformers often cite drug policy as the front lines of class and race warfare, arguing that drug-related incarceration has greater impact than hot button issues like affirmative action. Opposition to the War on Drugs, however, gains little traction because few politicians will risk appearing "soft on crime" or advocate for the criminal underclass that bears the brunt of these laws.[186] Drug sentences become longer, and we spend more resources incarcerating drug convicts. As the trends for the past thirty years indicate, an increasing percentage of public money goes into incarceration whereas a smaller percentage goes toward education.[187] According to Currie, we "have systematically depleted other public institutions to pay for our incarceration binge – a self-defeating course that helps to ensure that violent crime will remain high despite even more drastic efforts to contain it."[188] Imagine, in contrast, a criminal justice system that engaged apologetic drug offenders in the ways I suggest. Whether the offender has been sober for many years or asks for the state's assistance in treating addiction, her apology provides insights into the most effective path forward for her and her community. If I explain in my apology that I understand my drug activity as wrong and I turned to it in part because I lost my job and had trouble coping with the expenses of caring for a sick child, this does not excuse my crimes but does help diagnose the underlying conditions leading me toward offending. I stand the best chance of staying sober if I have a viable job as well as addiction treatment. Apologies bring to light these underlying conditions and resist the view that addiction is *pure and simple* the result of bad choices for which one must accept responsibility. The apologetic offender presents herself as both potentially capable of redemption and the product of an environment. Optimal treatment requires attending to the medical condition of her addiction, the moral condition of her blame, and the social condition of the underlying causes. A categorical apology works on all fronts. Given that about half of cases in the criminal justice system are drug related, these are not trivial examples. How we respond to apologetic drug offenders tests our core values of justice and models the guiding principles for the daily administration of those values. Apology reductions can advance leftist principles, and even a radical spirit, by combating individual and structural injustice.

Conclusion

Orthodox leftists may continue to view apology reductions as little more than an attempt to mollify bourgeois guilt because such reforms offer only superficial adjustments to the underlying relations to the means of production: superstructural smoke from the structural fire. For some, all such piecemeal reform becomes the enemy of the real change. Although I appreciate the unrelenting critical orientation of such views, I expect a majority of leftists will view apologies in criminal law as double-edged. On the one hand, they can provide a progressive alternative to the retributive incarceration boom. On the other, they can isolate the offender as solely culpable, thus directing attention away from the various social conditions that breed crime. I find hyperbole in Max Scheler's claim that "not utopianism but Repentance is the most *revolutionary* force in the moral world," but on balance I believe leftists should endorse apology reductions as valuable alternatives to the dominant current practices.[189] David Greenberg claimed in 1981 that the "role of Marxist criminologists as criminologists will be small in a socialist movement in this country in the near future" because crime seemed at that time secondary to other structural injustices.[190] Issues of criminal justice have undoubtedly become more central to social justice since the late 1970s because of skyrocketing incarceration rates. Apology reductions present one means of addressing these issues.

According to Retributive Justifications for Punishment
The Prima Facie Retributive Case against Apology Reductions

At first glance retributive theories appear unlikely to reduce punishments for voluntarily apologetic offenders. From the usual "eye-for-an-eye perspective," the person committing offense X *deserves* commensurate punishment Y. The offender must pay this debt in kind, and her actions after the offense – apologetic or otherwise – do not reduce the balance due on her moral account. Discounting this debt because of an offender's repentance fails to balance the scale of justice in the proper currency. A retributivist will likely argue that a rapist such as Beebe deserves to suffer the full punishment with all of the entailed hard treatment *regardless of his subsequent moral transformation*. In addition, retributivists will object to various ways that reducing sentences for apologetic offenders seem to violate the principle of proportionality. If an apologetic rapist serves only a short sentence but an unrepentant rapist spends life in prison, the justice system fails to meet equally serious crimes with equally severe sentences. Beyond the problem of disproportionate punishments, indexing penalties to the offender's post-offense moral transformation invites the sorts of inequalities between offenders that the sentencing guidelines sought to reduce through standardization. If two people commit similar crimes, from the retributive perspective they should receive similar punishments. Providing credit for apologies, in other words, requires indeterminate and discretionary sentencing repugnant to those who believe punishment should be administered according to an inflexible "do the crime, serve the time" metric. Retributivists worry that apology reductions provide pretexts for *lenience* – morally unjustified lenience – that minimizes the wrongness of the deed, fails to administer hard treatment sufficient to balance the scales of justice, and treats both victims and offenders unfairly. As J. D. Mabbott summarized in 1939, in the legal context "the punisher is not entitled to consider whether the criminal is penitent any more than he may consider whether the law is good."[191]

I now argue that apology reductions can meet these objections and that even a retributivist can and should support reducing sentences for apologetic offenders. To simplify the argument, presume the case of an offender offering a promissory categorical apology prior to suspicion, conviction, and sentencing. In addition, stipulate sufficient certainty that the offender is not attempting to game the system or otherwise deceive the relevant parties. Further, bracket all non-retributive concerns addressed elsewhere. Clearing the ground in this way allows me to argue that within the spirit of retributive theories of punishment, the categorically apologetic offender should be punished less than unapologetic offenders. In part for the reasons discussed earlier with respect to the powerful using mercy to appear morally upright while terrorizing the powerless with severe and unpredictable punishments, I do not consider such reductions of punishment as supererogatory acts of mercy.[192] By the spirit of retributive logic, the categorically apologetic offender *deserves* less punishment.

Dialectical Retributivism: Beyond Act and Character Retributivism
When retributivists consider apologies and repentance, the discussion tends to divide between "act retributivism" and "character retributivism." Act retributivism – sometimes referred to as classic or grievance retributivism – indexes the amount of punishment deserved to the badness of the deed at issue. Like the usual retributivist perspective to reduce wrongdoing to an individual's free choice rather than view the act as the byproduct of social conditions and circumstances, the act retributivist isolates the wrong as a singular moment in time. When the wrong is done, its wrongness crystallizes forevermore. Regardless of the changes in the offender's behavior or in social norms, the wrong committed will never be more or less wrong than it is at the moment of commission. Likewise, the commensurate punishment for that wrong remains fixed in time. Act retributivism tends toward absolutism in this regard, with courts meting out more or less universal justice. From this perspective an offender's apology – regardless of its power and evidence of a profound and demonstrable moral transformation – will probably have no bearing on the punishment she deserves. My remorse does not reduce my metaphysical debt. Accountants of cosmic justice do not accept apologies as legal tender.

Character retributivism, by contrast, makes a broader judgment about the whole of the offender's moral being.[193] Although it contains Aristotelian elements,[194] character retributivism typically takes inspiration from Kant's notion of "inner viciousness" and considers the offense in question as one data point in an offender's life.[195] Just as repeat offenses or lack of remorse provide additional insight into the subject's depravity, remorse and subsequent good deeds indicate improved character.[196] The character retributivist calibrates punishment according to the desert of the *person*, considered holistically, rather than merely her singular criminal act. Character retributivists therefore believe that "evil people are to be punished in proper proportion to their inner wickedness."[197] From this perspective, a categorically apologetic offender demonstrates a transformation that indicates an improvement in character from the time of offense. If two offenders commit the same crime but one is remorseless while the other achieves genuine moral improvement, the transformed offender has a better character than the unrepentant and thus *deserves* less punishment. Reducing the apologetic offender's punishment on this account would not be a matter of discretion or mercy. Justice would require it.

Kierkegaard bridges character retributivism, rehabilitation, and remorse in the Christian context. "Punishment itself becomes a blessing" for Kierkegaard because of the significance of remorse as a means to spiritual knowledge: "[T]he one who merely strives to get on does not learn to know the way as well as the remorseful man."[198] He asks:

So wonderful a power is remorse, so sincere is its friendship that to escape it entirely is a most terrible thing of all. A man can wish to slink away from many things in life, and he may even succeed, so that life's favored one can say in the last moment, "I slipped away from all the cares under which other men suffered." But if such a person wishes to bluster out of, to defy, or to slink away from remorse, alas, which is indeed the most terrible to say of him, that he failed, or – that he succeeded?[199]

Like Aquinas' general claim that "God allows evils to happen in order to bring a greater good therefrom," Kierkegaard views remorse as a kind of spiritual undergoing that teaches "the way." As quoted earlier, "if he has done wrong, then he must, if he really wills one thing and sincerely wills the Good, desire to be punished, that the punishment may heal him just as medicine heals the sick."[200] Kierkegaard suggests that all Christians should experience remorse and that those who do not experience it fully will ultimately be judged as inferior in character leading to "a most terrible thing of all."

Although character retributivism comfortably supports apology reductions, it raises several problems requiring resolution. Whereas act retributivists find reform irrelevant to sentencing, character retributivists face the burden of establishing with sufficient certainty that the offender has undergone a genuine moral transformation. Murphy – who has nuanced and changed his view on character retributivism throughout his distinguished career – finds this problem determinative: "It is hard enough – given human capacity for self-deception – to be very certain of one's own motives and fundamental desires, and there are staggering obstacles in the way of our making such judgments about others."[201] Given the difficulty of evaluating character, Murphy reluctantly inclines toward not giving "much weight to expressions of remorse and repentance at the sentencing stage of the criminal process" because he finds "too much chance of being made a sucker by fakery."[202] I appreciate Murphy's caution here, but several responses warrant consideration. First, if character retributivism presents the correct view, then we are morally obligated to undertake evaluations of the offender's character. The difficulty of such investigations would seem largely irrelevant for a Kantian, and he would probably advise us to devote more time and resources to such undertakings. Second – as "In Practice: Applying Apology

Reductions" discusses at length – although evaluating an offender's apology presents a complex task, several concrete questions and procedures can transform what might seem impossible into a relatively routine and reliable review process on par with other difficult but quotidian determinations in criminal justice. Peering into the soul of a criminal offender's apology may seem so difficult as to be foolhardy to even attempt it, but it only appears futile because of confused theories and hostile procedures. With some theoretical clarity and sensible protocols, we can determine the meanings of an offender's apology with a degree of confidence similar to what we experience in our judgments regarding an offender's mens rea.

The perceived "unanswerable" nature of such questions results, in part, from excessive expectations for character retributivism. As Murphy describes it via Michael Moore, "deep" or "whole" character retributivism "has its first and best home in the context of divine punishment – something that God might properly administer, on that final Day of Judgment, when he consults the ledger book of a whole human life and character."[203] If this is the proper standard for character retributivism, then it does indeed present questions unanswerable within the limits of a finite criminal justice system. Murphy correctly doubts whether we can accurately determine "the ultimate character of the individual," but can we ever determine the ultimate character of anyone in any circumstances?[204] I know my wife and children very well and would give my life for them, but could I successfully define their "ultimate characters"? Such absolutist and metaphysical language seems like unhelpful vestiges from earlier – and more simplistic – ways of classifying people. No matter how thorough, legal systems – and all human modes of inquiry for that matter – cannot achieve omniscience. It is dangerous folly to pretend that our imperfect findings regarding culpability and punishment mirror divine judgment. Even if legal officials could somehow overcome these epistemological obstacles, such an explicit analogue to casting comprehensive judgment on the offender's soul raises the previously discussed objections from liberal neutrality. Beyond evaluating whether an offender's apology bespeaks a genuine commitment to honor the moral principles underlying the law, deep character retributivism seems to require the state to uncover and evaluate our entire web of conscious and perhaps unconscious value systems to determine our punishments.[205]

In my view, act and character retributivism present a false dichotomy. We can synthesize the positions into "character of act" or *dialectical retributivism*. Metaphysical language can obscure the obvious fact that we punish the person rather than the act. The rapist, and not the act of rape, deserves to experience hard treatment. We imprison people, not crimes. But we find criminal acts embedded in lives, not served up as frozen slices of time on a scale of justice. One's acts and one's character stand in a dialectical relationship. What I do makes me who I am. Who I am determines what I do. How I respond when I err not only presents a strong indicator of my character but also provides opportunities to develop and define my identity in a kind of *felix culpa*. To the extent that we can isolate individual events in a person's life, we attribute meaning to these acts by triangulating that deed with the person's past and future.

If someone steps on my toe in anger and breaks it, her subsequent response tells me quite a bit about the nature of that act. She may taunt me and threaten to break more toes. She may go on a toe-breaking rampage, targeting only people of my ethnicity. She may apologize immediately, or years later. The nature of the initial assault changes depending on how it fits into a broader moral narrative. If I learn that the toe breaker either went to great lengths to find me and apologize or continued on to commit many more ethnically motivated assaults, I would retroactively feel less or more harmed. I would recalibrate desert accordingly. The story need not be so comprehensive that I must know everything about her character – her views on abortion, human relations, and the existence of God – to surmise her blameworthiness with regard to my toe. I do, however, better understand the badness of the event when placed in the context salient to this offense.

Scheler illuminates some of the phenomenological aspects of what I describe as dialectical retributivism. Responding to those who criticize repentance as a "useless deadweight" that "dwells morbidly on a past which is done with and unalterable," Scheler understands repentance as way of *endowing the past with new meaning*. Repentance, writes Scheler, "alters the 'unalterable' and places the regretted conduct or attitude in a new relation with the totality of one's life, setting it to work in a new direction."[206] As an "incursion into the past sphere of our life" and "encroachment upon it," Scheler claims that repentance "extinguishes the element of moral detraction, the quality of 'wickedness,' of the conduct in question" and thereby "relieves the pressure of the guilt which spreads in all directions from that wickedness, and at the same time deprives evil of that power of reproduction by which it must always bring forth more evil."[207] Repentance both revises the meanings of past wrongs and reduces the wickedness of such conduct with respect to the "totality" of the offender's life. Dialectical retributivism narrows this perspective to the badness of the offense: to the *character of the act*. When Scheler claims that repentance "bursts the chain of evil's reproductive power" and provides "the mighty power of self-regeneration of the moral world, whose decay it is constantly working to avert," we can understand certain forms of apology as

1. ending an ongoing harm, for instance by repaying a debt or retracting an insult (thus preventing it from becoming quantitatively worse in its perpetuation);

2. revising the badness of the harm, for instance by overwriting it with revised meanings in light of positive post-offense interactions (thus reducing the qualitative badness of the offense); and
3. preventing the worsening of the offense by averting a kind of downward spiral whereby unrepented offenses lead to revenge or other offenses that, in turn, cause the initial offense to feel even more contemptible as the seed of greater evil.[208]

Criminal desert lies not *either* in the inherent badness of the act stripped of all contexts *or* in the totality of the offender's being. We have no compelling reason to choose one or the other point of reference when both provide relevant information. Instead, considerations of the blameworthiness of an offender's deed should take into account how her prior and subsequent actions and mental states inflect the badness of that deed. Post-offense behavior and mental states should therefore influence our judgments regarding appropriate punishments. Whether regarding a broken toe or committing a sexual assault, we should judge desert with a temporally symmetrical view. Just as one's behavior and mental states before and after an offense alter culpability because they tell us relevant information about the nature of the act, so, too, one's mental states and behavior after an offense impart significance salient to desert. We can undertake such inquiries in a narrow sense indexed to the nature of the action over time rather than to the offender's entire character. Limiting the review in this way should reduce the temptation to speak in quasi-religious and absolutist terms of the offender's "wicked" or "evil" nature.[209] Dialectical retributivism also suggests how social injustice such as poverty or lack of opportunity might impact desert.

Dialectical retributivism also lends support to three strikes and similar laws. Instead of the consequentialist perspective that repeat offenders present greater risks and therefore should be met with increased sentences, a dialectical retributivist sees recidivism as data points in a longitudinal view of the offender. Prior crimes take on new meaning in the context of subsequent crimes, for instance as convictions plot a trajectory from minor to major offense and thereby increase the badness of the deeds. An earlier weapons charge becomes more sinister if we learn that the offender later used a gun to rob. However, although three strikes laws enjoy political favor, the notion that an offender's good deeds – whether through apologetic actions or otherwise – should reduce her punishment does not receive symmetrical support. If three "strikes" result in an "out" – typically a life sentence – then a certain number of "hits" should bring the offender home.

Considering potential objections to dialectical retributivism strengthens its appeal. In criticizing character retributivism generally, Tasioulas argues that "retributive desert is backward looking: it focuses on a past wrongdoing, and the hard treatment that is deserved communicates blame for that wrong-doing ... the gravity of the wrong is not influenced by anything that takes place subsequent to the wrong-doing, such as the offender's profound repentance."[210] The main exception, he argues, arises when "repentance occurs immediately upon the commission of the wrongful act and in such a way that it influences our estimation of the latter's very nature."[211] In a case in which the "offender is immediately appalled by what he has done, apologizes and seeks to make amends to the victim, and without delay turns himself in to the authorities despite having a perfectly good opportunity to evade capture – repentance is a factor mitigating culpability." Tasioulas finds such an exception permissible because we understand the offense as "as a lapse or aberration, a succumbing to temptation or the pressures of the moment, rather than the product of a settled determination to do wrong."[212] If an attacker immediately apologizes, on Tasioulas's reading, this indicates that we should interpret the offense through at least some of the offender's post-offense behaviors and mental states. Presumably a symmetrical logic would apply if the offender did something immediately after the offense that made it even worse, for instance adding a few insults or additional blows. Where, however, do we draw the temporal line? Strong emotions accompany many offenses, and whatever feelings cause me to attack you may continue to motivate my subsequent insults. Anyone involved in even minor arguments appreciates that once we break the levy, waves of negative emotions and actions often surge forward. Cooling-off periods vary by temperaments and injuries. Perhaps a few seconds, perhaps a day, perhaps a year may pass before we regret our offense, organize our thoughts, transform our behavior, and summon the courage to apologize. The cognitive, emotional, and behavioral elements of apologies are not like switches that can be flipped on and off. As I argue repeatedly, substantive apologies often take time. What happens during the period between offense and apology provides crucial chapters in the intertwined moral stories of the act and the character of the person committing the act.

Murphy once endorsed character retributivism more enthusiastically, in large part because in some crimes (Murphy uses rape as an example) the wrongfulness of the act results from the continued insult or degradation suffered by victims.[213] The pain and badness of this sort of offense continues beyond the moment of the act, but the enduring pain "may be withdrawn – and thus the hurt lessened – when the wrongdoer repents."[214] Murphy comes to doubt this point because he worries that he "overestimated the importance of symbolic messaging," especially for serious crimes.[215] I appreciate that in many offenses the material injury caused by the act, for example the destruction of property or crippling of a body part, will in some respect constitute the bulk of the injury. But even in the most irreversible crimes such as the murder of a loved one, however, the killer's post-offense behavior can certainly make matters worse. Although it may sound blasphemous to say so, a killer's post-offense behavior can also lessen the badness of the act of murder, at least to the extent to which she can reduce the fear, confusion, degradation, or future suffering that it causes. Apologies can, in these respects, revise the meanings of the offense and the punishment owed.

As I described it, dialectical retributivism strikes a balance between act and character retributivism by allowing knowledge of the narrowly salient aspects of the offender's character to inform the nature of the act. On this account some apologetic offenders will probably – although further arguments must be made – deserve reductions in punishment.[216] I hope to have shown that although character retributivists would naturally endorse apology reductions, those inclined toward act retributivism should accept that apologies can reduce the badness of deeds.

It warrants mention that the U.S. Supreme Court expressly determined that sentencers may consider an offender's character when determining punishment and that post-offense behavior can indicate the sorts of improvements in *character* that warrant reductions in sentencing. Writing for the majority in the 2010 case *Pepper v. United States*, Justice Sotomayor cited long-standing tradition back to 1937 that "justice generally requires consideration of more than the particular acts by which the crime was committed and that there be taken into account the circumstances of the offense together with the character and propensities of the offender."[217] *Pepper* also cited *Koon v. United States*: "It has been uniform and constant in the federal judicial tradition for the sentencing judge to consider every convicted person as an individual and every case as a unique study in the human failings that sometimes mitigate, sometimes magnify, the crime and the punishment to ensue."[218] Notice that the Court speaks here of unique circumstances magnifying *the crime itself*. "Permitting sentencing courts to consider the widest possible breadth of information about a defendant," writes Justice Sotomayor citing *Wasman v. United States*, "'ensures that the punishment will suit not merely the offense but the individual defendant.'"[219] According to the Court, the Sentencing Commission intended to afford judges "wide discretion in the sources and types of evidence used to assist him in determining the kind and extent of punishment to be imposed within limits fixed by law,"[220] and it incorporated this view in §3661 of the guidelines: "In determining the sentence to impose within the guideline range, or whether a departure from the guidelines is warranted, the court may consider, *without limitation*, any information concerning the background, character and conduct of the defendant, unless otherwise prohibited by law."[221] We should not necessarily read the Court's opinion as an endorsement of character or dialectical retributivism given that it makes no mention of underlying justifications for punishment – it would, for example, make sense to consider character and post-offense behavior from a strictly rehabilitative perspective. *Pepper* does, however, provide an authoritative foothold for the proposition that apology reductions honor the spirit of the guidelines as interpreted by the Supreme Court. The Court also recently noted Eighth Amendment concerns with failing to consider the evolution of an offender's character, ruling in *Graham v. Florida* that the offender's life sentence "guarantees he will die in prison without any meaningful opportunity to obtain release, no matter what he might do to demonstrate that the bad acts he committed as a teenager are not representative of his true character, even if he spends the next half century attempting to atone for his crimes and learn from his mistakes." Finding that Florida "denied him any chance to later demonstrate that he is fit to rejoin society based solely on a nonhomicide crime that he committed while he was a child in the eyes of the law," the Court concluded that "the Eighth Amendment does not permit" such punishments.[222]

Desert

If retributivists should consider post-offense behavior, does the apologetic offender *deserve* less punishment? Consider the many ways that an apology can mitigate the grievousness of the wrong, which in turn should reduce the punishment needed to provide equivalent justice. In corroborating the factual record, I confess my crime with all of its salient details. This spares the victim and community some degree of the pain associated with protracted efforts to learn what happened and why. Part of the evil of suffering serious injuries results from living with the specter of the violent unknown: Who did this? Why? Will they do it again? Will they ever be brought to justice? A detailed confession explaining what I did and why I did it goes some way toward reducing this particular badness associated with crime. It may help, within a retributivist perspective, to think in terms of the offender continually harming the victim in these respects until a confession or legal determinations resolve the issues. Every day that she awakes without the offender confessing, she experiences a new harm in coming to terms with the trauma and uncertainty. As Miguel de Cervantes describes this process, "[t]he very remembrance of my former misfortune proves a new one to me." Here we view the crime not in a metaphysically strict sense of "one act, one moment" but rather from a temporally looser perspective in which the offending unfolds over time along various vectors of harm. I do not mean this in the consequentialist sense that the act causes some future suffering, but rather along the retributive register that moral wrongs are often composed of a number of interrelated wrongs that manifest at different times. An apology has the power to stop some of these interrelated wrongs. Call this a *time-release theory of harm*. In cases of sexual violence, for instance, only some of the badness occurs during the physical attack. Other harms come in waves after the offender has fled and continue crashing against the victim.

Corroborating the factual record can end some of these vectors of harm and therefore lessen the overall badness of the offense.

Accepting blame can alleviate the pain not only of knowing who caused the injury – a relief compared to wondering which anonymous person did this – but also of exonerating the victim from thinking that she deserves fault for the injury. Part of the evil of rape, for example, stems from its tendency to lead the victim to ask whether she deserves some portion of the blame because she allowed herself to be vulnerable or did not sufficiently fight back. The perpetrator's clear acceptance of blame can reduce this psychological vector of harm.

Degradation constitutes a core aspect of the badness of many offenses: I harm you because I find you and your dignity subordinate to my interests. Whether understood as a violation of the practical imperative or as otherwise disrespecting the victim, this wrong endures from the moment of the initial crime (if not before) until the offender comes to see the victim as holding a certain kind of moral worth.[223] In the interim between an assault and an apology for the assault, the victim suffers a continued affront as the offender refuses to provide relief from this continued indignity. In this regard, justice delayed is justice denied. The longer it goes on, the worse it becomes. A categorically apologetic offender, by contrast, recognizes the victim as a moral interlocutor and thereby discontinues this aspect of the harm. In contrast to an offender who continues to refuse to recognize the victim as an equal, piles on the injuries, and makes things worse, the categorically apologetic offender puts an end to some aspects of the stream of harm. She therefore deserves less punishment. The significance of this recognition could increase if the offense causes the victim to suffer indignities from members of the community as well as from the offender. If a rapist initially claimed that the sex was consensual and thereby caused community members to question the victim's honesty, for example, the offender's eventual confession, acceptance of blame, and recognition of the victim as a moral interlocutor can prove especially important as a means of restoring the victim's status.

An apology's combination of identifying each harm, identifying the moral principles underlying each harm, and sharing a commitment to the moral principles underlying each harm also reduces the badness of the offense because one aspect of the harm lies in its undermining of community values and the fear and uncertainty this generates. An offense can, in other words, threaten the victim's and her community's overarching sense of justice and peace. This identifies an injury beyond concern for revictimization. Some see their sense of existential and moral order collapsed by trauma. To use an extreme example, the badness of the Nazi Holocaust lies not just in the deaths of millions but also in the horror of the disintegration of the moral order. Some offenses cause systems of meaning to teeter over an abyss. We worry that things have changed for the worse, that we will suffer like this forevermore. When a criminal categorically apologizes, she reinforces the legal and moral authority of the values in question. She ends the vector of generalized anxiety triggered by the belief that one's world is collapsing. Note that the voluntarily apologetic offender confirms these values not because legal threat bends her will but because she understands them as just. This secures their value beyond political regimes and distinguishes their value from court-ordered apologies.

Reform and redress provide the most obvious ways that apologies reduce the badness of offenses. An unreformed offender presents a continued threat. That threat amplifies the initial act: I beat you once and I may well do it again. Causing another to live in anticipation of such danger constitutes harm beyond the violence of the original offense. The reformed offender reduces this aspect of harm by forbearing from reoffending and repeatedly demonstrating this commitment by resisting opportunities and temptations to reoffend.

With respect to redress, imagine I steal a large sum of money from you and thereby harm you in a variety of ways from material deprivation to disrespect. In the simplest sense, the longer I keep the money, the *worse the offense*. Whether we frame this in terms of lost interest, lost opportunities, or an extended period of financial insecurity, one thing seems uncontroversial: the longer the duration, the greater the injury. Interest accumulates on moral debts, and therefore desert increases over time for the remorseless offender who does not provide redress. Again, justice delayed is justice denied. When an apologetic offender provides commensurate redress, she stops the clock. Desert along this vector of harm stops accruing. The offender providing redress deserves less punishment than the unapologetic because she commits a lesser offense. Pecuniary injuries best lend themselves to this sort of analysis, but the following guideline seems to apply to a broad range of injuries: the longer the offense goes without apologetic redress, the worse the offense becomes.

As restorative and restitutive theories point out, victims play a minor role in most criminal cases in the United States and they are unlikely to personally enjoy much relief or concrete redress from state-administered criminal proceedings. Victims who receive categorical apologies, by contrast, benefit from commensurate redress of the sort that can reduce the intensity and duration of their injuries. We should not, however, slip into metaphysical language that takes talk of commensurable redress too literally. For a crime such as murder, no amount of redress can "undo the harm" in its totality, even if an apology can to some extent reduce the offender's desert.

In addition, notice how apologies can inform our understanding of the offender's mental states not only after the crime but also before and during.

We have reason to believe that someone quick to apologize is more likely to have committed the crime without strong conviction or careful deliberation, as she quickly realizes her error. The remorseless offender, by contrast, appears to hold deeper convictions preventing her from recognizing her action as wrong. Although obviously a generalization – one could be certain during years of deliberate planning that she would be justified in killing someone but have a change of heart the moment she sees the victim's dying face – the inference that the remorseless offender possessed more culpable mental states at the time of the offense than an immediately remorseless offender seems about as reliable as most other accepted methods of reading the mens rea.

Note that an offender's continued post-offense failure to suffer the appropriate negative emotions increases harm to the offender and the badness of her acts. In Beebe's case, if he continued to happily socialize on campus or even found pleasure in his sexual assault, this probably worsens his offense against Seccuro in at least two respects: Beebe denies Seccuro the retributive "good" of seeing him suffer, and he causes her the pain of watching him continue to enjoy her degradation. I find emotions most relevant with respect to hard treatment as discussed later, and I consider issues of increasing punishment for unapologetic offenders in "Symmetry: Increasing Punishments for Unapologetic Offenders."

In summary, from the retributivist perspective – whether act, character, or dialectical retributivism – an offender deserves punishment in proportion to the gravity of her wrongdoing. The categorically apologetic offender deserves less punishment because her post-wrongdoing behavior reduces that gravity of her offense. Some may wonder about the propriety of reducing sentences for apologetic offenders: if they ought to apologize regardless of the benefits, should we reward them for satisfying their moral obligations? Retributive apology reductions do not reward the offender (as an act of mercy or generosity, for instance) but rather properly calibrate retributive responsibilities.[224]

Hard Treatment
If the categorically apologetic offender *deserves* less punishment, she requires less hard treatment to balance the scales of justices. I treat this issue independently in part because retributivists differ regarding the necessity of hard treatment as opposed to other forms of punishment that satisfy desert without emphasizing the need for the offender to suffer.[225] For some, however, the retributive belief that someone who commits a serious offense *deserves to suffer* presents its most powerful and instinctual appeal. Although this brings to mind Nietzsche's warning to "distrust all in whom the desire to punish is strong," the hard treatment requirement names the sense of injustice experienced when a murderer or rapist – regardless of their subsequent

transformation for the better – avoids full punishment. "They can't get away with this," some will think. "They deserve to suffer."

If someone like Beebe can cause such pain, get treatment, and become an improved person who offers a meaningful apology to his victim, we might imagine all of this unfolding without him suffering very much. Indeed, we could imagine an offender like Beebe feeling pretty good most of the time as he experiences the positive trajectory of his life. Perhaps he comforts himself by thinking "everything happens for a reason" and views the offense as a necessary evil allowing him to hit rock bottom and turn his life around. He may feel better than ever by the time he writes to Seccuro because he feels like he is turning a corner in his life. Happy remorse seems like an odd pairing, but a sense of accomplishment in moral improvement often mixes negative emotions with the positive.

On my account, a categorically apologetic offender suffers some degree of negative emotions and endures various sorts of hard treatment. Does she suffer enough? I should first block the common suspicion articulated by Tasioulas that there exist cases of "genuine repentance that do not involve undergoing anything remotely resembling a penance."[226] He offers the case of "the petty thief who comes to a sudden realization of the wrongfulness of his life of crime through a moral or religious conversion, then settles down to a perfectly decent family life, caring for his hitherto neglected wife and children." Although such a realization might cause negative emotions, "it is stretching things unduly to treat his feelings of guilt and remorse as a punishment."[227] Although I agree that various forms of transformation can occur without producing sufficient hard treatment to warrant consideration as commensurate punishment, the primary issue lies in the notion of "genuine repentance." Tasioulas's example clearly does not qualify as anything like a categorical apology. How does hard treatment measure against this higher standard?

The entire process associated with categorical apologies visits pain on the offender and entails various forms of hard treatment, so much so that Duff believes the very aim of punishment is "to bring offenders to suffer what they deserve to suffer – the pains of repentance and remorse."[228] But again we would benefit from a fine-grained account of where precisely this pain manifests and how this pain approximates the levels of suffering that retributivists believe offenders should feel. In general, the categorical apology seems to obviously entail pain at various stages. Recounting the details of one's wrongdoing, shouldering blame for the harm caused, explaining one's moral failures, facing the victim as moral equal, subjecting oneself to scorn, and generally participating in the rituals of remorse all occasion various kinds of pain. Apologizing categorically hurts, which in part explains its rarity. Two aspects seem to account for the bulk of the hard treatment: redress and emotions.

Regarding redress, first note that we should probably not describe the pains associated with not reoffending as retributive in nature – retributivists will probably understand such pains of deprivation constitutive of a general moral obligation. If Beebe suffers from not acting on impulses to rape, for instance, we probably should not understand such pain as punitive in nature and thus to be somehow subtracted from his total deserved hard treatment. This would look like double counting. Recall, however, my understanding of the redress required of a categorical apology: The offender takes practical responsibility for the harm she causes, providing commensurate remedies and other incommensurable forms of redress to the best of her ability. The offender provides a proportional amount of redress, but she need not meet excessive demands from victims with unreasonable or inappropriate expectations. I leave questions regarding what constitutes unreasonable or excessive demands to be determined in consideration of cultural practices, and I appreciate that such deliberations will often be contentious. One might be tempted to read the requirement that the offender provide proportionate redress as effectively building into the concept of the categorical apology sufficient punitive hard treatment. Such a reading, however, would elide distinctions between providing redress and enduring retributive hard treatment. We can imagine a variety of forms of redress that do not exactly seem like suffering. A wealthy offender can provide a large financial amount to the victim without feeling that loss given the size of her fortune. An offender can find such value in helping others that she views her community service as a welcome and satisfying activity. Both cases require sacrifice, but they hardly look like *suffering*. To further complicate matters, many people willingly perform community service not as a means of punitive redress but because they find the work meaningful or act from a sense of duty. In some cases apologetic redress will amount to hard treatment. In some cases it will not. We could say the same of any punishment in that some offenders welcome imprisonment because they see it as preferable to life beyond bars or as a simultaneously painful and cathartic means of cleansing their spirit. Although it may seem like only a decided minority would find such pleasure in pain, self-flagellation as a means of ecstatic penance has deeps roots across a range of cultures.

Setting aside unusual cases, apologetic redress typically constitutes hard treatment. If I wrongfully cause you $100,000 damage, compensating you will hurt. Even if I love my job, paying you back will consume a considerable amount of my time and require various sacrifices: I will spend years of summers teaching classes for extra pay and forgo vacations and other inessential expenditures as a sacrifice to meet my debt. It would be unpleasant and I think fair to describe this as a kind of hard treatment. Compensatory measures become more complex in matters regarding less obviously commensurable injuries. If I wrongfully render you a quadriplegic, how will my redress amount to proportional hard treatment? We need not resolve those problematic issues here. We must only establish that some apologetic redress – in the form of monetary awards or otherwise – can constitute the sort of hard treatment intended by retributivists. If my apology for your injury includes paying your medical expenses as well as spending considerable amounts of my time personally caring for you and others, such financial pain and emotional toil looks like hard treatment. It is not clear how much redress suffices – just how many hours and how much money must I sacrifice to suffer an amount of pain equivalent to rendering someone quadriplegic? – but my efforts should count for something on the scale of hard treatment. Compared to the offender who provides no such hard treatment through redress, such an apologetic offender appears to lessen her moral debt. Given enough time and enough hard treatment through apologetic redress, offenders could presumably clear her debt. Some evils may require more time to atone than is available in this life.[229]

We can also consider emotional suffering experienced by apologetic offenders as a form of hard treatment.[230] Distinguishing and measuring emotions presents immensely complex theoretical and empirical issues, and I attempted to identify these concerns at some length in *I Was Wrong*.[231] I ultimately argued that the categorically apologetic offender will experience an appropriate degree and duration of sorrow and guilt as well as empathy and sympathy for the victim. I left questions regarding what constitutes the appropriate qualitative and quantitative emotional components of categorical apologies to be determined in consideration of cultural practices and individual expectations. We should also keep in mind the difficulty of predicting how emotions will develop over time, as research suggests that forecasting affective states proves difficult and we often recover from negative emotions more quickly than expected.[232] For our purposes here, we only need to establish that the emotional pain associated with apologies should count in some respect toward the total hard treatment debt.

I am not willing to go as far as Murphy to claim that the "sincerely repentant person tortures himself" because a wide range of emotions and intensities can be at issue in these cases – from a mild and momentary pang of conscience to intense lifelong shame. The latter results in more suffering than the former, which explains why we often speak of someone who experiences great emotional pain associated with remorse as having "suffered enough." Inversely, I suspect that much of the folk psychological fascination with "remorseless criminals" relates not only to the worry that those who do not feel the proper negative emotions are more likely to reoffend but also to the notion that those who do not emotionally suffer enough are "getting away with" their crime by avoiding this form of hard treatment. As a kind of punishment already undergone, it seems that emotional suffering should count as hard treatment. I have enough experience with the slipperiness of these concepts that I will not claim that X amount of emotional suffering for Y duration should count for Z reduction in owed hard treatment. As a general proposition, however, negative emotions experienced by apologetic offenders should count for some reduction in their punitive debt. If the offender experiences the appropriate emotions given the offense, the greater the intensity and duration of these emotions, the farther she has gone toward meeting her quota of hard treatment.

One might argue that the sorts of hard treatment associated with apologies should not count against the suffering owed because such punitive measures must be administered by the state rather than self-inflicted. Note possible sources of hard treatment. I can freely undertake punitive activity through apology with its emotional and remedial hardships. A third party can exercise vigilante justice against me: beating me in the street. The victim can take revenge against me: personally collecting the debt by harming me in the manner she finds most suitable. In a sense that most of us no longer believe literally, "nature" can deliver punitive hard treatment by afflicting the offender with cancer or destroying her house in a tornado. Or politically legitimate authorities can administer justice through its procedures and officials. In my understanding, retributivists tend to prefer state administration of hard treatment primarily because the state's resources, procedures, and impersonal distance from the offense increase the likelihood that we identify the correct offender and deliver proportionate hard treatment. Emotional and vindictive mobs or victims, by contrast, seem comparatively more likely to punish innocents or over-punish the guilty. The state, in other words, is more likely to get it right. Self-inflicted punishment probably tends toward under-punishing, but not always. Particularly self-loathing wrongdoers, for instance, may take their own lives in a gesture of penitential self-sacrifice for a non-capital offense. Divine and omniscient authority would dispense justice more accurately, but democratic states lack such powers.

Once we control for these factors, what reasons remain for requiring the state rather than the offender to administer her hard treatment? We might object to the offender's retention of her freedom to choose her punishment given that her offense presumably denied her victim similar autonomy, creating a kind of unfairness where the offender retains control over the suffering of both the victim and herself.[233] This seems to capture some of our discomfort with Beebe's self-reform. However, why exactly might we find this problematic? Denying the offender the ability to self-punish could be either an additional amount of hard treatment, a distinct and incommensurable form of hard treatment, or something else altogether. If retributivists understand this to add the quantity of hard treatment, the offender could overcome this objection by adding X amount of hard treatment of her choice. If the state's imposition of punishment presents a distinct form of hard treatment and the offender cannot compensate with any amount of self-imposed suffering – and no other third party can fulfill this role – then the state will need to find ways to administer this particular form of hard treatment on top of an already completed self-directed punishment. This need not discredit the value of the self-imposed hard treatment that the repentant offender already tolled on the ledger of moral debt.

One might also object that self-inflicted hard treatment lacks sufficiently public meaning when contrasted with state-administered punishment, but I have argued at length that categorical apologies entail considerable publicity when appropriate.[234] I see no necessary reason why self-inflicted hard treatment – especially if the state recognizes such suffering as a legitimate consideration in the public sentencing process – cannot achieve comparable public benefits (setting aside for the moment whether such benefits should be viewed as retributive in nature). This seems especially important given the prominence of plea arrangements that diminish the public value of hard treatment. By contrast, self-inflicted punitive suffering pursuant to apologies will often be more visible than most state-administered punishments served behind prison walls and mostly invisible to the public eye. I consider this further in the context of communicative retributivism.

I worry that vengeful instincts motivate remaining arguments against crediting apologetic offenders for self-inflicted hard treatment: your suffering does not count unless we receive the sadistic pleasure of delivering cruelty ourselves. Nietzsche warned that retributivism generally arose from such vindictive instincts rather than from the window-dressing concern for human dignity, but I like to think that most retributivists would reject cruelty as a valued objective of punishment. Indeed, we might hope that an increased role for apologies in law might work to reduce – rather than amplify and legitimize – the desire for revenge.[235]

I should say a bit more about revenge, especially in light of Griswold's thoughtful work on vengeful anger.[236] Although it provides arguably the longest-standing argument for punishment, revenge garners little support from contemporary philosophers. Revenge now feels *dirty*, as when Nietzsche waxes aristocratic: "For this is your truth: you are too *pure* for the filth of the words: revenge, punishment, reward, retribution."[237] Revenge – setting aside whether it is best understood as an emotion or whether it describes an exclusively retributive phenomenon – holds a certain kind of power. Solomon finds the desire for revenge "the very foundation of our sense of justice, indeed, our very sense of ourselves, our dignity, and our sense of right and wrong."[238] Dennett even argues that we "ought to admit, up front, that one of our strongest unspoken motivations for upholding something close to the traditional concept of free will is our desire to see the world's villains 'get what they deserve.'"[239] Contrary to descriptions of revenge as a form of filthy resentment, Griswold finds an "air of moral purity and even sanctity" in feeling vengeful anger as "righteous."[240] Following Aristotle and Aquinas' shared sense that we should feel appropriate amounts of vengeful anger in certain situations, Griswold claims that a "virtuous person will feel vengeful anger as appropriate but will take revenge only after careful deliberation and in view of the additional considerations and conditions." This leads to situations in which one can be justified in "wishing ill for another" but not justified in personally taking revenge because "good reasons of a different order" – such as the duty to conform to the rule of law – proscribe vigilante justice.

Griswold argues, however, that it makes "no sense to desire vengeance against an offender who is contrite and has expressed contrition, taken responsibility, made amends, and taken every other conciliatory and emendatory step one could reasonably wish for."[241] We should therefore forswear vengeful anger when "faced with the appropriate forgiveness or excuse conditions." Griswold does not apply his position to cases of judicial punishment, nor does he consider the possibility of collective vengeful anger or criminal justice as a delivery mechanism for collective vengeance, but his account of personal cases of vengeful anger in private matters parallels my discussions of retributivism. If the offender undertakes the work of categorically apologizing, vengeful attitudes should wane. If not, vengeful anger transforms from expressing indignation as we rise up to defend our principles into indulging the "pleasures of fury."[242] Although much more could be said about the apologies in both cases, I am reminded of two situations in which expressions of remorse quelled thirst for revenge. In 2013, a California student went on a shooting spree seeking revenge against high school bullies. The student he most wanted to kill offered a tearful apology while cowering behind a desk. Somehow the words and display of emotions changed the shooter's heart. He dropped the weapon.[243] Jordan's King Hussein similarly prevented violence by personally visiting the homes of grieving Israeli parents of seven children killed on a school outing by a Jordanian soldier. Accompanied by his children, Hussein knelt before the parents and said, "I feel that I've lost a child." The parents, as well as Israelis watching the broadcasts of his visit, found Hussein's remorse meaningful and credited it with abating calls for revenge and with preserving a fragile peace agreement.[244]

In conclusion, the hard treatment associated with categorical apologies should count – and in some cases count quite a bit – toward the suffering deserved by offenders within retributivism. Failing to reduce hard treatment for apologetic offenders departs from proper retributive concerns and becomes cruelty. The amount that apologetic suffering should discount the state-imposed hard treatment will vary case by case and will – as is typical of retributive punishment – prove difficult to quantify.

Proportionality and Consistency

Proportionality, consistency, and equality present interrelated issues within retributivism. Proportionality relates to the punishment fitting the offense, such that the offender receives the amount and kind of punishment that she deserves given the nature of her wrongdoing. We should not punish parking tickets with execution or murders with small fines. Consistency relates to like offenders receiving like sentences, such that two people committing the same crime without salient distinctions will receive the same punishment. If offenders A and B commit similar crimes and provide similar apologies, it would be inconsistent to give A but not B credit for her remorse by reducing her sentence. Consistency also has a temporal component: if we reduced the sentence for a similar crime and apology last year, then consistency requires us to do it again. Of course one can be consistently unjust, for instance by regularly applying apology reductions only to rich, white offenders. Some commentators speak of reducing apologies for apologetic offenders as potentially violating "equal treatment"[245] or "horizontal equality," but separating the issues helps avoid conflation.[246] It seems clearest to speak of retributivist objectives to (1) determine proportionate sentences and (2) administer those punishments consistently.

The notion that an apologetic offender will receive a lesser sentence than an unapologetic offender committing the same crime confronts the objection that such a "downgrade in horizontal equality," in von Hirsch's terms, has "nothing to do with the conduct's being worse; but rather, only to do with the offender's personal degree of amenability to penitential regimes."[247] As I attempted to show earlier, apologies can reduce the gravity of the offense. We can therefore honor the principle of proportionality if we consider contrition when calibrating desert. Tasioulas further notes that "moral reasoning will not standardly single out one precise quantum of punishment as proportionate to the gravity of the wrong in each and every case; instead, it will be likely that a punishment falling within some fairly broad range of severity can be properly inflicted as deserved."[248] Once we allow for some leeway in proportionate punishments – and I am unsure how we can morally justify even one less iota of punishment within strictly retributive schemes unless the apology reduces the gravity of the offense and thus the appropriate desert – repentance provides a reason to come in high or low within that acceptable range.

Von Hirsch characterizes the problem as penalizing those with "thicker skin" and less likely to adopt a remorseful attitude. Although von Hirsch refers primarily to those moved to apologize as a result of their sentence – a scenario I consider in detail later – this applies to those who generally require "tougher penance before the message is likely to penetrate."[249] If we adopt the position that hard treatment primarily serves to *bring about* apologies, then some offenders may require more hard treatment than others to reach this result. Indeterminate sentencing systematically faces this problem, adjusting one's sentence and hard treatment according to one's response.[250] Respond to punishment with repentance and reduce your sentence; respond with defiance and increase your sentence. For the reasons noted, I find apologies relevant to desert and we should therefore particularize punishment to these characteristics.

The primary retributive issue here is not that offenders deserve particularized punishments in light of their apologies, but that granting officials excessive discretion in these complex matters invites inconsistent and unfair results. Without clear guidelines, we rightfully worry that disingenuous offenders will game the system and receive credit for staged apologies. We worry that disadvantaged but morally transformed offenders will fall victim to bad lawyering or systemic bias will prevent them from receiving the reduction in punishment that they deserve according to retributive logic. Many of the concerns discussed regarding bias, inequality, and social justice resurface here. Just as like crimes should be treated the same, like apologies should be treated the same. Retributivists should work to achieve consistency along with proportionality. Standardization in such review of apologies in criminal law therefore seems essential. I attempt to provide such guidelines in the section "In Practice: How to Reduce Punishment for Apologetic Offenders."

Dignity

Like the "two Kants" mentioned in the rehabilitative context – the humane and peaceful Kant *versus* the stern absolutist advocate for capital punishment – Kantian penal theory operates on two tracks that do not always appear to run in the same direction. One might identify Kant with hard treatment and deserved suffering. Those unsympathetic to retributivism may even believe he provides high-minded pretexts for justifying sadistic revenge and cite Nietzsche for the claim that we should view retributivism as the current bloom of deeply rooted traditions of cruelty. As contemporary theorists such as Duff argue, however, respect for human dignity guides retributivist theory even if this can be difficult to discern in practice. Braithwaite makes this point powerfully:

> Liberal retributivists like to say that punishment is more dignified than rehabilitation. This view has long been disparaged by those who question how dignified it can be to have one's head shaved, [be] put in prison fatigues, [be] subjected to rectal searches for drugs, live in daily fear of bashings and rape and countless more subtle humiliations. Actual punishment practices seem more plausibly described in terms of communal lusts for afflicting indignity on the evil.[251]

Apology reductions, I believe, can help reconcile retributive commitments to dignity with the administration of justice.

The conceptions of dignity present multifaceted and contested sets of ideas. In punishment, discussions of dignity often cite Kant and Hegel for their origins. Although some argue that we should view rehabilitation as the proper heir of the tradition of dignity developed within German idealism, orthodox readings view retributivism through Kant's practical imperative.[252] Bennett, for example, argues that "retributive reactions are necessary to do justice *to the offender.*"[253] Duff's argument that punishment should aim to generate repentance in offenders understands a criminal's dignity as inviolable. "My main aim," writes Duff, "is to explore the implications of the Kantian demand that we should respect other people as rational and autonomous moral agents – that we should treat them as ends, never merely as means – for an understanding of the meaning and justification of criminal punishment."[254] Duff elaborates this requirement:

[T]o respect another person as a rational and autonomous moral agent is to treat him and respond to him as one who is able, and should be allowed, to conduct his own life and determine his own conduct in light of his own understanding of the values and goals which command his allegiance. It involves a refusal to manipulate him, or to use him merely as an instrument for the attainment of social or individual goals; insofar as I may properly attempt to modify his conduct (or, more accurately, attempt to bring him to modify his own conduct), I should do so by bringing him to understand and accept the relevant reasons which justify that attempt.[255]

Duff's theory of moral communication – which I will discuss in further detail in the context of the state leading an offender to repent – "addresses [offenders] as moral agents" by appealing to their consciences and engaging them in moral dialogue meant to bring about their own autonomous understanding that their crimes are wrong and warrant repentance along with self-reform.[256] For Duff, such dialogue presents a "matter of moral or rational compulsion, as when a person cannot avoid recognizing a truth that stares her in the face or forces itself on her attention."[257] Because punishment addresses the offender as an "autonomous agent who must in the end accept or reject the message communicated by her punishment for herself... it still leaves her free to reject it."[258] Such an approach will "preclude any attempt to *force* a citizen to change her moral attitudes, or to bring about such a change by any means other than those of rational moral persuasion."[259] Punishment must afford "criminals the respect and concern due to them."[260]

Even when an effort to induce self-reform seems very likely to fail, according to Duff, we "owe it to victims and to offenders to make the attempt... since in making it we show that we do take crime seriously as a public wrong and address the offender as someone who is not beyond redemption."[261] Such a view bars use of psycho-surgical methods of transforming behavior[262] as well as – and contrary to Kant's own position – death as the "ultimately exclusionary punishment."[263] So long as they do not suffer from the kind of mental illness that Kant describes as being "morally dead,"[264] on Duff's account we must treat even one who commits "horrific crimes" as someone "who could, and who should be given the chance to, repent his crime and redeem himself."[265] Radzik similarly writes from a Kantian position that emphasizes rehabilitation of wrongdoers and their relationships as the proper method of recognizing the offender's dignity.[266]

Apology reductions offer a practical apotheosis of such a Kantian ideal of dignity in punishment regardless of whether we understand this imperative along retributive or rehabilitative registers. Consider Duff's vision:

[Punishment] addresses the criminal as a rational moral agent, seeking his understanding and his assent; it aims to bring him not merely to obey the law, but to accept its requirements as being justified: to recognize the wrongness of what he has done, to make his own condemnation which his conviction expresses, and to guide his future conduct in light of the relevant moral reasons which the law, his trial and punishment all offer him for obeying the law. It treats him not merely as a moral agent with whom we are engaged in a communicative process of argument and persuasion – it seeks his participation, not merely his submission: for its aim is that he should come to make the punishment, and the repentant understanding which it expresses, his own.[267]

The categorically apologetic offender achieves all of these objectives as she participates in a moral dialogue through which she confesses her deeds, recognizes the nature of her blameworthiness with depth and precision, views her victims as moral interlocutors, appreciates the harm caused and takes responsibility to redress them, exercises her will to consistently transform her behavior and undertake redress, experiences appropriately contrite emotions, and does all of this with the intention of advancing the victim's well-being and affirming the values in question rather than behaving out of fear and manipulation. Indeed, apology reductions arguably meet Kantian and Hegelian demands of recognizing the dignity of both offenders and victims better than any other theory of punishment. Contrary to punishments that treat "a man like a dog instead of with the freedom and respect due to him as a man," the categorically apologetic offender accepts her full humanity through her contrition.[268]

The offender's dignified response to her wrongdoing should presumably be met with an equally dignified response from the state, the victims, and the community. What might this entail? First, they must of course treat the offender with dignity in all of the usual ways required by Kantians and their ilk, including treating the repentant offender as a fellow citizen.[269] Some may extend the sort of argument Kant deploys in favor of capital punishment and claim that the best way to honor the dignity of those who voluntarily break the law is to punish them fully and not reduce their sentences because of their contrition. I do not find this compelling because, as stated previously, apologies can reduce desert and earn credit for hard treatment. Others might adopt a skeptical attitude toward the offender and her contrition, refusing to believe that she has the capacity to change despite all of the evidence to the contrary. This would commit just the sort of dehumanization of the offender warned against by contemporary Kantians. If the offender's contrition leaves a remainder of hard treatment that should be met with additional punishment, the state must administer that punishment in a spirit and manner that continues to treat her as an end rather than a mere means.

These discussions have tended toward examples wherein the offender enters the justice system fully repentant. Matters become more complicated when apologies occur sometime after the criminal process begins, and I now turn to such cases in the context of the communicative role of categorical apologies.

Communicative Retributivism

Philosophers from Plato to Hegel to McTaggart to Duff have understood moral reform of offenders to be the ultimate aim of punishment. Although such morally ambitious and arguably paternalistic hopes for punishment generate friction against commitments to liberal neutrality and skepticism toward punishment as an effective means of rehabilitation, the basic insight transcends these challenges: the morally transformed offender is at least one of the ultimate aims of punishment. Criminals who arrive at the gates already reformed – call these "already apologetic offenders" – bypass the means of the justice system to arrive directly at these ends.

Duff treats those who require punishment to bring about repentance as his primary subject, and I will address those who "become repentant" in the next section. Here we focus on the already repentant. Recall the general contours of Duff's argument. Given his commitment to the dignity of offenders, Duff views punishment as a kind of "moral communication" that persuades them via rational means to repent their crimes.[270] Punishment *communicates* in rational terms the wrongness of the offense, and this explanation should appeal to the offender's reason and initiate her transformation. Even though the system must initially force the offender to serve her penitential sentence, the sentence does not manipulate her but rather appeals to her ability to recognize the inappropriateness of her actions by concentrating her attention on the crime. Over time the offender comes to see the "truth that stares her in the face,"[271] changes her mind, and accepts the necessity of "secular penance" to bring about her transformation and just deserts.[272] The offender, in other words, eventually sees the punishment as justified and in her moral interest. She then wills the punishment for herself as a form of hard treatment that is deserved and essential to her now self-directed repentance.[273] The offender remains free to reject this message. If she refuses to repent or reform, we should treat her "as if [s]he has apologized" once she has completed – against her will – the sentence. Duff does not endorse extending sentences until offenders voluntarily repent because such a practice would violate proportionality and autonomy by attempting to "bully or manipulate [them] into submission."[274] In addition to not extending sentences of the unapologetic, Duff – like von Hirsch – would *not* reduce sentences for apologetic offenders.[275] Even though Duff hopes for repentance as the outcome of punishment, the offender should serve the deserved proportionate "penance" regardless of her attitude toward the punishment. Duff holds this view even for the "already repentant" offender who turns herself in, confesses, feels "the pangs of remorse," and determines to "reform her future conduct."[276] Even though such an offender "is already suffering what she deserves to suffer – the pain of remorse,"[277] Duff believes we should not reduce her punishment because

1. "a principle of proportionality between the seriousness of the crime and the severity of punishment is intrinsic to my account.... To impose a lighter sentence on a repentant offender is thus to imply that repentance renders the crime less serious"[278];
2. "repentance is not something that can be achieved and completed in a moment"[279];
3. "the whole sentence serves the dual purpose of inducing and expressing repentance," meaning that although remorse has been independently induced repentance has not yet been properly expressed;[280] and
4. "she has not done what is required to reconcile herself with the political community whose laws and values she has infringed."[281]

From my perspective Duff should – even if he indicates otherwise – support apology reductions for several reasons. I previously addressed the issue of proportionality identified in Duff's first point at some length, and with respect to the second point, I argue that categorical apologies and their approximations are best judged longitudinally because the passage of time can either amplify or diminish meanings in light of an offender's reform, redress, and other post-apology behavior and mental states. With respect to the third point, if communicative retributivism aspires to rationally persuade offenders of the wrongness of their actions, then categorically apologetic offenders present something of an ideal success in that regard. Not only does the categorically apologetic offender understand the wrongness of her actions, but also she does so with a degree of clarity and sophistication beyond what Duff seems to expect. The categorically apologetic offender understands how various behaviors lead to criminal offenses, and she identifies the moral arguments supporting the relevant principles. She finds those principles compelling, she promises to honor those principles, she in fact does honor those principles by changing her behavior and providing redress, and she communicates these values and intentions to the relevant parties. Moreover, she does all of this with the intentions of honoring the principles and the victim and at risk to her own legal interests by confessing to a crime. This process better communicates moral value and sanction not only to the offender but also to the community because the categorically apologetic offender does not merely participate in court-designed apologetic rituals but instead actively drives the process of contrition with internally motivated beliefs. Again, the principles and the suffering of the victim motivate the offender. This amplifies the expressive value of her apologetic actions – when the offender makes clear that she came to see the wrongness of her ways of her own volition, she testifies to the power of the principles rather than the coercive authority of the legal system. Voluntary recognition of wrongdoing also presents a more compelling example of a moral dialogue than most exchanges in the criminal context. As R. J. Lipkin points out, Duff's version of the criminal process hardly seems like a genuine moral dialogue because of the offender's very limited ability to convince state representatives that the state and its laws are on the wrong side of morality. Thus, Lipkin argues, there "is no true exchange of moral arguments in court."[282] These considerations address the third point, and I fail to see what the last point adds beyond the first three in conjunction with the other meanings and functions addressed herein.

These points seem especially salient when contrasted with an offender undergoing the sort of apology ritual endorsed by Duff or Bennett. When a court orders an offender to undergo "penance" in the form of fines, service work, or a prison term, the public may never know the spirit in which the offender undertakes these efforts. Such attitudes and motivations matter a great deal for all of the reasons I identify, and in this regard not all acts of penance are equal.[283] Begrudging community service, for example, conveys very different meaning from work undertaken out of an offender's sense that she owes a debt to her community and wishes to make amends to the best of her ability because this is the right thing to do. On Duff's account the offender may even deny guilt or contest the moral justification of the law, yet we should still treat her as if she conceives of the forced punishment as pursuant to sincere repentance. In the context of a criminal justice system in which we treat even the transparently defiant offenders as if they offer morally transformative and "symbolically adequate" apologies, we invite skepticism regarding the ability of criminal remorse to convey the sorts of thick meanings entailed by categorical apologies.[284]

Duff's position toward not reducing punishments for voluntary repentance appears to result from his limited attempts to unpack meanings potentially associated with apologies. This prevents him from understanding reform, redress, or negative emotions, for example, as intrinsic to apologies.[285] It is also unclear whether Duff believes apologies include confessions and acceptance of blame. All of this leaves considerable ambiguity regarding how apologies map onto communicative retributivism, leading Duff to reject the idea that apologies complete the retributive work he expects of punishment. As I attempted to demonstrate earlier, however, in addition to fulfilling the primary objective of communicative retributivism – moral reform through rational discourse – the categorically apologetic offender already satisfies the major retributive demands through the various forms of hard treatment intrinsic to the apology while honoring principles of desert, proportionality, consistency, and dignity. If Duff adopted a thicker conception of apology, then it appears that he should support apology reductions. As I argued throughout *I Was Wrong*, we have many compelling reasons for replacing binary notions with a standard like the categorical apology that accounts for a range of social, moral, and instrumental significance. Given the high stakes for offenders, victims, and their communities, it seems especially important to utilize a nuanced and comprehensive view of apologies within criminal justice systems. Despite Duff's commendable desire to treat all offenders as dignified agents capable of reform, his as if approach risks exacerbating already considerable confusion regarding the meanings of apologies in criminal law. We can better accomplish these objectives by parsing the substance conveyed by apologies and calibrating punishments accordingly.

My comments here may shed some light on tension in Duff's work. Despite his explicit rejection of reducing punishments for already repentant offenders, note how the following passage qualifies that view:

An offender who is truly contrite has already done part of the work of punishment for herself: she has recognized and repented her crime, and subjected herself to the pain of remorse; her confession, or her formal plea of "Guilty" in court, are appropriate expressions of her repentance – as too are such efforts at reparation or restitution she might make. Her contrition may not show her actual offense to have been any less serious (except if and insofar as it shows that her crime was not the act of one wholeheartedly committed to evil ends): but it may show that she is less in need of punishment, since she is already punishing herself. But contrition, however genuine, will not always render further punishment inappropriate or unjustified: at least in the case of more serious crimes we may say that the contrite offender should still receive, and should indeed accept, a punitive sentence from the court. For repentance is not simply something one does, and is then finished with; the task of coming to understand, to repent, and truly to disown my crime may be a long and arduous one.... The penitent perpetrator of a serious crime might, if left to herself, find and undertake an appropriate penance: but the court, whose proper task is to ensure that wrong-doers undergo suitable punishments, may properly specify her penance for her.[286]

Here Duff gestures various ways toward apology reductions: contrition can "do the work of punishment" in various ways, her apology "*may* show that she is less in need of punishment, since she is already punishing herself," contrition will "not always render further punishment inappropriate or unjustified," and the offender might of her own doing "undertake an appropriate penance." Duff also suggests that those who exercise "principled dissent" deserve lighter punishments, which further suggests his willingness to index punishment to an offender's mental states regarding her crime rather than simply the "badness" of the crime itself.[287] Duff leaves little role for the state beyond ensuring that the offenders' voluntary apologies rise to the levels of contrition, hard treatment, redress, and such expected by the state. As I explain later regarding the practical implementation of apology reductions, such oversight is not only compatible with but also essential to the position.

In addition, Duff's Kantian orientation and undeveloped view of apologies prevents him from appreciating the full consequentialist value of his own position.[288] When perceived as "unduly dominated by the idea of retributive desert," Duff's important theory appears off-putting to policymakers concerned with the practical significance of remorse for criminal justice.[289] Even if penance reduces recidivism rates, Duff's theory "does not make the justification of a penal system depend upon its contingent efficiency as a means to some independently identifiable end." He therefore resists empirical evidence supporting this claim because the theory ultimately rests on retributive principles rather than measurable effects.[290] Duff emphasizes that although his view "looks to the future" in that "punishment aims to induce a process of repentance, self-reform, and reconciliation," he warns that "this is not to say that it seeks to combine retributivist and consequentialist elements in a 'mixed' penal theory." Duff insists that

[w]hereas on a consequentialist account the relationship between punishment and the ends which justify it is purely *contingent* (punishment is justified if it is a contingently efficient means of securing some independently identifiable end), on my account that relationship is *internal*: for that end to be achieved (the offender's repentant understanding of her crime) is such that punishment (the attempt to induce such an understanding by the communication of censure) is an intrinsically appropriate way to achieve it.[291]

Duff specifically contrasts his view to Braithwaite and Petit in this regard.[292] Such a focused retributivist view becomes blind or indifferent to the many consequentialist reasons for reducing punishments for apologetic offenders.

Similar issues arise regarding Duff's treatment of underlying conditions. He appreciates that "persisting and systematic injustice" can exclude offenders from the political community and believes that such exclusion can undermine their obligations to the law.[293] Although he does not say whether contemporary justice systems reach this point or what to do when one – or millions – of criminal offenders stand on the other side of this point, he does recognize that underlying social conditions can dramatically impact the meanings of apologies from certain offenders.[294] From this recognition he concludes, however, "that once the defendant is brought to trial, such injustices will probably not be relevant, unless they generate what the law should recognize as a justification or excuse for what he did."[295] Thus "the court's decisions are properly isolated from the broader social and political context in which the law and the criminal process, as particular practices, are set."[296] Even "unjustly excluded offenders have still committed genuine wrongs, for which they must be called to account and punished," but their punishment "must include some recognition of the wrongs they have suffered and of the morally flawed character of their punishment," perhaps "expressed in the regretful or apologetic tones of the sentence."[297] "We owe it" to the offender, writes Duff, "to continue to treat him as someone who is not irrevocably cut off from the values he has flouted, who could still redeem himself – even if he will not do so."[298] Rather than prescribing some kind of assistance to the offender or reforming the structural conditions causing her exclusion, Duff offers punishment administered in "apologetic tones." I am uncertain what Duff means here by "apologetic tones," but this particularly unfortunate ambiguity highlights the importance for communicative retributivism to clearly articulate its concept of apology while explaining how such meanings relate to social justice. Doing so will strengthen Duff's already powerful position.

Becoming Apologetic versus Already Apologetic
Comparative Value

Unlike those rare cases of offenders who arrive at the gates of the justice system categorically apologetic, convicts tend to stumble toward contrition at various stages in the criminal process. I discussed the blurred boundaries between voluntary and involuntary apologies in the context of court-ordered apologies, and here I consider those who *voluntarily* grow to adopt apologetic attitudes during or after the formal criminal process. We can call these offenders those who "become apologetic."

Notice the infinite variations here, with the spectrum from voluntary to involuntary apologies overlaid with various degrees of coercion that produce a wide range of apologetic meanings. The first experience of being handcuffed, for example, may awaken a teenager to the seriousness of her offense and bring about a change of heart. A previously remorseless addict may experience a moment of clarity after a period of jail-cell sobriety powerful enough to illuminate a path toward contrition. An elderly inmate having spent much of her life in prison may gradually become apologetic after decades of maturation. An offender might sit through a trial and sentencing as her attorney directs her to deny all wrongdoing, all while vaguely knowing that she has done wrong and needs to turn her life around yet needing considerable help from the state to provide and maintain an apology indicating deep transformation.

These examples involve the law using its coercive authority – in applying restraints, detaining, or placing on trial – that steers the offender toward apology. As I noted in the context of court-ordered apologies, questions of voluntariness become increasingly complex as an offender undergoes deeper involvement with the more coercive aspects of the justice system's incentives and disincentives. *I Was Wrong* defined coerced apologies as those provided in circumstances in which a threat or offer significantly influences someone's ability to choose not to apologize and an ultimatum from someone with power over her – rather than the apologizer's recognition of her blameworthiness or desire to increase the well-being of the victim – drives a coerced decision to apologize. Contrast coerced apologies with the evolution envisioned by Duff wherein the state forces an offender to undergo punishment and through this process – perhaps *because of* this process – her attitude changes and she becomes voluntarily apologetic. Although she may have begun the process aiming primarily to avoid punishment, she comes to apologize for the sake of the victim, the community, and the breached principle.

Two kinds of issues require our attention when an offender becomes apologetic after state intervention: (1) the comparative value of such apologies and (2) the appropriateness of bringing about such repentance as a goal of the state. Regarding the first set of questions, do those who become apologetic within the system deserve different treatment – particularly different discounts in punishment – than those who arrive already repentant? Should the justice system treat an offender who becomes apologetic after her first night behind bars differently than one who becomes apologetic in the thirtieth year of her sentence? Should an apology warrant the same reduction in sentence regardless of the length of its gestation? If an offender requires intensive therapy, moral dialogue, or addiction treatment to become apologetic, should she receive the same reduction in punishment as those who come around more easily?

As a general baseline, categorical apologies will convey similar meaning regardless of how and when they come to fruition because the elements required of a categorical apology control for various issues of timing and generation. Two categorical apologies will be similar in the most salient respects irrespective of when they occur in the criminal process.

Distinctions between those who arrive in the criminal justice system apologetic and those who become repentant later in the process, however, offer practical and evidentiary insights. I work through these issues in more detail later, but we can note the obvious points here. If an offender denies all culpability during a trial, for example, but then undergoes an overnight transformation between the guilty verdict and the sentencing hearings, we have reason to suspect that she apologizes primarily as strategic means: deny wrongdoing before trial to maximize chances of a favorable plea or finding of innocence, but repent once the court finds guilt to maximize the possibility of a lenient sentence. A delay need not reduce the value of an apology. Apologies require the passage of time for an offender to become remorseful, undergo treatment, demonstrate reform, provide redress, experience hard treatment, communicate values, and so on. It is not as if an offender is remorseless one day, a switch flips, and the next day she apologizes categorically. These things take time. Courts will better understand and measure the meanings of apologies if they view them as treatments rather than cures for criminality. This is not to say that delayed apologies do not present costs. The justice system may expend considerable resources investigating a crime while the offender refuses to apologize and confess. An offender's denials of blame can increase the pain to the victim and her community, as well as prolong fear that the true offender remains at large. The unapologetic offender increases the duration that a victim suffers the indignity of not being recognized by the offender as a moral interlocutor. The victim waits for reform and redress while interest accumulates on moral debts. The sooner she apologizes, the sooner the offender begins experiencing the sorts of negative emotions that should count as retributive hard treatment. If an offender takes a long time to see the wrongness of her actions, this can provide this offers a measure of the depth of the moral hole from which she digs out. The victim may die waiting for an apology, foreclosing the possibility for certain kinds of meaning altogether. Thus the passage of time can cut both ways. The general principle holds that already apologetic offenders should receive similar reductions in punishment as those who become categorically apologetic, but this will vary somewhat depending on the underlying punishment theory emphasized. Considerations of how and when the acts of contrition materialize should, however, guide assessments of the authenticity and value of such apologies across the range of penological perspectives in the ways identified later.

Objections from Liberal Neutrality Revisited
As previewed in earlier discussions of restorative justice, one major difference between the already apologetic offender and the offender who becomes repentant lies in the role played by the state. With the already repentant offender, the state can more or less *respond* to and *evaluate* self-directed contrition. If she arrives at the gates well on her way toward a categorical apology, the state can adopt a reactive rather than active posture with respect to her contrition and recalibrate punishment accordingly. Such situations avoid the most powerful objections from liberal neutrality discussed and require little if any intervention into the offender's beliefs.

Most cases, however, will place the state in a more complicated position in which it receives offenders who become apologetic to varying degrees during their interactions with the criminal justice system. This can come about in two ways. The state could go about its punishment business without regard for apologies as possible or desirable outcomes – it simply administers justice in the form of fines, prison terms, or otherwise. If an offender becomes apologetic during this process, then the state might reduce punishment. Here contrition would be an unintentional – but perhaps welcome – byproduct of punishment. Alternatively, the state could view apologies as an explicit objective of criminal justice and conceive of punishment primarily as a soul-crafting "pump" for moving offenders toward contrition.[299] It could attempt to bring about apologies in ways that maximally honor the offender's dignity. It could work toward these goals by offering strictly voluntary addiction treatment, therapy programs, religious and moral education, or programs to convert offenders' labor into redress for victims, all while ensuring that neither these programs nor incentives for participating in these programs present even the appearance of state coercion. The goal could be to help the offender learn how to provide substantive apologies.

To what extent – if any – should the state serve as a midwife of contrition and encourage, coach, or induce voluntary apologies? Recall that objections from liberal neutrality tether around concerns that a state's consideration of an offender's apology requires it to cross a line from appropriately public punishment to excessively paternalistic moral reformation. According to these objections, the state should not use its coercive authority to manipulate an offender's value system: it can punish us, condemn us, deter our behavior, and appeal to our faculties of reason to explain why we should honor its law. Our values, however, stand beyond the proper purview of the state. As von Hirsch states it, "the state ought to have no such goal as inducing repentance" because "there is a difference between the state expressing condemnation and the state aiming to induce repentance in offenders." Von Hirsch therefore does "not advocate a penance theory, according to which the aim of the sanction would be actually to seek to generate in the offender specified sentiments of shame, repentance, and the like."[300] Expanding the role of apologies in law risks expanding the state's authority deep into our value systems, bringing to mind the various dangers associated with court-ordered apologies. Cases of those who "become apologetic" seem particularly susceptible to these criticisms if the state actively promotes and works on an offender's deep moral reform. These objections become stronger still if the offender rejects the state's moral authority, for example because she disagrees with the law or finds the state morally bankrupt.[301] Also recall how these issues can surface by imposing a certain conception of forgiveness on victims and communities by requiring them to participate in a system that seeks restoration rather than, for example, religiously motivated revenge.

In general, a few guidelines help frame how such objections apply to those who become apologetic within the criminal justice system:

1. If an offender arrives already repentant, then many of these objections appear less worrisome because the state did little to "interfere" with the offender's conscience – the state passively receives and evaluates apologies rather than promoting them.
2. The more potentially coercive the situation, the stronger the objections from liberal neutrality.
3. The harder the state works to bring about a categorical apology – and the more it intends to produce an apology – the stronger the potential objections from liberal neutrality.
4. The further the state "moves the needle" from remorseless to remorseful with an offender, the greater the concern that it violates liberal neutrality.
5. The more controversial the law violated – consider illegal marijuana possession or outlawed homosexual relations – the greater the concern.
6. The "deeper" the value at issue – contrast a speeding violation with a killing of a doctor providing abortions by a religiously motivated vigilante – the greater the concern.
7. Objections from liberal neutrality apply more strongly to adult than to juvenile offenders.

Several of these issues require further discussion. Liberalism commits to what Rawls might call a "thin" conception of justice that all citizens must honor.[302] Basic liberal notions of fairness, equality, rights, and so forth undergird criminal law.[303] We can assert these political values without presupposing "ultimate principles" regarding their origins and justification. Thicker notions of justice fill in a person's ultimate grounding for these thin values and how they relate to various other private beliefs such as one's religious views and notions of the good life. Criminal law in a secular liberal society requires its citizens to respect the state's thin notion of justice while allowing for great variance in thick conceptions of the good. Although an atheist and a religious fundamentalist may hold very different thick reasons regarding why we should not murder, the law equally commits them to a shared thin conception of justice while allowing for disagreement and dissent regarding thick beliefs. Apologies in criminal contexts will recognize the basic values of citizenship. It is well within the jurisdiction of the state to teach offenders that they should respect the law, for example by feeling remorse and providing redress for criminal activity. The crime's very illegality – as distinguished from legal but immoral behavior – places it squarely within the thin conception of justice that delimits the domain of public concern. The criminal justice system alters the behavior of its population, whether through appealing to moral reasoning, prescribing medication, or threatening with the sort of punishment that causes citizens to realign their self-interests with the public good. *How* we teach people that they should be apologetic for breaking the law is a legitimately contested moral and political question with practical ramifications. Kantians will likely find moral reasoning the only legitimate means of teaching such lessons. Consequentialists may consider other means. If "repentance training" became a state-sponsored religious program providing benefits to the born-again and penalizing everyone else, then we would have reason for concern. However, *that* the state should teach offenders to experience remorse for criminal activity – as opposed to merely immoral activity – should be less controversial. Including voluntary apologies – either from the already repentant or from those who come to apologize after time within the system – in the toolbox of criminal justice does not seem to cross into the authoritarianism of court-ordered apologies.[304] To repeat, how the state should best respond to such violations – as well as what the state should proscribe – presents a range of contested questions, but supporting, encouraging, and responding to voluntary apologies for criminal acts seems well within the remit of the liberal state.

Although apologies in criminal law will primarily address violations of the thin public notion of criminal wrongdoing, it can be difficult to disentangle an apology that addresses illegal behavior from those that speak to immoral but non-criminal behavior. Alcoholism, for example, is not illegal, but it contributes to various criminal activities. If we receive an apology from an alcoholic friend for insulting us during a drunken rage, the meanings of her contrition depend on the extent to which it includes a fulfilled promise to treat the addiction – so too with criminal matters. A justice system should evaluate an apology from an alcoholic who gets drunk and commits assaults in light of her commitment to reform her non-criminal behavior (drinking) as well as her criminal behavior (assaulting). Does this encroach too far into her conscience?

Before answering that question, note that illegal addiction presents somewhat simpler issues because both the addiction and the resultant illegal activity – stealing to support a methamphetamine habit, for example – fall within the purview of the criminal justice system. Moral and political debates continually contest the domain of the justice system, however, as the addiction examples demonstrate given the contested status of drug laws. Objections from liberal neutrality suggest clear boundaries distinguishing public/criminal and private/non-criminal, but these fronts run between contested moral and political territory. The percentage of criminal cases resulting from drug crime and the wide range of domestic opinion and international policies regarding the illegality of various controlled substances exemplifies the unsettled boundaries between thick and thin conceptions of justice.

With this in mind, a few rough guidelines may prove useful. A state reducing punishment because a convict accepts Christ as her savior would seem like an egregious violation of liberal neutrality. If we allow informal communities to take control of the restorative process and they advance inappropriately religious, objectionable, or patently unreasonable conceptions of punishments – by requiring the offender to attend religious ceremonies or be subjected to humiliating rituals, for example – the liberal state should not supervise or implicitly endorse such practices. Likewise, if the discourse around apologies in criminal law became a thinly veiled strategy for religious groups to make inroads into the justice system by using the state's threat of violence – Be Saved and Be Free! – to motivate spiritual conversion via repentance, this would clearly violate principles of liberal neutrality. The issue becomes less obvious if the offender becomes apologetic while participating in Alcoholics Anonymous and working through its steps to facilitate a "spiritual awakening" and a relationship with "God as we understand him."[305] Very thick religious, spiritual, and existential transformations will often drive the most substantive apologies, especially in the context of serious criminal violations. Although the justice system should not index punishment to such private beliefs, neither should it ignore the various ways that such commitments frame, motivate, and corroborate other aspects of apologies that fall within the properly "neutral" domain of the justice system. Viewing apologies as embedded within underlying thick commitments that inform the meanings of the apology need not, as Von Hirsh warns, "grant the community more sweeping authority over its members" by "giving it powers of deeper inquiry into members' moral attitudes."[306] These "moral attitudes" – thick as they may be – speak to an offender's mental state, culpability, likelihood to recidivate, and other attributes directly relevant to the state's thinner and "liberally neutral" charge.

I oppose court-ordered apologies in part for reasons akin to those identified by arguments from liberal neutrality that reject coercive methods of bringing about apologies. Whereas Duff and Bennett support requiring offenders to involuntarily participate in apology rituals, apology reductions should be considerably less vulnerable to such objections. Even when communicative retributivists such as Duff advocate for apology rituals, however, they take great care to avoid coercing offenders to apologize in any morally thick way. Although the thinness of their conception of apology leaves me to question its ultimate value – in part because they do not expect an apology to be offered "in a spirit of remorse or even to put on signs of such remorse" – it prevents them from overflowing into the sorts of private values safeguarded by liberal neutrality.[307] Duff's Kantian model strictly insists that "respect for autonomy will preclude any attempt to *force* a citizen to change her moral attitudes or to bring about such a change by any means other than those of rational moral persuasion."[308] When Duff seeks "not merely 'reform' but 'self-reform,'" communicative retributivism reaches deeply and "forcefully" into the offender's moral consciousness.[309] But it does not grab hold unless the offender reaches back. "We can try to force them to hear the message that their punishment aims to convey," Duff writes, "but we must not try to force them to accept it—or even to listen to it or to take it seriously."[310] Tasioulas offers the following helpful example in support of Duff here:

> When a judge... imposes a community service order on a teenaged offender convicted of damage to property, in preference to an equally severe fine or period of detention, and does so in the hope that by being required to remove illegal graffiti the offender will be confronted with, and led to reflect upon, the misery that criminal activity of the kind in which he engages causes to his own community, why should we suppose that disrespect must have been shown to the latter as a rational agent capable of reaching his own assessment of his past conduct? On the contrary, the punishment can only perform this communicative function if it respects the agent's self-determination: he is required to hear the message, but remains free to ignore it or reject it.[311]

Criminal sanction always risks violating an offender's autonomy and overreaching its proper domain, but a justice system can encourage apologies in ways that present less risk of violating liberal neutrality than most other forms of punishment. Consequentialists place less emphasis than do Kantians on dignity and rational agency in these discussions and will likely be less concerned with whether justice systems intend to induce apologies or whether contrition results as an unintentional byproduct of punishment. I do not, however, see reasons why sophisticated consequentialist analyses would reach different conclusions than Kantians regarding these issues.

Unless the state carefully restricts these options regarding appropriate punishment, however, it may be left to enforce inappropriate agreements. If the parties determine that the offender must attend particular religious services to achieve repentance or to undergo various forms of humiliation or abuse as penance, state agents will be expected to monitor – and thereby implicitly endorse – these practices. As an example that these face-to-face conferences might arrive at indefensible conclusions, Radzik imagines a sex offender receiving a mild sentence because those around the sentencing table believe that the victim deserves some of the blame for the assault because she wore revealing clothing.[312] If we add to this dynamic the victim's increased responsibility for fashioning the punishment and redress, how can we protect against various imbalances of power and fears of revictimization from distorting a process intending to better serve the needs and rights of the community? Are the benefits to the victim – as well as the offender, community, and state – worth the risks? Here again we should be mindful of the dangers of replacing excessively standardized justice with more particularized but inconsistent legal practices.

Radzik responds to these concerns with a compelling proposal. The liberal state, she argues, "has a broader constituency and a distinctive agenda that gives it an independent stake in the resolution of crime." Although she endorses the general principles of restorative justice, "the liberal state should not simply endorse whatever outcome the other parties to the conflict decide upon."[313] She elaborates:

> The state has a stake in the resolution of crime that is broader than its duty simply to aid particular victims, offenders, and even local communities in coming to a negotiated resolution. It has both a right and a duty to express its own views about what counts as an acceptable and satisfactory resolution. The state should not replace the victim, but neither should it be a neutral bystander or a mere servant.[314]

Radzik proposes what we might describe as a "happy medium": "[T]he tensions between restorative justice and liberalism can be resolved only by granting a greater role to the state than many advocates of restorative justice would find acceptable."[315] She suggests that the state might adopt procedural safeguards or veto powers, but she leaves the central practical issues unresolved.[316] Bennett promotes a similar view, arguing that the "state must retain the role of setting the level of the sentence" to express appropriate condemnation, but "it could set the level in fairly abstract terms: for instance, in terms of community service."[317] With the abstract level of punishment determined by the state, "the victim and offender could then consider how these hours should be spent, what the offender could meaningfully do to make amends for his crime."[318] This raises questions. Does restorative justice apply primarily to matters related to sentencing, or does it also play a role in determinations of guilt? Given the relationship between apologies and confessions at various stages of legal proceedings, limiting restorative practices to post-conviction would severely limit its value. Can the state simply hand over the sentencing process to communities, or must the state fulfill its duty to condemn crime with its own declarations and punishments? What sorts of issues will trigger state intervention? When do restorative justice practices cross the line that requires state intervention? How can the state protect principles or proportionality and ensure that crimes of equivalent seriousness receive similar punishments? How will the state police these standards? What role might judges, lawyers, mediators, juries, or other state agents play? How should the state exercise its authority? What are the penalties for rejecting the state's attempt to veto or otherwise control the outcomes of restorative justice? Even the most laissez-faire conceptions of restorative justice typically expect the state to participate in the process in some capacity, but precisely what "greater role" should it play? Bennett, for instance, argues that the state should "retain the role of setting the level of the sentence" but set the sentence in "fairly abstract terms" that would then be filled in and made more determinate via restorative justice practices.[319] Thus if the state determines a sentence of X amount of public service, the community could determine what sorts of activities would fill that time.[320] As long as the punishment advances and does not conflict with the state's thinner objectives, thicker arrangements within restorative process can avoid offending principles of liberal neutrality.

Questions regarding how the state can encourage apologies from criminal offenders without violating principles of liberal neutrality raise many practical issues best addressed in subsequent sections. A few theoretical considerations should oversee those discussions. Most basically, how we construct criminal justice can steer offenders toward or away from apologies. Some institutions tend to produce suffering and resentment. Others tend toward remorse. Institutions providing humane treatment, counseling, and addiction therapy will probably produce more apologies than will systems that deposit offenders into brutal conditions with little support or hope. Community service orders and other forms of punishment designed to bring the offender to reflect on the nature of her offense, confront its consequences, and provide commensurate redress should stimulate remorse without encroaching on the boundaries defended by liberal neutrality.

We should not, however, limit our consideration to whether criminal sentences and prisons are conducive to remorse. What happens after and – perhaps even more importantly – before a person enters the justice system will impact apologies. If we release an apologetic but tenuously sober addict from prison without access to quality health care, treatment programs, employment opportunities, or procedures to continue to provide redress, then even the most promising apology faces a high probability of seeing its significance erode over time.[321] The transition from criminal to civil society always presents challenges, and apologetic convicts face a particular set of opportunities and risks. Although it would clearly violate principles of liberal neutrality for the state to transition offenders from the counsel of prison therapists to the tutelage of clergy, we can appreciate the support various extrajudicial networks provide.[322] Likewise, an offender who comes from a community that takes apologies seriously enters the criminal process with stronger skills and support to see her through moral transformation. Such communities will likely include strong social bonds, quality child care and early education, widespread trust, and a deeply shared sense of values and fairness. When we contrast this with the fractured and skeptical communities in which many offenders are raised, we can appreciate the sorts of social transformations required to produce more apologetic populations.

Finally, Duff makes an important point regarding the practical difficulty of administering a system attempting to bring about meaningful apologies while honoring various moral and political constraints.

> It is, in moral terms, easy enough to administer a system of deterrent punishments, or a system of retributive punishments that aims simply to impose a suitably onerous burden on offenders: it is a very much harder task to administer communicative punishments which are to address offenders as responsible moral agents, and to persuade them to repent their crimes and to reform themselves–and to administer them in such a way and with such a spirit that they do not become either empty rituals or oppressive attempts at moral bullying. It is easy for those who are not directly involved in the penal system to leave the administration of punishments, whether as deterrent or as retribution, to the system's officials: it is much harder to treat offenders who have been punished as fellow citizens with whom we must be reconciled.[323]

Apology reductions require a lot of effort to apply fairly. I can appreciate the temptation to exclude considerations of apologies from punishment because of their complexities and the potential for abuse they invite. As I hope to have shown, however, we have very good reasons – and even duties – to undertake these efforts.

Symmetry: Increasing Punishments for Unapologetic Offenders

If we should reduce punishments for apologetic offenders, should we also increase punishments for the unapologetic? This presents an interesting test for the consistency of my position because it potentially identifies latent biases in my argument. Apology reductions might smell like a kind of bleeding heart leftist position – go easy on those unfortunate and sorry souls who need our help rather than punishment. Murphy notes in this regard that "those who want to count expressions of repentance and remorse in the criminal's favor are first in line to condemn the use in assigning punishment of claims that the criminal's character is 'cruel, heinous and depraved' or reveals a 'hardened, abandoned, and malignant heart' – phrases that have appeared in death penalty and other American homicide cases."[324] The very possibility that offenders could ever deserve *more* punishment makes some uncomfortable, as if reducing punishment provides the often unspoken general objectives from which academics should not deviate. Politicians increase punishments; academics must counter with arguments to decrease punishments. Given the current state of over-punishment in the United States, some will say, how could anyone argue for more punitive measures – with the possible exception of causes important to the left such as the elimination of hate crimes, sexual violence, or corporate misconduct? In addition, the idea that something as emotionally vulnerable and difficult to evaluate as apologies could lead to increased hard treatment may seem especially insidious to those in the helping professions or advocates for restorative justice. Although not as straightforward as arguing that if X mitigates the sentence then not-X must aggravate, a symmetrical position requires increasing punishments for unapologetic offenders presuming that the state does not already over-punish them.[325]

Robert Solomon expresses the mirror image of apology reductions, stating the popular sentiment that we "rightly insist on much greater punishment for those criminals who show no remorse."[326] This appears to be a widely held belief and requires some refining.[327] Consider first categorically *un*apologetic offenders, by which I do *not* mean those who may experience various degrees of contrition yet fail to rise to the level of a categorical apology. I have in mind those who fail or refuse just about every aspect of the categorical apology: they deny involvement in criminal activity despite overwhelming evidence against them, they refuse to accept blame for harm they obviously caused, they deny that they did anything wrong, they refuse to recognize the wrongness of the acts in question, they reject the underlying values, they continue to disrespect and express contempt for victims, they show no regret, they do not utter anything resembling apologetic words, they make no promises that they will not reoffend if presented with the opportunity, they undertake no reform, they offer no redress, and they express no emotions of contrition. Such a thoroughly unapologetic offender might appear sociopathic and we might wonder about her psychological fitness. Most remorseless offenders will not be so aggressively unapologetic, but for the sake of argument we can consider the categorically unapologetic as a touchstone.

A consequentialist perspective seems rather straightforward. A categorically unapologetic offender has made no progress toward rehabilitation nor has she made efforts toward restorative justice. She probably causes further injury to victims and communities. She seems undeterred, far from incapacitated, and likely to recidivate. The categorically unapologetic offender looks dangerous. Although three strikes laws and other considerations of prior record usually do not undertake a careful enough accounting of the costs and benefits of such legislation, their attention to remorselessness as demonstrated by repeat offending belongs within this line of justification of punishment.

Retributivists – especially dialectical retributivists – should find that categorically unapologetic offenders *deserve* more punishment because they *aggravate* the crime. *Black's Law Dictionary* defines aggravation as "any circumstance attending the commission of a crime or tort which increases its guilt or enormity or adds to its injurious consequences, but which is above and beyond the essential constituents of the crime or tort itself."[328] As I argued in the context of dialectical retributivism, behavior before or after the criminal act can increase or decrease the badness of that deed in various ways. Consider a few ways that this applies to unapologetic offenders deserving more punishment. The categorically unapologetic offender refuses to confess and thereby causes victims to suffer pain associated with not knowing what happened, why it happened, and its likelihood of happening again. If someone unapologetically commits many sexual assaults, this increases the likelihood that she possesses particularly culpable mental states and it will be more difficult to defend her actions as accidental or otherwise less blameworthy. The remorseless offender continues to disrespect the victim by disregarding her suffering and refusing to address her as a moral interlocutor. The longer the degradation persists, the greater the harm. The unreformed offender also continues to threaten the victim and community. Recall the example of theft: the longer I keep the money, the worse the offense, and the more punishment I deserve. Lack of remorse also speaks to the culpability of mental states before, during, and after the offense – all of which speak to the badness of the crime on the retributivist account. Although considerations of prior record typically speak to consequentialist concerns, a history of offending can inform a retributive perspective as it speaks to mental states before, during, and after criminal acts. The unrepentant offender thus causes a variety of harms to the victim to continue without relief or to grow in their badness, and this adds to the punishment deserved.

The remorseless offender also does not experience the sorts of suffering that I claimed should be discounted from the hard treatment she otherwise deserves. The unapologetic "get away with" the crime in the sense that they avoid the pain of guilt, and retributivists may therefore wish to pile on extra hard treatment to compensate for this lack of self-punishment. Nor does the remorseless offender experience the particular form of shameful labor experienced when undertaking self-motivated redress. Particularly sadistic unapologetic offenders may even experience pleasure from their wrongdoing and thus require additional punishment to negate this benefit to them and balance the scales.

Proportionality, consistency, and equality also point toward increasing sentences for categorically unapologetic offenders. If unapologetic offenders increase the gravity of their crimes, then they deserve more punishment to reach proportionate levels. As with consistently reducing punishment for contrite offenders and treating like apologies alike, we should take care to treat similarly remorseless offenders similarly. We often find great vitriol in denunciations of "evil-hearted" offenders, and we would benefit from parsing what we mean by such terms and how these meanings should map onto punishments. Rather than ad hoc determinations that a particular offender deserves maximum punishments because of her lack of contrition, we should apply consistent standards for apologetic and unapologetic offenders to ensure that excessive discretion in these complex and emotionally charged matters do not lead to unfair outcomes.

Some may continue to have difficulty believing that increasing punishment can honor anyone's dignity, including the remorseless. If we continue to assume the admittedly dubious stipulation of a morally justifiable baseline punishment, however, could increasing punishment for an unapologetic offender better honor her dignity than not doing so? If we take the position that thorough but noncoercive attempts to rehabilitate the offender best honor her dignity, then increased rehabilitative punishments for unapologetic offenders could be viewed as honoring or even advancing dignity. The leading retributive theories of dignity, however, tend toward viewing punishment not as a means to the end of reform – although the theory of moral communication can often seem rehabilitative in nature – but rather as a kind of inherently valuable moral discourse owed to the offender and to justice. Punishment may or may not induce reform but will be justified as punishment regardless of its rehabilitative success. Duff believes, therefore, that we must "morally communicate" with those who unapologetically commit even the worst crimes and address them as "not beyond redemption."[329] An unapologetic offender will require more forceful communication to concentrate her attention on her wrongdoing and to convey the wrongness of her deeds as well as the inappropriateness of her lack of contrition. On the communicative retributive account, such increased punishment does not reduce the offender's dignity but rather takes it even more seriously. Understanding various ways that an offender can be unapologetic increases the state's ability to understand the nature of the offender's resistance as well as how to overcome that resistance through rational discourse. It should recalibrate punishment accordingly.

With those general positions outlined, consider several caveats. First, for leftists the primary issue probably remains: establishing the correct baseline punishment and in particular a baseline that pays sufficient attention to the correlation between structural inequalities of various kinds and the commission of crime. Without this, many critics may be willing to speculate about increasing punishments for unapologetic offenders. Murphy's classic article on Marx and retributivism captures the concern here: retributivism may indeed provide a compelling theory of punishment, but it functions as an ideological justification for blaming and disempowering the poor in the context of such inequality.[330] The notion of owing an unapologetic indigent offender more punishment will therefore seem especially repugnant to those concerned with structural inequality.

Second, various issues complicate the aggravating effects of remorselessness. Mental illness or disability, for example, can inhibit certain kinds of apologetic meaning. If an offender suffers from any number of conditions that impede her ability to experience or express emotions, Justice Kennedy warns that "serious prejudice could result if medication inhibits the defendant's capacity . . . to demonstrate remorse or compassion." Kennedy worries that in capital cases such "assessments of character and remorse may... be determinative of whether the offender lives or dies."[331] If mental illness contributes to criminal activity, we should take into account how such conditions relate to post-offense behavior and mental states lest we compound the disadvantages of her illness. Retributivists and consequentialists will likely differ regarding how to respond to psychopathy or other mental states that reduce moral culpability yet increase dangerousness. In addition, some convicts may refuse to apologize because they maintain their genuine innocence. Increasing their punishment because of this insistence would pile one injustice atop another: not only do we wrongly convict you, but we punish you even more because you fail to express remorse for a crime you did not commit. Similar issues arise in cases of civil disobedience and principled refusal in which the offender admits breaking the law but refuses to apologize because she believes the law is unjust. Various legal excuses and justifications also present challenges of this sort.

Third, as with reducing sentences for apologetic offenders, it matters when we find the subject unapologetic. A remorseless offender at the outset of legal proceedings may evolve into a categorically apologetic offender, or she may remain defiant throughout the process. It seems likely that, all other salient variables equal, offenders should grow more remorseful over time even if only because they "age-out" of criminal activity. This would seem especially likely if the system somehow incentivizes remorse, for instance by viewing expressions of contrition as evidence of reform in support of a reduction or termination of punishment. A justice system that alienates, criminalizes, and degrades offenders, however, might increase remorselessness over time. We should be cautious not to fuel a downward spiral by sending unapologetic offenders through a system that increases their remorselessness, only to punish them even more for their worsening condition.

Finally, questions regarding *how much* more punishment unapologetic offenders should receive are just as numerous and complex as those regarding how much less punishment should be visited on apologetic offenders.

B. In Practice: Applying Apology Reductions

When you plead guilty, I think that's a sufficient apology.[332]

Marvyn M. Kornberg, attorney for Justin Volpe, the New York City officer who confessed – once evidence against him became overwhelming during trial – to forcibly sodomizing Abner Louima with the broken broomstick causing severe internal injuries.

I'm on appeal. You don't appeal if you think that you should be sorry.[333]

Martha Stewart

The Institutional Framework
An Adversarial Plea-Driven System

I have argued *why* we should support apology reductions. Moving from the abstract to the practical requires us to consider the who, where, and when of criminal procedure and institutional design. Administering a criminal justice system that gives apologies their proper due within the parameters of the liberal state presents a complex set of morally charged bureaucratic challenges. How do we carve out spaces in justice systems for apologies that allow for and recognize moral transformation without routinizing the process in ways that render most expressions of remorse perfunctory attempts to game the system? We cannot simply trust everyone to improvise in a spirit of reconciliation. It is also, as I hope to have convinced readers, worth the effort to reform the current system that allows state agents to wing it. Although generally supportive of something like apology reduction, Richard Lippke outlines the practical obstacles to implementing such policies and convincingly argues that current practices are not "remotely in the vicinity" of justifying remorse reductions for guilty pleas.[334] I leave the nuts and bolts of reform to those with far better working knowledge of criminal procedure. I can, however, sketch a rough blueprint of the general hydraulics of a well-functioning apology/punishment system.

To the contemporary ear, apologies and law sound like oil and water. Although it might seem that something about the essential properties of contrition and law do not mix, a different legal environment would render them much more compatible. If a justice system took reintegrating the offender into the community and repairing relationships as its primary objectives, then apologies would probably become central to its core mission. In the context of prevailing ideologies in the United States, however, apologies seem misplaced and even idealistic naiveté because criminal law is more about legal war than community peace. The privileged and disadvantaged take different paths through the system, and we expect all comers to battle tooth and nail with all of their resources to get out. Its timing seems surreal, with the imprisoned waiting for years for their "day in court" and then finding life-altering decisions rendered within seconds of plea bargaining. We sever the victim-offender relationship and replace it with the state-offender dynamic, thereby supplanting the possibility for interpersonal reconciliation with institutional coldness designed to process maximum punishment for the generic criminal. As the very title of the matter indicates – the State *versus* the Accused – this is an adversarial battlefield. Losers pay with years of their lives.[335] We train the combatants to fight accordingly. The accused will deny everything; prosecutors will accuse whatever they can and overcharge accordingly. The momentum of institutional procedures overruns moral reasoning. As in war, it is difficult to imagine a time or place for remorse when inside the trenches of contemporary punishment. I do not mean to overstate the adversarial nature of contemporary criminal law. The United States represents an extreme form of adversarial individualism. Other nations offer more collaborative models less driven toward incarceration. Even within the United States, various innovative restorative justice techniques have gained a foothold alongside established rehabilitative practices such as community service orders that have long sought to occasion reflection and apologies in the ways discussed earlier. These alternatives, however, remain the exception.

As Lippke explains in his excellent and much needed *The Ethics of Plea Bargaining*, 90 to 95 percent of criminal convictions in the U.S. result from guilty pleas rather than from jury trials.[336] Despite being "subject to withering scrutiny... the practice chugs along, more or less unaffected by the academic debate surrounding it."[337] Like the fast food of sentencing, pleas are quick and cheap – but only if we focus on short-term costs and benefits for social health. Questions regarding the role of apologies in jury trials and sentencing hearings may hold the most interest for philosophers, but they have considerably less practical import than issues related to plea bargaining. Plea agreements allow defendants to plead guilty to one charge typically in exchange for the prosecutor's agreement not to pursue more serious charges. Both prosecution and defense weigh odds in this process. For the prosecution, what are the chances that she can convict this defendant on the most serious charges given the available evidence, the general strength of the case, and other variables? If the prosecutor knows her case is weak, should she offer a plea with a lesser sentence rather than drop the case altogether? The defendant weighs the risks from her perspective. Is it worth accepting the plea and admitting guilt for the lesser charge – even if she is innocent – if this means that she will be released because of the time she already served waiting for this process to unfold? Should she go to trial, remain in prison for the duration of the proceedings if she cannot make bail, take her chances facing the more serious charge (often with a court-appointed attorney of uncertain ability and commitment to representing her), and try to prove her innocence? Will her defense attorney advise her to roll the dice and go to trial, thereby creating more work – in many cases without more pay – for her and for the prosecutor with whom she regularly negotiates? Or will she encourage her to accept the deal?

Consider the apologetic defendant within this culture of plea bargaining wherein prosecutors exercise increasing discretion regarding who to charge, what to charge, and how to punish.[338] Prosecutors functionally serve as the primary judge of acts of contrition within the justice system. They stand in a different relationship to offenses than civil plaintiff's attorneys because they represent the state rather than an aggrieved person.[339] Whereas a civil attorney is beholden to the wishes of her client because the client typically pays the bill for her legal services and can drop the issues if she wishes, the state employs prosecutors and they operate with considerable independence from the will of the victim. If an apology moves a civil plaintiff to settle, her attorney will serve her client's wishes accordingly. A criminal prosecutor, however, need not consult the victim regarding her perception of an offender's contrition. Victims rarely interact with criminal offenders given the run of the assembly line of criminal justice bureaucracies, but even if the offender found the opportunity to provide a promissory categorical apology to the victim and this moves her to want the charges dropped, the prosecutor can usually disregard the victim's desires.

Not only can prosecutors exercise discretion to ignore or discount apologies, but various reasons suggest that they are likely to do so. Unlike victims with emotional investments in the particularities of their injuries, prosecutors stand at a greater critical distance from the offense.[340] This "detachment" renders prosecutors less concerned with the reconciliation – emotional reconciliation or otherwise – of the specific parties and more focused on the state's interests.[341] Prosecutors can also develop a healthy skepticism for "handcuff apologies" that inexperienced victims may lack.[342] Instead of reducing penalties for contrite offenders, prosecutors may view apologies offered in early proceedings as evidence that they have a particularly strong case worthy of a trial or at least a defendant who has diminished her bargaining power in plea negotiations.[343] A victim may appreciate an apology at any stage in the proceedings and wish to reconcile or "drop the charges," but a prosecutor who builds a case for trial will likely want these sunk costs to produce a conviction and may see a defendant's late apology as a nail in her coffin.[344] An apologetic offender increases the prosecutor's return on her investment of trial preparation. Inversely, defense attorneys – especially overburdened public defenders – might consider apologetic clients bad investments of their efforts. As Robbennolt worries, a "defense attorney who is engaging in triage is likely to spend fewer resources investigating and researching a case with a statement by the defendant expressing responsibility or remorse."[345] Defense attorneys often use the possibility of trial to their advantage, threatening understaffed prosecutors with the prospect of hundreds of hours of preparation for an uncertain outcome.[346] With an apology on the table, that defendant's chances of being proven innocent at trial diminish significantly. An apologetic defendant may find herself doubly disadvantaged: prosecutors will pursue her more aggressively because they smell blood in the water while defense attorneys cut bait to devote their attention to more winnable cases. For several of these reasons, Robbennolt concluded that "contrary to the assertion that apologies might lead to more favorable plea bargained outcomes for defendants, the nature of plea negotiation renders this result unlikely."[347] Add to this the class dynamics of plea negotiations, with some uninformed defendants accepting the initial pro forma offer whereas those white-collar criminals with sophisticated attorneys engage in protracted negotiations that structure the indictment as well as the plea.[348] Inequality manifests at every stage of the process. All of this creates a hostile environment for fair apology reductions.

The Sentencing Guidelines

The oddities of the U.S. Federal Sentencing Guidelines begin to make sense within this adversarial and plea-driven system. Created with the intention of standardizing sentencing in federal courts, the guidelines appear to reduce punishments for apologetic offenders. Section 3E1.1 of the 2012 guidelines states:

Acceptance of Responsibility

(a) If the defendant clearly demonstrates acceptance of responsibility for his offense, decrease the offense level by 2 levels.
(b) If the defendant qualifies for a decrease under subsection (a), the offense level determined prior to the operation of subsection (a) is level 16 or greater, and upon motion of the government stating that the defendant has assisted authorities in the investigation or prosecution of his own misconduct by timely notifying authorities of his intention to enter a plea of guilty, thereby permitting the government to avoid preparing for trial and permitting the government and the court to allocate their resources efficiently, decrease the offense level by 1 additional level.[349]

Offenders who "accept responsibility" and thereby permit the government to "avoid preparing for trial" and thus to "allocate their resources efficiently" will receive a total of three level reduction in their sentences. A three-point reduction typically reduces a sentence by about 35 percent.[350] For less serious offenses, the "acceptance of responsibility" reduction can determine if the offender serves time in prison or on probation. For offenses at the top of the sentencing table, three points can equal decades of incarceration. The commentary to section 3E1.1 offers guidance for applying the adjustments. Defendants who exercise their right to a trial and require the government to meet its burden of proof typically do not qualify for the reduction.[351] Those who deny their guilt at trial but then "accept responsibility" after being found guilty and in order to earn the discount similarly fail to meet the spirit of the reduction. The comments resist describing the adjustment as an entitlement for anyone who enters a guilty plea and instead require the offender to establish beyond a preponderance of the evidence that she deserves the reduction.[352] Appellate judges grant "great deference" to the sentencing decisions regarding whether the offender deserves such a reduction because the "sentencing judge is in a unique position to evaluate a defendant's acceptance of responsibility."[353] Section 3E1.1 works in conjunction with section 5K1.1, which provides reductions for offenders who – based on the prosecutor's recommendation – "provide substantial assistance in the investigation or prosecution of another person who has committed an offense."[354] The guidelines do not explain why they provide such reductions beyond the assertion that doing so "recognizes legitimate societal interests" and that "for several reasons, a defendant who clearly demonstrates acceptance of responsibility for his offense by taking, in a timely fashion, the actions listed above (or some equivalent action) is appropriately given a lower offense level than a defendant who has not demonstrated acceptance of responsibility."[355] The only specific justification states that the defendant merits reduction because the acceptance of responsibility "ensures the certainty of his punishment in a timely manner."[356] At first glance the guidelines appear to roughly support apology reductions. Things are not as they seem.

Before addressing the specifics of how the "acceptance of responsibility" provision relates to categorical apologies, we should take seriously O'Hear's compelling evidence that such finer points may be irrelevant given that these sections of the guidelines have become a de facto automatic reduction for offenders accepting pleas. O'Hear argues that the guidelines allow for two distinct and conflicting understandings of "accepting responsibility." One understanding supports the "remorse paradigm," in which accepting responsibility means something like providing a categorical apology. Alternatively, the "cooperation paradigm" serves to "encourage and reward a defendant's behavior if it facilitates the efficient administration of the criminal justice system, contributes to the recovery and restoration of victims, or protects society at large from additional criminal activity."[357] Section (b) of 3E1.1 supports the cooperation paradigm as it speaks to the offender's assistance to the prosecution, which O'Hear describes as allowing the additional reduction for "exceptional cooperation, but not for exceptional remorse."[358] Application notes also support the cooperation paradigm: "[T]his adjustment is not intended to apply to a defendant who puts the government to its burden of proof at trial."[359] Conduct obstructing or impeding the administration of justice "ordinarily indicates that the defendant has not accepted responsibility."[360] O'Hear also points out that the provisions originated in the proposal to formalize typical pre-guidelines discounts of 30 to 40 percent for those accepting guilty pleas.[361] Practitioners understand these discounts for cooperation as a "practical necessity" to manage increasing case loads occasioned by the War on Drugs, and according to O'Hear, "all of the major institutional actors in sentencing in the district – defense lawyers, probation officers, prosecutors, and judges – possess a mutually reinforcing set of interests and expectations, the result of which is the effective transformation of section 3E1.1 into a more-or-less automatic discount for guilty pleas."[362] The cooperation paradigm therefore reigns in the work-a-day business district courts. The federal appellate courts, however, tend toward the loftier moral sentiments of the remorse paradigm.[363] Because of the extraordinary deference afforded to district court's 3E1.1 determinations, however, the cooperation paradigm prevails in the vast majority of applications. In other words, appellate courts imagine the district courts evaluating subjective evidence of the offender's remorse. Because the appellate courts typically lack evidence of the offender's mental states other than what appears in the record, they defer to the district court's impressions and "will generally uphold acceptance-of-responsibility findings on the slimmest of evidence on the record." District courts, however, do not usually attempt to evaluate remorse in most cases but instead rubber-stamp a reduction for anyone who accepts a plea. District courts find that offenders "accept responsibility" – nudge nudge, wink wink. Cases are processed. According to one national study, 88 percent of those who plead guilty receive a reduction. Of those who go to trial, 20 percent also receive the benefit.[364]

O'Hear argues that the commission left the plea versus remorse intentionally vague. Providing an automatic 10- to 15-percent discount for pleas would provide substantial administrative benefits and effectively codify ad hoc pre-guidelines practices, but the drafters understood that such an automatic discount could be viewed as an unconstitutional penalty for exercising one's right to trial. To gain the benefits of a plea discount without the disadvantages, the commission created the "acceptance of responsibility" provision. Instead of automatically discounting for pleas, the commission allows judges discretion to reduce punishment on a case-by-case basis for those who "clearly demonstrate responsibility." Although the guidelines do not promulgate constitutionally suspect rules allowing defendants to barter away – under the threat of an even longer sentence – their right to prove innocence at trial, in practice the reduction for pleading rather than going to trial is effectively automatic.[365]

This creates dishonesty in sentencing because "acceptance of responsibility" language suggests a determination regarding the offender's moral attitudes, but in fact it typically makes no such attempt to evaluate contrition but instead provides a quid pro quo for relieving prosecutors of the burdens of trial. O'Hear therefore finds that "the trial penalty is hidden in an acceptance-of-responsibility provision, and judges are largely free to set standards for the penalty on an *ad hoc* basis."[366] The ad hoc nature of review invites abuse, for instance by treating an offender's exercise of her right against providing self-incriminating testimony or her expressions regarding the unfairness of a law as evidence of lack of remorse.[367]

Now situate these dubious "acceptance of responsibility" determinations in the context of highly deferential review by federal circuit courts, or what was described by the Fifth Circuit as "even more deferential than clear error" to reverse. Federal appellate courts tend to treat findings of responsibility per

3E1.1 as factual determinations best left to district courts because of their direct access to the offender.[368] The very standard of deference indicates that the district court – a trial court with the opportunity to observe the defendant throughout the process – should evaluate the various indicia of remorse to determine whether the offender in fact accepts responsibility in some sense beyond offering a strategic plea. Because of the deferential standard of review, however, trial courts can rubber-stamp acceptance of responsibility reductions with little concern for being overturned on appeal.

Setting aside how 3E1.1 operates in practice as an automatic reduction for pleas, imagine that courts instead attempted to apply a remorse paradigm. What might the guidelines mean by "acceptance of responsibility"? The application notes identify a limited set of indicia. "In determining whether a defendant qualifies under subsection (a)," the commentary advises, "appropriate considerations include, but are not limited to, the following":

(A) truthfully admitting the conduct comprising the offense(s) of conviction, and truthfully admitting or not falsely denying any additional relevant conduct for which the defendant is accountable under §1B1.3 (Relevant Conduct). Note that a defendant is not required to volunteer, or affirmatively admit, relevant conduct beyond the offense of conviction in order to obtain a reduction under subsection (a). A defendant may remain silent in respect to relevant conduct beyond the offense of conviction without affecting his ability to obtain a reduction under this subsection. However, a defendant who falsely denies, or frivolously contests, relevant conduct that the court determines to be true has acted in a manner inconsistent with acceptance of responsibility;
(B) voluntary termination or withdrawal from criminal conduct or associations;
(C) voluntary payment of restitution prior to adjudication of guilt;
(D) voluntary surrender to authorities promptly after commission of the offense;
(E) voluntary assistance to authorities in the recovery of the fruits and instrumentalities of the offense;
(F) voluntary resignation from the office or position held during the commission of the offense;
(G) post-offense rehabilitative efforts (*e.g.*, counseling or drug treatment); and
(H) the timeliness of the defendant's conduct in manifesting the acceptance of responsibility.

Meeting each of these factors is not necessarily sufficient for a reduction; failing to meet all of these criteria does not necessarily prohibit a reduction. Again setting aside the underlying ambiguity regarding whether one should even bother attempting to evaluate remorse and instead just applying the automatic plea discount, this loose set of considerations hardly provides clear guidance even if we attempt to identify remorse. First note that the list of considerations does not mention apology, remorse, or contrition. The commentary notes mention remorse, but as a warning against frustrating the plea discount: "This adjustment is not intended to apply to a defendant who puts the government to its burden of proof at trial... and only then admits guilt and expresses remorse."[369]

In the absence of clear guidelines we find a patchwork of opinions built on judges' impressionistic evaluations of offenders. As noted, appellate courts tend to think that "accepting responsibility" requires a "moral element."[370] Like the confusion in the general public about the "true meaning" of apologies, however, circuit courts differ widely in their understandings of remorse. Most of the elements of the categorical apology have been litigated in the federal courts, with no clear consensus emerging regarding the nature of genuine remorse warranting a discount. I will avoid citing a litany of legal opinions pontificating on remorse in section 3E1.1 to demonstrate their imprecise and conflicting reasoning. The guidelines provide an ambiguous standard for "accepting responsibility"; case law adds layers of confusion with courts offering conflicting and overconfident assurances regarding the nature of remorse and its relation to the guidelines. Note a few of the most obvious questions considered, not considered, and intentionally ignored by federal appellate courts.

First, must the offender admit guilt for all of her criminal activity, or only for the offense to which she pleads? Given the prevalence of pleas, courts will often find defendants accepting pleas for conduct other than their actual offenses. In some cases they will admit guilt for something less than what they know they did, perhaps because the state lacks evidence to prove the more serious charge or because the offender traded cooperation in another matter for the reduction. Beebe, for example, confessed to rape but then pleaded guilty only to aggravated sexual battery. Defendants also accept pleas by admitting to something they did not do because they fear being found guilty of a more serious charge despite their innocence – I'll admit to possessing marijuana even though it wasn't mine, as long as you don't pursue the intent to sell charge with its potential seven-year sentence.

Imagine if we treated apologies like this in our private affairs. Suppose a spouse finds record of a call to her partner's former lover on a night when the partner does not come home until the next morning. The spouse suspects infidelity. An unreliable neighbor corroborates the spouse's suspicion. The partner denies infidelity, challenges the credibility of the neighbor, and says, "You can't prove I was unfaithful, but you can prove that I called my former lover and lied about it. I'll apologize for the call and for lying about it. Alternatively, I can admit to and apologize for that fling you suspected last year." Suppose the accusing spouse has a busy social docket, decides not to investigate further, and agrees to accept the apology for the lesser included offense of lying with the punishment of extra chores rather than divorce. Judges disagree about the correct reading of 3E1.1 in this respect. The First Circuit determined that constitutional protections against self-incrimination dictate that a "defendant who has made a plea agreement must accept responsibility solely for the counts to which he is pleading guilty,"[371] overturning the district court's view that "acceptance of responsibility means total candor by the defendant as to his total criminal conduct."[372] Application notes have not resolved the issue, permitting courts to consider as but one factor among others whether the offender admits or denies "additional relevant conduct" and allowing the defendant to "remain silent in respect to relevant conduct beyond the offense of conviction without affecting his ability to obtain a reduction under this subsection."[373]

In addition, notice the difficulty of mapping apologetic emotions into plea agreements. If I committed a greater offense but plead to the lesser offense – or if I am altogether innocent – what sorts of emotions should I experience? It seems absurd to index the appropriate emotions to the plea given the likelihood that the plea does not correspond to the defendant's wrongdoing. If everyone knows or strongly expects that the offender committed the more serious offense but accepts a plea for a lesser, should she experience the more intense negative emotions associated with the more serious offense? Should we expect Beebe to feel only as badly as one should feel for committing aggravated sexual assault, rather than require him to experience the full pain of being a rapist?

Further, when must remorse become apparent under 3E1.1? Is apologizing upon arrest too early? Is apologizing upon conviction necessarily too late? What if the offender apologizes a few months into the investigation and then again at sentencing? Section 3E1.1 indicates that expression of remorse after conviction – and perhaps at any stage during trial or even during preparations for trial – should not merit the reduction. Beyond the benefit of sparing the state the efforts associated with trial, are there compelling reasons in the remorse model to reject contrition that surfaces later in the process leading up to sentencing? Apologies after conviction but before sentencing should generally lead us to question the intentions motivating the acceptance of responsibility after the court has found guilt. I have argued throughout, however, becoming apologetic can take some time. Sitting through a trial, learning of the pain suffered by victims, living in prison and outside of one's usual environment, and undergoing various forms of counseling and treatment can all foster the sort of transformation that brings about meaningful apologies.[374] Uncooperative behavior early in the process can give way to genuine prison cell reckoning. The guidelines seem excessively skeptical to this possibility, perhaps because of their interest in preventing trials altogether. Similarly, contrition too early – immediately upon arrest, for instance – should raise different sorts of suspicion.

Intentions for "accepting responsibility" receive little attention within the remorse paradigm. Section 3E1.1 understands an offender's acceptance of responsibility as an indicator of likelihood of either recidivism or rehabilitation, but intentions seem paramount for such a presumption. If the offender pleads, as the Seventh Circuit put it, "for the apparent purpose of obtaining a lighter sentence" rather than from moral intentions, should courts deny the discount even though the offender provides an otherwise thorough apology satisfying A through H of the "appropriate considerations"?[375] An application note in the 1986 draft of 3E1.1 explained that the "sentencing judge is in a unique position to evaluate whether the offender's post-offense conduct is sincere or merely self-serving." As O'Hear reads this, "the 1986 draft suggests that no matter how beneficial post-offense conduct is, a judge may still deny the adjustment if the defendant is motivated by the wrong reasons."[376] References to intentions have since been removed, allowing individual judges to decide if they should consider the offender's reasons for accepting responsibility, and if so, what weight they should place on such motivations.

These examples suggest that even when courts attempt to evaluate the offender's remorse rather than simply provide an automatic plea discount, the guidelines and appellate courts promulgate confused and inconsistent standards. It remains far from clear that the guidelines or the courts have such intentions. Consider the Ninth Circuit's decision in *United States v. Vance*. The district court denied a 3E1.1 reduction because Vance "had taken the case through a suppression hearing, had refused to talk to the probation officer, had refused to assist law enforcement authorities, had not fully admitted his guilt, and had shown insufficient evidence of contrition."[377] The Ninth Circuit, against the grain of other appellate courts favoring the remorse paradigm, scoffed at the possibility that the offender's contrition is relevant at sentencing, contending that there "is no particular social purpose to be served by lenience toward those who cry more easily, or who have sufficient criminal experience to display sentiment at sentencing instead of restraining their emotions in public."[378] The "factual inquiry required by the guidelines does not require a penetrating judicial examination of the criminal's soul," explained the appellate court, because the "guidelines recognized that sentences have historically been reduced by fairly predictable percentages upon pretrial pleas of guilty, and came about as close as they could, without penalizing the exercise of constitutional rights, to codifying the percentage."[379] The Ninth Circuit therefore directs its district courts to look only to the "objectively ascertainable evidence" and offers guilty pleas as the exemplary and seemingly sufficient form of such evidence. This jurisdiction need not even attempt to address the complexities of remorse.

In the absence of uniform and clear standards guiding implementation of the reduction – is the reduction automatic for pleas, and if not, what constitutes the thicker conception of accepting responsibility? – section 3E1.1 has become one of the most appealed provisions of the sentencing guidelines.[380] The confused and inconsistent reduction also invites the sorts of disparities, inequalities, and discrimination discussed in previous sections. If two people commit the same crime, the one who plea bargains will probably receive a lighter sentence than the one found guilty at trial. This disparity may be justified for various reasons, but the reduction remains discretionary and can be dispensed at the caprice of the court.[381] If a judge wishes to withhold the reduction for any number of reasons – because the offender seems "unapologetic" or otherwise "uncooperative," for instance – appellate courts grant her exceptional deference to rule on these impressions. Judges with different conceptions of remorse will treat otherwise similar offenders differently. An apologetic offender might receive a reduction in one court but not another. In some cases the unrepentant offender who pleads will receive the reduction, but the genuinely remorseful offender will not. Add to this the likelihood that such vague standards applied impressionistically and behind a wall of considerable deference will compound the advantages of privileged offenders. Whether poorly coached in appearing remorseful or because they display a demeanor less likely to strike judges as contrite, minorities, the poor, the mentally disabled, and defendants from cultural backgrounds unlike those of reviewing judges will likely not fare as well as the advantaged under such a system for all of the reasons previously discussed. If a judge looks for signs of genuine contrition, an articulate, well-educated, and effectively represented offender with various resources at her disposal stands a better chance of making a case that she deserves the reduction. "As a perusal of the section 3E1.1 case law demonstrates," writes O'Hear, "concealment, dissimulation, [and] noncooperation' time and again constitute the basis for a denial of the two-point reduction."[382] He reasonably asks: "To what extent are the courts in these cases ultimately punishing defensive strategies that have been inculcated in an offender by virtue of membership in a subordinated racial, cultural, or economic group?"[383] It is not surprising that one study found that black offenders may have been denied the reduction considerably more frequently than non-black offenders who commit similar crimes.[384] In addition, all of this vague "acceptance of responsibility" language can prove especially dangerous for those with ineffective legal counsel because it invites the sort of open-ended confession that can prove disastrous for a legal defense.

I argued earlier that reducing punishments for apologetic offenders can effectively honor principles of proportionality and consistency, but the current administration of 3E1.1 systematically violates these values. This has raised various proposals for reform, including delinking automatic reductions for pleas and reductions for remorse, considering remorse more akin to other characteristics that are "not ordinarily relevant" to sentencing according to chapter 5 of the guidelines, and eliminating consideration of remorse altogether.[385] These proposals have considerable merits compared with current 3E1.1 practices. If we seek a compelling general approach to remorse and punishment – as I argue we should and as many will believe we *must* – we need to look beyond the Federal Sentencing Guidelines.

As the general picture of the climate of the criminal justice system in the United States comes into focus, we can appreciate just how hostile this environment is to substantive apologies. From the first interaction with the authorities, the wrongdoer encounters an adversarial system driven by lawyers who view the conflict in terms of state case-load management rather than interpersonal reconciliation. Defense attorneys advise clients to keep their feelings of remorse to themselves or risk providing prosecutors with an advantage. Even if the offender wishes to confess and apologize, defense attorneys will usually reformulate and channel these sentiments to achieve their maximal benefit within unaccommodating institutional structures such as the guidelines. Prosecutors cannot process cases fast enough, and pleas become the primary means of moving traffic through the bottleneck. Rather than seeking to reduce the inputs – by reforming drug policy, for instance – the system increasingly relies on pleas to accelerate output and thus seeks ways to incentivize their use via measures such as 3E1.1. In this respect, plea bargains extend the reach of the justice system by allowing prosecutors to get a "bite" on a broader portion of the population while juking the statistics to demonstrate high conviction rates, which in turn become evidence of the effectiveness and necessity of prosecutorial work.[386]

Responding to Skepticism

Two sorts of skepticism exist regarding whether apologies have a place in the justice system. The first generally doubts that apologies and law belong together. For many, the oil of moral transformation just does not mix with the ocean of social control via adversarial representation and plea bargaining. Some lobby this objection in terms of liberal neutrality. Bennett, for instance, claims that although "the world would be a better place if offenders did respond to expressions of condemnation with genuine repentance and reform," he doubts that "aiming to make this happen is the business of the state, let alone the justification for the criminal sanction."[387] I responded to these forms of skepticism throughout my defense of apology reductions.

The second form of skepticism remains to be addressed. Here the doubt lies not in the importance of apologies for the justice system but in our ability to distinguish genuine from staged repentance. If the system rewards apologies by reducing punishment, considerable incentives will encourage lying. How can we know the hearts of criminals with sufficient certainty and in a manner that does not further compound injustices, for example by finding the apologies of the disadvantaged less credible than remorse expressed by the privileged?[388] These are serious concerns, but we should not overstate the degree of skepticism warranted. Nor should we allow these worries to hamstring efforts to meet our responsibility to use sound judgment when responding to apologetic offenders. We continually evaluate appearances of vice and virtue in everyday life, and we do this with varying degrees of success. Criminal justice systems routinely determine culpability according to constellations of data points. This has long included reading mental states of offenders, victims, witnesses, and others. Deception is endemic to justice systems. Rather than throwing up our hands at the impossibility of mind reading, we develop methods for distinguishing truth from lies to an acceptable degree of certainty. Imagine that no evidence could ever satisfy our epistemological demands: video evidence could be doctored, the confession could have been given under hypnosis, and all 100 witnesses could be conspiring against the accused. We could be in the Matrix. Rather than responding to such worries by abandoning attempts to determine guilt, we establish procedures and standards that guide judgment. Prosecutors, judges, juries, and most everyone in the justice system has a nose for dishonesty. We design procedures that optimize the possibility that fallible humans can separate truth from lies. We certainly do not allow individual judges to make impressionistic decisions based on subjective, implicit, and unreviewable standards. We do not always succeed, but we can judge the meanings of apologies in legal environments just as we negotiate varying degrees of doubt regarding guilt.

Some speak as if apologies operate in some magical dimension of the soul inaccessible to the justice system. It appears this way in large part because we have never attempted to provide systematic guidelines for evaluating apologies in law. Like all sorts of human conditions, apologies can be tested, measured, and evaluated. With sufficiently sophisticated theoretical frameworks in place and applied with properly calibrated procedural tools, the justice system should treat apologies like other elements in sentencing and should have similar confidence in their findings. I now attempt to set out those guidelines.

A Practical Framework for Evaluating Apologies in the Criminal Context
Guiding Questions: How Should We Evaluate?
My colleagues and I first offered a version of these guidelines in the context of the bar admission process.[389] Evaluations of remorse play an important role in character and fitness reviews for applicants to the bar with

problematic records, but evaluations of remorse were often ad hoc applications of implicit principles applied impressionistically. Decisions regarding applicants' remorse were unpredictable and often contradicted each other within the same jurisdictions. We therefore enumerated thirteen questions that should guide review boards as they evaluate the apologies and remorse of bar applicants. Such principles, we argued, concentrate reviewers' attention on the variables most salient to evaluating the quality of the applicant's remorse. We argued that such a principled framework can lend rigor and consistency to the review process, which will, in turn, better serve both the bar and applicants to the bar.

I now attempt to demystify the process of evaluating apologies by setting out questions that should help orient reviewers in various legal contexts. Here I emphasize criminal matters. Apologies and remorse have been features of legal systems for thousands of years, and I doubt this fixture of human relations will change anytime soon. The following questions should better equip those who review apologies and remorse to systemically evaluate their relationships to desired outcomes. I address *who* should undertake reviews of apologies as well as *when* and *where* reviews should be undertaken. I first offer questions that should guide *how* we evaluate apologies across legal contexts.

1. Has the Offender Corroborated the Factual Record? Reviewers should first ask whether the wrongdoer explains what she did with an appropriate degree of specificity and thereby corroborates a detailed factual record of the events salient to the injury. Rather than offering vagaries such as "I used poor judgment" or "I failed to heed the warnings," reviewers should look for apologies that provide a clear account of what happened. This information may implicate others without excusing oneself. In conjunction with considerations regarding timing, offenders should generally "come clean" or "get it all out" early in the process rather than waiting for years of investigations and legal proceedings to disclose the extent of the transgressions. The offender will be exceptionally cooperative in helping authorities gather information and will not obstruct evidentiary process. Offenders who volunteer incriminating evidence increase their credibility, especially if prosecutors are unaware of the existence of such evidence or if it would have been particularly difficult to obtain. With the caveats noted later regarding not punishing defendants for protecting their rights, uncooperative offenders who make specious attempts to exclude evidence undermine their credibility.

Reviewers should also question the remorse of offenders who claim to have disclosed everything only to later release more incriminating information when pressure mounts. If possible, corroborated records should reach agreement among the victim, offender, and sometimes the community regarding what transpired and the relevant aspects of the context in which the injury occurred. In cases of collective crimes committed by multiple actors, contradictory stories raise doubts – especially if two offenders seek apology reductions while offering competing accounts of what happened.

The record will often include accounts of the mental states of the apologizer at the time of the offense, including motivations for committing the offense. If the offender took a calculated risk to maximize her personal wealth while endangering the well-being of others, she should not describe the consequence as unforeseeable. In addition to establishing the record, meeting this criterion goes some way toward demonstrating the offender's credibility and candor.

If a defendant continues to assert her innocence for a crime for which she entered into a plea bargain, we could find little significance in an expression of remorse for this crime. Indeed, we might expect a defendant of especially high character to refuse to apologize for a wrongdoing she did not commit despite the fact that such an expression of remorse might reduce her punishment.

2. Has the Offender Accepted Blame for the Crime? In accordance with notions of proximate causation, the offender accepts blame for causing the harm at issue. We can distinguish this from expressing sympathy for the injury, noting the difference between statements such as "I was wrong and I accept blame for X" and "I am so very sorry that we are experiencing this crisis." These discussions benefit from speaking precisely in terms of "accepting blame" rather than "accepting responsibility."[390] Accepting blame admits that I did something wrong and I deserve blame for the consequences. Accepting responsibility can mean any number of things. A maintenance worker can "take responsibility" for cleaning someone else's mess (an occupational responsibility) or an innocent bystander can take "moral responsibility" for a natural disaster by providing aid (an ethical duty). We can maintain a binocular view of wrongdoing that attributes individual blame while appreciating environmental and structural contributors to wrongdoing such as systemic inequality.

The offender need not accept blame for every charge if she is innocent of some of them. She may explain, with precision, the portion of the blame that she deserves. This might entail apologizing and accepting culpability for a minor offense while aggressively defending against a more serious and frivolous accusation. Such honesty can counter adversarial trends that encourage opposing parties to deny everything and accuse everything, hoping that years of attorneys' fees will produce truth somewhere in between.

Reviewers should pay especially close attention to acceptance of blame in cases of collective harms committed by multiple offenders. Offenders who shift culpability to peers, supervisors, institutional dynamics, or social structures diminish their own culpability.

Acceptance of blame should link to culpable mental states, with intentional, knowing, willful, negligent, reckless, and other mens rea requirements reflected in the acceptance of blame. Attempts to explain why the offender is not at fault often bespeak a failure to accept blame. Offenders who appear primarily to regret being caught or subject to review often fail to satisfy this element. Offenders also should not attempt to describe intentional offenses as accidental or otherwise deny that it was their intention to harm. Those who invoke insanity defenses or otherwise cast their behavior as excused or justified will typically not accept blame.

Felony murder cases present interesting examples here because the doctrine expands the legal definition of murder to include accidental killings committed during the commission of applicable felonies, as well as rendering all participants in such felonies liable for the murder committed in the commission of the crime.[391] If a driver sits in the getaway car while her accomplices unintentionally kill a bank teller during a robbery, the felony murder doctrine subjects the driver to felony murder charges. This can lead to counterintuitive convictions, such as the Missouri case of James Colenburg in which a man was convicted of murder because he struck and killed a toddler who darted in front of his car. The car had been stolen seven months earlier, thus providing the predicating offense for felony murder even though the child's death was accidental. In such cases the felony murderer may accept responsibility for the underlying offense and also for undertaking dangerous activities that should have been foreseen as potentially leading to such injuries but balk at assuming blame for intentional murder. When legal doctrine deviates from common conceptions of proximate causation, reviewers may need to afford apologetic offenders some latitude in their understanding of blame for convicted offenses.

3. Does the Offender Possess Appropriate Standing to Apologize and Accept Blame?

The offender accepts blame for the harm and she – rather than an attorney, proxy, or other third party – undertakes the work of apologizing described herein. This can become problematic in various ways. First, someone other than the defendant may attempt to apologize for her. Such third-party statements regarding the offender's apology will typically provide marginal insight into the offender's contrition. In situations where the offender has limited ability to express her apology – because of language barriers or disabilities, for example – a proxy can help the offender articulate her contrition. Translating an offender's statements, for instance, need not diminish their value. Such assistance differs from a proxy *apologizing for* the offender in the sense that a parent might apologize for a child by stating "she is very sorry and accepts blame for her actions." Although parents may have some insight into the offender's attitudes unavailable to the court and may perhaps add some credibility to the offender's own stated acceptance of blame, third parties cannot do the work of apologizing for her.[392] An attorney, for instance, cannot feel guilt for her client or complete her community service work on her behalf. Certain apologetic activities cannot be outsourced without altering their meanings.

Different issues arise when the state charges the defendant with an offense for which she believes she lacks standing to accept blame. This can result from perceived innocence: "Someone else should be apologizing because I didn't do it." The state might also pursue a crime different from or more serious than the defendant's actual offense. If a prosecutor charges a street-level drug dealer with money laundering but her low rank never brought her near such activity, then she lacks standing to accept responsibility for the money laundering. Given the prevalence of plea arrangements wherein defendants accept charges that may not reflect the spirit of their actual crime, the moral relation between offense, blameworthiness, charge, and apology can become divorced from the offender's perception of what actually happened and what deserves an apology. Reviewers should be mindful of these convoluted moral chains, both to require the offender to personally accept blame for her crimes and to allow contrite offenders some latitude when charges do not line up cleanly with actual wrongdoing for which she feels contrite.

4. Does the Offender Identify Each Harm? Crimes often result from the aggregation of many lesser wrongs. The apologetic offender should identify each harm, taking care not to conflate several harms into one general harm or apologize for only a lesser offense (the "wrong wrong"). In the criminal context, this will include elements of the crime. In Beebe's case, he could identify a range of offenses including drugging Seccuro, assaulting her, and concealing the crime. Volunteering non-criminal activity that contributed to the offense provides reviewers with additional insight into the offender's understanding of how various aspects of his life led to the crime. Offenders should also distinguish harms to various victims and constituencies. A sex offender such as Beebe, for instance, harms not only the direct victim but also the community, the families of both victim and offender, and many others.

Reviewers should maintain special mindfulness to objections from liberal neutrality here. Self-awareness of contributory but non-criminal activity provides insights into her understanding of her predicament as well as her likelihood of recidivism. Beebe's alcoholism, for example, relates to the harms he caused as well as his likelihood of recidivism. Alcoholism is not, however, a crime. State reviewers should be wary of allowing such information to effectively increase or decrease punishments. If an offender finds the primary harm caused by her commission of murder to be disobedience to her god, for instance, reviewers should take care to neither reward nor punish this view.

Given their prevalence and their status as what many consider "victimless crimes," drug offenses create tensions in this regard. If a marijuana grower does not view her illegal activity as harmful, then as a matter of political conscience she may refuse to apologize or accept blame. She may also carefully parse the harms, explaining that she does not find growing harmful but she appreciates that trafficking in such illegal activity visits various harms upon her family, her community, law enforcement, and others. Explicitly refusing to apologize can be a means of protest. Reviewers should understand such disputes regarding the proper nature of harm as probative of the offender's attitudes and predictive of her future behavior.

5. Does the Offender Identify Principles Underlying Each Harm? The offender should identify the moral principles underlying these harms with an appropriate degree of specificity, making explicit the values at stake. The offender explains *why* she is wrong. Someone who understands both the legal and the moral justifications for the criminalization of these activities provides reviewers with insights into their comprehension of the wrongness of their actions. An offender who merely views the activity as inappropriate because it is illegal demonstrates a kind of superficiality that reviewers should take into account, if only as an indicator that she lacks internal motivations for not reoffending and may recidivate when she believes she is unlikely to be caught. In some cases offenders may not understand the criminal nature of their activity or the seriousness of their crimes, for example white-collar criminals who knew that their fraudulent activities exposed them to civil claims but did not realize that they faced prison. Such a shock can trigger rapid reform.

Those who identify the principles underlying their harms provide insights into their character and the nature of their offenses. Notice that many of the relevant moral principles – avarice, lust, envy, and so forth – are not necessarily illegal. As discussed in the context of dialectical retributivism, again we tread close to objections from liberal neutrality. Offenders will hold diverse views regarding the ultimate source of the normative authority underlying laws. Some may cite Kant's *Groundwork*, some the Koran, and some their Baptist grandmother. It will prove tempting for reviewers to place more credence in the belief systems that come closest to their own views – an urge they should resist if we value liberal neutrality.

6. Does the Offender Share a Commitment to the Principles Underlying Each Harm? In addition to understanding the principles underlying the various harms at issue, the offender commits to these principles as just. The phrase "I was wrong" conveys this better than "I am sorry," as the former accepts blame for what the offender appreciates as wrongdoing whereas the latter may provide no more than an expression of sympathy or a displeasure with a state of affairs. As with all elements, reviewers may question offenders to ensure that they understand and commit to the values at issue. Perhaps more than any of the other aspects of the apology, an offender's expressed commitment to the violated principle can humanize her. Rather than just another malefactor to be processed, we see the offender as a person with shared values.

The offender may not share the underlying value, again with an advocate for drug legalization providing an obvious example. In such cases the offender may clarify that although she disagrees with the underlying principle, she understands the principle, she respects the law, and she will not violate it again. Reviewers can understand such an offender as simultaneously disagreeing with yet pledging obedience to the particular statute. Reviewers should evaluate the credibility of such a pledge in the context of other elements.

7. Does the Offender Recognize Victims as Moral Interlocutors?

Throughout this process the offender should recognize the victims of the underlying offenses as moral interlocutors. With this, she demonstrates that she considers the victims as moral agents worthy of engaging in moral discourse and abandons the belief that she can disregard the victim's dignity, humanity, or worth in pursuit of her own objectives. This process invites the victim and others to judge her. She makes herself vulnerable and cedes control. In her most vulnerable moments the offender turns not to her allies but to her victims, now welcoming them as peers in the struggle for meaning and justice. In the Kantian sense, she honors their dignity as fellow moral agents. In the Hegelian sense, she recognizes that her dignity depends on theirs.

Offenders can demonstrate this by reaching out to victims in various ways, including attempting to apologize to them directly. They might provide their direct contact information to victims, allowing victims to control the timing and other terms of interactions.

Occasions may arise in which reviewers credit offenders for not contacting victims because of the offender's considered judgment that contact might cause victims further harm, a sensitivity that Beebe arguably lacked. Reviewers should be wary of offenders who direct their apologies primarily to review committees and appear to disregard victims. Given the limited opportunities for offenders to address victims within many justice systems, reviewers should appreciate this limit and facilitate such exchanges whenever possible, as discussed later in the context of where and when such apologies can take place.

8. Has the Offender Expressed and Demonstrated Categorical Regret? The offender should demonstrate categorical regret for the actions in question, meaning she believes that she made a mistake that she wishes could be undone. Reviewers should distinguish categorical regret from the offender's continued endorsement of her actions (often accompanied by an expression of sympathy regarding what she perceives as the justifiable consequences of her actions). If an applicant claims that her conduct was "the best choice she had" given the circumstances, reviewers have reason to doubt if she would act differently if confronted with similar temptations.

Reviewers should note precisely what the offender regrets. Sentencing courts often confront sentiments similar to those expressed in *People v. McDade*, where the offender stated: "I would like to say due to the seriousness of the charges, it's forced me to look at myself, and I regret getting in the situation that I got in, which all I want to do is just get through this and return back to my family."[393] The appellate court found that this "statement indicated he was not sorry for what he had done to the victim, but rather he was sorry for what he had done to himself."[394] Reviewers should not discount the importance of an offender regretting the damage she causes to herself and to her family and her wishes that those effects could be undone. Self-interested regret has motivation power. If regret for harming victims does not accompany this regret for harms caused to oneself and one's immediate family, however, then reviewers should question the offender's appreciation for the nature of the variety of harms caused as well as her commitment to reform.

If the offender appears primarily to regret being caught – as McDade's "regret getting in the situation" suggests – reviewers can attempt to clarify the intended significance and adjust their evaluation accordingly. Inarticulate defendants may be especially prone to speak of regret in a general sense that appears to connote self-interest rather than regret for offending and causing harm to others, and reviewers should take precautions to prevent unfortunate phrasing from obscuring categorical regret for harming the victim.

9. Has the Offender Performed the Apology? When appropriate, offenders should express apologies to the victim rather than keeping thoughts of contrition to themselves or sharing them only with third parties such as the reviewers. Offenders should address apologies to victims as moral interlocutors. They should express the content required of a categorical apology explicitly. The apology should reach the victim or an appropriate proxy. The victim may exercise reasonable discretion regarding whether the offender should present the apology only to the victim or also to a broader community. The determination of whether the apology should be committed to writing, conferred to the victim in writing, or entered into the record also lies within the victim's and reviewer's reasonable discretion. Written statements will often prove valuable given the complexity of apologies. An apology can be a technical undertaking as it corroborates a record, identifies norms, parses causal moral responsibility, and commits to certain kinds of reform and redress. A written version of the apology allows the offender to construct a precise statement attending to these details. Oral apologies often occur in emotional fits and starts with garbled content. Rather than attempt to identify the contents of the apology amid an emotional and highly nuanced conversation, the victim, reviewers, and other parties can benefit from scrutinizing a stable written statement to identify the sorts of meaning the offender may or may not have offered. In addition, a written apology records the statement, allowing the victim to share it with others or produce it as evidence.[395] Some victims will also want to avoid being in the presence of their attackers. On the other hand, oral apologies afford victims and reviewers an opportunity to evaluate the offender's demeanor. They can also ask questions and engage the apologizer and read her cues when "off script" of a written apology. A written apology supplemented by face-to-face conversation is usually optimal. To repeat, reviewers should exercise appropriate skepticism toward apologies and remorse directed primarily at the reviewing body and should direct applicants to take steps toward reconciling with the offended. Given the dynamics of current criminal procedures in the United States, even those with the best intentions may find it difficult to apologize directly to victims rather than to the court and its officials. Consider in this respect subsequent discussions of where and when these apologies might be delivered. Barring exceptional circumstances, individual defendants should not receive reductions on the basis of apologies expressed by their organizations, for instance if a leader in a white-collar crime or drug organization expresses contrition but her underlings do not apologize for their role in the crimes.

10. Has the Offender Demonstrated Sufficient Reform? The categorically apologetic offender will reform and forbear from reoffending over her lifetime. She will demonstrate this commitment by resisting temptations to reoffend. Actions will speak louder than words. Resisting many such temptations over a considerable duration adds credibility. The shorter the record and the fewer temptations resisted, the less confidence committee members should feel in their ability to predict the trajectory of the offender's behavior.

This temporal aspect of reform creates obvious procedural challenges. If an offender in her twenties commits an assault and stands before a sentencing judge one year later, the court has a limited record of reform. If the applicant was incarcerated for much of the duration between offense and review, she may not have confronted similar opportunities to reoffend. Beyond having the chance to demonstrate reform, offenders need time to appreciate that they should reform. Whether because they deceive themselves about their culpability or because they fail to understand why they should reform, it takes time to undergo the sort of change of heart associated with a categorical apology. Offenders may require years of incarceration and treatment before they even begin to undertake internally motivated reform. Even then, they do not flip a switch from bad to good.

Reviewers have a better sense of reform when they possess longitudinal data on the offender's post-offense behavior. Again, the longer she goes without reoffending, the more credible her reform. In the context of most sentencing, however, courts have very little data that speaks credibly to the offender's reform. Given that the offender recently committed the crime and that she would likely return to similar temptations to reoffend, reviewers typically have to infer that she will recidivate unless they have compelling evidence establishing otherwise. Prima facie, reviewers face a serious problem: How can they judge reform before the offender has actually reformed? Convicts typically do not deserve the benefit of the doubt, so we need time to evaluate how they corroborate their words with actions.

For these reasons, *when* reviewers evaluate an offender's reform becomes especially important. Expressions of remorse that include concrete measures of reform will gain credibility. Different opportunities for reform are available from pre-crime, offense, arrest, allocution, trial, sentencing, incarceration, conditional release, execution, and the many points in between. In some cases the offender will commit the crime, be immediately arrested and detained, and remain incarcerated until sentencing. This affords her little opportunity to demonstrate reform, both because she probably lacks opportunity to undertake reform and she will find little if any occasion to resist the temptation to reoffend within prison because of the restricted environment and increased surveillance. Beebe's case, by contrast, presents more than twenty years of evidence of reform. If reviewers can corroborate Beebe's record of reform and resisting temptation, this provides powerful evidence of conversion. Although most cases will fall between these extremes, the scenarios are typical in that they both presume sentencing should be the occasion to consider remorse. The timing of sentencing, however, often prematurely judges remorse with insufficient data. I subsequently consider in more detail additional and potentially more appropriate opportunities for evaluating reform, including credit for serving "good time" in prison. Such a broader perspective on reform should afford a more accurate evaluation of the apology across more data points. Evaluations of apologies could then be more like clemency and pardon decisions, in which reviewers enjoy longer durations between offense and evaluation and therefore generate more confidence when determining the extent of reform.[396]

If reviewers consider conduct after the offense as relevant to reform, they should also consider conduct before the offense. Although not entirely symmetrical because the very notion of reform promises a break with the past, reviewers should consider all relevant information regarding the trajectory of the offender's record. A repeat offender who previously promised but failed to reform will lack credibility barring some reason for distinguishing the past from the future. Apologies from offenders with a record of deceiving, refusing to accept blame, failing to complete addiction treatment programs, or otherwise backsliding will appear unreliable. In this respect other elements of the apology illuminate reform; accomplishing reform of various degrees provides a lens through which to understand the meanings of other elements.

Reviewing bodies should consider the conditions that created temptations to offend. If the convict was impoverished at the time she committed a petty theft, for instance, a better financial situation may reduce the likelihood of recidivating. Addiction treatment should factor prominently in this regard; an applicant who offended while addicted and has been sober for years since committing the offense demonstrates that she has potentially reformed her conduct in part. Like reform accomplished within the controlled environment of prison, reviewers should similarly consider the probative value of reform completed under sentences that include conditions designed to reduce temptations to reoffend such as those barring sex offenses from living within a certain proximity to schools. For those who have had little opportunity to demonstrate reform at the time of review, a promising plan to utilize their post-conviction time – whether in prison or otherwise – offers a window into their imagined path toward reform. Such promises to reform will carry less weight than demonstrated records of change.

Reviewers should consider the age of the applicant at the time of the offense. Young offenders generally stand better chances of rehabilitation than more mature offenders. Young offenders able to resist temptation offer especially important evidence for reform when the duration amounts to a substantial portion of their lives. Apologies form older offenders – especially those who committed the crimes in their youth – can provide evidence of the "aging out" process.

Reviewers should take precautions not to compound advantages or disadvantages of offenders in this regard. Wealthy offenders, for instance, have resources to post bail and demonstrate reform by participating in top treatment programs at the counsel of elite attorneys who understand what sorts of activities will impress particular reviewers. Indigent offenders, by contrast, may languish in prison unable to do much to demonstrate reform other than staying out of further trouble. Realistic reviewers will appreciate the advantages of privileged offenders on release into money and opportunity when compared with those who return to poverty even worse off as a result of being branded with a criminal sentence, but this does not mean that the rich are necessarily more reformed than the poor.

Finally, recidivism rates vary considerably by offense. Reviewers should adjust their expectations for what sufficiently demonstrates reform accordingly.[397]

11. Has the Offender Provided Appropriate Redress for her Offenses? The offender should take practical responsibility for the harm she causes, providing commensurate remedies and other incommensurable forms of redress to the best of her ability. Redress can take many forms, pecuniary or otherwise. The applicant should provide a proportionate amount of redress, but she need not meet excessive demands from victims with unreasonable or inappropriate expectations. Questions regarding what constitutes excessive demands can be determined in consideration of cultural practices, and such deliberations will often prove contentious. She provides these remedies to the offended parties or a suitable proxy.

The apologizer should accept the legitimacy of some amount of legal punishment for her wrongs. An offender can remain contrite while protesting excessive sanctions, for instance if a high school student caught selling an ounce of marijuana demonstrates convincing remorse but argues that a seven-year prison sentence is too harsh for such a crime. The amount of punishment that offenders believe they deserve offers insight into the extent of their remorse.

Timing of the redress also provides probative value. Redress early in the process can indicate the offender's inclination to reform as well as her desire to reduce the harm to the victim as soon as possible. As the Federal Sentencing Guidelines recognize, redress prior to conviction can reinforce a willingness to accept blame.[398] The greater the portion of redress provided at the time of review, the more credible the apology.

Reviewers should not confuse limited resources or opportunities to provide redress with an absence of contrition. Indigent offenders will often lack the ability to offer redress as they wait in detention and struggle to find money to post bail, retain attorneys, and pay fines.[399] A small amount of redress provided through considerable efforts by an indigent inmate can provide more insight into contrition than a large check from a wealthy but unmoved offender.

Reviewers should also appreciate the potentially infinite forms of redress other than financial compensation. Consulting victims regarding their preferred methods of redress creates an opportunity to treat her as a moral interlocutor. Reviewers should avoid metaphysical language suggesting that redress can in every instance provide value commensurate with the injury, and they should watch for offenders who overstate the ability of redress to "pay their debt" or "put this behind" them. The victims or the state may reasonably contend that some injuries can never be sufficiently redressed despite offenders' best efforts.

Apologies from offenders who fail to redress harms or provide a credible plan for providing redress should be discounted accordingly.

12. Does the Offender Intend for the Apology to Advance the Victim's Well-Being and Affirm the Breached Value Rather than Merely Serve her Self-Interests?

Instead of merely promoting the apologizer's purely self-serving objectives, the offender should intend her apology as a good faith attempt to advance the victim's well-being and affirm the breached value. Benefits the offender receives from her apology – such as restored social standing, amelioration of guilt, or reduced punishment – should be the byproduct rather than primary objective of the apology. The offender should not offer the apology primarily as a means to the end of reducing punishment. Unlike the crime, the apology should not be an act of selfishness. We can understand the sentencing guidelines' refusal to reduce punishment for an offender convicted at trial and who "only then admits guilt and expresses remorse" as a way to evaluate intentions in this regard.[400] This provides a secular correlate to the common religious belief that "only redemptive acts carried out from a conviction of their intrinsic rightness should have the power to redeem."[401]

Behavior demonstrating a pattern of remorse will likely provide greater insight into the offender's mental states than will bare assertions of her intentions or demeanor evidence. Timing, placement, and method of apology can provide windows into motivations. Apologizing well before conviction can provide evidence of the offender's intentions because the confession and acceptance of blame suggests that the offender acts from moral principles despite the strategic disadvantages this likely causes her. Offenders who seek to advance the victim's well-being should demonstrate sensitivity to the impact of apologies on victims, for instance by taking precaution not to unnecessarily open old wounds or by heeding victims' requests that details of the confession remain private because of the harm publicity might cause. Here again offenders find opportunities to treat victims as moral interlocutors.

13. Does the Applicant Demonstrate Appropriate Emotions?

As a result of her wrongdoing, the offender should experience an appropriate degree and duration of sorrow and guilt as well as empathy and sympathy for the victim. Reviewers should determine what constitutes the appropriate qualitative and quantitative emotional components of apologies in consideration of cultural practices. Focusing reviewers on such evidence and requiring finding of fact on these points should discipline committees to value the emotional content of the apology as a discrete element, allowing them to attribute apologetic meanings to emotions without overvaluing dramatic displays of feeling. Emotions are only one aspect of apologies, and often one deceiving and problematic aspect. However distraught a convict, for example, these emotions alone do not necessarily accept blame or demonstrate reform.

Emotional content and intensity will vary over time. Immediately after committing a crime, adrenaline fueled fear and denial may limit the offender's ability to appreciate the harms she causes. She may come to appreciate the seriousness of her offense only after hearing a victim impact statement. For some, the sharp intensity of angry self-loathing on conviction may evolve into a somber acceptance of guilt. An offender's experience of seemingly conflicting emotions such as simultaneous guilt for committing the crime along with hope in her attempted self-improvement need not undermine the emotive force of her apology. Reviewers should also not underestimate offenders' cognitive and emotional bias toward denying guilt, especially early in the process as they come to terms with their situation. Offenders may require a considerable amount of guided reflection to process and express complex emotions, particularly those offenders with preexisting emotional and psychological challenges. The procedural environment can also influence emotions, with adversarial processes that isolate the offender differing from restorative practices that actively cultivate feelings as offenders interact with stakeholders in various ways. Reviewers should calibrate expectations for the offender's emotions accordingly.

Reviewers should not expect emotional amplifiers – "I am so very very deeply sorry" – to convey the central meanings of apologies.

When and Where Should We Evaluate?
For these guidelines to work to maximal effect, qualified reviewers should apply them at appropriate times. As noted throughout, forbearance, reform, and redress present ongoing projects: the categorically apologetic offender reforms and forbears from reoffending over her lifetime. With the possible exception of death, no single moment allows for final judgment of an apology's meaning. Apologies provide treatments, not cures. An offender resisting temptations to reoffend over a considerable portion of her life should be considered more reliably reformed than someone who lacks a similar record. Recidivating gives reason to reinterpret all preceding apologetic gestures and reduce their significance accordingly. All of these factors point toward what Lippke describes as a "wait and see" approach."[402]

Just as a sentencing hearing does not provide an especially telling occasion to judge an offender's recovery from addiction – and indeed it may be a particularly ineffective time to evaluate because of the likelihood that the addict will be on her best behavior – singular moments in the criminal process provide but a glimpse into remorse. If only judges could look into the present and future of the offender's soul and divine her remorse forevermore. They cannot, and believing otherwise is dangerous judicial occultism.

Shoehorning binary evaluations of remorse into preexisting sentencing procedures may appear to produce administrative efficiencies, but they ultimately prove hasty and counterproductive. The fact that justice systems are overburdened does not excuse such failures, and indeed thoughtfully administered reductions for apologetic offenders should reduce certain pressures. Instead of the current systems of singular, ad hoc, and impressionist declarations by sentencing judges who may lack a rudimentary understanding of the contours of apologetic meanings, we should instead aim to string together a series of data points gathered by well-informed reviewers. Patience would be rewarded with more just and effective treatment of offenders.

Although important, I do not wish to overstate the role of timing for apologies. Reviewers can identify promissory categorical apologies at specific moments, and promissory categorical apologies can convey considerable substance far beyond what currently passes in many jurisdictions for expressions of remorse. A promise made, however, differs from a promise kept. Actions over time convey more meaning than eloquent but fleeting expressions of contrition. Given this, where and when should reviewers evaluate apologies in order to clearly understand their many vectors of significance?

As we have seen, the criminal justice system in the United States affords little opportunity for anything like categorical apologies.[403] Markus Dubber describes modern penal institutions where "offenders and victims alike are irrelevant nuisances, grains of sand in the great machine of state risk management." Offenders find little opportunity for the intricacies of contrition within such an assembly line of justice.[404] Bibas and Bierschbach describe how even the most "genuinely remorseful offender who wishes to apologize to his victim and make amends usually has no readily available way to do so."[405] Offenders "almost never" encounter victims until sentencing, instead interacting primarily with attorneys who obviate attempts to apologize. Even during sentencing, an offender typically directs her statements to the court and must literally turn her back on the judge if she wishes to face her victim to apologize.[406] Considering this, what sorts of procedural mechanisms could create opportunities for offenders to recognize victims as moral interlocutors and convey the various forms of meaning expected from a categorical apology?

In the temporality of apologies, early and late expressions of contrition carry distinct and ideally reinforcing meanings. I discussed issues of timing in *I Was Wrong* with respect to non-criminal offenses, but many of those considerations apply with respect to legal disputes as well. Apologies that come soon after the offense provide various benefits. The sooner the apology, the sooner the victim experiences recognition as a moral interlocutor, acknowledgement of her suffering, and the discontinuation of various offenses. As discussed in the context of retributive arguments for reducing punishment for apologetic offenders, the apology reduces the badness of the offense by ending certain harms. If I steal money from you, the longer I keep it the worse the harm. Upon apology and restitution, I stop the interest from accumulating on those moral debts. The sooner I apologize, therefore, the better. Early apologies also allow the offender to begin the long process of apologizing and bringing about maximal benefits to victim, community, and herself while minimizing further harms.

An early apology can also indicate the offender's self-directed understanding that she should apologize. Apologies take on different significance if offenders volunteer them before victims or third parties request or command them. Recall the discussion of requiring children to apologize. If the child offers the apology before anyone points out the transgression, this indicates a degree of moral development because the child has internalized the relevant norms and has engaged in something like autonomous moral deliberation. When an offender independently realizes that she breached a value she endorses, this provides an indicator of her intentions.

Apologies soon after the offense can also provide a powerful indicator of intentions. If an offender confesses her crime early in the process – for instance, prior to conviction, arraignment, arrest, or even suspicion – this offers evidence that she apologizes for reasons beyond the legal strategy of playing to the remorse reduction. The value of such an early confession will in part be a function of the likelihood that the offender would ultimately be convicted. Although Beebe's confession was not early in the sense that it came decades after the crime, he seemed unlikely to ever be punished for his crime and his confession initiated his ultimate conviction. His apology seems especially remarkable because even though it resulted in reduced punishment, without it he would have received no punishment at all. Unlike offenders who apologize early in the process, those who apologize after conviction but before sentencing warrant appropriate suspicion regarding the motivation for their contrition. Such apologies will often look like attempts to maximize the benefits but reduce the risks of accepting blame. Offenders should be prepared to rebut prima facie suspicion against such apologies.[407]

For the sorts of intentional offenses that populate the criminal justice system, reviewers should appreciate that moral reform takes time. If I rob you, at the moment of the theft I presumably find my actions justified or find matters of justification irrelevant. I probably have a long way to go before seeing the need to apologize. If we expect offenders to search for their deepest values, undergo treatments of various kinds, demonstrate reform, provide redress, and generally reorient their lives by consistently practicing new habits, it would be naïve to expect them to complete such a transformation before sentencing. Even exceptionally reformed offenders will have difficulty establishing a credible record of reform between arrest and sentencing, especially if they are detained for much of this period and thus not facing temptations to reoffend. This is in part what makes Beebe's confession so notable – it took him decades to undergo the sort of reform that led him to confess. This lends credibility. Although we can question the value of his apology for various reasons, he does not feign a jailhouse conversion. Presuming that he understands the criminal consequences of his actions, he has come to value something more than his own legal interests.

Less immediate apologies provide reviewers with a longer record and thus more evidence. Unlike conflicts with friends and family in which we might be more inclined toward trusting the apologizer, a demonstrated record of reform is especially important in criminal contexts because offenders will typically lack credibility given their previous offenses and incentives to deceive reviewers. Like promises or declarations of love, the passage of time allows us to make more informed evaluations of apologetic utterances. Subsequent actions corroborate and build on initial apologetic behavior. A snapshot of an offender's contrition at any one moment does not convey a full picture. Longitudinal review of contrition allows reviewers to extrapolate behavior. Some will declare their remorse with great histrionics only to backslide and become far from apologetic. Others might begin the process appearing remorseless but, over time, reckon with their deeds so intensely that they become categorically apologetic. Some may be very late to experience contrition, only feeling pangs of conscience after many years of incarcerations and as they approach death.

Ideally reviewers should base major reductions in punishment for apologies upon longitudinal evaluation of an offender, with demonstrations of contrition over time deserving the greatest reductions. Reviewers can identify such data points at all stages of the process, including but not limited to pre-offense, immediately post-offense, pre-arrest, arrest, arraignment, plea negotiations, plea allocutions, trial, sentencing, various restorative processes, time served, parole, probation, and post-release. Reviewers can consider the following questions: Does the offender's previous record contain thin apologies and broken promises to reform? Do similar temptations to recidivate persist, or has the offender taken steps to distance herself from these conditions? Does the offender resist arrest, destroy evidence, or otherwise seem unmoved by her crime? Does she immediately attempt to help her victim, call the authorities, consistently demonstrate appropriately contrite emotions, and do everything within her power to take practical responsibility for her actions?[408] How does she comport herself in the intake process, while detained, during negotiations, and at trial? Does she appreciate the gravity of her offense and treat relevant parties respectfully or does she disdain the process?[409] Victim-offender mediation and other restorative practices provide obvious opportunities for offenders to express contrition and for reviewers to evaluate remorse. How does the offender behave in these contexts? Does she and attorneys use apologies as a kind of negotiating tool, for instance offering to apologize if and only if the prosecutor drops the charges or otherwise confers some benefit to the defense? Does she apologize strategically after criminal but before civil claims, a tactic allegedly contemplated by Kobe Bryant's defense?[410] Mindful judges can encourage plea allocutions that provide a clear accounting of the crime along with the appropriate apologetic elements. Does the offender offer more than a one-word utterance of "guilty" during allocutions? Does she plan to utilize her period of detention in a manner that adds credibility to her apology? Does she successfully participate in addiction and other treatment programs? Has the passage of time brought general maturity, suggesting that she may have "aged-out" of criminal activity? How does she provide redress over time? Is her commitment to taking responsibility nominal, or does it orient her life? Does she require prompting to meet her restitution schedule, or does she always remit payments on time? If the prosecutor enters into a diversionary agreement whereby the criminal charges will be dropped if the offender satisfies certain conditions, does the agreement require the offender to apologize? If so, does the agreement explain what the state expects of such an apology and does the offender satisfy the elements? To what extent is such an apology voluntarily provided rather than coerced, and what conclusions do reviewers draw from such conditions? Even if the "accepting responsibility" reduction has become primarily a means of rewarding pleas, the letter of the Federal Sentencing Guidelines seems attuned to many of these issues with its instructions to consider "voluntary termination or withdrawal from criminal conduct or associations," "voluntary payment of restitution prior to the adjudication of guilt," and "post-offense rehabilitative efforts."[411]

"Good time" served provides the most common post-sentencing data within many jurisdictions where judges impose sentences as theoretical maximums that they can reduce if the convict demonstrates cooperative behavior while incarcerated. The amount of reduction for good time varies widely, with the norm being a possible 25 to 40 percent.[412] Although some critics find such reductions a form of unjustified auxiliary sentencing in which convicts face additional punishment for doing things that would not be criminal outside of prison – such as failing to follow prison rules regarding personal grooming[413] – O'Hear argues that we should view such good time reductions as a means of recognizing, rewarding, and encouraging atonement.[414] For O'Hear, incarceration offers an extended period to evaluate remorse and we should view "good-time decisions as a continuation of the dialogue regarding the offender's atonement that has begun at sentencing."[415] O'Hear imagines formalizing the good time discount, with the judge explaining that the convict can serve either the upper or lower range of the sentencing depending on how she serves her time.[416] Contrary to the commonly held view that prisoners passively wait for their sentences to expire, O'Hear suggests explaining to convicts at sentencing, arrival at prison, and on release that they should actively choose to take advantage of educational, employment, and counseling opportunities.[417] Judges can explain that "acceptance of responsibility requires more than words; it must be demonstrated through positive conduct over a long period of time," and they can invite offenders to view prison as an opportunity "to give life to the words of apology you have spoken in this courtroom." In a gesture of reintegrative shaming, judges can explain that if "you do the hard work that is necessary to truly earn those credits, then you will indeed deserve an early return."[418] If good time discounts track apologetic meaning – rather than simple adherence to or violations of prison protocols – then they can provide fairly reliable insight into post-sentencing contrition. When triangulated with an offender's contrition at various stages of the process, reviewers would have a far more accurate means of evaluating whether the offender deserves an apology reduction.

Review of apologies can continue after release from prison as acts of contrition migrate to more natural post-custodial habitats. As socially situated practices, apologies benefit from bridges between the justice system and civil society. Religious organizations and twelve-step programs, for instance, provide a way to transition apologies within the confines of incarceration into the unstructured temptations of general society. Apologies in this environment also become more obviously motivated by desire other than reducing punishment.

States can indirectly encourage remorseful offenders attempting to reintegrate by supporting community institutions to the extent possible without running afoul of reasonable objections from liberal neutrality. In many ways this post-release environment may present one of the strongest indicators of the offender's chances of success. We should also remain mindful of the range of concerns from leftists regarding the various ways that gross inequality leads to both crime and recidivism.

Even the most apologetic offender might reoffend after decades of demonstrable reform that resulted in major reductions in punishment. Indeed, a convict can execute a well-orchestrated ruse and seek out the first opportunity to recidivate on release. Preventing this would require detaining all offenders for life. The point here is to minimize the likelihood of such deceptions by maximizing the data points available to reviewers at various stages. This information should then be evaluated according to coherent and consistent standards by qualified reviewers. I now turn to questions regarding who should conduct such review in the various contexts.

Who Should Evaluate?
In general, evaluations of apologies should be conducted by qualified reviewers who can consistently apply coherent and compelling standards for apologetic meanings that track the intended penological purposes. This raises several issues.

First, reviewers must understand the intricacies of apologies. Such meanings are complex, not obvious, subject to deception, and carry high stakes. States should not permit armchair moralizing with gut instincts regarding binary determinations of whether the offender "really means it." Just as we would not accept an unqualified correctional officer prescribing medication for an inmate's mental illness, those making judgments about apology reductions should be fluent in the languages of contrition. All information relevant to offenders' remorse should flow to an expert capable of synthesizing such data. This expert or panel of experts should follow the offender's contrition over time and evaluate the evolution of the offender's apology.

In addition to holding the appropriate expertise, reviewers should be neutral third parties without conflicts of interest in the outcomes. Prosecutors and defense attorneys can offer insights into offenders' apologies, but given their institutional roles as advocates to respectively maximize or minimize punishment, we should not entrust them with the final word on what sorts of reductions offenders deserve. Prosecutors' combination of power and discretion to charge and plea bargain coupled with their incentive to increase conviction rates creates a dangerous mix that leaves them especially ill-positioned to evaluate apologies. Prosecutors also invest considerable time and resources in the pretrial process. Such sunk costs can diminish prosecutors' estimation of offenders' contrition even when victims or other parties find apologies worthy of reductions or even dismissal.[419] All of this suggests that prosecutors should not serve as the primary reviewers of offender apologies despite the unfortunate fact that in the United States they currently play just such a role. Plea situations – which again comprise the vast majority of cases in the United States given the realities of drug case-load management – station prosecutors as the primary if not sole arbiter of apologies. Prosecutorial power may only increase in the near future, in which case it becomes especially important to provide guidelines for evaluating apologies. The guidelines should maximize the fairness of such decisions and institute rigorous appellate oversight to ensure that the state does not abuse such authority.[420] Expert witness testimony from either side of the conflict can also provide insights into apologies, but again the state should view their reliability in light of their incentives to distort the evidence.[421]

Related to concerns regarding potential conflicts of interest, reviewers should be appropriately detached from the crime to evaluate apologies free from excessive emotional distortions. Victims, for instance, may want an apology so desperately that they inflate the meanings conveyed and fail to understand the correlation between the apology provided and the penological objectives. Prosecutors, by contrast, may become so jaded that they discount all apologies as disingenuous.[422] Instead, reviewers should cultivate an unbiased attitude that allows them to evaluate the cognitive, behavioral, and emotive elements of apology.

Although apologies may seem most naturally suited to informal exchanges tailored to the particularities of situations, formality protects against abuse and inconsistency. The offender's informal activities may provide important insights into her apology, for instance as she expresses remorse to the family of the victims, adopts a suppliant attitude toward arresting police, undertakes reform with particular determination, or gains the trust of her prison warden. All of this information is important, but we should not entrust those who occupy these stations in the justice system with the authority to make on-the-fly judgments regarding how the offender's contrition warrants reductions in punishment. Instead, they should submit such evidence to a central officer of the state who synthesizes and evaluates the data over time to provide consistent and proportionate adjustments for apologetic offenders.

Contrast the often lauded practice in the Japanese criminal justice system of affording considerable discretion to police and other agents of the state to handle crimes differently according to an offender's perceived contrition. Braithwaite, for one, finds inspiration in the Japanese model. I discussed diverse cultures of contrition in *I Was Wrong*, explaining that in Japan apologies often serve as ennobling rituals of humility emphasizing collective bonds rather than individual wrongdoing. Japanese police exercise considerable discretion to direct apologetic offenders away from the formal justice system. Prosecutors in Japan enjoy similar discretion, allowing them to suspend sentences for apologetic offenders.[423] This results in a distinctive system, with low crime rates, a 99.5 percent conviction rate, and suspended sentences in two-thirds of all cases.[424] Without adequate supervision, affording such discretion to police in the United States could invite even more wildly inconsistent and biased outcomes.

We might think of juries as the conscience of the community and therefore good candidates for applying apology reductions, but in the United States juries have little role in sentencing except in capital trials.[425] We also have little reason to believe that jurors understand the nuances of apologies and how they apply to penological objectives. Jury instructions on the forms of apologetic meanings and their relevance to punishment might help guide their deliberations, but again, a jury's evaluation of an apology over a narrow window of time provides limited insight compared with longitudinal analyses. If a jury forms, rules on the apology, and then disbands, who reviews their determination if the offender recidivates soon thereafter? Continuity of review should anchor a more durable and responsive process.

Sentencing judges seem like obvious candidates for reviewing apologies, but they also typically lack training in the subject. Replacing ad hoc impressionistic review with judicial training on the nuances of apologetic meaning could improve this situation. Oversight by state experts coupled with less deferential appellate review would also help the process conform to more

APOLOGY REDUCTIONS IN CRIMINAL LAW 223

defensible standards. Judges – like victims, arresting officers, prosecutors, expert witnesses, social workers, or any other one of these reviewers – have a limited perspective on any particular offender's remorse. State experts who follow the development of an offender's remorse can synthesize more holistic views of how apology reductions should apply. Unlike guidelines section 3E1.1, review of reductions for apologies should not be afforded exceptional deference. An apology evolves over time, at each stage warranting de novo review. This is not to doubt the quality of previous decisions but to re-view – to look again – based on new evidence added to the record. The trajectory of apologetic meanings can go in opposite directions, with a remorseless offender radically transforming or an apparently model penitent being exposed as a fraud. We should retire the simpleminded legal fiction born from the epistemological limits of criminal procedure that judges can, in a single moment, see into the hearts of criminals. Replacing this metaphysical convenience requires rolling up our sleeves to do the gritty work of applying apology reductions.

In addition, deferential standards of review of apologies and remorse usually rest on a belief that trial judges and others benefit from "demeanor evidence" and direct insights not available at the appellate level. Although useful, courts have overstated the value of such evidence, perhaps in an attempt to preserve the myth of the trial judge's gift for peering into the offender's soul. Recidivating or years of successful participation in addiction treatment, for example, will tell reviewers far more about the meanings of the offender's apology than will her body language at trial.

Despite the importance of formalized expert-driven evaluations of apologies in the sentencing process, various opportunities exist for informal means to particularize punishments. Bennett, for instance, makes the compelling argument that although the "state must retain the role of setting the level of the sentence," it could do so in abstract terms while allowing considerable flexibility regarding the specifics of punishment.[426] After applying apology reductions, the state could delegate to victims decisions regarding which option from a variety of community service programs would prove most valuable for the parties.[427] Striking the optimal balance between standardizing apology reductions while realizing benefits of individually tailored and community sensitive responses to crime would require evaluating costs and benefits in light of emerging empirical research.

For these reasons, states utilizing apology reductions should (1) establish clear standards regarding the sorts of meanings expected of apologies to warrant reductions in punishment; (2) promulgate those standards widely and train experts to apply these standards; (3) rely on experts to gather longitudinal data and synthesize data provided and to make evaluations of offender apologies on the basis of this information, and; (4) provide rigorous oversight of these determinations to maximize accuracy and consistency.

This leaves two apparent options for who should occupy this institutional role: either better trained judges with expertise in apology reductions and who follow the apologies of individual offenders over time, or non-judicial state experts who specialize in evaluating apologies and report their recommendations to the judiciary and other state agents who control custodial and noncustodial punishments. Any number of permutations of these possibilities might also prove viable, for example both combining better training for judges and providing them with readily available access to state experts. Jurisdictions could divide labor and expertise, with only some judges specializing in cases of apologetic offenders. These judicial experts could oversee procedures specially tailored to such situations, for instance by emphasizing various restorative strategies early in the process. The viability of such practices will depend on various practical issues, including the ever-present issues of resource allocation in an overburdened system. There are many means to reach the ends of fairly reducing punishments for apologetic offenders.

Application Notes
General Considered holistically, the preceding questions offer reviewers some precision regarding the significance of apologies in criminal contexts. If reviewers can answer affirmatively to each of the questions, a strong case exists for reducing punishment. Categorical apologies provide many meanings, serve many functions, and indicate the sort of moral transformation worthy of a reduction in punishment. With these elements in mind, reviewers can work from a shared and consistent conception of apologies and remorse. Even if not all apologies must reach the categorical benchmark to deserve a reduction and if some believe we should adjust the standards, the benefit of simply having a consistent measure against which to evaluate particular examples provides a considerable and novel benefit to the practice of law. Such a fine-grained analysis of apologies should assist reviewers in understanding the range of meanings that an apology can convey so that they can compare the apologies they receive with the meaning they require for a reduction in punishment.

Just as it is presumably a legislature's roll to articulate the purposes of state punishment, how and how much courts should recalibrate punishments in light of contrition also fall within lawmakers' jurisdiction. Reasonable people will disagree about such things. These guidelines accommodate a range of views by clarifying the meanings conveyed by apologies even while arguments endure regarding how such substance should map onto socially and institutionally situated legal practices. Note that although the overall purpose of some legal frameworks will be opaque, confused, or otherwise unconvincing – the U.S. criminal justice system being an unfortunate example – this is not so in every context. The American Bar Association explicitly states that reviewers should view remorse of applicants to the bar who have committed potentially disqualifying acts as indicators of the likelihood that they will practice law according to the code of legal ethics. Despite the misnomer of "character and fitness reviews," the governing bodies make clear that reviewers in bar admissions contexts should not understand themselves to be engaged in a metaphysical exercise wherein they cast judgment on the character of the applicant and exact retributive punishment accordingly. Instead, these consequentialist reviews gather available evidence to predict whether the applicant will uphold standards of the bar.

Legislatures may wish to indicate that some offenses are of a nature that no remorse is sufficient to warrant apology reductions. In the context of bar admissions, my colleagues and I argued that the National Council of Bar Examiners should undertake a systematic review of potential disqualifying offenses and marshal all available theoretical and empirical evidence to evaluate the correlation between certain offenses and the ethical practice of law.[428] If some offenses provide an unacceptable likelihood of recidivism, governing agencies should set policies accordingly. Similar provisions can restrict apology reductions. States may, for example, wish to prevent those convicted of sex offenses against children from ever working in certain environments regardless of the quality of their remorse. In such cases states should clarify that the graveness of the offense and not the offender's insufficient apology drives the punishment and policy. Rather than leaving individual reviewers to wonder if some crimes "cross the line" and if the offender could ever be sufficiently apologetic to receive a reduction for such a severe offense, legislatures should provide clear direction regarding the limits of the apology reduction for even optimal apologies.

Weighing and Prioritizing Elements Reviewers will inevitably need to weigh and prioritize the various elements in light of the relationship between the meanings of the apologies provided and the objectives of the system. An offender who satisfies all thirteen elements will likely deserve a reduction in punishment regardless of the governing punishment theory. Apologies that fail to address each element will be common. How, for example, should reviewers treat an offender who satisfies all elements in an exemplary manner other than providing redress or establishing a lengthy record of reform? First, note that the elements present a mutually reinforcing structure of apologetic meaning because these gestures tend to appear in concert. Second, reviewers should investigate whether some justifiable reason prevents an offender from meeting all of the elements. One's failure to provide redress may result from her poverty, and reviewers should take care not to penalize offenders for lack of resources alone. Some offenders may lack the ability or otherwise find it disproportionately difficult to convey appropriate emotions. Reviewers can adjust expectations for particular offenders accordingly. Third, as discussed later, some of the elements naturally occur after others and therefore all might not be present at any given moment in the process. An offender who confesses may still need time to undergo reform and provide appropriate redress. If the offender jumps to expressions of sympathy and financial restitution, reviewers should wonder if she intends to accept blame and address the remaining elements. Generally, shortcomings regarding any of these elements should raise concerns. None of the thirteen elements is trivial. Reviewers should recognize red flags, understand the dangers they present, and judge accordingly based on the totality of the circumstances. Reviewers will not find guarantees that the offenders will not recidivate, but evaluating apologies according to these elements can achieve greater accuracy in predicting the correlation between past, current, and future behavior while treating offenders more fairly and consistently.

Scripted Apologies As standards for the sort of apology warranting a reduction in punishment become widely understood, how should reviewers respond to "scripted" apologies following the rulebook *too* closely? An apology structured by the categorical framework and rehearsed accordingly need not appear disingenuous. Apologies present complex issues, and we should not expect wrongdoers to develop their own conceptual frameworks. Twelve-step programs offer a useful analogy in that not every addict needs to design her own program for her recovery to be somehow more real. Instead, they participate in a time-tested process and devote their energies to completing its elements – so too with apologies. The elements require considerable efforts and their preexisting structure outlines this work one manageable step at a time. In the criminal context, the state's "scripting" of the apology according to the categorical standard and in consultation with the victim and community allows the public to express expectations regarding what merits reductions in punishment for public harms. Rather than imposing a hollow checklist, the process orients offenders toward desired outcomes.

Various safeguards exist within the categorical apology to identify those who simply rehearse clichéd apologetic language or who otherwise go through the motions without providing the desired meanings. These criteria should help reviewers identify glib offenders.

Although the categorical framework presents abstract guidelines, apologies will vary considerably in their respective contexts. In addition, parties may agree to depart from the standards for various justifiable reasons. They may, for example, wish to emphasize one aspect over another. For these reasons I doubt rote categorical apologies will inundate justice systems. Again, every expression of remorse need not satisfy the elements of a categorical apology. Nor is the best the enemy of the good such that "imperfect" apologies are necessarily flawed in some way. Instead, the categorical apology provides a benchmark against which reviewers can interpret expressions of remorse.

Having such explicit standards will create opportunities for those who seek to game the system. Every rule creates a new opportunity to test how far it can bend. Lawyers will attempt to control the process, and we should not be surprised if they draft and even perform as much of the apology as they can get away with to maximize the likelihood of the desired outcome. As reviewers repeatedly explain the meanings they seek, however, elements like standing, intentions, and reform should curb behaviors that flout the spirit of the reduction. Unlike the current murky and ad hoc standards in which deception thrives, the comparative clarity of apology reductions should shine light into the recess of contrition. These standards should help smoke out apologies calibrated to limit exposure to legal penalties and attempting to parlay undeserved moral credit into self-serving benefits. Reviewers should have a healthy skepticism for apologies that smell of the law office, but hopefully such standards allow them to parse the meanings without unduly discounting apologies that attempt in good faith to meet categorical standards.

Juvenile Offenders State punishment of children raises many thorny problems regardless of the underlying theory. Note a few issues specific to apologies. In some respects apologetic juvenile offenders present the most compelling cases for reduced punishment. Promises to and demonstrations of reform from young offenders take on added significance because of their superior chances of rehabilitation compared with adult offenders. Youthful offenders who repeatedly resist temptations to recidivate offer especially probative evidence of their reform.

Juvenile offenders may, however, lack a range of abilities and experiences that may cause their remorse to appear comparatively immature. They may lack the ability to articulate their beliefs and emotions. Providing redress can prove difficult for a child. Adults must overcome considerable difficulties in providing substantive apologies in the face of criminal punishment, but such pressure may prove debilitating for a juvenile offender. Child offenders can also be especially susceptible to heeding bad legal advice from their attorneys or parents. For these reasons juvenile offenders may require more guidance than their adult counterparts. As discussed in the context of the rehabilitative potential of court-ordered apologies, developmentally appropriate coaching of remorseful juvenile offenders can take a heavier hand without becoming unjustifiably coercive. Reviewers should keep these considerations in mind both when reducing punishments for apologetic juvenile offenders and when considering transferring "remorseless" youths from juvenile to adult jurisdictions.[429]

Zealous Representation If defense attorneys move to suppress wrongfully obtained evidence, might reviewers interpret this as a failure to confess and accept blame? Likewise, an attorney's defense of her client's innocence regarding some but not all of the charges might suggest that the defendant refuses to cooperate fully. Reviewers face such challenges when attempting to reconcile an attorney's aggressive advocacy for her client with an offender's remorse. Defense attorneys confront similar questions: How must I temper efforts to achieve the best possible outcome for my client to support rather than undermine her contrition? Apology reductions change the dynamics for both prosecution and defense.

Contemporary manifestations of zealous representation develop in an adversarial system wherein we expect our attorneys to play every angle. Apologies disrupt that system. If we grant reductions for contrition, effective attorneys will need to develop new ways to represent the interests of their clients. Beebe, for example, did not need an attorney to prove his innocence by any means available. He needed someone who understood his moral transformation, his objectives in confession, the legal and interpersonal landscape into which the confession would fall, and the most effective means of reaching those objectives. His lawyer's assertion that "it was not a rape" dramatically undermined his attempted remorse.[430] Such outright denials of illegal activity that the offender later admits (or in Beebe's case previously admitted) indicate a refusal to corroborate the factual record, and Beebe's attorney risked undoing the legal benefits of his decades of transformation.

The Federal Sentencing Guidelines do not require offenders "to volunteer, or affirmatively admit, relevant conduct beyond the offense of conviction in order to obtain a reduction," in part to protect rights against self-incrimination. If reviewers learn that the offender attempted to hide related uncharged offenses, however, this offers probative value. Establishing credibility is a delicate process for the accused, and they may get one bite at the apple. A white-collar criminal found concealing tax evasion while apologizing for fraud, for instance, can burn all of the goodwill her contrition established. Apology reductions will therefore test defense attorneys' instincts against volunteering incriminating information and require them to rethink the cost and benefits of coming clean. This will require more consultation with the offender than has been customary to discuss the option of apologizing, the risks and rewards, and the attitudes and approaches one should adopt if seeking to provide a maximally meaningful apology rather than a maximally aggressive defense. At a minimum, reviewers should heed the Seventh Circuit's opinion that courts should determine whether the offender understands and agrees with the attorney's strategy before citing this strategy as a basis for denying a remorse reduction.[431] Reviewers should exercise extra caution when attributing the legal tactics of an attorney to the will of juvenile, mentally disabled, and other offenders who are particularly unlikely to have control over legal strategies of their attorneys.

An attorney can zealously advocate for her client's interests, but for the categorically apologetic offender those interests are not simply defeating the prosecution. Although the apologetic offender will understand that she deserves punishment, she need not submit to every charge and punishment thrown at her by prosecutors who smell blood in the water.[432] A reduction for apology should not give prosecutors license to tear into defenseless offenders, and the state should exercise its authority and discretion with restraint given the increased asymmetry of power in such cases. Nor should the attitudes expected of apologetic offenders create a chilling effect on challenges to injustices and efforts for reform. Non-frivolous constitutional challenges can coexist with categorical apologies if such positions do not undermine the offender's acceptance of the underlying value. Nothing in the principle supporting apology reductions prevents offenders from defending against violations of their rights. Lines between frivolous claims and zealous advocacy are hardly obvious and vary considerably according to political views.[433] Reviewers should be careful here and resist regulating attorney behavior by refusing to reduce the sentence of her apologetic client: dare to question the state and we will be sure to deny an apology reduction.[434] Given the deference typically afforded to trial courts in factual findings of remorse, appellate courts should be wary of those claiming to deny reductions in punishment based on demeanor or similar evidence when, in fact, they take issue with the offender's exercise of constitutional rights or use of other good faith legal strategies.

The sort of sentence that the apologetic offender willingly accepts provides one measure of remorse. In Beebe's case, the maximum sentence for rape was life in prison. He served five months for aggravated sexual assault, thanks in large part to the aggressive advocacy of his attorney. This seems insufficient unless his years of public service before his sentence work count as a form of punishment. If Beebe is so eager to atone for his crimes against Seccuro however, why does he think this punishment sufficed – especially because she found the sentence offensively inadequate? The sentencing judge should have been much more explicit in his analysis of how these pieces add up to the sentence issued, and this case demonstrates the importance of reviewers showing their math regarding how the elements of apology equal the punishment so that appellate reviewers can check their conclusions.

Insistence of Innocence Particularly within adversarial systems, defendants have powerful incentives to claim innocence even when confronted with incontrovertible evidence against them. Assertions of innocence can take various forms with different ramifications for punishment and apologies. An offender might admit committing an offense but reject the law's moral authority in a principled act of dissent. Such a position would be consistent with a refusal to apologize because one rejects the underlying principle, for example in protesting the illegality of certain recreational drugs. A different kind of offender might admit even heinous offenses against others yet remain remorseless for any number of reasons, including sociopathology or other mental illnesses that impede acceptance of blame.

More typically, defendants will earnestly maintain that they did not commit the offense. Such a defendant would of course not accept blame, and therefore central meanings of apologies would not be available to her: she cannot simultaneously deny guilt and categorically apologize for the crime.[435] Again distinguish between an offender pleading innocence and a remorseless offender refusing to apologize despite guilt. Wrongful convictions will unfortunately remain a feature of the criminal justice system for the foreseeable future, and the disadvantaged will likely suffer disproportionately in this regard. A system that credits apologetic offenders can increase such injustice for the wrongfully convicted who maintain their innocence: not only do they face unjust punishment but they will be denied an apology reduction and may even be perceived as deserving more punishment because they refuse to accept blame and apologize.

For all offenders the incentive scales for and against apologizing tilt at a certain point, with the taboo against admitting guilt in the adversarial system giving way to contrition's ability to reduce punishment. The innocent face a distinct set of challenges in this regard. Within a system that rewards apologies, the wrongly convicted will face temptations at various stages to falsely admit guilt to gain those rewards. Once wrongfully convicted, for example, she might decide at sentencing or later hearings to cut her losses and try to apologize for something she did not do to gain the benefits of remorse. She might grow weary of her principled claims of innocence that result in increased hard treatment, from a maximum sentence as a result of her lack of remorse to the parole board's repeated denial of release because of her perceived lack of reform as she continues to deny guilt.[436] Under enough pressure, the accused commonly provide full confessions for crimes they did not commit.[437] Indeed, it might take exceptional integrity not to feign guilt and remorse in such situations to appear rehabilitated and receive the institutional benefits.[438] Temptations to apologize even though innocent also complicate the possibilities for post-conviction exoneration because reviewers doubt that anyone would confess to a crime they did not commit, thus the "innocent prisoner's dilemma": take advantage of the best chance of release by accepting blame during parole hearings even though innocent or maintain innocence and hold out for the remote possibility of post-conviction exoneration.[439]

We would also expect those wrongfully accused to endorse particularly zealous representation and to refuse findings of guilt with all available strategies. The notion of a frivolous legal claim will have a rather different moral tenor for a truly innocent defendant than for the guilty who seeks to avoid deserved punishment through legal tactics. Given that the system also levels the "trial tax" against such defendants who refuse to plea because of their innocence, defending against wrongful accusation comes with considerable risks.[440]

Those who earnestly maintain innocence throughout the criminal processes should not face increased punishments for their lack of remorse. Of course the innocent do not deserve punishment at all, and the apology reduction is one of many problems for the wrongly convicted. Rights against self-incrimination and the potential inscrutability of defendants who refuse to address their culpability notwithstanding, reviewers should, to the extent possible, distinguish credible from incredible denials of guilt in these regards.[441] Certainly considerations of remorse cannot supplant usual processes for determining guilt, but the continued insistence of innocence despite the benefits of apologies and confession at various stages in the process provides reviewers with a potentially important piece of evidence regarding the offender's culpability. Reviewers should understand such claims of innocence as potentially more than stubborn denials or remorseless pathology and pay special attention to situations in which the offender's self-interest points toward accepting guilt yet she continues to assert innocence, as these cases can be especially deserving of further investigation by innocence commissions and other reviewing bodies.[442] Such secondary review might mitigate the layers of bias – in terms of general social disadvantages as well as the lack of credibility afforded to convicts – against those who claim innocence despite the system's findings otherwise.[443]

Capital Cases The confusions regarding apologies in law discussed throughout this book can become life-and-death matters in capital cases. Studies repeatedly indicate that reviewers find a capital offender's remorse as one of the primary indicators of whether she will be sentenced to death, even as jurors lack basic understanding of distinctions between expressing remorse and accepting blame.[444] A few points deserve emphasis.

First, the death of the victim presents majors obstacles to categorical apologies in most cases, as offenders have limited ability to engage the dead in dialogue, to treat the dead as moral interlocutors, or to provide sufficient redress to them. Second, apologies from the gallows – like deathbed apologies – will likely prevent the offender from demonstrating reform or completing redress. Third, the innocent prisoner's dilemma is especially acute in capital cases. If the accused insists on denying guilt and thus refuses to accept blame, she risks appearing remorseless. Lack of remorse increases the likelihood that she will be sentenced to death. The lawyerly reflex to deny guilt can prove lethal in capital cases in which the prosecution mounts powerful evidence. All parties involved should understand that claiming innocence presents considerable risk. Defense attorneys should advise their clients of the special dynamics of these situations, requiring considerable trust between client and attorney.[445]

If a convict maintains her innocence throughout her execution even if confession and remorse could have spared her life, this offers potentially dramatic insights into her beliefs and values. Note in this regard the distinctions between a capital defendant who does not testify or otherwise address the salient parties and thereby leaves everyone wondering whether she actually maintains her innocence and the defendant who actively insists on her innocence. Impassioned defense from the accused as well as her attorney in the face of the risk of refusing to accept blame should place reviewers on notice that such an "all-or-nothing" attitude may have probative value.

Finally, if apologetic offenders deserve a reduction in punishment, questions arise regarding *how much* of a discount the state should grant. Settling on the percentage of reduction will prove difficult, but the preceding discussions of the underlying theories of punishment all point to a clean standard: offenders providing promissory categorical apologies in capital cases should be spared death.

Perjury and Intentionally False Apologies Intentionally deceptive apologies attempting to gain legal benefits can amount to committing perjury. This should not apply to cases in which a defendant suffers from confusion regarding the meanings of apologies and offers an expression of sympathy or otherwise ambiguous apology instead of a more categorical effort. Nor should it apply to good faith attempts to convey muddled understandings of complex beliefs and values, even when those understandings are demonstrably wrong (such as the offender who claims to have accepted responsibility for a charge while continuing to assert innocence for that same charge). An offender's interpretations of her own apologetic states deserve some deference. A party who while under oath before a reviewing body intentionally attempts to deceive relevant parties to receive the benefit, however, should be understood as lying to the state and punished accordingly. Attorneys and other third parties who encourage or attempt to induce such false apologies should be similarly penalized.

It may prove difficult to establish that someone lies under oath about their apology, but the legal system is accustomed to evaluating similar mental states. The threat of being charged with a separate punishable offense for deceptive apologies should offer some deterrent for the remorseless and their attorneys who might consider staging an apology an otherwise risk-free strategy.

Increasing Punishments for the Remorseless As argued earlier, if we presume just baseline punishments, then a consistent and symmetrical position requires increasing punishments for unapologetic offenders. Given that states tend to over-punish by most philosophically rigorous standards and therefore a just baseline of punishment rarely exists, there may seem to be less urgency in increasing punishment for the remorseless than for decreasing punishment for the apologetic. All of the considerations set forth regarding the practicalities of evaluating apologies, however, will allow states to identify categorically unapologetic offenders with greater accuracy and consistency.

Again, the categorically unapologetic offender denies involvement in criminal activity despite overwhelming evidence against her, refuses to accept blame for harm she obviously caused, not only denies that she did anything wrong but refuses to recognize the wrongness of the acts in question, rejects the underlying values, continues to disrespect and express contempt for victims, shows no regret, fails to utter anything resembling apologetic words, makes no promises that she will not reoffend if presented with the opportunity, undertakes no reform, offers no redress, and feels no emotions of contrition. Although few offenders will demonstrate all of these characteristics, the categorically unapologetic provides a measure more accurate than the far too common denouncements of offenders as evil, soulless, or otherwise generally villainous. As with evaluations of apologies, the state should not treat remorselessness as an interminable condition but rather one that evolves over time. Reviewers should also take special care not to confuse remorselessness with mental illness, manifestations of inequality, or other disadvantages that inhibit the offender's ability or desire to express and experience contrition.

Amount of Reduction Precisely how much should a state reduce punishment once an offender establishes various apologetic meanings? Previous commentators have understandably avoided this question. For Duff, "no determinate answer is forthcoming."[446] Others suggest that the apologetic offender should receive the minimum when offenses carry a range of punishments.[447] Although providing little more than a plea benefit, the guidelines offer a 35-percent reduction for "accepting responsibility." The difficulty of answering this question results in part from divergent views regarding why we punish, how much we should punish, and what kinds of punishment provide proportionate and commensurate responses to crime. Apologies add layers of complexity to this morass.

My basic advice here calls for legislative bodies to articulate the underlying objectives of punishment pursued by the judiciary and to correlate these objectives with apology reductions. Legislatures rarely indicate that X apology should equal Y reduction. If they wish to index punishments to remorse or remorselessness, legislatures should make these intentions as explicit as possible. Regardless of the amounts of reductions they allow, promulgating sensible guidelines would go some way toward reducing current injustices.

Of course legislators will debate apology reductions, and hopefully such debates will advance the analysis beyond anything proposed here. Publicly arguing about the amount of reduction due to apologetic offenders, promulgating rules, and providing guidance to state agents stands a far better chance of approximating justice than the current practices of expecting individual reviewers to figure out such difficult and important questions.

In general, reviewers should think in terms of a sliding scale, with more thorough apologies deserving greater reductions in punishment.[448] Reviewers should simultaneously keep in mind that the greater the reduction in punishment, the greater the temptations to feign apologies. Reviewers should heed all of the precautions set forth herein accordingly.

Whatever the amount of apology reduction, it should be consistent between offenders. Similar apologies for similar crimes should receive similar reductions. Reviewers should consider not only the amount of punishment but also how different forms of punishment can foster contrition. An offender showing early signs of remorse, for instance, may be more receptive to restorative techniques that build on her desire to make amends. The state can accomplish such particularity in sentencing while honoring principles of proportionality by attuning the *kind* of sentence to the offender's needs and maintaining deserved *amounts* of punishment.[449]

As an additional note of caution, legal agents should avoid overstating claims that reducing punishment "forgives" the apologetic offender or that the apology somehow "restores" the community to a pre-offense equilibrium. Forgiveness and reconciliation are every bit as nuanced as apologies. Our eagerness to put terrible events behind us can lead to excessive optimism, but Pollyanna attitudes present dangers in analyses of reconciliation between those who commit serious crimes and their communities. We may reduce punishments for apologetic offenders, for example, but this does not necessarily entail that they deserve blind trust. As Cheshire Calhoun has explained, "trust is scalar" and comes in various degrees for different activities.[450] One might resume friendly relations with a former spouse guilty of infidelity and trust her to safely drive the children to school, for example, without trusting her enough to restore the marriage. This speaks to an incapacitative element: I will not allow you to harm me again in that way. If one regenerates enough trust to warrant restoring the marriage, that trust will be different from pre-infidelity trust. Any evidence of a new infidelity would be viewed in the context of the former offense and would justify elevated suspicion. So too with criminal offenders – if the state and victims find an offender's apology convincing and reduce a prison term accordingly, this does not mean that we should act as if the offense never existed. Certain cautions may still be necessary, and the offender may still deserve close scrutiny. On the scale of trust, considerable distance can separate the need to incarcerate (minimal trust) from unconditional release (maximal trust).

I mention this here not because I wish to extend the carceral archipelago for apologetic offenders but rather to preempt the dueling threats of excessive skepticism and excessive belief in the power of an offender's reform. I worry about both those overeager to apply apology reduction – recall the Grosmaires as they heed Christ's call to forgive their daughter's murderer – as well as those who reject the possibility that criminals can undergo moral transformation and therefore deserve less suffering. As political currents rise and fall, reviewers should keep this practical beacon in view: the state can tailor sentences that reduce punishments for offenders while specifically moderating our trust with respect to the matter on which she previously proved untrustworthy. Taking measures to restrict an apologetic offender's ability to reoffend, therefore, can be consistent with generally reducing her punishment.

Bias I noted throughout ways that apology reductions can compound various disadvantages. Although one federal judge reports to have "heard extraordinarily sincere allocutions from folks who could not read or write and infuriatingly insincere nonsense from sophisticated, highly educated white-collar defendants," one would expect these to be exceptions to the rule.[451] Privileged offenders will typically sound more articulate, appear more likely to be members of the cultural ingroup of legal officials, receive better counsel on how to express remorse, enjoy greater opportunities for top rehabilitation programs, and have their reentry cushioned by money and opportunities.

The example of Anthony Warren resonates here. Warren fired a stray bullet that left three-year-old Kai Leigh Harriot paralyzed from the waist down. At the age of five, Kai Leigh stated at Warren's sentencing hearing: "I forgive you, Anthony Warren. What you did to me was wrong, but I still forgive you." Two years later from prison Warren videotaped an apology to the girl and her family as part of a Boston-area peace project. "To be blessed with the opportunity to be forgiven by a beautiful person like Kai, it made me want to change," Warren stated in the video filmed in the prison chapel. "It made me want to be less colder and harder. It made me really want to take a look at myself and take a look at my duties and responsibilities as a black man in my community." Warren continued: "I want to thank Kai Leigh; I want to thank her mother; I want to thank her family. I want to apologize to my community. I just appreciate the opportunity that you gave me." Although emotionally powerful in many ways, while watching the video one senses that Warren feels terrible but he does not know what to say to capture the subtleties of apologetic meaning. Parsing his spoken words tells us little, unlike an offender who receives elite legal counsel that coaches her how to translate the insights revealed in therapy into deliverables that hit all the right notes of contrition. Even as Warren exudes humility, a certain demeanor gap persists as phrasing, speech patterns, and dress. His apology bears the marks of criminal – and prison – culture. Even when exercising caution not to evaluate an apology unfairly, reviewers must maintain exceptional vigilance to prevent explicit and implicit biases from contaminating evaluations.

Privileged offenders will often receive optimal counsel regarding the where, when, and how of apologies as a legal strategy. The disadvantaged may consider the option only years later, as in Warren's case when a youth development group reached out in the context of making a thirty-minute video of inmates in Old Colony prison. In addition, reviewers should not confuse an offender's inability to provide redress as a result of poverty with a failure or unwillingness to take practical responsibility. Nor should they unfairly conflate one's access to programs that promote reform with a moral transformation while believing that those stuck in prison – because they cannot afford to post bail, for instance – will probably just get worse. As noted, however, there is unfortunately some truth in believing that privileged offenders face fewer obstacles to reform and therefore may stand better chances of fulfilling certain aspects of apologetic meaning. For all of these reasons, limited discretion combined with rigorous appellate review should work to identify biases in evaluations of apologies and work toward a standardized and fair process that treats like apologies alike.

Conclusion

According to my "kitchen sink" approach, the apology reductions should be compelling across a range of underlying justifications for punishment. Depending on numerous variables and beliefs, voluntary apologies can supplement the objectives of punishment. In some cases apologies can supplant traditional forms of punishment by independently and more effectively achieving their goals. Sometimes apologies can simultaneously advance objectives from conflicting traditions that might otherwise appear practically irreconcilable. A sophisticated understanding of these possibilities provides a powerful tool for a criminal justice system. Failure to appreciate the meanings of apologies results in injustices and inefficiencies. I should conclude by tying a few remaining loose ends.

First, I have not considered whether we should understand reductions in punishment for apologetic offenders as forgiveness, mercy, leniency, clemency, pardon, amnesty, or otherwise. These are contested terms and how one describes apology reductions will depend on one's underlying views on punishment.[452] I should repeat, however, a few claims about forgiveness made in *I Was Wrong* most relevant to criminal punishment.[453] Just as binary views of apologies prove too coarse to appreciate the intricacies of apologetic substance, binary views of forgiveness also oversimplify the range of meanings and functions of the practice. Thinking of forgiveness as an act that we can definitively complete misleads us in many cases. I also doubt that any set of criteria or scale of forgiveness that provides the "necessary conditions of forgiveness" will settle matters. You might, for instance, tell an unfaithful lover that you have forgiven her and trust her once again to restore a sense of security to the relationship; however, you may still experience nagging doubt, occasional bouts of anger, or even painful memories many years after reconciling. As Margaret Urban Walker puts it, "he may be unable not to feel many things when the memory of his wife's unfaithfulness is stirred; and there may be, for all his resolution, some vibrancy and hopefulness, some playfulness and silly freedoms that he will not recapture.[454] If we experience any of these thoughts or feelings to any degree, do we void our forgiveness? This seems like a rather ham-fisted question given the terribly complex moral and psychological issues it raises. Similar concerns arise in criminal contexts, for instance when judges consider the prior offenses of someone who reoffends after serving a full sentence. Like apologies, notions of forgiveness seem to identify a loose constellation of interrelated meanings among various beliefs, judgments, emotions, and actions. We may value and emphasize different aspects of forgiveness in different contexts. These various purposes of forgiveness may conflict. Truth and reconciliation tribunals, for example, often take forgiveness as an orienting principle while simultaneously minding a range of objectives including administering retributive justice, deterring future atrocities, granting amnesty to maximize stability, and creating a historical record to preserve the memory of the harm. These potentially conflicting goals do not render forgiveness impossible but rather require consideration of the relative values and meanings of the different elements of forgiveness.[455] This approach helps makes sense of the idea of "unforgivable" crimes by identifying certain aspects of forgiveness that cannot be met in certain cases, which in turn allows parties to work toward various kinds of reconciliation even if other wounds endure.[456] Additionally, notice a problem with construing reductions in punishment as a form of state-endorsed collective forgiveness. We typically do not think that a third party can forgive an offender on behalf of the victim, and we should question the extent to which the state possesses standing to forgive.[457]

An apology's reception creates a kind of dialectical or "feedback" meaning. Victims reject even the most thorough apologies, and this has consequences. If a victim refuses to hear words of apology or returns attempts at restitution, meanings go unrealized. Although my contrition may be transformative for me, it may fall on deaf ears in a manner similar to an apology to the deceased. A victim's refusal to forgive can amplify certain forms of meaning such as regret. A rebuff may also affirm the sanctity or inviolability of the breached value for the victim. By contrast, a victim can extend and compound its significance if she gratefully receives the apology. If an apology results in a form of forgiveness that prevents a death sentence, this resonates through the remainder of the life of the person given a "second chance." Responses to acts of contrition may seem unclear: our interlocutor may reply with a counter-apology, an expression of counter-forgiveness, a gesture of thanks, or some series of moves to diffuse the awkwardness common in such exchanges.

This raises the possibility that an apology from an offender creates a moral duty for the victim, state, or community to forgive her in the form of reduced punishment of otherwise.[458] Might, in other words, the victim *owe* the offender forgiveness if she apologizes properly? Can the offender justifiably demand for the victim to forgive her in such circumstances, as if the tables in the moral economy have turned and the victim must now discharge her debt to the offender by conferring forgiveness? Some of the previous discussions – particularly the retributive arguments – do suggest something like morally required forgiveness in the form of reduced punishment. We can restate this in terms of when victims, communities, or states should "accept" an apology and whether we should think of accepting an apology as synonymous with forgiveness. Before we can begin to respond to this issue, we face the recurring problem of what sort of apology creates conditions for what sort of forgiveness. Achieving conceptual tidiness in such an analysis is onerous, and cases of collective apology and collective forgiveness would compound the difficulty of such work. Just as complex issues arise regarding how apologies from collectives such as nations or corporations relate to punitive measures against these groups, reducing punishment for contrite offenders can look like a kind of state-sanctioned collective forgiveness. This raises many serious problems, including whether the state possesses the sort of standing that entitles it to forgive or whether thinking in this way stretches our moral concepts too thin.

Another issue straddles the theoretical and the practical. If a criminal offender undergoes the sort of moral transformation indicative of a categorical apology, do efforts on her behalf to reduce her punishment necessarily undermine her repentance?[459] Beebe's attorney, for example, cast doubt on his remorse not only by minimizing the badness of his acts but also by advocating for the lightest possible sentence. Seeking a reduction in punishment because of one's apology does not necessarily undermine one's claim for such a reduction. An apologetic offender need not passively accept all decisions of those she has wronged or those with authority over her.[460] A retributivist, for instance, could believe that she deserves less punishment because her remorse decreases her desert. An offender might also protest the proportionality of the penalty, for example if a sober and apologetic offender convicted of possession of crack cocaine admits her blameworthiness but finds the mandatory minimum sentence excessive. An apologetic offender might also reasonably believe that she can better undertake reform and redress outside of prison, making her appeal for a shorter sentence not necessarily a self-serving reduction in punishment but rather a more socially productive means to "pay her debt" than passing time in prison on public expense. How we should view an apologetic offender or her legal counsel's request for a reduction of punishment will depend on the context and various practical issues. Certain details may provide particular insight into the offender's motivations. She may remain unapologetic throughout the trial, for example, but once found guilty she may offer a histrionic apology along with other strategies to reduce her sentence. When triangulated with these other facts, "asking for" lenience will probably warrant reasonable inferences toward undermining the apology's credibility. Within the context of a criminal justice system with questionable laws and punishments and in the legacy of the dark history of rituals of contrition, however, we should exercise care to avoid allowing the system to take advantage of apologetic offenders. We should counsel offenders to accept what is deserved but not more.

As we have seen, criminal procedures are the pumps and hydraulics driving these conversations. Experts in these areas – both practitioners and academics – will surely have much to add to the previous discussions. I am especially grateful for insights from those fluent in international practices such as active remorse (*tätige reue*) in Germany and neighboring jurisdictions.

Finally, one might object that apologies in the criminal context – especially something like categorical apologies – are so rare that we should not build, in von Hirsch's words, "a whole penal strategy" around them.[461] Categorical apologies are indeed exceptional, whether in the criminal context or in everyday family relationships. For many offenders the very drives and social conditions that propel them toward crime simultaneously repel them from experiencing contrition. Whatever compels us to commit misdeeds, in other words, probably also drives us away from conscientiously apologizing for those offenses. It seems especially unlikely that someone guilty of a grave criminal offense can transform from a wrongdoer to an exemplary penitent. The criminal justice system appears to further decrease the likelihood of offenders becoming remorseful rather than further alienated. With that said, a few points support my approach. I do not propose anything as ambitious a "whole penal strategy" built around apologies. I only seek a means of valuing apologies that fairly assigns them appropriate worth. A moral transformation that results in a categorical apology from a criminal offender achieves something approximating exemplary success across a range of punishment theories. Although rare, categorically apologetic offenders present a regulative ideal transcending partisan views regarding the ultimate purpose of the justice system. As such, their rarity only increases their value and significance. The criminal justice system confronts an endless variety of remorseful and remorseless actors. I hope to provide some guidance for evaluating such offenders fairly and consistently.

PART TWO

Apologies in Civil Law

CHAPTER FOUR

The Institutional Framework: Economic Outcomes and Noneconomic Values

Introduction

As we transition into apologies in civil law, consider the case of Donna Bailey. The outdoor education instructor and mother of two had been studying to become a physical education teacher when a rollover crash while riding in a Ford Explorer equipped with Bridgestone/Firestone tires left her paralyzed below the neck.[1] This combination of vehicle and tire resulted in an estimated 250 fatal rollover crashes and as many as 3,000 additional serious injuries. Bailey sued for $100 million. Three Ford attorneys visited Bailey at her hospital bed, where she had been confined and breathing through a ventilator for ten months. Ford negotiated to apologize to Bailey and record the hospital visit on video, but only without audio. According to Bailey's attorney, Ford insisted on this silencing condition because "they didn't want anyone hearing what they say."[2] We do not know why the attorneys sought to limit access to their words, nor do we know what they said to Bailey. Their gestures satisfied Bailey nonetheless. "The gist of the whole thing was that they were truly sorry for what... happened to me," Bailey recounted, "and I felt like it was very sincere."[3] Bailey settled for an undisclosed amount that very day. Ford's spokesperson issued a statement: "We are pleased to have resolved this case with Donna Bailey and we extend our sympathies to her and her family."[4]

Because organizations cause so many civil injuries, governments are the boogeyman of the right, corporations the boogeyman of the left. Concerns addressed in *I Was Wrong* regarding collective apologies resurface here. We can only speculate about many of the meanings of Ford's apologies without a transcript of the interactions. Ford and Firestone had been entwined since 1906 when Henry Ford outfitted the Model T with Firestone tires, but disagreements regarding culpability effectively ended their relationship. Ford publicly blamed Bridgestone. Bridgestone blamed Ford. It seems unlikely that Ford's attorneys accepted blame in their apology to Bailey. Bailey characterizes their statements as an expression of sympathy ("they were truly

243

sorry for what... happened to me"), echoing the spokesperson's expression of "sympathies" for the injuries without acknowledging a role in causing those injuries. I also doubt that this semiprivate apology explained how and why Ford had done something wrong, which specific individuals deserved blame, or how they would prevent it from happening again. Instead, the attorneys probably either avoided the topic of blame altogether or deflected misdeeds into the abstract collective of the corporation. Neither apology explains who deserves blame for paralyzing her and killing hundreds of others. The attorneys may even have described these injuries as *accidents*, unforeseeable and unintended harms for which no one deserves blame. Court documents, however, established that Ford engineers and executives knew about rollover problems for some time and even redesigned the vehicle without addressing the problem. Bridgestone was also well aware of the dangers. None of these individuals appear to accept blame.

In addition, Bailey's attorneys explained that she did "not want her case to stand merely for someone who wanted a monetary award" but rather "wanted to advance public safety and protect lives." If Ford does not admit to doing anything wrong, why would they change their practices? Why should we correlate expressions of sympathy with increased safety, especially because – even after Ford's apology to Bailey – Bridgestone refused to recall the model of tires that allegedly caused her accident? The settlement included public release of internal documents and promises to undergo further reviews of the tires that might lead to additional recalls, but that is quite different from promising to increase safety standards and keeping those promises.

Those most directly responsible for Bailey's injury could have admitted their wrongdoing, experienced appropriate emotions, undergone a moral transformation, promised not to reoffend, kept those vows, and provided redress. Instead, it seems that Ford paid attorneys to express sympathy in a manner that minimized legal exposure and brand damage while maximizing benefit in negotiations. In this case, that meant having attorneys say what Bailey wanted to hear to settle while concealing the content of the apology from the public by turning off the sound in the video.

An eyes-wide-open view sees a rather conflicted series of events: a semipublic apology offered pursuant to multimillion dollar settlement negotiations that refuses to admit wrongdoing and seems unlikely to initiate reform, but that is accompanied by a negotiated release of information that might lead to increased public safety. It also looks like a corporation buying a victim's silence in the context of a public relations crisis and ongoing litigation with other parties. Ford can assert that it "apologized" and gain credit for doing so – both in the settlement negotiations and in the public opinion – without admitting wrongdoing or otherwise undertaking legal risk. Ford and Bridgestone's intent seems clear. The accidents left Firestone facing a 20-percent decline in sales and a 40-percent decline in stock value.[5] Ford did not want another Pinto-style crisis damaging its reputation and sought to settle as many cases as quickly as possible, including six cases like Bailey's in a single day.[6] We can hardly fault Ford for its legal strategy, but reducing Ford's actions to a plain and simple apology fails to appreciate the dynamics at work and distorts important issues of social justice and public policy.

A pattern becomes evident when studying civil cases. A victim suffers harm. She wants something like an apology. She may not know what a sufficient apology would entail, but something like a categorical apology often motivates her: she wants to know what happened, she wants someone to admit wrongdoing, she does not want to stand by while someone "gets away with" violating a moral principle she cares about, she wants to be respected and recognized as wronged, she wants the wrongdoer to feel badly, she wants to know this is not going to happen again to her or to anyone else, and she wants the wrongdoer to take practical responsibility for redressing her injury. The law does not seem like the obvious venue for such meanings – in part because of the monetary rather than moral tenor of civil proceedings – but for various reasons the victim finds herself embroiled in adversarial litigation. Like the hammer that sees every problem as a nail, lawyers do as they are trained and process the claim into legal currency. The victim who enters the process seeking something like a categorical apology often leaves with a settlement, a rather ambiguous expression of sympathy, and sum of money minus legal fees.

Cases like Bailey's are not exceptional examples of obsessively moral complainants forcing square pegs of apologies into round holes of civil litigation. Victims recurrently seeking apologies give a pulse to the moral heart of civil law. Imagine the situation faced by Anne Anderson. Evidence mounts that your child's leukemia was caused by a factory unlawfully dumping toxic waste in your neighborhood. A legal battle ensues, as made famous by Jonathan Harr's *A Civil Action*. What would you want if someone profited while knowingly endangering children, and your child now suffers as a result? The horror of this is almost unimaginable for a parent: as terrible as it may be to have a seriously ill child, to learn that someone benefits by causing this suffering adds infuriating injustice to devastating misfortune. There is no remedy, only redress. What would you seek from the law if this were your child? Money, of course, would help. Given that money might be considered a root cause that motivated the offense, pecuniary damages also seem appropriate. Many readers would want what Andersen sought: for those responsible for her child's cancer "to come to her front door and apologize."[7] Similarly imagine yourself as the grieving Wisconsin mother with a child killed by a surgeon's error during a routine appendectomy. After the hospital offered to settle for $150,000 – the maximum medical liability in the state – the mother objected: "it isn't the money." "I want my day in court," she explained, "I want to hear them tell me what went wrong.

I want to hear them admit guilt and tell me they're sorry."[8] The father of Ron Goldman similarly claimed that he would trade any damages won in a civil trial for a confession from O. J. Simpson for killing his son.[9] Lee Taft describes how he believed "something was missing" in the cash awards he won for his clients:

> I made this observation firsthand in the early 1980s when I represented a young widow in a medical negligence case. Her husband had been seriously injured, and the medical team in charge of his care failed to discern the extent of the injuries he had sustained. He died a slow and agonizing death. She was left with small children, few financial resources, and deep feelings of resentment against the doctors in charge of her husband's care. The case was eventually settled, and because there were minor children involved, a hearing was held to apportion the settlement proceeds between the widow and the children. As we left the courthouse after the hearing, she began to rage. I thought she was disappointed in the apportionment ordered by the court or that she regretted settling rather than trying the case. But she denied that either of these feelings was the source of her hostility. She was angry that none of the doctors had ever said he was sorry that his conduct had contributed to her husband's death. She experienced this omission as another injury, moral harm added to professional malpractice. She said that if the doctors had apologized, she would have felt more able "to heal."[10]

For this litigant, an apology admitting fault would have conveyed meaning distinct from any amount of money.

In contrast to cases in which victims receive private expressions of sympathy accompanied by cash awards, consider an international example of an apology that provided the linchpin for broad social transformations. From 1932 to 1968, Japanese chemical manufacturer Chisso Corporation discharged wastewaters containing mercury into Minamata Bay. As evidence mounted in 1959 that its pollutants caused lethal and disfiguring Minamata disease, Chisso denied the connection even though its own scientists knew they were to blame. Chisso claimed that explosives from World War II contaminated the water and refused to stop dumping mercury. They offered nominal "sympathy" payments to victims. In the pro-business and anti-environmentalist climate of the era, Chisso held off further evidence of the connection between its pollution and increasingly widespread illness, even hiring *yakuza* in 1972 to attack and seriously injure photojournalist W. Eugene Smith for publishing images of deformed victims in *Life* magazine.[11] Chisso continued dumping, believing that it had so defeated the claimants that it reduced its sympathy payments to one-tenth of the original offered.[12] Activists in the devastated fishing community persisted, and in the late 1960s political winds began to favor environmentalists. Chisso could no longer suppress the international consensus that their mercury caused the harms. One of Chisso's own doctors provided a deathbed confession that he produced convincing evidence in 1959 that their pollutants caused the disease

THE INSTITUTIONAL FRAMEWORK

but destroyed the evidence at Chisso's demand.[13] Victims – who had been ostracized from their community, banned from stores and restaurants, and treated like contagious lepers who sought to destroy the Japanese economy with their radical environmental agenda – were granted a meeting with chief executives. When company president Kenichi Shimada claimed that Chisso could not afford the damages, one victim stood and proclaimed: "If I don't get the indemnity money, I can't live." He then shattered a glass ashtray on the negotiating table and slit his wrists with it. Shimada conceded: "Yes, yes, yes – we will pay."[14]

Victims insisted on an apology, requiring Shimada to supplicate himself on his knees before victims and accept blame for injuries to thousands.[15] Japanese courts sentenced two Chisso executives to two-year prison terms. Extensive reform followed the gestures of contrition. Payments to victims were so extensive that the Japanese government needed to bail out Chisso in 1978 to ensure that it could continue "accepting its burden of shame" and compensating victims.[16] Chisso stopped dumping. It paid for the majority of the multibillion-dollar remediation. Chisso paid fishermen, whose livelihood it had destroyed, to catch poisoned fish and deliver them to its toxic incinerators for disposal. In 1973, the Japanese government, which had earlier been complicit in the cover-up, officially recognized 3,000 Chisso victims. In addition to transforming Japan from environmental catastrophe into a land of comparatively clean land and water, the reforms associated with Minamata influenced industrial pollution policies around the world.[17] The victims' demands for an apology that provided reform and redress changed the world.

The death of a loved one may elicit the strongest demands for contrition, but the phenomenon appears across the range of civil litigation. In her sexual harassment claims against Bill Clinton, for example, Paula Jones broke with her team of attorneys over her insistence that she seek not only a financial award but also an apology that accepted blame.[18] Even intellectual property disputes between corporations that should view litigation as purely economic transactions create impassioned pleas for apologies.[19] Apologies pervade civil law, with many victims wanting their meanings even when they do not know exactly what they seek or understand how such desires render them vulnerable. This chapter aims to reduce, or at least organize, these confusions.

The following sections first explain the conflicted cultural and legal dynamics that allow for apologies in civil law to convey considerable economic value, in part because of their appearance as transcending economic value. Second, I outline how this economic value creates incentives to distort apologies. Defense attorneys and tort reformers, for example, claim that apologies have "nothing to do with fault" because such an understanding best advances their interests by gaining the benefit of appearing contrite while not exposing wrongdoers to the liability associated with accepting blame. Clarifying these dynamics should contribute to several objectives. Legal agents who understand the uses – and occasionally the abuses – of apologies in civil law should be better equipped to identify deceptive apologies and insist on and negotiate for the meanings they desire. In particular, awareness of these tactics should empower less-privileged victims in their conflicts with sophisticated legal actors who use ambiguities surrounding the substance of apologies to further compound their advantages. I am especially concerned with raising awareness of the deceptive acts of contrition from collectives – often corporations and governments – that appear to suggest reform and redress but that in fact do little to prevent future injury and may even continue to endorse the harmful behavior. These critical views of apologies in civil law should not diminish the potentially profound role that they can play in dispute resolution. Rather than throwing out the baby with the bathwater here, we should recognize the meanings that apologies can convey in civil law, cultivate these meanings, identify where apologies do not mean what they claim to mean, and inform various legal agents of the complex dynamics at work. To achieve this perspective we must maintain a binocular view of both individual and collective aspects of apologies in civil disputes.

This chapter identifies what I consider the most significant issues regarding the role of apologies in civil proceedings and suggests methods for addressing these concerns. Many of the issues salient to apologies in criminal law also apply to civil matters, but here I attempt to identify features of modern civil law – especially in the United States – deserving particular attention. Determining what constitutes a matter of civil rather than criminal law presents questions that invoke a community's underlying social and political views. Rarely are these beliefs obvious or uncontested. Why, for instance, does the U.S. federal government consider marijuana violations criminal offenses while relegating the sorts of wrongdoing that led to the Deepwater Horizon disaster as largely civil matters?[20] Which harms are more serious? Which are more "public"? Lines become still more blurred as restorative justice practices shift the emphasis in criminal law toward conflict resolution and away from punishment. Thankfully, I need not address those issues here other than to consider how the centrality of financial outcomes in civil litigation creates a life for apologies quite different from their existence in criminal matters.

Civil law covers a range of diverse practices. An apology in divorce proceedings differs considerably from a corporation's expressions of remorse for a toxic tort or a bank's admission to misrepresenting assets. I address contrition in civil law in a general manner that allows specialists in respective fields to extrapolate specific applications. Different parties in these varied contexts – whether the injured or the liable, defense or plaintiffs' counsel, or tort-reform legislatures or victim's rights advocates – will approach these dynamics from their respective views, especially as financial incentives color their respective interests. Civil law also complicates the usual one-to-one relationship of an apology from an offender to a victim. Whereas criminal law typically finds a single offender offering apologies to the victims and the state, civil matters present various arrangements beyond two-party litigation. Class actions, for instance, introduce layers of complexity in litigation, and multiparty settlements often require oversight by judges to evaluate the fairness of agreements. This places the state in a rather different role in evaluating apologies in criminal and civil law. I therefore devote considerable attention to collective apologies throughout the following discussions.

A. A Prominent Distinction Between Civil and Criminal Law: Money

Money explicitly structures the existence of apologies in contemporary civil law to a much greater extent than it does in criminal law. Although inequality undoubtedly plays a significant role in contemporary punishment, criminal law does not explicitly recognize financial outcomes as the primary objective of its processes. Law and economics perspectives and restitutive approaches to criminal law might conceive of punishment more like financial transactions, but I suspect that the majority of participants in the criminal justice system do not strictly equate money with justice. Commitments to substantive principles of justice endure even as we appreciate that personal wealth often translates into favorable outcomes in criminal matters, most obviously by one's ability to afford elite defense attorneys. "Buying justice" offends intuitions even if we do little to change the current practice of distributing legal representation on the basis of the ability to pay. In civil law, however, money enjoys a far less conflicted existence as the prize of litigation.

I Was Wrong discussed the importance of shared values for categorical apologies and the difficulty of reaching such agreements within and between pluralistic cultures. I also noted the uncontroversial fact that, for better or for worse, money serves as the prevailing common denominator of value between diverse world views. This is the case in both culture generally and law specifically, and the law and economics movement has refined the ability of legal institutions to convert injuries into financial metrics. Although the thought may seem disconcerting, attorneys have become accustomed to legal handbooks such as *Valuing Children in Litigation: Family and Individual Loss Assessment*. Here we find tables with titles such as "Benefits from a Child to Parents from Ages 19–58 Based on a Child Born in 1977," "Lost Earnings Capacity and Contribution," and "Investment Value of Indirect Costs of Generic and Marginal Children for Working and Non-Working Mothers by Level of Mother's Education."[21] These grim studies determine the legal value of deceased children in the language of U.S. dollars. As courts and settlements routinely reduce the particularities of one's flesh, bone, thoughts, and emotions to a monetary value, it seems as if everything now has a price in civil law. Simmel worried in 1900 that capitalism creates not only a market economy but also a market culture in which "money becomes the central and absolute value."[22] Commodification debates too often swing between rhetorical flourishes, with Marxist "root of all evil" claims countering Randian "root of all good" faith in money and free markets.[23] By classifying the different types of arguments against commodification, distinguishing these issues to the extent possible, and identifying how the normative criteria typically deployed may in fact bootleg pro-market bias into the discourse, I previously argued that critiques of commodification in law face problems of ideology, intractability, and hyperbole.[24] These issues, I find, tend to generate highly partisan reactions. Providing an evenhanded evaluation of the relative costs of commodification against its benefits would require multiple volumes of analysis. I therefore ask readers – to the extent possible – to set aside for the moment normative questions regarding the increasing prominence of commodification in justice systems other than to note how such features give shape to apologies in civil law.[25]

Tendencies toward commodification in law do not develop in isolation. Culture influences law, law influences culture, and Pierre Schlag has rendered any clear separation between law and culture deeply problematic.[26] The inextricable intertwinement of culture, society, politics, and markets creates a feedback loop.[27] Regardless of whether law and economic theories *cause* us to think of injuries in financial terms or merely *reflect* the economic mindset prevalent outside of legal institutions, money exists in both spheres as something of an "ultimate value." This results, in part, because traditionally dominant moral codes founded on conceptions of religious or secular universality fall out of favor in the liberal state. Individualist "rational choice" within marketplaces ascends as the preferred conception of legal agents. Although critics often contest its neutrality and its very presence in certain spheres, money becomes the most widely accepted indicator of value. Financial sensibilities inflect our traditionally noneconomic evaluative concepts. "Responsibility" takes on increasingly monetary connotations and moral trespasses come to be seen as economic injuries. If I wish to admit blame and accept responsibility, I should be mindful that within this culture I may become vulnerable to litigation and economic damages in addition to any moral debt I intend to pay. Even if a litigant seeks primarily moral rather than economic redress, she may seek a cash award because she appreciates that her culture measures significance in dollars. A large award conveys that the courts have taken a claim seriously and speaks most directly to the sorts of cost-benefits analyses that drive policy. In civil law – as in the culture at large – success often becomes synonymous with receiving money. Plaintiffs exercising mercy in this context face Shylockian choices whether to release apologetic civil wrongdoers from their debts.[28]

B. Why We Would Not Expect Apologies in Civil Law

We might expect contrition to play central roles in collectivist cultures that emphasize collaborative conflict resolution, but apologies seem out of place within an adversarial legal system coevolved to fit hand in glove within competitive markets. An apology will look, prima facie, like a concession in such a culture. Law schools train attorneys to argue and advocate. Attorneys build reputations fighting on behalf of their clients; they do not wish to be known for apologetic surrenders in battle.[29] Conciliatory behavior such as what I describe as a categorical apology seems outside the bounds of the adversarial practice. If one wished to apologize, litigation would seem largely unnecessary because parties could resolve the conflict via informal means.

The insurance industry presents another apparent barrier to apologies in civil law. Many activities that carry high risks of causing injuries – consider driving an automobile or practicing medicine – exist within an *insurance culture* that shapes behaviors and expectations around these practices. Any community that relies on automobiles will suffer traffic accidents, and how we respond to resultant injuries says a lot about our social and political beliefs regarding who should bare these costs. In Japan, for instance, a collision might result in both drivers emerging from their vehicles to promptly apologize to each other to affirm social bonds threatened by the accident.[30] In those stressful post-accident moments, the community ties – rather than economic self-interest – tend to take precedence in Japan. Such parties might resort to litigation if the other party does not apologize because the failure to apologize causes an offense deeper than an automotive accident.[31] In the United States, by contrast, we typically emerge from accidents with our insurance papers in hand. My Amica insurance card envelope states in bold letters: "IF AN ACCIDENT HAPPENS: Stay calm. Do not admit liability." Insurance companies have voided policies when the insured provided an unauthorized apology because admissions of blame can violate terms of coverage.[32] Although voiding coverage because of an apology is rare and courts have been more likely to allow insurers to void coverage when post-accident apologies not only admit fault but also offer to pay for the damages, most of us do not appreciate the legal nuances of our coverage. We only see the prominent "do not admit liability command" on the papers in our hand.[33] At the scene of the accident with potential damages unknown and terms of coverage in fine print somewhere in our files back home, apologizing feels risky.

Physicians face similar uncertainties with their liability insurance. As of 2003, United Medical Protection's Australian Medical Insurance Limited policy warned that physicians "must not make any admission, offer or promise in relation to any claim covered by this policy without our prior written consent."[34] If breaching this vague and broad provision might leave the doctor uninsured, offering an apology to a victim for a mistake amounts to a serious risk. Indeed, within the current climate of tort reform, doctors may feel more eager to please their insurers than their patients. The insurance culture, nested within the culture of adversarial litigation, appears – and we will add a layer to this momentarily – to systematically discourage wrongdoers from accepting responsibility for their actions.

Moreover, apologies seem professionally out of place and character for attorneys. As noted, we train attorneys to advocate, not to concede. Admissions of guilt run counter to the very spirit of the litigator's attitude. An attorney who suggests that her client should apologize risks appearing disloyal and offending client expectations: I come to you for legal advice, not moral guidance.[35] If the conflict has reached the stage in which the plaintiff seeks legal counsel, the defendant has probably already denied wrongdoing. Defense attorneys face an uphill struggle explaining why apologizing offers an effective strategy in the context of previous denials. If the attorney is not careful, ineffective counsel in advising a client to take the unorthodox path of apologizing can prove disastrous for her reputation and raise claim of legal malpractice.[36] The very idea of apologizing seems not only against the grain but also downright risky for defense attorneys.

Plaintiffs' attorneys have an especially significant practical disincentive: a fulfilling apology for a client may undermine their fees. Consider the role of contingency fee arrangements in which attorneys take on matters under the condition that they will receive a percentage of their clients' winnings rather than a flat fee or an hourly rate.[37] Few plaintiffs' attorneys, in my experience, will be motivated by the prospect of receiving one-third of an apology.[38] Contingency fee arrangements enfranchise litigants who otherwise could not afford access to the courts, but they also encourage attorneys to steer clients toward economic remedies. Contingency fee arrangements in part account for how readily the law can process so many seemingly noneconomic injuries into pecuniary awards. The more plaintiffs' attorneys can process injuries of various kinds into financial awards, the more they stand to profit. The larger the economic award, the more the plaintiffs' counsel earn. In this regard, attorneys have economic incentives to avoid conciliatory behaviors that deflate hostilities, wind down conflicts, and reduce financial settlements.[39] Apologies risk siphoning off some of the value of legal work into noneconomic spheres. A settlement proposal in a case like that of Paula Jones, for instance, might offer $750,000 plus a certain kind of apology or alternatively $1,000,000 and no apology. If her attorneys stand to receive one-third of the award, we can appreciate why her first legal team quit when they learned that she demanded the apology from Clinton. If Jones sought only an apology and refused money, she would need to either find pro bono representation or cover the legal fees herself.

Apologies from collectives face additional barriers. Beyond potential insurance and fiduciary duties preventing admissions of wrongdoing, some groups feel under siege by legal attackers. Walmart was sued 4,851 times in 2000 alone, about 13 claims per day.[40] Social psychologists provide a litany of reasons why what William White calls "organizational men" will descend into unapologetic groupthink when embroiled in protracted conflicts.[41] Leaders unconsciously amplify information that corroborates their justification while attacking or ignoring evidence suggesting that their group deserves blame. As conflicts endure over time and leaders prejudge incoming claims as adding to the mountain of frivolous litigation, the group reinforces its position as innocent.[42] Members of the group rally around their perceptions of the just as justified. Individuals feel their own identities and justifications entwined with those of the group. Members seek and share evidence corroborating their justification, creating an echo chamber reinforcing their views. They uncritically internalize supporting information while attacking anything dissonant with their world view.[43] Emotions rather than cognitive reflection drive most of this process, with those most informed and invested in issues often being the most biased.[44] Neuroscientific research piles on studies suggesting that "reward circuits" light up when we suppress information that conflicts with what we believe.[45] For group leaders – or individuals generally – to recognize the need to apologize, mountains of counterevidence or an emotional experience powerful enough to overwrite existing commitments are often required.[46] Even if one person has a change of heart, peers, superiors, and institutional momentum will pull her back to old views. Placing these obstacles in the context of potentially heavy exposure to liability by admitting wrongdoing, we can see why corporations have been historically reluctant to apologize.

Considering all of this, one would not expect to find many apologies within such a legal environment unless contrition – rather counterintuitively – conferred a strategic advantage. Increasingly, apologies do seem to confer a benefit in civil litigation. This tactical use of remorse, I argue, results in part from an apology's ability to appear as something more than tactical. One of the primary sources of an apology's economic value, in other words, lies in its tenuous identity as something that cannot be bought.

C. The Economic Value of the Semblance of Noneconomic Value: The Enduring Desire for More than Money

Consider Bailey's demand for an apology from Ford and the significance this held for her. Bailey did "not want her case to stand merely for someone who wanted a monetary award," and the apology – presumably in addition to the information released as a condition of the settlement – satisfied her desire for something more than a financial transaction. The apology spoke to the *moral* nature of her claim, which resonates with the common intuition that apologies provide value along different registers than a cash payment. If a cheating lover refused to apologize but instead offered money to compensate for the harm suffered because of her infidelity, the betrayed would likely take offense because the offender appears to fail to understand the nature of the harm and the appropriate means to redress those harms. She would cross between two distinct realms of value. Despite living in a world in which we seem comfortable with an increasing range of goods entering the stream of commerce, we still maintain some sense of the separation – even if only as a form of nostalgia – between commodities and goods that should not be bought and sold. In part because of their historical associations with traditions of repentance and thus our deepest spiritual values, apologies strike us as one of those ceremonies that convey meaning in ways that money cannot.[47]

Scott Atran and Jeremy Ginges document how this dynamic unfolds in the Palestinian conflict, the "world's great symbolic knot."[48] For many of the thousands of Palestinians and Israelis interviewed, sacred values oriented their views of various resolutions to the conflict. Suggestions that these values could be bartered away for money – "sweetening the pot" by supplementing a compromise regarding land with substantial cash payments, for example – caused respondents to recoil from negotiations as if they had been asked to sell their children: "[T]he greater the monetary incentive involved in the deal, the greater the disgust from respondents."[49] Contrary to rational choice economic approaches that might undermine negotiations regarding issues so fundamental to "who we are and who we want to be," Atran and Ginges found that apologies from the opposition would make both Palestinians and Israelis more inclined to accept settlements. Deputy chairman of Hamas Mousa Abu Mazook, for example, rejected financial incentives to settle, angrily objecting, "No, we do not sell ourselves for any amount." The possibility of an Israeli apology for the 1948 catastrophe produced a more favorable reaction: "Yes, an apology is important, as a beginning. It's not enough because our houses and land were taken away from us and something has to be done about that."[50] If an apology can have more significance than "any amount" of money in such a conflict, we can appreciate its potentially deep spiritual resonances.

A belief that apologies transcend money goes some way toward making sense of the economic value of contrition in civil law. Consider the 2009 study conducted by a team at the Nottingham School of Economics claiming that even the most transparently tactical apologies conferred rather astonishing benefits to wrongdoers. In this controlled experiment, eBay sellers responded to disgruntled customers with either a boilerplate e-mail apology that did not accept blame or a cash payment. According to their findings, 45 percent of the aggrieved parties withdrew their complaints after receiving the electronic apology. Only 23 percent withdrew their complaints after being offered cash payment to withdraw their grievance.[51] Attempting to explain why customers would be moved by a "cheap talk" e-mail denying responsibility and obviously sent for the purpose of convincing them to retract their negative comments, researchers speculated that "apologizing triggers a heuristic to forgive that is hard to overcome rationally."[52] They concluded: "[A]pologies are a powerful and at the same time cheap tool to influence customers' behavior."[53] Notice the dramatic conclusion suggested by the study: even when we recognize that an apology is provided to manipulate us, we still feel a strong urge to give the apologizer what she wants because of the deep roots of reconciliation traditions that these strategies manipulate. This brings to mind situations in which someone offers an obviously poor excuse for her behavior, yet we reflexively respond with conciliatory clichés such as "don't worry about it." Whether from a desire to minimize social conflict or a sense that it would be somehow impolite not to release the transgressor from our negative evaluations, studies suggest that in some respects our impulse to reconcile runs deeper than our ability to rationally evaluate whether reconciliation is deserved.[54] Other studies have found, rather incredibly, that we disapprove of victims who do not accept even "unconvincing" apologies.[55] Within some contexts, in other words, apologetic language confers credit and triggers responses that probably should not withstand close evaluation.

Civil litigators have begun to internalize these points. What was once considered a radical strategy of the Toro Company – the subject of many personal injury claims given the dangerousness of lawn equipment – and the Lexington, Kentucky Veteran's Affairs Hospital has inspired many industries seeking to reduce legal damages. According to Toro's general counsel, their traditional "litigate everything" attitude produced a pattern over hundreds of claims: Toro would spend between $60,000 and $100,000 on legal fees in typical cases and then settle just before trial for about $15,000.[56] Management had an idea: "Why not take that $15,000 and maybe a little more and quit making these defense lawyers rich?"[57] Toro decided to institute a practice in which they would send a "good listener" to the injured person's home along with a team of investigators to document the injury and details regarding the person's financial situation. The representative would then offer sympathy and a settlement offer without admitting guilt and would cloak the exchange behind a mandatory confidentiality agreement.[58] This strategy saved Toro approximately $54,000 per claim, $900,000 in annual settlement costs, and $1.8 million in annual liability insurance premiums.[59] Toro estimates saving more than $75 million between 1991 and 1999 thanks to this strategy.[60] At least one plaintiff's attorney took issue with these tactics: "Although Toro tries to come off as though alternative dispute resolution is good for everybody.... They are not nice guys.... They will leave you with four cents on the dollar.... Watch out for those guys. They are real snakes in the grass."[61]

In part as a result of Toro's return rate, academic and corporate interest in the economic value of apologies in litigation exploded. Consider a few of the claims in this emerging field. Robbennolt found that receiving an apology that accepted responsibility increased the likelihood that a respondent would accept a settlement offer by 21 percent.[62] In the area of medical malpractice,[63] Michael Woods claims that the "likelihood of a lawsuit falls by 50-percent when an apology is offered and the details of a medical error are disclosed immediately."[64] In one study, 91 percent of cases in which the defendants offered an apology settled, whereas only 38 percent settled when the defense did not apologize.[65] Given the high stakes of tort reform and the powerful interests behind reducing civil damages awards, the minutia of these dynamics become objects of research – all the way to evaluating the optimal facial structures for those delivering corporate apologies for various kinds of damages.[66] A 2009 study led by a Cornell economist found that "safe apology" legislation for medical malpractice cases could "increase the number of settlements by 15% within 3 to 5 years of adopting the laws."[67] Under pressure from tort-reform lobbyists seeking to capitalize on the benefits of apologies without facing the legal risks of admitting blame, lawmakers have been busy rewriting evidentiary laws.[68] It can feel at times like "apology mania."

We should temper our enthusiasm. Robbennolt's empirical studies find that only apologies that accept responsibility increased the likelihood that parties will accept settlement offers.[69] Expressions of sympathy, by contrast, served primarily to increase uncertainty about an offer.[70] Although apologies might help settle claims already in motion, it is not clear that such a strategy does not invite more legitimate claims: "I had not thought of suing you, but now that you have apologized, perhaps I should discuss this with my attorney." This leads one author to doubt that preemptively disclosing medical errors will reduce legal costs: "[T]he vast majority of patients who sustain medical injury never sue" because they fail "to recognize their condition or attribute it to an external cause."[71] Given the "huge reservoir of potential claims," the paper calculated a 95-percent chance that full disclosure policies would increase the number of claims, a "60% chance that comprehensive disclosure of severe injuries would at least double the annual number of claims nationwide, and a 33% chance that volume would increase by threefold or more."[72] Any number of independent variables could have contributed to Toro's positive results, such as particularly effective negotiators who exercised good judgment regarding when to try the apology strategy and when to adopt more adversarial attitudes. Meanwhile, the University of Michigan Health System claims it saves $2 million per year because of its Disclosure, Apology, and Offer program. Stanford University's hospitals claim $3.2 million in savings. Seven Massachusetts hospitals launched a similar program in 2012.[73] An administrator from a participating Massachusetts hospital explained that they were "impressed with the evidence coming out of the University of Michigan and Stanford that suggests they have achieved a more satisfying experience for patients and providers, and lowered costs." The state's three largest insurers funded the program.[74] Anyone arguing that the meaning of these dynamic and ambiguous trends is obvious is either not paying close enough attention or trying to sell something.

To review, disincentives deter both plaintiffs and their attorneys from pursuing apologies as a primary remedy, yet this very rarity of acts of contrition in law appears to increase their value. In what can seem like a sea of cold economic self-interest, an apology appears like a beacon of compassion. For those who seek specifically moral redress for their injuries or experience discomfort with the idea of converting their suffering into financial damages, apologies can resonate loudly along a different register of meaning. We adjudicate a variety of claims in civil proceedings, and something is lost in the translation when the law struggles to reduce such a range of injuries to a monetary common denominator. Within this context, an apology can offer distinct kinds of value for those who seek more than money from their civil actions. Here is the irony. As we find with many goods described as priceless – consider a master work of art – the very notion that something has value beyond price renders it very expensive. Because apologies seem spiritually rich, confessional, even sacred, they convey near magical power in litigation. The sense that an apology within law conveys exceptional noneconomic significance, in other words, creates an especially valuable commodity. Recall Bailey's settlement agreement with Ford. Three corporate defense attorneys – who might each bill upwards of $1,250 per hour – travel to Bailey's bedside to deliver undisclosed apologetic language. This was enough to convince the paralyzed claimant that the settlement was not just "about the money."[75] Ford settled her case – along with numerous others – on the day of the apology. Again, what appears from a plaintiff's perspective like the magical key unlocking the hearts of corporate self-interest looks like an effective cost-saving strategy to the defense.

The picture of evil corporations fleecing innocent plaintiffs by twisting sacred traditions of repentance is a caricature. To what extent are injured parties duped by sophisticated legal strategies that parlay the semblance of moral substance into economic advantage? Many victims understand the dynamics. Sometimes victims seem to proclaim the moral value of the apology they receive even when they know that it conveys little other than money and appearances. Richard Wolffe claims that attitudes have changed over recent decades in the context of reparation for Holocaust survivors. Whereas survivors initially shunned compensation as "blood money," Wolffe found that "now the consensus among people who've suffered this kind of thing is you have to pay money. Without the money there's no sincere apology."[76] "There's something about the process of compensation that we kind of expect in today's society," Wolffe explained. "We expect to be paid for our suffering."[77] The plaintiffs' bar, a powerful lobby in its own right, cashes in on these evolving sentiments.

The media throws gas on these ambiguities. After the 1960s, corporations enjoyed less deference as because their image as do-no-wrong job creating post-war demigods became suspect.[78] Environmental disasters, in particular, required executives to engage in crisis management. Corporate apologies came into fashion, providing viewers with spectacular television as industry giants bowed before the disfigured poor. Reporters relish calling for apologies from the powerful, perhaps as means of channeling their reformist impulses after funds for investigative reporting dried up. Media figures get two bites at the moralizing apple, calling for the apology and then evaluating it with questionable and undeservedly confident standards.[79] Such good versus evil narratives seem to only increase confusion about the meanings actually conveyed by apologies or not.[80]

In the subsequent sections I hope to render these dynamics a bit more explicit as they play out in various civil contexts. My primary objectives are twofold. First, I want to empower legal agents with the understanding of the meanings of apologies in civil law. I want them – particularly those who already suffer from various disadvantages in civil law – to be aware of the sorts of significance that apologies can convey and to measure the apologies they seek with the apologies they receive. Second, I aim to demonstrate how civil litigation can and should cultivate the meanings associated with categorical apologies.

CHAPTER FIVE

A Practical Framework for Evaluating Apologies in Civil Contexts

A. Guiding Questions: How Should We Evaluate Apologies in the Civil Context?

Apologies in civil and criminal law share many features. Notice a few distinctions. First, in criminal matters the state – for better or for worse – typically holds the authority to determine how much punishment an offender deserves and how an apology does or does not impact that punishment. Even though contemporary justifications for punishment rest on deeply conflicted foundations and lack coherent objectives, the state dominates the discussion regarding justifications for punishment. I argue that the *state* should apply apology reduction in criminal cases. In civil matters, by contrast, injured parties typically have exclusive control over the sorts of meanings they seek from an apology, whether they believe the offender satisfied those expectations and how those meanings or lack of meanings impact the dispute. A seriously injured party in a civil matter can decide not to pursue legal recourse if she finds the offender sufficiently apologetic, but in criminal cases the state will usually prosecute its case regardless of the victim's sentiments concerning remorse or forgiveness. Just as the state's discretion in criminal matters presents various challenges and opportunities, I hope to identify various points where injured parties should be aware of their options as well as the potential advantages and disadvantages of such freedom. In general, I hope the following discussions allow victims to understand better what they seek from apologies and to evaluate the apologies they receive accordingly. The *four corners of apologies* offer touchstones throughout this process: Did the offender explain what happened with sufficient detail, accept blame as deserved, not reoffend, and provide appropriate redress?

Second, civil matters require systematic attention to collective apologies. For reasons mentioned earlier, contemporary legal systems tend to consider harms caused by collectives such as corporations to be civil rather than criminal matters. Although criminal law addresses various kinds of coordinated actions between individuals, it typically views its jurisdiction as one-on-one situations in which it can attribute blame to a single individual or a number of single individuals working in concert. As organizations cause harm and blame becomes more difficult to pin on individuals, legal systems usually classify these injuries as civil matters. This may overstate it, but when the wealthy cause harm in groups, we consider the offense civil and levy fines against the organization as such; when the poor form groups and commit harm, we attribute blame to individuals and charge them individually. Compare, for instance, how we typically punish members of a drug cartel (individual and criminal charges) with how we fine illegal activities of pharmaceutical companies (collective and civil charges). For those skipping to these chapters seeking abbreviated guidance regarding collective apologies in civil matters, I recommend reviewing part II of *I Was Wrong* in addition to this book. I see no way around it: collective apologies are more difficult to understand, to deliver, and to evaluate than individual apologies. The following sections attempt to flag the most significant issues regarding collective apologies in civil law.

Standing and consensus require particular attention in the context of collective apologies in civil matters. I address standing with regard to who accepts blame, but consensus-related concerns pervade the ensuing discussions. I argued in *I Was Wrong* that groups of people can categorically apologize if each member of the group *individually* satisfies each required element, agreeing on the factual record, admitting shared culpability, identifying and committing to the same moral principles, finding the victim's suffering legitimate and proportionate, expressing categorical regret, undergoing parallel reform, providing commensurate redress, and so on. Individual contributions to the apology may differ, for example because members accept blame for different aspects of the wrongdoing, but their apologies will aggregate into a coherent narrative for the group expressing shared commitments to personal and institutional reform. Many obstacles can impede this process, but the problem of consensus deserves special attention. Return to the Ford rollover example. Imagine Ford's attorneys provide something like a categorical apology to Bailey and admit blame for her accident and describe in detail the moral failings that caused executives to choose profits over safety. Setting aside for a moment issues regarding standing – how much value should we place in apologies from attorneys who may have had little if any role in the proximate cause of the injuries? – we should ask the following: How do the apologies represent the actual beliefs and attitudes of members of the organization? Imagine Ford's president holds a "buyer beware" libertarian view, privately rejecting "all of this touchy-feely political correctness apology nonsense" and maintaining that those buying its mid-priced vehicles should not expect luxury-level safety. Suppose a junior executive talks her into the economic benefits of apologizing. Further imagine that a little more than half of Ford's leadership supports an apology and a little less than half does not believe they have done anything wrong. Suppose the anti-apology minority includes the obvious heir to Ford's presidency. Some who support the apology feel grave remorse for their role in the accidents and actively seek jobs elsewhere because they disagree with the values of the heir. One rising star objected all along to Ford's failure to take proper safety precautions. She refuses to apologize and tarnish her reputation because she believes that she did everything within her power and, in her view, all of the blame should fall on the chief executives. Several of the most junior executives do their best to remain silent to avoid internal political repercussions from aligning with the losing side in the developing feud thereby damaging prospects for promotion. Imagine Ford's leadership publicly blames line workers, mechanics, or safety consultants such that everyone knows that executives intend for the blame to fall on their underlings when they announce that "*we* must do a better job." Imagine some attorneys going off script when apologizing to victims, placing blame where they think it belongs or where they think the victims want to see it placed. Meanwhile, laborers know executives ordered them to sacrifice safety for profit. A whistle-blower apologizes to the media, explaining that she "knew following orders was wrong." She releases incriminating documents that undermine the narrative constructed by executives and their crisis management consultants. Back channel discussions in the office sometimes leak to the media. The president retires to "spend more time with family." Her successor adopts an even less apologetic approach to the ongoing rollover litigation. She undoes much of the remorse provided across private settlement agreements. She moves on after three years to be replaced by the rising star junior executive who had been the loudest voice objecting to Ford's safety failures all along. She issues a new apology, excoriating and placing all of the blame on her predecessors. She undertakes an aggressive program to reform safety protocols, but a recession limits her ability to implement the program and she is replaced after losing favor with board members and shareholders.

What should a victim make of such a convoluted yet typical timeline of collective apologies? In most cases, victims are unaware of conflicts beneath the façade of collective apologies, including disagreements about what happened, who deserves blame, and what should be done about it. Lack of consensus may have led to intentional ambiguity in the apologies. The views of some executives may remain inscrutable even to their colleagues because they played their cards close. Whether I am a rollover victim or simply considering buying an automobile, the more I know about the consensus underlying Ford's apologies, the better I am able to read its institutional moral compass. The larger the organization – consider Bill Clinton's apology on behalf of "the international community" for the Rwandan genocide – the more complex the issues of consensus. Even if we do not expect consensus, how much agreement is enough? Rather than asserting some percentage of agreement suffices to grant definitive authority to apologize for an organization, it seems better to hold both the majority and minority positions in view. If only a slight majority support an apology, this is important information. We also better understand the dynamics if we appreciate the relative power, composition, and trends in those camps. If a minority contains a few powerful operatives who appear to be gaining support, we should nuance our understanding accordingly. Simplifications in this regard can be deceptive and dangerous.

Membership also raises questions. Who exactly belongs to the group apologizing: Only current executives who had some authority over the process? Executives hired after the relevant decisions had already been made? Any living person who has worked for Ford or any of its subsidiaries and contractors? If those primarily responsible for the injuries have moved on to other organizations, does a consensus require their input and acceptance of blame? What if Ford fires those who refuse to endorse the apology? These questions help us appreciate how problems of consensus often defy simple declarations such as "Ford Apologizes to Victims." As we see throughout this book and its predecessor, apologies operate in gray areas. Collective apologies darken these gray areas, and seeing into their significance requires two virtues often hard to come by: evenhandedness and patience. I now take the third pass through the elements of apologetic meaning, this time as relevant to civil matters. Hopefully this new context justifies any redundancies, and readers' eyes have become focused to see the issues in this landscape before I point them out.

1. Has the Civil Offender Corroborated the Factual Record?

As with criminal matters, we should ask whether the offender explains what she did with an appropriate degree of specificity to establish a record of the events salient to the injury. "What happened" may be obvious, but the victim desires a public admission confirming her account. In other cases the story may be opaque to the victim: You defrauded me, but how exactly did this scheme work? How many others did you harm? Did you know that you were selling a worthless product or that you were poisoning my children? Apologies in civil contexts can answer these questions. Vague assertions that "mistakes were made" will typically not provide the explanations offenders seek.

Those who volunteer information regarding adverse events early in the process gain credibility, especially if such evidence would have been difficult to obtain through the discovery process; those who concede damaging facts only after they can no longer deny them lose credibility. If the dispute reaches legal action, offenders have probably withheld information and victims have brought the claim in part to compel discovery and require the offender to provide information. Refusals or delays disclosing information justifiably create doubts regarding underlying motivations. If Ford had publicly admitted the dangers as soon as they learned of a pattern of rollovers rather than waiting for plaintiffs to force their hand, this could have bespoken intentions to reform and provide redress. Instead, their apology looks like a legal tactic. Civil offenders who admit everything by "getting it all out" as early in the process as possible establish credibility and set the tone of the apologetic narrative. Institutional offenders who claim in their apologies that they are unaware of the harmful activities can further undermine their image because such admissions imply inadequate supervision and negligent leadership.[1]

Having said that, civil harms caused by collectives can present challenging factual investigations because webs of causation weave throughout the organization such that even leaders of the group may be unclear as to exactly how they came to be causing such harms. Leaders may not know of the wrongdoing within their organization's past or present and only learn the extent of a problem after reading reports from investigators. Just as we would not entrust criminal defendants to gather information about their own cases, civil offenders gain credibility by allowing external reviewers to access to the relevant information. Establishing a record may take time to conduct research and institutional self-study. Documenting large-scale harm over a prolonged period – consider Chisso Corporation's pollution of Minamata Bay – can occupy teams of historians. Many modern products bring together pieces from around the world. Determining exactly what caused the problem and where blame falls can require technical investigations. Even after congressional hearings, Ford and Firestone debated what caused the combination of vehicle and tire to malfunction and tried to shift blame to each other. "We've spent nine exhaustive months looking at the issue, sharing the information with Ford," said Firestone executive, "But when we ask Ford: 'What have you been doing on the vehicle side? What information will you share with us from the vehicle standpoint?' it's like butting your head up against a brick wall.'" Such adversarial dynamics over complex products and organizational structures make it especially challenging to learn what happened, leaving the person behind the wheel an easy target for blame.[2]

Many of the cases discussed throughout these sections require technical findings to identify fault in the entangled chain of events. Whether investigating Ford rollovers, Chisso pollution, thalidomide deaths and deformities, or fraudulent banking practices, lone plaintiffs will rarely have sufficient resources to undertake this work. This can create David versus Goliath dynamics dramatized by *A Civil Action* and *Erin Brockovich* in which victims find themselves outgunned by legions of corporate defense attorneys doing everything in their power to obscure facts.[3] Such battles can threaten the very existence of small practices, and class actions can forge alliances that even the sides a bit. Government investigations can also help undertake discovery, establishing a public record on which individual plaintiffs can bring meritorious claims. Some prosecutors insist, for this reason, that settlements include public admissions of facts and blame uncovered by government investigations.[4]

Cataloguing a full record may no longer be possible, for example because the names and stories of many victims of the African slave trade are lost to history. Here we can combine the desire to recognize victims and their suffering with the realization that the possibilities for some apologetic meanings expire as time passes. Some vectors of significance die with the victims or offenders. If someone goes to her grave with a secret regarding what actually happened, no apology from the living can resurrect that particular form of meaning. Plaintiffs should be especially wary of representatives assuring that they will "get to the bottom of what happened," yet they never actually report sufficient findings or provide a schedule for when they will report such facts.

Here we can also appreciate the importance of identifying victims other than the claimant, as this notifies others of potential claim. If the victim is deceased – perhaps even long deceased in cases of harms that occurred long ago – identifying as much of the class of victims as possible draws heirs and community members into the discourse.

Some civil offenders confess certain facts only to later deny them, perhaps because they initially spoke too freely and now legal counsel denies earlier admissions. In the hypothetical extension of the preceding Ford example, we see the danger of collectives retracting earlier accounts of events as leadership and other dynamics change over time. We could imagine such a scenario in the United States if a Democratic administration provided an apology for any number of wrongs only to have a subsequent Republican administration adopt a "No Apology" – the title of Mitt Romney's autobiography – attitude purging admissions of wrongdoing from the record.[5] The Japanese government's undoing of its apology for its use of Korean sex slaves during World War II provides a particularly shocking example of this dynamic, with the prime minister undermining previous expressions of remorse by claiming that there was "no evidence to prove that there was coercion" of the wartime sex slaves.[6] History, in this sense, can be temporary. Such telling and un-telling of wrongs can cause renewed pain for victims and they should maintain awareness of the tenuousness of such historical accounts.

Establishing a factual record will often include explanations of the offenders' mental states at the time of offense, including accounts of the intentions motivating the harmful actions. When collectives cause harm, this may include various forms of internal documentation recording the process and deliberations leading to the offense. Minutes of board meetings, written communications relevant to the decision-making process, accounts of relevant conversations, and other materials can provide insight into the facts and intentions underlying the harmful behavior. Victims should be wary of offenders who explain harms as unforeseeable or unintentional when consequences of their actions seem predictable.

Apologies within legal contexts have an advantage over more informal expressions of remorse thanks to the fact-finding mechanisms native to legal disputes. Although a battle in its own right in litigation wars, the civil discovery process has evolved to establish procedures to create a record of information salient to the claims at issue. Whether a contract dispute between two individuals or an intergenerational toxic tort, an optimal discovery process uncovers *what really happened* without overreaching. This can include a wide range of information and media such as incriminating photos and e-mails. Chisso's attempt to suppress photos of its victims by beating photographer W. Eugene Smith offers an egregious example of excluding information from public review. In large-scale injuries, such investigations can be immensely time-consuming and expensive. They also may require research expertise. Gathering such information can extend beyond the reach of individual victims, making class actions or interdisciplinary commissions often better equipped to establish a record.

By getting out the facts prior to or during the legal discovery process, the offender builds a foundation on which the remaining aspects of her apology stand. As discussed in the following section, legislative efforts to exclude evidence provided in the context of an apology seems particularly misguided. If I offer an apology explaining that I deserve blame, why do I move to exclude this information from the legal process? If I explain in detail what happened and why I deserve blame during settlement negotiations but later deny that I ever said this or move to render what I said inadmissible, my victims should understand that I will revise that story subject to my interests. Ford might privately admit to Bailey, for instance, that leaders intentionally decided to compromise safety to increase profits after conducting a cost-benefit analysis and that they took precautions not to document this process so that it would not work against them in future litigation. If Bailey then refused the settlement offer, they could claim publicly that they did not foresee the risks while seeking to suppress anything they said to Bailey.

If Bailey accepted the offer and agreed to a confidential settlement, she would not know if Ford would have turned on her by adopting a "deny everything" strategy had she insisted on a trial. Whether a confidential settlement agreement protects the facts or they trickle out through contentious litigation, either of those scenarios differ from what we should expect from a categorical apology: a voluntary explanation of the salient facts that does not limit the apology's audience because of the offender's desire to conceal her wrongdoing.[7] If the victim seeks public disclosure of the record at issue for various reasons, she should evaluate the apology received accordingly and review confessions veiled by confidentiality agreements with appropriate skepticism.

Finally, victims hoping their legal actions will create a public record fostering reform should attend to the terms of agreements, lest they miss the sort of clause that Facebook inserted into its settlement with the Federal Trade Commission for failing to protect the privacy of its users: Facebook "expressly denies the allegations set forth in the complaint."[8] Attorneys negotiate such clauses, and defendants will often trade them for larger restitution payments: "I'm offering X but I'll pay 2X if I can deny all allegations." Victims should be clear about their objectives here: Do they seek maximum payout for themselves, or do they want the offender to admit facts and accept blame for this claim and others?[9]

2. Has the Civil Offender Accepted Blame?
The Fundamentals of Individual and Collective Blame in Civil Matters

The acceptance of blame constitutes a core meaning of apologies. It also presents some of the most complex challenges, especially when applied to groups that commit mass injuries and in which tenuous chains of command obscure moral networks. As subsequent sections explain, powerful forces go to great lengths to compound and benefit from these confusions in civil law. *I Was Wrong* devoted considerable space to debates regarding collective responsibility, for instance the extent to which it makes sense to blame an organization such as Ford or Goldman Sachs *as organizations* rather than distributing culpability to individuals within the organization. Pettigrove explains it well: "[W]hile it makes sense to speak of a collective as an *agent*, it does not make sense to speak of a collective as a *person*."[10] Apologies from organizations therefore raise issues distinct from apologies from persons. I will not revisit those debates in any detail here, but I find these questions immensely important given the increasing role of institutions in our interconnected lives and the massive harms that institutions can cause.

Compelling reasons point toward holding collectives responsible for civil harms. We commonly speak as if collectives deserve blame and praise, as I did earlier gathering the culpability of all of its employees into an assertion that Ford – rather than particular decision makers within the organization – caused the injuries. Leftists in particular like to attribute responsibility to non-individuals, partly because of their sympathy toward arguments for structural causation – Blame Capitalism! – and because within such a world view corporations stand as the fountainhead of so many social ills. Even those on the right who recite the absolute inviolability of "individual responsibility" help themselves to notions of collective blame when they speak of "The Government" or "The Liberal Media" as the proximate cause of various negative phenomena. A practical argument also looms large: collectives such as corporations and governments have deeper pockets than individuals.

By holding such groups responsible we can tap their resources for redress. When we speak of collective blame in the context of civil law, however, we should not lose sight of a few key points.

Most basically, a categorically apologetic civil offender accepts that the injury is her fault. She does not offer mere sympathy for the harm, nor does she view herself as an innocent or even heroic person "taking responsibility" for solving problems not of her making. Rather, and in accordance with commonsense notions of proximate causation, she admits to unjustifiably causing the harm. This does not require her to concede guilt for every exaggerated claim against her, and in many cases it will be important to clarify which actors deserve blame for which harms. Ford and Bridgestone, for example, deserve blame for distinct roles in causing the injuries.

The expectation that wrongdoers should accept blame seems obvious, yet we commonly find remarkably stubborn refusals to admit fault. A group of leading British bankers claimed that they provided a "profound and unqualified apology" after the 2008 financial crisis while offering three hours of testimony explaining why they were not to blame. It took Grünenthal Pharmaceuticals sixty years to offer its first self-described apology for the death and birth defects it caused thousands of children with its anti-morning sickness drug thalidomide, but even then Grünenthal admitted no fault for causing the harms.[11] Coca-Cola paid $156 million to settle a class of discrimination claims, all the while admitting no fault. As Jonathan Cohen puts it, corporations "don't pay that kind of money when they are innocent."[12]

Wrongdoers sometimes claim that no one deserves blame because the harm was somehow accidental or unintentional. Too many historical examples demonstrate how wrongdoers bury villainous intentions deep within faceless institutional forces to deflect blame away from themselves and into faceless institutions or what Werner Herzog describes as the "overwhelming and collective murder" of nature. The soldier claims she did not intend genocide. The executive claims that she did not will the deaths. Consider what some described as Lloyd Blankfein's apology for Goldman Sachs' role in the 2008 banking crisis: "While we regret that we participated in the market euphoria and failed to raise a responsible voice, we are proud of the way our firm managed the risk it assumed on behalf of our clients before and during the financial crisis."[13] Blankfein's statement of regret for "participating in market euphoria" seems especially galling because Goldman Sachs led the charge into subprime mortgages and their actions were a *primary cause* of the collapse.[14] Matt Taibbi provides this analogy for Goldman's conversion of high-risk loans into AAA-rated investments: "Imagine a meat company that bred ten billion rats, fattened them on trash and sewage, ground their bodies into chuck, and then sold it all as grade-A ground beef to McDonald's and Burger King, right under the noses of the USDA." Goldman's actions, according to Taibbi, are "exactly the same thing, only with debt instead of food. We're eating it, they're counting the money."[15] Goldman profited – billions by some estimates – from flooding the market with these toxic assets. Goldman enjoyed these winnings in part because it bet against the products it sold to others. Blankfein's regret for "participating in market euphoria" makes it sound as if a tsunami washed over the banking ecosystem, sweeping up his institution in its rising tides. By his account the financial crisis sounds like a natural disaster: unforeseeable, beyond our control, and leaving no one to blame. The record indicates the opposite, as Goldman Sachs foresaw the market's volatility, threw gas on it, sold highly combustible products while fire-proofing its own assets, and then collected on its fire insurance. Those who grew rich from this system look rather suspicious when they help themselves to Marxist claims of structural victimization as they attempt to deny their personal responsibility. In the same sentence that Blankfein deflects blame, he expresses pride for "the way our firm managed the risk" for our clients, bespeaking shocking insensitivity to the downstream consequences for those who lost their jobs, homes, and life savings in part as a result of Blankfein's actions.[16]

Because we view those who intend to harm us as the most culpable and those who do not intend to cause harm as less so, another common strategy denies culpable intentions by casting the harms as accidental. Determining the mental states of offenders at the time of the offense, however, often proves difficult. Most wrongdoers take advantage of our inability to read their minds, spinning any evidence that might suggest plausible deniability. Some will rationalize themselves into believing that they did not intend to cause harm even though they engaged in blatantly hurtful activities, claiming that "we did not mean to harm anyone" even when this obviously belies the facts.

Intentions become still more opaque when speaking of collectives. When referring to collective intentions, do we identify an aggregation of the mental states of individuals or something located within the institution as such and irreducible to members?[17] Did Ford, as a collective rather than as a few individuals, intend to sacrifice safety for profit? Did Chisso Corporation, as an institution rather than as a collection of individuals, intend to poison its neighbors? Should we, in a normative sense, view collectives as if they possess mental states even if that view seems metaphysically suspect?[18] I will not consider these issues other than to notice how they inflect civil apologies from collectives. Individuals typically do not articulate their intentions to cause civil harms – "I am going to defraud these people" – because they usually need not issue directives to themselves. In addition, they know enough to keep such thoughts private. Evidence of various sorts may betray their assertions that they did not intend to cause harm, but typically investigators must piece together implicit clues to construct an account of the offender's mental states. Institutions, however, often outline their principles and objectives in plans, charters, minutes, and other statements of objectives to coordinate efforts of multiple actors. If we learn that Goldman Sachs leadership knew their actions could harm others but would likely lead to great profits with little risk for the firm, it becomes increasingly difficult to describe the consequences as accidental.

Collective intentions can be even more inscrutable than individual motivations. Within organizations individuals may hold conflicting intentions, with some deviously scheming to profit by causing suffering while others in the group remain ignorant of the potential consequences or work tirelessly to prevent these consequences. Some individual members may experience a variety of intentions, some days being unaware of potential consequences, some days working to avoid potential consequences, and at other times feeling like they should do whatever it takes to make money. Some may settle into apathy, not intending to cause harm but thinking that there is not much they can do to stop it so they might as well make some money. This wide spectrum of intentions within organizations points toward the importance of apologies that capture the specific roles played by individuals. Although groups of people can act together in various respects, victims should be wary of those who attempt to shift blame from the individual to the collective. In many cases we can rather easily identify who within a collective deserves blame for their specific contributions. Some will intentionally order underlings to value profit over life. Others will execute those orders. Some will look the other way. Others should have paid more attention. Some will lie to cover it up. Several individual people committing multiple interlocking wrongs can cause great harm. Collective apologies often allow individuals to disappear into the collective, as if the institution had a will entirely of its own, or as if the corporation – or perhaps "market forces" – took the wheel and no one could do anything about it. This is often a lie shrouded in a metaphor. The hypocrisy of allowing the collective to shoulder one's culpability becomes especially odious when we see it from those who are first in line to demand recognition – especially in the form of pay raises – when things go well. Executives eagerly accept credit for their work when demanding high salaries; when the pendulum of accountability swings, they should be equally willing to accept blame.

This does not entail that every overzealous mortgage lender or defaulting homeowner must bear the full weight of the financial crisis. It is best to explain, with precision, the portion of the blame that one deserves. The banking example demonstrates how individuals may deserve blame for contributing to the situation in distinct ways and how we can identify who, in particular, deserves blame for which offenses. Who, for instance, called the shots that resulted in the most harmful deregulation or the most damaging accounting practices? Do they apologize for their personal failures, the failures of their banks, or for capitalism run amuck generally? Do they conceal their personal wrongdoing by speaking in terms of the institution or the "financial community" as such? Do individuals who should apologize for their own mistakes allow the collective to shoulder responsibility that they should bear? Do apologies from institutional leaders avoid naming those who deserve blame?

Civil complainants should use extra caution when those who injured them avoid providing individual apologies that accept personal blame and instead offer some form of collective apologies in which no one in particular admits culpability. Many victims know full well who caused their suffering. Watching the guilty outsource their moral work to the corporate mantel can add insult to injury. Apologies from collectives can provide important meanings, but these should not supplant or be provided in lieu of the meanings that can only emerge from the individual wrongdoer's acceptance of blame.

Demanding precision in attributions of blame allows us to identify what went wrong, where it went wrong, and how it can be avoided in the future. Who, for instance, made the decision to grant high-risk loans such favorable ratings? One might claim that the ratings guidelines, rather than those who applied the guidelines, deserve blame. These standards and their interpretations did not materialize from market ether: they resulted from contested historical battles in which individuals took sides and lobbied for the policies that contributed to the crisis. Rather than treating the collapse as some sort of freak unforeseeable economic natural disaster, we should be clear about how a series of bad decisions added up to cause such consequences. If we know where to place blame and whom to hold accountable, we stand a chance of preventing it from happening again. When future generations read of the 2008 economic collapse or the Fukushima nuclear disaster, apologies that detail how the individual failures aggregated to cause such damage will provide far greater insight into how to prevent similar injuries than will nonspecific declarations of a collective's guilt.

Requiring a degree of specificity in the distribution of blame for civil harms relates to aforementioned issues regarding consensus. Tallying how many members hold which intentions, establishing a majority view, and then declaring that X group intended Y will misrepresent important subtleties. If some leaders of Goldman Sachs intended to defraud investors while others risked their careers objecting to these tracts, we can parse blameworthiness accordingly. Such refinements in moral causation can also help shatter claims that victims should view large-scale events caused by human agents as somehow accidental. Victims can demythologize stories of institutional demons that disfigure good intentions into wicked deeds by tracing institutional behavior to the acts and intentions of individuals where appropriate and expecting acceptance of blame, reform, and redress accordingly. Rather than viewing the harms as accidents for which we can prepare but not prevent, precise attributions of blame identify the need for reform at various levels: executives must take fewer risks of these sorts, employees should not look the other way, regulatory bodies must remain impartial, legislatures need to adequately fund regulatory agencies, and so on. Differentiating culpability in these senses offers a much greater awareness of how individual actions aggregate to cause large-scale harm. Such understanding should increase our chances of preventing further harm.

How we assign blame and the extent to which we consider something blameworthy again raises asymmetries between civil and criminal law. Although the law may tend to treat serious harms caused by individuals as criminal but injuries and even deaths caused by collectives as civil matters, victims often reject the idea that a corporation's cost-benefit determination exposing them to harm should be redressed with money alone. Even those who would never identify as leftists may come to agree with Engels if they lose a loved one in a civil injury:

> If one individual inflicts a bodily injury upon another which leads to the death of the person attacked we call it manslaughter; on the other hand, if the attacker knows beforehand that the blow will be fatal we call it murder. Murder has also been committed if a society places hundreds of workers in such a position that they will inevitably come to premature and unnatural ends. Their death is as violent as if they had been stabbed or shot.... Murder has been committed if society knows perfectly well that thousands of workers cannot avoid being sacrificed so long as these conditions are allowed to continue. Murder of this sort is just as culpable as the murder committed by the individual.[19]

I raise this point here because compelling apologies in civil law sometimes require looking beyond legal constructs regarding who deserves blame for what. If I oversaw a factory and knowingly allowed it to release carcinogens that caused your child to die from leukemia, I may understand that I am not subject to the same penalties as I would be if I killed her with a bullet. How different, really, is my degree of blame? Does my apology put the legal cart before the moral horse in order to minimize my culpability, or do I accept unmitigated blame for killing your child? Does the apology hide behind legalities, or does it stand in guilt before moral law?

Even unsuccessful legal complaints can result in victims continuing to expect apologies accepting blame. The law draws rather sharp distinctions regarding culpability, but legal actions can expose morally blameworthy behavior that does not warrant remedy under the law. Perhaps in the eyes of the law I was not negligent when I harmed you, but I realize that I should have done more to protect you and I deserve blame accordingly. Situations of sovereign immunity present a similar dynamic: legal protections may immunize me from liability in the eyes of the law, but I understand that I deserve blame. I was wrong and should apologize, even if the law rules in my favor.

Inversely, one can be legally liable yet morally innocent. Consider how strict liability claims depart from the usual correlations of intentions with culpability. As Joel Feinberg explains it, strict liability applies to cases in which legal doctrine holds agents responsible for harm even though "the contributory fault condition is weakened or absent."[20] Laws occasionally stipulate that businesses engaged in ultrahazardous activities should absorb the costs of resultant injuries even when they are not at fault and no matter how much care they take to prevent injuries.[21] If I manufacture explosives and my product causes an injury, I can be held "liable without fault." I may not deserve blame for the injury and I may have been exceptionally scrupulous to create the safest possible explosives, but my jurisdiction structures the law such that people like me who profit from this business bear the burden of paying for such harms. This arrangement provides additional incentive for me to do everything within my power to make the hazardous product as safe as possible. Feinberg emphasizes an important distinction here: although vicarious liability makes sense – someone assumes liability for damages even if they lack blame for the harm – "*there can be no such thing as vicarious guilt.*"[22] Victims should probably not, therefore, expect those found vicariously liable to provide apologies that accept blame.

Unlike criminal law's usual black-and-white palette of guilty and not guilty, tort law paints victims and offenders in many shades of gray. Between its constructions of strict liability and various forms of immunity, there exists a range of doctrines that protect against findings of fault, divide blame between plaintiffs and defendants, or otherwise nuance how law assigns responsibility for injuries. Consider assumption of risk, comparative negligence, contributory negligence, and standards of care. Like criminal law, analytic traditions of assigning blame in civil law provide conceptual tools far more refined – although perhaps no less controversial – than commonsense notions of responsibility populating apologies in more informal conflicts. The legal analysis of blame will sometimes conflict with the commonsense view; sometimes it informs the commonsense view and causes the injured party to appreciate that she deserves some of the blame. Imagine I am late for a concert and hastily pull out of my driveway while a bit distracted trying to find the tickets in my bag. I had two drinks with dinner, but I am under the legal limit. An intoxicated driver – just over the legal limit – crashes into me. Would the accident have happened if I had paid closer attention to oncoming traffic or if I did not have any alcohol in my system? Even if the drunk driver deserves all of the legal blame and I seek an apology from her that admits fault, this does not erase my carelessness. My subcriminal behavior has consequences for her. I may appreciate that her wrong was worse than mine, but I may also owe her an apology for my role in this life-changing accident. Informal conflicts often take this form of "I'm sorry for X" followed by the injured party sharing some blame with a statement such as, "Well, I shouldn't have Y and maybe if I had Z none of this would have happened." Fair-minded sharing of responsibility that avoids overstating one party's blame and the other's innocence can be quite effective in repairing relationships, but legal conflicts tend toward the adversarial approach of shifting as much blame as possible to the opposition.

I consider apologies within settlement agreements more fully later, but note here that offenders who condition their acceptance of blame on acceptance of settlement conditions – "I will concede fault if you agree to X redress and Y confidentiality agreement" – provide limited value. Most obviously, failing to accept or violating the conditions of the settlement nullifies the admission of fault. If the settlement requires that its terms remain confidential, will the offender deny fault publicly? How will this impact efforts to reform? Expressions of remorse conditioned on settlement terms also provide insights into the motivations behind the apology: the offender seems to apologize not because she undergoes a moral transformation and wishes to confess, but because she seeks to gain some benefit from an expression of contrition.

Institutional apologies and admissions of guilt can have considerable value. Collective apologies can, for instance, declare or renew a group's core values. They can provide examples for individuals within the group to follow when confessing their own role in the wrongdoing, in part by ensuring that blame is shared and that no individual will be scapegoated or blamed disproportionately to her actions. Collectives can also synthesize apologies from many individuals into a coherent narrative that pieces together how many minor failings added up to major harms. A binocular view that simultaneously appreciates how individual blame and structural causation combine to result in harm provides the best vantage for understanding what happened, who deserves blame, and how to best fix the problem. Too often, however, collective apologies in civil law are comprised of *neither* individuals taking personal responsibility for the harm and changing their ways accordingly *nor* institutions undertaking the sorts of structural reform that would prevent similar harms. Collective apologies often actively avoid attributing blame in order to insulate wrongdoers – often the most powerful leaders who initiate and benefit most from the behavior – from the consequences of their actions.

This creates problems down the line of apologetic meanings. If no one in particular deserves blame, for example, who gets punished? Does anyone need to feel negative emotions, or can everyone in the institution avoid experiencing guilt or shame? Who in particular needs to change their behaviors? Who pays for the redress? Who do we consult if redress stalls or if the injurious behavior continues? These considerations all warrant attention.

Obfuscation as Tactic: Apology as "Nothing to Do with Fault"
One litigation tactic involves wrongdoers offering expressions of empathy or sympathy without accepting blame: "I am sorry that you had the wrong leg amputated" differs from "I mistakenly amputated the wrong leg because

I failed to X, Y, and Z." Equivocating between expressions of sympathy and admissions of fault takes many forms and results from differing motivations. Some civil defense attorneys understand and exploit the ambiguities, advising clients to say just enough to maximize the appearance of contrition without undermining their claims of innocence.[23] To give the appearance of offering a "sincere" apology, thereby receiving the strategic benefits of being perceived as remorseful, an offender can express sympathy without admitting responsibility, corroborating the factual record, or even acknowledging the legitimacy of the victim's injury. Tanick and Ayling, for instance, recommend that the apology be "carefully crafted to avoid admission of wrongdoing."[24] Levi advises in the *New York University Law Review* that "lawyers protective of their clients' interests might serve those interests by encouraging clients to apologize short of admitting liability."[25] Levi suggests that "lawyers might allow their clients to express empathy and regret while avoiding formulations that would make liability undeniable, such as 'I neglected my duty,' 'my actions caused your injury,' or 'if only I hadn't done X, you would never have been injured.'"[26] Cohen similarly describes how to offer a "partial apology": express "sympathy for the injured party's condition, but not admit fault or express regret for the defendant's actions." Following an injury, Cohen explains, "the offender might visit the injured party in the hospital and state simply, 'I am very sorry that your leg is broken, and I hope that you feel better soon.'"[27] Apologies of this sort probably do not identify the nature of the moral harm suffered by the plaintiff and may fail to express a shared commitment to honoring those values. The apologizing party may continue to commit the same harm against the plaintiff or others as she apologizes, stating to a victim that she is "sorry for your suffering" while continuing to visit similar injuries on others and refusing to accept that she has done anything wrong.

Some clarification regarding *empathy* and *sympathy* may be helpful here, as the terms are not synonymous as this literature sometimes suggests. Empathy typically refers to one's ability to recognize, understand, and feel another's emotions.[28] The better we can comprehend another's beliefs, desires, and life situations through empathic understanding, the more we can ascertain and relate to her emotional states.[29] Sympathy relates more closely to compassion, wherein we perceive a subject suffering or in an otherwise undesirable state and wish for the alleviation of the negative condition. We can think of sympathy as "feeling sorry for," not necessarily in the sense of having pity but rather in hoping that another will be relieved from hardship or offering our companionship while she endures a negative experience. Whereas empathy understands one's mental states but may not evaluate whether they are appropriate or justified, sympathy judges those states and hopes for their alleviation. We often use compassion not only as a way to express the passive sympathetic wish for relief but also as an active effort to provide such relief. Empathy and sympathy interact in a variety of disputed ways, and one can seemingly be empathic but not sympathetic (I understand your feelings but believe you deserve to experience them on retributive grounds) or sympathetic but not empathetic (I generally want to help you feel better even though I lack basic understanding of how you feel or what caused it).[30] Empathy and sympathy feature prominently in apologies because they connect cognitive and emotional aspects. Although explaining wrongdoing, affirming the breached value, and admitting fault all play important roles in apologizing, standing alone these recognitions can appear cold and abstract. Empathy triggers an appreciation of the victim's pain: "I caused a particular person to suffer." The apology, as I discuss at length, creates connections between victim and offender across emotional as well as cognitive spheres. Empathy and sympathy speak to an apologizer's recognition of her wrongdoing as such as well as revealing her motivations for redressing the harm. When I empathize with the offended, I better appreciate the consequences of my acts because I am attuned to what it feels like to suffer such harm. If I cause you to incur medical expenses, for instance, instead of thinking of the injury in strictly economic terms, empathy provides an understanding of the less visible damages. If I understand that you experience considerable physical pain, anger, anxiety, and fear, I may be more likely to appreciate why my actions were unjustifiable. Hume and Schopenhauer found sentiments essential to moral judgment for just these reasons. If we can relate to a victim's mental states and recognize them as undesirable, this triggers a sympathetic desire to ameliorate such suffering with remedial actions.

Expressing empathy or sympathy in this manner without admitting guilt presents a low-risk strategy for the defense: such gestures cost nothing in terms of money or litigation strategy, yet some victims may find them so meaningful that they reduce their demands or otherwise soften their positions. The defense risks little and can gain considerable advantage. The more the gestures look like whatever the victim understands as an apology – keeping in mind that she may suffer from considerable confusions that cause her to overvalue the empathy, perhaps by conflating an emotional display with acceptance of blame and believing that the offender "lets down her guard" by her statements – the better the chances of the defense leveraging such gestures to its advantage. Within an adversarial context it can seem foolish not to at least try such a low-risk/high-reward tactic.

Of course not all expressions of empathy or sympathy attempt to manipulate the opposition, and they can set a genuine tone of concern and cooperation: we all wish this did not happen and we hope to resolve the issues respectfully. Indeed, the wrongdoer's attitude toward the offense often serves as the primary reason the victim brings a formal claim. Various studies suggest that a doctor's post-injury behavior plays a larger role in the patient's decision to bring a claim than does the injury itself. Of patients who have colorable claims against their doctors, 80–90 percent pursue legal action,[31] and patients described the doctor as "not caring, or delivering the news in a dysfunctional way, or not keeping people up to date, or abandoning the family or the patient" in 70 percent of those cases resulting in legal action.[32] Good bedside manner, in other words, includes not adding insults to injuries doctors cause. Expressions of empathy without accepting blame can also avoid the downward spiral of offender's stonewalling victims for fear that anything they say that even remotely sounds like an apology will be used against them. This avoidance in turn offends the victim to the extent that she brings legal action primarily because of the stonewalling rather than because of the original injury.[33] In cases of large organizations causing injuries, expressions of empathy can go some way toward countering their cold, calculating, faceless images.[34] I suspect class dynamics often frame these interactions as comparatively disadvantaged victims feel disrespected by the wealthy attorneys, executives, and doctors. If a victim already feels somehow exploited by elites and the injury is the last straw that precipitated legal action, expressions of empathy become especially important.

Efforts to improve the tone by expressing empathy, however, can of course result from very different objectives. Some offer sympathy as an expression of genuine emotions: I really do feel terrible for you, I hope I can provide some relief, and I offer these sentiments out of respect and concern for you. One can accomplish all of this in earnest while not accepting blame for the harm and still reap financial benefits from this attitude – honest and virtuous behavior need not necessarily conflict with financial interests.[35] However, more nefarious intentions can motivate expressions of sympathy that do not accept blame. In addition to the hope that some victims may mistake sympathy for an apology accepting blame, some may view the very process of setting a respectful tone as little more than an "attitudinal structuring tactic" designed to manipulate victims' behavior and gain an upper hand by appearing to soften the adversarial setting. This also allows the defense to attempt to gather information while in "friendly mode," only to switch back to scorched Earth litigation once it obtains necessary documents and concessions.[36] From this perspective empathy tricks the victim into letting down her guard. Intentions present complex issues, and frankly an actor may not know exactly why she offers empathy. She may simultaneously feel badly and know that expressing empathy presents strategic advantages, hoping that good business practices and noble values coincide.[37] Her motivations may be opaque to her. The intent to deceive, however, motivates some strategies. We should treat these like other matters of professional responsibility in which attorneys advise clients to lie.[38]

Consider the tactic of offering expressions of sympathy first as a test to determine if that alone will be "sufficient to quell a purported 'victim.'"[39] If claimants expect more than sympathy, one can dole out a little apologetic meaning at a time to determine how much is needed.[40] Bartering away apologetic meaning in this regard allows attorneys to reserve admissions of guilt as the trump card if negotiations stall.[41] Parties approaching the apology from a fully instrumental perspective can index the blame accepted to the likelihood that guilt will be established for various offenses. If the established record makes denial implausible, then confession will seem a more effective mitigation strategy.[42] If some wrongdoing will be difficult to prove, then the defense with this instrumental attitude will structure the acceptance of blame narrowly or vaguely enough to gain maximum advantage while not unnecessarily conceding ground. Cohen describes this as "spin control."[43] Given the skill required to calibrate the apology to deliver just the right amount of substance without giving too much away, some advise that offenders should leave the act of apologizing to their attorneys "in order to prevent unwitting exposure to liability or inadvertent admitting of guilt."[44] If "a full apology is to be made," Pavlick suggests, "a mediation session preceded by a confidentiality agreement may often be the best place for it since apologies made in that forum are protected by federal law."[45] Victims should understand all admissions of guilt are not legally equal. Admissions contained within confidentiality agreements or in statutorily protected venues – as discussed later – have considerable restrictions on their significance. The offender could, for instance, confidentially accept blame in your case because she knows that this will cause you to reduce your demands for compensation. She can adopt this strategy while simultaneously refusing to admit blame in a parallel case with another party.

Perhaps the boldest tactic involves a straightaway assertion from defense attorneys and those who share their interests that apologies do not require accepting blame. Some make an even stronger claim that apologies "have nothing to do with fault." I defend at length in *I Was Wrong* and throughout this book that traditions of apologies and repentance share core meanings grounded in thousands of years of history across a wide range of cultures: the most significant kinds of apologies admit wrongdoing and signify moral transformation. This largely explains why they convey such substance. Without explaining how they arrive at this position, many legal commentators claim that apologies have only accidental relationships to confessional guilt. Cornell, Warne, and Eining assure readers that "an apology is *not* synonymous with an admission of guilt or fault."[46] Pavlick believes "clients should be counseled not to make an admission of fault, especially since such an admission is not a requirement of an authentic apology."[47] A 2009 study claims that apologizing may lead to favorable verdicts while explicitly claiming that apologies express sorrow "without admitting guilt."[48] Others warn that even if reserving the apology for a confidential mediation session, "clients should be counseled not to make an admission of fault, especially since such an admission is not a requirement of an authentic apology."[49] One partner at a large firm frames the divorce of apologies and blame as a matter of courtesy: "Not to say, 'I'm sorry' is rude and arrogant. It has nothing to do with fault."[50] "Moreover," this practitioner continues, "'I'm sorry' in everyday speech usually means 'I'm sorry we find ourselves in this current situation.' It is not about fault."[51] Such examples crystallize vague moral language and economic incentives into a powerful example of confirmation bias: I want to believe that apologies do not require accepting blame, so I will disregard thousands of years of moral traditions and all countervailing contemporary arguments to adopt the belief that affirms my interests. In such a case it becomes difficult to ascertain if the attorney really believes that apologies have nothing to do with fault or if he advocates for this position professionally even though he would never accept it personally, for example if one of his family members owed him an apology.

Note an additional form of equivocation suggested by Michael Woods: "Bear in mind that taking responsibility does not necessarily imply acknowledging that you made a mistake."[52] Woods suggests the following: "I am responsible for your care and will find out what happened. If possible why it happened. I will keep you posted of what I learn and how it can be used to prevent future errors. At this point, I'm not sure if I would have done anything differently, but I intend to explore this thoroughly." As Woods explains, this assertion of responsibility does not admit wrongdoing. Instead, the doctor asserts responsibility for caring for a wound as a matter of professional duty even, which would be the case whether the physician or a stranger on the street caused the injury. Responsibility to treat an injury differs from responsibility for causing an injury, but adding the words "responsible for" along with "sorry" to a statement of empathy creates an appearance of accepting blame. A physician well-schooled in risk management can choose her words carefully to deceive a distraught victim hearing these words through a haze of emotion and amid other important information – for instance regarding prognosis and treatment options.

The rather incredible assertion that apologies have "nothing to do with fault" could result from the presuppositions of the context: apologies only have a place in civil law if we understand them as something other than admissions of fault. Otherwise there is no place for them within adversarial legal institutions, like there is no place for giving away goals in a soccer match. The dissonance we experience from this perspective is like forcing a square peg into a round hole – rounding apologies by removing the aspect of confession distorts them beyond recognition.

These dynamics call for rather different approaches from victims seeking apologies and those alleged to have caused injuries. If you want an apology that admits blame, be certain this is what you receive. Take caution not to accept statements of sympathy for admissions of fault. Victims should make explicit – to themselves, their counsel, the offenders, or their communities – why they desire offenders to accept blame. An acceptance of blame typically provides the linchpin around which many other aspects of apologetic meaning turn, from understanding what happened to undertaking reform and providing redress. With a mere expression of sympathy the offender need not admit to having done anything wrong, she may not commit to proving remedy, she may not see any reason to change her behavior, and she may continue injuring others in the same manner. As discussed later, victims should also be clear regarding who they wish to accept responsibility. If they believe blame should fall to a specific executive, they should be wary if the leader only expresses empathy while leaving underlings, attorneys, or the institution in the abstract to shoulder the guilt.

From the defense's perspective, it appears that the most thoughtful parties have arrived at something of a consensus regarding the optimal strategies for navigating the dangers and benefits of apologies. This does not require a scorched Earth approach to litigation but instead seems – at least within this incredibly convoluted universe of meaning – like a rather honest and humane approach. Although I will not speak to the specifics of the programs and their differences, emerging patterns surface across Stanford's PEARL (Program for Early Assessment and Resolution of Loss), Sorry Works!, Lee Taft's *Taft Solutions*, and others. Medical injury cases occupy most of the literature, and certain principles recur. Sorry Works!, for example, works to teach physicians the difference between expressions of empathy and admissions of fault to help overcome the fear that all uses of "sorry" will "buy the hospital, practice, or insurance company a lawsuit."[53] Advising that "empathy is appropriate 100% of the time, while apology is appropriate only [if] an investigation has proven a mistake," Sorry Works! recommends "an empathetic I'm sorry immediately after an adverse event coupled with a promise of an investigation and customer service assistance such as food, lodging, phone calls, transportation, etc."[54] Providing the disclaimer that insurers may require consulting with them prior even to expressing empathy, Sorry Works! advises that one should not admit fault at the empathy stage and should instead consult risk managers, insurance companies, and defense counsel for assistance with the investigation. Depending on the results of the investigation, the physicians may then provide "a real apology (I'm sorry I made a mistake) coupled with fair, upfront compensation (paid for by your insurer), or more empathy if no error occurred."[55] Sorry Works! also emphasizes the role of nurses and staff in this process and the importance of teaching them to convey empathy rather than creating a wall of silence around adverse events.[56]

Stanford University Medical Center's PEARL program adopts similar strategies. The PEARL process provides "around-the-clock" consultants to advise and initiate "rapid initial assessments" of "concerning outcomes."[57]

The investigations determine whether events are "anticipated" or "unpreventable adverse outcomes" – commonly understood as complications – or a "preventable unanticipated outcome" for which fault can be attributed. In either case, Stanford providers "fully disclose" the information to the patients. If they find that the adverse outcome was preventable, providers "offer a fault-admitting apology for the outcome and the PEARL team works to arrive at a fair accommodation with the patient."[58] The process includes determining the causes of the events and "implementing lessons learned" so that "other similarly situated patients will not experience similar adverse outcomes."[59] Stanford's "underlying philosophy is that the benefits to patients and caregivers from full disclosure and prompt remedial action outweigh the possibility of creating additional risk or claims." PEARL's proactive approach serves their objectives of "improving patient safety and the quality of care, treating patients with dignity and respect, and ensuring staff learns and corrects" mistakes.[60] PEARL also claims to reduce costs for the Stanford Medical Center, saving $3.2 million per year and reducing claim frequency by 36 percent over one 42-month period.[61] In addition to the benefits of reducing future mistakes by disclosing and correcting errors, the PEARL program claims to improve the mental health of doctors who risk falling into the "cycle of addiction, burnout, and suicide" after committing a medical mistake.[62]

These full disclosure programs evolve toward practices that make a good deal of sense from various and often opposed perspectives. Especially within medical contexts, injuries occur frequently. Previous generations of "deny and defend" risk management strategies are giving way to the new wave of full disclosure protocols that identify wrongs, offer a fault-admitting apology, settle early rather than litigating and accumulating attorney's fees, and correct errors to prevent future injuries and their various costs to both victims and offenders. Given the turbulent climates of modern medicine and litigation, these programs bespeak progress toward balanced and commonsensical conflict resolution.

Optimism here should remain cautious for a few reasons. Those advocating for these programs have incentive to inflate their value. Sorry Works!, for example, still helps itself to equivocating between "sorry" and accepting blame when inflating the value of its for-profit services. Consider its assertions that "we know absence of sorry is one of the chief drivers of medical malpractice litigation" and that "seasoned med-mal litigators say patients and families often mention it during depositions: 'Nobody ever said sorry.'" Sorry Works! similarly claims "sorry is one thing patients and families want most post-event, and it's not necessarily 'Sorry we screwed up' but 'Sorry this happened, and we still care about you.'"[63] Such claims beg the central question: Does the absence of empathy or the refusal to accept blame cause litigation? Moreover, how often do wrongdoers actually provide the sorts of "fault-admitting apologies" that victims deserve? Accounts of these apologies tend to come from hospitals, defense attorneys, and risk management consultants. All of these parties have incentive to overstate the quality of their apologies and to feed the misconception of apology as something other than admitting blame. I once attended a symposium where the general counsel for a major care provider touted the highest ethical principles guiding his organization's use of apologies in litigation. A plaintiff's attorney in the audience promptly raised his hand to claim that he was currently involved in a conflict with the speaker's organization and had experienced nothing of the sort. We should review any claims from the medical industry – and those serving its interests – regarding the apologies they provide and the benefits of those apologies with appropriate scrutiny lest we leave the foxes guarding the henhouse.

The disruptive innovators in full disclosure and fault-admitting apologies operate in a broader context in which legislators and defense attorneys continue to insist that apologies do not admit fault. Powerful interests exert disproportionate control over language usage and believe the no-fault conception of apologies serves them best. Winners write not only the histories but also the legislation defining the terms that govern us. For those with the most power over legal discourse, incentives point toward redefining apologies as something other than moral transformations that admit guilt and promise reform. I do not mean to suggest that civil defense attorneys intentionally conspire to distort language to their advantage, but a critical mass of power can sway accepted definitions of legal terminology. We need only consider how *Citizens United* defines corporations as legal persons.[64] We can now consider the role of tort reform in statutorily defining apologies according to lobbying interests.

Obfuscation as Law: Sympathy as Apology Legislation

One might fairly question the significance of a few bare assurances from attorneys and legal scholars claiming that apologies do not admit wrongdoing, but the situation becomes considerably more conspicuous when legislation systematically codifies these counterintuitive beliefs across national and international jurisdictions. I leave summarizing the nuances of this rapidly changing legislation to those with a boots-on-the-ground perspective, but the long view captures the dynamics. Commentators often trace the origins of "safe apology" statutes – laws providing evidentiary "safe havens" for certain types of gestures by rendering them inadmissible to prove liability – to Massachusetts's pioneering laws in this area. Early advocates for safe apology legislation cited the emotional and spiritual value of an apology and therefore sought to carve out protected legal spaces for conversations like the one desired by the Massachusetts legislator who sought an apology from the driver who killed his daughter.[65] As jurisdictions followed Massachusetts's example, definitions of "apology" evolved. Some states protect expressions of sympathy from admission into evidence but do not cover statements of fault.[66] Some statutes protect apologies described vaguely as "general benevolence."[67] Some protect even admissions of wrongdoing, fault, errors, or mistakes.[68] Some statutes provide general protection for apologies while leaving the term ambiguous.[69] Members of the Texas legislature unsuccessfully attempted to make definitions of safe apologies *more obfuscatory* by repealing provisions clarifying that acknowledgements of fault remained admissible.[70] Statements made during mediation of settlement negotiations receive the greatest protections. Some statutes only apply to cases of medical error,[71] in part to coordinate with legislative requirements for disclosing adverse outcomes as well as American Medical Association (AMA) instructions stating that providers "are ethically required to inform the patient of all the facts necessary to ensure understanding of what has occurred."[72] According to the AMA, fears "regarding the legal liability which might result following truthful disclosure should not affect the physician's honesty with a patient."[73] Some of these safe haven laws impact when the clock starts for statute of limitations purposes. Most of the discussions take place at the state level, but some argue for reforming federal rules of evidence as well.[74] These trends have gained traction internationally, for example with New South Wales, Australia, adopting the following maddeningly inexact definition of apology: "[A]pology means an expression of sympathy or regret, or of a general sense of benevolence or compassion, in connection with any matter whether or not the apology admits or implies an admission of fault in connection with the matter."[75] It goes on to provide considerable protections for such gestures, stating that such

> apology made by or on behalf of a person in connection with any matter alleged to have been caused by the fault of the person... does not constitute an express or implied admission of fault or liability by the person in connection with that matter, and is not relevant to the determination of fault or liability in connection with that matter.[76]

It further states that "evidence of an apology made by or on behalf of a person in connection with any matter alleged to have been caused by the fault of the person is not admissible in any civil proceedings as evidence of the fault or liability of the person in connection with that matter."[77] These are deep and broad exclusions.

Why has all of this legislative attention turned to apologies over the past fifteen years? Like so many concepts taken up in law, political and economic conflicts shape apology legislation. Just as *Citizens United*'s understanding of corporate personhood did not result from breakthroughs in the philosophical concepts of self, powerful forces seek to control the pen when states define apologies and their interests color this contested term that references our deepest values and ancient moral traditions. Tort reform provides the primary battleground for these fights.[78] In a simplified sense, tort reform debates who should bear the costs of personal injuries: wrongdoers, victims, or taxpayers. From the perspective of the "business community" – to use the term favored by tort reformers over "corporate interests" – costs for liability insurance have become excessive because they risk paying large amount when they harm someone in the course of business. From this perspective, injured parties – and "frivolous" plaintiffs seeking to fleece deep-pocketed corporations – receive so many large awards that liability threatens business. Insurers, of course, have an obvious interest in limiting potential damages because this reduces the amount they need to pay out. Thus, they argue, we find ourselves in a "litigation crisis" that requires reforms of tort laws in various ways that reduce costs for businesses. These include initiatives such as capping noneconomic damages, reducing punitive damage awards, expanding mandatory arbitration, and requiring losing parties in civil litigation to pay the winner's attorney's fees. All of these objectives defang plaintiff's attorneys by limiting victims' access to courts and curtailing the rights of injured parties: if my child suffers a disabling injury because of a defective product or medical negligence, for instance, as a result of tort reform my family may be required to arbitrate the claim with the paid official of the business' choosing rather than adjudicating the claim in civil court. We may also find the amount we can recover "capped" such that we are limited to $250,000 in noneconomic damages in some states even though it will cost millions to care for the child and taxpayers via Medicare – rather that the wrongdoers – will pay the costs of a lifetime or care for a disabled child. George W. Bush and Karl Rove leveraged tort reform to great political success in Texas and beyond.[79]

Tort reformers often bundle apology legislation within these other initiatives on the basis that providing protections for apologies will generally advance the interests of those defending against claims. When apologetic statements become inadmissible for determining liability, this bars plaintiffs from utilizing an important piece of evidence. If receiving an apology causes victims to expect lower damage awards because they find the offender contrite and if apologies do not carry a strategic risk for the defense because the law prevents construing apologies as confessions, then apology legislation provides a double benefit for civil defendants. As Woods's *Healing Words: The Power of Apology in Medicine* proclaims: "[C]onsidering the near-anarchy over tort reform to limit jury awards, you'd think doctors would be eager to adopt a risk management strategy that offers a 50-percent reduction in litigation."[80] All four recommendations on the back cover of Woods's book come from insurance companies or risk management firms. For these reasons, Cohen suggests that apology legislation passes "because large organizations such as insurance companies, medical associations and

Fortune 500 companies will lobby for them."[81] Apology legislation disproportionately advances the interests of the rich.

Tort reform holds most political currency with the right, and the perceived crisis received most attention during the administrations of Ronald Reagan and George W. Bush. In addition to pro-business economic conservatism, the apology legislation also strikes a chord with social conservatism. The very mention of apology, ironically, conjures both "personal responsibility" and spiritual traditions of repentance – even when the law defines apologies as something other than admissions of fault. Like many tensions in allegiances between social and economic conservatism, the spiritual values and economic interests of apologies in law coexist on the same political platform even as they seem at cross-purposes. Lobbyists and legislators can cite reduced litigation costs when speaking to the corporations providing their umbilical cords of financing but then proselytize to their religious base about how apology laws enable parties to "reach out to others in a humane way without fear" even as they know that in practice the laws provide another way to protect wrongdoers from liability.[82] Apology safe havens could in principle open spaces that allow parties to informally reach some degree of moral reconciliation via apology, but the informality usually allows the powerful to gain further advantages and co-opt the process as they have done with similar alternative dispute mechanisms such as binding arbitration.[83] Confusing, informal, and inadmissible apologies advance business interest on this account, which begins to explain why Texas legislators would take the remarkable measure of trying to *un-define* apologies within a tort reform package.[84] Vagueness, like discretion, tilts toward power.

The plaintiffs' bar presents the most organized resistance to apology laws and tends to view the legislation as contrary to patients' rights. For plaintiffs' trial lawyers, tort reform generally looks like a form of corporate welfare as it shifts costs of injuries to victims by limiting their compensation. By protecting corporations from the cost of injuries they cause, plaintiffs' attorneys argue that such laws allow businesses to be less concerned with the safety of their products than they would be if legislation did not artificially reduce potential legal damages. For consumer rights advocates, large tort awards drive product safety and help protect populations from especially dangerous products such as asbestos because potential litigation exposure outweighs potential profits. Although some members of the plaintiffs' bar understand their efforts as a form of consumer protection, we should be careful not to demonize defense attorneys as hired guns for corporate interests while idealizing plaintiffs' attorneys fighting for the public good. For some trial lawyers, apology laws seem problematic primarily because they give wrongdoers an evidentiary advantage and arguably reduce settlement awards and even prevent litigation altogether. As noted earlier, reduced awards mean reduced payments for trial lawyers taking a percentage. For many plaintiffs' attorneys, apology laws undermine their business mantra: more litigation and higher settlements. The plaintiffs' bar therefore presents countervailing interests to corporate-backed safe apology legislation, but in its current form this is hardly a lobby that one should uncritically support if seeking to achieve the sorts of substantive apologies in civil law that would advance the general interests of victims and communities.

These legislative dynamics confuse rather than clarify apologetic meanings. "Safe apology" laws effectively promote conflating expressions of sympathy with admissions of guilt, and this distortion primarily benefits the guilty and the powerful. If a core meaning of an apology resides in the apologizer's rendering herself vulnerable – I admit that I was wrong, I deserve blame, I must change, and I owe you redress – legal safe havens undermine the basic attitudes and consequences of contrition. Contrary to those who argue that legal protections will somehow encourage contrition, in my view the very willingness to accept the fair consequences is a hallmark of apologies. This vulnerability accounts for why apologies can convey such gravitas. Although she need not accept unreasonable punishments, the apologizer lets down her defenses and submits to appropriate redress. She corroborates her words with deeds, sometimes paying redress. We can bifurcate legal actions accordingly: I admit fault, but we disagree about – or at least we need a legal process to determine – appropriate damages.[85] With safe apology legislation, by contrast, "I am sorry" goes the way of "not guilty" as a legal utterance that one offers even when just about everyone – including the speaker – understands that she does not really mean the phrase in a substantively rich sense. It becomes, in other words, a legal cypher divorced from thick moral substance. Imagine if, by comparison, a family's house rules defined apologies as mere expressions of sympathy that did not entail admissions of culpability and that required no change of behavior or redress. Such a family would attribute rather limited value to apologies and would seek other means of expressing the sorts of meanings excluded from the definition.

I also doubt that safe apology legislation excluding statements from evidence will, as some suggest, somehow promote more benevolent behavior after accidents or result in more effective redress for injured parties via prompt settlements. If the wrongdoer seeks to admit fault and provide redress, she may do so even prior to the commencement of a civil claim. Perhaps an apology then satisfies the victim and resolves the matter without recourse to legal proceedings. If the wrongdoer refuses to provide a remedy that satisfies the victim and a legal action ensues, however, excluding the apology from evidence primarily seems to encourage strategic apologizing – cast a line of sympathy and see what legal benefit you catch – without consequence. If the wrongdoer seeks to offer an apology that admits fault, legislation can encourage this behavior while also enforcing the consequences of such admissions. Law should not attempt to sever the relationship between accepting blame and its repercussions, especially when doing so disproportionately advantages those who cause injuries by excluding evidence against them and potentially deceiving victims who mistake a litigation tactic for a morally transformative apology. If the law codifies conceptions of apologies, it should provide clear and defensible definitions.

Because the privileged can more easily afford – socially and financially – to avoid expressing remorse, some argue that apology safe havens protect disadvantaged groups inclined to apologize because their lack of power causes them to be subordinately apologetic.[86] I discussed various aspects of this important concern, including worries about the legacy of contrition as a means of humiliating the disadvantaged. I explained how apology exclusions benefit the powerful, but whether apology safe havens disproportionately advantage the rich or poor presents an empirical question. As I noted with regard to unsettled questions of whether women apologize more than men, we should be careful about how we measure and not simply code for ambiguous utterances of the word "sorry." As crisis management experts advise, "complexity is the apologist's friend."[87] Rather than blinkering everyone – confuse the meanings of apologies, add layers of distorting legislation, compound the mystery with unsupported but sympathetic claims about demographic tendencies to utter ambiguous terms, and then bury the apologies in settlement agreements – we should be specific about what apologies mean and do not mean in particular civil proceedings and parse their value accordingly.

3. Does the Civil Offender Possess Appropriate Standing to Apologize and Accept Blame?

On the twentieth anniversary of a gas leak injuring half a million people in Bhopal, India, *BBC World News* aired Dow representative Jude Finisterra's apology to victims. He explained that Dow was liquidating subsidiary Union Carbide to fund $12 billion in remediation and redress costs. Dow lost $2 billion in market value in the following twenty-three minutes as investors reacted. Finisterra turned out to be activist Andy Bichlbaum, staging a hoax to draw attention to Dow's refusal to accept responsibility for the disaster.[88] Markets corrected when traders realized that Bichlbaum lacked authority to apologize for Dow, a multibillion-dollar lesson in standing to apologize for civil harms.

A categorically apologetic wrongdoer accepts blame and provides the apology herself rather than outsourcing the work of contrition to a proxy such as an attorney or spokesperson. The difference between the spokesperson and the wrongdoer delivering the apology is often readily apparent, as the Ford example demonstrates. We do not know what the attorneys said during the bedside meeting. Perhaps they verbalized blame-accepting statements from those responsible for Bailey's injury. Perhaps the attorneys spoke of their own blameworthiness, admitting that they had personally crafted, contributed to, reviewed or failed to meet their duties to prevent the policies that caused the injuries. They may have simply expressed sympathies on behalf of Ford Motor Company without admitting anything like personal blame for her injuries.

Third parties can express important meanings, for instance by corroborating the victim's account of the event, apportioning blame, vindicating moral principles, legitimating suffering, and providing redress. In most cases, however, apologies from third parties fail to convey certain kinds of important meanings. Just as my attorney cannot exercise for me, she cannot undergo moral transformation on my behalf. I cannot offload my blame to her. I cannot delegate my penance and the entailed negative emotional experiences. We often have a clear sense of who needs to apologize. The offender's corroboration of the factual record sharpens this sense as it explains who did what. Civil injuries committed by collectives add layers of complexity. Who deserves blame and for what exactly? Will that person or those people apologize, or will they deflect culpability and leave it to public relations to express contrition?

Two kinds of issues arise here. First, did the person apologizing cause the harm at issue? If not, did those who should shoulder the blame somehow legitimately delegate authority to her? We can imagine situations in civil injuries in which the person offering the apology stands in various relationships to the blameworthy actors. A current executive can blame former executives, thereby converting the apology into an act of self-promotion. A current executive can blame employees other than herself. A line worker can blame an executive. A spokesperson can blame the institution in its most abstract sense. A leader from one institution can apologize for a competitor: imagine a General Motors president taking the opportunity to elevate his own brand by "apologizing on behalf of the automotive industry for the diminished safety reputation of American-made vehicles as a result of the Ford rollover crashes." A leader can blame deceased leaders of previous generations, a particularly painless and often self-aggrandizing path as the living walk over the dead. I might apologize on behalf of Ford regardless of whether I have any connection to the accidents and regardless of whether they asked me to do so because I think "those victims deserve a real apology and I'm going to give it to them." In all of these examples we see the limits of apologies from those who lack standing because they do not commit the offense at issue. As much as people desire apologies – and sometimes desire as many apologies as they can get and from as many sources as possible – we should be clear about a few kinds of meaning that are only possible when the apologies come from those who personally accept blame.

Imagine victims of Ford or Chisso know that specific executives decided to risk causing catastrophic injuries to maximize profits. The victims feel personally attacked and demeaned by these particular executives. They have seen their faces in glossy promotional materials. They know the offenders became wealthy in part by endangering others. Now the corporation, after deliberation about what best protects its brand, sends contrite-looking representatives to deliver an apology. Those executives who haunt the victims can blithely deflect blame. Insurance covers the costs of redress with "no skin off the back" of the responsible parties. Perhaps most importantly, however, the offenders do not have to look the victims in the eye. They need not see and feel the damage they have caused. They can avoid, literally and symbolically, bowing their heads to their victims and recognizing them as moral interlocutors. Offenders can remain aloof and untouched when sending representatives, a particularly problematic attitude in civil cases in which wealthy institutional offenders harm comparatively poor victims who are especially sensitive to being treated as second-class citizens. All of this adds insult to injury for many victims. By personally delivering the apology, the offender shows respect, makes herself vulnerable to the victim, attaches blameworthiness to her identity, and subjects herself to all of the unpredictable emotions that may follow.

Some apologetic meanings require the offender's participation. If offenders go to their graves unrepentant, certain meanings cannot materialize no matter how badly we want them or how much others may try. If culpable Ford executives defend to the death their view of caveat emptor and argue that customers bear the responsibility for ensuring their safety, then those victims will never receive relief from the insult that they caused their own injuries. Others – perhaps even the next generation of Ford executives – may assure victims that they do not deserve blame for killing their own children by driving recklessly or failing to maintain the vehicle properly. This differs from hearing it from the offender. They are the right words, but from the wrong person – like your spouse telling you that you deserve millions in research funding after the National Science Foundation rejects your proposal. Similarly, victims may justifiably wish to judge offenders' emotions for themselves. Perhaps they want to be sure that the offender really does experience shame and that these feelings reinforce a promise not to reoffend. Perhaps the victim holds retributive attitudes and wants as many people as possible to witness the offender's suffering in order to increase the humiliation and maximize their deterrent value. Offenders who prefer to delegate the apologies to spare themselves the pain might also view sending delegates as a preferable legal strategy: rather than allowing emotions to run high and risking further insult in a face-to-face exchange that could "easily obstruct settlement," better to send a calm and experienced proxy to handle the transaction.[89] In such situations I suggest asking victims from whom they desire an apology.

I Was Wrong distinguished a few kinds of attempts to assert standing for collectives: (1) standing for nonmembers of the collective; (2) standing for individual members of the collective without authority to represent the collective as such; and (3) standing for an individual as a member of the collective with authority to represent the collective, including the various ways that delegation might endow an individual with such authority.[90] These categories can help sort through the kinds of issues confronted in civil matters regarding both individual and collective apologies.

First, consider standing for nonmembers of the collective. Given the financial stakes of conveying the proper emotions, leveraging those sentiments into favorable outcomes, and avoiding further exposure, paying someone to apologize for you might seem like money well spent. *I Was Wrong* discussed Jay Rayner's fictional story of Marc Basset, the United Nation's Chief Apologist. After a term of service for the UN apologizing to various constituencies for a range of historical injuries – apologies in which Bassett does not accept personal blame for the suffering and does not commit to personally reforming or providing any redress – Bassett founds a private firm that delivers apologies for multinational corporations and other deep-pocketed institutions. In both his work for the UN and for private entities, Bassett sought to establish membership in the group to increase the plausibility of his claim to possess standing to apologize. While working for the UN, his family lineage remotely connected his bloodlines to atrocities around the world. In the corporate setting, ownership of one stock established membership.[91] Such claims to membership stretch credibility. The sort of symbolic membership asserted by Bassett thus lacks the substantive standing required to convey various kinds of meaning associated with categorical apologies. If one did not act culpably to cause the harm at issue, for example, she cannot personally accept blame. Truth being stranger than fiction, a Tianjin attorney runs a team of "emissaries of regret" who provide apologies on behalf of even unrepentant clients willing to pay their fees.[92] Commentators suggest that this provides a valuable service in China, where apologies make people feel especially vulnerable as they carry stigmas of the legacy of the Cultural Revolution and the sorts of mandatory expression of regret demanded of transgressors against the state.[93]

I should disclose here that I sometimes advise individuals and groups seeking to apologize. I perform much of this work pro bono, but I occasionally receive payment for these services. Because of the aforementioned issues regarding standing, however, I am not an apologist-for-hire. I do not apologize *for* clients. Instead, I guide those intending to apologize through the many nuances of the ritual. This may entail commenting on drafts and warning against common errors that cause apologies to appear disingenuous or otherwise render them ineffective. Sometimes I discuss the potential legal, political, economic, or personal consequences of certain kinds of apologies. My role varies depending on the situation, but I usually interview the offender, learning her perspective on the events and what she hopes to accomplish with an apology. Sometimes I meet with offended parties to understand their perspectives on the events and what they would like an apology from the offender to convey. I lead discussions regarding the sorts of apologetic meaning that may be most significant given the nature of the offense, the desires of the parties, and the cultural context. This is often the most important step, as such exchanges cause parties to fundamentally rethink the objectives of their apology. I then help parties break down the elements of their apologies, encouraging them to draft one section at a time while I provide feedback to help them navigate the moral, political, and legal landscape. Because a substantive apology consists of much more than the words spoken, we discuss nonverbal aspects of apologizing. Sometimes I consult with attorneys regarding the consequences of apologies in civil and criminal matters. For those who seek or have received apologies, I help interpret their significance. If an apology is calibrated to avoid accepting blame or providing redress, I try to detect this. If someone receives an apology pursuant to a settlement, I help decode it. I offer lectures, seminars, and longer courses on various aspects of apologizing, tailoring these sessions to the needs of the group.

None of this work requires me to assert standing for an offender or to apologize for anyone. Some might argue that even by coaching offenders on how to apologize I do too much of the work for them, perhaps because the truly repentant offender should have full command of her contrition without guidance from an expert. According to that view, an offender who even needs to read books like mine lacks genuine contrition because the path through remorse should be self-evident to anyone who has seen the light. I admit to finding some truth here. Some offenders lack apologetic instincts to the extent that I wonder if they might be sociopaths. I sometimes encourage offenders to explain how little they understood about apologies within the eventual and hopefully much improved apology, as I find that victims appreciate knowing the baseline from which the offender begins her process of transformation. Victims also appreciate insight into which elements of the apology come easily to the offender and which require the most effort. As I have argued, the meanings of apologies are far from obvious. Few people have spent as many hours as I have thinking about apologies, and even I need to refer back to the signposts staked out by the categorical apology. In addition, organizations benefit from outsider advice on these matters because management can slip into self-justifying yes-men groupthink where they have difficulty believing that they did anything wrong. Civil defense attorneys tend to adopt the biases of their clients and may genuinely believe that the opposition is obviously wrong even when the rest of the world thinks otherwise. Outsider perspectives can help offenders appreciate why victims demand apologies. In my view, the assistance I offer to apologizers does not raise the sorts of standing issues that make apologizers-for-hire so problematic. Apology mills contribute to the farce of apologies and undermine the credibility of remorse generally. Many of our public and private conversations about our shared values now occur in the context of someone apologizing or demanding an apology, and I find thoughtful apologies essential for the health of our pluralistic society. It pains me to see public figures botch apologies and squander the opportunity to enrich our discussions about our collective values. I hope that my advising work, like my research, enriches public moral discourse in some small way by helping us be clear about this practice.

Questions of standing in collective apologies become more challenging when, rather than hiring an outsider to perform the deed, the apologizer occupies a position that allows her to make a more credible claim to have contributed to causing the harm. Modern institutions interrelate in baroque organizational charts, with some entities overseeing hundreds of large subsidiaries. Each of these subsidiaries has its own clusters of departments, branches, and other subgroups over which it exercises various degrees of control and oversight. Consider but a few of the standing issues that arise regarding apologies from and claims against these groups.

If standing to provide certain kinds of apologetic meaning requires membership in that group, of which group must the apologizer be a member? In the Chisso example, a janitor with a lifetime of service to the corporation may wish to apologize. If she played no role in the decision-making process, however, her ability to accept blame is clearly limited because she cannot claim membership in the operative group of decision makers. A high-ranking executive who played no role in the mercury emissions might have standing to accept blame for some things, for instance failing to investigate sufficiently once members of the community raised the issue. Only those who decided to release the toxins into the bay, however, can claim standing to accept blame for those particular actions. Here, standing tracks previous discussions regarding precision in attributions of blame within collectives.

Consider if the apologizer holds not only horizontal membership in the group but also vertical authority over it, as would be the case if the chief executive at Ford apologizes for the failures of its safety team. Imagine that although the executive could have fired the safety team or intervened in their work at any time, she knew very little about vehicular safety and allowed the group to operate with near complete autonomy. Imagine that leaders of the safety team refuse to accept blame for the accidents, but the executive states: "On behalf of the entire Ford family, we apologize for the mistakes made by our safety team. We promise to never make those mistakes again." In one respect the executive speaks for the safety team whether they want her to or not, and her statements can indicate Ford's intention to produce safer vehicles in the future. As a promise to do better from someone presumably with the authority to make good on that promise, we would not want to minimize the significance of the statement. Victims are left to wonder if the members of the safety team – those most directly responsible for the harms – believe that they deserve blame or experience any sorts of remorse. The executive may possess the authority to change the institution, but she cannot undergo moral transformations for those proximately responsible for the harm. Those safety engineers may even leave Ford and take their unbowed beliefs and practices to another auto manufacturer. Instead of accepting blame by trying to cast herself as a member of the offending group, we can read the executive's apology as an act of distancing herself from the wrongdoers. Firing these employees casts out the offenders and their blameworthiness, severing their membership to purify the moral status of the organization.

Generally speaking, individuals with both obvious membership in the organization as well as a high rank in that organization – what I call "membership with rank" – make the strongest claims to possess standing to apologize for the organization. Even this risks oversimplifying. President Obama has membership with rank to speak for the United States, but to say he "speaks for me" regarding any number of positions overstates his authority. Issues of consensus surface here: for many controversial issues, only about half of U.S. voters agree with Obama. If it becomes important for another to know that I disagree with Obama – if I am traveling in the Middle East and wish to make clear to my hosts that I reject his policy on drones, for instance – then my own statements clarifying my views override what my hosts might expect to be my "American" view. Many forms of collective membership do not require a member to endorse the views of its leaders. Thus when a member with rank asserts standing to apologize on behalf of the group, we understand the leader's contrition most clearly if we appreciate how her assertions track the actual views of her constituencies. The degree of disagreement tolerated within the organization should also inform our understanding. Disagreeing with a leader's apology could be considered a grave offense in some regimes. Publicly challenging your boss's contrition might get you fired. In such authoritarian situations it can therefore prove difficult for victims to discern how members actually view the apology. If Obama apologizes for something, by contrast, commentators in the United States will have little reservations about expressing their opinions and identifying when the president speaks for them or not.

After establishing the relevant group to which the apologizer should belong to hold a credible claim to standing, additional questions arise regarding the temporal nature of the collective. We often act as if leaders occupy unbroken chains of causation, for example as if the president of the

United States is effectively one moral agent from Washington to Obama. This metaphor strains credibility. Although apologies from current leaders for the mistakes of past leaders convey important meanings regarding the contemporary values and intentions of the institution, this differs considerably from an executive accepting blame on behalf of her predecessors. We can stretch notions of group membership and moral causation too thin. I might assert standing to accept blame for the destruction of Carthage because I share membership in humanity – and perhaps also my wife's Italian-American heritage – with the Romans of 146 BCE. If modern Tunisians learn of my apology and file a claim against me to recover their ancient losses, I would be quick to explain that I did not intend to imply that I deserved blame for the ancient genocide.

Notice how this temporal dynamic played out when Grünenthal chief executive Harald Stock offered what was described as an apology sixty years after the initial thalidomide injuries. Grünenthal does not accept blame for the injuries, instead stating:

The thalidomide tragedy took place 50 years ago in a world completely different from today. The international scientific community, the pharmaceutical industry and governments, legislators and administrations have had to learn a lot from it. Throughout the world the tragedy influenced the development of new authorization procedures and legal frameworks, which seek to minimize the risks of new medicines for patients as much as possible. Grünenthal has acted in accordance with the state of scientific knowledge and all industry standards for testing new drugs that were relevant and acknowledged in the 1950s and 1960s. We regret that the teratogenic potential of thalidomide could not be detected by the tests that we and others carried out before it was marketed.[94]

Stock asserts that even the former leaders of the company do not deserve blame because the dangers "could not be detected." This is a dubious claim because by 1965 international scientists accused Grünenthal of "hoodwinking" safety reviewers, and a German court found Grünenthal's testing "negligent, misleading, inexcusable, very inadequate by the standards of the day."[95] Some accuse Grünenthal of knowingly targeting pregnant women with drugs that they knew would cause deformities and bribing reviewers in order to sell more pills, but current leadership continues to deny these findings and refuses to admit that previous leaders deserve blame. Instead, Grünenthal emphasizes current mental states by expressing "sincere regrets about the consequences of thalidomide" and "deep sympathy for all those affected, their mothers and their families."[96] If we assume for a moment that Stock can speak for a consensus of the collective in its present membership, then we can also assume that he can comfortably claim standing to express their current sympathy for what happened in the past. Similarly, Stock's statement, "[w]e are aware of our responsibility and will continue to fulfill it in demand-oriented projects and initiatives," speaks of prospective responsibility rather than retrospective acceptance of blame. Temporal issues become muddied when Stock further states: "We also apologize for the fact that we have not found the way to you from person to person for almost 50 years. Instead, we have been silent and we are very sorry for that."[97] Here the harms related to failing to acknowledge, engage, and provide redress to victims continued under Stock's leadership. Such continuity over fifty years introduces important ambiguities. The wrong of "being silent" sounds like a euphemism for many harms, including denying that they caused severe birth defects, ignoring victims, and failing to provide redress to those in dire need of help for their disabled children. Does Stock or current executives assert standing to accept blame for their own contributions to these failures that happened on their watch? Did they, personally, fail to acknowledge the victims as moral interlocutors? Or, do they allow the temporal ambiguity of their statements to conceal their own wrongdoing? If a victim felt disrespected and otherwise harmed by Stock – if Stock failed to return her letters pleading for assistance and otherwise made her life with thalidomide injuries even worse, for instance – having him personally accept such blame confers very different meanings than the nonspecific statement he provides. As one victim expressed his dissatisfaction, Grünenthal provides "some kind of statement that they are emotionally connected to our suffering. They've had 50 years to make billions of dollars while we struggled and our parents committed suicide. And now, they're apologizing for not saying anything. How dare they do that and think it's going to be enough."[98]

Issues regarding delegating the work of apologizing for civil harms also deserve attention. *I Was Wrong* identified a few ways delegation might occur: (1) an individual delegating to another individual; (2) an individual delegating to a collective; (3) a collective delegating to an individual; (4) a collective delegating to a collective; and (5) variations on these arrangements in which members delegate to nonmembers or nonmembers delegate to members. I will not analyze the many possible nuances here other than to point out a few general features of these dynamics.

Less controversial claims to standing benefit from a process whereby members explicitly and unanimously agree that a group leader may express specific apologetic sentiments on their behalf. Imagine, for example, a small company of five employees coordinating to compose an apology and unanimously electing the longest tenured member of the group to deliver it for them. Notice again, however, that I cannot delegate certain forms of apologetic work. I cannot, for example, delegate my emotional states or outsource my moral transformation. In the same sense I might hire someone to deliver a loving note and gift to my mother on her birthday, but I cannot hire someone to love my mother for me because I am too busy to feel it or because I actually feel rather negative toward her but want her to think otherwise. Notice also that the dead rarely delegate authority to apologize for them to third parties, and even if they did, such apologies would suffer from various weaknesses. A promise not to reoffend, for instance, seems redundant if the offender is already dead.

Situations will arise wherein victims do not place much importance in whether the apologizer possesses standing to accept blame or speak on behalf of the wrongdoers. If the Ford, Chisso, or Grünenthal victims primarily seek to prevent others from suffering similar harms, they should focus on the prospective statements of executives and regulators with the power to make those changes. Current members with rank may lack culpability but have the more important ability to make the future different from the past. If victims primarily seek redress, they may not care who writes the checks so long as they clear. Attempting to attribute blame and attach it to individuals long dead or otherwise indisposed to admit guilt can hinder the process of eliminating dangers and gaining relief. Despite this, some victims of civil harms will tirelessly demand that those responsible for their suffering admit guilt. Civil claimants enter disputes with a range of objectives. Sometimes these objectives conflict. Hopefully the proceeding discussions help clarify the costs and benefits of such expectations and how the apologies provided measure up to the meanings sought.

Standing in civil matters typically concerns not whether the *offender* has standing to accept blame but whether the *claimant* has standing to bring the claim because she suffered an injury. In most situations one cannot simply be an abstractly interested third party to bring a civil claim, but instead one must assert that she has suffered or will imminently suffer harms recognized by law. She is, in other words, directly involved in the action rather than possessing a purely academic interest. Issues of claimant standing raise noteworthy concerns for individual and collective apologies in civil actions, especially as related to a victim's ability or desire to forgive an offender. Imagine that although I did not suffer injuries from the Ford rollover, I am so deeply moved by the suffering of victims that I take up the cause and campaign for a blame-accepting apology from Ford. The civil courts provide my battleground, and I go so far as to adopt one of the injured children to establish standing. Suppose my legal team prevails, and Ford agrees to settle and privately accept blame. To what extent do I have authority to forgive them? To what extent can my adopted child forgive them on behalf of all of the victims?

Suppose my legal team had brought a class action against Ford, and Ford provided a public apology accepting blame to all of us. Some members of the class forgive and some do not. Those who died in the crashes have no say; it would seem rather presumptuous to assume that they would have forgiven the offender had they experienced the apology. Forgiving raises as many questions as apologizing. I will not begin to address those issues here other than to note that the standing concerns facing collective offenders also apply to collective victims. Sometimes questions of victim standing can be even more controversial, for instance as one group claims to have forgiven the offender while another group of victims finds such purported reconciliation to be an insulting betrayal. Imagine that you were disabled in a rollover accident and have battled Ford in the courts with little success while they deny wrongdoing. Imagine watching Donna Bailey on television, describing Ford's representatives as "very sincere" in their remorse. Bailey receives a settlement award. Your bills accumulate. Ford leverages Bailey's example to undermine your demands that Ford publicly admit fault. Imagine that Ford strikes a deal with a safety advocacy group started by one of the victims, and Ford very publicly contributes large amounts to the group and describes this as redress "paying their debt to society." You get nothing from this pool, and Ford maintains that it has now exhausted its remediation budget so all the more reason to surrender your legal battles. Such examples draw attention to how the standing of individual and collective victims can raise potentially serious considerations.

4. Does the Civil Offender Identify Each Harm?

For individual civil offenders, concerns here parallel those in criminal contexts. Does she identify all of the harms at issue rather than collapsing multiple wrongs into an undifferentiated assertion that she somehow acted badly such that we cannot discern precisely what she admits? Does she name only the most undeniable offense in light of the accumulated evidence? Does she apologize for only the lesser offense, perhaps because doing so maximizes strategic advantages of contrition while minimizing legal risks?

Consider how this might unfold in a divorce proceeding in which infidelity destroyed a marriage. If the unfaithful partner apologizes, which harms does she name? Does she identify lying, betraying, or subjecting the children to emotional pain? These harms may have persisted over decades, manifested across a range of behaviors. Perhaps the marriage had undergone a long deterioration, and she does not regret finding a new partner but does recognize the wrongness of the deceptions she committed to hide the extramarital relation. As the betrayed spouse, it may be important to understand if the partner sees lying as the only harm requiring an apology because she embraces the relationship with her new partner. If contributory behaviors such as alcoholism provide the root cause of infidelity, she may most desire her spouse to recognize drinking as the underlying issue most requiring treatment.

In criminal cases, lines between illegality and immorality trigger questions regarding liberal neutrality. In civil matters, however, injured parties rather than the state hold authority to bring claims. If a victim believes that those who harmed her have since taken Jesus into their hearts and view their wrongdoing primarily as harms against God, she may decide against bringing a claim against her fellow born-again Christians. State prosecutors cannot judge offenders so explicitly in terms of faith, but nothing prevents civil litigants from allowing religious beliefs to motivate their legal actions.

Collectives identifying harms in civil contexts often require considerably more scrutiny because the offenses may unfold over years and across the span of the institution's reach. Chisso would require volumes to document the history and ongoing suffering across a region. These harms would touch every aspect of the lives of some victims, as well as the lives of their children and grandchildren: physical pain, emotional suffering, disregard for their humanity, social exclusion, financial collapse across generations, destruction of traditional fishing jobs, environmental degradation, tax burdens to Japanese citizens to remediate its waters, distrust of corporate as well and governmental bodies, and more. Such large-scale harms typically involve collusion from multiple actors: managers who released mercury into the bay, Chisso scientists who kept quiet despite knowing the dangers, executives who promoted unfounded claims that the injuries resulted from dumped World War II explosives, government officials who looked away or actively papered over Chisso's lies, thugs who beat the protesters and those who dared to photograph the deformed victims, and so on.

Apologizing for the "wrong wrong" also surfaces in the collective context. With so many harms to choose from, representatives can decide on which of many swords to fall. Blankfein's apology for "participating in market euphoria," for instance, reminds one of the priests who apologized for breaching his vow of chastity after molesting children. Whatever Blankfein means by "participating in market euphoria," it does not describe the behavior that concerns most of us.

Note how insufficiently specific apologies allow leaders to obscure their own culpable actions under an umbrella of overly generalized harms. If a Chisso executive speaks only of "harms we caused the community," he does not specify the damage he personally caused and deflects blame onto an impersonal collective.

5. Does the Civil Offender Identify Principles Underlying Each Harm?

Here we seek to determine whether the offender understands *why* the offense is harmful. This can occur at two levels: comprehending the prevailing state of the law or registering the offense according to deeper moral codes. Offenders may recognize various authorities for such prohibitions, from the laws of the State of New Hampshire to the Old Testament. Note the difference between a legalistic understanding of the wrong ("Article XYZ, Section 3.1 requires disclosing the presence of asbestos in residential real estate") and a moral understanding ("Lying to people about the presence of carcinogens in a home and thereby exposing them to danger to make profit is immoral because it treats people as a mere means to making money"). Tanaka provides an example of a Japanese meat distributor that falsely labeled the origins of their products. The managers first saw their crime as "violating labeling laws," which sounds like a rather banal offense against bureaucratic regulations. Such laws exist, however, to protect consumers from potentially deadly illnesses such as mad cow disease. To apologize effectively, the executives needed to understand why the public perceived them as attempted murders rather than incompetent bookkeepers.[99]

Offenders who understand the principle at issue can identify other behaviors falling within its provenance. The scope of the recognized value can be narrow or broad, for example limiting the requirement to disclose asbestos in real estate transactions or broadening the principle to apply to lying generally. Ford might identify a narrow principle ("Tires on Explorers must meet X criterion"), an intermediate principle ("The safest tires should be used on all vehicles"), or a broad principle ("All manufacturers should meet the highest safety standards regardless of cost").

Collective civil harms cluster around the sorts of vices more commonly found within institutions, including negligence, complicity, breaches of fiduciary duties, failure to adequately train or supervise, and refusal to promote justice or prevent injustice. Civil apologies can accentuate some principles while ignoring others, calibrating its meanings accordingly. Grünenthal, for example, apologizes "for the fact that we have not found the way to you from person to person for almost 50 years. Instead, we have been silent and we are very sorry for that." If executives regret "being silent," what would they have said given that they deny any culpability for the harms caused by thalidomide? Some may be insulted by Grünenthal's silence, perhaps because they feel rejected as moral interlocutors. I doubt this amounts to the central principle at issue for most when considered alongside the birth defects, the marketing of a deceptively tested drug, and the refusal to provide redress. I suspect that many victims and members in the broader community believe the root moral failure in this case, like many mass torts, lies in valuing profit over safety. Offenders rarely name that principle, making it unlikely that they will reform to honor it.

Imagine in this regard if a group of bankers accepted responsibility for the 2008 economic collapse and sought to explain why their actions deserve blame. Why were they wrong? Were they merely negligent accountants, or were they driven by greed? Did they lie, steal, or otherwise violate trust and abuse power? Did they violate laws or unscrupulously vitiate them? Is their primary failure, in their eyes, getting caught? These are all rather different offenses, and moral failings often result from the aggregation of many lesser wrongs. Such an accounting would provide insights into the characters of the offenders and the nature of their offenses, and their contrition will probably seem unsatisfying until they address these transgressions with some precision. Notice here that avarice, like many of the relevant moral principles, is not necessarily illegal.

The process of identifying the principles at issue can bring substantial benefit for a community, even if the offender ultimately refuses to endorse the value.[100] Whether through internal discussions or in public discourse surrounding the harms, the process of understanding why actions invoke the demand for an apology can occasion self-reflection and institutional review regarding first principles. Sometimes this occasions institutional reflection on norms endorsed by its predecessors that have since become unacceptable.

6. Does the Civil Offender Share a Commitment to the Principles Underlying Each Harm?

Identifying the principles at issue differs from endorsing those principles. Chik-fil-A, for example, may appreciate that some customers oppose its stance against same-sex marriage. Chik-fil-A executives explained their views and defended themselves against exaggerations of their position:

The Chick-fil-A culture and 66-year service tradition in our locally owned and operated restaurants is to treat every person with honor, dignity and respect – regardless of their beliefs, race, creed, sexual orientation or gender. We are a restaurant company focused on food, service and hospitality; our intent is not to engage in political or social debates.[101]

Meanwhile, chief executive Dan Cathy confessed to being "guilty as charged" regarding his views on homosexual marriage.[102] This illustrates the crucial distinction between recognizing a value and endorsing that value as legitimate. If the offender rejects the principle at issue, she will not think that she has done anything wrong. Vocal opposition may lead her to double down in defense of her beliefs. Rather than repudiating its views with an apology, Chik-fil-A executives attempted to disengage from the political issue to minimize boycotting and negative economic impact. Substituting interracial marriage – "we're guilty as charged that we oppose interracial marriage but our intent is not to engage in political or social debates" – helps sharpen the distinction between understanding and endorsing the principles at issue.

By contrast, awareness of and commitment to the underlying principle provides reason to speak the signature phrase of the categorical apology: I was wrong. My actions *deserve blame* because they violate values I share with the victims. An offender who explains why she commits to the principles provides a glimpse into her character and motivations. If an employer explains that she should not have discriminated against you in the workplace because she now realizes that doing so conflicts with her religious or moral views, this differs from a boss realizing she cannot legally fire you for being homosexual. In some cases legal motivations for endorsing values may have more predicative power than strictly moral motivations, as the offender may not have understood that she could get into so much trouble for being homophobic. The law provides an effective deterrent, and she will not make that mistake again. She might, however, aggressively lobby to repeal the applicable laws. You should exercise caution if you encounter her in a forum that does not provide protections against homosexual discrimination. Such an apology differs from a similar situation in which the offender comes to view her legally prohibited homophobia as morally problematic as well. If she describes why she no longer wishes to be homophobic, she provides additional insight into both her character and her likelihood of reoffending. Again, notice that nothing prevents civil litigants from bringing claims or dropping claims on the basis of whether they find the offender's reasons for apologizing and endorsing the value at issue satisfactory – no matter how personal those reasons.

Apologies responding to civil charges can serve as declarations of institutional policy. A group might update its charter to conform to evolving social norms or to reflect changes in leadership. A declaration can also restate and emphasize a commitment to long-held values from which members have deviated. Again, the process of discussing, revising, and renewing commitments to core values supports important objectives even if the collective or individual does not accept blame for the harm at issue. Here we could imagine Grünenthal leadership responding to demands for an apology by declaring product safety as its highest value and honoring that value, all while refusing to admit culpability for thalidomide-related harms. Perhaps in the wake of public concern over pharmaceutical safety – on the anniversary of thalidomide's release, for instance – other corporations and governing bodies join in Grünenthal's safety pledge, and as a result Grünenthal's gestures have considerable impact even while not accepting guilt.

Regarding standing and delegation, declarations of executives and spokespersons may not reflect the values of everyone in the collective. Future members may retract the declaration or otherwise reject the principles. As discussed later, intentions motivating an offender can also inform our understanding. It makes a difference if a corporation endorses a value primarily to brand itself as principled in a manner that will appease – or at least not repel – its market base. Endorsing a value in principle differs from honoring that value in practice. Subsequent sections consider that gap.

7. Does the Civil Offender Recognize Victims as Moral Interlocutors?

When civil offenders treat victims as moral interlocutors, they afford them respect. They treat them as humans deserving dignity rather than as mere means to some end such as profit maximization. They understand and interact with the injured not as abstractions – numbers on a balance sheet or statistical liabilities – but as individuals who think and feel. Wrongdoers understand the need to reach out and apologize specifically to the victims rather than expressing contrition to the media, regulators, or stakeholders with the most power over them.[103] When I harmed you, I saw you as unworthy of sufficient consideration, but now I turn to you in humility to discuss the values that give meaning to my life.

Unlike the state-driven procedures of criminal prosecution, civil victims often remain present throughout the civil process and can read offenders for the sorts of significance they convey. Whereas criminal procedures can tempt offenders to apologize to a judge or another representative of the state because such officials evaluate remorse for credit toward reducing punishment, a civil victim typically maintains authority to discharge an offender from liability. The victim may exercise this option if satisfied that the offender now treats her with respect, and therefore the offender has considerable incentive to direct the apology toward her. Some civil cases seem like a pretext for pursuing one unspoken desire: victims want offenders to show them respect. Collective civil harms present various challenges and opportunities in this regard. Often in cases of large-scale civil injuries the offense stems not from an aberrant misdeed somehow out of character for the offender but rather from systematic disregard of the interests of a group of people. Sometimes this disregard is callous and intentional, as when Enron employees took delight in the suffering of the vulnerable victims during the California blackouts because such misfortune translated into company profits. Recognizing victims and members of the community with equal worth can be especially significant in the aftermath of such degradation. Timothy George argues in this regard that protests against Chisso and demands for redress facilitated the democratization of postwar Japan.[104]

I have worked on cases with tens of thousands of civil victims. How in such situations do offenders – whether living individuals or large institutions – treat specific victims as moral interlocutors and as something more than a statistic? Certainly this presents challenges, but when one injures so many people, one should realize the scale of the damage caused and the enormity of work required to make amends. Naming victims can provide a step toward recognizing victims, although whether this recognition should be public depends on the context. Someone defrauded, for example, may not want everyone – especially other scammers – to know that she fell for a scam. A child of a parent who died from mercury poisoning may very much want Chisso to publicly recognize her deceased parent. Mass mailings and e-mailings individualized to the extent possible can help personally recognize victims. Video of the offenders performing the apology attached to such mailings can add a layer of presence. Offenders can arrange – and when suitable pay for the cost of travel and attendance – an "open forum" where they can meet with victims. Press conferences also invite victims and the general public to engage in open-ended discussions and to judge the offenders' responses to the crises, thereby ceding power to those harmed.

All of these occasions can provide mechanisms for victims to speak to the offenders and for offenders to respond. This can include any number of face-to-face or technologically mediated processes, but all methods should expect those who deserve blame to subject themselves to the interlocutions of their victims. The channels for conversation should flow in both directions rather than affording the offender full control over the form and context of the exchanges. Honoring so many victims as civil interlocutors can become an offender's full-time work, and personally undertaking this work differs from hiring a public relations firm to field comments from disgruntled customers. Consider, in this regard, if culpable Chisso executives state that they respect all of their victims as moral interlocutors but then avoid meeting them or otherwise claim to be too busy. Such behaviors would provide important data points in evaluating their priorities and the meanings of their apologies.

A few additional subtleties deserve attention. In some cases interlocution with the victim will not be possible. She may be long dead. She may refuse to participate in dialogue. Offenders may be left to recognize an interlocutor who rejects them. Victims may desire that recognition come not from those to blame for the harm but rather from their replacements or superiors. If I suffered employment discrimination at your hands, I may want you fired as well as an apology not from you but from the highest-ranking person in the organization who will declare that I am a person of equal worth and who has the power to ensure that this never happens again. Some may desire the recognition from the highest-ranking official in the collective because this confers the greatest elevation of their status. When Bill Clinton offered his apology for the Tuskegee experiments, he lacked certain kinds of standing to accept blame for the atrocities. As a standing president publicly recognizing the moral status of poor black Southerners, however, he probably does more to elevate their standing and bring attention to the injustices against them than would actions from lower-ranking officials better positioned to accept blame for their own roles in authorizing or conducting the experiments.

These challenges should not obscure the damage that can be done when apologizers fail to recognize victims. Even if the injury is minor, the victim may seek assurance that offenders cannot disregard her rights – she is a person and she brings a civil claim in part to demand that she be treated as such. Failing to recognize her as a moral interlocutor in the apology can cause greater harm than the underlying offense. Again, imagine that I am victim of employment discrimination. The media catches wind of the allegation and the accused company issues a public apology as a tactic to control the damage. Meanwhile, the company refuses to acknowledge me or return my calls. Perhaps I was planning on leaving that job anyway, I found the offense largely symbolic, and I bring the claim primarily to call attention to future harm potentially suffered by my similarly situated colleagues. Being treated like a prop in a public relations strategy would leave me feeling even more intensely disrespected. I fear that the politics and economics of collective apologies often escalate injuries by failing to recognize victims in these ways.

Lastly, I would like to provide an explanation for those who view these issues along a more Continental axis. Levinas and Adorno were my first philosophical loves, and they lurk beneath the surface of my treatment of apologies. For Levinas and Adorno, the ethical relation is always between singulars: the face or the nonidentical other and the "subject."[105] As soon as we introduce collectives – the nation, an ethnicity, any group of faces – we lose sight of the concrete singularity and vulnerability that both Adorno and Levinas believe must anchor ethical life. Both contrast this with abstract Kantian ethical law or the like. Levinas offers a distinctive treatment of apologies as a kind of perpetual undoing of conceptual violence or, in his terms, the apology of unsaying the said. As he writes in his distinctive way: "Apology, in which the 'I' at the same time asserts itself and inclines before the transcendent, belongs to the essence of conversation."[106] Part of my caution with respect to collective apologies rests in their abstraction from individuals who have been harmed into impersonal conceptual clusters. Collective apologies risk losing sight of individual victims in all of their vulnerability.

In this light I find Pope John Paul II's contrition regarding the Church's role in the Holocaust especially interesting.[107] In many ways the Church's response is remarkable: remarkably effective and remarkably ineffective. As Raymond Cohen has written, the Church's apology spans forty years of penitential acts culminating in the Pope's dramatic placement of a note in the Western Wall.[108] The note stated:

God of our fathers, you chose Abraham and his descendants to bring your Name to the Nations: we are deeply saddened by the behavior of those who in the course of history have caused these children of yours to suffer, and asking your forgiveness we wish to commit ourselves to genuine brotherhood with the people of the Covenant.

Although high theater for the 2000 Jubilee, this fails to provide meaning on many levels. It does not accept blame, either on behalf of the Pope or his predecessors. It is painfully general and ambiguous. It speaks to the Almighty rather than to victims. By some accounts, however, it transformed relations between Christians and Jews. There are many reasons for this impact, but one seems especially suggestive with respect to recognizing victims as interlocutors. Prior to the event at the Western Wall, the Pope's pilgrimage offered several gestures of contrition, including a stop at Holocaust memorial Yad Vashem.[109] Here, among his hosts in a reception line of Holocaust survivors, stood Edith Zierer. In 1945, the Pope found the thirteen-year-old Zierer in a Polish train station, huddled in a corner wearing a striped labor camp uniform and near death.[110] He fed her, wrapped her in his cloak, and got her on the train to Krakow so that she could search for her parents, who, unbeknownst to her, had already been killed. Fifty-five years later the Pope shared a few bittersweet moments with this survivor in Yad Vashem as she gave thanks for providing a small island of kindness amid a sea of utter horror. In addition to his abstract and universal appeal for forgiveness at the Wall, he also confronted a singular elderly woman in all of her complexity. While the Pope bowed in shame for the massive failures of his institution, this singular being thanked him for saving her life – two humans, face to face. This contrast of the universal and the singular brings into focus the overlapping layers of meaning. Nothing the Pope can do or say is enough. Genuflecting before this singular victim can only remind him that he should have done this and more for every victim. Many of those victims are dead. Certain kinds of meaning are forever lost and can only be mourned. Institutional apologies do not neutralize historical wrongdoing by magically discharging their predecessors' debts. The most effective collective apologies must often resist the language of closure to articulate and respond to enduring pain.

8. Does the Civil Offender Express and Demonstrate Categorical Regret?

A categorically regretful offender understands that she has committed a moral error that she wishes she could reverse. Categorical regret differs from empathy for the consequences of a justified decision. If an employer says she regrets firing her employee while explaining that "this is my only option because I can't have pregnant women working here," she still endorses the difficult choice even though she empathizes with the employee. By contrast, the employer might experience categorical regret after the termination. Perhaps she faces a discrimination claim brought by the former employee, and in the process she begins to understand the harm she caused. Perhaps she had not given issues regarding gender equality in the workplace much thought, but this crash course via litigation causes her to see the light. She understands that she would not want someone to do this to her or her children. She comes to feel guilty for the harm she has caused, recognizes her choices as wrong, and wishes she could turn back the clock and make the better choice. Rather than wishing she did not *get caught* wrongfully terminating or realizing that she should have better concealed her illegal intentions to fire the woman because she was pregnant, she becomes categorically apologetic when she internalizes the wrongness of her actions. Unlike criminal cases wherein the state incapacitates offenders and "shuts them down" in various ways, civil offenders often remain in business after wrongdoing. If they continue to commit similar offenses while claiming to experience regret, this provides powerful evidence that their regret is something other than categorical.

Revisit Grünenthal's explanation that it "acted in accordance with the state of scientific knowledge and all industry standards for testing new drugs that were relevant and acknowledged in the 1950s and 1960s. We regret that the teratogenic potential of thalidomide could not be detected by the tests that we and others carried out before it was marketed." What does Grünenthal "regret"? Rather than recognizing a mistake of some kind, Grünenthal claims to regret that the standard tests utilized at the time did not detect the dangers. As we saw earlier, however, they have been widely accused of distorting their research and flouting safety standards even of that era. Grünenthal continues to deny this. Even if they had met those standards, Grünenthal still faced a choice: apply the lowest acceptable legal standards or exceed those conventions to establish a degree of certainty that thalidomide would not injure fetuses. Like many manufacturers who release products into the stream of commerce once they clear rather low and contested safety standards and before the scientific community can reach consensus with longitudinal data regarding the potential consequences of a product, Grünenthal decided that thalidomide was safe enough to sell and generate profits. Instead of regretting this decision, Grünenthal executives endorse it: we met the standards at the time, those standards were too low to catch the likelihood that X children would suffer server deformities, and we do not regret failing to achieve a higher degree of certainty regarding product safety. Grünenthal, in other words, stands by its decision. Victims and potential customers should take note: despite causing some of the most horrific injuries in the history of civil law, Grünenthal endorses the industry standard of 1950 as good enough for the time. This suggests that Grünenthal continues to endorse releasing products so long as they satisfy the minimum safety conditions established within a given market. This differs considerably from an institution so transformed that it becomes the leader of industry reform and the standard bearer for consumer safety.

Categorical regret can raise complex issues when organizations look back on their multivariable cost-benefit analyses. Surely consumer safety is important for Grünenthal executives, either because they genuinely care about other people's suffering or because they realize that injuries tarnish their brand. In retrospect, they should have waited to release thalidomide. At the time and in the context of many other drugs being developed, how many tests must be done? How long must a drug developer wait? Such questions invoke long-standing debates regarding the regulation of markets. As institutions balance competing objectives – in this case the tension between getting a product to market and waiting for more certainty regarding the product's safety – what looked like a reasonable decision at the time can look disastrous once we know its consequences. Grünenthal's decisions look particularly egregious because they appear to have intentionally distorted the research and then aggressively marketed thalidomide to pregnant women. Ford, Chisso, and the Tuskegee experimenters all undertook similar cost-benefit analyses. We now want them to understand that they made unacceptable choices. From the broader perspective, the waves of civil actions against corporations since the mid-twentieth century has reduced the amount of risk that we allow institutions to take with individual well-being: recalibrate risk assessment or face the legal consequences.

Institutions often attempt to invoke exculpatory background facts to mitigate the wrongness of their decisions. Grünenthal's "everyone was doing it" argument orients its moral compass by industry standards, even as it appears to have violated those norms. Others invoke praiseworthy objectives that unintentionally contributed to the harm – imagine if Ford cited a desire to provide low-cost vehicles as the reason for not devoting more resources to safety or if Chisso invoked its zeal to advance the postwar Japanese economy as contributing to its neglect of environmental concerns. We should distinguish between those who offer this information as an excuse and those who demonstrate increased self-awareness by reconstructing the decision-making process in a manner that helps them understand the wrongness of their choice so that they can avoid similar mistakes going forward: I clearly understand why I did it, I see why it was wrong, and this knowledge allows me to explain how I will avoid those pitfalls in the future.

This can lead to interesting tensions. If the underlying error can be traced to something so general as valuing profit over safety, a categorically apologetic executive may have difficulty finding a place to work. Apologetic white-collar criminals sometimes retire because they cannot reconcile their business instincts with their newly invigorated value for people over money. Like individuals, governments can also undergo deep renovations to their values with changes in administrations, laws, and norms. Corporations, however, may find that certain changes to their value systems will amount to organizational suicide. If Grünenthal stated that thalidomide injuries sparked a commitment to never again release pharmaceuticals without knowing for certain they would not cause harm, this would strongly suggest categorical regret. It would also effectively put them out of business.

Sometimes the harm at issue will be the proximate cause of the apologizers' power and identity. In the case of categorical regret for African slavery or genocide against Native Americans, we can trace much of the United States' current wealth to those events. Undoing such injustices implies wishing the nonexistence of the nation in its current form.[111] Would Chisso have survived as an organization if it had borne the costs of properly disposing of its wastes? Do Chisso stakeholders really wish they had made choices that would have put them out of jobs or money?

We should also appreciate that the accused sometimes stand by their decisions and make it clear that they do not regret their actions because they would make the choice again if confronting the same variables. Grünenthal victims may not like it, but when executives appear to endorse the judgment of their predecessors, they stake out a position about which reasonable people may disagree. They wish the decision did not produce such unintended *consequences*, but they do not believe they committed a moral error in making that decision. Perhaps we think they should have done more and erred more on the side of caution. Perhaps we find them cold-hearted and deluded. They disagree, believing they made the best possible choice given the circumstances. Current executives may even believe that casting blame on their predecessors would be a disingenuous betrayal. We should evaluate the substance of their apology accordingly.

9. Has the Civil Offender Performed the Apology?
Reviewers should not look too narrowly at apologies as speech acts, but the features clustered around the utterances lay foundations for the meanings they promise. A few aspects deserve special attention in civil contexts. First, note the limits of someone stating that she "owes you an apology" and acting as if uttering that phrase alone accomplishes the task. "I think I may owe you an apology" adds further opacity, as if she has not yet determined what sort of apology – if any – you deserve. Just as "I think I may owe you money" differs considerably from actually paying a debt, statements suggesting that one might apologize in the future leave meanings indeterminate and unrealized. For what do you admit blame? Why do you think that was wrong? Are you promising to never do it again and to redress the damage you caused? Ambiguity defines the gesture in the absence of clear statements articulating these commitments. Some of the most theatrical gestures of contrition suffer from such inscrutability. Willy's Brandt's gesture of kneeling at the monument to victims of the Warsaw Ghetto Uprising comes to mind. Brandt explained: "On the abyss of German history and carrying the burden of the millions who were murdered, I did what people do when words fail them."[112] Without the words, we are left to interpret the implications of his ritualistic genuflection. Sometimes such rituals seem to curate their ambiguity rather carefully, as when Grünenthal unveiled a statue of a thalidomide victim while refusing to admit wrongdoing. We just do not know what the gestures signify without further explanation.

Rather than apologizing to a third party or keeping the apology to themselves via internal statements within the organization, offenders should express the contents of the apology to the victims and community as appropriate. Given the complex and precise range of content to be conveyed, written exchanges will often express these meanings more clearly and permanently than oral statements. Written records also transfer to the victim the power to share, publicize, or otherwise make legal or non-legal use of the information in the apology. Some civil victims may also desire a spoken apology for various reasons, including the desire to evaluate the offender's emotions and engage her in conversation that may provide insight into her mental states. Some may wish to avoid face-to-face confrontations with the person who harmed them, in part for fear of further manipulation or harm. Collective apologies for large-scale harms occurring over long periods magnify these benefits of written apologies as institutions sort out the substance they seek to convey. Such apologies may require a great deal of internal discussion and necessitate disclosing considerable amounts of information to various constituencies.

The extent to which offenders perform apologies publicly or privately presents one of the most contested issues in the context of civil harms. Public apologies for civil harm can accomplish many objectives, including explaining to the community what happened, removing suspicions that the victim deserves blame, honoring and reaffirming the breached values, elevating the status of historically subordinated classes of victims, and triggering a process of reform across similarly situated institutions. Victims may have good reasons for wanting to keep apologies provided to them private, perhaps because public knowledge of the apology would bring undesired attention and cause further pain. Victims may find an offender's desire to broadcast an apology to amount to moral grandstanding that serves offenders' interests at the expense of the victims' desire for discretion: "Look at me. I am apologetic. I am good. Recognize my goodness and confer benefits." In rare cases, offenders might want to publicize their apology because they genuinely desire to accomplish some public benefit by doing so, yet their victims desire personal privacy over public good.

In most civil contexts, however, offenders are motivated to limit public exposure to and scrutiny of their apologies. The majority of civil cases in the United States end in settlement agreements, and confidentiality provisions within these agreements provide the most common means of actively suppressing public awareness of apologies. Toro, the company credited with innovating corporate apologies as a means of reducing litigation costs, requires that confidentiality agreements exclude statements made during mediation from admission in court.[113] Commentators widely recognize mediation as a "natural place for apology" because "a main goal of mediation is to help the parties work out their differences."[114] Confidentiality of mediation proceedings and agreements vary by jurisdictions, with some protections preventing victims from disclosing to the public or to other victims that the offender has apologized.[115]

Why would an offender want to limit public review of its apology? Consider a few examples. Imagine that a surgeon operated under the influence of illegal stimulants and in an act of gross negligence caused a child to suffer debilitating injuries. The parents bring a malpractice claim against her. She admits her addiction. She accepts blame. The family agrees to a large and confidential settlement, in part because caring for the injured child will be expensive. They fear the unknown of a trial that could leave them with nothing, so they take the settlement money. They agree to an amount that their attorneys think is about all they can hope for from a trial, but at the price of signing a confidentiality agreement preventing them from discussing the case. The surgeon and the hospital are especially keen to avoid publicly admitting blame because, unbeknownst to the family, the doctor also injured other children. Those families, however, have not filed claims because they never thought to suspect negligence. A public apology could alert these other families to the surgeon's wrongdoing and result in numerous claims. Those multiple claims could cost the doctor her license. The hospital might need to overhaul their supervisory protocols, addiction treatment programs for physicians, and sanctions for offending doctors. Instead, the confidential settlement leaves the community in the dark. New patients presume the surgeon's competence. She continues to operate on children. The hospital and the surgeon are left to self-police. If other injuries come to light, the family receiving the confidential apology can only watch from the sidelines. Gagged from discussing how their child's suffering relates to the new victims, they may feel as though they bargained away their status as moral interlocutors. While the doctor and hospital deny culpability, such lies would justify them in feeling as if they are again mere means to others' ends.

In the Ford situation, a public declaration admitting wrongdoing and committing to reform would have occasioned public discussion. Ford would be on the record describing what it did, why it was wrong, and how it would correct the problem. The public could then evaluate Ford's future behavior in light of these declarations. Instead, Ford limits its apology to whatever ambiguous meanings the public might glean from Bailey's statements to the media – statements she may have been required to utter per the settlement agreement. Ford achieves its objective of settling with Bailey and others without publicly admitting guilt and thereby weakening its legal position against other victims. Ford also refused to concede in the court of public opinion that it deserves blame for producing unsafe vehicles. Without the ability to evaluate what Ford said to Bailey, whether anyone accepted blame, what the representatives promised her, and how the company plans reform its practices, the media reports that "Ford Apologizes." Ford also potentially gains another significant benefit: "[B]y preemptive measure and apology, corporations have become increasingly able to avoid class certification and to avoid severe financial crisis."[116] Civil defense attorneys have strategic reasons to offer confidential apologies in settlement agreements if doing so carries little risk (both within that particular negotiation and with respect to exposure to future litigation) and softens demands for damages. Defense attorneys can divide and conquer in this respect, agreeing with individual claimants to terms that would not satisfy a unified class of victims who publicly state their demands and collectively scrutinize offers.

Some describe settlements contingent on confidentiality a form of "hush money" whereby victims "prostitute" their injury and its potential to precipitate reform for the sake of negotiating the most favorable settlement terms for themselves.[117] The quid pro quo becomes undeniable: offenders trade money or other goods because this is a price they are willing to pay to limit public scrutiny of their apology. It can prove expensive when a plaintiff insists that her claim is "not about the money" and instead demands a public apology as the primary form of remedy because she most wants to create awareness and prevent similar injuries from happening to others. Her attorneys may expect one-third of her settlement. By refusing to trade silence for personal compensation, she may need to pay her legal fees out of pocket. This high road is especially difficult to walk for victims who lack such resources, especially if their injuries have caused them financial difficulties such as caring for a disabled family member.

As discussed in the criminal context, informalized justice can exacerbate inequalities by sidestepping many of the protections that formal processes afford vulnerable parties.[118] Apologies rendered confidential by mediation, arbitration, or other settlement agreements generally risk compounding inequality by conferring disproportionate advantages to powerful offenders. Sophisticated defense teams can manipulate the nuances of safe apology legislation to convince naïve victims that their apologies amount to a sort of "coming clean" and acceptance of blame, when in fact they have no impact other than placating victims.[119] This leads to the rather obvious suspicion that Ford shields its apology from public scrutiny because it would not withstand analysis.

Public apologies also can suffer in various ways from failing to address the victims directly. Some civil offenders seem to apologize to the media, regulatory bodies, or other third parties rather than to victims. Failing to acknowledge victims in this way can cause new harms by denying victims status as moral interlocutors. In cases with thousands of victims, reaching individuals presents logistical challenges noted earlier. A victim's death forecloses certain kinds of significance.[120]

Note an additional caution. Once the media calls for an apology, offenders may find microphones thrust into their faces if they do not comply with requests for interviews or hold press conferences addressing the issues. Such confrontations rarely reflect well on the offender and can create poor first impressions. Whatever British Petroleum does to remedy the Deepwater Horizon disaster, Tony Hayward's statement after eleven people died in the explosion encapsulated what many saw as the corporation's callous incompetence: "The first thing to say is I'm sorry. We're sorry for the massive disruption it's caused their lives. There's no one who wants this over more than I do. I would like my life back."[121]

10. To What Extent Does the Civil Offender Demonstrate Reform?

Here we return to the mantra: apologies are treatments not cures, beginnings not conclusions. Apologies make promises. The categorically apologetic offender forbears from reoffending over her lifetime. Apologies that identify the principles at stake provide specific criteria to determine if the offender continues to honor those values. The offender demonstrates reform with a record of resisting temptations to reoffend. The more temptations she overcomes over a longer duration, the more evidence we have of her reform and the more confidence we can have in our ability to predict her behavior. The process of publicly or privately performing an apology sets a stage. The lifetime of behavior enacts the moral transformation. Such covenants set forth the conditions of future relations and can lay the foundations for large groups to live in peace rather than retribution and fear.

Who makes and keeps the promise to reform in civil claims? Standing to undertake reform correlates to standing to accept blame in cases of individual offenders. If corporate free agency causes executives to regularly change teams, who or what assumes responsibility for reforming? Current leadership may endorse reform, but over time new executives with less resolve to honor those commitments may replace them. If an institution changes status through merger, acquisition, bankruptcy, dissolution, or otherwise, does the promise to reform transfer to the new entity? A systematically corrupt institution may funnel all of its blame into a single individual, acting as if firing her solves the problem. Here an institution might argue that all reform falls on that lone bad apple. Once it removes her, the organization has completed its corrective actions. Alternatively, collectives may deflect blame so deeply into the collective as such that no particular members believe they have personally done anything wrong or that they must personally reform.

If the apologizing institution will soon cease to exist, it shares the limited ability of deathbed apologies to undertake reform because it will not be around long enough to fulfill its promises. Imagine an apology from leaders of Enron assuring the public that they will undertake aggressive reform and promise that Enron will never again engage in such activities. The apology amounts to a one-foot-in-the-grave plea to try to keep the organization alive and to elicit some sympathy. Enron soon files for bankruptcy, and most of the executives run for the door and go on to lead other institutions. The promise to reform would amount to little unless those executives carried the commitments to their new institutions. Chisso reorganized itself into JNC Corporation in 2011, so we should evaluate the extent to which JNC takes on Chisso's commitments.

Promises to reform can be either too collective such that no one takes responsibility or too individual such that the need to reform falls entirely on one scapegoat who can be ritually excised. A sufficiently precise accounting of moral causation and blame – identifying individual actors as well as those who promulgate blameworthy policies – affords the best perspective on who should undertake which reforms. The binocular approach of individual reform as well as structural renovation offers the most effective means of achieving and sustaining institutional reform.

This makes attempts to dissociate apologies from blame especially problematic. If the law construes an apology as something other than an admission of guilt, the apologizing party need not admit to having done anything wrong. If they have not transgressed, they need not reform their behavior. Thus a party can simultaneously offer a "safe apology" while reoffending against the plaintiff or others. Ford could offer a safe apology without taking any actions to fix the problem. Indeed, Ford could offer a safe apology while simultaneously launching a public relations campaign denying wrongdoing and asserting the safety of vehicles they know to be faulty. Cost-benefit analyses may conclude that offering safe apologies and settling claims in this manner provides a cost-effective alternative to recalling or improving a dangerous product. Whether in cases of pharmaceutical misrepresentations, mass telemarketing scams, environmental catastrophes, or other mass torts, injuries result from systems set into motion by actors within collectives. If laws and various legal agents construe apologies as primarily a matter of expressing empathy for individual victims, the harmful underlying conditions remain unreformed. Lest anyone perceive me as paranoid to suggest that someone would apologize while knowingly committing the same harm against others, consider Chisso's purported redress. In 1959, the Japanese government ordered Chisso to install a wastewater treatment system. The company complied and held a ceremony to commemorate the event, leading the public to believe that the water was now safe. The Chisso president even drank a glass. Court proceedings later established that Chisso knew all along that "the purification tank was installed as a social solution and did nothing to remove organic mercury."[122] They continued dumping. When new victims came forward, Chisso assured the public that their wastewater could not be to blame because they had installed the filter.

Notice how this operates on both individual and collective levels. For an individual tort-feasor – a surgeon who operates on the wrong limb while intoxicated, for example – an ambiguous apology expressing sympathy for the injury does not necessarily commit her to reform. She may refuse to admit fault, perhaps blaming a nurse for confusing her. She may think she does her best work after a few drinks. She may view the adverse event as an inevitable cost of doing business: "I'm really sorry this happened to you. I've performed thousands of these procedures. This was bound to happen sooner or later, and this is why I pay so much for insurance." She gives no indication that she will change her behavior. Consider the hospital's perspective. Imagine the hospital's chief executive states, "[w]e deeply regret this terrible incident and apologize for any suffering this has caused. We will make every effort to get to the bottom of this and to make the patient healthy and whole again." The hospital then waives all fees for treatment and provides a cash settlement to the patient that exceeds her demands. Beyond the promise to "get to the bottom of this" – a vague assurance that may or may not be explained and followed up pursuant to the settlement agreement – we know nothing about how members of the organization view their culpability or the need for institutional change. Does the hospital have a sufficient disciplinary program to respond to such offenses? Did it willfully ignore warnings regarding this particular surgeon? Does it properly train its nurses and assistants to provide appropriate safeguards to ensure that the proper procedures are performed on the correct patients? Does it have effective programs in place to treat stress and addiction in its staff? Does the hospital tolerate a culture of addiction among its staff? Do the long hours and difficult work breed exhaustion, addiction, and mistakes? Does it have a history of attributing blame to individual surgeons when it should instead reform its policies to foster a less mistake-prone environment? These questions all address the extent to which individual caregivers should shoulder all of the blame for harms or whether underlying structures such as hospital policies or insurance protocols cause or contribute to the injuries in some respect. If apologies from neither the individual doctor nor the hospital speak to these issues, they avoid committing to individual and collective reform.

This is not to say that doctors and care facilities must be infallible and that mistakes always result from negligence. In medicine and elsewhere, people make mistakes. As Leape argues, professional standards that insist on infallibility pressure doctors to cover up negative events. According to Waller, the attitude that all injuries result from individual blameworthy doctors causes caregivers to hide negative outcomes because they believe they will be held culpable. The excessively individualistic view of medical harm focuses on "the last link in the chain" by attributing the fault to a single doctor and creating a white wall of silence among doctors.[123] The system goes unreformed. We should instead encourage doctors to report problems and fix the system.[124]

An apology that does not commit to correcting the root cause of the problem may resolve the issues for one plaintiff while failing to correct the conditions that will likely injure others.[125] This leads Waller to adopt a controversial position "against moral responsibility": "Blaming the unfortunate individual in whom the flawed process reached its fulfillment fails to fix the deeper systemic causes and does nothing to prevent other persons from developing similar flaws and making the same mistakes."[126] I discussed in the criminal context why I believe eliminating individual responsibility from apologies overcompensates for the lack of attention to structural causation, but we can appreciate a crucial point: many apologies in civil law fail on both fronts by refusing to accept individual blame and ignoring the need for structural reform. Instead they offer ambiguous empathy and financial redress for individual claimants.

By contrast, consider how Chisso's eventual apology galvanized a nascent environmental movement in Japan. I do not mean to suggest that every civil apology must trigger global social reform, but I do believe expectations for reform in civil actions often go unarticulated. A deeply held objective drives many plaintiffs toward litigation: this must never happen again. Victims often seek apologies not only to address their personal needs but to incite reform by requiring those with the power to institute changes that will prevent their injuries from being visited on someone else. As in Minamata Bay and many cases like it, suffering can beget activism. If victims seek apologies that animate such reform, they should evaluate the apology they want against the apology they receive.

Victims should ensure that apologizers honor promises to reform. Just as we should exercise a healthy skepticism toward criminal offenders who promise change, victims should not overvalue bald assurances from civil wrongdoers that they will "look into the situation" or "do everything within their power to make sure it never happens again." Ford's Jacques Nasser assured that "you have my personal guarantee that no one at Ford will rest until every recalled tire is replaced."[127] Firestone said "we'll do whatever it takes, however long it takes, to regain your trust."[128] Surely workers at Ford will and should rest while attempting to replace the problematic tires, so what should we take from Nasser's hyperbolic cliché? If Ford takes longer than it should, how will Nasser back his guarantee? Additionally Firestone will not do whatever it takes. Like every tire manufacturer, they will continue to conduct cost-benefit analyses that factor the often competing objectives of profit and safety. Perhaps they will invest more in safety in response to this crisis, but that seems rather different than making safety their sole objective regardless of cost. The mother of the murdered student depicted in the infamous Kent State photo that captured his grieving classmate kneeling over his body recounted her outrage with the settlement agreement awarding her $15,000 and what she described as a "pseudo-apology." Kent State officials did not admit blame and stated that "better ways must be found to deal with these confrontations."[129] Rather than accepting such ambiguous and noncommittal assertions at face value, reviewers can evaluate the commitment. Have they begun the reform? How do they plan to undertake the changes? What measures ensure that they will complete the changes? How will they audit individual behavior and institutional design, culture, and decision-making processes? Should we trust internal audits? Would transparent external reviews be more reliable? How will they evaluate progress toward reform on individual and collective levels? How do they incentivize desired behaviors? What happens if they fail because of changes in leadership or corporate dissolution? How will the institution punish those who fail to honor the principles? Will the institutions report their failures to external regulators? What sanctions will apply, and do these penalties provide sufficient deterrent rather than amounting to little more than fines absorbed as a cost of doing business? Does anyone take personal responsibility for overseeing the reform? What if she leaves? We can answer these questions with increasing confidence over time as offenders demonstrate or undermine their commitment to reform.

Unlike criminal cases in which the state arrests and removes offenders from opportunities to reoffend, in civil cases wrongdoers often remain in business during the dispute in question. This sometimes affords a good look into the offenders' hearts through their post-offense behavior. They may continue to commit the very same offenses against others. They may have fundamentally changed their policies and practices years ago. With Chisso we had decades of records demonstrating a reluctant and slow transformation, but a transformation nonetheless. Given that Chisso/JNC now operates under intense public scrutiny, it seems unlikely that the organization would reoffend. Actions speak louder than words, and a lifetime of actions speaks loudest. As an individual claimant against Chisso wondering what to make of its apologies, one can extrapolate from its rather long record to judge the current status of reform efforts. Chisso executives can explain with some precision their plan to transform: what steps do they take to ensure that this never happens again, how will they incentivize and enforce their plan, how far along have they come in that process, and what evidence can they produce that they engage in a good faith process of transformation? One can count and discount Chisso's apology accordingly.

Whatever value I attribute to the apology, I would reevaluate if Chisso reoffended. Victims of those new offenses could bring claims to hold Chisso accountable, and they would hopefully view any fresh apologies with a healthy skepticism given that Chisso failed to honor previous promises not to reoffend. If Chisso buried earlier apologies within confidential settlements, however, new victims would lack this insight. Also note difficulties related to knowing whether a collective has reoffended. Some recidivism may hide deep within the institution's black boxes. These offenses may not come to light without aggressive discovery demands in the context of new legal claims. Uncertainty can arise if only one or a few members transgress, for example if a single Chisso distributor improperly disposes of a few barrels of toxic waste. Rather than taking a binary view where any recidivism nullifies the apology, reviewers benefit from a nuanced approach that considers Chisso's response to the infraction, the extent of the infraction, the incidence of similar offenses, and the rank of the offender. Infractions will also hold different value depending on their relation to the scope of the principles of reform: releasing mercury into Minamata Bay would undermine the apology in a manner different than would an accounting scandal. Both activities fail the public trust and lie in pursuit of profit – values Chisso should identify in an apology – but only one causes the sort of environmental damage central to Chisso's original apology.

11. Has the Civil Offender Provided Appropriate Redress?

The categorically apologetic offender provides appropriate redress for the harms she caused. In most cases the sooner she provides this redress the better because the victims will typically continue to suffer the unmitigated effects of the harm until some form of redress assuages the injury. Returning property, for example, shortens the duration of the deprivation. Prompt redress can also provide insight into an offender's mental states including her recognition of the illegitimacy of her actions.

Determining what constitutes appropriate redress often proves contentious. Many disputes become civil claims precisely because the victim and offender disagree on what is owed. Qualitative and quantitative issues arise: What kinds of redress are appropriate? How much redress suffices? Japanese Americans received $20,000 as redress for internment during World War II, leading one victim to state: "[T]he American government stole 4 years of my life and has now put a price of $5000 on each stolen year.... It would have been better to receive no financial settlement."[130] Here we can separate issues regarding wrongful use (no amount of money will suffice, money may add insult to injury, and other forms of redress are more appropriate) and disparity of value (I should receive more money to compensate for the harms).

The most obvious kind of redress ends the harm at issue. Reform and redress intertwine: if you apologize for taking something, you return it. The obvious, however, does not always prevail in legal arguments. Consider the U.S. Supreme Court's 2008 ruling in *Hawaii v. Office of Hawaiian Affairs* in which it considered the U.S. Congress' 1993 apology for the overthrow of the Hawaiian government 100 years earlier.[131] After considerable debate in which senators claimed that "logical consequences of this resolution would be independence"[132] for Hawaii and that the apology would "finally acknowledge Queen Liliuokalani's plea for justice,"[133] a rare congressional apology materialized. The apology resolved "to acknowledge the historic significance of the illegal overthrow of the Kingdom of Hawaii, to express its deep regret to the Native Hawaiian people, and to support the reconciliation efforts of the State of Hawaii ... with Native Hawaiians."[134] The apology went on to recognize "the suppression of the inherent sovereignty of the Native Hawaiian people," to "apologize[ ] to Native Hawaiians on behalf of the people of the United States for the overthrow ... with the participation of agents and citizens of the United States, and the deprivation of the rights of Native Hawaiians to self-determination," and to express a "commitment to acknowledge the ramifications of the overthrow of the Kingdom of Hawaii, in order to provide a proper foundation for reconciliation between the United States and the Native Hawaiian people."

The Supreme Court of Hawaii interpreted the apology as endorsing native Hawaiians' claims to 1.2 million acres of land, finding that "based on a plain reading of the Apology Resolution ... Congress has clearly recognized that the native Hawaiian people have unrelinquished claims over the ceded lands, which were taken without consent or compensation."[135] Writing for a unanimous U.S. Supreme Court, Justice Alito reversed the Hawaiian Supreme Court, explaining that the apology provided no more than "conciliatory or precatory" language. "Such terms are not the kind that Congress uses to create substantive rights," and therefore the apology did not impact the status of the contested land. As Justice Ruth Bader Ginsburg previewed the ruling at oral argument: "Why isn't it sufficient just to say that this resolution has no substantive effect, period?"[136] Thus in the Supreme Court's view, even though Congress' apology declared the illegality of the overthrow and taking of the land, this did not entail that they meant to return it or otherwise admit that they lacked legitimate ownership of it. On the court's reading, we can paraphrase the congressional apology as "we're sorry we took it from you and we know that was wrong and illegal, but we're keeping it."[137] If an apology in civil law does not explicitly promise the most basic redress, therefore, even the highest courts may find that it is of strictly "symbolic" value. If the U.S. Congress can formally and publicly describe itself as apologizing without even intending to discontinue committing one of the central harms adjudicated, we can imagine the sorts of apologies that pass muster in confidential settlement agreements and avoid simply returning what was illegitimately taken. In apologies for the 2008 banking crisis, for example, Blankfein and others could have returned their personal bonuses or a portion of their institutional profits and directed those funds toward victim redress. Although "returning" the Hawaiian land presented many complexities, it offered a fairly simple solution compared to other collective harms. Imagine returning to Native Americans or African Americans everything the United States wrongfully took from them and their ancestors. As I argued elsewhere, something like full reparations for African slavery might require redistributing resources to an extent that it would shift the balance of global power from the northern to the southern hemisphere.

Recompense alone may prove insufficient because the process of engaging the victim as a moral interlocutor reveals an infinite variety of kinds of redress. Some victims may seek personalized redress, with the offenders devoting their time rather than their money to reparative efforts. A parent, for instance, may want Grünenthal executives to personally care for a child disabled by thalidomide. She may desire this because she not only wants the assistance it provides – she could probably receive more effective treatment from a professional caretaker funded by Grünenthal – but also wants those responsible to better understand and feel the daily suffering they caused. Returning to something like the Levinasian perspective, such face-to-face care for others differs considerably from responsibility taken from a distance via proxies and payments.

Just as it becomes increasingly difficult to treat victims as moral interlocutors as the number of victims increases, appropriately individualized redress for collective harms presents challenges. Even if we set aside issues regarding caring for the dead or for those who suffered harm long ago, personally attending to large classes of victims can require more than a lifetime of work. Caring for even a single victim can seem like an infinite amount of work. How, then, can we decide when an executive has discharged her duties to a person she caused to be severely disabled? Where do we draw the line? If we multiply this by tens of thousands of victims, what could ever be enough? What would discharge the moral and economic debt of Swiss banks for their role in the Holocaust?[138] When has Chisso finished making amends? Redress would probably include sufficient funds to provide a lifetime of care for the special needs of thalidomide victims, needs which only become more acute as victims age and their caretaking parents pass away. Even death seems like a contentious moment to consider redress complete. Here we confront an unfortunate reality: redress for some injuries may never erase or fully compensate for the loss.

In part because of these difficulties, financial compensation often emerges as the best of flawed methods of redress as it provides a near universal common denominator of value that offenders can distribute widely and with relative ease. Money conveys a certain kind of gravity, in some respects more powerful than the softer meanings conveyed by other elements of apologies. Like many complex problems, the temptation is strong to throw money at victims and act as if this repairs the situation. As Desmond Tutu stated: "None of us labours under any delusions – you cannot put a monetary value to a person's suffering."[139] Tutu argues, however, that although reparations "can never bring back the dead, nor adequately compensate victims for pain and suffering, they can and must improve the quality of [victim's] lives." I have written in some detail on commodification in law and do not wish to understate the value of monetary compensation, but victims should be wary of offenders who reflexively favor monetary compensation over engaging in a process that requires them to directly participate in the remediation.[140] Some offenders want to remain in control and aloof. Money can keep them at a comfortable distance from the unpleasant consequences of their actions, and they would rather overpay a disfigured claimant than look into her eyes and dress her sores. Offenders insulating themselves from the harms they cause with a wall of gold seem less likely to be transformed by the remediation process. Such distancing also provides insights into their emotions and intentions. Although financial redress can provide certain kinds of meaning, it may avoid others desired by victims. Payment alone, for instance, will typically not provide strong evidence of moral transformation.

We should also be mindful of the extent to which monetary awards supplant other forms of redress, particularly in settlement contexts wherein apologies exist as one of many remedies subject to negotiation. Consider a case such as *Dukes v. Walmart* in which attorneys sought to pursue a class action sexual discrimination claim on behalf of 1.6 million women.[141] As noted earlier, compensation structures in civil law steer plaintiffs' attorneys toward financial payments so that they can receive one-third of the largest possible monetary award. If the attorneys had negotiated to maximize payment for their clients and thus themselves, this would have produced rather different social consequences than if they had sought something like a collective categorical apology from Walmart executives who promised to reform their policies and otherwise promote gender equality.

Given that apologies – even if understood as expressions of sympathy rather than admissions of guilt – become economically valuable in part because they signify something more than economic value, some argue that the adversaries should bargain for them like other legal goods. When arguing for Hong Kong courts to utilize apologies as a remedy in disability discrimination cases, for instance, Peterson suggests that courts "should ask the defendant whether he is willing to give the apology, making it clear that if he is unwilling to do so the court will increase the award of monetary damages by a specified amount."[142] Although this example invokes the diverse cultural conceptions of apologies addressed in *I Was Wrong*, such reduction of an apology to a cash equivalent makes explicit many of the concerns raised throughout this work.

Unsatisfied by all other remedies, some victims may seek punitive redress sufficient to provide stronger deterrents or more retributive punch. Contrite offenders may appreciate that they should provide damages beyond what the court expects as compensable damages. They may also understand that their redress should deter others tempted to commit similar harms. In other words, parties may agree that redress should exceed the cost of the harms to prevent future offenders from viewing potential civil damages as costs of doing business that can be recouped by raising prices or otherwise passing along the penalties to consumers.

Punitive conceptions of redress for institutional offenders also raise concerns regarding collective punishment, famously captured by Thurlow's remark: "Did you ever expect a corporation to have a conscience, when it has no soul to be damned, and no body to be kicked?"[143] Collective punishment lacks popularity, in part because of deontological fears that it entails causing suffering to innocent members of a group – by jailing the parents of a murderer or forcing subordinate members of a group to pay for the sins of their superiors, for example – as well as consequentialist concerns that it hinders deterrent effects of penalties. It also runs counter to favored notions of individual moral responsibility that locate blame in the choices of free agents. Punitive redress from collectives, however, can take many forms beyond fines. Courts might order the institution to transform its charter or operating procedures, submit to periodic external reviews, or expend considerable resources publicizing its wrongdoing to raise awareness and hopefully change the behaviors of peer institutions.[144] Such penalties invoke concerns discussed in the context of court-ordered apologies.

Similar to how we would find it problematic if a murderer's child served her parent's prison sentence, redress conveys different significance depending on who provides it. Some civil claimants may consider this point irrelevant: as long as I get a check to cover the damages, it does not matter who signs it. One's position here will depend on the meanings sought, but the strictly economic view – "They want someone to dress their wounds? Then send a nurse" – tends to have blind spots. Unlike throwing money at the problem, working on the front lines of remediation offers several kinds of substance. Taking practical responsibility requires the offender to directly confront the harm she caused and to invest her own life in caring for her victim. She has existential skin in the game. She subjects herself to the emotional pain of grappling with the consequences of her actions. Victims may consider this pain retributive because the offender deserves to take a hard look and be haunted by the suffering. Offenders should not, in other words, enjoy the psychological comforts of their offices while others endure post-offense trauma. If we understand civil redress as a means to the end of their moral transformation – or as some essential element of their moral transformation – then delegating redress frustrates that objective. The offender's direct participation in providing redress also reinforces her treatment of the victim as moral interlocutor, enacting the understanding that her time is not too valuable to care for the person she harmed.

Where the money comes from should matter even for those who maintain a strictly financial view of redress. Those who profited from causing suffering should take the loss. If former executives who grew rich from blameworthy activity leave their successors holding the bag, this parallels punishing the child for the parent's crime. Culprits sometimes offload the burden of redress to taxpayers. The Japanese government, for example, diverted public funds to Chisso so that it could continue compensating victims.[145] Victims must have found state subsidy of Chisso's damage payments rather complicated because the response to the disaster contributed to Japanese democratization, but the government contributed to the problem. Regardless of whether the Japanese government should accept fault and pay damages, the sources for redress followed circuitous paths that did not necessarily track culpability in any careful sense. Similarly, whatever apologies Blankfein and others provided for the 2008 financial crisis, much of the redress pursuant to the bailouts came not from the banks but from the government via taxpayers. Some therefore view the bailouts as but another means of channeling funds from victims to offenders rather than vice versa.

Consider this in regard to offenders who cite their redress payments as evidence of the sincerity of their contrition while they receive tax windfalls by deducting those costs. British Petroleum, for example, enjoyed a $10 billion tax benefit by writing off $37.2 billion in Deepwater Horizon cleanup expenses.[146] Typically offenders cannot deduct settlement amounts intended as punitive penalties, but they can deduct business expenses used to compensate victims or remediate injuries. Because most settlements do not distinguish between penalties and compensatory damages – and because sophisticated offenders know to negotiate for such ambiguity – the IRS rarely challenges such deductions even when they amount to billions in losses.[147] The offender will announce the full amount of its redress hoping to maximize the appearance of contrition and "accepting responsibility." Government regulators will probably not explain that actual redress is about one-third less because the larger the award, the bigger the perceived "win" for regulators. Inflating settlement amounts allow the offenders to avoid expenses and negative publicity of trial, offenders look maximally contrite when paying large sums, and government officials tout how they held feet to the fire without having to try the case.[148] According to Public Interest Research Group, tax-deductible settlements cause the public a fourfold loss:

First, the public suffers the direct impact of corporate wrongdoing. Second, taxpayers are forced to shoulder part of the amount of the penalty because the public must cover the forgone revenue by raising tax rates, cutting public programs, or adding to the national debt. Third, future deterrence of corporate wrongdoing is weakened. And fourth, the absence of a trial eliminates opportunities for a public airing of evidence about corporate misdeeds and the lax regulations that can lead to them.[149]

We can add a fifth problem: if victims intend the penalties to serve retributive ends, ambiguities that allow for tax deductions also lessen the pain of the damages. Whatever portion of the $1.1 billion settlement for the 1989 Valdez disaster was intended to cause Exxon the pain it deserved, the corporation felt less than two-thirds of it.[150] For these reasons several legislative movements advocate for disallowing the deductibility of settlements, eliminating ambiguities between punitive and compensatory damages, and disclosing the after-tax amounts of settlements to prevent inflating public perceptions of the value of settlements.[151] Offenders may pass whatever they cannot deduct onto shareholders and insurers, further insulating decision makers from deterrents that might cause them to take fewer risks with other people's well-being.[152] If I grow rich from harming you and liability insurance covers the costs associated with apologetic redress, what lesson have I learned?

As discussed earlier, it can prove challenging to identify the proximate cause of harms within institutions, especially when leaders intentionally deflect blame into their nebulous bureaucracies. Victims will find it exceptionally galling that those who both caused their harm and profited from doing so walk away without having to provide redress of any kind. Some leaders will even cause the harm, profit from the harm, apologize for the harm, promise that the institution will redress the harm, and then leave others to pay for and undertake the work of providing redress. We can reserve a specific kind of scrutiny for a departing president leaving the bill for the successive administration or an executive strapping on a golden parachute while promising to do "everything within my power to make things right." Apologies come too easily when they do not cost the apologizer anything, and we can watch for those whose enthusiasm for redress wanes once they realize that a collective apology impacts them personally. Hypocritical views of moral causation abound. When things go well, we use narrow conceptions of causation: I deserve credit, and I expect commensurate compensation. When things go badly, we hide behind veils of immunity that prevent blame from reaching us personally or following us after we jump ship. This asymmetry stacks the deck in favor of powerful wrongdoers, allowing them to profit from risking other people's lives without exposing themselves to much more than a failed business venture. Victims should keep these considerations in mind when evaluating the actual value and cost of apologetic redress. Otherwise they may unwittingly subsidize egregious offenses with their own tax payments and insurance premiums while reducing deterrent and retributive impacts of redress.

The temptation to seek redress from the collective rather than the individual sometimes makes strategic sense because institutions tend to hold greater resources than individuals. Especially in cases with massive damages, even the world's wealthiest individuals lack sufficient funds to adequately compensate the injured. This practical matter influences the metaphysics of collective responsibility: we often act as if institutions deserve blame because this belief affords the best chance of collecting. Victims should keep in mind, however, that such "deeper pockets" arguments may in fact take from the innocent. If the Japanese government directs funds to Chisso victims, what social programs does it cut to make up the difference? While the architects of the 2008 financial crisis enjoy new corporate, academic, and governmental leadership positions, U.S. citizens endure "austerity" and "sequestration" cuts designed in part to clean up the mess created by bank executives. The deeper pockets arguments also tend to equate redress too narrowly with economic compensation. As in criminal cases in which indigent offenders lack resources to redress the harms they caused, institutional leaders who cannot cover the entire bill to fix the problem they caused can still contribute quite a bit. Rather than throwing up their hands because they could never possibly unscramble the eggs, culpable leaders can take practical responsibility by devoting the time and resources – limited and insufficient though they are – toward making amends. Instead we often find culpable leadership untouched and moving on to the next stage of their careers.

In addition to determining the kinds of redress, the amount of redress, and who should undertake that redress, civil claims raise standing questions regarding who *receives* the benefits. What, precisely, must recipients suffer to qualify for redress?[153] Do we provide reparations to only the directly injured, or do we include spouses, children, or others? The unborn – sometimes described as "fourth party victims" – can suffer the most, particularly in toxic torts.[154] In cases involving harms against classes such as African or Native Americans, do we determine compensation according to race, ethnicity, citizenship, social and economic status, biology, self-identification, or some other criteria?[155] Do all victims deserve the same amount, or do we index redress to the amount of harm? Do we go so far as to adjust for relative cost of living, or does this become too fine-grained? These are significant questions best addressed according to the nuances of particular situations.[156]

All of this invites a lot of lawyering. As I repeatedly note, plaintiff's attorneys working under contingency fee arrangements steer the process, and they have incentives to channel redress toward financial compensation so that they can pocket one-third of that amount. Contingency arrangements steer plaintiffs away from noneconomic forms of redress and reduce the award victims receive by the deducted attorney fees. In many cases, therefore, I recommend that apologetic offenders offer – as soon as possible – to pay for the plaintiff's legal fees. Such a gesture can fundamentally change the adversarial dynamic and bespeak genuineness in intention to resolve the conflict to the victim's benefit. Offenders who balk at "funding the enemy" in this regard miss an opportunity to rebut skepticism toward their contrition.

Finally, offenders who voluntarily provide commensurate redress establish their credibility more effectively than those who wait for a court to order compensation or fight for every dime in settlement negotiations. Determining redress sometimes requires intricate findings and lengthy discussions to design the optimal methods and amounts. Regulators, attorneys, judges, and various parties require time and effort to structure such redress. Tensions and disagreements often arise even for categorically apologetic civil offenders. Once the parties set redress, however, offenders who provide redress graciously and without needing compulsion or threats provide windows into the intentions motivating their apologies.

12. What Intentions Motivate the Civil Offender's Apology?
The categorically apologetic offender undertakes the work of apologizing for the sake of the offender, the community, and the breached value. This differs from an apology provided primarily if not exclusively for self-serving objectives. Consider, for instance, a spouse apologizing during divorce

proceedings not because she regrets mistreating her partner but because she believes the gesture will improve her leverage in alimony and child support negotiations. Imagine an executive apologizing for her organization's systematic racial discrimination because the marketing department claimed that this would increase sales to minority groups.[157] Contrast a board of trustees that undergoes a wave of retirements, fills vacated board seats with minorities, hires a new chief executive in part because of her progressive views on race relations, and rewrites its charter to express racial equality, and this new board and executive issue an apology declaring their genuinely heartfelt disdain for the organization's previous racism. Even if all of the other aspects of the apology remain the same, intentions matter.

Within most legal contexts the objective seems obvious: the intention underlying all adversarial law – whether criminal or civil – is *winning*. Legal apologies in civil contexts look prima facie like means to the end of gaining advantage. Moreover, corporate institutional DNA seeks to minimize losses and maximize profits. Just as we harbor suspicions that criminal offenders feign contrition to reduce their punishment, we doubt that corporations view apologies as more than a means to the end of profit. Beyond the short-term cost-benefit analysis determining whether and what sort of apology to offer in a particular conflict, consumers appreciate that organizations view their brand – their corporate "character" – as their most lucrative asset.[158] A reputation as a trusted brand pays dividends not only in sales but also in political influence and credibility in future litigation.[159] Apologies that accept short-term losses can provide good long-term investments; only short-sighted executives "underinvest" in apologies.[160] We default to a skepticism toward corporate apologies for this reason and set the burden of credibility appropriately high.

Governmental apologies suffer from a similar crisis of credibility as candidates and parties consult focus groups and pollsters to decide the extent to which various kinds of apologies confer strategic advantages. Determining intentions usually requires fallible inferences as we look for clues revealing mental states, but sometimes organizations leave a smoking gun by explaining in internal documents precisely why they apologize. The debate over an apology for the Chinese head tax – a fee levied against Chinese immigrants to Canada beginning in 1888 – has been a political battleground for decades with conservatives and liberals spinning the issue and leaving the victimized group perennially unsatisfied. In 2013, a leaked memo from British Columbia's liberals outlined a campaign strategy of using public funds to apologize to Chinese and Indian voters to secure "quick wins" with those ethnic groups.[161] Outrage ensued. The now transparent attempt to use expressions of contrition for historical injustice to gain political support led one community leader to express his disgust: "This attitude behind this document – it really stinks. That's what we object to. It doesn't give us any respect. It uses us as a commodity, that we are simple-minded people."[162] The president of the Union of British Columbia Chiefs added that the intention expressed in the memo "represents a deep sense of betrayal and we find it highly offensive that now the moves on the part of the B.C. provincial Liberals are tainted by this revelation, and it brings into question their efforts at reconciliation with respect to historical wrong doings." The president of the Head Tax Families Society of Canada summarized his position: "Don't pander to me by saying that 'Hey we have a strategy. We are going to apologize.' Well you know what? Take your apology and shove it where the sun don't shine."[163] Again, intentions matter.

Others expressed less concern regarding the political maneuvering and focused instead on securing payments for the thousands of families impacted by the head tax. The executive director of the Chinese Canadian National Council equated a "genuine apology" with one providing substantial financial compensation to victims. "If we wanted just an apology," he explained, "we would have got it back in 2011."[164]

Certainly reform and redress can occur begrudgingly, for instance as the result of court-ordered punishments or remediation programs. Whether a civil court orders the offender to publicize her offense, she publicizes the wrong as a strategic ploy to reduce damages, or she publicizes the offense out of a sense of remorse and concern with public interest, such actions can all have positive impact regardless of the underlying intentions. Some victims may not care very much about the motivations for apologizing, so long as they get what they seek. As I hope to have shown, however, some meanings central to categorical apologies rely on specific intentions. Parties interested in those sorts of meanings must pay especially close attention to the civil apologizer's mental states.

The notion that collectives as such can intend anything – as opposed to aggregating the mental states of members – adds another layer of complexity that I will not consider here other than to note questions regarding consensus. One member of an organization might apologize from the purest and most self-sacrificing of intentions. Others in the same organization might support the apology for cynical and purely self-interested instrumental reasons. Perhaps everyone in the organization shares the same motivations for apologizing. Standing issues discussed earlier resurface here, and those evaluating the intentions motivating a collective apology for a civil offense should parse meaning accordingly. A consensus of membership apologizing for the sake of the victims and the values breached provides the ideal motivation, but this sets a difficult standard to meet for large organizations with diverse memberships.

Although we cannot yet directly observe a civil offender's mental states, we can read multiple data points for patterns. Treating apologies as commodities subject to negotiation provides evidence that the offender views contrition as a quid pro quo. Just as we would view with disdain a spouse offering to admit and apologize for infidelity only if her estranged partner agrees to increase alimony payments, we would find limited significance in a corporation agreeing to apologize and accept responsibility only if settlement terms remain confidential. If an apology appears calibrated to avoid admitting wrongdoing and limit exposure to legal penalties, it will look like an attempt to parlay undeserved moral credit into self-serving benefits. As with criminal offenders, accepting blame early in the process compares favorably with waiting until evidence becomes undeniable. An early confession can throw the offender at the mercy of the victims, abandoning legal gambits for the sake of contrition. Morally transformed offenders may need to apologize against the advice of attorneys who view early admissions as legal suicide and advise repentant clients to visit a member of the clergy rather than the victim. Offenders providing redress only when compelled by the courts or when they have exhausted means of avoiding paying do not inspire confidence that their actions flow from a sense of responsibility. Firing or otherwise punishing those deserving blame and installing new leadership can demonstrate an institution's intention to change course. Taking advantage of tax deductions for redress paid, as well as negotiating for ambiguities that allow for such deductions, gives the appearance of intending to resolve the problem as cheaply as possible even if that means foisting the costs on taxpayers. Likewise, those who avoid personally providing redress limit opportunities to evaluate their motivation to treat victims as moral interlocutors. Demonstrating respect for the victims by reducing their anxieties and not causing them further injury can be a simple but important indicator that offenders view the well-being of others above their own interests. The offender's demeanor and emotional presentations can offer some insight into mental states. Reviewers should take precautions not to overemphasize potentially superficial displays, especially when conflicting with other evidence. This is particularly important where collectives delegate the work of appearing contrite to spokespersons, as we see when Ford sent its attorneys to Bailey's hospital bed. Difficult as it may be to read emotional cues of individuals, institutional apologies do not even offer a glimpse at the faces of those who should be accepting blame. We should make little of histrionic attorneys paid to emote remorse while leaders who called the shots obscure their intentions behind confidential documents. Again, beware of apologies that smell of the law office.

13. Does the Civil Offender Demonstrate Appropriate Emotions?
As we saw with criminal cases, the emotional content of apologies in civil matters presents important but nebulous issues. The offender should experience an appropriate degree of the relevant kinds of emotion, typically including sorrow, guilt, empathy, and sympathy. An offender who fails to

experience the proper apologetic emotions does not provide certain kinds of meaning and is unable to demonstrate an understanding of and a disgust with the pain she caused. Negative emotions can also bespeak deserved suffering. Beyond this baseline recognition that emotions play essential roles in apologies, questions abound. Which emotions, in what quantity, and for how long should the offender experience them? How should the emotions evolve over time as offenders better understand the extent of the damage? How do cultural differences regarding emotional expression nuance any answers we provide?

Criminal defense attorneys understand that appearing remorseless results in heavy punishments and they coach defendants accordingly. Civil defense attorneys, however, may view client emotions as irrelevant or even a nuisance to be contained lest they impair legal strategy.[165] Plaintiffs' attorneys may likewise view their clients' desire for emotional payout as competing with financial compensation for both the victim and her counsel.[166] On the other hand, civil procedures do not present the obstacles that make it so difficult to foster emotional bonds between criminal offenders and their victims. An emotionally powerful apology at just about any time or place between parties can transform a civil action.

Collectives are ill-suited to experiencing or communicating emotional content. Even though we may speak of corporations as persons in the eyes of the law, the idea that institutions *as such* experience emotions strains the metaphor. Members of the collective may feel grief, regret, remorse, or shame, and in the aggregate all of these emotions may add up to meaningful expressions. The notion that the collective experiences negative emotions in some sense irreducible to the mental states of its members, however, humanizes organizational structures too much. It would be as if we expected an animated corporate mascot to somehow embody the mind of the organization; as if a de profundis Ronald McDonald entails that McDonald's Corporation suffers negative emotions and therefore should be viewed as appropriately contrite even if the blameworthy executives remain unmoved. Such dissociation between the individual feelings and collective harms leads some to view modern corporations as sociopathic.[167]

The idea that human spokespersons can embody the emotions of a collective faces similar problems. The spokesperson can presumably feel emotions, and we are fairly accustomed to humans outsourcing emotional work to other humans. The spokesperson might actually feel any number of apologetic pangs. Even if she does not deserve blame or feel guilt, she can sympathize with plaintiffs. Many organizations employ customer service representatives to do just this.[168] Problems of standing arise here: Is she the person who should be experiencing the negative emotions on account of her blameworthiness? Does she distinguish between her own emotional states and those allegedly attributable to the organization? If we expect the civil offender to suffer retributive punishment via experiencing negative emotions – recall Kant's example of humiliating the wealthy defamer – expressions of shame from her paid ambassador cause pain to the wrong person. Acting as if we can emotionally punish a collective as such allows individual offenders to deposit their moral debts into soulless institutions. Likewise, if the spokesperson can absorb the organization's shame or humiliation this would seem to significantly diminish whatever deterrent threat or rehabilitative impact of such negative emotions.

Even if a leading executive who deserves blame expresses the requisite emotions, does she speak for her own emotions or for the group's? Do other blameworthy individuals also experience these emotions? What if only a few members of the group really *feel bad*, some felt terribly guilty for a while but now experience occasional sadness for the victims, some give it no thought, and others think the victims deserve to suffer? Again, issues of consensus complicate matters, especially in apologies from the state when so many issues divide across party lines. As noted previously, emotions provide one way to read the intentions of the apologizer. Deciphering the mental states of individuals via outward appearance is an inexact science; reading the face and emotions of a spokesperson to determine the feelings of an institution approaches folly.

A collective might address the emotional component of its apologies not by trying to channel feelings through a delegate but rather by working to cultivate the appropriate attitudes in its members. Chisso, for example, could require its employees to care for those suffering from Minamata disease. Beyond assisting those in need, such service can sensitize employees to the plight of victims such that Chisso workers will feel sympathy and remorse rather than ignoring the emotional costs of their pollution. Various means of keeping the suffering of victims present – whether though memorials, seminars, documentaries, or otherwise – can similarly guide a group's emotional state. Institutions can also punish those demonstrating callousness or otherwise expressing inappropriate sentiments.[169]

The difficulty of mapping negative emotions onto collectives can have the benefit of forcing victims and offenders to evaluate apologies according to other, more substantive aspects of apologies. Rather than fixating on the emotional fits and starts that too often guide evaluations of apologies or expecting institutions to drum up pain for events long in the past and to which leaders have little emotional connection, recognizing that emotions have a limited role in collective civil wrongdoing can concentrate attention on whether the institution provides salient facts, accepts blame, provides redress, and hits various other notes that do not require controversial attributions of collective mental states.

Although emotions play important roles, victims should exercise caution not to overvalue emotional displays. Given their intensity, emotional outbursts can overshadow more telling aspects of apologies. We should not, for instance, be duped into thinking that convulsive tears somehow compensate for failing to accept blame or refusing to provide sufficient redress.[170] Here again we can warn against making too much of emotional amplifiers – "I am so very terribly deeply sorry" – as if an abundance of adverbs somehow compensates for other deficiencies in the apology.

Conclusion

I introduced discussions of apologies in civil law by embedding them within broader cultural dynamics, and I conclude by reinforcing that the tincture of modern life colors all of this analysis. As long as defending a legal action feels more natural than apologizing – and as long as accepting blame feels more shameful than brazenly denying it – treadmills of contrition will churn out perverse injustices.[171] As long as claimants treat civil courts like casinos – disdained as dens of greed and vice but overcrowded with the disillusioned seeking to cash in – offenders will do everything they can to stack the apology deck in their favor. When we measure sincerity in dollars, apologies will trade like an antiquated currency.

Hopefully the preceding analysis sheds some light on this situation. Perhaps a more eyes-wide-open perspective on apologies in civil law will provide a toolkit for offenders who seek to offer substantive apologies while empowering victims to pursue the apologetic meanings they desire. Perhaps this might lead to less duping, less excessive denying, and less excessive claiming. I admit to dreaming of pro bono centers devoted to providing legal services for victims seeking apologies – victims who might not otherwise have access to justice when plaintiffs' attorneys work for a percentage of speculated financial winnings. I hope to have shown that apologies in civil law are a powerful force, capable of directing the global zeitgeist and bringing the most powerful organizations in the world to their knees. They are, however, only one force among many.

Concluding Call for Collaboration

Niels Bohr defined an *expert* as someone "who has made all the mistakes which can be made in a very narrow field."[1] I have surely made many mistakes. Ten years ago, for example, it seemed like a good idea to think a single article could provide a comprehensive theory of apologies. Now that I have written two books on apologies, I am still hardly an expert on Bohr's account. Many, many mistakes remain to be made. We are only beginning to understand the complexity of apologies and remorse, and as we inch toward lucidity we discover how these concepts entwine with other equally intricate, contested, and rapidly evolving ideas. Consider, for instance, how neuroscience overwrites understandings of blameworthiness or emotions, or how "big data" revolutionizes how we predict crime and recidivism. Both of these increasingly quotidian bodies of knowledge will challenge current conceptions of apologies and their relation to law. Many of the suggestions in this book will eventually look like quaint folk knowledge, but hopefully some of the questions of the future will grow from the seeds planted here.

Those who expect the power of logical argumentation to finish the job of understanding apologies may reach this conclusion dissatisfied or even anxious. Apologies are highly context dependent creatures; their shape shifting defies static classification. As this book – along with *I Was Wrong* – struggles to apply a *theory* of categorical apologies to *concrete cases*, the cumulative effect should help readers develop the sort of *phronesis* that improves their judgments of the particularities of apologies as they find them in different legal habitats. Practical wisdom is an ongoing process of coalescing insight through practice, and it does not typically result from cribbing someone else's arguments.

Thankfully all of us researching these genuinely interdisciplinary issues make our mistakes in public. With a few notable exceptions of the most durable specimens of thinking, over a long enough view of history most theories become obsolete. Individual humans tend to be pretty bad at theorizing, but when we aggregate our efforts into science – in the old sense of the term – we do a bit better. We learn from each not only over time but also across disciplines.

Clearly this book is overambitious and cannot answer many questions that it raises. I hand off many issues to those more qualified to address and defend the various bridges too far. Empirical questions arise throughout this book; new findings could undermine or support many of my central arguments. The categorical apology is an unwieldy instrument, but it captures a high-resolution image of the substance of remorse with all of its pumps and hydraulics. Given that apologies are treatments rather than cures, we face the added challenge of measuring fluid processes rather than static utterances. Hopefully my theories can add some precision to coding such that the data gathered illuminates rather than obscures the meanings at stake.

In addition, some of the most useful insights about the relationships between apologies and law will come not from professorial interlopers in the justice system but from boots on the ground practitioners. Procedures vary widely across disputes and jurisdictions. Experts in victim impact statements, pretrial diversions, or class action settlement agreements, to name but a few, will possess knowledge about apologies and the fine-grained details of practicing law beyond anything I could offer. Hopefully academic research in these areas continues to integrate the practical wisdom of those who live on the front lines of justice.

The optimal viewpoint should include not only interdisciplinary research spanning innumerable areas of practical microexpertise but also international perspectives on apologies and law. Little is written about it in English, but Germany, Russia, Turkey, Estonia, and Austria are but a few of the jurisdictions accommodating for variants of "active remorse" or "manifested repentance" – *tätige reue* in German.[2] We would benefit from close study of these examples, mining their datasets and learning from their trials and errors.

Apologies have been embedded in legal institutions for thousands of years and across many civilizations. Their importance only increases in modernity, in part because they serve as something of a last stand for debating values. How a culture understands and institutionalizes apologies provides a fingerprint of its moral struggles. We argue whether public institutions should engage in soul crafting by encouraging and sustaining apologies because we know so much is at stake: the role of the state in defining the good, the encroaching attacks on traditions of individual moral agents deserving blame, the value of something other than money, and so on. We tend not to teach how to apologize in schools, in part because such training invokes illiberal traditions of repentance and does not advance favored STEM initiatives. Apologies are not our strongest subject. We struggle to square the humility and vulnerability of apologies with a litigious culture that expects perfection from others while helping ourselves to exceptionalism. We worry that apologies compound pervasive structural inequalities. Apologies, in other words, reflect our abstractions about justice back to us in the most concrete and intimate situations.

As with all theories of justice, we should be suspicious of claims to definitively solve these problems. Thus I have one final note of caution: I hope this book provides some illumination, but gray areas will remain however much we may desire to drive out all darkness. People tend to find uncertainty in law especially uncomfortable, as if guilt and innocence should always break cleanly and leave no doubts regarding on which side of the bright lines of justice one stands. Studying the relationship between apologies and law requires a high tolerance for nuance and uncertainty, and therefore I join Murphy's call for humility when evaluating offenders. "Even though the necessities of maintaining civilized life and schemes of cooperation require that we sometimes make and act on our best judgments of wrongdoing and criminal responsibility," warns Murphy, "we should be very cautious about overdramatizing and overmoralizing what we must (regretfully) do here by portraying it as some righteous cosmic drama – as a holy war against ultimate sin and evil."[3] Those who treat Beebe's punishment like a math problem and claim to know with certainty what he deserves probably understand little about the issue beyond their dogmas. Attempting to gain clarity about these issues requires abandoning low-resolution oversimplifications to survey the layers of complexity in the terrain. Then we can chip away at our illusions, spend years working toward a few increments of clarity, and subject our theories to as many critical eyes that will look with us in the same directions.

Notes

Introduction

1. Liz Seccuro, *Crash into Me: A Survivor's Search for Justice* (New York: Bloomsbury, 2011), 8.
2. Ibid., 109.
3. Ibid., 230–31.
4. Ibid., 232.
5. Kristen Gelineau, "Rape Victim Gets Justice 23 Years After the Attack," *Los Angeles Times*, March 18, 2007.
6. Seccuro, *Crash into Me*, 237.
7. Lauren Glaze and Erika Parks, "Correctional Populations in the United States, 2011," *Bureau of Justice Statistics*, November 29, 2012, available at http://www.bjs.gov/index.cfm?ty=pbdetail&iid=4537.
8. Thanks to my friend Sara McKinstry Cleaves for this term.
9. See Liz Seccuro, "A Plea Deal for George Huguely," *Huffington Post*, December 16, 2010.
10. Liz Seccuro, "A History of Violence: Not Huguely, But the University of Virginia," *Huffington Post*, May 27, 2010.
11. "He Raped as a Teenager and Now Works to Stop Sexual Violence in South Africa," *CNN.com*, May 7, 2012.
12. Paul Tillis, "Can Forgiveness Play a Role in Criminal Justice," *New York Times Magazine*, January 4, 2013.
13. Rebeccah Cantley, "Ann, Conor's Relationship Brings up Issues of Teen Dating Violence," *Tallahassee.com*, August 27, 2011.
14. Tillis, "Can Forgiveness Play a Role in Criminal Justice."
15. Nick Smith, *I Was Wrong: The Meanings of Apologies* (New York: Cambridge University Press, 2008).
16. See, for example, Deborah Levi, "The Role of Apology in Mediation," *New York University Law Review* 72 (1997): 1165–220, 1186–87: "If a party asks for an apology, the opposing lawyer is likely to regard that party as intransigent and to protect her client from the risk that evidence of apology could become a basis for assigning liability in a subsequent legal proceeding."

17. American Medical Association, Office of the General Counsel, Division of Health Law, "Medical Professional Liability Insurance" (1998), 133. I learned of this resource from Cohen, "Advising Clients to Apologize," note 60.
18. Michael Woods, *Healing Words: The Power of Apology in Medicine* (Santa Fe: Center for Physician Leadership, 2007), 52–53.
19. Sir William Blackstone, *Commentaries on the Laws of England*, Volume II (Philadelphia: Lippincott Company, 1908), 339.
20. Lesek Kolakowski, *My Correct Views on Everything* (South Bend: St. Augustine's Press, 2005), 188.
21. See Lee Taft, "Apology Subverted: The Commodification of Apology," *Yale Law Journal* 109 (2000): 1135–60, 1150: "This competition is captured in a lawsuit, the purpose of which is to establish the fault of one party and offer relief to the other. This is hardly an atmosphere that encourages expressions of remorse."
22. For examples of discussions of apologies in criminal law by social scientists, see Howard Zehr, *Changing Lenses: A New Focus for Crime and Justice* (Scottsdale, PA: Herald Press, 1990); Howard Zehr, "Why Can't We Just Apologize?" *Crime Victims Report* 11-3 (2007): 38; Gordon Bazemore and Mark Umbreit, "A Comparison of Four Restorative Sentencing Models," in *A Restorative Justice Reader: Texts, Sources, Context*, ed. G. Johnstone (Cullompton: Willan Publishing, 2003), 225–44; Anthony Bottoms, "Some Sociological Reflections on Restorative Justice," in *Restorative Justice and Criminal Justice: Competing or Reconcilable Paradigms*, ed. Andrew von Hirsch et al. (Portland: Hart Publishing, 2003), 79–113; H. Strang, "Justice for Victims of Young Offenders: The Centrality of Emotional Harm and Restoration," in *A Restorative Justice Reader*, 286–93; Carrie Petrucci, "Apology in the Criminal Justice Setting," *Behavioral Sciences and the Law* 20 (2002): 337–62; Keith Niedermeier, Irwin A. Horowitz, and Norbert L. Kerr, "Exceptions to the Rule: The Effects of Remorse, Status, and Gender on Decision Making," *Journal of Applied Social Psychology* 31 (2001): 604–23; Robert R. Weyeneth, "The Power of Apology and the Process of Historical Reconciliation," *The Public Historian* 23-3 (Summer 2001): 9–38; Susan Alter, "Apologizing for Serious Wrongdoing: Social, Psychological, and Legal Considerations," *Final Report for the Law Commission of Canada* (1999); Walter J. Dickey, "Forgiveness and Crime: The Possibilities of Restorative Justice," in *Exploring Forgiveness*, eds. Robert D. Enright and Joanna North (Madison: University of Wisconsin Press, 1998), 106–20; Randolph B. Pipes and Marci Alessi, "Remorse and a Previously Punished Offense in Assignment of Punishment and Estimated Likelihood of a Repeated Offense," *Psychological Reports* 85 (1999): 246–48; M. H. Gonzales, J. A. Haugen, and D. J. Manning, "Victims as 'Narrative Critics': Factors Influencing Rejoinders and Evaluative Responses to Offenders' Accounts," *Personality and Social Psychology Bulletin* 20 (1994): 691–704; D. Robinson, L. Smith-Lovin, and O. Tsoudis, "Heinous Crime or Unfortunate Accident? The Effects of Remorse on Responses to Mock Criminal Confessions," *Social Forces* 73 (1994): 175–90; C. Kleinke, R. Wallis, K. Stalder, "Evaluation of a Rapist as a Function of Expressed Intent and Remorse," *Journal of Social Psychology* 132-4 (1992): 525–37; Christy Taylor and Chris L. Kleinke, "Effects of Severity of Accident, History of Drunk Driving, Intent, and Remorse on Judgments of a Drunk Driver," *Journal of*

Applied Social Psychology 22 (1992): 1641–55; G. S. Schwartz et al., "The Effects of Post-Transgression Remorse on Perceived Aggression, Attribution of Intent, and Level of Punishment," *Journal of Social and Clinical Psychology* 17 (1987): 293–97; Michael G. Rumsey, "Effects of Defendant Background and Remorse on Sentencing Judgments," *Journal of Applied Social Psychology* 6 (1976): 64–68; Harry S. Upshaw and Daniel Romer, "Punishment For One's Misdeeds as a Function of Having Suffered from Them," *Personality and Social Psychology Bulletin* 2 (1976): 162–65; W. Austin, E. Walster, and M. K. Utne, "Equity and the Law: The Effects of a Harmdoer's 'Suffering in the Act' on Liking and Assigned Punishment," in *Advances in Experimental Social Psychology*, ed. L. Berkowitz (New York: Academic Press, 1976), 217–59; Jerry I. Shaw and James A. McMartin, "Perpetrator or Victim? Effects of Who Suffers in an Automobile Accident on Judgmental Strictness," *Social Behavior and Personality* 3 (1975): 5–12; and Dana Bramel, Barry Taub, and Barbara Blum, "An Observer's Reaction to the Suffering of his Enemy," *Journal of Personality and Social Psychology* 8 (1968): 384–92.

23. For discussions of the role of apologies in criminal law by legal scholars or appearing in law reviews, see Brent White, "Saving Face: The Benefits of Not Saying I'm Sorry," *Law and Contemporary Problems* 72 (2009): 261–69; Daniel Medwed, "The Innocent Prisoner's Dilemma: Consequences of Failing to Admit Guilt at Parole Hearings," *Iowa Law Review* 93 (2008): 491–557; Margareth Etienne and Jennifer K. Robbennolt, "Apologies and Plea Bargaining," *Marquette Law Review* 91 (2007): 295–322; Abigail Penzell, "Apology in the Context of Wrongful Conviction: Why the System Should Say its Sorry," *Cardozo Journal of Conflict Resolution* 9 (2007): 145–61; Stephanos Bibas, "Transparency and Participation in Criminal Procedure," *New York University Law Review* 81 (2006): 911–66; Candace McCoy, "Plea Bargaining as Coercion: The Trial Penalty and Plea Bargaining Reform," *Criminal Law Quarterly* 50 (2005): 67–107; Susan Szmania and Daniel Mangis, "Finding the Right Time and Place: A Case Study Comparison of the Expression of Offender Remorse in Traditional Justice and Restorative Justice Contexts," *Marquette Law Review* 89-2 (2005): 335–58; Stephanos Bibas and Richard A. Bierschbach, "Integrating Remorse and Apology into Criminal Procedure," *Yale Law Journal* 114 (2004): 85–148; Sherry Colb, "Profiling with Apologies," *Ohio State Journal of Criminal Law* 1 (2004): 611–25; Erin Ann O'Hara, "Apology and Thick Trust: What Spouse Abusers and Negligent Doctors Might Have in Common," *Chicago Kent Law Review* 79-3 (2004): 1055–89; Robert Weisberg, "Apology, Legislation, and Mercy," *North Carolina Law Review* 82 (2004): 1415–40; Cheryl Bader, "Forgive me Victim for I have Sinned: Why Repentance and the Criminal Justice System Do Not Mix – A Lesson from Jewish Law," *Fordham Urban Law Journal* 31 (2003): 69–97; Margareth Etienne, "Remorse, Responsibility, and Regulating Advocacy: Making Defendants Pay for the Sins of Their Lawyers," *New York University Law Review* 78 (2003): 2103–76; S. Garvey, "Restorative Justice, Punishment, and Atonement," *Utah Law Review* 1 (2003): 303–17; Elizabeth Latif, "Apologetic Justice: Evaluating Apologies Tailored Toward Legal Solutions," *Boston University Law Review* 81 (2001): 289–319; S. Garvey, "Punishment as Atonement," *UCLA Law Review* 47 (1999): 1801–58; Theodore Eisenberg, Stephen Garvey, and Martin Wells,

"But Was He Sorry? The Role of Remorse in Capital Sentencing," *Cornell Law Review* 83(1998): 1599–637; Scott Sundby, "The Intersection of Trial Strategy, Remorse, and the Death Penalty," *Cornell Law Review* 83 (1998): 1557–98; Charles R. Calleros, "Conflict, Apology, and Reconciliation at Arizona State University: A Second Case Study in Hateful Speech," *Cumberland Law Review* 27 (1997): 95–137; Lisa Orenstein, "Sentencing Leniency May Be Denied to Criminal Offenders Who Fail to Express Remorse at Allocution," *Maryland Law Review* 56 (1997): 780–93; Michael O'Hear, "Remorse, Cooperation, and 'Acceptance of Responsibility': The Structure, Implementation, and Reform of Section 3E1.1 of the Federal Sentencing Guidelines," *Northwestern University Law Review* 91 (1997): 1507–73; Ellen Bryant, "Section 3E1.1 of the Federal Sentencing Guidelines: Bargaining with the Guilty," *Catholic University Law Review* 44 (1995): 1269–305; Richard Delgado and Jean Stefancic, "Apologize and Move On?: Finding a Remedy for Pornography, Insult, and Hate Speech," *University of Colorado Law Review* 67 (1994): 93–111; John H. Langbein, "Torture and Plea Bargain," *The Public Interest* 58 (1980): 43–46. For an exchange on remorse, apology, and mercy, see Sherry Colb, "Retaining Remorse," Stephanos Bibas, "Invasions of Conscience and Faked Apologies," Susan A. Bandes, "Evaluating Remorse is Here to Stay: We Should Focus on Improving its Dynamics," Lisa Kern Griffin, "Insincere and Involuntary Public Apologies," Janet Ainsworth, "The Social Meaning of Apology," and Jeffrie Murphy, "Reply," all appearing in *Criminal Law Conversations*, eds. Paul Robinson, Stephen Garvey, and Kimberly Kessler Ferzan (New York: Oxford University Press, 2009). For a recent symposium on mercy in criminal law, see Stephen Gravey, "Questions of Mercy," Stephanos Bibas, "Forgiveness in Criminal Procedure," David Dolinko, "Some Naïve Thoughts about Justice and Mercy," R. A. Duff, "The Intrusion of Mercy," Heidi Hurd, "The Morality of Mercy," Jeffrie Murphy, "Remorse, Apology, and Mercy," John Tasioulas, "Mercy and the Liberal State," all appearing in a special volume of the *Ohio State Journal of Criminal Law* 4-2 (2007). For discussions of "shaming sanctions," see Andrew von Hirsch, *Censure and Sanctions* (New York: Oxford University Press, 1996): 82–83; Stephen Garvey, "Can Shaming Punishments Educate?" *University of Chicago Law Review* 65 (1998): 733–93; James Q. Whitman, "What Is Wrong with Inflicting Shame Sanctions?" *Yale Law Journal* 107 (1998): 1055–92; Dan Kahan, "What Do Alternative Sanctions Mean?" *University of Chicago Law Review* 6 (1996): 591–652 (Kahan has since revised views. See "What's Really Wrong with Shaming Sanctions," *Texas Law Review* 84 (2006): 2075–95).

24. The central sections of Federal Sentencing Guidelines pertaining to remorse can be found at 18 U.S.C.S. app. § 3E1.1. See the *2012 Guidelines Manual* at http://www.ussc.gov/Guidelines/2012_Guidelines/Manual_HTML/3e1_1.htm.
25. *Riggins v. Nevada*, 504 U.S. 127, 144 (1992) (concurring opinion). See Eisenberg, Stephen Garvey, and Martin Wells, "But Was He Sorry? The Role of Remorse in Capital Sentencing"; Pipes and Alessi, "Remorse and a Previously Punished Offense in Assignment of Punishment and Estimated Likelihood of a Repeated Offense"; Sundby, "The Intersection of Trial Strategy, Remorse, and the Death Penalty"; Kleinke, Wallis, and Stalder, "Evaluation of a Rapist as a Function of Expressed Intent and Remorse"; Rumsey, "Effects of Defendant Background and Remorse on Sentencing Judgments," 64–68.

26. For discussions of apologies in civil law in law reviews and by law faculty, see J. Robbennolt, "Apologies and Medical Error," *Clinical Orthopedics and Related Research* 467 (2009): 378–82; J. Robbennolt, "Apologies and Reasonableness: Some Applications of Psychology to Torts," *DePaul Law Review* 59 (2010): 489–513; Michael Runnels, "Apologies All Around: Advocating Federal Protection for the Full Apology in Civil Cases," *San Diego Law Review* 45 (2009): 137–60; Robin Ebert, "Attorneys, Tell Your Clients to Say They're Sorry: Apologies in the Health Care Industry," *Indiana Health Law Review* 5 (2008): 337–70; Carole Houk and Lauren Edelstein, "Beyond Apology to Early Non-Judicial Resolution," *Hamline Journal of Law and Public Policy* 29 (2008): 411–22; Aaron Lazare, "The Healing Forces of Apology in Medical Practice and Beyond," *DePaul Law Review* 57 (2008): 251–64; J. Robbennolt, "Attorneys, Apologies, and Settlement Negotiation," *Harvard Negotiation Law Review* 13 (2008): 349–97; Mitchell Stephens, "I'm Sorry: Exploring the Reasons Behind the Differing Roles of Apology in American and Japanese Civil Cases," *Widener Law Review* 14 (2008): 185–204; Prue Vines, "Apologies and Civil Liability in the UK: A View from Elsewhere," *Edinburgh Law Review* 12-2 (2008): 200–30; Colin Jones, "Apologies and Corporate Governance in the Japanese Context: Tatsumi Tanaka's *Sonna Shazai De Wa Kaisha Ga Abunai (Apologizing that Way Will Endanger Your Company)*," *BYU International Law and Management Review* 3 (2007): 303–17; Prue Vines, "The Power of Apology: Mercy, Forgiveness or Corrective Justice in the Civil Liability Arena," *Public Space* (2007): 1–51; Ashley A. Davenport, "Forgive and Forget: Recognition of Error and Use of Apology as Preemptive Steps to ADR or Litigation in Medical Malpractice Cases," *Pepperdine Dispute Resolution Law Journal* 6 (2006): 81–107; J. Robbennolt, "Apologies and Settlement Levers," *Journal of Empirical Studies* 3 (2006): 333–73; Brent T. White, "Say You're Sorry: Court-Ordered Apologies as a Civil Rights Remedy," *Cornell Law Review* 91 (2006): 1216–312; D. Hyman and C. Silver, "Medical Malpractice Litigation and Tort Reform," *Vanderbilt Law Review* 59 (2006): 1085–136; Ilhyung Lee, "The Law and Culture of the Apology in Korean Dispute Settlement (with Japan and the United States in Mind)," *Michigan Journal of International Law* 27 (2005): 1–53; Virginia L. Morrison, "Heyoka: The Shifting Shape of Dispute Resolution in Health Care," *Georgia State University Law Review* 21 (2005): 931–62; Jennifer Robbennolt, "What We Know and Don't About the Role of Apologies in Resolving Health Care Disputes," *Georgia State Law Review* 21 (2005): 1009–27; Lee Taft, "Apology within a Moral Dialectic: A Reply to Professor Robbennolt," *Michigan Law Review* 103 (2005): 1010–17; Prue Vines, "Apologising to Avoid Liability: Cynical Civility or Practical Morality?" *Sydney Law Review* 27-5 (2005): 483–505; Prue Vines, "Apologies in the Civil Liability Context," *Australian Civil Liability* 2-1 (2005): 6–7; J. Brown, "The Role of Apology in Mediation," *Marquette Law Review* 87 (2004): 655–72; Sidney Kanazawa, "Apologies and Lunch: Strategic Options for Every Litigator," *For the Defense* 46-7 (2004): 29–34; Donna Pavlick, "Apology and Mediation: The Horse and Carriage of the Twenty-First Century," *Ohio St. Journal of Dispute Resolution* 18 (2003): 829–66; J. Robbennolt, "Apologies and Legal Settlement: An Empirical Examination," *Michigan Law Review* 102-3 (2003): 460–516; Erin O'Hara and Douglas Yarn, "On Apology and Consilience," *Washington Law Review* 77 (2002): 1121–92; R. Cohen, "Legislating Apologies: The Pros and Cons,"

University of Cincinnati Law Review 70 (2002): 1–29; Latif, "Apologetic Justice,"; Dai-Kwon Choi, "Freedom of Conscience and the Court-Ordered Apology for Defamatory Remarks," *Cardozo Journal of International and Comparative Law* 8 (2000): 205; Max Bolstad, "Learning from Japan: The Case for Increased Use of Apology in Mediation," *Cleveland State Law Review* 48-3 (2000): 545–78; William K. Bartels, "The Stormy Sea of Apologies: California Evidence Code Section 1160 Provides a Safe Harbor for Apologies Made after Accidents," *Western State University Law Review* 28 (2001): 141–57; D. Shuman, "Role of Apologies in Tort Law," *Judicature* 83-4 (2000): 180–89; Taft, "Apology Subverted"; Jonathan R. Cohen, "Advising Clients to Apologize," *Southern California Law Review* 72 (1999): 1009–69; Jonathan R. Cohen, "Nagging Problem: Advising the Client Who Wants to Apologize," *Dispute Resolution Magazine* (Spring 1999): 19–38; Steven Keeva, "Does Law Mean Never Having to Say You're Sorry?" *American Bar Association Journal* 85 (1999): 64–68; Aviva Orenstein, "Apology Excepted: Incorporating a Feminist Analysis into Evidence Policy Where You Would Least Expect It," *Southwestern University Law Review* 28 (1999): 221–75; Levi, "The Role of Apology in Mediation"; Marshall Tanick and Teresa Ayling, "Alternative Dispute Resolution by Apology: Settlement by Saying 'I'm Sorry,'" *Hennepin Lawyer* (1996): 22–25; Peter Rehm and Denise Beatty, "Legal Consequences of Apologizing," *Journal of Dispute Resolution* (1995): 115–30; R. Korobkin and C. Guthrie, "Psychological Barriers to Litigation Settlement: An Experimental Approach," *Michigan Law Review* 93 (1994): 107–27; John Soloski, "The Study and the Libel Plaintiff: Who Sues for Libel?" *Iowa Law Review* 71 (1985): 217–20.
27. For social scientific discussion of apologies in civil law, see Johannes Abeler, Juljana Calaki, Kai Andree, and Christoph Basek, "The Power of Apology," available at http://www.nottingham.ac.uk/economics/cedex/papers/2009-12.pdf; Robert Cornell, Rick Warne, and Martha Eining, "The Use of Remedial Tactics in Negligence Litigation," *University of Utah Contemporary Accounting Research* 26-3 (2009): 767–87; A. Wu et al., "Disclosing Medical Errors to Patients: It's Not What You Say, It's What They Hear," *Journal of General Internal Medicine* 24-9 (2009): 1012–17; Michael B. Rainey, Kit Chan, and Judith Begin, "Characterized by Conciliation: Here's How Business Can Use Apology to Diffuse Litigation," *Alternatives to High Cost Litigation* 26-7 (2008): 131–34; Hyman and Schechter, "Mediating Medical Malpractice Lawsuits Against Hospitals: New York City's Pilot Project," *Health Affairs* 25 (2006): 1394–99; L. Kaldjian et al., "An Empirically Derived Taxonomy of Factors Affecting Physicians' Willingness to Disclose Medical Errors," *Journal of General Internal Medicine* 21 (2006): 942–48; Aaron Lazare, "Apology in Medical Practice: An Emerging Clinical Skill," *Journal of the American Medical Association* 296 (2006): 1401–04; K. Mazor et al., "Disclosure of Medical Errors: What Factors Influence How Patients Respond?" *Journal of General Intern Medicine* 21 (2006): 704–10; Hearit, *Crisis Management by Apology*; C. B. Liebman and C. S. Hyman, "Medical Error Disclosure, Mediation Skills, and Malpractice Litigation: A Demonstration Project in Pennsylvania," *The Project on Medical Liability in Pennsylvania* (2005), available at http://www.pewtrusts.org/pdf/LiebmanReport.pdf; C. Sparkman, "Legislating Apology in the Context of Medical Mistakes," *AORN* 82-2 (2005): 263; Douglas Frenkel and

Carol Liebman, "Words that Heal," *Annals of Internal Medicine* 140 (2004): 482–83; C. Liebman and C. S. Hyman, "A Mediation Skills Model to Manage Disclosure of Errors and Adverse Events to Patients," *Health Affairs* 23–4 (2004): 22–32; K. Mazor, S. Simon, and R. Yood, "Health Plan Members' Views about Disclosure of Medical Errors," *Annals of Internal Medicine* 140–6 (2004): 409–18; Thomas H. Gallagher et al., "Patients' and Physicians' Attitudes Regarding the Disclosure of Medical Errors," *Journal of the American Medical Association* 289 (2003): 1001–07; R. Lamb et al., "Hospital Disclosure Practices: Results of a National Study," *Health Affairs* 22 (2003): 73–83; Ameeta Patel and Lamar Reinsch, "Companies Can Apologize: Corporate Apologies and Legal Liability," *Business Communication Quarterly* 66–1 (2003): 9–25; Brian H. Bornstein, Lahna M. Rung, and Monica K. Miller, "The Effects of Defendant Remorse on Mock Juror Decisions in a Malpractice Case," *Behavioral Sciences and Law* 20 (2002): 393–409; Latif, "Apologetic Justice"; Jonathan Cohen, "Apology and Organizations: Exploring an Example from Medical Practice," *Fordham Urban Law Journal* 27 (2000): 1447–82; Carl Schneider, "What It Means To Be Sorry: The Power of Apology in Mediation," *Mediation Quarterly* 17–3 (2000): 265–80; S. Kraman and G. Hamm, "Risk Management: Extreme Honesty May Be the Best Policy," *Annals of Internal Medicine* 131–12 (1999): 963–67; A. Wu, "Handling Hospital Errors: Is Disclosure the Best Defense?" *Annals of Internal Medicine* 131–12 (1999): 970–72; A. Witman, D. Park, and S. Hardin, "How Do Patients Want Physicians to Handle Mistakes? A Survey of Internal Medicine Patients in an Academic Setting," *Archives of Internal Medicine* 156 (1996); 2565–69; H. S. Farber and M. J. White, "A Comparison of Formal and Informal Dispute Resolution in Medical Malpractice," *Journal of Legal Studies* 23–2 (1994): 777–806; C. Vincent, A. Phillips, and M. Young, "Why Do People Sue Doctors? A Study of Patients and Relatives Taking Legal Action," *Lancet* 343 (1994): 1609–13; G. Hickson et al., "Factors that Prompted Families to File Medical Malpractice Claims Following Perinatal Injuries," *Journal of the American Medical Association* 267 (1992): 1359–63; M. May, and D. Stengel, "Who Sues Their Doctors? How Patients Handle Medical Grievances," *Law and Society Review* 24–1 (1990): 105–20; D. Novack et al., "Physicians' Attitudes Toward Using Deception to Resolve Difficult Ethical Problems," *Journal of the American Medical Association* 261–20 (1989): 2980–85; Ann J. Kellett, "Healing Angry Wounds: The Roles of Apology and Mediation in Disputes Between Physicians and Patients," *Journal of Dispute Resolution* (1987): 111–32; Stephen B. Goldberg, E. Green, and F. Sander, "Saying You're Sorry," *Negotiation Journal* 3 (1987): 221–24; John O. Haley, "The Implications of Apology," *Law and Society Review* 20 (1986): 499–507.

28. Woods, *Healing Words*, 3.
29. See Hyman and Schechter, "Mediating Medical Malpractice Lawsuits Against Hospital." Robbennolt also notes methodological concerns regarding this study in "Attorneys, Apologies, and Settlement Negotiation," note 36.
30. See Robbennolt, "Apologies and Legal Settlement," 485–86: "When no apology was offered 52% of respondents indicated that they would definitely or probably accept the offer, while 43% would definitely or probably reject the offer and 5% were unsure. When a partial apology was offered, only 35% of respondents were

inclined to accept the offer, 25% were inclined to reject it, and 40% indicated that they were unsure. In contrast, when a full apology was offered, 73% of respondents were inclined to accept the offer, with only 13–14% each inclined to reject it or remaining unsure."
31. See Abeler et al., "The Power of Apology."
32. Gerald Gorn, Yuwei Jiang, and Gita Venkataramani Johar, "Babyfaces, Trait Inferences, and Company Evaluations in a PR Crisis," *Journal of Consumer Research* 35-1 (2008): 36–49.
33. Cornell, Warne, and Eining, "The Use of Remedial Tactics in Negligence Litigation," 767. See also Kanazawa, "Apologies and Lunch," 32.
34. Tanick and Ayling, "Alternative Dispute Resolution by Apology," 22.
35. Ibid. See also Levi, "The Role of Apology in Mediation."
36. In addition to the literature discussing apologies in civil law generally, for examples of specific discussions of the role of apologies in medicine see Abeler, Calaki, Andree, and Basek, "The Power of Apology"; Cornell, Warne, and Eining, "The Use of Remedial Tactics in Negligence Litigation"; Robbennolt, "Apologies and Medical Error"; Runnels, "Apologies All Around"; Wu et al., "Disclosing Medical Errors to Patients"; Ebert, "Attorneys, Tell Your Clients to Say They're Sorry"; Lazare, "The Healing Forces of Apology in Medical Practice and Beyond"; Rainey, Chan, and Begin, "Characterized by Conciliation"; Kevin Sack, "Doctors Say 'I'm Sorry' Before 'See You in Court,'" *New York Times*, May 18, 2008, at A1; F. Bender, "I'm Sorry Laws and Medical Liability," *Virtual Mentor: American Medical Association Journal of Ethics* 9-4 (2007): 300–04; John Kleefeld, "Thinking Like a Human: British Columbia's Apology Act," *University of British Columbia Law Review* 40 (2007): 769–808; Laura Landro, "The Informed Patient: Doctors Learn to Say 'I'm Sorry'; Patients' Stories of Hospital Errors Serve to Teach Staff," *Wall Street Journal*, January 24, 2007; C. Schmidt, "We're Sorry: The Healing Power of Apology – and How Two Little Words Can Make Medicine Safer," *Harvard Public Health Review* (2007); Woods, *Healing Words*; *Medical Justice: Making the System Work Better for Patients and Doctors: Hearing Before the S. Comm. on Health, Educ., Labor and Pensions*, 109th Cong. 3 (2006); R. Boothman, "Apologies and a Strong Defense at the University of Michigan Health System," *Physician Executive* (2006): 7–10; Davenport, "Forgive and Forget"; Peter Geier, "Emerging Med-Mal Strategy: I'm Sorry," *National Law Journal*, July 17, 2006, 1; Hyman and Schechter, "Mediating Medical Malpractice Lawsuits Against Hospitals"; Hyman and Silver, "Medical Malpractice Litigation and Tort Reform"; Kaldjian et al., "An Empirically Derived Taxonomy of Factors Affecting Physicians' Willingness to Disclose Medical Errors"; Aaron Lazare, "Apology in Medical Practice"; Lucian Leape, "Full Disclosure and Apology – An Idea Whose Time Has Come," *Physician Executive* 32-2 (2006): 16–18; Katherine Mangan, "Acting Sick: At Medical Schools, Actors Help Teach Doctors How to 'Fess Up to Mistakes – and How to Avoid Them," *Chronicle of Higher Education*, September 15, 2006, 8; K. Mazor et al., "Disclosure of Medical Errors"; Gail Garfinkel Weiss, "Medical Errors: Should You Apologize?" *Medical Economics*, April 21, 2006, 50; Lucian Leape, "Understanding the Power of Apology: How Saying 'I'm Sorry' Helps Heal Patients and Caregivers," *Focus on Patient Safety* (2005): 1–3; Liebman and Hyman, "Medical Error Disclosure, Mediation Skills, and

Malpractice Litigation"; Morrison, "Heyoka"; Robbennolt, "What We Know and Don't About the Role of Apologies in Resolving Health Care Disputes"; Sparkman, "Legislating Apology in the Context of Medical Mistakes," 263; Lee Taft, "Apology and Medical Mistake: Opportunity or Foil?," *Annals of Health Law* 14 (2005): 55–94; Vines, "Apologising to Avoid Liability"; Frenkel and Liebman, "Words that Heal"; R. Lamb, "Open Disclosure: The Only Approach to Medical Error," *Quality and Safety in Health Care* 13-1 (2004): 3–5; Liebman and Hyman, "A Mediation Skills Model to Manage Disclosure of Errors and Adverse Events to Patients"; Mazor, Simon, and Yood, "Health Plan Members' Views about Disclosure of Medical Errors"; Lindsey Tanner, "Doctors Eye Apologies for Medical Mistakes," *Associated Press*, November 8, 2004; Rachel Zimmerman, "Medical Contrition: Doctor's New Tool to Fight Lawsuits: Saying I'm Sorry," *Wall Street Journal*, May 18, 2004; Gallagher et al., "Patients' and Physicians' Attitudes Regarding the Disclosure of Medical Errors"; Lamb et al., "Hospital Disclosure Practices"; Cohen, "Legislating Apologies"; Bornstein, Rung, and Miller, "The Effects of Defendant Remorse on Mock Juror Decisions in a Malpractice Case"; Latif, "Apologetic Justice"; Cohen, "Apology and Organizations"; Taft, "Apology Subverted"; Chantal Brazeau, "Disclosing the Truth About a Medical Error," *American Family Physician* 60 (1999): 1013–14; Kraman and Hamm, "Risk Management"; Wu, "Handling Hospital Errors"; Witman, Park, and Hardin, "How do Patients Want Physicians to Handle Mistakes?"; J. Stratton Shartel, "Toro's Mediation Program Challenges Wisdom of Traditional Litigation Model," *Inside Litigation* 9 (1995): 10; Farber and White, "A Comparison of Formal and Informal Dispute Resolution in Medical Malpractice"; Vincent, Phillips and Young, "Why Do People Sue Doctors?"; Hickson et al., "Factors that Prompted Families to File Medical Malpractice Claims Following Perinatal Injuries"; May and Stengel, "Who Sues Their Doctors?"; D. Novack et al., "Physicians' Attitudes Toward Using Deception to Resolve Difficult Ethical Problems"; and Kellett, "Healing Angry Wounds." See also the materials from Doug Wojcieszak's Sorry Works! project at http://www.sorryworks.net/home.phtml.

37. Mass. Gen. Laws. ch. 233, 23D (1999): "[S]tatements, writings or benevolent gestures expressing sympathy or a general sense of benevolence" are inadmissible "as evidence of an admission of liability in a civil action." For all of the notes identifying relevant legislation, I aggregated findings of various authors working in the area and added them to my own findings. Particular thanks to Jennifer Robbennolt for identifying many of these statutes in her excellent articles. For examples of various forms of "safe apology" legislation," see Ariz. Rev. Stat. Ann. § 12-2605 (2005): "Any statement, affirmation, gesture or conduct expressing apology, responsibility, liability, sympathy, commiseration, condolence, compassion or a general sense of benevolence that was made by a health care provider...to the patient, a relative of the patient, the patient's survivors or a health care decision maker for the patient and that relates to the discomfort, pain, suffering, injury or death of the patient as the result of the unanticipated outcome of medical care is inadmissible as evidence of an admission of liability or as evidence of an admission against interest"; Cal. Evid. Code § 1160(a) (2000): "The portion of statements, writings, or benevolent gestures expressing sympathy or a general sense of benevolence relating to the pain, suffering, or

death of a person involved in an accident and made to that person or the family of that person shall be inadmissible as evidence of an admission of liability in a civil action. A statement of fault, however, which is part of, or in addition to, any of the above shall not be inadmissible pursuant to this section"; Colo. Rev. Stat. § 13–25–135 (2003): covering statements "expressing apology, fault, sympathy, commiseration, condolence, compassion, or a general sense of benevolence"; Conn. Gen. Stat. § 52–184(d) (2005); Del. Code Ann. tit. 10, § 4318 (2006); D.C. Code Ann. § 16–2841 (2007); Fla. Stat. Ann. § 90.4026(2) (West 2005): "The portion of statements, writings or benevolent gestures expressing sympathy or a general sense of benevolence relating to the pain, suffering, or death of a person involved in an accident and made to that person or to the family of that person shall be inadmissible as evidence in a civil action. A statement of fault, however, which is part of, or in addition to, any of the above shall be admissible pursuant to this section"; Ga. Code Ann. § 24-3-37.1 (2006): covering statements "expressing benevolence, regret, apology, sympathy, commiseration, condolence, compassion, mistake, error, or a general sense of benevolence"; Haw. Rev. Stat. § 626–1 (2006); Idaho Code § 9–207 (2008); Ill. Comp. Stat. 5/8–1901 (2005); Iowa Code § 622.31 (1999); Ind. Code Ann. § 34-43.5-1; La. Rev. Stat. Ann. § 13:3715.5 (2005); Me. Rev. Stat. Ann. tit. 24, § 2907 (2005); Md. Cts. & Jud. Proc. Code Ann. § 10–920 (2004); Mont. Code. Ann. § 26-1-814 (2005); Mo. Rev. Stat. § 538.299 (2007); Neb. Rev. Stat. § 27–1201 (2007); N.H. Rev. Stat. Ann. § 507-E:4 (2005); N.C. Gen. Stat. § 8C-4, Rule 413 (2004); N.D. Cent. Code § 31–04-12 (2007); Ohio Rev. Code Ann. § 2317.43 (2004); Okla. Stat. Ann. tit. 63, § 1-1708.1H (2004); Ohio Rev. Code Ann. § 2317.43; Or. Rev. Stat. § 677.082 (2003); S.C. Code Ann. § 19-1-190 (2006); S.D. Codified Laws § 19–12–14 (2005); Tenn. R. Evid. § 409.1 (2003); Tex. Civ. Prac. & Rem. Code Ann. 18.061(a) (1) (West 1999): covering expressions of "sympathy or a general sense of benevolence relating to the pain, suffering, or death of an individual involved in an accident"; Utah Code Ann. § 78–14–18 (2006); Vt. Stat. Ann. tit. 12, § 1912 (2006); Va. Code Ann. § 8.01–581.20:1 (2005); Wash. Rev. Code § 5.66.010(1) (2002); W. Va. Code § 55-7-11(a) (2005); Wyo. Stat. Ann. § 1-1-130 (2004).

38. Contrast, for example, Cal. Evid. Code § 1160(a); Fla. Stat. § 90.4026(2); Tenn. R. Evid. § 409.1; Tex. Civ. Prac. & Rem. § 18.061; and Wash. Rev. Code § 5.66.010(1) with Colo. Rev. Stat. § 13–25–135 and Ga. Code Ann. § 24-3-37.1.
39. See, for example, Colo. Rev. Stat. § 13–25–135; Ga. Code Ann. § 24-3-37.1; 735 Ill. Comp. Stat. 5/8–1901; Ohio Rev. Code Ann. § 2317.43; Okla. Stat. Ann. tit. 63, § 1-1708.1H; Or. Rev. Stat. § 677.082; Wyo. Stat. Ann. § 1-1-130.
40. See, for example, Ohio Rev. Code Ann. § 2317.43; Okla. Stat. Ann. tit. 63, § 1-1708.1H; Or. Rev. Stat. § 677.082; Wyo. Stat. Ann. § 1-1-130.
41. Jeff Bailey, "Airlines Learn to Fly on a Wing and an Apology," *New York Times*, March 18, 2007.
42. Ian Ayres, *Super Crunchers: Why Thinking by Numbers is the Way to Be Smart* (New York: Bantam, 2008), 63–65.
43. For more elaboration, see *I Was Wrong*, 7–9.
44. For discussions of apologies, repentance, and related matters in the history of philosophy, see John Searle, *Speech Acts: An Essay in the Philosophy of Language* (Cambridge: Cambridge University Press, 1969); J. L. Austin, *How to Do*

Things with Words (Oxford: Oxford University Press, 1962); John Searle, "A Classification of Illocutionary Acts," *Language in Society* 5 (1976): 1–24; Moses Maimonides, *Hilchot Teshuvah: The Laws of Repentance* (New York: Moznaim, 1987); Michel de Montaigne, "Of Repentance," in *Montaigne: Essays*, ed. and trans. John M. Cohen (New York: Penguin, 1993), 235–49; Michel de Montaigne, *Apology for Raymond Sebond*, trans. M. A. Screech (New York: Penguin, 1988); Immanuel Kant, *The Metaphysical Elements of Justice*, trans. John Ladd (Indianapolis: Hackett, 1999), 101.

For extended conversations about apologies in philosophical literature in addition to *I Was Wrong*, see Linda Radzik, *Making Amends: Atonement in Morality, Law, and Politics* (New York: Cambridge University Press, 2009); Christopher Bennett, *The Apology Ritual: A Philosophical Theory of Punishment* (New York: Cambridge University Press, 2008); Margaret Urban Walker, *Moral Repair* (New York: Cambridge University Press, 2006); R. A. Duff, *Trials and Punishments* (New York: Cambridge University Press, 1986); Luc Bovens, "Apologies," *Proceedings of the Aristotelian Society* 108 (2008): 219–39; Bruce Waller, "Sincere Apology without Moral Responsibility," *Social Theory and Practice* 33-3 (2007): 441–65; Glen Pettigrove, "Unapologetic Forgiveness," *American Philosophical Quarterly* 41-1 (2004): 187–204; Pettigrove, "Apology, Reparations, and the Question of Inherited Guilt," *Public Affairs Quarterly* 17-4 (2003): 319–48; Trudy Govier and Wilhelm Verwoerd, "The Promise and Pitfalls of Apology," *Journal of Social Philosophy* 33-1 (2002): 67–82; Trudy Govier and Wilhelm Verwoerd, "Taking Wrongs Seriously: A Qualified Defense of Public Apologies," *Saskatchewan Law Review* 65 (2002): 157; Paul Davis, "On Apologies," *Journal of Applied Philosophy* 19-2 (2002): 169–73; Nicolaus Mills, "The New Culture of Apology," *Dissent* (Fall 2001): 113–16; Kathleen Gill, "The Moral Functions of an Apology," *Philosophical Forum* 31-1 (2000): 11–27; Jana Thompson, "The Apology Paradox," *Philosophical Quarterly* 55-201 (2000): 470–75; Richard Joyce, "Apologizing," *Public Affairs Quarterly* 13-2 (1999): 159–73; Jeffrie Murphy, " Repentance, Punishment, and Mercy," in *Repentance: A Comparative Perspective*, eds. Amitai Etzioni and David Carney (Lanham, MD: Rowan and Littlefield, 1997); Jean Harvey, "The Emerging Practice of Institutional Apologies," *International Journal of Applied Philosophy* 9-2 (1995): 57–65; John Wilson, "Why Forgiveness Requires Repentance," *Philosophy* 63-246 (1988): 534–5; and Louis Kort, "What is an Apology?" *Philosophical Research Archives* 1 (1975): 78–87.

45. For an overview of the history of the terms *apology* and *apologize* in English, see Marion Owen, *Apologies and Remedial Interchanges: A Study of Language Use in Social Interactions* (Berlin: Mouton de Gruyter, 1985), 109–13.

46. The 2005 edition provides the following definitions of apology: "1. The pleading off from a charge or imputation, whether expressed, implied, or only conceived as possible; defence of a person, or vindication of an institution, etc., from accusation or aspersion; 2. Less formally: Justification, explanation, or excuse, of an incident or course of action; 3. An explanation offered to a person affected by one's action that no offence was intended, coupled with the expression of regret for any that may have been given; or, a frank acknowledgement of the offence with expression of regret for it, by way of reparation; 4. Something which, as it were, merely appears to apologize for the absence of what ought to have been there; a poor substitute."

47. See Mitch Simon, Nick Smith, Nicole Negowetti, "Apologies and Fitness to Practice Law: A Practical Framework for Evaluating Remorse in the Bar Admission Process," *ABA Journal of the Professional Lawyer* 37 (2012): 37–78.
48. Proeve and Tudor treat remorse as an emotion rather than, for example, a cognitive state or a series of behaviors. See Michael Proeve and Steven Tudor, *Remorse: Psychological and Jurisprudential Perspectives* (Burlington: Ashgate, 2010), 29–30: "In this book we are primarily concerned with a particular emotion: remorse."

Chapter One: The Categorical Apology Revisited

1. Note that *I Was Wrong* combined reform and redress into one element but I now separate them.
2. Iris Murdoch, "The Sublime and the Good," in *Existentialists and Mystics: Writings on Philosophy and Literature*, ed. Peter Conradi (New York: Penguin, 1997), 206. Glen Pettigrove applies the terms to examples of forgiveness in "The Forgiveness We Speak," *Southern Journal of Philosophy* 42–3 (2004): 373.
3. The classification systems for reconciliation developed by social scientists such as Jens Meierhenrich are also valuable in this regard. See Jens Meierhenrich, "Varieties of Reconciliation," *Law and Social Inquiry* 31–1 (2008): 195–231.
4. See *I Was Wrong*, 114–26.
5. See Zohar Kampf, "Journalists as Actors in Social Dramas of Apology," *Journalism: Theory, Practice, and Criticism* 12 (2011): 71–87. See also Kampf's "Public (non) Apologies: The Discourse of Minimizing Responsibility," *Journal of Pragmatics* 41–11 (2009): 2257–70.
6. Max Scheler, *On the Eternal in Man* (New Brunswick: Transaction Publishers, 2010), 54.
7. For examples of sociolinguistic discussions of apologies, see William Benoit, *Accounts, Excuses, and Apologies: A Theory of Image Restoration Strategies* (Albany: SUNY Press, 1995); Deborah Tannen, *You Just Don't Understand: Women and Men in Conversation* (New York: Ballantine Books, 1990); S. Blum-Kulka, J. House, and G. Kasper, eds., *Cross-cultural Pragmatics: Requests and Apologies* (Norwood, NJ: Ablex, 1989); Owen, *Apologies and Remedial Interchanges*; Albert Mehrabian, "Substitute for Apology: Manipulation of Cognitions to Reduce Negative Attitude Toward Self," *Psychological Reports* 20 (1976): 687–92; G. Kasper and S. Blum-Kulka, eds., *Interlanguage Pragmatics* (New York: Oxford University Press, 1993); Malgorzata Susczynska, "Apologizing in English, Polish and Hungarian: Different Languages, Different Strategies," *Journal of Pragmatics* 31 (1999): 1053–65; R. R. Mehrotra, "How to be Polite in Indian English," *International Journal of the Sociology of Language* 116 (1995): 99–110; M. Lipson, "Apologizing in Italian and English," *International Review of Applied Linguistics in Language Teaching* 32–1 (1994): 19–39; Janet Holmes, "Apologies in New Zealand English," *Language in Society* 19 (1990): 155–99; Janet Holmes, "Sex Differences and Apologies: One Aspect of Communication Competence," *Applied Linguistics* 10–2 (1989): 194–213; Anna Trosborg, "Apology Strategies in Natives/Non-natives," *Journal of Pragmatics* 11 (1987): 147–67; A. Cohen and E. Olshtain, "Comparing Apologies Across Languages," in *Scientific and Humanistic Dimensions of Language*, ed. Kurt

Jankowsky (Amsterdam: John Benjamins, 1985): 175–83; S. Blum-Kulka and E. Olshtain, "Requests and Apologies: A Cross-Cultural Study of Speech Act Realization Patterns (CCSARP)," *Applied Linguistics* 5 (1984): 196–213; Olshtain and Cohen, "Apology: A Speech Act Set"; Coulmas, "'Poison to the Soul'"; A. Cohen and E. Olshtain, "Developing a Measure of Socio-Cultural Competence: The Case of Apology," *Language Learning* 31 (1981): 113–34; and A. Borkin and S. Reinhart, "'Excuse Me' and 'I'm Sorry,'" *TESOL Quarterly* 12 (1978): 57–70.

For examples of general (distinguished from specific treatments of apologies in law) discussions of apologies in psychology, see Aaron Lazare, *On Apology* (New York: Oxford University Press, 2004); C. Ward Struthers et al., "The Effects of Attributions of Intent and Apology on Forgiveness: When Sorry May Not Help the Story," *Journal of Experimental Social Psychology* 44-4 (2008): 983–92; J. Eaton et al., "When Apologies Fail: The Moderating Effect of Implicit and Explicit Self-Esteem on Apology and Forgiveness," *Self and Identity* 6-2 (2007): 209–22; J. L. Risen and T. Gilovich, "Target and Observer Differences in the Acceptance of Questionable Apologies," *Journal of Personality and Social Psychology* 92-3 (2007): 418–33; Cynthia McPherson Frantz and Courtney Bennigson, "Better Late than Early: The Influence of Timing on Apology Effectiveness," *Journal of Experimental Social Psychology* 41 (2005): 201–7; D. P. Scarlicki, Robert Folger, and Julie Gee, "When Social Accounts Backfire: The Exacerbating Effects of a Polite Message or an Apology on Reactions to an Unfair Outcome," *Journal of Applied Social Psychology* 34 (2004): 322–41; Holley S. Hodgins and Elizabeth Liebeskind, "Apology Versus Defense: Antecedents and Consequences," *Journal of Experimental Social Psychology* 39 (2003): 297–316; Dale T. Miller, "Disrespect and the Experience of Injustice," *Annual Review of Psychology* 52 (2001): 527–53; Seiji Takaku, "The Effects of Apology and Perspective Taking on Interpersonal Forgiveness: A Dissonance-Attribution Model of Interpersonal Forgiveness," *Journal of Social Psychology* 141 (2001): 494–508; Gregg J. Gold and Bernard Weiner, "Remorse, Confession, Group Identity, and Expectancies About Repeating a Transgression," *Basic and Applied Social Psychology* 22 (2000): 291–300; Steven J. Scher and John M. Darley, "How Effective Are the Things People Say to Apologize? Effects of the Realization of the Apology Speech Act," *Journal of Psycholinguistic Research* 26 (1997): 127–40; H. S. Hodgins, E. Liebeskind, and W. Schwartz, "Getting Out of Hot Water: Facework in Social Predicaments," *Journal of Personality and Social Psychology* 71-2 (1996): 300–14; Mark Bennett and Christopher Dewberry, "I've Said I'm Sorry, Haven't I? A Study of the Identity Implications and Constraints that Apologies Create for Their Recipients," *Current Psychology* 13 (1994): 10–21; Mark Bennett and Deborah Earwaker, "Victims' Responses to Apologies: The Effects of Offender Responsibility and Offense Severity," *Journal of Social Psychology* 134 (1994): 457–64; Gonzales, Haugen, and Manning, "Victims as 'Narrative Critics': Factors Influencing Rejoinders and Evaluative Responses to Offenders' Accounts"; Ken-ichi Ohbuchi and Kobun Sato, "Children's Reactions to Mitigating Accounts," *Journal of Social Psychology* 134 (1994): 5–17; M. H. Gonzales, D. J. Manning, and J. A. Haugen, "Explaining our Sins: Factors Influencing Offender Accounts and Anticipated Victim Responses," *Journal of Personality and Social Psychology* 62-6 (1992): 958–71;

Barry R. Schlenker and Michael F. Weigold, "Interpersonal Processes Involving Impression Regulation and Management," *Annual Review of Psychology* 43 (1992): 133–68; Bernard Weiner et al., "Public Confession and Forgiveness," *Journal of Personality* 50 (1991): 281–312; Bruce W. Darby and Barry R. Schlenker, "Children's Reactions to Transgressions: Effects of the Actor's Apology, Reputation, and Remorse," *British Journal of Social Psychology* 28 (1989): 353–64; Ken-ichi Ohbuchi et al., "Apology as Aggression Control: Its Role in Mediating Appraisal of and Response to Harm," *Journal of Personality and Social Psychology* 56 (1989): 219–27; T. Holtgraves, "The Function and Form of Remedial Moves: Reported Use, Psychological Reality, and Perceived Effectiveness," *Journal of Language and Social Psychology* 8-1 (1989): 1–16; Robert A. Baron, "Attributions and Organizational Conflict: The Mediating Role of Apparent Sincerity," *Organizational Behavior and Human Decision Processes* 41 (1988): 111–27; Schwartz et al., "The Effects of Post-Transgression Remorse on Perceived Aggression, Attribution of Intent, and Level of Punishment"; Jennifer F. Orleans and Michael B. Gurtman, "Effects of Physical Attractiveness and Remorse on Evaluations of Transgressors," *Academic Psychology Bulletin* 6 (1984): 49–56; Bruce W. Darby and Barry R. Schlenker, "Children's Reactions to Apologies," *Journal of Personality and Social Psychology* 43 (1982): 742–53; Barry Schlenker and Bruce W. Darby, "The Use of Apologies in Social Predicaments," *Social Psychology Quarterly* 44 (1981): 271–78; J. T. Tedeschi and C. A. Riordan, "Impression Management and Prosocial Behavior Following Transgression," in *Impression Management Theory and Social Psychological Research*, ed. J. T. Tedeschi (New York: Academic Press, 1981), 223–44; and Austin, Walster, and Utne, "Equity and the Law."

For examples of general discussions of apologies in sociology Nicholas Tavuchis' *Mea Culpa: A Sociology of Apology and Reconciliation* (Palo Alto: Stanford University Press, 1991) remains the most frequently cited work by a sociologist on apologies. See also Charles Tilly, *Credit and Blame* (Princeton: Princeton University Press, 2008); Erving Goffman, *Relations in Public* (New York: Basic Books, 1971); Marvin B. Scott and Stanford M. Lyman, "Accounts," *American Sociological Review* 33 (1968): 46–62; and Erving Goffman, "On Cooling the Mark Out," *Psychiatry* 15 (1952): 451–53.

For examples of general discussions of apologies in social sciences other than linguistics, psychology, or sociology, see Melissa Nobles, *The Politics of Official Apologies* (New York: Cambridge University Press, 2008); Martha Minow, *Between Vengeance and Forgiveness: Facing History after Genocide and Mass Violence* (Boston: Beacon, 1998); Jens Meierhenrich, "Varieties of Reconciliation," *Law and Social Inquiry* 31-1 (2008): 195–231; Edward C. Tomlinson, Brian Dineen, and Roy Lewicki, "The Road to Reconciliation: Antecedents of Victim Willingness to Reconcile Following a Broken Promise," *Journal of Management* 30 (2004): 165–87; Sim B. Sitkin and Robert J. Bies, "Social Accounts in Conflict Situations: Using Explanations to Manage Conflict," *Human Relations* 46 (1993): 349–70; D. C. Barnlund and M. Yoshioka, "Apologies: Japanese and American Styles," *International Journal of Intercultural Relations* 14 (1990): 193–206; and Jerald Greenberg, "Looking Fair vs. Being Far: Managing Impressions of Organizational Justice," *Research in Organizational Behavior* 12 (1990): 111–58.

8. I discuss the relation between apologies and gender in *I Was Wrong*, 108–13. For further examples of discussions of apologies and gender, see Tannen, *You Just Don't Understand*, 233; Tannen, *The Argument Culture*, 47; Janet Holmes, *Women, Men, and Politeness* (New York: Longman, 1995), 182; Tannen, *Talking from 9 to 5: Women and Men at Work* (New York: Harper Collins, 1994), 46; Sara Mills, *Gender and Politeness* (Cambridge: Cambridge University Press, 2003), 231; Jeffrey Z. Rubin and Bert R. Brown, *The Social Psychology of Bargaining and Negotiation* (New York: Academic Press, 1975), 173–74; Levi, "The Role of Apology in Mediation," 1186; Orenstein, "Gender and Race in the Evidence Policy"; Erin O'Hara and Douglas Yarn, "On Apology and Consilience," *Washington Law Review* 77 (2002): 1121–92; Miriam Meyerhoff, "Sorry in the Pacific: Defining Communities, Defining Practices," *Language in Society* 28 (1999): 225–38; M. Timmers, A. H. Fischer, and A. S. R. Manstead, "Gender Differences in Motives for Regulating Emotions," *Personality and Social Psychology Bulletin* 24 (1998): 974–85; Janet Holmes, "Sex Differences and Apologies: One Aspect of Communication Competence," *Applied Linguistics* 10-2 (1989): 194–213; Judith Mattson Bean and Barbara Johnstone, "Workplace Reasons for Saying You're Sorry: Discourse Task Management and Apology in Telephone Interviews," *Discourse Processes* 17 (1994): 59–81; J. M. Stoppard and C. D. Gruchy, "Gender, Context, and Expression of Positive Emotion," *Personality and Social Psychology Bulletin* 19 (1993): 143–50; Nessa Wolfson, "Pretty Is as Pretty Does: A Speech Act View of Sex Roles," *Applied Linguistics* 5-3 (1984): 236–44.
9. See, for instance, Etienne and Robbennolt, "Apologies and Plea Bargaining," note 102:

   In assessing the role of apologies in plea bargaining, we must be mindful of the various alternatives. Most cases do not present a binary choice between "an apology" and "no apology." Cases fall into various categories. In some cases, the defendant makes no admission of guilt or expression of remorse whatsoever. In other instances, the defendant may confess or make a partial admission of guilt without expressing remorse. A third possibility is that a defendant may make an apology that expresses both guilt and remorse. It is certainly possible that a prosecutor would respond to each of these alternatives differently.

   See also Robbennolt, "Apologies and Legal Settlement: An Empirical Examination," 419.
10. Robbennolt, "Attorneys, Apologies, and Settlement Negotiation," 352.
11. Robbennolt, "Apologies and Settlement Levers," note 104.
12. See Robbennolt, "Apologies and Plea Bargaining," 302.
13. Diane Rehm devoted her March 18, 2008, broadcast to discussing the issues with me after the Spitzer scandal raised interest in apologies. The program is archived at http://thedianerehmshow.org/shows/2008--03--18#20034.
14. Rachel Sklar, "Ex-NYSE Director Langone on Spitzer: 'We All Have Our Own Private Hells. I Hope His Private Hell Is Hotter than Anybody Else's,'" *Huffington Post*, March 28, 2008.
15. Danny Hakim and William Rashbaum, "No Federal Prostitution Charges for Spitzer," *New York Times*, November 6, 2008.
16. Ibid.

17. For a thoughtful discussion of Clinton's remorse, see Laura Miller's "Forgive Me, America, for I Have Sinned," *Salon*, October 15, 2008. Miller reviews Susan Wise Bauer's *The Art of the Public Grovel: Sexual Sin and Public Confession in America* (Princeton: Princeton University Press, 2008).
18. See *I Was Wrong*, 62.
19. Hakim and Rashbaum, "No Federal Prostitution Charges for Spitzer."
20. See Miller, "Forgive Me, America, for I Have Sinned" and Wise Bauer, *The Art of the Public Grovel*.
21. Kenneth Woodward, "The Road to Repentance," *Newsweek*, September 28, 1998, 18.
22. Dany Hakim, "Gilded Path to Political Stardom, with Detours," *New York Times*, October 12, 2006. Wise Bauer makes these points powerfully with regard to Clinton's religion. See Wise Bauer, *The Art of the Public Grovel*.
23. See Wise Bauer, *The Art of the Public Grovel*, 217: "Scandal-marked politicians cannot preserve a dignified silence; they must prove, through humble confession, that they are willing to acknowledge the power of the voters at whose pleasure they serve."
24. Ibid., 3: "Behind the demand that leaders publicly confess their sins is our fear that we will be overwhelmed by their power."
25. Danny Hakim, "Spitzer Spends Time with Lawyers and Family," *New York Times*, April 14, 2008.
26. Danny Hakim, "Six Months Later, Spitzer is Contrite, Yes, but Sometimes Still Angry," *New York Times*, September 28, 2008.
27. This section paraphrases *I Was Wrong*, 155–252.
28. Charles Tilly, *Credit and Blame* (Princeton: Princeton University Press, 2008), 127.
29. See *I Was Wrong*, 148.
30. Jana Thompson describes political apologies as "forward- rather than backward-looking" in "The Apology Paradox," 473–74. Peter Digeser argues for a forward-looking account of political forgiveness in *Political Forgiveness* (Ithaca: Cornell University Press, 2001).

Part One: The Penitent and the Penitentiary: Apologies in Criminal Law

1. Friedrich Nietzsche, *The Genealogy of Morals*, in *The Portable Nietzsche*, trans. Walter Kaufmann (New York: Penguin, 1977), 516.
2. Roy Walmsley, "World Prison Population List," *International Center for Prison Studies* (9th ed., 2011). Rwanada is a distant second with 595 per 100,000.
3. Ibid.
4. As of June 2013, the Federal Bureau of Prisons has 47.0% of inmates incarcerated for drug offenses. Federal Bureau of Prisons, "Quick Facts about the Bureau of Prisons," June 29, 2013, available at http://www.bop.gov/news/quick.jsp.
5. Marc Mauer and Ryan King, *A 25 Year Quagmire: The "War on Drugs" and its Impact on American Society* (Washington, DC: Sentencing Project, 2007), 2.
6. Michelle Alexander, *The New Jim Crow* (New York: The New Press, 2010), 6.
7. For an excellent general overview, see Antony Duff's *Stanford Encyclopedia of Philosophy*'s entry on "Legal Punishment" available at http://plato.stanford.edu/entries/legal-punishment/.

8. See Guyora Binder and Nick Smith, "Framed: Utilitarianism and Punishment of the Innocent," *Rutgers Law Journal* 32 (2000): 115–224.
9. See Francis Allen, *The Decline of the Rehabilitative Ideal* (New Haven: Yale University Press, 1981), and Jeffrie Murphy, *Punishment and Rehabilitation* (New York: Wadsworth Publishing Company, 1994).
10. For the history of punishment in the United States, see Norval Morris and David Rothman, *The Oxford History of Punishment: The Practice of Punishment in Western Society* (Oxford: Oxford University Press, 1997), and David Rothman, *The Discovery of the Asylum: Social Order and Disorder in the New Republic* (Boston: Little Brown, 1971).
11. As Duff puts it: "'Positive' retributivism holds not merely that we must not punish the innocent, or punish the guilty more than they deserve, but that we should punish the guilty, to the extent that they deserve: penal desert constitutes not just a necessary, but an in principle sufficient reason for punishment (only in principle, however, since there are very good reasons – to do with the costs, both material and moral, of punishment – why we should not even try to punish all the guilty). A striking feature of penal theorising during the last three decades of the twentieth century was a revival of positive retributivism – of the idea that the positive justification of punishment is to be found in its intrinsic character as a deserved response to crime."
    Duff, "Legal Punishment."
12. Although commentators often repeat the "framing the innocent" criticism, Guyora Binder and I argue that it does not appear to raise serious problems. Utilitarianism originated as a legal theory that demanded several institutional conditions for the public pursuit of utility, including security of person and property, legality, legislative supremacy, democratic accountability, publicity, and transparency. These utilitarian political procedures would preclude framing an innocent person. See Binder and Smith, "Framed."
13. Karl Marx, "The German Ideology," in *Karl Marx: Selected Writings*, 201.
14. Currie, Crime and Punishment in America, 65–66.
15. George Fletcher, "Material Poverty – Moral Poverty," in *From Social Justice to Criminal Justice: Poverty and the Administration of Criminal Law*, eds. William Heffernan and John Kleinig (New York: Oxford University Press, 2000), 240.
16. Ibid.
17. Ibid.
18. Angela Davis, *Are Prisons Obsolete?* (New York: Seven Stories Press, 2003).
19. Duff makes a similar point in *Punishment, Communication, and Community* (New York: Oxford, 2001), 32.
20. Jeffrey Reiman and Paul Leighton, *The Rich Get Rich and the Poor Get Prison: Ideology, Class, and Criminal Justice*, 9th ed. (Boston: Pearson, 2010), 4.
21. John Tasioulas, "Punishment and Repentance," *Philosophy* 2 (2006): 279.
22. Ibid., 283.
23. In this regard Tasioulas writes: "On this "two-pronged" justification for punishment, the moral reason to desist from crime grounded in the blameworthiness of the conduct, which is expressed by the reprobative function of the sanction, is backed up by a prudential reason created by the threat of hard treatment. In virtue of our susceptibility to the force of moral reasons, we are fit objects of

censure, but given the temptations we can experience to rebel against those reasons, we are given a prudential reason to stiffen our resolve to be law-abiding." Ibid., 290.
24. H. L. A. Hart, "Prolegomenon to the Principles of Punishment," *Proceedings of the Aristotelian Society* 60 (1959–60): 1.
25. Ibid., 3.
26. Ibid., 4.

Chapter Two: Against Court-Ordered Apologies

1. "Off Roader Calls Ordered You Tube Apology 'Baloney,'" *Columbian*, July 28, 2010.
2. See the discussion at *Adventure Rider*, http://www.advrider.com/forums/showthread.php?t=605039.
3. Radzik, *Making Amends*, 18.
4. See Michel Foucault, *The History of Sexuality: An Introduction*, Volume I, trans. Robert Hurley (New York: Vintage Books, 1978), 58.
5. Michel Foucault, *Discipline and Punish: The Birth of the Prison*, trans. Alan Sheridan (New York: Vintage Books, 1995), 38.
6. Ibid.
7. Ibid., 42.
8. Ibid., 38–39.
9. Ibid., 46–47.
10. Foucault, *The History of Sexuality*, Volume I, 59.
11. As Foucault puts it:

> The obligation to confess is now relayed through so many different points, is so deeply engrained in us, that we no longer perceive it as the effect of a power that constrains us; on the contrary, it seems to us that truth, lodged in our most secret nature, "demands" only to surface; that if it fails to do so, this is because a constraint holds it in place, the violence of power weighs it down, and it can finally be articulated only at the price of a kind of liberation. Confession frees, but power reduces one to silence; truth does not belong to the order of power, but shares an original affinity with freedom: traditional themes in philosophy, which a "political history of truth" would have to overturn by showing that truth is not by nature free – nor error servile – but that its production is thoroughly imbued with relations of power. The confession is an example of this.

Ibid., 60.

12. According to Foucault:

> [C]onfession is a ritual of discourse in which the speaking subject is also the subject of the statement; it is also a ritual that unfolds within a power relationship, for one does not confess without the presence (or virtual presence) of a partner who is not simply the interlocutor but the authority who requires the confession, prescribes and appreciates it, and intervenes in order to judge, punish, forgive, console, and reconcile; a ritual in which truth is corroborated by the obstacles and resistances it has had to surmount in order to be formulated; and finally, a ritual in which the expression alone, independently of its external consequences, produces intrinsic modifications in the person who articulates it: it exonerates, redeems, and purifies him; it unburdens him of his wrongs, liberates him, and

promises him salvation. For centuries, the truth of sex was, at least for the most part, caught up in this discursive form.

Ibid., 61–62.
13. See Martin Wright, *Justice for Victims and Offenders: A Restorative Response to Crime* (Philadelphia: Open Press, 1991), 17–18.
14. Lawrence Friedman, *Crime and Punishment in American History* (New York: Basic Books, 1993), 25–26. See also Bibas, "Forgiveness in Criminal Procedure."
15. Friedman, *Crime and Punishment in American History*, 26. See also Foucault, *Discipline and Punish*, 49–50.
16. See Harvey Fireside, *Soviet Psychoprisons* (New York: Norton, 1982).
17. See Robert Jay Lifton, *Thought Reform and the Psychology of Totalism: A Study of "Brainwashing" in China* (Chapel Hill: University of North Carolina Press, 1989).
18. David Rothman, *The Discovery of the Asylum: Social Order and Disorder in the New Republic* (Boston: Little Brown, 1971), 107.
19. For an overview of these historical trends, see Peter Scharff Smith, "The Effects of Solitary Confinement on Prison Inmates," *Crime and Justice* 34 (2006): 441–528.
20. Ibid., 45.
21. Murphy, "Repentance, Punishment, and Mercy," 146.
22. Radzik, *Making Amends*, 17.
23. See Ibid., discussing Magdalen asylums in detail.
24. Elliott Curie, *Crime and Punishment in America* (New York: Henry Holt, 1998), 21.
25. See Bennett, *The Apology Ritual*, 13: "[P]enal justice can be described as a set of institutions in search of a narrative or a 'practice without a policy'.... It seems that for many victims and officials who run the institutions, it is not clear what they system is actually meant to be doing, what the overall purpose of criminal justice is – or whether the officially given purposes are compelling ones."
26. Thanks to William Heffernan for helping me formulate these thoughts.
27. Although she subscribes to a "broadly Kantian approach to moral theory," Radzik distances herself from retributivism. Radzik, *Making Amends*, 21. Bennett describes his view as a punitive theory of restorative justice: "[U]nlike many proponents of restorative justice, I believe that the right theory of the importance of apology will lead us to understand properly the importance of *punitive* responses to wrongdoing. On my view, understanding apology will give us an answer to the question of why hard treatment is a necessary part of a response to wrongdoing. Thus I will depart from those who think of restorative justice as being a non-punitive response to crime."

Bennett, *The Apology Ritual*, 7.
28. Duff, *Trials and Punishments*, 6.
29. Kant, *The Metaphysical Elements of Justice*, 139. The preceding passages – and perhaps the most quoted in all of punishment theory – state:

Judicial punishment ... is entirely distinct from natural punishment. In natural punishment, vice punishes itself, and this fact is not taken into consideration by the legislator. Judicial punishment can never be used merely as a means to promote some other good for the criminal himself or for civil society, but instead it must in all cases be imposed on him only on the ground that he has committed a crime; for a human being can never be manipulated merely as a means to the purpose of someone else and can never be confused with the objects of the Law of things.... His innate personality [that is, his right as a person] protects him against such treatment, even though he may indeed be condemned to lose his civil personality. He must first be found to be deserving of punishment before any consideration is given to the utility of his punishment for himself or for his fellow citizens. The law concerning punishment is a categorical imperative, and woe to him who rummages around in the winding paths of a theory of happiness [utilitarianism] looking for some advantage to be gained by releasing the criminal from punishment of by reducing the amount of it – in keeping with the Pharisaic motto: "It is better that one man should die than that the whole people should perish." If legal justice perishes, then it is no longer worthwhile for men to remain alive on this earth. If this is so, what should one think of the proposal to permit a certain criminal who has been condemned to death to remain alive, if, after consenting to allow dangerous experiments to be made on him, he happily survives such experiments and if doctors thereby obtain new information that benefits the community. Any court of justice would repudiate such a proposal with scorn if it were suggested by a medical college, for [legal] justice ceases to be justice if it can be bought for a price.

What kind and what degree of punishment does legal justice adopt as its principle and standard? None other than the principle of equality (illustrated by the pointer on the scales of justice), that is, the principle of not treating one side more favorably than the other. Accordingly, any undeserved evil that you inflict on someone else among the people is one that you do to yourself. If you vilify him, you vilify yourself; if you steal from him, you steal from yourself: if you kill him, you kill yourself. Only the Law of retribution (jus talionis) can determine exactly the kind and degree of punishment; it must be well understood, however, that this determination [must be made] in the chambers of a court of justice (and not in your private judgment). All other standards fluctuate back and forth and, because extraneous considerations are mixed with them, they cannot be compatible with the principles of pure and strict legal justice.

30. Some might be surprised to learn that Kant argued for apologies to the dead. He provides this example in *Metaphysical Elements of Justice*:

If someone spreads a rumor about a dead person's crime that when alive would have made him dishonorable or at least despicable, anyone who can provide evidence that this accusation is intentionally false and a lie can then openly declare that he who cast aspersions on the dead man's character is a calumniator, which [in turn] makes [that person] himself dishonorable. He [the defender of the dead man] would be unable to do all of this if he did not rightfully assume that the dead man was insulted thereby, even though he was dead, and then he [the dead man] was owed an apology from him [the rumor monger], even if he no longer exists.

If one takes a deontological view of apologies, the death of your victim does not discharge you from your duty to apologize. Ibid., 101.
31. See *Minneapolis v. Richardson*, 239 N.W.2d 197, 206 (Minn. 1976).
32. I discuss the relationship between apologies and emotion in *I Was Wrong*, 96–107. For additional examples of philosophical discussions of emotions relevant

to apologies, see John Rawls, *A Theory of Justice* (Cambridge, MA: Harvard University Press, 1971). See also R. J. Wallace, *Responsibility and the Moral Sentiments* (Cambridge, MA: Harvard University Press, 1998); J. P. Tangney and K. Fischer eds., *Self-Conscious Emotions: The Psychology of Shame, Guilt, Embarrassment, and Pride* (New York: Guilford Press, 1995); Bernard Williams, *Shame and Necessity* (Berkeley: University of California Press, 1994); G. Taylor, *Pride, Shame, and Guilt: Emotions of Self-Assessment* (Oxford: Oxford University Press, 1985); Herbert Morris, ed., *Guilt and Shame* (Belmont: Wadsworth Press, 1971); Calhoun, Cheshire, "An Apology for Moral Shame," *Journal of Political Philosophy* 12-2 (2004): 127–46; and J. Deigh, "Shame and Self-Esteem: A Critique," *Ethics* 93 (1983): 225–45.
33. See Radzik, *Making Amends*, 30.
34. Ibid., 101.
35. Ibid., 36.
36. Ibid., 35.
37. Ibid., 36.
38. See Herbert Morris, "Persons and Punishment," *The Monist* 52 (1968): 475–501.
39. Bennett, *Apology Ritual*, 196–97.
40. Ibid., 9.
41. Ibid., 112.
42. Ibid., 149.
43. Ibid., 196.
44. Ibid., 154–55.
45. Christopher Bennett, "Taking the Sincerity Out of Saying Sorry: Restorative Justice as Ritual," *Journal of Applied Philosophy* 23-2 (2006): 130 (citing von Hirsch, *Censure and Sanctions*, 82–83).
46. Bennett, *Apology Ritual*, 173.
47. Ibid., 148.
48. Ibid., 154
49. Ibid., 7.
50. Ibid., 112.
51. Etzioni uses a similar example in *Repentance*, 152.
52. Duff, *Punishment, Communication, and Community*, 110.
53. Ibid., 111–12.
54. Ibid., 109.
55. Duff, *Trials and Punishments*, 260.
56. Duff, *Punishment, Communication, and Community*, 107.
57. Ibid.
58. Ibid., 116–17. See also: "This is not to deny that her punishment is coercive. It is inflicted on her or she is required to undergo it, whether or not she is willing to be punished: she is confronted by a probation officer who insists on talking to her about her crime or by a victim who insists on talking to her about her crime or by a victim who insists on telling her just what she did. It addresses her forcefully, seeking to get her attention, to make her attend to what she has done. We can even hope that she will be 'compelled'; to face up to what she has done and to recognize it as a wrong. But this is a matter of moral or rational compulsion, as when a person cannot avoid recognizing a truth that stares her in

the face or forces itself on her attention. It still addresses her as an autonomous agent who must in the end accept or reject the message communicated by her punishment for herself, in the light of her own conscience; and it still leaves her free to reject it."
Ibid., 116.
59. Duff, *Trials and Punishments*, 251.
60. Duff, "Punishment, Communication, and Community," in *Debates in Contemporary Political Philosophy: An Anthology*, eds. Derek Matravers and Jonathan Pike (New York: Routledge, 2003), 397. See also Duff, *Punishment, Communication, and Community*, 116: "[W]hat matters is not just that, but how, she is brought to repent her crime. If she is simply bullied or coerced into submission, she might come to a kind of repentance, but her punishment has not succeeded as a mode of moral communication."
61. Duff, *Punishment, Communication, and Community*, 121–2.
62. Ibid., 123–24 (emphasis added).
63. For an excellent bibliography and overview of philosophical conceptions of coercion, see Scott Anderson's "Coercion" entry for the online *Stanford Encyclopedia of Philosophy*, available at http://plato.stanford.edu/entries/coercion/.
64. See *Riggins v. Nevada*, 504 U.S. 127, 144 (1992) (concurring opinion).
65. Michael Moore, "Causation and the Criminal Law," in *The Oxford Handbook of Criminal Law*, eds. John Deigh and David Dolinko (New York: Oxford University Press, 2011), 169.
66. On coercive offers, see Anderson, "Coercion."
67. Andrew von Hirsch, *Proportionate Sentencing: Exploring the Principles* (New York: Oxford University Press, 2005), 122.
68. Duff, *Punishment, Communication, and Community*, 108: "To recognize and repent the wrong I have done is also to recognize the need to avoid doing such wrong in the future. Truly to disown that wrong is also to commit myself to avoid trying to repeat it. A process of censure or punishment aimed at inducing repentance thus also aims to induce reform: not to re-form the wrongdoer as an object that we must mold to our wishes, but to persuade her of the need to reform herself."
69. Ibid., 119: "[R]epentance is not something that can be achieved and completed in a moment. At least with serious wrong, it requires time and effort."
70. Nietzsche, *Genealogy of Morals*, 502.
71. Ibid.
72. Ibid., 499. For a succinct overview of Nietzsche's layered theory of punishment, see Mark Tunick, *Punishment Theory and Practice* (Berkeley: University of California Press, 1992), 20–28.
73. Ibid., 115.
74. Ibid., 124.
75. For Bennett, "the fundamental job of the criminal sanction is not to induce repentance or to achieve moral reconciliation between offender and community: its job is simply to express proportionate condemnation, and that is done perfectly well regardless of how the offender receives that condemnation." Bennett, *The Apology Ritual*, 148.
76. Ibid., 196.

77. G. W. F. Hegel, *The Philosophy of Right*, trans. T. Knox (Oxford: Oxford University Press, 1942), 246.
78. For an excellent analysis of ethical issues related to plea bargaining, see Richard Lippke, *The Ethics of Plea Bargaining* (New York: Oxford, 2011).
79. Seccuro, *Crash Into Me*, 205.
80. Ibid., 197.
81. Ibid., 236.
82. White, "Say You're Sorry: Court-Ordered Apologies as a Civil Rights Remedy," 1281.
83. See Latif, "Apologetic Justice," 314: "A judge's coercion of an apology can give rise to a full apology in the same way a parent's command to a child to apologize often produces an effective, and even genuine, apology."
84. Emily Bazelon, "Say You're Sorry. Is Forcing Your Kids to Apologize a Bad Idea?" *Slate*, January 8, 2008.
85. See Murray Straus, *Beating the Devil Out of Them: Corporal Punishment in American Families and its Effects on Children* (San Francisco: Lexington, 1994).
86. John Braithwaite, *Crime, Shame, and Reintegration* (New York: Cambridge University Press, 1989), 67.
87. Ibid., 163
88. Martha Nussbaum, *Upheavals of Thought* (New York: Cambridge University Press, 2001).
89. Alexander, *The New Jim Crow*, 57: "Ninety percent of those admitted to prison for drug offenses in many states were black or Latino, yet the mass incarceration of communities of color was explained in race neutral terms, an adaptation to the needs and demands of the current political climate."

    See also ibid., 97: "People of all races use and sell drugs at remarkably similar rates. If there are significant differences in the surveys to be found, they suggest that whites, particularly white youth, are more likely to engage in illegal drug dealing than people of color. One study, for example, published in 2000 by the National Institute on Drug Abuse reported that white students use cocaine at seven times the rate of black students, use crack cocaine at eight times the rate of black students, and use heroin at seven time the rate of black students. That same survey revealed that nearly identical percentages of white and black high school seniors use marijuana. The national Household Survey on Drug Abuse reported in 2000 that white youth aged 12–17 are more than a third more likely to have sold illegal drugs than African American youth."
90. Reiman and Leighton argue that giving police broad discretion "would assure us that a good portion of the prison population would experience their confinement as arbitrary and unjust and thus respond with rage, which would make them more antisocial, rather than respond with remorse, which would make them feel more bound by social norms." Reiman and Paul Leighton, *The Rich Get Richer and the Poor Get Prison*, 3.
91. Federal Bureau of Prisons, "Quick Facts about the Bureau of Prisons."
92. See Haya El Nasser, "Paying for Crime With Shame," *USA Today*, June 25, 1996, 1A.
93. Murphy, *Getting Even*, 149.
94. See Latif, "Apologetic Justice," 313.

95. Ibid.
96. El Nasser, "Paying for Crime With Shame," 1A.
97. "Malaysian to Tweet Apology 100 Times in Defamation Case," *Guardian UK*, June 2, 2011.
98. David Sussman, "What's Wrong with Torture?" *Philosophy and Public Affairs* 33–1 (2005): 1–33.
99. For a variety of such examples, see Garvey, "Can Shaming Punishments Educate?"
100. Contrast my view with Lazare, *On Apology*, 118.
101. See White, "Say You're Sorry," 1296: "[P]laintiffs like to hear defendants say they're sorry, and sometimes feel satisfaction in seeing a defendant make an apology that she did not want to make."
102. White, "Say You're Sorry," 1297.
103. Ibid., 1302.
104. Latif, "Apologetic Justice," 311.
105. *Fischer v. Byrnes*, Queensland Anti-Discrimination Tribunal 33 (Aug. 8, 2006).
106. White, "Say You're Sorry," 1296.
107. *De Simone and Ors v. Bevacqua*, (1993) P92–516 (1996). Cited in Carol Peterson, "The Failure of the Hong Kong Court of Appeal to Recognise and Remedy Disability Discrimination," *Hong Kong Law Journal* 30 (2000): note 17.
108. *Skellern v. Colonial Gardens Resort Townsville & Anor*, (1996) EOC P92–792. See also *Krepp v. Valcic*, (1993) EOC P92–520; and *Woomera Aboriginal Corporation v. Edwards & Ano*, (1994) EOC P92–653.
109. *Bull & Anor v. Kuch & Anor* (1993) EOC P92–518.
110. *R v. D & E Marinkovic* (1996) EOC P92–841.
111. *Imperial Diner v. State Human Rights Appeals Bd.*, 417 N.E.2d 525, 529 (1980).
112. *Ma Bik Yung v. Ko Chuen*, CACV 267/99, 9 (2000).
113. See *I Was Wrong*, Part Two: Collective Apologies.
114. *Wooley v. Maynard*, 430 U.S. 705, 714 (1977): "The right of freedom of thought ... against state action includes both the right to speak freely and the right to refrain from speaking at all."
115. See, for example, *Griffith v. Smith*, 30 Va. Cir. 250 (1993); *Imperial Diner, Inc. v. State Human Rights Appeal Bd.*, 417 N.E.2d 525 (NY 1980); Andrew Horwitz, "Coercion, Pop-Psychology, and Judicial Moralizing: Some Proposals for Curbing Judicial Abuse of Probation Conditions," *Washington and Lee Law Review* 57 (2000), 114.
116. See generally White, "Say You're Sorry," 1298–300.
117. See ibid., 1300: "The First Amendment simply does not bar a court or legislative body from directing public officials to make certain public statements in carrying out their official duties."
118. Stanley Fish, *There's No Such Thing as Free Speech* (New York: Oxford, 1994), 104.
119. Ibid., 111.
120. David van Mill, "Freedom of Speech," *Stanford Encyclopedia of Philosophy*, available at http://plato.stanford.edu/entries/freedom-speech/.
121. Choi, "Freedom of Conscience and the Court-Ordered Apology for Defamatory Remarks," 309.

122. Ibid., 309–10.
123. Bennett, *Apology Ritual*, 154.
124. *Kicklighter v. Evans County School District*, 968 F. Supp. 712, 719 (S.D. Ga. 1997).
125. See *I Was Wrong*, 17–27.
126. White, "Say You're Sorry," note 224.
127. Hence I disagree with White's claim that "requiring unrepentant officials to endure a small amount of psychological discomfort is a small price to pay to help injured individuals get the apology that they need to begin to put their lives back together." White, "Say You're Sorry," 1297.
128. *R. v. Northwest Territories Power Corporation* (1990), 5 C.E.L.R. (N.S.) 67, 75–77.
129. See, for example, cases collected in Robyn Carroll, "You Can't Order Sorriness, So Is There Any Value in an Ordered Apology?: An Analysis of Ordered Apologies in Anti-discrimination Cases," *University of New South Wales Law Journal* 33-2 (2010): 360–85.
130. Promotion of Equality and Prevention of Unfair Discrimination Act 2000 (South Africa), section 21(2)(j) (my emphasis).

Chapter Three: Apology Reductions in Criminal Law

1. Sören Kierkegaard, *Purity of Heat Is to Will One Thing*, trans. D. Steere (New York: Harper and Row, 1956), 35.
2. Nietzsche, *The Genealogy of Morals*, 81–82.
3. Richard Lowell Nygaard, "On the Role of Forgiveness in Criminal Sentencing," *Seton Hall Law Review* 27 (1997): 1014.
4. Gelineau, "Rape Victim Gets Justice 23 Years After the Attack."
5. *United States v. Vance*, 62 F.3d 1152, 1158 (9th Cir. 1995).
6. Proeve and Tudor, *Remorse*, 115.
7. See 18 U.S.C.S. app. § 3E1.1 (Law. Co-op. 2000).
8. See, for example, Eisenberg, Garvey, and Wells, "But Was He Sorry?"; Pipes and Alessi, "Remorse and a Previously Punished Offense in Assignment of Punishment and Estimated Likelihood of a Repeated Offense"; and Sundby, "The Intersection of Trial Strategy, Remorse, and the Death Penalty."
9. For an excellent overview of these and related concerns, see Bibas and Bierschbach, "Integrating Remorse and Apology into Criminal Procedure."
10. Simon, Smith, Negowetti, "Apologies and Fitness to Practice Law."
11. See Darby and Schlenker, "Children's Reactions to Apologies."
12. Jean Hampton, "The Moral Education Theory of Punishment," *Philosophy and Public Affairs*, 13-3 (1984): 234.
13. Murphy states: "It would be quite irresponsible, for example, to put – unsupervised – a convicted child molester in an environment of small children in order to make sure that he has his pedophilia under full control." *Remorse, Apology, and Mercy*, 163, note 42.
14. Murphy uses the O'Connor example in ibid., note 43.
15. See Jean Hampton, "The Moral Education Theory of Punishment," 234, in which she offers the analogy that "like a bad but repentant child who will conclude, if he is not punished by his parents, that his action must not have

been so bad, the repentant criminal might well need to experience his complete sentence in order to 'learn his lesson' effectively."
16. See sources collected in G. Sweeten, A. R. Piquero, and L. Steinberg, "Age and the Explanation of Crime, Revisited," *Journal of Youth and Adolescence* 42–6 (2013): 921–38.
17. See the sources collected in Proeve and Tudor, *Remorse*, 209.
18. Daniela Hosser, Michael Windzio, and Werner Greve, "Guilt and Shame and Predictors of Recidivism: A Longitudinal Study with Young Prisoners," *Criminal Justice and Behavior* 35–1 (2008): 138–52.
19. Raffaele Rodogno, "Shame and Guilt in Restorative Justice," *Psychology, Public Policy, and Law* 14 (2008): 155.
20. See, for example, Thomas Scheff, "Shame and Conformity," *American Sociological Review* 53–3 (198): 395–40.
21. See, for example, John Haley, "Apology and Pardon: Learning from Japan," *American Behavioral Scientist* 41–6 (1998): 842–967.
22. For a thoughtful discussion of these issues, see Michael O'Hear, "Appellate Review of Sentences: Reconsidering Deference," *William and Mary Law Review* 51 (2010): 2123–67.
23. Ibid., note 90.
24. See discussion in ibid., 2147–48.
25. See R. A. Duff, "Virtue, Vice, and Criminal Liability: Do We Want an Aristotelian Criminal Law?" *Buffalo Criminal Law Review* 6–1 (2002): 169.
26. Braithwaite, *Restorative Justice and Responsive Regulation* (New York: Oxford University Press, 2002), 16.
27. Radzik, *Making Amends*, 21.
28. Ibid., 143–45.
29. Ibid., 83.
30. Ibid., 79.
31. Ibid., 83.
32. As Margaret Urban-Walker puts it: "It is not then the few words of apology, or even the bowed head or the tears of remorse, that magically mend a torn fabric of relationship but what deep reservoirs of trust and still flowing springs of hope can be tapped." *Moral Repair*, 199.
33. Braithwaite, "Repentance Rituals and Restorative Justice," 120.
34. Braithwaite, *Restorative Justice and Responsive Regulation*, 249.
35. Ibid., 250.
36. See Bibas and Bierschbach, "Integrating Remorse and Apology into Criminal Procedure." 247.
37. Bibas, "Forgiveness in Criminal Procedure," 337.
38. See sources collected in ibid., 335.
39. See sources collected in Bibas and Bierschbach, "Integrating Remorse and Apology into Criminal Procedure," notes 260–65.
40. See, for example, Ken-ichi Ohbuchi, "Apology as Regression Control," *Journal of Personality and Social Psychology* 56–2 (1989): 219–27.
41. See George Kelling and Catherine Coles, *Fixing Broken Windows: Restoring Order and Reducing Crimes in Our Communities* (New York: Touchstone, 1996).
42. See chapter nine of Proeve and Tudor, *Remorse*, for a discussion of remorse in restorative justice conferencing.

43. George Fletcher, *With Justice for Some: Protecting Victims' Rights in Criminal Trials* (Reading, MA: Addison-Wesley, 1996), 248.
44. See, for example, Bennett, *Apology Ritual*, 144, and Radzik, *Making Amends*, 156. See also Duff, "Legal Punishment": "Such an insistence on the need for a public criminal process reflects two aspects of the concept of crime: first, it is sometimes important to recognise that a situation involves not just people in 'conflict', but a victim who has been wronged and an offender who has done the wrong; second, some such wrongs are 'public' wrongs... wrongs that properly concern not just those directly affected, but all members of the political community."
45. Bibas, "Forgiveness in Criminal Procedure," 330.
46. Ibid., 338.
47. Braithwaite, *Restorative Justice and Responsive Regulation*, 12–13.
48. Ibid.
49. Braithwaite, *Crime, Shame, and Reintegration*, 18.
50. Ibid., 163.
51. Ibid., 179.
52. Ibid., 55.
53. Ibid.
54. Ibid., 63 (citing D. H. Bayley, *Forces of Order: Police Behavior in Japan and the United States* [Berkeley: University of California Press, 1976], 156).
55. Braithwaite enumerates the following "facts a theory of crime ought to fit":
    1. Crime is committed disproportionately by males.
    2. Crime is committed disproportionately by 15–25 year olds.
    3. Crime is committed disproportionately by unmarried people.
    4. Crime is committed disproportionately by people living in cities.
    5. Crimes is committed disproportionately by people who have experienced high residential mobility and who live in areas characterized by high residential mobility.
    6. Young people who are strongly attracted to their school are less likely to engage in crime.
    7. Young people who have high educational and occupational aspiration are less likely to engage in crime.
    8. Young people who do poorly at school are more likely to engage in crime.
    9. Young people who are strongly attached to their parents are less likely to engage in crime.
    10. Young people who have friendships with criminals are more likely to engage in crime themselves.
    11. People who believe strongly in the importance of complying with the law are less likely to violate the law.
    12. For both men and women, being at the bottom of the class structure... increases rates of offending for all types of crime apart from those for which opportunities are systematically less available to the poor.

    Crime, Shame, and Reintegration, 44–50.
56. Ibid., 70.
57. Ibid., 55: "[T]he nub of deterrence is not the severity of the sanction but its social embeddedness; shame is more deterring when administered by persons

who continue to be of importance to us; when we become outcasts we can reject our rejectors and the shame no longer matters to us."
58. Ibid., 89.
59. Ibid., 81–83.
60. Braithwaite, *Restorative Justice and Responsive Regulation*, 10.
61. Braithwaite, *Crime, Shame, and Reintegration*, 100.
62. Ibid., 100–1.
63. Ibid.
64. Ibid., 57–58.
65. Ibid., 77.
66. Eliza Ahmed, Nathan Harris, John Braithwaite, and Valerie Braithwaite, *Shame Management through Reintegration* (New York: Cambridge University Press, 2001), 52.
67. Braithwaite, "Repentance Rituals and Restorative Justice," 129.
68. Braithwaite seems well aware of the dangers of insincere apologies. See, for example, Braithwaite, *Restorative Justice and Responsive Regulation*, 152: "Apology, when communicated with a ritual solemnity, is actually the most powerful cultural device for taking a problem seriously, while denial is a cultural device for dismissing it. In turn feminists rightly contend that insincere apology is endemic in attempts to regulate family violence: the apology becomes a tactic, a way station toward the ultimate reassertion of violence and domination."
69. Radzik, *Making Amends*, 166.
70. Ibid., 171.
71. Ibid., 171–72. See Martha Nussbaum, "Adaptive Preferences and Women's Options," *Economics and Philosophy* 17 (2001): 67–88.
72. Bennett also appreciates this difficulty. See Bennett, *Apology Ritual*, 179.
73. Ibid., 121.
74. Radzik, *Making Amends*, 161.
75. See Bennett, *Apology Ritual*, 166, and von Hirsch, *Censure and Sanctions*, 74.
76. See, for example, Proeve and Tudor, *Remorse*, 117. See also Bennett, *The Apology Ritual*, 196: "[T]he state has no duty forcibly to rehabilitate the offender, or even to aim to induce repentance in any way other than through the symbolically adequate expression of condemnation."
77. Braithwaite appreciates the deterrent value of shame in this regard. See *Crime, Shame, and Reintegration*, 75.
78. See ibid.: "[S]haming and repentance build consciences which internally deter criminal behavior even in the absence of any external shaming associated with an offense. Shaming brings into existence two very different kinds of punishers – social disapproval and pangs of conscience."
79. Hampton, "The Moral Education Theory of Punishment," 218.
80. *United States v. Beserra*: 29. 967 F.2d 254, 256 (7th Cir. 1992) (Posner, J.).
81. Murphy, *Getting Even*, 42.
82. See Amitai Etzioni, *Civic Repentance* (Lanham, MD: Rowman & Littlefield, 1999), 31: "[N]o matter how painstaking the inquiry, it is impossible to determine whether a person has internalized community values or has, during the period of scrutiny, experienced a 'jailhouse conversion.'"
83. See Bibas and Bierschbach, "Integrating Remorse and Apology into Criminal Procedure," 84.

84. Bennett, for example, offers an "ideal theory of punishment" and "as such it does not adequately explain how we might deal with the more messy and more challenging cases that tend to come up in the real life of the criminal justice system." Bennett, *Apology Ritual*, 197.
85. Hart, "Prolegomenon to the Principles of Punishment," 18.
86. Ibid.
87. As Reiman puts it, "demeaning and emasculating criminals by placing them in an enforced childhood characterized by privacy and no control over their time or actions, as well as by the contrast threat of rape or assault, is sure to overcome any deterrent effect by weakening whatever capacities a prisoner had for self-control. Indeed, by humiliating and brutalizing prisoners, we can be sure to increase their potential for aggressive violence." *The Rich Get Richer and the Poor Get Prison*, 3.
88. Currie, *Crime and Punishment in America*, 172–73.
89. Murphy, "Remorse, Apology, and Mercy," 452–53.
90. Glaze and Parks, "Correctional Populations in the United States, 2011": "Adult correctional authorities supervised about 6,977,700 offenders at yearend 2011, a decrease of 1.4% during the year."
91. Walmsley, "World Prison Population List."
92. Reiman, *The Rich Get Richer and the Poor Get Prison*, 14.
93. "Quick Facts about the Bureau of Prisons."
94. Karl Marx, *Capital: Volume I*, trans. Samuel Moore and Edward Aveling and ed. Frederick Engels (London: Swan Sonnenschein, 1906), 736–37.
95. See ibid., 775: "The discovery of gold and silver in America, the extirpation, enslavement and entombment in mines of the aboriginal population, the beginning of the conquest and looting of the East Indies, the turning of Africa into a warren for the commercial hunting of black-skins, signalised the rosy dawn of the era of capitalist production. These idyllic proceedings are the chief momenta of primitive accumulation. On their heels treads the commercial war of the European nations, with the globe for a theatre."
96. Alexander, *The New Jim Crow*, 6.
97. Rosalind Peetchesky, "At Hard Labor: Penal Confinement and Production in Nineteenth Century America," in *Crime and Capitalism*, ed. David Greenberg (Palo Alto: Mayfield, 1981), 341.
98. Randall Sheldon, "Convict Leasing: An Application of the Rusche-Kircheimer Thesis to Penal Changes in Tennessee, 1830–1915," in Greenberg, *Crime and Capitalism*, 358–66.
99. See Rakesh Kochar, Richard Fry, and Paul Taylor, "Wealth Gaps Rise to Record Highs Between Whites, Blacks, Hispanics," *Pew Social and Demographic Trends*, July 26, 2001, available at http://www.pewsocialtrends.org/2011/07/26/wealth-gaps-rise-to-record-highs-between-whites-blacks-hispanics/.
100. Alexander, *The New Jim Crow*, 57.
101. Ibid., 97.
102. Ibid., 101.
103. Ibid., 200.
104. Ibid., 130.
105. Ibid., 159.

106. Reiman, *The Rich Get Richer and the Poor Get Prison*, 101: "[T]he criminal justice system does not protect us against the gravest threats to life, limb, or possessions. Its definitions of crimes are not simply a reflection of the dangers that threaten us.... A government really intent on protecting us would enforce work-safety regulations, police the medical profession, require that clean air standards be met, and devote sufficient resources to the poor to alleviate the major disabilities of poverty. But it does not. Instead we hear a lot of cant about law and order and a lot of rant about crime in the streets. It is as if our leaders were not only refusing to protect us from the major threats to our well-being but also trying to cover up this refusal by diverting our attention to crime, as if this were the real threat."
107. Ibid., 209.
108. Ibid., 110.
109. Karl Marx, "Letter from Marx to Arnold Ruge," available at http://www.marxists.org/archive/marx/letters/ruge/.
110. See Christine Sypnowich, "Law and Ideology," *Stanford Encyclopedia of Philosophy*, available at http://plato.stanford.edu/entries/law-ideology/.
111. Richard Quinney, *Bearing Witness to Crime and Social Justice* (Albany: State University of New York, 2000), 115.
112. Davis, *Are Prisons Obsolete?*, 15.
113. Currie, *Crime and Punishment in America*, 185–86.
114. Ibid., 65.
115. Nick Smith, "Commodification in Law: Ideologies, Intractabilities, and Hyperboles," *Continental Philosophy Review* 42-1 (2009): 101–29.
116. Evgeny Pashukanis, *The General Theory of Law and Marxism*, trans. Barbara Einhorn (New Bruswick: Transaction, 2007), 180–81.
117. Georg Simmel, *The Philosophy of Money*, trans. Tom Bottomore and David Frisby (London: Routledge, 1978), 445.
118. Ibid., 446.
119. George Simmel, "The Metropolis and Mental Life," in *Simmel on Culture*, ed. David Frisby (London: Sage, 1997), 176.
120. Karl Marx, *Grundrisse*, trans. M. Nicolaus (New York: Vintage, 1973), 222.
121. Karl Marx, "On James Mill," in *Karl Marx: Selected Writings*, ed. David McLellan (New York: Oxford University Press, 2000), 128.
122. Karl Marx, "The German Ideology," in *Karl Marx: Selected Writings*, 201.
123. Bruce Waller, *Against Moral Responsibility* (Cambridge: MIT Press, 2011), 309.
124. See Lee Ross, "The Intuitive Psychologist and His Shortcomings: Distortions in the Attribution Process," in *Advances in Experimental Social Psychology*, ed. L. Berkowitz (New York: Academic Press, 1977), 173–220.
125. Willem Bonger, *An Introduction to Criminology* (London: Methuen, 1936), 75–76.
126. Jeffrie Murphy, "Marxism and Retribution," in *A Reader on Punishment*, eds. Antony Duff and David Garland (New York: Oxford, 1994), 61–62.
127. Ibid., 62.
128. Ibid., 65.
129. Ibid., 64 (citing Bonger).
130. Greenberg, *Crime and Capitalism*, 8.

131. Reiman, *Rich Get Richer*, 200: "The elimination of poverty is the most promising crime fighting strategy there is, and, in the long run, the most cost-effective."
132. Currie, *Crime and Punishment in America*, 108: "[Effective crime reduction programs]... have a number of things in common. They are preventative, rather than simply reactive; they emphasize building the strengths and capabilities of young people and their families, rather than simply treating their deficiencies or preaching virtues at them; they encourage productivity and responsibility; and they tackle concrete, real-world problems that undercut life chances and breed hostility, stress, and demoralization. Most of the successful programs are comprehensive – or what some would call 'ecological': they address multiple problems of children, youths, or families wherever they arise – in the family, the community, the health-care and school systems, and the housing and labor markets. They tend, insofar as possible, to deal with the roots of the problems, rather than just the symptoms."
133. Ibid., 159–60: "As a society we want to have it both ways. We want competent, caring families that can do a good job of socializing and supervising children, but we refuse to provide the social supports that would make that possible. We force many parents to choose between draining overwork in the low-wage economy and demoralizing poverty outside of it. We want parents to work, but we balk at providing the child care that would allow them to do so without jeopardizing the well-being of their children. We want parents to spend quality time with their children, but we reject the paid work leaves or shorter hours that would make it possible. Then we blame families for the consequences. We understand that childhood traumas may lead to violence, but we draw the line at reliably providing the preventative health care that could address them. We acknowledge the link between child abuse and violent crime, but we starve our child protective systems."
134. Reiman, *Rich Get Richer*, 206.
135. Currie, *Crime and Punishment in America*, 81: "[F]our priorities seem especially crucial: preventing child abuse and neglect, enhancing children's intellectual and social development, providing support and guidance to vulnerable adolescents, and working intensively with juvenile offenders."
136. See Duff, *Punishment, Communication, and Community*, 179–83.
137. Radzik, *Making Amends*, 18.
138. Ibid., 17.
139. Murphy, "Marxism and Retribution," 64.
140. See Murphy, "Repentance, Punishment, and Mercy," 155: "[T]hose who flout those values feel so alienated (perhaps because of poverty or racial injustice or cultural exclusion) that they could not reasonably see reintegration into the community as a good to be secured by their punishment because they never felt truly integrated into the community in the first place."
141. See ibid.
142. See Ronald S. Everett and Barbara C. Nienstedt, "Race, Remorse, and Sentence Reduction: Is Saying You're Sorry Enough?" *Justice Quarterly* 16-1 (1999): 117–18: "[A] judge in a region with a large Hispanic population commented on Hispanic males' difficulty in openly and publically admitting guilt, 'to look you in the eye and say they're sorry'. Cultural values inculcated in certain racial/ethnic minorities may prohibit such required displays of remorse, just

as a judge's cultural values may preclude him or her from perceiving a valid expression of remorse from a member of a different racial/ethnic group."
143. James Doyle, "The Lawyer's Art: 'Representation' in Capital Cases," *Yale Journal of Law and the Humanities* 8-2 (1996): 431.
144. Ibid., 438.
145. Joseph Rand, "The Demeanor Gap: Race, Lie Detection, and the Jury," *Connecticut Law Review* 33-1 (2000): 1-4.
146. See Doris James and Lauren Glaze, "Mental Health Problems of Prison and Jail Inmates," *Bureau of Justice Statistics Special Report*, revised December 14, 2006. See also O'Hear, "Remorse, Cooperation, and 'Acceptance of Responsibility,'" 1550-52.
147. "Saving Face with a Baby-Face? Shape of CEO's Face Affects Public Perception," *University of Chicago Press Journals*, May 30, 2008.
148. *U.S. v. Edwards*, 595 F.3d at 1016 (9th Cir.) (*en banc*).
149. Kenneth Mann et al., "Sentencing the White-Collar Offender," *American Criminal Law Review* 17 (1980): 500.
150. *Edwards*, 595 F.3d at 1016.
151. See Bibas, "Forgiveness in Criminal Procedure," 347.
152. *U.S. v. Vance*, 62 F.3d 1152, 1158 (9th Cir. 1995).
153. Pashukanis, *The General Theory of Law and Marxism*, 178.
154. Karl Marx, "Capital Punishment," *New York Daily Tribune*, February 18, 1853.
155. Ibid.
156. David Green, *When Children Kill Children: Penal Populism and Political Culture* (New York: Oxford, 2008), 35.
157. As Murphy puts it: "Start with a bourgeois model of rationality and you will, of course, wind up defending a bourgeois theory of consent, a bourgeois theory of justice, and a bourgeois theory of punishment." Murphy, "Marxism and Retribution," 61.
158. For this sort of criticism of liberal reform, see Tony Platt, "Prospects of a Radical Criminology in the USA," *Crime and Social Justice* 1 (1974): 2-10.
159. Tilly, *Credit and Blame*, 20.
160. Murphy, "Marxism and Retribution," 63.
161. Ibid.
162. These passages paraphrase longer arguments from *I Was Wrong*, 38-46.
163. P. F. Strawson, "Freedom and Resentment," *Proceedings of the British Academy* 48 (1962): 1-25.
164. Marion Smiley considers how our judgments of culpability track our social, political, and economic conditions in *Moral Responsibility and the Boundaries of Community* (Chicago: University of Chicago Press, 1992).
165. Daniel Dennet, *Freedom Evolves* (New York: Penguin, 2004), 289.
166. On these issues, see R. J. Wallace, *Responsibility and the Moral Sentiments* (Cambridge: Harvard University Press, 1994); Dennett, *Freedom Evolves*; and Dennett, *Elbow Room: The Varieties of Free Will Worth Wanting* (Cambridge, MA: MIT Press, 1984).
167. See Derk Pereboom, *Living without Free Will* (New York: Cambridge, 2001) and *Four Views on Free Will* (New York: Blackwell, 2007).
168. See *I Was Wrong*, 173-221.

169. Lucian Leape, "Error in Medicine," *Journal of the American Medical Association* 272 (1994): 1851–52.
170. Ibid.
171. Waller, *Against Moral Responsibility*, 290.
172. Ibid.
173. Ibid., 90–91.
174. Waller, "Sincere Apology without Moral Responsibility."
175. Ibid., 463.
176. Waller, *Against Moral Responsibility*, 191.
177. See Penzell, "Apology in the Context of Wrongful Conviction."
178. Thanks to Sarah Scott at John Jay for pointing out how frequently wrongfully convicted people desire apologies, especially from detectives and district attorneys. See David Eggers and Lola Vollen, *Surviving Justice: America's Wrongfully Convicted and Exonerated* (San Francisco: McSweeneys, 2005).
179. See Robert Weisberg's highly original and insightful "Apology, Legislation, and Mercy," 1427: "[T]he Supreme Court's suspension of the death penalty in the 1972 *Furman* decision constitutes an act of apology and pardon. Of course, some might insist on definitionally excluding a judicial decision, at least a decision rendered on a legal question, from the category of extra-jurisprudential mercy. But *Furman* invalidated the entire death penalty structure of the United States in one gesture and, in so doing, permanently released hundreds from death row. Moreover, it did so in an implicit holding that confessed nothing so simple as legal error at trial, but rather, the moral failure of the whole history of capital punishment in the United States. *Furman* itself was preceded, though not necessarily motivated by, gubernatorial pardons of death sentences in the late 1960s, at a time when the civil rights movement had shamed the United States over the random but, more importantly, racially imbalanced administration of the death penalty. Thus, I suggest viewing the decision as a parallel to those gubernatorial pardons, or indeed as harmonizing them into a national act of amnesty. Indeed, *Furman* is the second of two major apologies for historical racism in the modern Supreme Court – the other, of course, being the singular Warren opinion in *Brown v. Board of Education*."
180. As Weisberg puts it, "we normally think of the apology as what the criminal offers in hope of, or as a condition of, obtaining mercy. This Essay proposes the opposite – the notion that in extending mercy, the state, or the society for which it acts, itself apologizes to the criminal, or, as is made clear below, to the set of citizens who by historical fact or social category are most likely to have been condemned for the crime in question. In doing so, the apologizing authority also in some way confesses error." Ibid., 417. Notice how this proposal offers a means of responding to earlier discussions regarding dim prospects for reintegrating offenders into communities that treat them unfairly.
181. Douglass Hay, "Property, Authority, and Criminal Law," in Douglas Hay et al., *Albion's Fatal Tree: Crime and Society in Eighteenth-Century England* (New York: Pantheon, 1976), 17–63. See Weisberg's discussion of Hay in "Apology, Legislation, and Mercy," 1422–25.
182. Hay, "Property, Authority, and Criminal Law," 48.
183. Ibid., 49.
184. See Reiman, *The Rich Get Richer*, 72.

185. Ibid., 66.
186. See Alexander, *The New Jim Crow*, 83 and 214.
187. Robert Gangi, Vincent Schiraldi, and Jason Ziedenberg, *New York State of Mind: Higher Education vs. Prison Funding in the Empire State, 1988–1998* (Washington, DC: Justice Policy Institute, 1998); James Sterngold, "Prisons' Budget to Trump Colleges': No other Big State Spends as Much to Incarcerate Compared with Higher Education Funding," *San Francisco Chronicle*, May 21, 2007.
188. Currie, *Crime and Punishment in America*, 34.
189. Scheler, On the Eternal in Man, 56.
190. David Greenburg, *Crime and Capitalism*, 493.
191. J. D. Mabbott, "Punishment," *Mind* 48 (1939): 157.
192. Contrast Tasioulas, "Repentance and the Liberal State," 505: "[A]ntecedent repentance can have significance under a norm of mercy. This norm is distinct from the norm of retributive desert, whether in its character or grievance forms, which is a norm of justice. Mercy expresses charitable concern for the wrongdoer, and it generates *pro tanto* reasons to punish him less severely than he deserves. Not being a norm of justice, there is no implication that mercy is a basis for concluding that the offender deserves to be punished less severely because of his repentance or that he has a right to less severe punishment. Desert and rights fall within the domain of justice, not charity. But, in appropriate cases, there may be an obligation to show mercy, one that stands in a potentially conflictual relationship with the obligation of justice to impose the deserved punishment."
193. Proeve and Tudor suggest a version of character retributivism in *Remorse*, 133: "A censuring practice is, then, not just about the crime committed in the past but it is also made to a particular human being in the 'narrative unfolding' of her life since the crime."
194. See Duff, "Virtue, Vice, and Criminal Liability," 169.
195. See Murphy, *Punishment and the Moral Emotions*, 160.
196. For a discussion of character in conviction and in sentencing, see James Landon, "Character Evidence: Getting to the Root of the Problem through Comparison," *American Journal of Criminal Law* 24 (1997): 581–615.
197. See Murphy, *Punishment and the Moral Emotions*, 29.
198. Kierkegaard, *Purity of Heart is to Will One Thing*, 11.
199. Ibid., 10.
200. Ibid., 35.
201. Murphy, *Punishment and the Moral Emotions*, 35–36. See Murphy's earlier view in "Retributivism, Moral Education, and the Liberal State."
202. Murphy, *Punishment and the Moral Emotions*, 161.
203. Ibid., 29.
204. Ibid., 37.
205. See Tasioulas, "Repentance and the Liberal State," 504: "[T]here remains the basic problem that character retributivism is highly intrusive in its implications for state action. It requires the state to delve into the innermost moral condition of its citizens, to make an exhaustive accounting of all those features of our lives – desires, wishes, deeply-held convictions, many of them unspoken, hidden and even sub-conscious – that form part of our moral characters. But this sort

of activity runs foul of the requirement that the liberal state should respect the autonomy of its citizens. After all, how can we be autonomous centers of decision-making if every aspect of our thoughts, motivations and character traits is liable to be held up to public scrutiny with the severity of the sentence hanging in the balance?"

206. Scheler, *On the Eternal in Man*, 42.
207. Ibid., 44.
208. Ibid., 55.
209. See Joshua Dressler, *Understanding Criminal Law* (New York: Matthew Bender, 1987), 461.
210. Tasioulas, "Punishment and Repentance," 308.
211. Ibid.
212. Ibid.
213. See Murphy, *Getting Even*, 43–44.
214. Ibid.
215. Murphy, *Punishment and the Moral Emotions*, 76.
216. Note that Duff hints at something similar: "Perhaps we would hope that, at least with very serious crimes, the offender would be led to a profound re-examination and re-orientation of his entire being: but criminal punishment, as an exercise in penitential communication, need not be *that* ambitious; it need not aspire to the kind of 'deep character retributivism' against which Murphy rightly warns us. It focuses on the wrongfulness of the criminal deed, on the wrongful attitudes or concerns directly manifested." Duff, "Penance, Punishment, and the Limits of Community," 304.
217. *Pepper v. United States*, 131 S. Ct. 1229 (2011) (citing *Sullivan v. Ashe*, 302 U S. 51, 55 (1937)).
218. 518 U.S. 81, 113 (1996).
219. *Pepper* (citing *Wasman v. United States*, 468 U.S. 559, 564 [1984]).
220. *Pepper* (citing *Williams v. New York*, 337 U.S. 241, 247 [1949]).
221. *Pepper* citing 18 U.S.C. §3661. USSG §1B1.4 (2010) (emphasis added by the Court).
222. *Graham v. Florida*, 130 S. Ct. 2011 (2010).
223. See Pettit, "Indigence and Sentencing in Republican Theory," in Heffernan and Kleinig eds., *From Social Justice to Criminal Justice*, 238: "The offender can withdraw the assumption of a dominating position over the victim, acknowledging the victim's standing and admitting the mistake made in the original challenge. The offender can help to rectify the challenge to the victim's freedom, in a word, by an act of apology and recognition."
224. Contrast Tasioulas' thoughtful views on merciful reductions articulated in "Mercy" and "Punishment and Repentance."
225. Contrast, for example, views on hard treatment endorsed by von Hirsch, "Punishment, Penance, and the State" and as stated by Robert Nozick, *Philosophical Explanations* (Cambridge: Harvard, 1983), 385: "Consider next a person who (before capture) sincerely repents of his wrongful act and, on his own, makes amends to the victims, goes off and does extraordinarily good deeds – works in a leper colony or whatever – from a desire to add good to the world. Does such a person now deserve to be punished, should he be punished?... [S]ince the person already is connected up with correct values qua correct values, since

these already have a significant effect in his life, there is nothing for punishment to do. The further consequence the teleological retributivist hopes for already is present, the link to be effected already holds. It is important, though, that the link with correct values make a significant alteration in his life, in what his life otherwise would have been, that it alter his life significantly, and negatively according to his previous view.... It is not necessary, though, that this person feel or suffer pain."

226. Tasioulas, "Punishment and Repentance," 310.
227. Ibid.
228. Duff, *Punishment, Communication, and Community*, 107.
229. See Richard Swinburne, *Responsibility and Atonement* (New York: Oxford, 1989), 81.
230. Social psychologists have suggested this possibility. See Gold and Weiner, "Remorse, Confession, Group Identity, and Expectancies about Repeating a Transgression," 291: "[T]he emotional suffering that a defendant experiences as a result of remorse may diminish the need for externally imposed punishment in order to achieve the retributive goal of just deserts."
231. *I Was Wrong*, 96–107.
232. See Jeremy Blumenthal, "Law and the Emotions: The Problems of Affective Forecasting," *Indiana Law Journal* 80 (2005): 166–72.
233. Murphy, "Remorse, Apology, and Mercy," 431: "[W]hatever suffering one imposes on oneself is a result of one's own choices-something that victims cannot say of themselves with respect to the suffering imposed on them. Even in extreme self-imposed penance, penance of great suffering, one still retains an autonomy that one has denied to one's victims. Thus, no matter what one might do, one could never fully get right with victims of this nature."
234. See Tasioulas, "Repentance and the Liberal State," 504–5.
235. Sayre-McCord, "Criminal Justice and Legal Reparations as an Alternative to Punishment," 522: "[A]t least sometimes apologies, and efforts at making amends, and recognition of another's right to take offense, all work to extinguish (rather than satisfy) the desire for revenge."
236. Charles Griswold, "The Nature and Ethics of Vengeful Anger," in *Passion and Emotions*, ed. James Fleming (New York: NYU Press, 2013), 77–126.
237. Nietzsche, *Thus Spake Zarathustra*, in *The Portable Nietzsche*, ed. Walter Kaufmann (New York: Penguin, 1976), 206.
238. Robert Solomon, *In Defense of Sentimentality* (Oxford: New York, 2004), 37.
239. Daniel Dennett, "Some Observations of the Psychology of Thinking about Free Will," in *Are We Free? Psychology and Free Will*, eds. John Baer, James Kaufman, and Roy Baumeister (New York: Oxford, 2008), 258.
240. Griswold, "The Nature and Ethics of Vengeful Anger," 86.
241. Ibid., 103.
242. Ibid.
243. "Cries of 'Sorry' Halted Gunman's Rampage," *Associated Press*, January 12, 2013.
244. Gwen Ackerman, "Jordan's King Touches Israelis by Joining Them in Mourning," *Associated Press*, March 16, 1997.
245. See Dan Markel, "Against Mercy," *Minnesota Law Review* 88 (2004): 1453–73.

246. Von Hirsch, *Proportionate Sentencing*, 103.
247. Ibid.
248. Tasioulas, "Repentance and the Liberal State," 498.
249. Von Hirsch, *Censure and Sanctions*, 75.
250. See Duff, *Trials and Punishments*, 278.
251. Braithwaite, "Repentance Rituals and Restorative Justice," *Journal of Political Philosophy* 8-1 (2000): 116.
252. See Jean-Christophe Merle, *German Idealism and the Concept of Punishment*, trans. Joseph J. Kominkiewicz with Jean-Christophe Merle and Frances Brown (New York: Cambridge, 2009), 13: "It is not retributivism, but instead solely rehabilitation, that takes the responsibility truly seriously that a human being – and especially a criminal – has for his or her actions."
253. Bennett, *Apology Ritual*, 8.
254. Duff, *Trials and Punishments*, 6
255. Ibid. See also ibid., 52, 59, and Duff, *Punishment, Communication, and Community*, 124
256. Duff, *Punishment, Communication, and Community*, 116–17.
257. Ibid., 116.
258. Ibid.
259. Ibid.
260. Ibid., 113.
261. Ibid., 115.
262. Duff, *Trials and Punishments*, 262: "If someone suggested, for instance, that we might hope to develop some kind of drug or psycho-surgical technique which would provide a more efficient and less painful method of securing the kind of reformative change at which punishment aims, we would not need to question the empirical plausibility of her suggestion: for the suggestion itself is incoherent. No such technique could, logically, produce the results at which punishment aims: such techniques do not address the criminal, as punishment must address her, as a responsible moral agent who can and should come to understand the moral implications of what she has done; they are not, as punishment must be, attempts to solicit and arouse her repentant understanding of her crime; and the acquisition of such an understanding must of its nature be beneficial to the criminal."
263. Duff, *Punishment, Communication, and Community*, 153: "My account thus has no room for the death penalty, which is the ultimately exclusionary punishment." On life imprisonment for "dangerous offenders," see Duff, *Punishment, Communication, and Community*, 170–74.
264. See discussion in Murphy, *Punishment and the Moral Emotions*, 132–33.
265. Duff, "Penance, Punishment, and the Limits of Community," 307. Avishai Margalit offers a similar argument in *The Decent Society* (Cambridge: Harvard University Press, 1996), 75: "Even the worst criminals are worthy of basic human respect because of the possibility that they may radically reevaluate their past lives and, if they are given the opportunity, may live the rest of their lives in a worthy manner. . . . Even though it is likely that she will continue living this way, this likelihood should not be turned into a presumption, because in principle an evildoer has the capacity to change and repent. This capacity implies that she deserves basic respect as a human being who should not be

'given up on,' precisely because there is a chance, no matter how small, that she will repent."
266. Radzik, *Making Amends*, 83.
267. Duff, *Trials and Punishments*, 262–63.
268. Hegel, *The Philosophy of Right*, 246.
269. See Duff, *Punishment, Communication, and Community*, 114.
270. Ibid., 115: "Punishment should be understood, justified, and administered as a mode of moral communication with offenders that seeks to persuade them to repent their crimes, to reform themselves, and to reconcile themselves through punishment with those they have wrong."
271. Ibid., 116–17.
272. Ibid., 106.
273. Ibid., 111–12.
274. Ibid., 122.
275. Ibid., 120: "[M]y account does not imply that repentance should entitle the offender to a lighter sentence."
276. Ibid., 118.
277. Ibid.
278. Ibid., 121.
279. Ibid., 119.
280. Ibid., 121.
281. Ibid., 119.
282. R. J. Lipkin, "Punishment, Penance, and Respect for Autonomy," *Social Theory and Practice* 14 (1988): 96.
283. Von Hirsch raises similar concerns in *Proportionate Sentencing*, 94.
284. Bennett, *Apology Ritual*, 8 and Duff, *Punishment, Communication, and Community*, 124.
285. Duff does suggest, however, that repentance is a process that requires reflection and reform rather than a singular speech act. See, for example, *Punishment, Communication, and Community*, 108 and 119.
286. Duff, *Trials and Punishments*, 289.
287. See Duff, *Punishment, Communication, and Community*, 122.
288. See ibid., 115: "For while my account is non-consequentialist, in that it does not make the justification of a penal system depend upon its contingent efficiency as a means to some independently identifiable end, it is not a purely retributivist account that justifies punishment solely in terms of its relationship to the past crimes for which it is imposed. Punishment is justified as a legitimate attempt to protect citizens from crime and to preserve the political community by persuading offenders to repent their crimes."
289. Tasioulas, "Punishment and Repentance," 286.
290. See Duff, *Punishment, Communication, and Community*, 115. Duff warns: "[T]here might be a temptation to rely on such a deterrent effect in justifying their punishment: to think that it is still worth punishing them and that their punishment can still be an effective way of protecting citizens against crime, because even if they are not morally persuaded, they (or others like them) might nonetheless be deterred. We must resist this temptation if we are to take seriously the conception of punishment as an enterprise of moral communication and the objections to using punishment as a deterrent... using punishment as

a deterrent is inconsistent with a proper regard for actual potential offenders as members of the normative political community." Ibid., 124.
291. Duff, "Punishment, Communication, and Community," 52.
292. Duff, *Punishment, Communication, and Community*, 118: "Braithewaite and Petit locate shame within a strictly consequentialist perspective, as a useful technique for achieving the goods at which punishment should aim. But the value of remorse on my account is not a consequentialist value."
293. Ibid., 183.
294. Ibid., 183 and 188.
295. Ibid., 186–87.
296. Ibid.
297. Ibid, 200.
298. Ibid., 123.
299. Thanks to Winston Thompson for this formulation.
300. Von Hirsch, *Proportionate Sentencing*, 92
301. See discussion in von Hirsch, *Censure and Sanctions*, 74: "Duff's examples assume that the person punished acknowledges the moral authority of the punishing agent. In the context of the criminal sanction, that assumption becomes problematic. Consider the disaffected defendant who (for reasons of radical opinion, previous bad experience with the criminal justice authorities, or whatever), does not think that the State possesses any particular moral authority over him. Whatever regrets he may have about his action he does not wish to respond to any demand by the *State* that he feel penitent."
302. For a similar and more explicitly Rawlsian view, see Tasioulas, "Repentance and the Liberal State," 511.
303. As Radzik puts it: "While it is true that the liberal state is committed to freedom of conscience and the pluralism of reasonable conceptions of the good, there is no point or value in denying that liberalism is committed, at its core, to certain moral values – specifically the freedom and equality of persons." *Making Amends*, 163.
304. Bibas and Biershbach agree with a version of this argument: "Encouraging offenders to learn the value of the rights they have violated by asking them to acknowledge and repudiate their crimes hardly seems a totalitarian invasion of conscience. This is particularly true because the lesson taught is limited to that narrow set of acts that society has defined as crimes. Offenders and victims, moreover, are always free to refuse to participate." "Integrating Remorse and Apology into Criminal Procedure," 147.
305. See *A Brief Guide to Alcoholics Anonymous*, available at http://www.aa.org/pdf/products/p-42_abriefguidetoaa.pdf.
306. Von Hirsch, *Proportionate Sentencing*, 106.
307. See Bennett, *Apology Ritual*, 148: "The reason for this is partly that requiring offenders to put on a show of remorse would be incompatible with their integrity. But it is also because the fundamental job of the criminal sanction is not to induce repentance or to achieve moral reconciliation between offender and community: its job is simply to express proportionate condemnation, and that is done perfectly well regardless of how the offender receives that condemnation."
308. Duff, "Punishment, Communication, and Community," 397.

309. Duff, "Penance, Punishment, and the Limits of Community," 303.
310. Ibid.
311. Tasioulas, "Repentance and the Liberal State," 510–11.
312. Radzik, *Making Amends*, 161.
313. Ibid., 173.
314. Ibid., 172.
315. Ibid., 174.
316. Ibid., 167.
317. Bennett, *Apology Ritual*, 180.
318. Ibid.
319. Ibid.
320. Ibid., 148.
321. Tasioulas makes an interesting suggestion in this regard: "[I]t might well be advisable for offenders to be granted the opportunity to carry on with some elements of their legally-imposed penance on a voluntary basis, even after their sentence has been served. Thus, an offender who, as part of a community service order, is required to undertake work in a soup kitchen, might be given the opportunity to carry on working there even after he has served his sentence." "Repentance and the Liberal State," 520.
322. See ibid., 541: "[T]he state's facilitation of repentance can be indirect, by supporting various institutions in civil society-such as churches, charities, schools and so on-that provide ex-offenders with ritualized means of repentance. This indirect strategy has the benefit that the state disengages from any further direct involvement with the offender. This enables respected individuals involved in the running of these institutions to form a close enough relationship with the offender to vouch for the genuineness of their remorse and improved character. An official of the state, by contrast, might find it harder to form such a relationship given his association with the body that meted out the punishment. Moreover, in thus marking a clear contrast between the offender's punishment and his subsequent voluntary penance, doubts about the value of repentance in a punitive setting can be quelled. But the suggestion also faces problems. One is the difficulty of supporting these institutions in civil society without necessarily endorsing the broader ideology to which they subscribe, a problem that is particularly acute in relation to faith-based institutions."
323. Duff, "Penance, Punishment, and the Limits of Community," 306.
324. Murphy, *Punishment and the Moral Emotions*, 35.
325. See Proeve and Tudor, *Remorse*, 138 and 146.
326. Robert Solomon, *True to Our Feelings* (New York: Oxford, 2007), 95.
327. See sources collected in Robbennolt, "Apologies and Legal Settlements," note 74.
328. *Black's Law Dictionary*, 6th edition (St. Paul, MN: West, 1991).
329. Duff, *Punishment, Communication, and Community*, 115.
330. Murphy, "Marxism and Retribution."
331. *Riggins v. Nevada*, 504 U.S. 127, 143–44 (1992).
332. David Barstow, "Officer, Seeking Some Mercy, Admits, to Louima's Torture," *New York Times*, May 26, 1999.
333. "Stewart Stays Defiant," *Washington Times*, July 5, 2005.

334. Lippke says it well in the *Ethics of Plea Bargaining*, 117: "The most defensible form of remorse-based sentence reductions appears to be one in which they are awarded by state officials who deem an offender's progress toward moral reform substantial enough to warrant some easing off of his sentence. There are numerous problematic tasks such that a policy would necessitate state officials to perform: separation of the genuinely remorseful from those who feign it or exhibit one of its simulacra, figuring out why those who do not exhibit it have this failing, and discerning the strength of an offender's reattachment to the good life in the form of progress at moral reform. We might reasonably doubt the abilities of state officials to perform any of these tasks adequately and responsibly, let alone all of them. Moreover, performance of these tasks would require these same officials to conduct potentially intrusive inquiries into the lives of offenders, their thinking about their conduct, and their emotional reactions to it. Offenders who failed to cooperate with these inquires could not, for a variety of reasons, simply be deemed unremorseful and ordered to serve their full sentences. State officials would have to inquire into the reasons for non-cooperation, to ensure that they did indeed reflect poorly on offenders, and thus were legitimate bases for denying them sentence reductions. My conclusion is not that a policy of sentence reduction for remorse cannot in principle, be defended, though I have underscored the many difficulties in mounting such a defense. But it should be apparent that defending such a policy does not place us remotely in the vicinity of a defense of the kinds of waiver rewards offered criminal defendants in exchange for their guilty pleas."
335. See Bennett, *Apology Ritual*, 4.
336. Lippke, *Ethics of Plea Bargaining*, 1. See also George Fisher, *Plea Bargaining's Triumph: A History of Plea Bargaining in America* (Palo Alto: Stanford University Press, 2003).
337. Lippke, *Ethics of Plea Bargaining*, 2.
338. See Etienne and Robbennolt, "Apologies and Plea Bargaining," 300.
339. Ibid.: "[T]he principal reason to expect a diluted impact of apologies is the near absence of victims and (often) defendants from the negotiating table. Put another way, the prosecutor's role as the negotiator for the state alters the negotiation dynamic in significant ways. Criminal prosecutors represent the state, not the crime victim, and are not required to follow the wishes of the victim in resolving the case. The degree to which a crime victim has control over the prosecutor varies from limited to non-existent."
340. See sources collected in Ibid., 315–16.
341. See ibid., 316–17.
342. See ibid., 307–8.
343. See ibid, 320: "A defendant who desperately wants to plead is more likely to accept the plea offer presented. Following an admission of guilt, her attorney will have little leverage to obtain a more favorable plea offer. The primary leverage that defendants have is the threat of trial, and this threat may become far less credible after an apology."
344. Ibid., 319.
345. Ibid., 320.
346. Ibid.
347. Ibid., 301.

348. See ibid., 311–12: "On one end of the plea bargaining spectrum, agreements are struck with little or no negotiation. In the context of large numbers of misdemeanors or low-level felony cases, plea agreements are often the result of an assembly line model of case processing in which prosecutors – based largely on police reports – assign a preliminary plea offer to each case. This preliminary offer is often the final offer. In many of these cases, the prosecutor has had no prior contact with the defendant, victim, law enforcement officer, or defense attorney before the opening negotiation offer is made. Unrepresented defendants often accept the plea offer without discussion.... On the other end of the negotiation spectrum, plea deals are the result of lengthy and drawn out bargaining processes.... In white-collar and large criminal conspiracy cases, much of the plea bargaining occurs prior to indictment. Defendants typically know well before they are charged that they are a target of a criminal investigation. Defense attorneys advocate on behalf of their clients early in the process and play a central role in framing the charges to be indicted. It is not unusual in such cases for defendants to express remorse."

349. See 18 U.S.C.S. app. § 3E1.1.

350. See *2012 Guidelines Manual* § 3E1.1. See also sources collected in Bibas and Bierschbach, "Integrating Remorse and Apology into Criminal Procedure," notes 18–20.

351. *2012 Guidelines Manual* § 3E1.1: "2. This adjustment is not intended to apply to a defendant who puts the government to its burden of proof at trial by denying the essential factual elements of guilt, is convicted, and only then admits guilt and expresses remorse. Conviction by trial, however, does not automatically preclude a defendant from consideration for such a reduction. In rare situations a defendant may clearly demonstrate an acceptance of responsibility for his criminal conduct even though he exercises his constitutional right to a trial. This may occur, for example, where a defendant goes to trial to assert and preserve issues that do not relate to factual guilt (*e.g.*, to make a constitutional challenge to a statute or a challenge to the applicability of a statute to his conduct). In each such instance, however, a determination that a defendant has accepted responsibility will be based primarily upon pre-trial statements and conduct."

352. Ibid.: "3. Entry of a plea of guilty prior to the commencement of trial combined with truthfully admitting the conduct comprising the offense of conviction, and truthfully admitting or not falsely denying any additional relevant conduct for which he is accountable under §1B1.3 (Relevant Conduct) (*see* Application Note 1(A)), will constitute significant evidence of acceptance of responsibility for the purposes of subsection (a). However, this evidence may be outweighed by conduct of the defendant that is inconsistent with such acceptance of responsibility. A defendant who enters a guilty plea is not entitled to an adjustment under this section as a matter of right."

353. Ibid.: "5. The sentencing judge is in a unique position to evaluate a defendant's acceptance of responsibility. For this reason, the determination of the sentencing judge is entitled to great deference on review."

354. *2012 Guidelines Manual* § 5K1.1.

355. *2012 Guidelines Manual* § 3E1.1.

356. Ibid.

357. O'Hear, "Remorse, Cooperation, and 'Acceptance of Responsibility,'" 1511.
358. Ibid., 1517.
359. *2012 Guidelines Manual* § 3E1.1.
360. Ibid.
361. O'Hear, "Remorse, Cooperation, and 'Acceptance of Responsibility,'" 1512–13.
362. Ibid., 1534.
363. See cases collected ibid., notes 76–77.
364. See sources collected in ibid., 1539–42.
365. Ibid., 1514: "The Commission identified the underlying purposes of rewarding guilty pleas and developed a mechanism to achieve those purposes, thus converting a bright-line rule proposal – always give a discount for guilty pleas – into a discretionary open-ended test – does the defendant accept responsibility? Such a discretionary test can overcome the difficulties of the automatic plea discount by permitting judges to avoid unseemly or inappropriate downward adjustments, by preserving an opportunity for defendants who go to trial to earn the same adjustment as those who plead guilty, and by retaining uncertainty in the system."
366. Ibid., 1553.
367. See ibid., 1556–60.
368. See ibid., 1526–29.
369. *2012 Guidelines Manual* § 3E1.1.
370. See *United States v. Fagan*, 162 F.3d 1280, 1284 (10th Cir. 1998): "Several circuits have specifically held that a moral element is implicit in acceptance of responsibility and is satisfied by the defendant's expression of contrition and remorse."
371. *United States v. Franco-Perez* 873 F.2d 455 (1st Cir. 1989), 463.
372. Ibid., 457–58.
373. *2012 Guidelines Manual* § 3E1.1.
374. O'Hear, "Remorse, Cooperation, and 'Acceptance of Responsibility,'" 1518: "[N]othing is implausible about a defendant turning over a new leaf during or after a trial, perhaps as a result of hearing testimony from victims or receiving counseling or drug rehabilitation prior to sentencing. Nonetheless, the section 3E1.1 commentary expressly excludes from its ambit the defendant who challenges the factual elements of his guilt at trial and 'only then admits guilt and expresses remorse,' regardless of the sincerity or degree of that remorse."
375. See *United States v. Hammick*, 36 F.3d 594, 600 (7th Cir. 1994): "[A] fundamental principle underlying the acceptance of responsibility reduction" is "that in the absence of evidence of sincere remorse or contrition for one's crimes, a guilty plea entered for the apparent purpose of obtaining a lighter sentence does not entitle a defendant to a reduction for acceptance of responsibility."
376. O'Hear, "Remorse, Cooperation, and 'Acceptance of Responsibility,'" 1521.
377. See O'Hear's discussion of *Vance*. Ibid., 1532–34.
378. *United States v. Vance*, 62 F.3d 1152, 1159–60 (9th Cir. 1995), 1159.
379. Ibid., 1160.
380. See O'Hear, "Remorse, Cooperation, and 'Acceptance of Responsibility,'" 1543.
381. See ibid., 1543–44.

382. Ibid., 1552.
383. Ibid.
384. Ibid., 1541.
385. Ibid., 1563.
386. McCoy, "Plea Bargaining as Coercion," 12: "The prosecutor gets his or her 'bite' on a higher number of offenders, primarily those at low levels of offence severity including ever-higher numbers of people arrested for drug offences and 'quality of life' crimes. Thus, the old assumption that caseload causes plea bargaining probably misunderstands the direction of causation in the modern era. Perhaps *plea bargaining causes high caseload*, not the other way around. Plea bargaining facilitates the widening of social control through criminal sanctioning."
387. Bennett, *Apology Ritual*, 197.
388. See, for example, Etienne, "Remorse, Responsibility, and Regulating Advocacy," 2162; Etzioni, *Civic Repentance*, 31; and Proeve and Tudor, *Remorse*, 110.
389. Simon, Smith, Negowetti, "Apologies and Fitness to Practice Law." I owe special thanks to Mitch Simon for helping me frame theoretical concerns – both in that article and throughout this book – in a manner that might be useful for practitioners.
390. See *I Was Wrong*, 33–38.
391. For an evenhanded evaluation of the controversial doctrine, see Guyora Binder, *Felony Murder* (Palo Alto: Stanford University Press, 2012).
392. Note the distinction between a parent attempting to accept blame for the actions of a child and a parent accepting blame for her own behavior, perhaps apologizing for abandoning the child years ago, which the parent believes has in turn contributed to the child's criminal development.
393. *People v. McDade*, 579 N.E.2d 1173, 1183 (Ill. App. Ct. 1991).
394. Ibid., 1184.
395. See *I Was Wrong*, 78, 142, and 232.
396. See discussion in Murphy, *Punishment and the Moral Emotions*, 163.
397. See the *Bureau of Justice Statistics*' reports on recidivism, available at http://www.bjs.gov/index.cfm?ty=tp&tid=17.
398. *2012 Guidelines Manual* § 3E1.1.
399. See Michael O'Hear, "Solving the Good-Time Puzzle: Why Following the Rules Should Get You Out of Prison Early," *Wisconsin Law Review* 1 (2012): 217.
400. *2012 Guidelines Manual* § 3E1.1.
401. See Jon Elster, "Redemption for Wrongdoing: The Fate of Collaborators after 1945," *Journal of Conflict Resolution* 50-3 (2006): 336.
402. Lippke, *The Ethics of Plea Bargaining*, 109: "We have good reason to adopt a 'wait and see' attitude toward her, to determine whether she truly understands the wrong she has done and is chastened by her remorse. This is not something we can discern at the point at which she first expresses remorse, even if it is heartfelt. Nor is it clear from her efforts to repair whatever damage she has done."
403. For an illuminating overview of these and related concerns, see Bibas and Bierschbach, "Integrating Remorse and Apology into Criminal Procedure." See also Szmania and Mangis, "Finding the Right Time and Place," 356.

404. See Markus Dubber, "Policing Possession: The War on Crime and the End of Criminal Law," *Journal of Criminal Law and Criminology* 91 (2001): 829–996, 849.
405. Bibas and Bierschbach, "Integrating Remorse and Apology into Criminal Procedure," 97.
406. Ibid., 136.
407. See cases collected in Ward, "Sentencing without Remorse," notes 110–25. See, in particular, *State v. Butler*, 462 S.E.2d 485, 489 (N.C. 1995): "[T]he fact that the defendant showed remorse while in jail carries little weight with this Court. It is relatively easy for one facing life behind bars to be remorseful"; *Wilkie v. State*, 813 N.E.2d 794, 800 (Ind. Ct. App. 2004): "I really don't consider remorse . . . a mitigating circumstance. I mean, quite frankly, everyone when they get to this point is going to be sorry. You are sorry for all sorts of reasons, you know, most of all, probably, what's going to happen to you, and that's only natural" (quoting trial court); *State v. Wilmoth*, No. C3-01-1884, 2002 WL 1325613, 3 (Minn. Ct. App. June 18, 2002): "You profess remorse now and at the time of your plea, but I think that's simply to affect your sentence. . . . Only now when he is worrying about his sentence does he profess any concern regarding the victims of the crime" (quoting trial court); and *State v. Smith*, 687 P.2d 1265, 1267 (Ariz. 1984): "I'd get a little remorseful too, after spending a few years in prison" (quoting trial court).
408. See cases collected in Ward, "Sentencing without Remorse," notes 83–91.
409. See cases collected in ibid., notes 94–106.
410. See Marc Boccaccini et al., "I Want to Apologize, But I Don't Want Everyone to Know: A Public Apology as Pretrial Publicity between a Criminal and Civil Case," *Law and Psychology Review* 32 (2008): 50–51.
411. *2012 Guidelines Manual* § 3E1.1.
412. O'Hear, "Solving the Good-Time Puzzle," 200: "The amount of good time available varies considerably by jurisdiction, and within some jurisdictions based on offense type and other considerations. Seven states offer day-for-day credit or better to at least some classes of inmates; in these states, a sentence might effectively be cut in half based on good conduct. Other states are much stingier, awarding only three or four days of credit per month. Still other states have quite elaborate systems that defy easy characterization. The norm, however, seems to be in the range of ten to twenty days per month, or a reduction in sentence length of twenty-five to forty percent."
413. Ibid., 203–4.
414. Ibid., 198.
415. Ibid., 219.
416. See ibid., 226: "[T]he sentencing judge might be instructed to announce the prison term in two ways, both with and without whatever acceptance discount the judge concludes is appropriate. The difference would constitute a contingent sentence credit that could be partially or fully withdrawn by prison officials as a sanction for serious, willful rule violations, on the theory that prison misconduct constitutes something of a repudiation of acceptance."
417. Ibid., 225.
418. Ibid., 226.
419. See Etienne and Robbennolt, "Apologies and Plea Bargaining," 300.

420. Bibas and Bierschbach, "Integrating Remorse and Apology into Criminal Procedure," 130: "[P]rosecutorial discretion raises the dangers of discrimination and abuse of power. But these dangers are inherent in existing prosecutorial discretion; remorse and apology make them no worse."
421. See Proeve and Tudor, *Remorse*, 104.
422. See Etienne and Robbennolt, "Apologies and Plea Bargaining," 316–17.
423. See Etzioni, *Civic Repentance*, 106: "The three most critical institutional features of Japan's criminal justice system are thus the authority given to the police not to report minor offense (*bizia shobun*) in cases where they deem appropriate; the authority of prosecutors to suspend prosecution where warranted by the nature and circumstances of the crime and the offender's attitude; and the courts' broad authority to suspend execution of sentences."
424. See ibid., 105–6.
425. See Morris Hoffman, "The Case for Jury Sentencing," *Duke Law Journal* 52-5 (2003): 951–1010.
426. Bennett, *Apology Ritual*, 180.
427. Ibid.
428. Simon, Smith, and Negowetti, "Apologies and Fitness to Practice Law."
429. See Martha Grace Duncan, "So Young and So Untender: Remorseless Children and the Expectations of the Law," *Columbia Law Review* 102 (2002): 1471: "In many jurisdictions, the presence of contrition is a legitimate argument for retaining juvenile jurisdiction, whereas its absence militates in favor of 'binding the child over' to the criminal system."
430. Seccuro, *Crash Into Me*, 109.
431. *United States v. Purchess*, 107 F.3d 1261 (7th Cir. 1997): 1266–67: finding that the sentencing court should have determined whether "the defendant understands and agrees with his attorney's argument before using counsel's challenge as a basis for denying the defendant a reduction for acceptance of responsibility."
432. See Etienne, "Remorse, Responsibility, and Regulating Advocacy," 2162: "The notion that a defendant lacks contrition when she challenges the government's evidence, alleges violations of her rights, or disagrees with her sentence is baseless.... It assumes that because a truly remorseful person exhibits some degree of self-reproach or even self-condemnation, she would accept whatever punishment is coming to her rather than seek to protect herself with the machinations of a fast-talking lawyer."
433. Ibid., 2173.
434. Ibid.
435. See *State v. Hardwick*, 905 P.2d 1384 (Ariz. Ct. App. 1995): 1391: "As contrition or remorse necessarily imply guilt, it would be irrational or disingenuous to expect or require one who maintains his innocence to express contrition or remorse."
436. See Medwed, "The Innocent Prisoner's Dilemma," 542: "[I]nnocent prisoners face a daunting dilemma when confronting parole boards. Refusing to acknowledge guilt will likely hinder an inmate's chance for parole, whereas taking responsibility for the underlying criminal act may paradoxically enhance the prospect of release and impair any future attempt at exoneration given that the contents of the parole file are often readily available to prosecutors. Merely

expressing remorse for the victim's predicament – short of taking individual responsibility for the crime – could damage a prisoner's subsequent efforts to clear his name through the courts, depending upon the prosecutorial interpretation (or characterization) of the statement."

437. See *PBS Frontline*'s haunting documentary "The Confessions," available at http://www.pbs.org/wgbh/pages/frontline/the-confessions/.
438. See *Hightower v. State Bar*, 666 P.2d 10, 14 (Cal. 1983): "[R]efusal to retract his claims of innocence and make a showing of repentance appears to reinforce rather than undercut his showing of good character.... An individual's courageous adherence to his beliefs, in the face of a judicial or quasi-judicial decision attacking their soundness, may prove his fitness to practice law rather than the contrary. We therefore question the wisdom of denying an applicant admission to the bar if that denial rests on the applicant's choosing to assert his innocence regarding prior charges rather than to acquiesce in a pragmatic confession of guilt, and conclude that [he] should not be denied the opportunity to practice law because he is unwilling to perform an artificial act of contrition."
439. See Medwed, "The Innocent Prisoner's Dilemma," 556.
440. Medwed, "Innocent Prisoner's Dilemma," 535.
441. See *Brown v. State*, 934 P.2d 235, 245–46 (Nev. 1997): "The district court violated Troy's Fifth Amendment rights by considering his 'lack of remorse' when he still had a constitutional right to maintain his innocence and by threatening to impose a harsher sentence if Troy refused to admit his guilt. Troy was unable to express remorse sufficient to satisfy the judge without foregoing his right to not incriminate himself, and the fact that he took the stand at trial does not change this analysis because Troy maintained his innocence. As such, requiring Troy to either express remorse or receive a harsher sentence violated Troy's Fifth Amendment rights and constituted an abuse of discretion."
442. See Medwed, "Innocent Prisoner's Dilemma," 556.
443. See ibid., 556–57.
444. See Sundby, "The Intersection of Trial Strategy, Remorse, and the Death Penalty"; Eisenberg et al., "But Was He Sorry? The Role of Remorse in Capital Sentencing"; Rumsey, "Effects of Defendant Background and Remorse on Sentencing Judgments"; and Garvey, "Aggravation and Mitigation in Capital Cases."
445. See Sundby, "The Intersection of Trial Strategy, Remorse, and the Death Penalty," 1596–97: "When the defendant is maintaining that he is in fact innocent, an attorney legitimately may be concerned that raising the possibility of admitting the killing will undermine any sense of trust. This possibility certainly argues for waiting until a relationship with the defendant has developed before broaching the subject and for laying out the strengths and weaknesses of the prosecution's case in a nonjudgmental and clear-eyed fashion. If done in this manner, the defendant is more likely to understand that the attorney is speaking to him out of a concern for the defendant's best interests."
446. Duff, *Punishment, Communication, and Community*: 134.
447. Murphy, "Repentance, Punishment, and Mercy," 157.
448. Bibas, "Forgiveness in Criminal Procedure," 339.
449. See Tasioulas, "Repentance and the Liberal State," 497: "[W]hen faced with a choice among punishments of equal severity, any one of which would convey

the requisite measure of justified censure, the sentencing authority may be guided by their relative efficacy as instrumental and constitutive means of repentance."

450. Calhoun puts it well in her review of Radzik's *Making Amends* in *Notre Dame Philosophical Reviews*: "[O]ne might resist the conclusion that victims are obligated, upon full atonement, to trust the former wrongdoer *with respect to the very matter* on which she was previously untrustworthy. Moral trust is scalar as are good will and moral competence. We may owe everyone, in the absence of evidence of untrustworthiness, some minimal level of moral trust. Further, we may owe fully atoning wrongdoers a general trust in their goodwill, their capacity to recognize authoritative norms, and their willingness to accept responsibility and make amends if they err in the future. We do not, however, owe it to everyone to trust them with our personal information, door keys, pets and the like. Atonement for betrayal cannot make it the case that we now owe a level of moral trust that wasn't owed in the first place." The review is available at http://ndpr.nd.edu/news/24115-making-amends-atonement-in-morality-law-and-politics/.

451. Mark Bennett, "Heartstrings or Heartburn: A Federal Judge's Musings on Defendants' Rite and Right of Allocution," *Champion* 35 (2011): 28.

452. To capture a sense of the diverse and thoughtful views, see K. D. Moore, *Pardons: Justice, Mercy, and the Public Interest* (New York: Oxford University Press, 1989); Jeffrie Murphy and Jean Hampton, *Forgiveness and Mercy* (Cambridge: Cambridge University Press, 1988); Meir Dan-Cohen, "Revising the Past: The Metaphysics of Repentance," in *Forgiveness, Mercy, and Clemency*, eds. Austin Sarat and Nassar Hussain (Palo Alto: Stanford, 2007): 117: "The three revisionary practices differ primarily in the subject of this reorientation: the subject of repentance is the wrongdoer; of forgiveness, the victim, and of pardon, an official acting on behalf of society or the state"; Cheshire Calhoun, "Changing One's Heart," *Ethics* 103 (1992): 76–96; P. Twambley, "Mercy and Forgiveness," *Analysis* 36 (1976): 84–90; 87: "[J]udges have no right to be merciful because it is not to them that any obligation is due. And they have an obligation to impose the sentence the law prescribes"; Claudia Card, "Mercy," *Philosophical Review* 81 (1972): 182–207.

453. See *I Was Wrong*, 132–39.

454. Urban-Walker, *Moral Repair*, 155

455. See Minow, *Between Vengeance and Forgiveness*, 16.

456. Consider Hannah Arendt, *The Human Condition* (Chicago: University of Chicago Press, 1968), 241: "It is ... a structural element in the realm of human affairs, that men are unable to forgive what they cannot punish and that they are unable to punish what has turned out to be unforgivable. This is the true hallmark of those offenses which, since Kant, we call 'radical evil' and about whose nature so little is known, even to us who have been exposed to one of their rare outbursts on the public scene. All we know is that we can neither punish nor forgive such offenses and that they therefore transcend the realm of human affairs and the potentialities of human power, both of which they radically destroy whenever they make their appearance. Here, where the deed itself dispossesses us of all power, we can indeed only repeat with Jesus: 'It were better for him that a millstone were hanged about his neck, and he cast into the sea.'"

457. Minow, *Between Vengeance and Forgiveness*, 17–20.
458. Contrast H. Rashdall, *A Theory of Good and Evil* (London: Oxford University Press, 1924); Murphy and Hampton, *Forgiveness and Mercy*; and D. Heyd, "Beyond the Call of Duty in Kant's Ethics," *Kant-Studien* 71 (1980): 308–24.
459. Others have raised this issue. See Proeve and Tudor, *Remorse*, 125 and 131; Murphy, "Repentance, Punishment, and Mercy," 158; and Tasioulas, "Punishment and Repentance," 308–09.
460. See *I Was Wrong*, 62–63.
461. Von Hirsch, *Censure and Sanctions*, 75.

Chapter Four: The Institutional Framework: Economic Outcomes and Noneconomic Values

1. "Tire Victim: Apology Seemed Sincere," *CBS News*, January 9, 2001.
2. Ibid.
3. Ibid.
4. Ibid.
5. Hearit, *Crisis Management by Apology*, 147.
6. "Tire Victim: Apology Seemed Sincere."
7. Jonathan Harr, *A Civil Action* (New York: Vintage, 1996), 452.
8. "Tragic Story Marks Debate over Limits on Suing Doctors," *Wisconsin State Journal*, October 15, 1997.
9. Tannen, *The Argument Culture*, 149.
10. Taft, "Apology Subverted," 1136–37.
11. Andrew Jenks, *Perils of Progress: Environmental Disasters in the 20th Century* (Upper Saddle River, NJ: Pearson, 2010), 19.
12. Ibid., 20.
13. Ibid., 19–20.
14. Ibid., 25. See also Robert Emmet Hernan, *This Borrowed Earth* (New York: Palgrave, 2010), 9–30.
15. Chisso provided the following statement in its settlement:

> Clause 2: Because Chisso did not take sufficient measures to prevent the spread of Minamata disease after its official discovery in 1956, did not undertake to investigate the cause of the disease, and did not provide patients with sufficient relief aid, the extent of the damages increased even further. Moreover, even when the causal substance had been confirmed and the disease became a social problem, Chisso continued to maintain a regrettable attitude toward its solution. Chisso will reflect upon these actions with heartfelt sincerity.
>
> Clause 3: Chisso deeply apologizes to those patients and their families, already in great poverty, who experienced further suffering from contracting Minamata disease, who suffered from a result of Chisso's attitudes, and who experienced various types of humiliation and, as a result, suffered from discrimination by local society.
>
> Furthermore, Chisso deeply apologizes to all of society... for its regrettable attitude of evading its responsibility and for delaying a solution, as this caused more inconvenience to society.
>
> Frank Upham, *Law and Social Change in Post-War Japan* (New York: Cambridge, 1987), 47–48.

16. Jenks, *Perils of Progress*, 32.
17. Bolstad, "Learning from Japan," 559: "Both the Thalidomide and Minamata cases show that apology is used in Japan not only to restore harmonious relationships to their previous smoothly functioning condition but to actually institute social change. The Minamata victims sought not only compensation, but a new order in which companies would be held accountable for negligent polluting in a nation which was at the time the most polluted in the world. The Minamata litigation resulted in the creation of a special dispute resolution system for the investigation and resolution of environmental pollution cases as well as stricter laws, which transformed Japan into one of the cleanest industrialized countries in the world. The issuing of apologies by the defendants in both cases did not maintain the social order or the status quo. The apologies acknowledged the legitimacy of the plaintiffs' protests, thereby paving the way for a revised social ordering."
18. David Savage and Robert Jackson, "Paula Jones's Lawyers Quit, Citing Disagreement," *L.A. Times*, September 9, 1997, A7.
19. Edmund Andrews, "None Prove So Stubborn as a Giant Spurned; G.M. Never Wavered in Its 4-Year Fight Over Executive Who Defected to VW," *New York Times*, January 11, 1997.
20. Duff finds it "notoriously difficult to give a clear and plausible account of the distinction between civil and criminal law." See Duff, "Legal Punishment."
21. Thomas Ireland and John Ward, *Valuing Children in Litigation: Family and Individual Loss Assessment* (Tucson: Lawyers and Judges Publishing Co., 1995).
22. Simmel, *The Philosophy of Money*, 279.
23. See Ayn Rand, *Atlas Shrugged* (New York: Vintage, 1957), 410–15.
24. See Smith, "Commodification in Law."
25. These issues include a complex range of debates regarding the presuppositions of liberalism; the background conditions of global inequality; commodification as a cause of poverty; objectification and offenses against dignity, exploitation, consent, and coercion; instrumentalizing tendencies; reductionism and identity thinking, concrete particularities, and cognitive errors of economic logic; contested notions of violence and domination; intertwined matters regarding commensurability, fungibility, and homogenization; the expressive force of commodification in law; the "gateway" theory of commodification in law; the role of legal institutions as locations for substantive justice; the state of inherent value and sacredness; the metaphysical status of money; and the features of market cultures and market personalities. See ibid.
26. Pierre Schlag, "The De-Differentiation Problem," *Continental Philosophy Review* 42–1 (2009): 35–62.
27. Ibid., 35.
28. See Twambley, "Mercy and Forgiveness," 85–86.
29. See Cohen, "Advising Clients to Apologize," 1046.
30. Bolstad, "Learning from Japan," 560–61: "American drivers are usually instructed by their insurance companies to say nothing after a fender-bender so as to avoid admitting fault. For American drivers, an apology is out of the question. Conversely, when a fender-bender occurs in Japan, *both* drivers typically emerge from their cars, bow to each other, claim responsibility and apologize. In one instance, when an American living in Japan was involved in a car

accident with a Japanese driver, the American simply exchanged information with the Japanese driver but did not express regret or apologize, consistent with American social custom. The Japanese driver was so enraged by the American's Failure to express regret over the accident that he actually sued him, an action rarely resorted to in Japan."

31. Ibid., 500: "Failure to apologize in Japan increases the likelihood of litigation and other forms of legal sanction."
32. See Bartels, "The Stormy Sea of Apologies," 153, and Cohen, "Advising Clients to Apologize," 1026.
33. Cohen, "Advising Clients to Apologize," 1026–27.
34. Cited in Vines, "Apologising to Avoid Liability," 487.
35. See Cohen, "Advising Clients to Apologize," 1043: "'If I wanted someone to tell me to apologize,' says the client, 'I would have gone to my minister, not my lawyer. What I want from you is to help me win.'"
36. See ibid., 1046.
37. See ibid., 1045.
38. On this general point, see Jean Sternlight, "Lawyers' Representation of Clients in Mediation: Using Economics and Psychology to Structure Advocacy in a Non-Adversarial Setting," *Ohio State Journal of Dispute Resolution* 14 (1999): 271.
39. Cohen, "Advising Clients to Apologize," 1046: "Lawyers derive much income from creating and maintaining litigation. Lawyers generally benefit when disputes escalate. Apologies help bring disputes to an end, and in so doing limit the lawyers' fees. A defendant's lawyer might fail to counsel a client to apologize, for, if an apology occurred, that attorney's hourly fees could end."
40. Richard Willing, "Lawsuits a Volume Business at Wal Mart," *USA Today*, August 13, 2001.
41. For an excellent overview, see Roger Conner and Patricia Jordan, "Never Being Able to Say You're Sorry: Barriers to Apology by Leaders in Group Conflicts," *Law and Contemporary Problems* 72 (2009): 233–82.
42. Ibid., 240–46.
43. See sources collected in ibid., note 47.
44. See ibid., 244.
45. See sources collected in ibid., notes 57–59.
46. See ibid., 246.
47. Of course even within some religious traditions, repentance could be bought through indulgences and similar practices. See *I Was Wrong*, 114–25.
48. Scott Atran and Jeremy Ginges, "How Words Could End a War," *New York Times*, January 24, 2009.
49. Ibid.
50. Ibid.
51. See Abeler, Calaki, Andree, and Basek, "The Power of Apology."
52. Ibid., 5.
53. Ibid., 6.
54. See William Ian Miller, *Faking It* (New York: Cambridge University Press, 2003), 92: "The victim is as often forced by social pressure to forgive no less than the wrongdoer is forced to apologize. Or he forgives because it is embarrassing not to once the wrongdoer has given a colorable apology." See also Risen and

Gilovich, "Target and Observer Differences in the Acceptance of Questionable Apologies," 418–33, and Bennett and Dewberry, "I've Said I'm Sorry, Haven't I?" 10–21.
55. See Bennett and Dewberry, "I've Said I'm Sorry, Haven't I?," 14–16, and Risen and Gilovich, "Target and Observer Differences in the Acceptance of Questionable Apologies," 426.
56. Shartel, "Toro's Mediation Program Challenges Wisdom of Traditional Litigation Model," 10.
57. Ibid., 11.
58. See sources collected and discussion in Cohen, "Apologies and Organizations," 1460–64.
59. Shartel, "Toro's Mediation Program Challenges Wisdom of Traditional Litigation Model," 13.
60. See Cohen, "Apologies and Organizations," 1461.
61. Shartel, "Toro's Mediation Program Challenges Wisdom of Traditional Litigation Model," 13.
62. See Robbennolt, "Apologies and Legal Settlement," 485–86: "When no apology was offered 52% of respondents indicated that they would definitely or probably accept the offer, while 43% would definitely or probably reject the offer and 5% were unsure. When a partial apology was offered, only 35% of respondents were inclined to accept the offer, 25% were inclined to reject it, and 40% indicated that they were unsure. In contrast, when a full apology was offered, 73% of respondents were inclined to accept the offer, with only 13–14% each inclined to reject it or remaining unsure."
63. See sources collected in note 37 of the "Introduction."
64. Woods, *Healing Words*, 3.
65. See Hyman and Schechter, "Mediating Medical Malpractice Lawsuits Against Hospitals." Robbennolt notes methodological concerns regarding this study in "Attorneys, Apologies, and Settlement Negotiation," n. 36.
66. Jiang and Johar, "Babyfaces, Trait Inferences, and Company Evaluations in a PR Crisis."
67. See Benjamin Ho and Elaine Liu, "The Impact of Apology Laws and Medical Malpractice," available at http://www.aeaweb.org/aea/conference/program/retrieve.php?pdfid=375.
68. See sources collected in note 37 of the "Introduction."
69. See Robbennolt, "Apology and Legal Settlement," 485.
70. See ibid., 491.
71. David Studdert, Michelle Mello, Atul Gawande, Troyen Brennan, and Y. Claire Wong, "Disclosure of Medical Injury to Patients: An Improbable Risk Management Strategy," *Health Affairs* 26 (2007): 216.
72. Ibid.
73. Alicia Gallegos, "Massachusetts Hospitals Launch Patient Apology Program," *American Medical News*, May 21, 2012.
74. Ibid.
75. "Law Firm Fees Defy Gravity," *National Law Journal*," December 8, 2008.
76. Suzy Hansen, "The Price of Pain," *Salon*, July 15, 2002.
77. Ibid.
78. See Hearit, *Crisis Management by Apology*, 13.

79. Ibid.
80. Ibid.

Chapter Five: A Practical Framework for Evaluating Apologies in Civil Contexts

1. See Jones, "Apologies and Corporate Governance in the Japanese Context," 305.
2. See Hearit, *Crisis Management by Apology*, 24.
3. Harr, *A Civil Action* and *Erin Brockovich*, dir. by Stephen Soderbergh (2000; Universal Pictures).
4. See Gretchen Morgenson, "Making Them Pay (and Confess)," *New York Times*, January 26, 2013.
5. Mitt Romney, *No Apology: The Case for American Greatness* (New York: St. Martin's Press, 2010). Also recall the words of G. H. W. Bush: "I will never apologize for the United States of America, ever. I don't care what the facts are." Atler, "High Stakes in New Orleans," 15.
6. See "Japan's Official Responses to Reparations," in *When Sorry Isn't Enough: The Controversy over Apologies and Reparations for Human Injustice*, ed. Roy Brooks (New York: New York University Press, 1999), 127–28. On Abe's subsequent denials, see "Sex Slave Denial Angers S. Korea," *BBC News*, March 3, 2007.
7. See *I Was Wrong*, 78–80.
8. Morgenson, "Making Them Pay (and Confess)."
9. See ibid.
10. Pettigrove, "Hannah Arendt and Collective Forgiving," *Journal of Social Philosophy* 37-4 (2007): 483–500.
11. "Thalidomide Apology Insulting, Campaigners Say," *BBC News*, September 1, 2012.
12. Cohen, "Legislating Apologies," 854.
13. "Goldman Regrets 'Market Euphoria' that Led to Crisis," *New York Times*, June 16, 2009.
14. Matt Taibbi, "The Greatest Non-Apology of All Time," *True/Slant*, June 18, 2009.
15. Ibid.
16. Ibid.
17. See John Searle, *The Social Construction of Reality* (New York: Free Press, 1995), and Michael Bratman, *Faces of Intention* (New York: Cambridge University Press, 1999):109–29.
18. See Margaret Gilbert, *On Social Facts* (Princeton: Princeton University Press, 1992).
19. Frederick Engels, *The Condition of the Working Class in England*, trans. W. O. Henderson and W. H. Chaloner (Palo Alto: Stanford University Press, 1958), 108–09.
20. Joel Feinberg, "Collective Responsibility," in *Collective Responsibility*, eds. May and Hoffman, 54.
21. Ibid.
22. Ibid., 60–61 (italics in original).

23. See Robin Topping, "Attorneys Balance 'Safe' with 'Sorry,'" *New York Newsday*, February 4, 2004.
24. Tanick and Ayling, "Alternative Dispute Resolution by Apology," 22.
25. Levi, "The Role of Apology in Mediation," 1188.
26. Ibid.
27. Cohen, "Advising Clients to Apologize," 1030.
28. See discussion in *I Was Wrong*, 99.
29. For an excellent treatment of the complex subject, see Markus Dubber's *The Sense of Justice: Empathy in Law and Punishment* (New York: NYU Press, 2006). For additional treatments of empathy from diverse theoretical orientations, see Karsten Stueber, *Rediscovering Empathy Agency, Folk Psychology, and the Human Sciences* (Cambridge: MIT Press, 2006); N. Eisenberg, "Empathy-related Emotional Responses, Altruism, and Their Socialization," in *Visions of Compassion: Western Scientists and Tibetan Buddhists Examine Human Nature*, eds. R. J. Davidson and A. Harrington (London: Oxford University Press, 2002), 131–64; J. Håkansson and H. Montgomery, "Empathy as an Interpersonal Phenomenon," *Journal of Social and Personal Relationships*, 20-3 (2003): 267–84; Stephanie Preston and Frans B. M. de Waal, "Empathy: Its Ultimate and Proximate Bases," *Behavioral and Brain Sciences* 25 (2002): 1–72; M. L. Hoffman, *Empathy and Moral Development* (New York: Cambridge University Press, 2000); and N. Eisenberg and J. Strayer eds., *Empathy and its Development* (Cambridge: Cambridge University Press, 1987).
30. See Stephen Darwell, *Welfare and Rational Care* (Princeton: Princeton University Press, 2004), 3; Michael Stocker and Elizabeth Hegeman, *Valuing Emotions* (Cambridge: Cambridge University Press, 1996), 214–17; and Nussbaum, "Equity and Mercy," *Philosophy and Public Affairs* 22 (1993): 83–125.
31. Studdert et al., "Disclosure of Medical Injury to Patients," 221.
32. See sources collected in Orenstein, "Apology Excepted," note 260.
33. See Cohen, "Apology and Organizations," 1458–59: "Often a 'vicious cycle' exists where following an error, an injurer (e.g., physician) wants to apologize but refrains from doing so out of fear of legal liability, and it is precisely this absence of an apology that triggers the lawsuit."
34. See ibid., 1461.
35. See Woods, *Healing Words*, 26: "[F]iscal rewards are a natural byproduct of authentic apology."
36. See, for example, the discussion of such strategies in Stephen Goldberg, Eric Green, and Frank Sander, "Saying You're Sorry," *Negotiation Journal* 3 (1987): 222–23.
37. See Cohen, "Advising Clients to Apologize," 1066: "While some may argue that telling people that they may receive financial benefits from apologizing is ethically questionable, I do not."
38. See Bolstad, "Learning from Japan," 576–77, and ibid., 1065.
39. Patel and Reinsch, "Companies Can Apologize," 22.
40. See ibid., 23: "Thus, one potential strategy would be to issue a sympathy statement at the initiation of any news of claim of wrongdoing. The statement can be structured to express only sympathy, allowing the corporation to wait until a later stage to make a full apology that admits fault and expresses remorse. If such a full apology is to be made, a mediation session preceded by a confidentiality

agreement may often be the best place for it, since apologies made in that forum are protected by federal law."
41. Ibid., 23.
42. Ibid., 22: "If a finding of guilt is inevitable, the corporation's focus should be on mitigating the damages of the act, and minimizing settlement and/or litigation costs and awards."
43. See Cohen, "Advising Clients to Apologize," 1060.
44. Pavlick, "Apology and Mediation," 863.
45. Ibid.
46. Cornell, Warne, and Eining, "The Use of Remedial Tactics in Negligence Litigation," 767.
47. Pavlick, "Apology and Mediation," 863.
48. Cornell, Warne, and Eining, "The Use of Remedial Tactics in Negligence Litigation," 767. See also Levi, "The Role of Apology in Mediation," 1188: "[R]ather than discouraging apology altogether, lawyers protective of their clients' interests might serve those interests by encouraging clients to apologize short of admitting liability. For example, lawyers might allow their clients to express empathy and regret while avoiding formulations that would make liability undeniable, such as 'I neglected my duty,' 'my actions caused your injury,' or 'if only I hadn't done X, you would never have been injured.'"
49. Pavlick, "Apology and Mediation," 863. See also Cohen, "Advising Clients to Apologize," 1058: "A more cautious approach would have been to write a note expressing sympathy for the injury without admitting fault ('Dear Ms. Reardon, I write to express my wishes that you are feeling well following our accident several days ago. Sincerely yours, Mr. Trendle.') and to wait until later to admit fault (but not assume liability), ideally in a 'safe' channel such as mediation. In the off event that Ms. Reardon's injuries proved severe, this would pose less of a risk, albeit what I would assess as a very slight risk, of voiding his insurance coverage."
50. Kanazawa, "Apologies and Lunch," 32.
51. Ibid.
52. Woods, *Healing Words*, 42.
53. See "Empathy vs. Apology," available at http://sorryworkssite.bondwaresite.com/empathy-vs-apology-cms-32.
54. "5 Key Facts about Disclosure," available at http://sorryworkssite.bondwaresite.com/five-key-disclosure-facts-cms-33.
55. Ibid.
56. Ibid.
57. "PEARL – Program for Early Assessment and Resolution of Loss," *PEARL*, available at http://src.stanfordhospital.org/products/pearl.html.
58. *Taft Solutions*, "Case Study: Healthcare," available at http://www.taftsolutions.com/healthcare-case-study/. See also "PEARL – Program for Early Assessment and Resolution of Loss": "PEARL distinguishes between anticipated or unpreventable adverse outcomes (known complications) and preventable unanticipated outcomes. In both cases, the policy is full disclosure to patients. However, if the adverse outcome was preventable, PEARL recognizes that the patient is entitled to 'full disclosure, apology, compensation, and conversation about the lessons learned – what will be different so that others are not similarly harmed.'"

59. *Taft Solutions*, "Case Study: Healthcare."
60. "PEARL – Program for Early Assessment and Resolution of Loss."
61. Ibid.
62. *Taft Solutions*, "Case Study: Healthcare."
63. "Empathy vs. Apology."
64. *Citizens United v. Federal Election Commission*, 558 U.S. 310 (2010).
65. See National Conference of State Legislatures, "Medical Malpractice Tort Reform," February 8, 2007, available at http://www.ncsl.org/standcomm/sclaw/medmaloverview.htm. In addition to the literature cited in note 37 discussing apologies in civil law generally, for examples of further specific discussions of "safe apology legislation" see Runnels, "Apologies All Around"; Vines, "Apologies and Civil Liability in the UK"; Bender, "'I'm Sorry" Laws and Medical liability"; Edward Dauer, "Apology in the Aftermath of Injury: Colorado's 'I'm Sorry' Law," *Colorado Lawyer* (April 2005): 47–55; C. Sparkman, "Legislating Apology in the Context of Medical Mistakes," 263; Latif, "Apologetic Justice"; Bartels, "The Stormy Sea of Apologies"; Taft, "Apology Subverted"; Cohen, "Advising Clients to Apologize"; Cohen, "Nagging Problem: Advising the Client Who Wants to Apologize"; Cohen, "Legislating Apologies: The Pros and Cons"; Keeva, "Does Law Mean Never Having to Say You're Sorry?"; Orenstein, "Apology Excepted"; and Rehm and Beatty, "Legal Consequences of Apologizing."
66. Jennifer Robbennolt compiled many of these statutes, and I am indebted to her findings. The subsequent notes draw from her notations in "Attorneys, Apologies, and Settlement Negotiation" as well as "Apologies and Settlement Levers." See Fla. Stat. § 90.4026(2) ("The portion of statements, writings, or benevolent gestures expressing sympathy or a general sense of benevolence relating to the pain, suffering, or death of a person involved in an accident and made to that person or to the family of that person shall be inadmissible as evidence in a civil action. A statement of fault, however, which is part of, or in addition to, any of the above shall be admissible pursuant to this section"). See also Cal. Evid. Code § 1160(a); Tenn. R. Evid. § 409.1; Tex. Civ. Prac. & Rem. § 18.061; Wash. Rev. Code § 5.66.010(1).
67. See Ariz. Rev. Stat. Ann. § 12–2605 (2005): "Any statement, affirmation, gesture or conduct expressing apology, responsibility, liability, sympathy, commiseration, condolence, compassion or a general sense of benevolence that was made by a health care provider . . . to the patient, a relative of the patient, the patient's survivors or a health care decision maker for the patient and that relates to the discomfort, pain, suffering, injury or death of the patient as the result of the unanticipated outcome of medical care is inadmissible as evidence of an admission of liability or as evidence of an admission against interest."; Colo. Rev. Stat. § 13–25–135 (2003): protecting statements "expressing apology, fault, sympathy, commiseration, condolence, compassion, or a general sense of benevolence"; Conn. Gen. Stat. § 52–184(d) (2005); Ga. Code Ann. § 24-3-37.1 (2006): protecting statements "expressing benevolence, regret, apology, sympathy, commiseration, condolence, compassion, mistake, error, or a general sense of benevolence"; S.C. Code Ann. § 19-1-190 (2006).
68. See Colo. Rev. Stat. § 13–25–135; Ga. Code Ann. § 24-3-37.1: "In any civil action brought by an alleged victim of an unanticipated outcome of medical

care, or in any arbitration proceeding related to such civil action, any and all statements, affirmations, gestures, or conduct expressing apology, fault, sympathy, commiseration, condolence, compassion, or a general sense of benevolence which are made by a health care provider or an employee of a health care provider to the alleged victim, a relative of the alleged victim, or a representative of the alleged victim and which related to the discomfort, pain, suffering, injury, or death of the alleged victim as the result of the unanticipated outcome of medical care shall be inadmissible as evidence of an admission of liability or as evidence of an admission against interest."

69. See Ohio Rev. Code Ann. § 2317.43; Okla. Stat. Ann. tit. 63, § 1-1708.1H; Or. Rev. Stat. § 677.082; Wyo. Stat. Ann. § 1-1-130.
70. H.R. 4, 78th Leg., Reg. Sess. (Tex. 2003) (March 28, 2003, version).
71. See, e.g., Colo. Rev. Stat. § 13-25-135; Ga. Code Ann. § 24-3-37.1; 735 Ill. Comp. Stat. 5/8-1901; Ohio Rev. Code Ann. § 2317.43; Okla. Stat. Ann. tit. 63, § 1-1708.1H; Or. Rev. Stat. § 677.082; Wyo. Stat. Ann. § 1-1-130.
72. See Robbennolt, "What we Know and Don't Know about the Role of Apologies in Resolving Health Care Disputes," 1011.
73. See ibid, 1011-12: "The American College of Physicians' Ethics Manual provides that 'physicians should disclose to patients information about procedural or judgment errors made in the course of care if such information is material to the patient's well-being. Errors do not necessarily constitute improper, negligent, or unethical behavior, but failure to disclose them may.' Similarly, the American Medical Association (AMA) instructs physicians that when 'a patient suffers significant medical complications that may have resulted from the physician's mistake or judgment, . . . the physician is ethically required to inform the patient of all the facts necessary to ensure understanding of what has occurred.' Moreover, the AMA counsels that '[c]oncern regarding the legal liability which might result following truthful disclosure should not affect the physician's honesty with a patient.'"
74. See, for example, discussions in Cohen, "Advising Clients to Apologize," 1034-35; Ebert, "Attorneys, Tell Your Clients to Say They're Sorry," 342; Orenstein, "Apology Excepted"; and Pearlmutter, "Physician Apologies and General Admissions of Fault," 692.
75. New South Wales Civil Liability Act of 2002, Sections 68-9.
76. Ibid.
77. Ibid. The Apology Act 2006 of British Columbia parallels the New South Wales legislation. See also Howard Kushner, "The Power of an Apology: Removing the Legal Barriers," a Special Report by the Ombudsman of the Province of British Columbia, Special Report Number 27 to the Legislative Assembly of British Columbia (2006), and Alter, "Apologising for Serious Wrongdoing."
78. Robbennolt gathered several sources claiming that safe apology legislation would advance the objective of tort reform. See Robbennolt, "Apologies and Legal Settlement," note 214. These sources include Cal. Assembly Comm. on Judiciary, Comment to Cal. Evid. Code 1160: "The author introduced this bill in an attempt to reduce lawsuits and encourage settlements by fostering the use of apologies in connection with accident-related injuries or death."; S.B. 1477, 21st leg. (Haw. 2001): legislation will allow parties to "reach out to others in a humane way without fear of having such a communication used subsequently

as an admission of liability"; and Tennessee Advisory Comm. Comment on Tenn. R. Evid. § 409.1: legislation was "designed to encourage the settlement of lawsuits." For media coverage, see Arthur Kane, "GOP Pushes Tort Reform in Colorado," *Denver Post*, April 6, 2003, at B4; Peggy Lowe, "'Sorry' Bill Advances," *Rocky Mountain News*, April 2, 2003, at 22A; Al Lewis, "Malpractice Measure is 'Sorry' Protection," *Denver Post*, April 13, 2003, at K1; and also the materials at SorryWorks!, which claim many benefits of apologies for medicine.

79. For an exposé of tort reform generally, see *Hot Coffee*, dir. by Susan Saladoff (2011: HBO Films).
80. Woods, *Healing Words*, 3.
81. Cohen, "Legislating Apologies," 856.
82. See, for example, S.B. 1477, 21st leg. (Haw. 2001).
83. See Cohen, "Legislating Apologies," 856–57.
84. H.R. 4, 78th Leg., Reg. Sess. (Tex. 2003) (March 28, 2003, version).
85. See Taft, "Apology Subverted," note 94: "Trials can be bifurcated so that liability can be considered separately from damages. This means that the admission of wrongdoing can be made while the offender maintains the opportunity to dispute differing perceptions of the consequences of the wrongful act. Some might argue that conceding liability while contesting damages is the equivalent of a botched apology. I disagree. A botched apology overlooks fault; it refuses to accept responsibility. In an admission of liability, the offender accepts fault and responsibility for the wrongful act. By separating liability issues from those regarding damages, the offender says only that he disagrees with the quantitative assessment of the harm caused. In accepting liability, the wrongdoer is 'owning up' to the fact that harm has been caused by a moral transgression, and by trying damages, he asks help from outsiders in evaluating the cost of that harm." See also ibid., 1156: "If apology is to be authentic, the offender must clearly admit his wrongdoing; he must truly repent if the apology is to be considered a moral act. When an offender says, 'I'm sorry,' he must be willing to accept all of the consequences-legal and otherwise-that flow from his violation. If a person is truly repentant, he will not seek to distance himself from the consequences that attach to his action; rather, he will accept them as a part of the performance of a moral act and the authentic expression of contrition."
86. See, for example, Orenstein, "Apology Excepted."
87. Hearit, *Crisis Management by Apology*, 135.
88. See http://theyesmen.org/.
89. See discussion in Cohen, "Apology and Organizations," 1478.
90. See *I Was Wrong*, 211.
91. Jay Rayner, *Eating Crow* (New York: Simon and Schuster, 2004), 254.
92. Elisabeth Rosenthal, "For a Fee, This Chinese Firm Will Beg Pardon for Anyone," *New York Times*, January 3, 2001.
93. Ibid.
94. See John Burns, "German Drug Maker Apologizes to Victims of Thalidomide," *New York Times*, September 1, 2012.
95. Sir Harold Evans, "Thalidomide's Big Lie Overshadows Corporate Apology," *Reuters*, September 12, 2012.
96. Burns, "German Drug Maker Apologizes to Victims of Thalidomide."

97. Ibid.
98. Ibid.
99. See discussion in Jones, "Apologies and Corporate Governance in the Japanese Context," 314.
100. See Mihaela Mihai, "When the State Says 'Sorry': State Apologies as Exemplary Political Judgments," *Journal of Political Philosophy* 21-2 (2013): 200-20, and Ernesto Verdeja, "Official Apologies in the Aftermath of Political Violence," *Metaphilosophy* 41-4 (2010): 563-81.
101. "Chick-fil-A: Who We Are," August 15, 2012, available at http://www.chick-fil-a.com/media/pdf/who-we-are.pdf.
102. Tiffany Tsu, "Is Chick-fil-A Anti-Gay Marriage? 'Guilty as Charged,' Leader Says," *Los Angeles Times*, July 18, 2012.
103. The public relations community is onto this point. See Roy Hutcheson, "How to Deliver a Good Corporate Apology," *PRWeek*, January 4, 2013.
104. Timothy George, *Minamata: Pollution and the Struggle for Democracy in Postwar Japan* (Cambridge: Harvard University Press, 2001).
105. See my "Questions for a Reluctant Jurisprudence of Alterity," *Essays on Levinas and Law: A Mosaic*, ed. Desmond Manderson (New York: Palgrave Macmillan, 2008), 55-75, and "Adorno vs. Levinas: Evaluating Points of Contention," *Continental Philosophy Review* 40/3 (2007): 275-306.
106. Emmanuel Levinas, *Totality and Infinity*, trans. Alphonso Lingis (Pittsburgh: Duquesne University Press, 1969), 40.
107. See discussion in *I Was Wrong*, 74-80.
108. Raymond Cohen, "A Time to Heal: Pope John Paul II's Penitential Gesture at Jerusalem's Western Wall," in *Public Apology Between Ritual and Regret*, eds. Daniel Cuypers, Daniel Janssen, Jacques Haers, and Barbara Segaert (Amsterdam: Rodopi, 2013), 65-78.
109. Roger Cohen, "The Polish Seminary Student and the Jewish Girl He Saved," *New York Times*, April 6, 2005.
110. Ibid.
111. Thompson, "The Apology Paradox," 476.
112. Cited in John Borneman, *Political Crime and the Memory of Loss* (Bloomington: Indiana University Press, 2011), 50.
113. See Cohen, "Apology and Organizations," 1461-64.
114. Cohen, "Advising Clients to Apologize," 1038. See also the forthcoming conference proceedings in the *Pepperdine Dispute Resolution Law Journal* from the symposium on "Rescuing Relationships: A Symposium on Apology, Forgiveness, and Reconciliation."
115. See Cohen, "Apology and Organizations," 1036-37: "Mediation offers a second possible avenue toward a 'safe' apology, and here the protection is much stronger. As mediation confidentiality provisions are created by state statutes and court rules, they vary widely; however, where they do afford protection, often the protection they afford is quite strong. Accordingly, lawyers must know the particular mediation statute applicable in a case. As most lawyers are repeat players in one locale, this should not be burdensome."
116. See Patel and Reinsch, "Companies Can Apologize," 18: "[B]y preemptive measure and apology, corporations have become increasingly able to avoid class certification and to avoid severe financial crisis. Revealing its blunders

before others do so can put a corporation in the position to shape public responses. It also provides an opportunity to initiate defensive measures by providing context of history and future commitments to responsibility. Thus, an apology can help a corporation to preempt accusations and negative publicity, diffuse public anger, and even prevent litigation."

117. Lazare, *On Apology*, 132.
118. See sources collected in Delgado and Stefancic, "Apologize and Move On?," 106–07: "One of the most insistent critiques of alternative dispute resolution holds that deformalized justice exacerbates power differentials among disputants."
119. See Cohen's dialogue in "Legislating Apologies," 857: "Sophisticated defendants are going take advantage of naive injured parties through these laws. They'll issue apologies knowing that there's no real risk involved, but naive injured parties will think these apologies are meaningful – that they do involve risk. Injured parties will think the injurers are putting their necks on the line when in fact they aren't."
120. See *I Was Wrong*, 75–77.
121. Richard Wray, "Deepwater Horizon Oil Spill: BP Gaffes in Full," *Guardian*, July 27, 2010.
122. Masazumi Harada, *Minamata Disease*, trans. Tsushima Sachie and Timothy George (Minamata Disease Patient's Alliance, 2004), 56.
123. Waller, "Sincere Apology without Moral Responsibility," 459.
124. See Leape, "Error in Medicine."
125. Waller, "Sincere Apology without Moral Responsibility," 462.
126. Waller, "Against Moral Responsibility," 199.
127. Hearit, *Crisis Management by Apology*, 136.
128. Ibid., 148.
129. Elaine Miller Holstein, "... And Still No Honest Apology Her Son Was Killed At Kent State," *New York Times*, May 4, 1990: "A 1974 criminal trial in which we contended that the students' civil rights had been infringed was thrown out of court. Our civil suit in 1975 ended in defeat when the jury found no one responsible for the deaths and injuries. We appealed and were granted a new trial. In 1979, our battles finally ended in a financial settlement. When settlement was first suggested, I was outraged: this case was not about money. We wanted a judicial finding or an admission by the defendants that they bore responsibility for the killings. We demanded a statement of apology. Several days were spent negotiating this apology in a series of scenes more appropriate to writing a movie contract than to our struggle for wording that would clearly express the defendants' acceptance of blame. They kept hedging. The final version was a watered-down pseudo-apology that, expressing deep regret, stated, 'Better ways must be found to deal with these confrontations.' I think we accepted it in part out of sheer exhaustion. (I received $15,000 and paid no court costs.)"
130. Lazare, *On Apology*, 131.
131. *Hawaii v. Office of Hawaiian Affairs*, 129 S. Ct. 1436 (2009).
132. Cited in "The Supreme Court, 2008 Term: Leading Cases," *Harvard Law Review* 123 (2009): 310.
133. Ibid.

134. Joint Resolution of Nov. 23, 1993, Pub. L. No. 103-150, 107 Stat. 1510-13.
135. *Office of Haw. Affairs v. Hous. & Cmty. Dev. Corp. of Haw.*, 177 P.3d 884, 922 (Haw. 2008).
136. Transcript of Oral Argument at 6, *Hawaii*, 129 S. Ct. 1436 (2009) (No. 07-1372), 2009 WL 462660.
137. As the editors of *Harvard Law Review* put it: "We apologize for stealing your land, but it's still our land." "The Supreme Court, 2008 Term," 310.
138. See Alexandra Herfroy-Mischler, "Post-Transitional Apology: Expressing Contrition Whilst Addressing the Holocaust Transitional Justice Failure," in *Public Apology Between Ritual and Regret*, 167-88.
139. Eric Yamamoto and Susan Serrano, "Healing Racial Wounds? The Final Report of South Africa's Truth and Reconciliation Commission," in *When Sorry Isn't Enough*, 498.
140. See "Commodification in Law."
141. 131 S. Ct. 2541 (2011).
142. Peterson, "The Failure of the Hong Kong Court of Appeal to Recognize and Remedy Disability Discrimination."
143. John Poynder, ed., *Literary Extracts from English and Other Works 1* (1814), 268.
144. See Christopher Stone, *Where the Law Ends: The Social Control of Corporate Behavior* (New York: Harper and Row, 1975); David Risser, "Punishing Corporations: A Proposal," *Business and Professional Ethics Journal* 8-3 (1989): 83-92; and Peter French, "The Hester Prynne Sanction," *Business and Professional Ethics Journal* 4-2 (1985): 19-32.
145. Andrew Jenks, *Perils of Progress: Environmental Disasters in the 20th Century* (Upper Saddle River, New Jersey: Pearson, 2010), 32.
146. Gretchen Morgenson, "Paying the Price, but Often Deducting It," *New York Times*, January 12, 2013.
147. See Phineas Baxandall and Ryan Pierannunzi, "Subsidizing Bad Behavior: How Corporate Legal Settlements for Harming the Public Become Lucrative Tax Write Offs, with Recommendations for Reform," *U.S. PIRG Education Fund* (2013), 1.
148. Morgenson, "Paying the Price, but Often Deducting It."
149. Baxandall and Pierannunzi, "Subsidizing Bad Behavior," 4.
150. Ibid., 6.
151. See Morgenson, "Paying the Price, but Often Deducting It."
152. See Morgenson, "Making Them Pay (and Confess)": "The S.E.C. routinely lets companies and individuals settle cases against them without admitting or denying its findings. This lets bad actors pretend that they've done nothing wrong. It also makes it harder for investors to mount successful lawsuits against them. Regulators say this is the best approach. The practice, they contend, helps the S.E.C. and other agencies avoid costly, time-consuming litigation that would tax already-stretched resources. Quick settlements, rather than long trials, mean victims get restitution faster. And there's always the possibility that the S.E.C. might lose in court. But these no-admission settlements can be little more than a wrist slap – and certainly do not qualify as punishment. Most financial penalties end up being paid for by the company's shareholders or its insurance policies. That's not much of a deterrent."

153. For a discussion of the difficulties of being "certified" as a recognized victim of Minamata disease, see Harada, *Minamata Disease*, 156–57.
154. See Charles Perrow, *Normal Accidents: Living with High-Risk Technologies* (Princeton: Princeton University Press, 1999), 69–70: "Fourth-party victims potentially constitute the most serious class of victims. Chemical or radioactive contamination of land areas could have far-reaching effects upon the health of future generations in other ways, including adding the burden of lifetime care and treatment of victims. Future generations carry the burden; the present generation reaps whatever rewards there may be from the activity."
155. See Alan Ray, "Native American Identity and the Challenge of Kennewick Man," *Temple Law Review* 79 (2006): 89–154.
156. See, for example, the essays in Jon Miller and Rahul Kumar, eds., *Reparations: Interdisciplinary Inquiries* (New York: Oxford University Press, 2007).
157. Consider Patel and Reinsch, "Companies Can Apologize," 18: "[A] corporation may also re-integrate itself with the community of consumers by offering an expression of remorse of sympathy to those harmed by its actions."
158. See ibid., 15–16: "Perhaps the most essential, intangible asset a corporation possesses is its public image. Accurately assessing the public's view of a corporation is vital when the corporation faces the prospect of defending a lawsuit in court. And, furthermore, corporate executives should be concerned not only about the potential impact of litigation on business operations but also about the potential impact of litigation on corporate reputation."
159. Ibid., 16: "A corporate apology can be an important element in perceived goodness because issuing an apology (or refusing to do so) can affect the opinions of citizens (potential customers and potential jurors) with regard to the fundamental ethics of a company." See also ibid.: "[T]he company's current image (based on perceptions of past behavior) can either help or hinder the company in future litigation by affecting the opinions of judge and jury. In fact, in complex civil cases, corporate image may be one of the most important factors influencing the juror's ultimate decision."
160. Cohen, "Apology and Organizations," 1476: "Legal expenses paid in compensation of injuries will typically appear on most organizations' balance sheets. However, many of the non-pecuniary benefits of apology (e.g., to organizational morale, loyalty, communication, productivity, reputation, and customer loyalty) will not typically appear on an organization's balance sheet. Hence, organizations that overly focus on short-term profits as reflected in balance sheets may tend to neglect apology. In some ways, a policy of apologizing for errors is like an investment: though the immediate price may be clear, the long run economic benefits, though real, are less defined. If the current CEO cares primarily about short-run profits, he may 'underinvest' in an approach of apology that may financially benefit a future CEO."
161. "First Nations and Cultural Groups Reject Political Apologies: Leaders Reject B.C. Liberal's Plan for 'Easy Wins' with Ethnic Groups," *CBC News*, March 7, 2013.
162. Ibid.
163. Ibid.
164. "Head Tax Apology Advocates Tell B.C. Premier Not to Delay," *Canadian Press*, March 10, 2013.

165. See Robbennolt, "Attorneys, Apologies, and Settlement Negotiation," 351: considering "how attorneys respond to apologies offered in litigation as they advise claimants about settlement, and compares the reactions of attorneys to those of lay litigants." See also Sternlight, "Lawyers' Representation of Clients in Mediation," 321–22: "Because the attorney does not share her client's nonmonetary interests, she may regard these interests as having little or no value. She therefore may not present them or certainly not emphasize them as part of the settlement package. Yet, if these nonmonetary interests are important to the client, their absence may well prevent a settlement from being reached. Some examples should help to clarify the point. A client in an employment discrimination case might seek not only monetary compensation but also nonmonetary relief including an apology, establishment of a training program intended to discourage future discrimination, or reinstatement. More generally, the client may seek dignity and respect. Yet, these nonmonetary goals likely have little appeal for the attorney who, after all, cannot take a one third contingency of an apology."
166. See Melissa Nelkin, "Negotiation and Psychoanalysis: If I'd Wanted to Learn About Feelings, I Wouldn't Have Gone to Law School," *Journal of Legal Education* 46 (1996): 420–29, 423: "Clients inevitably suffer when their lawyers insist on divorcing the professional encounter from the emotional underpinnings of the dispute involved. Client dissatisfaction with legal representation often results from the lawyer's inability to see the client's emotional self as anything but an impediment to sensible, rational management of the legal problem."
167. Joel Bakan, *The Corporation: The Pathological Pursuit of Profit and Power* (New York: Free Press, 2004).
168. See Hutcheson, "How to Deliver a Good Corporate Apology": "It can be good to apologize, even if you haven't done anything wrong. Showing concern for another person's problems always helps. Airline ticket agents don't cause storms that delay flights, but they can ease passenger frustration with an apology and a caring attitude. Frustration can easily escalate to anger if a company appears to be oblivious to the problems and indignities faced by customers, suppliers, and other stakeholders."
169. See Pettigrove's discussion of these possibilities in the context of collective forgiveness in "Hannah Arendt and Collective Forgiving," 492–93.
170. See Cohen, "Advising Clients to Apologize," 1171: "[I]f a plaintiff settles because she's emotionally fulfilled by an apology, isn't she being duped out of her legal entitlement – an entitlement that the apology itself makes concrete?"; O'Hara and Yarn, "On Apology and Consilience," 1186: "[A]pology can be used as a tool for organizations to strategically take advantage of individual victims' instincts to forgive in the face of apology"; and O'Hara, "Apology and Thick Trust."
171. Etzioni, *Repentance*, 34.

Concluding Call for Collaboration

1. Alan Mackay, *A Dictionary of Scientific Quotations* (London: Taylor and Francis, 1991), 35.

2. See, for example, discussions in Christian Knütel, *Tätige Reue im Zivilrecht* (Berlin: Duncker and Humblot, 2000); Laura Feldmanis, "Abandonment of Attempt to Commit Offence: Challenge to Penal Law Principle?" *Juridica* 2 (2013): 128–38; Oznur Sevdiren, *Alternatives to Imprisonment in England and Wales, Germany and Turkey: A Comparative Study* (New York: Springer, 2011); Olga Semukhina and Michael Reynolds, "Plea Bargaining Implementation and Acceptance in Modern Russia: A Disconnect Between the Legal Institutions and the Citizens," *International Criminal Justice Review* 19 (2009): 400–32, 417; and Marianne Löschnig-Gspandl and Michael Kilchling, "Victim-Offender Mediation and Victim Compensation in Austria and Germany – Stocktaking and Perspectives for Future Research," *European Journal of Crime, Criminal Law and Criminal Justice* 5-1 (1997): 58–78.
3. Murphy, *Punishment and the Moral Emotions*, 39.

Index

Abu Ghraib, 139
accidents, 5, 6, 8, 13, 17, 20, 22, 59, 138, 142, 187, 205, 244, 251, 267, 268, 269, 270, 272, 291
Adorno. T. W. A., 303
adversarial justice systems, 9, 10, 54, 105, 109, 118, 190, 191, 201, 204, 215, 228, 229, 230, 245, 251, 256, 263, 273, 276, 278, 323, 324
age of offender, 212. *See* Juvenile offender
aging out, 212
Alcoholics Anonymous, 3, 100, 181, 220
Alexander, Michelle, 40, 121–22
alienation, 2, 61, 82, 84, 94, 130, 132, 134
American Bar Association, 97, 224
Andersen, Anne, 245
Anderson, Anne, 245
anger management, 6, 7
Apartheid, 40, 120
apology reductions, 49, 98, 99, 100, 101, 103, 104, 105, 109, 111, 113, 114, 116, 117, 118, 123, 125, 127, 129, 131, 132, 133, 134, 136, 137, 145, 147, 148, 150, 155, 156, 159, 166, 169, 171, 173, 181, 186, 190, 193, 194, 201, 204, 220, 221, 222, 223, 224, 225, 227, 229, 230, 231, 233, 234, 235, 236, 259
apology, definition
  elements of categorical apology, 17–23
appealing determinations of remorse, 3, 196, 200
Aquinas, St. Thomas, 150, 165
Aristotle, 81, 104, 165
Atran, Scott, 254

Bailey, Donna, 243–45, 253, 257, 260, 265, 286, 296, 309, 326

bar admissions, 97, 225
Beccaria, Cesare, 41
becoming apologetic, 175–77
Beebe, William, 1–4, 6, 7, 8, 16, 58, 72–74, 81, 94, 95, 97, 99–101, 102, 103, 112, 114, 148, 159, 160, 161, 163, 197, 198, 206, 208, 211, 217, 218, 228, 229, 238, 332
Bennett, Christopher, 59, 63–65, 67, 70, 71, 90, 93, 97, 111, 112, 168, 172, 181, 183, 201, 223, 351, 354, 359, 360, 361, 371
Bentham, Jeremy, 42, 117, 124
Bhopal, India, 286
Bibas, Stephanos, 106, 107, 216
Bichlbaum, Andy, 286
big data, 330
Blackstone, William, 10
blame, accepting, 73, 74, 77, 85, 93, 104, 123, 136–45, 157, 204–05, 244, 293, 295. *See* proximate causation
  as liberal ideology, 136–45
  as not element of apologies, 277
  blaming the dead, 295
  collective blame, 35, 266–73
Blankfein, Lloyd, 267, 268, 297, 317, 320
Bonger, Willem, 130, 131
brainwashing, Maoist, 56
Braithwaite, John, 82, 84, 103, 105, 106, 107–11, 167, 174, 222
Brandt, Willy, 307
Bridgestone/Firestone, 243–44, 267
British Petroleum, 16, 139, 141, 310, 321. *See* Deepwater Horizon
Brown v. Board of Education, 120, 143
Bryant, Kobe, 219
Bush, George W., 283, 284

397

Calhoun, Cheshire, 234
Calhoun, Chesire, 380
capital punishment, 10, 56, 59, 85, 86, 113, 163, 167, 169, 222, 231, 232
capitalism, 119, 120, 124, 130, 137, 139, 141, 250, 266, 269. See Marx Karl
Chik-fil-A, 299
children, ordering to apologize, 74–83
Chinese head tax controversy, 324
Chisso Corporation, 36, 246, 247, 263, 265, 268, 287, 291, 295, 297, 301, 302, 305, 306, 311, 312, 313, 315, 318, 320, 322, 328, 381
Choi, Dai-Kwon, 90
civil discovery process, 265
class, 47, 57, 59, 60, 61, 111, 119, 122, 123, 125, 133, 134, 136, 145–47, 192, 212, 236, 276, 286, 288, 302, 308
Clinton, Bill, 26, 27, 29, 140, 141, 247, 261, 302
Cohen, Jonathan, 267
Cohen, Raymond, 303
collective apologies, 9, 14, 15, 34–37, 139, 140, 143, 144, 145, 243, 249, 259, 260, 261, 270, 273, 289, 291, 295, 303, 304
colonialism, 120
commodification, 127, 129, 250, 318, 325, 382
confidentiality agreements, 13, 255, 266, 277, 308, 309, 310, 315, 326
consensus, 35, 197, 246, 258, 260, 261, 262, 270, 292, 293, 305, 325, 328
consequentialism, 7, 14, 46, 49, 53, 67, 71–72, 74, 81, 82, 84, 86, 87, 88, 92, 97, 99, 105, 112, 114, 117, 124, 153, 156, 174, 182, 186, 187, 225, 319, 370, 371
consistency. See proportionality
Continental Airlines, 12
contingency fee arrangements, 252, 260, 323
corporations, apologies from, 10, 11, 12, 84, 135, 140, 141, 244, 256, 257, 258, 267, 288, 289, 300, 306, 314, 319, 321, 324, 326, 327. See Toro Company, Chisso Corporation
court-ordered apologies, definition of, 53
Currie, Elliot, 47, 118, 126, 127, 147, 363

Darfur, 141
Davis, Angela, 47, 125
de Cervantes, Miguel, 156

dead, apologies from the, 295
dead, apologies to the, 60, 231, 302, 304, 318, 352
deathbed apologies, 21, 231, 246, 311
Deepwater Horizon, 35, 122, 248, 310, 321. See British Petroleum
delegating apologies, 287, 288, 289, 294, 300, 320, 326, 328
demeanor evidence, 214, 223
Dennett, Dan, 138, 164
Dershowitz, Alan, 26, 34
desert, 45, 46, 67, 119, 149, 152, 153, 156–59, 166, 167, 170, 173, 174, 238
determinism, 124, 138, 139
deterrence, 42, 49, 83, 85, 113
deterrence and apology reductions, 113–17
dignity, 15, 18, 30, 45, 59, 62, 63, 64, 70, 82, 95, 97, 105, 112, 136, 157, 164, 167–70, 173, 178, 182, 188, 208, 280, 299, 300, 382, 395
discretion, 2, 5, 18, 89, 111, 122, 134, 136, 145, 150, 155, 167, 187, 191, 192, 195, 209, 221, 222, 229, 236, 259, 284, 308, 355, 378, 379
disenfranchisement, 45, 48, 121
domestic violence, 6, 7
drug and alcohol abuse and treatment, 2, 44, 69, 73, 81, 100, 104, 180, 181, 206, 272, 296
drug and alcohol treatment, 212
Dubber, Markus, 216
Duff, R.A., 59, 65–71, 74, 82, 83, 86, 105, 112, 160, 167, 168, 169, 170, 171, 172, 173, 174, 175, 176, 181, 182, 185, 188, 233, 369, 370, 371, 382

embourgeoisment of language, 138
emotional amplifiers, 33, 215, 329
emotions, 61, 66, 75, 104, 105, 144, 154, 162, 164, 188, 214–15, 225, 274, 275, 276, 281, 288, 326, 330. See negative emotions, humiliation
  collective emotions, 74–83
  conflicting, 215
  delegating emotional states, 289, 294
  difficulty expressing, 20, 227
  evaluating emotions, 3
  in civil cases, 326–29
  in court-ordered apologies, 62, 63
  in plea agreements, 198
  negative emotions. See hard treatment
Engels, Frederick, 271
Enron Corporation, 301, 311

ethical pluralism, 48
excuse, 35, 165, 205, 306

fault. *See* blame, accepting
Federal Trade Commission, 266
Feinberg, Joel, 272
felony murder, 205
financial crisis of 2008, 139, 267, 268, 269, 298, 309, 320, 322
Fish, Stanley, 89
Fletcher, George, 47, 107
Ford Motor Company, xi, 243–45, 253, 257, 260–68, 286, 287, 288, 291, 292, 295, 296, 298, 305, 306, 309, 310, 312, 314, 326
forgiveness, 5, 6, 7, 8, 57, 78, 106, 107, 108, 109, 110, 111, 112, 113, 165, 178, 234, 235, 236, 237, 238, 255, 259, 295, 296, 303, 304
Foucault, Michele, 54, 55, 56
four corners of apologies, 20, 259
Friedman, Lawrence, 56
Fukushima nuclear disaster, 270

gender, 4, 15, 22, 88, 111, 136, 304, 319
Gibney, Alex, 24
Ginges, Jeremy, 254
Goldman Sachs, 266, 267, 268, 269, 270
Goldman, Ron, 246
good time served, 211, 219, 220, 377
Greenberg, David, 147
Griswold, Charles, 164, 165
Grosmaire, Ann, 4–8, 106, 235
Grünenthal Pharmaceuticals, 267, 293, 294, 295, 298, 300, 304, 305, 306, 307, 317

hard pose, 134
hard treatment, 31, 44, 49, 64, 66, 100, 101, 111, 116, 118, 148, 151, 153, 159, 160, 161, 165, 166, 167, 170, 173, 174, 177, 185, 187, 230, 351, 367
Harr, Jonathan, 245
Harriot, Kai Leigh, 235
Hart, H. L. A., 49, 117
Hawaii v. Office of Hawaiian Affairs, 316
Hay, Douglas, 145
Hayward, Tony, 310
Hegel, G.W.F., 63, 72, 97, 137, 168, 169, 170, 208
Herzog, Werner, 267
Hogshire, Edward, 2–4
Holocaust, 157, 258, 303, 307, 318
Hume, David, 275

humiliation, 33, 52, 58–62, 64, 65, 66, 70, 71, 72, 81, 82, 83, 84, 86, 87, 88, 90, 92, 93, 167, 181, 182, 286, 288, 328
Hussein, King of Jordan, 165

I Was Wrong, 8, 9, 10, 11, 12, 13, 15, 17, 19, 20, 22, 23, 34, 35, 53, 58, 68, 69, 85, 138, 139, 142, 162, 173, 176, 216, 222, 236, 243, 249, 260, 266, 277, 289, 294, 319, 330
ideology, 124, 127, 133, 136, 137, 145
incapacitation, 42, 43, 46, 49, 86, 113, 114, 125, 186, 234, 304
  and apology reductions, 113–17
  and court-ordered apologies, 86
incommensurability, 46, 161, 163, 213
individualism, 136, 137, 140, 191
innocence, insistence of, 229–31
insurance, 13, 251, 253, 255, 268, 279, 283, 312, 321, 322, 382, 387, 393
intentions, 17, 19, 20, 32, 36, 53, 58, 62, 69, 76, 98, 116, 144, 171, 198, 199, 210, 214, 217, 227, 233, 263, 264, 267, 268, 269, 270, 272, 276, 293, 300, 304, 318, 323–26, 328
  collective intentions, 268
  intentionally deceptive apologies, 232
intergenerational justice, 119, 120, 132, 265

Japanese culture, apologies in, 103, 222, 251, 297. *See* Chisso Cporporation,
Japanese internment, 316
JNC Corporation. *See* Chisso Corporation
Jones, Paula, 247
juries, 3, 8, 10, 51, 117, 183, 191, 202, 222, 283, 394
juvenile, 363, 378
juvenile offenders, 15, 46, 81, 126, 131, 179, 227, 229

Kant, Immanuel, 45, 59, 60, 61, 62, 63, 65, 66, 67, 70, 71, 97, 105, 112, 124, 136, 150, 167, 168, 169, 174, 180, 181, 207, 208, 303, 351
  "two Kants", 167
  on "moral death", 169
  on apologies to the dead, 352
Kent State shootings, 314
Kierkegaard, Sören, 94, 150
King, Martin Luther, 64
Kolakowski, Lesek, 10
Korean sex slaves, 264

law and economics, 46, 249, 250
Leape, Lucian, 141, 313
Levinas, Emmanuel, 303, 317
liberal neutrality, objections from, 111, 112, 131, 151, 170, 177–85, 201, 206, 207, 220, 296
Lipkin, R. J., 172
Lippke, Richard, 190, 191, 215
Love, Yeardley, 4

Mabbott, J. D., 148
Maimonides, Moses, 31
Marx, Karl, 46, 111, 119, 120, 121, 123, 124, 128, 129, 130, 133, 134, 136, 137, 138, 147, 188, 250, 268
McBride, Conor, 4–8, 16, 102, 106, 111
McCain, John, 51
McDonald's Corporation, 327
McGreevey, Jim, 27
medicine and medical malpractice, 10, 11, 12, 23, 141, 142, 245, 246, 251, 256, 275, 279, 280, 281, 282, 283, 293, 308, 313
membership in collective, 35, 144, 145, 262, 289, 291, 292, 293, 325. See standing
mens rea, 101, 151, 159, 205
Minamata disease, 246, 328. See Chisso Corporation
Moore, Michael, 68, 151
moral interlocutor, recognizing victim as, 18, 21, 29, 36, 66, 68, 73, 76, 97, 104, 107, 109, 157, 177, 187, 208, 213, 216, 231, 288, 294, 298, 300, 302, 303, 309, 310, 317, 318, 320, 326
moral responsibility. See blame, accepting
moral transformation, 8, 10, 13, 15, 19, 23, 34, 49, 63, 64, 65, 67, 90, 112, 116, 148, 149, 150, 184, 190, 201, 224, 228, 235, 236, 238, 239, 244, 273, 277, 287, 294, 311, 318, 320
Murphy, Jeffrie, 57, 82, 83, 115, 118, 130, 133, 150, 151, 154, 162, 185, 188, 332, 367, 368

Nasser, Jacques, 314
Native Americans, 120, 306, 317, 323
negative emotions, 21, 33, 60, 61, 62, 64, 114, 154, 159, 160, 162, 172, 177, 198, 273, 327, 328
Nelson, Jane, 78
neuroscience, 50, 68, 139, 253, 330
Nietzsche, Friedrich, 39, 70, 94, 159, 164, 167

Nixon, Richard, 40
Nussbaum, Martha, 82, 111
Nygaard, Richard Lowell, 94, 96

O'Connor, Flannery, 102
O'Hear, Michael, 103, 194, 195, 199, 200, 219, 375, 377
Obama, Barack, 292, 293
organizational men, 253

Pashukanis, Evgeny, 127, 128, 129, 136
Pereboom, Derk, 139
perjury, 232
Petchesky, Rosalind, 120
Pettigrove, Glen, 266
phronesis, 330
Plato, 12, 170
plea bargaining, 106, 191–201, 204, 221
Poe, Ted, 82, 84
Pope John Paul II, 303
Posner, Richard, 115
prison abolition, 47, 125
Program for Early Assessment and Resolution of Loss, 279
promissory categorical apology, 21, 115, 148, 192
proportionality, 44, 59, 67, 100, 101, 111, 134, 136, 148, 166, 167, 171, 173, 183, 200, 234, 238
prosecutor, 2, 23, 32, 96, 103, 143, 190, 191, 192, 194, 195, 201, 203, 221, 223, 229, 264, 296, 373, 374, 378
prosecutors, 202
proximate causation, 17, 68, 124, 138, 139, 143, 204, 205, 260, 266, 267, 306, 321
psychoprison, Soviet, 56

Quinney, Richard, 125

race, 4, 82, 111, 119, 121, 122, 134, 136, 145–47, 236, 302, 323, 324
Radzik, Linda, 54, 57, 59, 62, 71, 105, 111, 112, 132, 169, 182, 183, 351, 371
Rawls, John, 179
Rayner, Jay, 289
Reagan, Ronald, 40, 284
Rebombo, Dumisani, 4
recidivism, 15, 23, 71, 74, 82, 97, 99, 102, 103, 104, 113, 114, 115, 117, 123, 131, 153, 174, 181, 186, 199, 206, 207, 211, 212, 213, 215, 218, 220, 222, 223, 225, 226, 227, 315, 330

INDEX

redress, 8, 16, 19, 20, 21, 22, 30, 31, 32, 35, 36, 41, 53, 59, 63, 65, 72, 74, 76, 81, 86, 88, 90, 96, 99, 101, 102, 107, 109, 114, 129, 132, 135, 158, 160, 161, 169, 171, 172, 174, 177, 178, 179, 182, 184, 186, 187, 210, 213, 214, 215, 217, 219, 225, 227, 231, 233, 236, 239, 244, 245, 247, 248, 250, 254, 257, 259, 260, 263, 267, 270, 273, 279, 285, 286, 287, 288, 289, 290, 294, 295, 296, 298, 301, 307, 312, 313, 316, 317, 318, 319, 320, 321, 322, 323, 325, 326, 328, 329
    duducting as business expense, 321
reform, 3, 7, 9, 18, 21, 22, 23, 28, 31, 32, 33, 35, 37, 44, 49, 53, 57, 61, 64, 65, 66, 68, 69, 72, 77, 81, 86, 98, 99, 100, 101, 102, 107, 108, 109, 113, 114, 121, 130, 131, 132, 137, 141, 142, 143, 144, 146, 147, 150, 163, 168, 170, 171, 172, 174, 177, 178, 180, 182, 185, 186, 188, 189, 190, 201, 207, 209, 210, 211, 212, 213, 215, 217, 218, 220, 222, 225, 227, 229, 230, 231, 233, 235, 236, 239, 244, 247, 248, 249, 260, 263, 266, 270, 273, 279, 281, 298, 305, 308, 309, 310, 311, 312, 313, 314, 315, 319, 325, 354, 370, 373
regret, 18, 30, 209, 274, 282, 304
rehabilitation, 10, 42, 43, 44, 45, 47, 50, 52, 56, 63, 64, 71, 74–83, 92, 97, 99–104, 110, 114, 117, 118, 126, 127, 131, 132, 133, 150, 155, 167, 168, 169, 170, 186, 188, 191, 196, 199, 212, 219, 227, 230, 235, 328, 369, 375
    contrasted with restorative justice, 105
Reiman, Jeffrey, 48, 119, 122, 123, 136, 146
reintegrative shaming, 103, 108, 110, 111, 220
religion, 2, 5, 7, 43, 57, 112, 139, 150, 151, 181, 207, 214, 220, 296, 299
remedy. *See* redress
remorse
    contrasted with apology, 16
repentance, 19, 31, 54, 55, 56, 57, 63, 65, 66, 67, 69, 94, 115, 147, 152, 154, 160, 162, 169, 170, 171, 173, 174, 178, 181, 277, 326
    already repentant offenders, 69, 104, 170, 171, 173, 176, 177, 180
    contrasted with apology, 16
    manifested repentance, 331
    repentance training, 180
repentant
    already repentant offenders, 179
responsibility, personal, 47, 68, 93, 123, 137, 138, 142, 143, 268, 273, 284, 314
restitution, 5, 21, 46, 56, 77, 107, 173, 196, 217, 219, 226, 237, 266, 393. *See* redress
restorative justice, 5, 6, 7, 46, 57, 58, 59, 62, 64, 68, 71, 98, 103, 105–13, 114, 118, 133, 158, 177, 181, 183, 186, 191, 248
retributivism, 7, 14, 31, 33, 34, 44, 45, 46, 47, 48, 49, 52, 57, 58–62, 63, 64, 65, 70, 71, 72, 74, 80, 81, 83, 85, 86, 90, 93, 97, 99, 100, 101, 105, 112, 118, 136, 147, 148, 149, 150, 151, 152, 153, 154, 155, 156, 159, 160, 161, 162, 163, 164, 165, 166, 167, 168, 169, 171, 173, 174, 175, 177, 181, 182, 185, 186, 187, 188, 189, 207, 216, 225, 237, 238, 275, 288, 311, 319, 320, 321, 322, 328, 351, 352, 366, 367, 368, 369, 370
    communicative retributivism, 170–75
    dialectical retributivsm contrasted with act and character retributivism, 156
    jusitifications for apology reductions, 175
    justifications for court-ordered apologies, 62
revenge, 41, 43, 125, 153, 163, 164, 165, 167, 178
Robbennolt, Jennifer, 11, 22, 23, 192, 256
Romney, Mitt, 264
Rothman, David, 57
Rove, Karl, 283
Rwanda, 140, 141, 261

safe apology laws, 281–86
Scheler, Max, 21, 147, 152
Schlag, Pierre, 250
Schopenhauer, 275
scripted apologies, 226–27
Seccuro, Liz, 1–4, 72–74, 95, 100, 159, 160, 206, 229
sentencing judges, 34, 58, 136, 155, 193, 199, 210, 216, 222, 229
settlement agreements, 10, 11, 13, 84, 244, 245, 246, 252, 253, 255, 256, 257, 261, 265, 266, 273, 282, 284, 286, 288, 290, 296, 308, 309, 310, 312, 313, 314, 316, 317, 318, 321, 323, 326, 331, 381, 387, 390, 392, 395
shame, 69, 82, 103, 108, 109, 110, 162, 273
    collective shame, 327, 328
shared responsibility, 273
Sharratt, Rickey, 51, 52, 84

Sheldon, Randall, 120
Shimada, Kenichi, 247
Simmel, Georg, 128, 250
Simpson, O. J., 246
slavery, 120, 121, 264, 306, 317
Solomon, Robert, 164, 186
Sorry Works!, 279, 280
Southwest Airlines, 12
sovereign immunity, 271
speech act, 8, 22, 53, 86, 91, 370
speech, freedom of, 88–91
Spitzer, Elliot, 23–34
standing to apologize, 17, 27, 36, 205, 206, 260, 286–96, 300, 302, 311, 323, 327
standing to bring claim, 295
standing to forgive, 238
Stewart, Martha, 189
Stock, Harald, 293
Strawson, P. F., 138
strict liability, 272

Taft, Lee, 246, 279
Taibbi, Matt, 267
Tannen, Deborah, 22
Tasioulas, John, 48, 153, 154, 160, 166, 182, 372
tätige reue, 239, 331
Tavuchis, Nicolas, 22
temptation, resisting, 7, 18, 30, 31, 43, 49, 57, 70, 102, 103, 113, 114, 135, 158, 209, 210, 211, 212, 215, 218, 227, 311
thalidomide, 36, 263, 267, 293, 298, 300, 305, 306, 307, 317, 318
third parties. *See* standing
time-release theory of harm, 156
timing of apologies, 30, 102, 176, 190, 203, 208, 211, 213, 214, 216
Toro Company, 255, 256, 308

tort reform, 12, 247, 252, 256, 281–86
torture, 55, 68, 70, 84
truth and reconciliation tribunals, 144, 237
Tuskegee experiments, 302
Tutu, Desmond, 318

U.S. Federal Sentencing Guidelines, 3, 10, 97, 129, 148, 155, 193–201, 213, 214, 219, 223, 228, 233
U.S. Supreme Court, 3, 143, 155, 156, 316
unapologetic offenders, 185–89, 200, 233
unforgivable harms, 82, 237
Union Carbide, 286
Urban Walker, Margaret, 237
utilitarianism, 42, 43, 46, 72, 84, 99, 124. *See* consequentialism
origins of, 42

value-declaring apology, 36, 85, 144
victimless crimes, 41, 88, 122, 207
vigilante justice, 163, 165, 179
von Hirsch, Andrew, 63, 69, 112, 166, 171, 178, 239, 367, 371

Waller, Bruce, 130, 141, 142, 313
Walmart, 253, 319
War on Drugs, 40, 119, 121, 146, 194
Warren, Anthony, 235
White, Brent, 87, 91
White, William, 253
Wolffe, Richard, 257
Woods, Michael, 11, 256, 278, 283
"wrong wrong," apologizing for, 18, 28, 206, 297

Yad Vashem, 303

zealous representation, 228–29
Zierer, Edith, 303